Solution Behavior of Surfactants

Theoretical and Applied Aspects

Volume 1

This book is to be returned on or before
the last date stamped below.

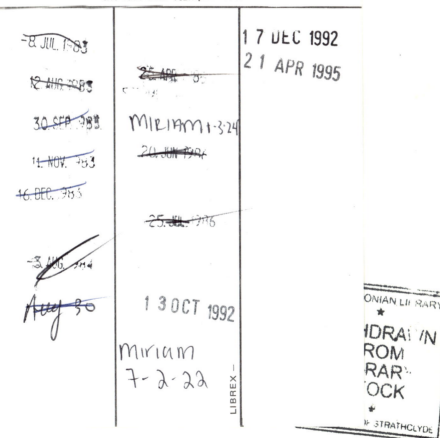

Solution Behavior of Surfactants

Theoretical and Applied Aspects

Volume 1

Edited by

K. L. Mittal

IBM Corporation
Hopewell Junction, New York

and

E. J. Fendler

The Standard Oil Company (Ohio)
Cleveland, Ohio

Plenum Press • New York and London

Library of Congress Cataloging in Publication Data

International Symposium on Solution Behavior of Surfactants: Theoretical and Applied Aspects (1980: Clarkson College of Technology)
  Solution behavior of surfactants.

  "Proceedings of the International Symposium on Solution Behavior of Surfactants: Theoretical and Applied Aspects, held under the auspices of the Eleventh Northeast Regional Meeting of the American Chemical Society, at Clarkson College of Technology, between June 30–July 3, 1980, in Potsdam, New York"—Verso t.p.
  Includes bibliographical references and indexes.
  1. Surface active agents—Congresses. 2. Solution (Chemistry)—Congresses. I. Mittal, K. L., 1945–   . II. Fendler, Eleanor J. III. Title.
  TP994.I58 1980   668'.1   82-10120
  ISBN 0-306-41025-8 (v. 1)   AACR2
  ISBN 0-306-41026-5 (v. 2)

Proceedings of the International Symposium on Solution Behavior of Surfactants:
Theoretical and Applied Aspects, held under the auspices of the Eleventh Northeast
Regional Meeting of the American Chemical Society, at Clarkson College of Technology
between June 30 – July 3, 1980, in Potsdam, New York

© 1982 Plenum Press, New York
A Division of Plenum Publishing Corporation
233 Spring Street, New York, N.Y. 10013

Printed in the United States of America

PREFACE

This and its companion Volume 2 comprise the proceedings of the International Symposium on "Solution Behavior of Surfactants - Theoretical and Applied Aspects" organized under the auspices of the 11th Northeast Regional Meeting of the American Chemical Society held in Potsdam, N.Y., June 30-July 3, 1980. This Symposium represented the third event in the series of symposia dealing with the topic of surfactants in solution. The first Symposium was held in Albany, N.Y., in 1976 under the title "Micellization, Solubilization and Microemulsions",[1] the proceedings of which have been documented in a two-volume set[1]. The second was held under the title "Solution Chemistry of Surfactants" in 1978 in Knoxville, TN, and the proceedings of this event have also been properly chronicled[2]. Apropos, the fourth biennial Symposium in this series is entitled "International Symposium on Surfactants in Solution" (K. L. Mittal and B. Lindman, Cochairmen) and is scheduled to be held from June 27 to July 2, 1982 in Lund, Sweden. Since these biennial events have been very successful and important in bringing researchers with varied interests together and in stimulating interdisciplinary communication, so the plans are to continue these on a regular basis with a change in venue for each meeting.

In this symposium a number of ramifications of surfactants were covered and the final program contained a total of 85 papers by 148 authors from 18 countries, and the papers were divided into 11 sessions. It should be added that both aggregation and adsorption of surfactants were covered, and the applications of surfactants were given due cognizance. A number of speakers were specifically asked to provide state-of-the-art overviews of certain topics and those were augmented by unpublished original research contributions. Consequently, the program reflected a blend of overviews and research papers - such a blend seems to be the best way to present the state of knowledge of any topic under consideration.

With regard to these proceedings volumes, it should be pointed out that, for a variety of reasons, nine papers (out of 85) are not included; however, 8 papers are included which were not presented. So these proceedings volumes contain a net total of 84

papers by 166 authors from 19 countries. The papers have been re-
arranged (from the order in the program) in a more logical manner
for the reader and have been grouped in nine parts. Volume 1 contains Parts I – II and Parts III–IX constitute Volume 2. The
topics covered include: thermodynamics and kinetics of micellization in aqueous media, hydrophobic interactions, aggregation in
non-aqueous media, aggregation behavior of biological surfactants,
mixed micelles, solubilization, micellar catalysis and inhibition,
reactions and interactions in micellar media, use of surfactants in
analytical chemistry, technological applications of surfactants,
tertiary oil recovery, adsorption of surfactants, historical aspects of surfactant adsorption, bilayer lipid membranes, and environmental and health aspects of surfactants.

    We sincerely hope that this two-volume set (circa 1500
pages) will be a useful source of information to both veteran
researchers and those who are contemplating taking a maiden
research voyage in the wonderful area of surfactants.[1,2] As a matter
of fact, this set coupled with the earlier two sets (a total of
circa 3500 pages) should provide a comprehensive compilation of
contemporary research and thinking anent surfactants in solution.

    Even a casual glance at the Table of Contents of these
volumes will reveal clearly that there is brisk activity taking
place in the arena of surfactants and all signals indicate that
there is going to be heightened interest in investigating both the
basic and applied aspects of surfactant aggregation and adsorption.
Surfactants play a major role in many human endeavors and the interest in reactions and interactions in surfactant media has gained
considerable momentum in the recent past, as these media provide a
fertile land for conducting a variety of interesting chemistry. It
should be pointed out that the papers were properly reviewed and in
many cases the authors were asked to make minor revisions. As for
discussion, an edited version is appended at the end of each part,
but it should be recorded here that there were very brisk and en-
lightening discussions both formally in the auditorium as well as
in corridors. In other words, discussion recorded here represents
only a fraction of total discussion which took place during the
Symposium.

    Acknowledgements. First of all, we are grateful to the
organizing committee (particularly Drs. J. Kratohvil and P. Zuman)
of the 11th Northeast Regional Meeting for sponsoring this event.
One of us (KLM) is thankful to the appropriate management of IBM
Corporation for permitting him to participate in the organization
of the symposium and in the editing of the volumes. EJF gratefully
achnowledges encouragement by the administration and management of
Texas A & M University and Kimberly-Clark Corp., respectively, to
organize the symposium and edit the proceedings. Our sincere thanks

are due to the unsung heroes (reviewers) for their fine and valuable comments, as comments of the peers are very important in maintaining the quality of scientific publications. One of us (KLM) would like to acknowledge the cooperation of his wife, Usha, particularly for letting him use the dining table as a desk and tolerating, without much complaint, the legion of folders strewn all over the house; and his kids (Anita, Rajesh, Nisha and Seema) for letting their Daddy use those hours which rightfully belonged to them. EJF would like to express her sincere gratitude to Natalie M. Ross and Manfred H. Fleschar for their valuable assistance in the organization of the symposium. Also she would like to acknowledge the patience, consideration and support of her children (Michael T. J. and Lisa A. M. Fendler).

Special thanks are due to Mr. Jim Busis (Plenum Publishing Corp.) for his continued interest in this project and for providing whatever help was needed. Last, but not least, the cooperation, enthusiasm and patience of the contributors is gratefully acknowledged.

K. L. Mittal
IBM Corporation
Hopewell Junction, New York 12533

E. J. Fendler
The Standard Oil Company (Ohio)
Warrenville, Ohio 44128

1.   K. L. Mittal, Editor, Micellization, Solubilization and Microemulsions, Vols. 1 & 2, Plenum Press, New York, 1977.

2.   K. L. Mittal, Editor, Solution Chemistry of Surfactants, Vols. 1 & 2, Plenum Press, New York, 1979.

CONTENTS OF VOLUME 1

PART I: GENERAL OVERVIEWS

CONTENTS OF VOLUME 2

PART III: MICELLES IN NON-AQUEOUS MEDIA

PART IV: SOLUBILIZATION PHENOMENON

PART V: REACTIONS IN MICELLES AND
              MICELLAR CATALYSIS

PART VI: MICROEMULSIONS AND REACTIONS
IN MICROEMULSION MEDIA

PART VII: USE OF SURFACTANTS IN
ANALYTICAL CHEMISTRY

PART VIII: MISCELLANEOUS APPLICATIONS
OF SURFACTANTS

Part 1

General Overviews

STRUCTURE AND DYNAMICS OF MICELLES AND MICROEMULSIONS

Björn Lindman and Håkan Wennerström
Physical Chemistry 1 and 2
Chemical Center, University of Lund
P.O.B. 740, S-220 07 Lund, Sweden

The surface of amphiphilic aggregates consists of amphiphilic head-groups, counterions and water molecules while the interior mainly contains the hydrocarbon chains. A review of the structure and dynamics of different parts of a micelle is presented; in particular, recent results obtained by NMR spectroscopy and tracer self-diffusion are discussed. Among problems considered are: alkyl chain conformation and flexibility mainly on the basis of recent ^{13}C NMR studies; hydration of micellar aggregates, inter alia global hydration number, counterion hydration and the concept of water penetration; counterion binding and counterion specificity, effect of concentration, head-group and competing ions on counterion binding; mobility and exchange kinetics of water molecules and counterions; sites of solubilization and influence of solubilizates on hydration and counterion binding. Special emphasis is on a comparison of these features for micelles with those of other amphiphilic aggregates, i.e. reversed micelles and liquid crystalline phases. The relation between microemulsions and other amphiphilic aggregates is also briefly considered.

INTRODUCTION

Due to both experimental and theoretical studies, there has been a considerable progress in our understanding of amphiphile association into normal and reversed micelles and into various liquid cyrstalline structures. Fundamental aspects of the primary micelle formation of surfactants in aqueous solution are now in general well understood while much still has to be learnt about the surfactant aggregates at high concentration and in the presence of a third component. However, it is becoming increasingly clear that many features at the molecular level remain practically unchanged at the transition from one type of aggregate to another, a finding that has been astonishingly little applied; it would be expected, for example, that many conflicting points regarding so-called micro-emulsions could be resolved by making systematic use of the analogies between different surfactant aggregates.

In this article we will review current ideas about the structure and dynamics of micelles in aqueous solution. We will start with a few basic statements about micelle formation and then discuss separately the alkyl chain conformation and flexibility, counterion binding to micelles, and micelle hydration. After discussing solubilization in micelles and relations between different phases, the article is terminated with some thoughts about surfactant aggregates of the microemulsion type formed in four-component systems of surfactant, water, hydrocarbon and short-chain alcohol (so-called cosurfactant). We have previously reviewed the present subject [1,2] but here some emphasis will be placed on recent developments. Although the results are in general applicable also to non-ionic amphiphiles, we will mainly consider the case of ionic surfactants.

SOME BASIC ASPECTS OF MICELLIZATION

The self-association of an amphiphilie occurs in a <u>stepwise</u> manner with one monomer added to the aggregate at a time, [3,4] i.e.

$$A_{n-1} + A_1 \leftrightarrows A_n \qquad\qquad (1)$$

For a long-chain amphiphile the association is <u>strongly cooperative</u> and results in large aggregates, micelles. Many thermodynamic, transport and spectroscopic properties show a distinct change in behaviour with concentration around a rather well-defined <u>critical micelle concentration</u> (cmc)[5-7].

In a typical case, the micelles have a closely <u>spherical shape</u> in a rather wide concentration range above the cmc, and in many cases there is no marked change in shape until at the surfactant solubility limit where a liquid crystalline phase generally

separates out. In other cases there is a marked transition to long
rod-like aggregates at higher concentrations.[8] This leads to
dramatic increases in solution viscosity [9] and other effective
methods to monitor the evolution of micelle shape are quasi-elastic
light scattering [10-12] and proton NMR line-shapes. [13] The formation of
rod micelles is promoted not only by increasing surfactant concentration but also by addition of salt and lowering the temperature[10],
and it can also be very sensitive to the counterion. Rod micelles
have been much studied; however, other non-spherical shapes, like
oblates have also been considered but they seem to occur only under
rather special conditions.

Micelle _size_ is an important quantity in the characterization
of amphiphile association but is not straight-forwardly obtained
mainly due to strong intermicellar interactions. Experimental
methods include classical and quasi-elastic light scattering (QLS)
and tracer self-diffusion studies. The best information available at
present stems from QLS [10-12] in the presence of added salt (ca. 0.4
-0.6 M) to suppress electrostatic interactions. From the diffusion
coefficient obtained, the micelle radius may be computed using
simple hydrodynamic theory (Stokes-Einstein equation). There is also
a great interest in methods that monitor the aggregation number
rather than micelle size. Potentiometric titrations[15] in the presence of very high amounts of salt (to minimize variations in the
activity coefficients) have been employed for short-chain
alkanoates. Spectroscopic methods which observe directly the surfactant in an unperturbed medium (i.e. avoiding adding salt or a
spectroscopic probe) are, of course, especially attractive since
corrections for intermicellar interactions etc. are not required. In
^{13}C NMR chemical shift studies[16] (Figure 1) of nonylammonium bromide
the data could be fitted with good precision to an association of
the monomers into a single micelle size, i.e.

$$nA_1 \rightleftharpoons A_n$$

with n = 35 ± 2. The method is not yet developed to give information
on the width of the micelle size distribution. If one considers the
information presently available for the size of spherical micelles,
a rather simple picture emerges, namely, that the radius is close to
the length of the extended amphiphile. For sodium dodecyl sulfate,
for example, r $\simeq$ 22Å corresponding to n $\simeq$ 60.[10]

Already from the step-wise formation process, (Equation (1)),
it can be deduced that a micellar solution will contain aggregates
with all values of n from 2 to far above the average value. However,
it has been difficult to quantitatively determine the _micelle_ _size_
distribution curve, an important reason being that aggregates of
intermediate size may be present in extremely low concentrations. A
decisive step in obtaining quantitative information on micelle size

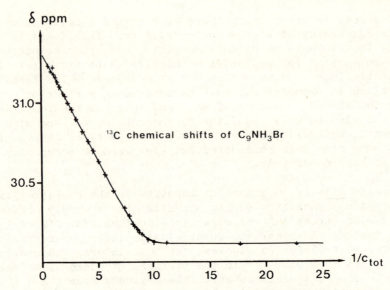

Figure 1. Chemical shift of carbon 4 from the polar head in nonylammonium bromide as a function of the inverse surfactant molality.
Curve theoretically calculated for a micelle aggregation number of
33. (From Ref. 16 after correction).

distribution was the development of a correct interpretation of
kinetic data. [4] Thus the kinetic work has clearly demonstrated the
presence of a very deep minimum in the size distribution curve as
well as quantified the width of the curve around the optimal value.
For $C_{12}SO_4Na$ (C_n is a n-alkyl chain with n carbon atoms) the minimum is located at n $\simeq$ 7 (concentration of the order of $10^{-10}M$ at
the cmc) while the standard deviation characterizing the width is
ca. 13. While in the region of spherical micelles, the solutions
are "low-disperse"; there is a very pronounced polydispersity,[12,17]
with rod micelles.

      Micelles are involved in a highly dynamic equilibrium, being
constantly formed and dissolved, as demonstrated in recent kinetic
studies.[4] It is essential to recognize this dynamical nature of the
system in experimental studies. The entering or leaving of monomers
one at a time in combination with the deep minimun in the size
distribution curve (acting as an effective "resistance" to a change
in the number of micelles) gives a large difference between the

average residence time of a monomer in a micelle and the average
micelle life-time.[4] Both these times increase strongly with
increasing length of the amphiphile alkyl chain. For $C_{12}SO_4Na$, for
example, the monomer resides on the average ca. 10^{-5} s in a micelle
which has a life-time of ca. 10^{-3} s.[4] In addition to this, there
are partial exits occurring on a much shorter time-scale.[18] As
regards water molecule and counterion kinetics, no definite information is available but the dynamics of these species are very rapid;
unpublished NMR experiments indicate that both counterions and water
molecules have life-times on a micelle in the nanosecond range.

THE NON-POLAR REGION

It was recognized by Hartley[19] already more than forty years
ago that there is a liquid-like interior of surfactant micelles and
recent studies giving quantitative information on various motional
processes within micelles fully support this.

^{13}C NMR chemical shifts of alkyl chains are mainly determined
by conformation equilibria, the chemical shift change form gauche to
all-trans being ca. 4 ppm. For a monomer being transferred from an
aqueous environment to a micelle, there is a change in the same
direction for all methylene carbons but the change is much lower
than the given figure. It is in the range 0.2 - 1.2 ppm for C_9NH_3Br
and C_7CO_2Na, the change being largest in the middle of the chain and
decreasing progressively towards the ends[20] indicating that the
difference in average conformation between monomers in the aqueous
region and in the micelles is largest for the central carbons.

The flexibility of the hydrocarbon chain can be conveniently
studied by NMR relaxation techniques without any labelling, which
perturbs the system. In several studies using NMR methods as well as
other methods one has, however, not taken into account that motion
within the micelle does not lead to local isotropy; this is directly
demonstrated by the occurrence of dipole-dipole and quadrupole
splittings for the corresponding liquid crystalline systems as well
as for solutions of rod micelles. In several determinations of the
"microviscosity" or "microfluidity" this effect has been neglected,
as well as the possible perturbation by the probe, and the dynamics
in the micellar interior seems to be considerably faster than indicated by these studies. Analysis of the ^{13}C T_1 data for sodium
octanoate given in Figure 2 in terms of fast local motion and slower
motion over the dimensions of the micelles gives the result that
there is no significant change in the fast motion on micelle
formation.[21] This motion which involves rotation about the C - C
bonds is thus extremely rapid in the micelles.

That the rotation of the amphiphile molecule about its long
axis is rapid in amphiphile aggregates was demonstrated in early NMR

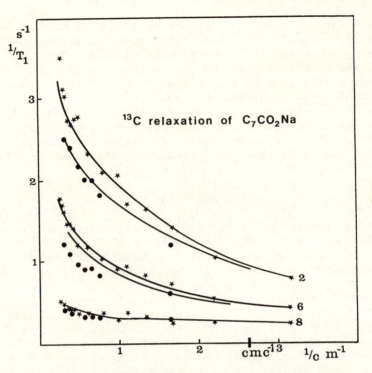

Figure 2. ^{13}C NMR relaxation of sodium octanoate is concentration and frequency dependent. T_1 data are shown for carbons $2(\alpha-CH_2)$ $3(\beta-CH_3)$ and $8(-CH_3)$. Upper ponts obtained at 15 MHz and lower ones at 25 MHz. (After Ref. 21.)

studies of liquid crystals (reviewed in Ref. 22). Evidence for a very rapid <u>lateral</u> <u>diffusion</u> is of more recent data[23], and now it has been shown for several different mesophase systems[24] to be of the order of 10^{-10} m^2/s, i.e. of the same order of magnitude as in weakly associated pure liquids. The ^{13}C variable frequency T_1 studies[21] support a similar later diffusional rate in micelles, because of the larger area per polar group for the latter case one may expect it even to be slightly more rapid.

For anisotropic liquid crystalline phases the order parameter characterizing the degree of orientation of a certain bond in a molecule and obtainable from <u>inter alia</u> NMR quadrupole splittings demonstrates the extent of motion to be large and to increase from the polar head.[25]

   Observations demonstrating further a liquid interior of
micelles are

a) The partial molar volume and compressibility of the amphiphile in
   micelles are large and similar to those of liquid hydrocarbons.[26]
b) The low temperature limit of existence of micelles is close to
   that of liquid crystalline phases,[1,2] where "liquid" chains have
   been unequivocally demonstrated.[22]

   In conclusion, it is evident that the state of the alkyl chains
in micelles is close to that of liquid alkanes. The average conformation is only slightly more extended than for the free monomer, and
concerning dynamics no demonstration of any change on micelle formation seems to be available.

COUNTERION BINDING

   The cooperative association of an ionic amphiphile into
micelles results in a concentration of charge on the aggregate
surface. This leads to the binding of a large fraction of the
counterions to the micelles, and as a result the combined effects of
micelle-counterion attraction, counterion-counterion repulsion and
amphiphile ion-amphiphile ion repulsion cancel to a considerable extent. Recent theoretical and experimental studies have revealed many
aspects of the counterion binding and as we will review it is best
characterized as a non-specific electrostatic interaction of very
mobile counterions with the micelle as a whole rather than with
discrete groups on the micelle surface. It is difficult to characterize the process by a stoichiometric counterion binding in a
conventional chemical equilibrium description. Although a continuous
counterion distribution is at hand,it is both useful and theoretically justifiable to introduce a counterion association degree,
denoted β, as the ratio between counterions and amphiphile ions in a
micelle, i.e.

$$\beta = \frac{[M_{mic}]}{[A_{mic}]} = \frac{[M_{mic}]}{[A]_{tot} - [A_{free}]} \qquad (2)$$

   In many experimental studies, the observable quantity, X, is a
weighted average over different environments the ion samples, i.e.
if we assume a two-site model

$$X_{obs} = P_{free}X_{free} + P_{mic}X_{mic} \qquad (3)$$

with

$$P_{free} = \frac{[M_{free}]}{[M]_{tot}}$$

$$P_{mic} = \frac{[M_{mic}]}{[M]_{tot}} = \frac{\beta[A_{mic}]}{[M]_{tot}}$$

The various experimental methods that monitor counterion binding can be divided into thermodynamic (e.g. ion activity, osmotic coefficient), transport (e.g. ion self-diffusion, conductivity) and spectroscopic (mainly various NMR and ESR methods) ones. Because of the nature of the counterion association, β is not a well-defined quantity, and different experimental techniques weigh the ion distribution differently. Thus thermodynamic methods monitor the free counterion concentration, transport ones the amount of counterions diffusing with the micelles, and spectroscopic methods the counterions in close contact with the micelle surface. (The counterion association degree has also been obtained from studies of the cmc as a function of added salt. It seems, however, that the slope in plots of log cmc versus log (cmc + C_{salt}) has no direct relation to β.[27]

In studies of the counterion self-diffusion, β is obtained from

$$\beta = \frac{[M]_{tot}}{[A_{mic}]} \cdot \frac{D_{obs} - D_{free}}{D_{mic} - D_{free}} \qquad (4)$$

where D_{free}(after possible correction for obstruction effects etc.) is obtained from studies in the absence of micelles and D_{mic} from micelle diffusion studies. [A mic] can be calculated from amphiphile diffusion (or from activity meas urements); for studies far above the cmc, [A mic] is not needed. As examples of self-diffusion results[28-31] β is found to be 0.6 for C_7CO_2Na, 0.6 for $C_8(C_6H_4)SO_3Na$, 0.60 for $C_{12}SO_4Na$, 0.74 for $C_{16}N(CH_3)_3Br$, and 0.57 for $C_{16}N(CH_3)_3Cl$. β is found to be essentially independent of concentration. The self-diffusion results are generally in close agreement with ion activity measurements.[32]

Among NMR techniques, counterion chemical shifts, relaxation rates and quadrupole splittings have a wide general applicability in studies of counterion binding to amphiphilic aggregates.[33] Of these we will consider here only chemical shifts and quadrupole splittings since they respond rather directly to the fraction of counterions in

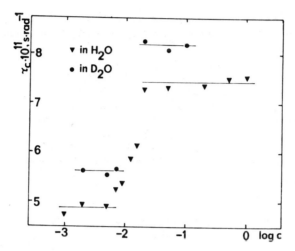

Figure 3. The reorientational correlation time (from ESR studies) of
VO^{2+} in sodium dodecyl sulfate solutions is independent of micelle
concentration. (From Ref. 38.)

direct vicinity of the aggregate surfaces; of these the quadrupole
splitting method[34] is applicable only to anisotropic mesophases.
Just to exemplify the results obtained it may be mentioned that β
(as well as the intrinsic chemical shift of bound counterions) is
independent of both n and concentration for micellar solutions[35] of
C_nSO_4Na, that β is independent of concentration for lamellar phase
of Aerosol OT and water as well for some other systems[36], that β is
independent of temperature and of added salt, the latter meaning
that added ions influence with good approximation only the
concentration of free ions.[37]

    A demonstration of the constancy in ionic interactions is shown
in Figure 3 giving ESR reorientation times of the VO^{2+} ion bound to
SDS micelles.[38] (The VO^{2+} ion was present in small amounts compared
to the SDS concentration). The conditions at the micelle surface can
be seen to remain unchanged on changing the amphiphile concentration
by several orders of magnitude.

Contenting with these exemplifications, we list below some general features of the counterion binding for simple hydrophilic counterions:

a)   For most cases β lies in the range 0.5 - 0.8.
b)   The three types of experimental methods give results in good agreement.
c)   Ion competition effects are small among monovalent ions while divalent ions replace monovalent ions effectively.
d)   Ion specificity is small for the cmc and for β , but may be very important for micelle size and shape.
e)   β is approximately independent of amphiphile concentration, temperature and alkyl chain length.
f)   There is a slight increase in β at the change in aggregate shape from sphere to rod and from rod to lamellae.
g)   β is only slightly affected by added salt.

Several of these observations are contrary to expectation for a conventional chemical equilibrium

$$qM + nA \ \rightleftharpoons \ M_qA_n$$

For example, one would expect β to change with temperature (as a result of an enthalpy change) and added salt and in particular one would expect the counterions to be dissociated on diluting the system. On the other hand, the observations point to a polyelectrolyte behaviour such as has been observed for linear polymers with a high charge density.[39] Here the ion condensation model, in which counterion binding occurs to reduce the effective charge density to a certain critical value independent of temperature and added salt, has been found to be in approximate agreement with many experimental observations.[39] Recent theoretical calculations using the Poisson-Boltzmann equation considering the amphiphile aggregates as uniformly charged and the counterions as point charges have identified an ion condensation behaviour for different aggregate geometries and have predicted all the general observations listed above.[2,27]

Counterion specificity effects always occur to a smaller or larger extent and we will here mention briefly two examples. (For organic counterions, ion specificity effects are, not unexpectedly, often of great importance.) For sodium ion binding to alkylcarboxylate and alkylsulfate aggregates both the chemical shift and the quadrupole splitting of bound counterions are very different and also (although the effects are small) alkali ion binding sequences appear to be different in the two cases.[2,33,35] It has been suggested that hydrogen-bond interactions between surfactant head-group and water of counterion hydration plays a role for carboxylate.

For $C_{16}N^+(CH_3)_3$ (CTA) micelles, Br^- binds preferentially to Cl^- both for spherical and rod-like micelles.[14] Around 30°C, the CTABr gives rods while CTACl does not (except at very high concentrations) In mixtures of CTABr and CTACl, the [81]Br quadrupole relaxation corresponds to rod micelles but [35]Cl[-] relaxation to spheres.[40,41] An unambiguous interpretation to this has not yet been found, but it appears[14] that either there are both spheres and rods with a strong preferential binding of Br^- to rods or there are two classes of binding sites on the micelles with one inner tighter one preferentially binding Br^-.

It appears from the numerous experimental studies carried out by various techniques that counterion binding to amphiphilic aggregates shows a surprisingly simple pattern, a pattern which can be well rationalized from a theoretical treatment[2,27] solving the Poisson-Boltzmann equation for uniformly charged bodies of idealized geometry interacting with counterions treated at point charges. Also the thermodynamic properties related to the ion distribution are well described by the Poisson-Boltzmann equation.[27] Ion specificity effects exist and should be a field of further study. Even if they are small they can have profound influence on micelle size and shape, phase equilibria, etc.; thus generally there are quite small energy differences between different geometrical forms of amphiphile aggregates.

HYDRATION

Amphiphile aggregation in aqueous systems involves a spatial separation of polar and non-polar molecules and groups which results from the entropically unfavourable water-hydrocarbon contact. The traditional picture of micelle formation assumes, therefore, the micelle structure to be such that water-alkyl chain contacts are minimized. The disordered and dynamic character of a micelle as well as restrictions in packing the alkyl chains makes it necessary to infer some alkyl chain-water contact. It is well established that at a small distance in from the micelle surface, water is almost completely excluded and also that the polar part of the amphiphile retains a considerable water contact.[42,43] For our proper understanding of several aspects of micellization, it is important to have quantitative information on hydration and to have detailed information on the location of the water molecules and on dynamic processes.

Even though a micelle hydration number, because of the non-specific and non-stoichiometric nature of the amphiphile-water interaction, is not uniquely defined and depends on the experimental approach chosen, it may illustrate well the general features of

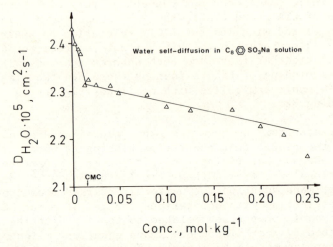

Figure 4. Water self-diffusion is influenced much less by the micelles than by the surfactant monomers. (Tracer self-diffusion studies of solutions of sodium octyl-benzenesulfonate (From Ref.42).

micelle hydration. In water self-diffusion studies, a general observation is that the non-micellized surfactant retards water translational mobility much more than the surfactant in micelles (Figure 4), thus directly demonstrating that the water-amphiphile contact is almost completely lost when the amphiphile enters a micelle.[28,29,31,42] Using certain assumptions one may deduce a global hydration number corresponding to the number of water molecules moving with the micelle as a kinetic entity. For a number of cases, the hydration number per amphiphile has been found to be 5-12 (a figure also found in viscosity studies) corresponding approximately to the hydration of the counterions and the polar head-groups.[42-44] For lamellar phases, deuteron NMR has shown that no more than 5-6 water molecules per polar head-group are oriented appeciably with respect to the amphiphile aggregates.[45]

An important water penetration deep into micelles (and thus a questioning of the classical picture of micelles) has been proposed at several occasions (reviewed in Ref. 42) mainly on the basis of spectroscopic studies. Mukerjee[46] and Stigter[47] as well as ourselves[42,43] have presented arguments against the concept of water penetration. In a typical spectroscopic approach to this problem one monitors a parameter of a probe, intrinsic or added, and correlates its value with that found in a pure solvent of a given polarity. Such a procedure presupposes firstly independent information on the distribution of probe molecules over the micelle and secondly a reliable relation between the employed spectroscopic parameter and the nature of the molecular environment. It seems clear that the results taken in support of water penetration have alternative reasonable interpretations and that there is little reason to abandon the picture of a micelle as an aggregate with an apolar interior and a polar surface in contact with the surrounding aqueous medium. Some arguments against "water penetration" are:

1) Global hydration number mentioned above.
2) According to partial molar volumes and compressibilities of the surfactant, the interior of micelles resembles liquid hydrocarbons. Furthermore, the partial molar volumes and compressibilities of solubilized alkanes are close to the values of liquid alkanes but considerably higher than those in water.[26,48]
3) The H/D isotope effect in ^{19}F NMR relaxation for partially fluorinated and flurorcarbon surfactants disappears on micelle formation[49] and an analogous observation was made using ^{1}H NMR relaxation for nonionic surfactant micelles.[50]
4) The stability ranges of different phases with distinct hydrophilic and hydrophobic domains are not consistent with an extensive degree of water penetration.
5) There is a low-rate of water diffusion between reversed micelles[31,51] as well as over lipid bilayers.[52]
6) It is possible to build micelles from space-filling molecular models without water in the interior[1,2]; on the other hand, the outermost one or two methylene groups must have an appreciable contact with water.
7) The thermodynamic properties of amphiphile-water systems can be rationalized using the assumption of no water penetration.[27]

SOLUBILIZATION

Solubilization is one of the most important features of surfactant solutions and an essential question is to establish the site of solubilization for different types of solubilizates. Although a given solubilized molecule certainly as a function of time samples all different parts of the micelle, it can be shown that some solubilizates are mainly found in the interior of micelles and others close to the surface.[46,53,54] Alkanes belong to the former group while long-chain alcohols have their hydroxyl group close to the sufactant head-groups and the alkyl group towards the interior. For aromatic compounds it has been more difficult to establish the solubilization site, which may also vary with surfactant polar head. A very useful technique to study solubilization, based on "ring current" effects in NMR, was introduced by Eriksson and Gillberg[55] who demonstrated that certain aromatic compounds are mainly located in the head-group region of CTABr micelles. At high solubilizate concentrations, a location in the interior parts grows in importance. Solubilization of aromatic compounds in the interfacial region has been confirmed in recent studies using different spectroscopic approaches. [40,53,54]

Depending on solubilization site, solubilization is expected to have different effects on counterion binding, hydration and size and shape of micelles. Effects on the degree of counterion binding have been demonstrated to be small and complex and difficult to document. From diffusion studies,[56] β is approximately constant on solubilization of benzene, octanol and cyclohexane in CTABr solutions while there is a small increase in β on solubilization of decanol in sodium octanoate solutions. For $C_{12}SO_4Na$, β is approximately unchanged on solubilization of several different compounds and the same applies to sodium octylbenzenesulfonate, although significant complex effects can be inferred. For sodium decanoate solutions, Vikingstad[48,57] has recently made some interesting observations of β from ion activity measurements. He finds a small increase in β on solubilization of alkanes (C_8 and C_{10}) and a small decrease on solubilization of alkandiols, while with alkanols β is essentially constant. As an interpretation, one may suggest that alkane solubilization by increasing the nonpolar part permits the formation of somewhat larger spherical micelles which have a higher surfactant charge density while the diols by being located at the surface reduce this quantity.

As regards the influence of solubilization on hydration, we have very little information. For approximately spherical CTABr micelles, there is according to self-diffusion studies[56] a reduced hydration on solubilization of octanol and hexanol but not on solubilization of cyclohexane. According to ^2H NMR studies[58] on hexagonal mesophases of water and sodium octanoate or sodium octyl sulfate a more polar solubilizate decreases water bining while a nonpolar one give a small effect or an increase in water binding.

Some interesting observations on solubilization were recently reported by Vikingstad and Hoiland.[48,59] Firstly, the partial molar volumes and compressibilities of n-alkanes and n-alcohols in sodium alkanoate (C_8, C_{10}, C_{12}) micelles are higher than those in water but close to those in liquid alkanes and alcohols, respectively; and secondly, n-alcohols (and even more so n-alkandiols) are found to decrease the amphiphile ion activity while n-alkanes give a very slight increase in amphiphile ion activity. For the latter case, it may be that an increased repulsion between head-groups connected with a growth of spherical micelles (and thus a closer packing at the surface) outweighs the general stabilization of micelles due to solubilization.

The calculations presented in this symposium volume by Jönsson et al. on the preferred aggregate sizes have interesting implications for the understanding of the solubilization process. Not counting the entropy factor for the micellar aggregates, the radius corresponding to an extended chain corresponds roughly to the optimal aggregate size where the hydrophobic and electrostatic interactions balance each other. In such a case, there is little energy to be gained by transferring an alkane from the pure liquid into a micelle. Addition of an alcohol or of salt changes the balance between the two main interactions so that the micelles have a larger tendency to grow and thus a larger solubilizing capacity.

Solubilization may have a marked <u>influence on micelle size and shape</u> and may induce the formation of another phase, generally a lamellar liquid crystal. It seems that the growth of micelles to long rods is connected with solubilization in the head-group region, for example, the solubilization of alcohols or of aromatic compounds in CTABr solutions;[40,41,55] such solubilization may have very dramatic effects on rheological properties, for example, induce viscoelasticity.[40,60,61] Phase equilibria for three-component surfactant systems, which have a wide theoretical, biological and technical interest have been extensively studied by Ekwall, Fontell and Mandell (reviewed in Ref. 62). Their work shows qualitative features which are common to many systems but also that the extension of different phases may vary dramatically with subtle variations in chemical structure of the components. This leads to marked differences in many macroscopic properties and it is an important task of future research to examine to what extent differences at the molecular level exist between different systems as well as between different phases in a particular system. As will be argued below, there are astonishingly small differences in local molecular dynamics and interactions that accompany dramatic changes in aggregate geometry and macroscopic properties.

SIMILARITY IN MOLECULAR INTERACTIONS AND DYNAMICS BETWEEN DIFFERENT AGGREGATE STRUCTURES

In a three-component system, surfactant-water-solubilizate, several different phases with different aggregate geometry generally occur.[62] Structures include normal and reversed micelles, normal and reversed hexagonal phases, lamellar phase and different cubic phases which may have a rather complex structure. It is natural to consider amphiphile association as a continuously progressing process over most of the composition range and to try to elucidate the molecular background to the changes in aggregate structure by spectroscopic and other techniques. Several different molecular interactions and dynamic processes need to be considered and systematic studies of this problem are sparse. However, a number of observations reported in the literature tend to give an overall picture of quite small

changes in local molecular interactions and dynamics with changes in
aggregate geometry and size. We list here a few pertinent examples:

1) Counterion chemical shifts and quadrupole relaxation rates show
   regular changes at phase transitions, for example, micellar-to-
   reversed micellar and micellar-to-liquid crystal, demonstrating
   that the fraction of bound counterions as well as the instrinsic
   chemical shifts and relaxation rates of these are quite
   insensitive to phase structure.[33,63,64]

2) The factor of two change in counterion quadrupole splitting
   observed at transitions hexagonal-to-lamellar liquid crystal
   likewise demonstrates that the counterion association degree
   changes very little.[34]

3) The counterion association degree, from diffusion studies,
   changes very little at the sphere-to-rod transition of micelle
   shape.[14,31]

4) According to ^{2}H quadrupole splitting studies, aggregate hydration
   changes very little between hexagonal and lamellar phase.[65]

5) ^{13}C T_1 results indicate that the alkyl chain conformation does
   not change substantially between micellar solutions and lamellar
   phase[21] and similarly from ^{2}H order parameters there is no
   appreciable change between hexagonal and lamellar phase.[25]

6) The lateral diffusion coefficient of the amphiphile is approximately the same in different liquid crystalline phases[24] and
   ^{13}C T_1 data are consistent with a similar value in micelles as
   well.[21]

7) The orientation of amphiphile[13] and solubilizate[66] molecules has
   been observed to be closely the same in rod micelles and in
   hexagonal phase.

8) Enthalpy changes at phase transitions are small.[67]

MICROEMULSIONS

These points on the similarity between molecular interactions
and dynamics in different phases may be useful in considering so-
called microemulsions, i.e., isotropic solutions which may contain
at the same time high amounts of both water and a hydrocarbon (or
another non-polar compound). It seems appropriate in this context to
consider both the "surfactant phase" found in three-component
systems non-ionic surfactant-hydrocarbon-water,[68] classical microemulsions in four-component systems with ionic surfactant[69], and
also the very extensive solution regions found in some "atypical"

three-component systems like sodium octanoate-octanoic acid-water[70] and sodium cholate-decanol-water.[71] The most important aspects to consider seem to be the following:

1) <u>Thermodynamic stability.</u> Here the important work of Friberg for ionic systems and by Shinoda for non-ionic ones has clearly established that microemulsions are thermodynamically stable.[69,72] Theoretical work to further understand the background of the stability seems particularly important. It is then particularly necessary to consider the stability with respect to <u>alternative phases</u>, mainly the lamellar phase, which form under similar conditions in other systems.

2) <u>Aggregate structure.</u> Progress here has been slow because of a lack of suitable experimental methods; many experimental techniques which work well for micellar solutions cannot be used for typical microemulsions because of strong interaggregate interactions at the high aggregate concentrations which are of particular interest. Interesting work on this problem has been presented <u>inter alia</u> by Shinoda[68,69,73], Friberg[69,72,74], Taupin[75] and co-workers, Scriven[76], Ruckenstein[77] and Talmon and Prager[78]; however, the views differ considerably due to in sufficient experimental information. Shinoda considers a lamellar-type structure with both water and hydrocarbon layers, while Friberg and Scriven consider more indefinite geometries of the hydrophilic-hydrophobic interface. Talmon and Prager discuss small hydrophobic and hydrophilic polyhedra which are randomly arranged. Taupin considers small water droplets in a hydrocarbon continuum with a transition to a water continuous structure at high water contents. To account for quite high conductivity well below the transition, she proposes a "percolation" mechanism taken from solid state physics. In Talmon and Prager's approach the high conductivity results from the statistical creation of extended water paths through random interchange of the hydrophilic and hydrophobic regions.

The differences between different authors are to a considerable extent only apparent, resulting from different starting points to the problem. Certain treatments[72,73] refer directly to amphiphile aggregation in other parts of the phase diagram and it seems that the above description gives very strong arguments in favour of such a view. Most authors suppose that there is a quite distinct separation of hydrophobic and hydrophilic domains, i.e. that one has hard sphere water droplets. This description has been shown to apply with good approximation for surfactant systems where the third component is a hydrocarbon or a long-chain alcohol[51] but is more questionable for typical microemulsion systems with a short-chain alcohol like pentanol or butanol; the solubility of these in aqueous domains can probably not be neglected. We will return to this below.

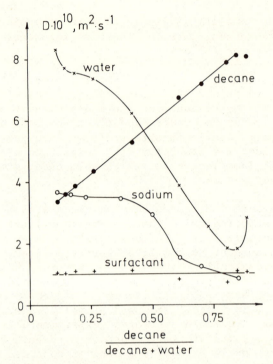

Figure 5. Both water, hydrocarbon and counterion ion self-diffusion are rapid over wise composition ranges for four-component systems surfactant-cosurfactant-hydrocarbon-water. Data for the system sodium octylbenzenesulfonate-pentanol-decane-water-sodium chloride. For further information see Ref. 79 from where the figure is taken.

In attempts to shed some light on microemulsion structure, tracer self-diffusion studies have been undertaken in collaboration with N. Kamenka and B. Brun in Montpellier. Self-diffusion coefficients of surfactant (subscript a), water (w), counterion (c) and hydrocarbon (s) were determined. For solutions of normal micelles, being water- but not hydrocarbon-continuous, one finds [28-31] generally $D_w > D_c \gg D_a > D_s \simeq D_{micelle}$, while for typical reversed micellar solutions, being oil- but not water-continuous, one finds [51] $D_s > D_a \gg D_w > D_c \simeq D_{micelle}$. For the system sodium octylbenzene-sulfonate-decane-pentanol-sodium chloride-water, a "typical" ionic surfactant microemulsion system, one finds over wide composition ranges rapid diffusion of water, hydrocarbon and counterion (cf. Figure 5).[79] NMR self-diffusion studies on several systems have confirmed this picture. [80] There seem to be two possible explanations for these findings, or perhaps best a combination of these, i.e.,

a) microemulsions are bicontinuous, i.e. both water and
   oil-continuous,
b) the internal interfaces are easily deformable or otherwise not
   well-defined.

3) <u>Molecular structure and dynamics of internal interfaces</u>. It
follows directly from several points above that an intriguing
problem concerns a detailed characterization on a molecular level
of the internal interfaces. One needs to know then local order
parameters and correlation times as well as distribution of the
different components over the water and hydrocarbon regions.
Experimental studies of these aspects should be able to tell to
what extent the presence of short-chain alcohol as co-surfactant
influences the internal interfaces and thus be rewarding in attempts
to understand the general basis of microemulsion formation.

It is not possible to discuss these matters further here but we
should like to round off with a few ideas on microemulsions. In our
opinion typical microemulsions consist of aggregates which are not
well-defined either geometrically or as regards to component distribution. Eicke[81,82] has presented evidence for the presence of
badly defined aggregates. Badly defined flexible aggregates, which
are easily opened up and fuse together would explain the rapid
transport of ions and water molecules. Such a picture of easily
deformable aggregates is also consistent with the low viscosities
observed and with the narrow lines in proton NMR spectra, most
significant observations for microemulsions. NMR studies show that
the linewidths are small indicating the surfactant molecules do not
experience a particularly ordered structure extending over larger
distances (unpublished work).

Thus we are led to the tentative conclusion that in the typical
microemulsion region there is
   i) polydispersity in "aggregate" size
  ii) polydispersity in "aggregate" shape
 iii) relatively low order at the polar - apolar "interface"
  iv) rapid changes in aggregate size and shape.
As a consequence of this there sould be a very rapid transfer of
molecules and ions between different aggregates which is in line
with the diffusion results. As one approaches either the water-rich
region with normal micelles or the water-poor region with inverted
micelles there occurs a gradual change to more well-defined
aggregates in the system.

ACKNOWLEDGMENTS

This article reviews results obtained in collaboration with several persons in Lund and elsewhere (see reference list). In particular B.L. wants to acknowledge the fruitful collaboration with B. Brun, H. Fabre, N. Kamenka in Montpellier on self-diffusion studies of surfactant association. This work was supported in part by travel grants from Centre National de la Recherche Scientifique and project grants from the Swedish Natural Sciences Research Council.

REFERENCES

1. H. Wennerström and B. Lindman, Phys. Reports, $\underline{52}$, 1 (1979).
2. B. Lindman and H. Wennerström,"Topics in Current Chemistry", $\underline{87}$, 1, (1980).
3. E.A.G. Aniansson and S.N. Wall, J.Phys.Chem., $\underline{78}$, 1024 (1974).
4. E.A.G. Aniansson, S.N. Wall, M Almgren, H. Hoffman, I. Kielmann, W. Ulbricht, R. Zana, J. Lang and C. Tondre, J. Phys. Chem., $\underline{80}$, 905 (1976).
5. K. Shinoda, T. Nakagawa, B.-I. Tamamushi and T. Isemura, "Colloidal Surfactants, Some Physico-Chemical Properties", Academic Press, New York, 1963.
6. C. Tanford, "The Hydrophobic Effect", John Wiley, New York, 1973.
7. P. Mukerjee and K.J. Mysels, "Critical Micelle Concentrations of Aqueous Surfactant Systems", NSRDS-NBS-36, Washington, D.C., 1971.
8. F. Reiss-Husson and V. Luzzati, J. Phys. Chem., $\underline{68}$, 3504 (1964).
9. P. Ekwall, L.Mandell and P. Solyom, J. Colloid Interface Sci., $\underline{35}$, 519 (1971).
10. N. A. Mazer, G.B. Benedek and M.C. Carey, J. Phys. Chem., $\underline{80}$, 1075 (1976).
11. C. Y. Young, P.J. Missel, N. A. Mazer, G.B. Benedek and M.C. Carey, J. Phys. Chem., $\underline{82}$, 1375 (1978).
12. P. J. Missel, N. A. Mazer, G. B. Benedek, C. Y. Young and M. C. Carey, J. Phys. Chem., $\underline{84}$, 1044 (1980).
13. J. Ulmius and H. Wennerström, J. Magn. Resonance, $\underline{28}$, 309 (1977).
14. H. Fabre, N. Kamenka, A. Khan, G. Lindblom, B. Lindman and G. J. T. Tiddy, to be published.
15. I. Danielsson and P. Stenius, J. Colloid Interface Sci., $\underline{37}$, 264 (1971); P. Stenius, Thesis, Åbo, 1973.
16. B. O. Persson, T. Drakenberg and B. Lindman, J. Phys. Chem., $\underline{83}$, 3011 (1979).

17. P. Mukerjee, J. Phys., Chem., 76, 565 (1972).
18. E. A. G. Aniansson, J. Phys. Chem., 82, 2805 (1978).
19. G. S. Hartley, J. Chem. Soc., 1938, 1968.
20. B. O. Persson, T. Drakenberg and B. Lindman, J. Phys. Chem., 80, 2124 (1976).
21. H. Wennerström, B. Lindman, O. Söderman, T. Drakenberg and J. B. Rosenholm, J. Am. Chem. Soc., 101, 6860 (1979).
22. Å. Johansson and B. Lindman in "Liquid Crystals and Plastic Crystals", G. W. Gray and P. A. Winsor, Eds., Vol. 2, p. 192, Ellis Horwood, Chichester, England, 1974.
23. J. Charvolin and P. Rigny, J. Chem. Phys., 58, 3999 (1973).
24. G. Lindblom and H. Wennerström, Biophys. Chem., 6, 167 (1977).
25. U. Henriksson, L. Odberg and J. C. Eriksson, Mol. Cryst. Liq. Cryst., 30, 73 (1975); T. Klasson, personal communication.
26. T. S. Brun, H. Hoiland and E. Vikingstad, J. Colloid Interface Sci., 63, 89 (1978).
27. G. Gunnarsson, B. Jönsson and H. Wennerström, J. Phys. Chem. in press; B. Jönsson, G. Gunnarsson and H. Wennerström, to be published.
28. B. Lindman and B. Brun, J. Colloid Interface Sci., 42, 388 (1973).
29. N. Kamenka, B. Brun and B. Lindman, Tr.-Mezhdunar Kongr. Poverkhn.-Akt. Veshchestvam., 7th 1976 2(II), 1019 (1978).
30. N. Kamenka, M. Chorro, H. Fabre, B. Lindman, J. Rouviere and C. Cabos, Colloid Polymer Sci., 257, 757 (1979).
31. H. Fabre, Thesis, USTL, Montpellier, 1980.
32. E. Vikingstad, A. Skauge and H. Høiland, J. Colloid Interface Sci., 66, 240 (1978).
33. B. Lindman, G. Lindblom, H. Wennerström and H. Gustavsson, in "Micellization, Solubilization and Microemulsions", K. L. Mittal, Ed., Vol. 1, p. 195, Plenum Press, New York, 1977.
34. B. Lindblom, H. Wennerström and B. Lindman, ACS Symposium Ser. 34, 372 (1976).
35. H. Gustavsson and B. Lindman, J. Am. Chem. Soc., 100, 4647 (1978).
36. H. Wennerström, B. Lindman, S. Engström, O. Söderman, G. Lindblom and G. J. T. Tiddy in "Magnetic Resonance in Colloid and Interface Science", J. P. Fraissard and H. A. Resing, Eds., D. Reidel, Dordrecht, in press.
37. H. Wennerström, B. Lindman, G. Lindblom and G. J. T. Tiddy, J. C. S. Faraday I, 75, 663 (1979).
38. P. Stilbs, J. Jermer and B. Lindman, J. Colloid Interface, 60, 232 (1977).
39. F. Oosawa, "Polyelectrolytes", Marcel Dekker, New York, 1971; G. S. Manning, Ann. Rev. Phys. Chem., 23, 117 (1972).
40. J. Ulmius, B. Lindman, G. Lindblom and T. Drakenberg, J. Colloid Interface Sci., 65, 88 (1978).
41. G. Lindblom, B. Lindman and L. Mandell, J. Colloid Interface Sci., 42, 400 (1973).

42. B. Lindman, H. Wennerström, H. Gustavsson, N. Kamenka and
     B. Brun, Pure Applied Chem., $\underline{52}$, 1307 (1980).
43. H. Wennerström and B. Lindman, J. Phys. Chem., $\underline{83}$, 2931 (1979).
44. P. Mukerjee, J. Colloid Sci., $\underline{19}$, 722 (1964).
45. N. O. Persson and B. Lindman, J. Phys. Chem., $\underline{79}$, 1410 (1975).
46. P. Mukerjee, J. R. Cardinal and N. R. Desai, in "Micellization,
     Solubilization, and Microemulsions"; K. L. Mittal, Ed., Vol. 1,
     p. 241, Plenum Press, New York, 1977.
47. D. Stigter, J. Phys. Chem., $\underline{78}$, 2480 (1974).
48. E. Vikingstad, Thesis, University of Bergen, 1980.
49. J. Ulmius and B. Lindman, unpublished study.
50. F. Podo, A. Ray and G. Némethy, J. Am. Chem. Soc., $\underline{95}$, 6164
     (1973).
51. H. Fabre, N. Kamenka and B. Lindman, to be published.
52. J. Andrasko and S. Forsén, Biochem. Biophys. Res. Commun.,
     $\underline{60}$, 813 (1974).
53. P. Mukerjee, Pure Applied Chem., $\underline{52}$, 1317 (1980).
54. P. Mukerjee, in "Solution Chemistry of Surfactants", K. L.
     Mittal, Ed., Vol. 1, p. 153, Plenum Press, New York, 1979.
55. J. C. Eriksson and G. Gillberg, Acta Chem. Scand., $\underline{20}$, 2019
     (1966).
56. N. Kamenka, H. Fabre, M. Chorro and B. Lindman, J. Chim. Phys.,
     $\underline{74}$, 510 (1977).
57. E. Vikingstad, J. Colloid Interface Sci., $\underline{73}$, 260 (1980).
58. N. O. Persson and B. Lindman, Mol. Cryst. Liquid Cryst., $\underline{38}$,
     327 (1977).
59. E. Vikingstad and H. Høiland, J. Colloid Interface Sci., $\underline{64}$,
     510 (1978); E. Vikingstad, J. Colloid Interface Sci., $\underline{64}$, 287
     (1979).
60. S. Gravsholt, J. Colloid Interface Sci., $\underline{57}$, 575 (1976).
61. J. Ulmius, H. Wennerström, L. Johansson, G. Lindblom and
     S. Gravsholt, J. Phys. Chem., $\underline{83}$, 2232 (1979).
62. P. Ekwall, Adv. Liquid Cryst., $\underline{1}$, 1 (1975).
63. H. Gustavsson, G. Lindblom, B. Lindman, N. O. Persson and
     H. Wennerström in "Liquid Crystals and Ordered Fluids", J. F.
     Johnson and R. S. Porter, Eds., Vol. 2, P. 161, Plenum Press,
     New York, 1974.
64. B. Lindman and P. Ekwall, Mol. Cryst. $\underline{5}$, 79 (1968).
65. H. Wennerström, N.-O. Persson and B. Lindman in "Colloidal
     Dispersions and Micellar Behavior," K. L. Mittal, Ed., pp. 253-
     269, ACS Symposium Ser. No. 9, American Chemical Society,
     Washington, D. C., 1975.   "
66. U. Henriksson, T. Klasson, L. Odberg and J. C. Eriksson, Chem.
     Phys. Lett., $\underline{52}$, 554 (1977).
67. J. B. Rosenholm, M. R. Hakala and P. Stenius, Mol. Cryst. Liq.
     Cryst., $\underline{45}$, 285 (1978).
68. K. Shinoda and H. Saito, J. Colloid Interface Sci., $\underline{26}$, 70
     (1968).
69. K. Shinoda and S. Friberg, Adv. Colloid Interface Sci., $\underline{4}$,
     281 (1975).

70. P. Ekwall and L. Mandell, Kolloid-Z.Z. Polym., 233, 938 (1969).
71. K. Fontell, Kolloid-Z.Z. Polym., 250, 825 (1972).
72. S. Friberg in "Microemulsions", L. M. Prince, Ed., p. 133, Academic Press, New York, 1977.
73. H. Saito and K. Shinoda, J. Colloid Interface Sci., 32, 647 (1970).
74. S. Friberg, I. Lapczynska and G. Gillberg, J. Colloid Interface Sci., 56, 19 (1976).
75. M. Laguës, R. Ober and C. Taupin, J. de Physique Lettres, 39, 487 (1978).
76. L. E. Scriven in "Micellization, Solubilization, and Micro-emulsions:, K. L. Mittal, Ed., Vol. 2, p. 877, Plenum Press, New York, 1977.
77. E. Ruckenstein, Chem. Phys. Lett., 57, 517 (1978).
78. Y. Talmon and S. Prager, J. Chem. Phys., 69, 2984 (1978).
79. B. Lindman, N. Kamenka, T.-M. Kathopoulis, B. Brun and P.-G. Nilsson, J. Phys. Chem., in press.
80. P. Stilbs, M. E. Moseley and B. Lindman, J. Magn. Resonance, in press and unpublished results.
81. M. Zulauf and H.-F. Eicke, J. Phys. Chem., 83, 480 (1979).
82. H.-F. Eicke, Pure Appl. Chem., 52, 1349 (1980).

HYDROPHOBIC INTERACTIONS, AN OVERVIEW

Arieh Y. Ben-Naim*
Bell Telephone Laboratories
Murray Hill, New Jersey 07974

Hydrophobic interaction is basically a potential
function that governs the attraction (or repulsion)
between two (or more) solute particles in aqueous
solutions. A variety of simple model-systems have
been suggested to study the nature of these interactions.
There exists today a considerable amount of information
on the effect of temperature, pressure and addition of
solutes on the strength of the hydrophobic interactions.
Unfortunately there are many discrepancies between the
results obtained by the different methods. Some of
the models used in the study of the hydrophobic interactions are described and their relevance to the understanding of the micellization processes are discussed.

The term "Hydrophobic Interactions" (HI) has been used in the
biochemical literature to describe a variety of biochemical
processes such as conformational changes of biopolymers, the
binding of a substrate to an enzyme, the association of subunits
to form a multisubunit enzyme, the formation of membranes and
higher order of organization of biological molecules to form a
functional unit in a living system. [1-4]

---

*Permanent address: Department of Physical Chemistry,
the Hebrew University of Jerusalem, Jerusalem, Israel

All of these processes have two features in common. They
all involve the association of a number of nonpolar molecules, or
groups within larger molecules, and they all occur in aqueous
media·   Of course every <u>real</u> biochemical process is very complex
in the sense that many factors combine to determine their rate and
equilibrium constants. We shall focus our attention on one of
these factors: the so-called HI.

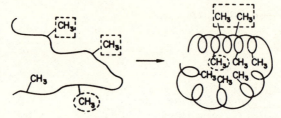

Figure 1.   A schematic description of a conformational change of a
biopolymer. One methyl group (circled) is transferred from an
essentially aqueous environment to the interior of the polymer.
Two methyl groups (in squares) approach each other and form a
"Dimer."

Figure 1 shows a schematic conformational change of a biopolymer; from a random coil form to a more compact form. Ignoring,
for the moment, all other factors that are involved in this
process, we focus our attention on the relocation of the side-
chain non-polar groups. Specifically, we find that some of these
groups have been transferred from an essentially aqueous environment into the interior of the biopolymer. This process is demonstrated by the methyl group which is encircled in Figure 1. Another typical process, also indicated in this Figure, is the
association of two methyl groups, i.e. they are far apart in one
conformation, and are brought close together in the final conformation.

In order to study the relative importance of these processes
it was found necessary to isolate them and study their thermodynamics in model systems [1-5] The appropriate model for the first
process was the transfer of a non-polar solute from water into a
non-polar solvent. The standard free energy of this simple
process provides an idea of the magnitude of one of the contributions to the driving force for the conformational change, depicted
in Figure 1. This model has been discussed extensively in the
literature and will not be discussed any further here [4]. We proceed next to the "dimerization" process that is indicated in
Figure 1. An appropriate "model system" for this case is not easy
to find. Of course there have been many studies of dimerization
equilibria of various solutes (e.g. carbocyclic acids) in water.
However those solutes, for which the study of the dimerization

equilibria is feasible, always contain some polar functional group. Therefore, the extraction of the contribution due to the non-polar groups to, say, the equilibrium constant, is not simple.

In what follows we shall describe two experimental methods of studying the thermodynamics of the HI, i.e. the process of "dimerization" between two simple non-polar solutes in water.

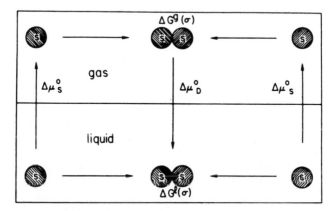

Figure 2. A cyclic process leading to equation (2). Two solutes S are brought from infinite separation to a small separation σ within the liquid. The corresponding free energy change is $\Delta G^1(\sigma)$. The second route is first to transfer the two solutes to the gaseous phase, then bring them to the separation σ, and finally introduce the "dimer" into the liquid.

We start by referring to Figure 2. The fundamental process in which we are interested is the one shown in the liquid phase. Namely, two solute molecules are brought from an initial state, when their distance is $R = \infty$, to a final state in which they are at $R \approx \sigma$, σ being roughly the molecular diameter of the solute particles. The free energy change for this process (carried out within the solvent at some specified temperature T and pressure P) is

$$\Delta G(\sigma) = G(T,P,N;R=\sigma) - G(T,P,N:R=\infty) \qquad (1)$$

In order to relate $\Delta G(\sigma)$ to experimentally measurable quantities we use either some elementary statistical mechanical arguments, or use the cyclic process as depicted in Figure 2. Clearly, since the change of free energy along the two routes must be the same we have the equality

$$\Delta G(\sigma) = \Delta \mu_D^0 - 2\Delta \mu_S^0 + U(R=\sigma) \qquad (2)$$

where U(R) is the direct interaction energy between the two solute particles, and $\Delta \mu_D^o$ and $\Delta \mu_S^o$ are the standard free energies of solution of the "dimer" and of the monomer respectively. We next define the indirect part of the free energy change by

$$\delta G^{HI}(\sigma) = \Delta G(\sigma) - U(R=\sigma) \quad (3)$$

This quantity will be referred to as the solvent-induced interaction, or simply the HI between the pair of solute molecules at a distance R = σ. Combining (2) and (3) we obtain the useful relation

$$\delta G^{HI}(\sigma) = \Delta \mu_D^o - 2\Delta \mu_S^o \quad (4)$$

The importance of this relation is that it connects our quantity of interest, δG^{HI}, with two, almost-measurable, quantities. Clearly $\Delta \mu_S^o$ is measurable for a real solute S. On the other hand $\Delta \mu_D^o$ is only formally the standard free energy of solution of the "dimer". But a "dimer", formed by two solutes at R = σ, is not a real solute, hence we cannot obtain $\Delta \mu_D^o$ from experiments. In order to proceed from Equation (4) we note that the quantity $\delta G^{HI}(\sigma)$ is independent of the direct, solute-solute interaction. (This was eliminated explicitly in (3)). Therefore we can modify Equation (4), by replacing the contact distance σ by the distance σ_1 = 1.53 A which is the carbon-carbon distance in ethane. With this modification, relation (4) may be transformed into an approximate relation.[4]

$$\delta G^{HI}(\sigma_1) \simeq \Delta \mu_{Et}^o - 2\Delta \mu_{Me}^o \quad (5)$$

Where on the rhs of (5) we have the standard free energies of solution of ethane and methane, two quantities that are available from experimental sources.

Figure 3 shows δG^{HI} in water and in some non-aqueous solvent as a function of the temperature. It is clear that there are two prominent differences between water and all the other liquids (for which the relevant experimental data is available). In the first place the absolute magnitude of $\delta G^{HI}(\sigma_1)$ is larger in water than in all the other solvents. (This, of course, does not exclude the possibility that other solvents, not represented in this Figure, would not exhibit even a larger value of δG^{HI}). Note also that the typical difference, say between water and ethanol at 25°C is about 0.5 kcal/mol, which is of the order of magnitude of kT at this temperature. This implies that a pair of methane molecules in water is expected to spend, on the average, more time being close to each other than in the other liquids (provided that the temperature, T, the pressure, P, and the solute density ρ_S, are the same in the various solvents). This is another way of describing the phenomenon of HI.

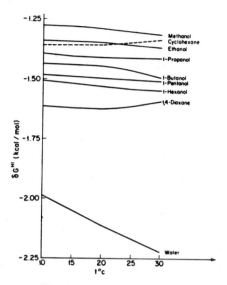

Figure 3.   Values of $\delta G^{HI}(\sigma_1)$ as a function of temperature, for two methane molecules in various solvents.

The second important difference between water and all the other solvents shown in Figure 3 is the temperature dependence of $\delta G^{HI}(\sigma_1)$. We observe that in all of the non-aqueous solvents the temperature dependence of $\delta G^{HI}(\sigma_1)$ is very small, whereas in water we find a clear-cut large and negative slope of $\delta G^{HI}(\sigma_1)$ as a function of temperature. Thermodynamically this is equivalent to a large <u>positive</u> entropy change associated with the HI-process, which in turn may be interpreted as arising from the breakdown in the structure of water. Some characteristic values of δG^{HI}, δS^{HI} and δH^{HI} are shown in Table I.

Table I.   Values of $\delta G^{HI}(\sigma_1)$, $\delta S^{HI}(\sigma_1)$, $\delta H^{HI}(\sigma_1)$ for Bringing Two Methane Molecules to the Separation $\sigma_1 = 1.533$ Å at 10°C.

Solvent	δG^{HI} (kcal/mol)	δS^{HI} (cal/mol deg)	δH^{HI} (kcal/mol)
Water	-1.99	12	1.40
Heavy water	-1.94	13	1.74
Methanol	-1.28	0	-1.3
Ethanol	-1.34	0	-1.3
1-Propanol	-1.39	2	-0.8
1-Butanol	-1.44	-1	-1.7
1-Pentanol	-1.49	0	-1.5
1-Hexanol	-1.51	2	-0.9
1,4-Dioxane	-1.61	3	-0.8
Cyclohexane	-1.36	1	-1.1

To the best of our knowledge the quantity δG^{HI} as defined
above is the only experimental measure of the HI between two
simple non-polar solutes. It is true though, that the distance at
which the HI is measured is not a physically realizable one. Hence
δG^{HI} is not directly related to the probability of finding two real
methane molecules at any realizable distance. However, from a
theoretical point of view δG^{HI} is still a useful quantity,
especially for comparing the strength of the HI in various solvents.
In addition this is a convenient "experimental" quantity with which
one can compare theoretically computed values of the HI.

We now turn to a second measure of the HI, which as will be
explained below, may be better referred to as an intramolecular HI
(IHI). The most important feature of the new measure is its relevance to the HI between two groups at more realizable distances.

Consider a "carrier" molecule, such as benzene, naphthalene
etc., and two alkyl chains at large separation from each other, say
the 1,4 dialkylbenzene. We now perform a "thought experiment".
We "cut" the molecule into four radicals; a phenyl, two alkyl and
one hydrogen atom. The exact location of the "cut" and its energetics will not concern us here, since in our final expression we
shall recombine the radicals and form a real molecule. For convenience we shall assume that the "cut" is done at the center of
the C-C and the C-H bonds. The process we shall be concerned with
is depicted in Figure 4. Namely, we start with the solute at a

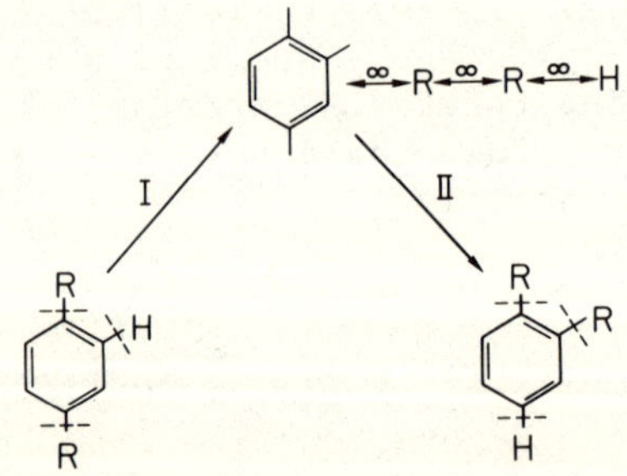

Figure 4. I is a schematic process of breaking 1,4-dialkylbenzene
into four radicals: benzyl ring ϕ, two alkyl groups R, and a hydrogen atom H. These radicals are recombined in process II to
form the new molecule 1,2-dialkylbenzene. In the intermediate
stage all the radicals are at fixed configurations and at infinite
separation from each other.

fixed position and orientation in the solvent (for simplicity we
assume that the molecule as a whole is rigid. Otherwise we should
take averages over all possible conformations of the molecule).

Having cut the molecule into four radicals we remove them to fixed
locations and orientation but at infinite separation from each
other. The process is carried out within the solvent at some
fixed temperature T and pressure P. Next we recombine the four
radicals to form a new isomer, namely the 1,2-dialkylbenzene, as
indicated in Figure 4. The net free energy change associated with
the entire process may be written, using classical statistical
mechanics, as

$$\exp\{-\beta\Delta G[(1,4)\rightarrow(1,2)]\} = \exp\{-\beta[U(1,2)-U(1,4)]\} \times$$

$$\frac{<\exp[-\beta B(1,2)]>_o}{<\exp[-\beta B(1,4)]>_o} \tag{6}$$

where the first factor includes the total change of the energy in
the process. Since we may assume that all the bond energies in
the two isomers are the same, we may simplify this term into

$$U(1,2) - U(1,4) = U_{RR}(1,2) - U_{RR}(1,4) \tag{7}$$

where U_{RR} is the direct alkyl-alkyl interaction energy at the
specified configuration. The quantity $B(1,2)$ is the "binding
energy", or the solute-solvent interaction of the solute (1,2)
with all the solvent molecules at some specific configuration X^N.
The average $< >_o$ is over all the configurations of the solvent
molecules, and over all possible volumes, in the T, P, N ensemble.

We may now identify each of the average quantities on the rhs
of (6), with the corresponding standard free energy of solution,
namely

$$\Delta \mu_{1,2}^o = - kT \ln<\exp[-\beta B(1,2)]>_o \tag{8}$$

and rewrite (6) as

$$\Delta G[(1,4)\rightarrow(1,2)] = U_{RR}(1,2) - U_{RR}(1,4) \tag{9}$$

$$+ \Delta \mu_{1,2}^o - \Delta \mu_{1,4}^o$$

Again, since we are interested in the indirect, or in the solvent
contribution to ΔG of the process, we define the following quantity

$$\delta G^{HI}[(1,4)\rightarrow(1,2)] = \Delta G[(1,4)\rightarrow(1,2)] - \Delta U[(1,4)\rightarrow(1,2)]$$

$$= \Delta \mu_{1,2}^o - \Delta \mu_{1,4}^o \tag{10}$$

The remarkable feature of the last relation is that it enable us to compute the HI between the two alkyl groups from experimentally determinable quantities. Note that since the benzene ring is present during the entire exchange process, the quantity δG^{HI} may not be identified as the HI between the two alkyl groups in the solvent. The more appropriate description would be the conditional HI, where the condition is the presence of the benzyl radical. Alternatively we may refer to δG^{HI} define in (10) as the intramolecular HI.

The basic idea of using a model for an IHI is that in biopolymer we do have two alkyl groups, mounted on a "carrier", which may be far apart in one conformation and at close distance in another conformation. In this case we certainly may talk about IHI. The model system used above only reduces the complexity of the process, by choosing a relatively simple carrier, which is assumed to be unaffected by the process.

Note also that a realization of the form (10) may not be obtained by purely thermodynamical arguments. Although free energies of processes are involved on the two sides of the equation, the process of transferring an alkyl group from one position to another (the molecule as a whole is devoid of translational and rotational freedom) is a molecular process not a macroscopic process. Thus δG^{HI} is essentially a molecular quantity, which through relation (10) is computable from experimentally measurable quantities.

We now present some numerical examples where relation (10) has been used to compute δG^{HI}. First we present in Table II some results for dialkylbenzene. Because of difficulties in synthesis we have results only for the methyl and the ethyl derivatives.

Table II. Values of the Indirect Part of the Work Required to Transfer an Alkyl Group from Position 4 to Position 2 at Two Temperatures.

Alkyl group	$t(°C)$	$\delta G^{HI}[(1,4) \to (1,2)]$ (cal/mol) in water	$\delta G^{HI}[(1,4) \to (1,2)]$ (cal/mol) in n-hexane
Methyl	10	−238	+69
	20	−300	−28
Ethyl	10	−603	+359
	20	−616	+445

The Figures for δG^{HI} [(1,4)$\to$(1,2)] in n-hexane are either positive or very small (and probably within the limits of the experimental error). On the other hand, in water we find a negative value of δG^{HI}, which seem to increase with the chain length of the alkyl group. [A value of the order of kT is important for a reinterpretation of δG^{HI} in terms of probabilities, this will be discussed below]. Note also that $|\delta G^{HI}|$ in water slightly increases with the temperature, a behavior which is consistent with previous conclusions on the temperature dependence of the HI.

We now turn to reinterpret the values in Table II in terms of probabilities of certain events.

Suppose we have a dialkylbenzene molecule at some fixed position and orientation in the solvent. Let us fix one alkyl group at position 1, and assume that the second group can attain either position 2 or position 4 (more precisely the assumption is made that the second alkyl group can exchange positions with the hydrogen atom at either position 2 or position 4). We may now ask: what is the ratio of the probabilities of finding the second group in these two positions. The general relation between probabilities and free energies is

$$\frac{P(2)}{P(4)} = \exp[-\beta U_{RR}(1,2)+\beta U_{RR}(1,4)]$$

$$\exp[-\beta\delta G^{HI}[(1,4)\to(1,2)]] \qquad (11)$$

However, since we are interested only in the solvent contribution to this ratio we define

$$\frac{y(2)}{y(4)} = \exp[-\beta\delta G^{HI}((1,4)\to(1,2))] \qquad (12)$$

The quantity in (12) may also be interpreted as the ratio of the ratios of the probabilities of the two events in the liquid relative to the gaseous phase, namely

$$\frac{y(2)}{y(4)} = \left[\frac{P(2)}{P(4)}\right]^{\ell} \left[\frac{P(2)}{P(4)}\right]^{g} \qquad (13)$$

Clearly by dividing by $[P(2)/P(4)]^g$ we have eliminated the contribution due to the direct interactions between the two alkyl groups.

Table III shows the values of $y(2)/y(4)$ that correspond to the same cases as in Table II. We see that the entries for n-hexane are either close to unity or smaller than unity, indicating a relative preference of the (1,4) configuration in this solvent.

Table III. Ratios of the (Solvent-Induced) Probabilities of
Finding an Alkyl Group in Positions 2 and 4 in a Molecule with a
Fixed Alkyl Group at Position 1.

Aklyl group	t(°C)	y(2)/y(4) in water	y(2)/y(4) in n-hexane
Methyl	10	1.527	0.885
	20	1.675	1.049
Ethyl	10	2.924	0.528
	20	2.878	0.465

On the other hand, in water there is a clear-cut preference for
the (1,2) configuration. For the ethyl radical the (1,2) configuration is about three times more probable than the (1,4) configuration [more precisely this is only the solvent contribution to
the relative probabilities]. Note also that for the ethyl radical
the probability ratio slightly decreases with the increase in the
temperature, whereas from Table II we have seen that $|\delta G^{HI}|$
increases with temperature. The reason becomes clear if we write
the relation between δG^{HI} and y(2)/y(4), namely

$$\delta G^{HI} = - kT \ln[y(2)/y(4)] \tag{14}$$

Hence the temperature coefficient of δG^{HI} has two contributions:

$$\frac{\partial \, \delta G^{HI}}{\partial T} = - k \ln[y(2)/y(4)] - kT \frac{\partial}{\partial T} \ln[y(2)/y(4)] \tag{15}$$

These terms correspond to the entropy and the enthalpy change, for
the HI-process, namely

$$\delta S^{HI} = - \frac{\partial \, \delta G^{HI}}{\partial T} \tag{16}$$

$$\delta H^{HI} = \delta G^{HI} + T \delta S^{HI} \tag{17}$$

An estimate of δS^{HI} and δG^{HI} for the ethyl radical, between the two
temperatures shows that

$$\delta S^{HI} = - \frac{\partial \, \delta G^{HI}}{\partial T} \simeq + 1.3 \text{ e.u} \tag{18}$$

$$\delta H^{HI} = kT \frac{\partial}{\partial T} \ln[y(2)/y(4)] \stackrel{\sim}{\sim} - 225 \text{ cal/mol} \qquad (19)$$

we see that the <u>total</u> temperature dependence of δG^{HI} is related to the entropy change, whereas the temperature dependence of the probabilities is connected with the enthalpy change for the process. In this particular example we see that δS^{HI} and δH^{HI} have opposite signs, though their magnitudes are quite small and might be well within the experimental error.

Before turning to other molecular models for measuring IHI it is instructive to note that the same experimental data may be processed in a slightly different way. We refer to Figure 5 where two disproportionation reactions are shown. The molecular "reactions" are the exchange of an alkyl group from one monoalkyl-benze, with a hydrogen atom on a second molecule, to form a dialkyl-benzene and a benzene molecule. These reactions are "thought experiments" in the sense that they are carried out between a pair of molecules <u>fixed</u> in their locations and orientations, but far apart from each other.

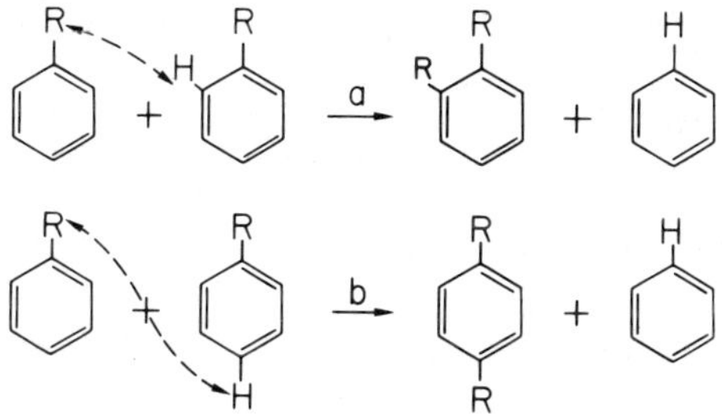

Figure 5. Two disproportionation reactions: In (a) two monoalkyl-benzenes are used to form a 1,2-dialkylbenzene and a benzene mole-cule. In (b) a 1,4-dialkylbenzene and benzene are formed from the same initial molecules.

Using a similar argument, as the one used to obtain relation (10), we get for the two "reactions" in Figure 5 the following expressions for the indirect parts of the total free energy changes,

$$\delta G^{HI}(a) = \Delta \mu^{o}(1,2) + \Delta \mu^{o}(B) - 2\Delta \mu^{o}(\psi-R) \qquad (20)$$

$$\delta G^{HI}(b) = \Delta \mu^{o}(1,4) + \Delta \mu^{o}(B) - 2\Delta \mu^{o}(\psi-R) \qquad (21)$$

Table IV. Values of $\delta G^{HI}(a)$ and $\delta G^{HI}(b)$ (in kcal/mol) as Defined
in Equations (20) and (21), respectively.

Aklyl group	t(°C)	In water		In n-hexane	
		$\delta G^{HI}(a)$	$\delta G^{HI}(b)$	$\delta G^{HI}(a)$	$\delta G^{HI}(b)$
Methyl	10	−0.205	+0.033	+0.007	−0.062
	20	−0.276	+0.024	+0.040	+0.068
Ethyl	10	−0.619	−0.016	−0.160	−0.411
	20	−0.609	+0.007	+0.304	−0.141

In Table IV we present values of $\delta G^{HI}(a)$ and $\delta G^{HI}(b)$ for the reactions (20) and (21). Perhaps the most important finding is that
for the ethyl radical reaction (a) is more favorable in water,
whereas in n-Hexane reaction (b) is the more favorable one. This
is again a different manifestation of the IHI.

A slightly similar model for measuring the IHI is the dialkoxynaphthalene molecule, where the two alkoxy groups are at
positions (2,3) and 2,7) respectively. We have used this as well
as the previous model to examine the difference in IHI in light
and heavy water. The results are shown in Table V. We see that
all the results for $\Delta \delta G^{HI} = \delta G^{HI}(D_2O) - \delta G^{HI}(H_2O)$ are positive.

Table V. Values of the Difference of the HI Between Light and
Heavy Water

$$\Delta \delta G^{HI} = \delta G^{HI}(D_2O) - \delta G^{HI}(H_2O)$$

MODEL USED	$\Delta \delta G^{HI}$ at 20°C
Dimethyl benzene	18. cal/mol
Diethyl benzene	183. cal/mol
Dimethoxynaphthalene	611. cal/mol
Diethoxynaphthalene	448. cal/mol
Dipropoxynaphthalene	486. cal/mol

This means that the IHI in H_2O is <u>stronger</u> than in D_2O. There
have been some comflicting reports in the literature regarding the
relative strength of the HI in these two liquids. We believe that
the results reported here are consistent with most of the conclusions reached from different sources. These have been recently
reviewed in a monograph on HI[4].

The dialkoxynaphthalene model was found useful to the study of the variation of the IHI in mixtures of water and ethanol[5] (at 20°C and atmospheric pressure). Figure 6 presents the results for the diethoxy naphthalene in mixtures (n) relative to pure water.

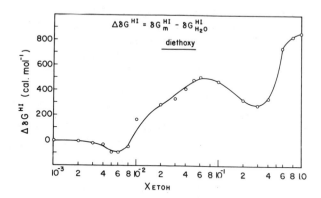

Figure 6. The difference $\Delta \delta G^{HI} = \delta G^{HI}_{M} - \delta G^{HI}_{H_2O}$ for various mixtures (n) of water and ethanol, as a function of the mole-fraction of the ethanol.

Perhaps the most interesting finding reported in this Figure is the minimum in δG^{HI} in the water-rich region which has never been studied before.

In previous studies there have been several conflicting reports on the "initial" effect of ethanol (or other added solutes) on the HI. One reason for such inconsistencies is the application of different experimental techniques (such as conductivity, chemical kinetics, thermodynamics etc.) which do not always convey the same information on the solute-solute interaction. The second reason is the difficulties encountered in carrying out measurements at very low alcohol concentrations. Thus the "initial" effect of the alcohol is usually identified with the initial concentration of alcohol at which the measurements were carried out. This, of course, does not necessarily coincide with the mathematical initial effect of the alcohol. We believe that, in this particular set of measurements, we have reached this mathematical limit, where we might safely conclude that the initial effect of ethanol on the IHI is negative. Namely, adding small amounts of ethanol increases the strength of the IHI. This is followed by a maximum and a minimum before it reaches the limiting value in the alcohol rich region. Note that the maximum at about $X \approx 0.05$ and the minimum at about $X \approx 0.2$ has been reported previously using the model discussed earlier (Equation 5).

It should be noted also that in both models discussed above we had made measurements only with short alkyl chains. Synthetic difficulties have forced us to preclude the use of larger alkyl groups. Also the solubilities of these compounds become exceedingly low and hence the determination of their standard free energies of solution becomes less accurate. In spite of these difficulties we believe that further effort should be expended to carry out such measurements with longer alkyl chains or longer and branched chain alkyl groups. The larger the alkyl groups, the lesser will be the effect of the carrier group on the HI. Also other carriers, especially those with a negligible effect on the structure of water in their surroundings, should be investigated.

Once a convenient model has been found, it will be desirable to study both the temperature and the pressure effects on the HI. These will provide interesting information on the entropy, enthalpy and volume changes for the hydrophobic interaction processes.

REFERENCES

1. W. Kauzmann, Adv. Protein Chem. 14, 1 (1959).
2. C. Tanford, "The Hydrophobic Effect: Formation of Micelles and Biological Membranes," 1st edition, John Wiley, New York, 1973; and references cited therein.
3. C. Tanford, "The Hydrophobic Effect: Formation of Micelles and Biological Membranes," 2nd edition, John Wiley, New York, 1980; and references cited therein.
4. A. Ben-Naim, "Hydrophobic Interactions," Plenum Press, New York, 1980; and references cited therein.
5. J. Wilf and A. Ben-Naim, J. Phys. Chem. 83, 3209 (1979).

PRESSURE STUDY ON SURFACTANT SOLUTIONS

M. Tanaka, S. Kaneshina*, G. Sugihara
N. Nishikido and Y. Murata
Department of Chemistry, Faculty of Science
Fukuoka University
Nishi-ku, Fukuoka 814, Japan
* College of General Education
Kyushu University
Chuo-ku, Fukuoka 810, Japan

A great many studies of the properties of surfactant solutions, for example studies of the surface tension, micelle forming
properties, solubility and solubilization, have been performed extensively using various methods, but for the most part they have
been performed at atmospheric pressure, due to the restriction of
the practical use of surfactant, and presumably due to the apparent difficulty in constructing the apparatus necessary for measurement under high pressure. Nevertheless, some researchers who
have recognized the usefulness of the application of pressure to
solution systems of surfactants have dealt successfully with these
difficulties in their contributions to the field. In order to describe the thermodynamic properties of a given solution system,
three variables are needed: these are temperature, pressure and
composition. Complete thermodynamic information can be obtained
by studying what happens to the solution under changes in pressure,
as well as under changes in temperature and composition. The most
important specific information afforded by studying the effect of
pressure is the change in volume, which is the conjugate extensive
thermodynamic variable with respect to pressure. Similarly, varying the temperature gives information regarding the change in entropy, which is the conjugate thermodynamic variable with respect
to temperature. From this perspective, new ground has been broken
as follows:

i) By measuring the solubilities of ionic surfactants under
pressure, the critical solution pressure, CSP, was found, which is

the pressure dependency of the Krafft temperature. Data of the CSP together with data of the critical micelle concentration, CMC, at various temperatures, T, allows construction of a three dimensional (T,P, and concentration) phase diagram. The partial molal volume change of surfactant accompanying micelle formation and dissolution was estimated using thermodynamic considerations from curves of the effect of pressure on the CMC and solubility.

ii) The effect of added salt, chain length, and temperature on the CMC of sodium alkylsulfates and alkyltrimethylammonium bromides under high pressure were investigated, and the mechanism of micelle formation was discussed.

iii) From the compression measurement the partial molal volumes of ionic surfactants and their homologous salts [sodium alkylsulfate, $R_n SO_4 Na$, n = 2-12, and alkyltrimethylammonium bromide, $R_n Me_3 NBr$, n = 2-12] under high pressure were determined.

iv) Also from the same method the apparent molal volumes of nonionic surfactants [poly (oxyethylene) dodecylethers, $C_{12}E_n$, n = 6-23.9, and poly ethyleneglycol, PEG, oligomers with various degrees of polymerization] in aqueous solutions have been measured as a function of pressure.

v) The effect of pressure on the behavior of aqueous solutions of nonionic surfactants has been studied (for example, CMC, cloud point, association number) and the phase diagram of nonionic surfactant-water system has been constructed.

vi) We have designed and assembled a laser light scattering apparatus for a measurement under high pressure. By means of this apparatus the pressure dependence of the micellar size in aqueous solutions of ionic and nonionic surfactants have been investigated. It is felt that such studies will lead to a better understanding of the complex factors involved in micelle formation or association.

In this paper pressure studies on surfactant solutions as mentioned above will be overviewed.

1. THE BEHAVIOR OF IONIC SURFACTANT SOLUTIONS
UNDER HIGH PRESSURE

1.1 The Effect of Pressure on the Solubility of Ionic
Surfactants in Water

With respect to the effect of pressure on the solubility, which is one of the most important characteristics of surfactants, Hamann observed that the solubility of dodecylamine hydrochloride

decreased with increasing pressure[1]. We determined in more detail
the solubilities of sodium dodecylsulfate (SDS) and dodecylamine
bromide (DAB) by measuring the electric conductivity at pressure
up to 3,000 atm and at several temperatures in the range 7 to 35°C[2]
(See Figure 1). It should be noted that the solution is easily superpressed under high pressure.

    Measurements of the CMC of ionic surfactants under pressure
were made by the same method as described by other workers [3][4][5].
The CMC vs pressure curve for SDS, curve DE in Figure 2, has a maximum at ca 1,000 atm. The effect of pressure on CMC will be discussed later in detail. The solubilities of SDS and DAB at various temperatures and pressures are plotted in Figure 1. The solubility of
DAB is much less than that of SDS, but the effects of pressure and
temperature on solubility are similar for these two surfactants.
The solubility of each detergent was found to depend upon temperature in the following way. At low temperatures the solubility decreases slowly with pressure. At high temperatures, the solubility
decreases very rapidly with pressure below a certain pressure P_c in
Figure 2, but at higher pressures than P_c it decreases slowly in a
manner similar to that at low temperatures.

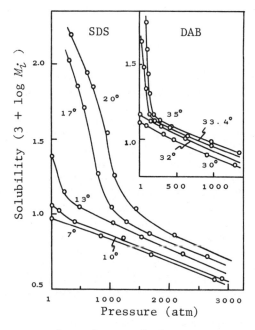

Figure 1. The pressure dependence of the solubility of SDS and DAB
at several temperatures. M_i is the solubility in molality[2].

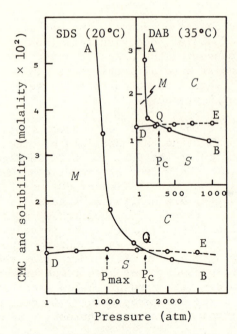

Figure 2. The variation of solubility with pressure (curve AQB), and the variation of the CMC with pressure (curve DQE). SDS (20°C), DAB (35°C). M is the area for micellar solution, S is the area for singly dispersed solution, and C is the area for hydrated sólid.[2]

Changes of the solubility and of the CMC with pressure at constant temperature, for example at 20°C for SDS and 35°C for DAB, are illustrated in Figure 2. Curves of the solubility vs pressure and of the CMC vs pressure intersect at Point Q which is at pressure, P_c. The area in Figure 2 is divided into the three regions S, M and C. It can be easily understood that the regions of S, M and C correspond to the regions in which respectively the singly dispersed solution, the micellar solution and the hydrated solid are stable, and that the singly dispersed solution, the micelles and the hydrated solid are in equilibrium at Point Q. It may be concluded from Figure 2 that the rapid decrease of solubility with pressure along AQ is due to the transfer of surfactant molecules from micelle to hydrated solid resulting in the effective deposition of solid. The slow decrease of solubility along QB is due to the absence of micelles in solution, the line QB being located below the line QE, along which there exist superpressed, metastable micelles.

It is well known that at atmospheric pressure the solubility of ionic surfactant increases abruptly at a certain temperature,

called the Krafft temperature. Discussion of the Krafft point has
been limited to atmospheric pressure. However, Figure 3 indicates
clearly that the Krafft temperature T_k can be defined also under
high pressure, i.e., the T_k under high pressure is the crossing
point of the solubility vs temperature curve and CMC vs temperature
curve at each pressure. It is obvious that, if the Krafft temperature at a pressure, for example P_c, is T_k, the solubility vs pressure curve at constant temperature T_k changes its slope abruptly
at the very pressure P_c. If the Krafft temperature is called the
Critical Solution Temperature (CST), the pressure P_c may be called
the *Critical Solution Pressure* (CSP).

The Krafft temperature rises almost linealy with increasing
pressure as shown in Figure 4.

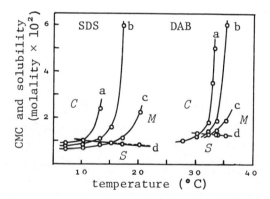

Figure 3. The variation of solubility with temperature (curves a,
b, and c), and the variation of the CMC with temperature (curve d).
For SDS, a = 1, b = 500, and c = 1000 atm. For DAB, a = 1, b = 64,
and c = 142 atm. Solubility values at each pressure were found by
use of the curves of Figure 1. *M* is the region for micellar solution, *S* is the region for singly dispersed solution, and *C* is the
region for hydrated solid. Regarding the curve d, the pressure
dependence of the CMC vs temperature curve is far less than that of
the solubility vs temperature curve. The CMC vs T curves for the
other higher pressure are very close to the curve d at 1 atm, and
it would be difficult to distinguish between these curves if all of
them were drawn. Only an additional curve (broken) for SDS at 1000
atm is drawn[2].

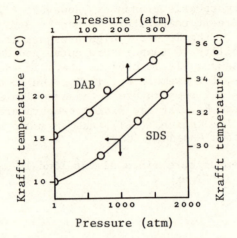

Figure 4. The correlation of the critical solution temperature
(Krafft temperature, CST) with the critical solution pressure
(CSP) for SDS and DAB.[2]

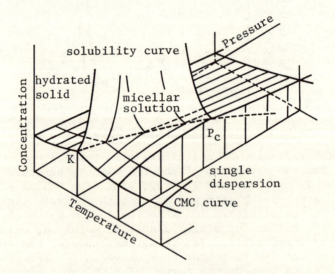

Figure 5. Three-dimensional phase diagram for the ionic surfactant
and water. K and P_c refer to the Krafft point and the CSP,
respectively. A dotted line indicates the critical solution line.[7]

On the basis of these results a three-dimensional phase diagram can be constructed as shown in Figure 5. Two curved surfaces,
the solubility-temperature-pressure surface and the CMC-temperature-
pressure surface, divide the space into three regions, in which the
singly dispersed solution, the micellar solution and the hydrated
solid are stable, respectively. This diagram may be valid for other
ionic surfactants in general. As is seen from Figure 5, the Krafft
temperature increases with increase in pressure. In other words,
the CSP increases with a rise in temperature. Once the temperature
(or pressure) is fixed, the CSP (or the CST) would be fixed. Thus
a *critical solution line* is drawn by a dotted line.

It should be noted that the meta-stable micelles can exist in
the regions of pressure and temperature considerably higher and
lower, respectively, than those of the critical solution line. This
metastable region is not drawn in Figure 5 to avoid complication.

1.2 The Effect of Pressure on CMC of Ionic Surfactants in Water

So far several studies have been made on the effect of pressure
on the CMC of surfactants in aqueous solutions.[1,3-8] All of them
have reported that the CMC vs pressure curve for ionic surfactants
in aqueous solutions exhibits a maximum at a certain pressure, usually near 1000 atm. All methods used for determining the CMC under
high pressures have been based on electroconductivity measurements,
in which a specific conductance vs concentration plot shows a break
at the CMC. Recently, we received a paper that insisted on the absence of the maximum in the CMC vs pressure plot, a conclusion which
was reached by the method of the differential absorbance of solubilized naphthalence as a function of pressure.[9] But we subsequently
presented further evidence for the CMC-pressure maximum for dodecylpyridinium bromide (DAB) solutions by means of both the optical and
electroconductivity methods.[10] Here the effects of added salt,
chain length and temperature on the CMC under high pressure will be
discussed.

Effect of added salt on the CMC under high pressure. The CMC's
of SDS in solutions of several NaCl concentrations at 35°C were determined as a function of pressure.[6] The pressure at which the CMC
becomes maximum is about 1200 atm and seems to be independent of the
concentration of NaCl up to 0.04 mole/Kg-H_2O. Using these results,
plots of the logarithm of the CMC vs the logarithm of the counterion
concentration are linear over the entire pressure range studied.[6]

The CMC's of dodecyltrimethylammonium bromide (DTAB) in solutions of various KBr concentrations at 25°C are shown in Figure 6
as a function of pressure. The addition of increasing amounts of
KBr lowers the CMC. In respective concentration of added salts up
to 0.05 mole/Kg-H 0, the CMC vs pressure curves are characterized
by a maximum point at ca 800 atm.[7]

48   M. TANAKA ET AL.

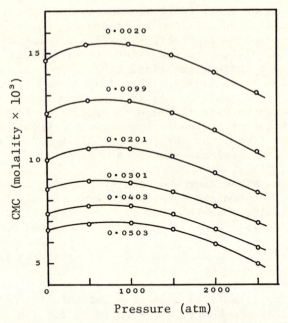

Figure 6. The CMC of DTAB in the presence of KBr at 25°C as a
function of pressure. The concentration of KBr in molality is
presented for each curve.[7]

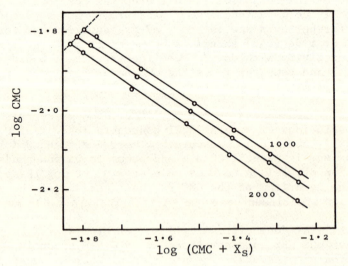

Figure 7. Plots of the logarithm of CMC versus the logarithm of
counterion concentration at various pressures. The numerical
values indicate the pressure in atm.[7]

Figure 7 shows plots of the logarithm of the CMC versus the logarithm of the concentration of counterion to be linear, as well as those for SDS. Thus the following familiar relation is found to hold for the system of DTAB-KBr under high pressure.

$$\log CMC = - \beta \log (CMC + X_s) + const. (T,P),\qquad (1)$$

where X_s is the concentration of KBr, and β is the degree of counterion association. The values of β, the slope in Figure 7, which were determined by the least-square method, are shown in Figure 8 as a function of pressure. Equation (1) holds also for the system of decyltrimethylammonium bromide (DeTAB) - KBr, thus, β's determined for DeTAB are shown in Figure 8 together with those for SDS. As mentioned elsewhere[6], Equation (1) indicates that the solubility product of micelle-forming species is constant if the CMC is taken as the solubility of the micelle in water.

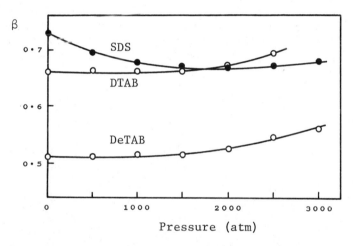

Figure 8. Pressure dependence of β for DeTAB and DTAB at 25°C, and for SDS at 35°C.[6,7]

The values of β for DTAB are always higher than those for DeTAB over the pressure range studied. It has been observed at atmospheric pressure that β increases with an increase of alkyl chain length in a series of sodium alkylsulfates.[11] The value of β for DeTAB and DTAB is almost independent of pressure up to 1500 atm and then increases with an increase in pressure, while β for SDS has a slight minimum at ca 1500 atm. This means that compression to 1500 atm does not change the degree of association of Br- ions on the micelle,

while compression to higher pressures above 1500 atm promotes an
association of Br- ions to the micelle. It is interesting to note
that the dissociation of electrolytes into ions is generally accompanied by a negative volume change and that compression promotes the
dissociation of ion pairs.

   Effect of Chain Length on the CMC under High Pressure. The
CMC's for a homologous series of alkyltrimethylammonium bromides[7]
and those of sodium alkylsulfates[6] were determined at various
pressures, and at 25°C and 35°C, respectively. The CMC of octyl-
trimethylammonium bromide (OTAB) was undeterminable because the
specific conductivity vs concentration curve showed gradual change
of its slope in the vicinity of the CMC at each pressure. As is
shown in Figure 9, the CMC increases initially with increasing
pressure and then decreases with pressure via the maximum at ca
800 atm. (In the case of sodium alkylsulfates the CMC becomes
maximum at about 1000 to 1500 atm, and this pressure is slightly
shifted to lower pressures with increasing alkyl chain length.)
The CMC's of DeTAB and DTAB under high pressures are in fair agreement with those reported previously by Tuddenham and Alexander.[4]
From the effect of chain length on the CMC under high pressure, the
partial molal volume change upon micellization per methylene group
and head group will be described later.

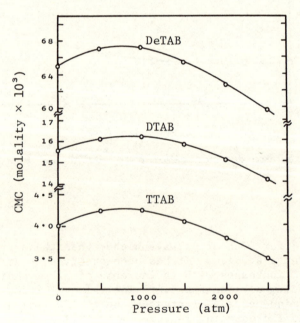

Figure 9. The CMC of alkyltrimethylammonium bromides at 25°C as a
function of pressure.[7]

1.3   The Partial Molal Volume and Its Change under High Pressure

It is well known that two main approaches have hitherto been
used for the thermodynamic analysis of micelliztion, i.e., one is
the phase-separation approach, which regards the micelle in a solution as a pseudo-phase, and the other approach is to apply the law
of mass action to micelle formation. Because of its simplicity and
convenience of application and its considerable authenticity we will
take the former approach here. The pseudo-phase separation model
leads to the following equation for the partial molal volume change
involved in the formation of micelles from singly dipersed surfactants.

$$\Delta \bar{V}m = (1 + \beta) \ RT \left(\frac{\partial \, ln \, CMC}{\partial \, P} \right)_{T,} \tag{2}$$

where β is a constant which represents the ratio of the number of
counterions to that of surfactant ions in the micelle, and the CMC
is in mole fraction units.[2 6 8 12 13 14] Equation (2) along with
the specific curve of CMC vs pressure, which has a maximum, suggests
that $\Delta \bar{V}_m$ decreases gradually with increasing pressure, and above the
pressure which gives the maximum in the curve of CMC vs pressure,
$\Delta \bar{V}_m$ becomes negative, as shown in Figure 10.

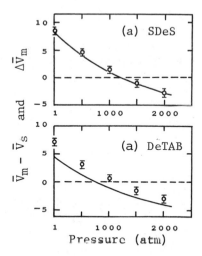

Figure 10.   Partial molal volume change on micellization.   (a)
sodium decylsulfate, (b) decyltrimethylammonium bromide, difference
between the partial molal volumes in micellar and singly dispersed
state (Φ) partial molal volume change on micellization calculated
from the pressure dependence of the CMC by using Equation (2)
(————)

With respect to solutions of a homologous series of surfactants, the CMC at 1 atm is known to decrease logarithmically with an increase in the number of carbon atoms, N, in the alkyl chain.[15]

$$\log CMC = A - BN \tag{3}$$

where A and B are constants. If the values of A and B are obtained as a function of pressure, we can get following relations by substituting Equation (3) into (2).

$$\Delta \bar{V}_m = 2.303 \ (1 + \beta) \ RT \left[\left| \frac{\partial A}{\partial P} \right|_T - \left(\frac{\partial B}{\partial P} \right)_T N \right]$$

$$= \Delta \bar{V}_{ion} + \Delta \bar{V}_{me} N \tag{4}$$

where, $\Delta \bar{V}_{me}$ is the partial molal volume change on micellization per methylene group, and $\Delta \bar{V}_{ion}$ may be assumed to be the contribution of ionic head group to the volume change on micellization. Equation (4) indicates that $\Delta \bar{V}_m$ varies linearly with N. This linear relationship has been established at 1 atm for sodium alkylsulfate and alkyltrimethylammonium bromide.[16] The values of $\Delta \bar{V}_{me}$ and $\Delta \bar{V}_{ion}$ at various pressures, which were calculated from the pressure dependence of A and B through Equation (4), are shown in Table 1, together with the resulting $\Delta \bar{V}_m$ for N = 12.

Table I. The Contribution of Hydrocarbon Tail and Ionic Head to the Partial Molal Volume Change on Micelle Formation[6]

Pressure (atm)	$\Delta \bar{V}_{me}$ (ml/mol)	$\Delta \bar{V}_{ion}$ (ml/mol)	$\Delta \bar{V}_m$ (N = 12) (ml/mol)
1	1.24	-4.74	10.1
500	0.47	-2.54	3.1
1000	0.10	-0.30	0.9
1500	-0.236	2.00	-0.8
2000	-0.394	3.24	-1.5
3000	-0.585	3.53	-3.5

It can be seen from Table I, that $\Delta \bar{V}_{me}$, the volume change on hydrophobic bonding, decreases from a positive value to a negative value with increasing pressure. This means that compression breaks

down hydrophobic bonding at lower pressure and promotes it at higher
pressure and that hydrophobic bonding contributes predominantly to
$\Delta\bar{V}_m$. We obtained 1.24 ml for $\Delta\bar{V}_{me}$ at 1 atm, which is comparable to
the value for the transfer of hydrocarbon part from an aqueous to a
nonpolar environment. The effect of the concentration of ionic head
groups on micellization has a negative contribution to $\Delta\bar{V}_m$, which
seems unlikely considering the fact that the ionic association
causes an increase in volume. Therefore, it is possible that the
methylene groups adjacent to the hydrophilic head make a much
smaller contribution to $\Delta\bar{V}_m$ than those far from this region.[6]

As mentioned above the difference in partial molal volume between the micellar and singly dispersed states could be estimated,
however, the pressure dependence of the partial molal volume in
each of these states is still unknown. If the *compression* of the
solution of surfactants is determined under different pressures,
the partial molal volumes of the various surfactants in the singly
dispersed and micellar states can be determined respectively. The
relation between the compression k and the partial molal volume of
a salt is expressed as

$$\bar{V}_p - \bar{V}_1 - \Delta\bar{V}_p, \qquad \Delta\bar{V}_p = \frac{\partial(\ V_1 k\ )}{\partial m} \qquad\qquad (5)$$

where $\bar{V}_p$ and $\bar{V}_1$ are the partial molal volume under pressure P and
atmospheric pressure, respectively; V_1 is the volume of solution
per 1000g of solvent, and m is the molality of salt. For sodium
alkylsulfates (R_nSO_4Na) and alkyltrimethylammonium bromides
(R_nMe_3NBr) the values of $\bar{V}_p$ were determined at 1000 and 2000 atm by
the interpolation of the curve of $\bar{V}_p$ vs pressure. The partial molal
volumes of the singly dispersed state ($\bar{V}_s$) and those of micelle-
forming species in the micellar state ($\bar{V}_m$) are given in Reference 14.
(Vikingstad et al. determined those of sodium decanoate in the
singly dispersed state and in the micellar state as a function of
pressure at 25°C through the method of ultrasound measurements.[17])

The $\bar{V}_s$ for R_nSO_4Na increases with increasing pressure up to
2000 atm, while V_s for R_nMe_3NBr decreases with increasing pressure.
In order to elucidate whether the different behavior between $\bar{V}_s$'s
of R_nSO_4Na and R_nMe_3NBr is attributed to the hydrophobic or hydrophilic part of these salts, the split of $\bar{V}_s$ into the contributions
of the ionic and hydrocarbon parts was attempted as follows. Plotting $\bar{V}_s$ versus the length of the alkyl chain N, straight lines were
obtained for R_nSO_4Na and R_nMe_3NBr under various pressures as shown
in Figure 11. Then the relation between $\bar{V}_s$ and N can be satisfactorily represented by the following relation.

$$\bar{V}_s = \bar{V}_{ion} + \bar{V}_{me}N, \qquad\qquad (6)$$

where $\bar{V}_{me}$ is the partial molal volume per methylene group and

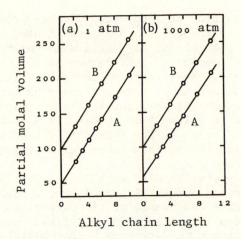

Figure 11. Partial molal volumes of R_nSO_4Na and RMe_3NBr as a function of alkyl chain length. (a) 1 atm, (b) 1000 atm; A: R_nSO_4Na, B: R_nMe_3NBr.

$\bar{V}_{ion}$ may be assumed to be the contribution of the ionic part which is obtained by extrapolating N to zero in a linear plot of $\bar{V}_s$ vs N. The values of V_{me} and $\bar{V}_{ion}$ determined for two homologues are presented in Table II. The values of $\bar{V}_{me}$ for R_nSO_4Na and R_nMe_3NBr agree with each other at atmospheric pressure, and decrease with increasing pressure, but there is a slight difference in the rate of decrease with pressure for the two homologues. On the other hand, $\bar{V}_{ion}$ of R_nSO_4Na increases clearly with increasing pressure, while $\bar{V}_{ion}$ of R_nMe_3NBr remains constant within the error of experiment. Thus, it can be concluded that the increase of $\bar{V}_s$ of R_nSO_4Na with pressure is attributed to the contribution of the increase of $\bar{V}_{ion}$ in preference to the decrease of $\bar{V}_{me}$ with pressure, on the other hand, the decrease of $\bar{V}_s$ of R_nMe_3NBr with pressure is controlled by the decrease of $\bar{V}_{me}$.

The decrease of $\bar{V}_{me}$ with pressure is a known phenomenon. It is known that the transfer of hydrocarbons from a nonpolar environment to water results in a negative volume change[18], which is considered to reflect the ordering of water molecules around the hydrocarbon chains, or *iceberg* formation.[19] Hence, the promotion of iceberg formation around the hydrocarbon chain by the application of pressure seems to participate in the decrease of $\bar{V}_{me}$.

Again concerning the change of partial molal volume on micelle formation, the values of $\bar{V}_m$ and $\bar{V}_s$ of SDeS and DeTAB are shown in Figure 12 as a function of pressure.[14] As is seen from Figure 12, two curves of $\bar{V}_m$ vs pressure and $\bar{V}_s$ vs pressure intersect each other at ca 1200 atm for both surfactants. Thus,

Table II. Counterion of Hydrophobic and Hydrophilic Groups to Partial Molal Volume under Pressure[14].

Pressure (atm)	R_nSO_4Na		R_nMe_3NBr	
	$\bar{V}_{me}$	$\bar{V}_{ion}$	$\bar{V}_{me}$	$\bar{V}_{ion}$
1	15.4	50.0	15.5	100.0
1000	14.9	56.0	15.2	100.5
2000	14.6	59.0	14.9	99.5

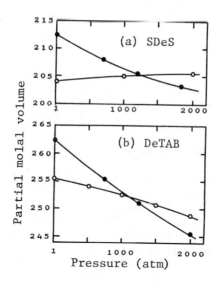

Figure 12. Partial molal volumes of micellar and singly dispersed states as a function of pressure. (a): sodium decylsulfate, (b): decyltrimethylammonium bromide:micellar state (●), singly dispersed state (○).

the change of the partical molal volume on micellization, i.e., $\bar{V}_m - \bar{V}_s$, changes its sign from plus to minus at ca 1200 atm. The initial compression causes the dissociation of micelles, i.e., the increase in the CMC, whereas the successive compression above 1200 atm causes the aggregation of monomers into micelles, i.e., the decrease in the CMC with compression, resulting in the decrease of the total volume of the solution. The present behavior of $\bar{V}_m$ and $\bar{V}_s$ versus compression is consistent with thermodynamic considerations of the pressure dependence of the CMC.

It is interesting to compare the $\Delta\bar{V}_m$ obtained from $\bar{V}_m$ and $\bar{V}_s$ data with the $\Delta\bar{V}_m$ estimated by applying Equation (2) to the pressure dependence data of the CMC. The value of $\Delta\bar{V}_m$ for SDeS at atmospheric pressure, 8.0 ml/mole, which was calculated from the pressure dependence of the CMC, is in fair agreement with that from the partial molal volume measurements, 8.4 ml per mole. Further, the values of $\Delta\bar{V}_m$ under high pressure are also in satisfactory agreement with those of $\bar{V}_m - \bar{V}_s$ obtained at various pressures as is shown in Figure 11 (a). On the other hand, in the case of DeTAB, a significant difference was observed (2.3 ml per mole at 1 atm) between $\Delta\bar{V}_m$ from Equation (2) and $\bar{V}_m - \bar{V}_s$ as shown in Figure 11 (b). Even if β were taken to be unity, which is unlikely in ionic micelles, the above difference becomes 1.7 ml per mole at 1 atm which seems to be beyond the experimental error. Further, it is clearly shown from the extensive work for homologous series of surfactants that the values of $\Delta\bar{V}_m$ calculated from the pressure dependence of the CMC for a homologous series of alkyltrimethyl-ammonium[4] are found to be smaller than the results of partial molal volume measurements.[18] Further detailed examination and discussion about these inconsistencies are necessary.

1.4 Effects of Temperature and Pressure on the CMC

The CMC's of SDS at various temperatures (17-40°C) and pressure up to 3000 atm were determined. The CMC is found to reach a maximum at about 1000 - 1500 atm over the entire temperature range studied. On the other hand the CMC - temperature curve passes through a minimum at a certain temperature, which tends to shift toward lower values as the pressure increases. When no salts are added, the changes in partial molal entropy and enthalpy on micelle formation are expressed as

$$\Delta\bar{S}_m = \frac{\Delta\bar{H}_m}{T} = -(1 + \beta)\ RT\left(\frac{\partial \ln\ CMC}{\partial T}\right)_p \qquad (7)$$

From this equation and temperature dependence of the CMC, $\Delta\bar{S}_m$ and $\Delta\bar{H}_m$ were estimated[6]. The temperature dependence of $\Delta\bar{H}_m$ at various pressures, the pressure dependence of $\Delta\bar{S}_m$ at different temperatures and the temperature dependence of $\Delta\bar{V}_m$ at various pressures were invesitgated, and interrelation among these quantities were discussed. Thermodynamic considerations of micelle formation from these studies can be summarized as follows. The decrease of $\Delta \bar{V}_m$ with pressure is due primarily to the large compressibility of the micelle[16], and the decrease of $\Delta \bar{S}_m$ and $\Delta \bar{H}_m$ with an increase in temperature is attributed to the increase of partial molal entropy and enthalpy in the singly dispersed state. Hence, the thermodynamic quantities of micellization may be grouped into four classes by means of temperature and pressure, as listed in Table III. P_{max} stands for the pressure at which the CMC becomes maximum, and T_{min} for the temperature at which the CMC becomes minimum. In the region of low temperature and pressure (class I), temperature and pressure affect the CMC oppositely. Compression causes the dissociation of the micelle, and elevation of temperature promotes aggregation to the micelle. In this region, *iceberg* formation is a predominant factor governing the process of micelle formation. In the region of high temperature and pressure (class IV) temperature and pressure also affect the CMC oppositely. In this temperature range, there is a breakdown of the *iceberg* structure. Thus $\Delta \bar{S}_m < 0$ is primarily due to the decrease of the stoichiometric number on micellization, and $\Delta \bar{V}_m < 0$ is due to highly compressed micelles. Class II is the region in which the *iceberg* structure is broken down and the micelle is not sufficiently compressed. In Class III, the entropy effect of the water structure contributes markedly to $\Delta \bar{S}_m < 0$, and the highly compressed micelle to $\Delta \bar{V}_m < 0$.

Table III. Thermodynamic Quantities on Micelle Formation of SDS[6].

Pressure	Temperature	Class	$\Delta \bar{H}_m$	$\Delta \bar{S}_m$	$\Delta \bar{V}_m$
$P < P_{max}$	$T < T_{min}$	I	+	+	+
	$T > T_{min}$	II	−	−	−
$P > P_{max}$	$T < T_{min}$	III	+	+	−
	$T > T_{min}$	IV	−	−	−

2. EFFECT OF PRESSURE ON THE SOLUTION BEHAVIOR OF NONIONIC SURFACTANTS IN WATER

So far, few studies have dealt with the effect of pressure on the solution behavior of nonionic surfactants. This chapter deals with the pressure-temperature-composition phase diagrams, specifically, the effect of pressure on the clouding phenomena and the solubility[20], and on the apparent molal volumes of micellar solution.[21] In this chapter, we used polyoxyethylene dodecyl ethers as nonionic surfactants and abbreviate them as $C_{12}E_n$ (n: the number of oxyethylene (OE) groups).

2.1 Pressure-Temperature-Composition Phase Diagrams of Nonionic Surfactant and Water Systems

Many authors have reported extensive studies concerning the temperature-composition phase diagram of nonionic detergents at atmospheric pressure[23-30]. We have constructed the pressure-temperature-composition diagrams of $C_{12}E_n$ (n=4, 5, 6)-water systems[20]. In Figure 13 the temperature-pressure diagrams of $C_{12}E_5$-water systems are shown in which the concentrations of $C_{12}E_5$ are 1, 5, 10 and 20 wt %. The diagrams for the concentrations of $C_{12}E_5$ less than 1 wt % (0.04 - 0.23 wt %) exhibited the similar features. The phase boundary was detected by the change of transmittance of the solution[20]. In Figure 13, the curve AB represents the cloud temperature (CT) vs pressure curve. In the region of two phases between the curve AB and CD, the water phase contains the low concentrations of surfactant and the liquid surfactant phase contains an amount of water. The area of the micellar solution becomes wider for the system containing the $C_{12}E_n$ of longer OE groups and no liquid crystalline phase forms below 100°C for $C_{12}E_6$-water systems[20]. The CT increases with an increase of pressure (curve AB).

The hydrogen bonding of OE groups of surfactant with water solvent, i.e. the hydration of OE groups, is a main factor controlling the stability of dissolved species, monomer and micelle, in the micellar solution. The volume change of hydrogen bonding is -4 to -7 cm^3 $mole^{-1}$ at atmospheric pressure and its sign does not change at least up to ca 400 MPa[33,34]. Then, the compression as well as an addition of OE groups into surfactant enhances the hydration of OE groups and thereby stabilizes the dissolved state of the species in the micellar solution. As a result, the area of the micellar solution is wider for the system containing the surfactant of longer OE groups, and the CT increases with pressure. However, the second derivative of CT with respect to pressure decreases with increasing pressure. This suggests that another factor, hydrophobic bonding, also plays an important role in the appearance of two phases, i.e., the clouding phenomenon.

By taking into account the fact that the CT vs composition curve is equivalent to a liquid--liquid (liquid surfactant and water) mutual solubility curve[23,26], we obtain the following relations among the CT, composition and pressure[20]:

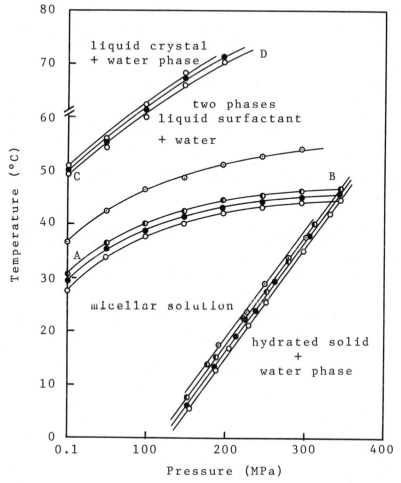

Figure 13. Temperature-pressure phase diagrams of the $C_{12}E_5$-water systems containing 1 wt % (○), 5 wt % (●), 10 wt % (◐) and 20 wt % (◎) of $C_{12}E_5$.

$$\left(\frac{\partial T}{\partial x_2}\right)_P \sim - \frac{RT\ (\ y_2 - x_2\ )}{\Delta \overline{H}}\ [\ \frac{1}{x_1} + \frac{1}{x_2}\ ], \qquad (8)$$

$$\left(\frac{\partial P}{\partial x_2}\right)_T \sim \frac{RT\ (\ y_2 - x_2\ )}{\Delta \overline{V}}\ [\ \frac{1}{x_1} + \frac{1}{x_2}\ ], \qquad (9)$$

$$\left(\frac{\partial P}{\partial T}\right)_{x_2} = \frac{\Delta \overline{S}}{\Delta \overline{V}}, \qquad (10)$$

where T is the cloud temperature, P is the pressure at the cloud
temperature, x_1, x_2 are the mole fractions of water and surfactant
in the water phase, respectively; y_1, y_2 are the mole fractions of
water and surfactant in the liquid surfactant phase, respectively;
$\Delta\bar{H}$, $\Delta\bar{V}$, $\Delta\bar{S}$ are the enthalpy, volume and entropy changes accompanied
by the separation of the liquid surfactant phase from the water
phase, respectively. The termodynamic quantities, $\Delta\bar{H}$, $\Delta\bar{S}$ and $\Delta\bar{V}$,
can be estimated by applying Equations (8-10) to the phase diagrams.
$\Delta\bar{S}$ and $\Delta\bar{H}$ are found to be positive and nearly independent of pressure for the $C_{12}E_5$ water systems. $\Delta\bar{V}$ is shown in Figure 14 as a
function of pressure at various compositions of the water phase.
It is seen from Figure 14 that $\Delta\bar{V}$ is positive and decreases, tending
to zero value, with pressure.

The entropy and enthalpy changes of dehydration and of hydrophobic bonding are known to be positive[35]. The volume change of hydrophobic bonding is positive at atmospheric pressure and changes its
sign near 100-150MPa except at higher temperature.[22, 35, 36]

That of dehydration is positive and does not change its sign
at least up to ca 400 MPa[33, 34]. For another system of polyoxyethy-

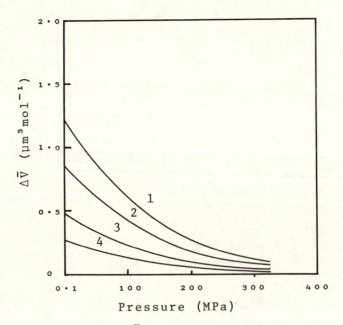

Figure 14. Volume change $\Delta\bar{V}$ accompanied by the separation of the
liquid surfactant phase from the water phase of various compositions; (1) 0.04, (2) 0.11, (3) 0.15, (4) 0.23 wt % of $C_{12}E_5$, for
the $C_{12}E_5$-water system.

lene nonylphenyl ether and water, it has been found that the CT vs
pressure curves exhibit maxima near 150 MPa in the pressure range
of 0.1–500MPa[31], [32], [35]. According to Equations (8–10), $\Delta\bar{H}$ and
$\Delta\bar{S}$ for this system are positive up to 500 MPa and $\Delta\bar{V}$ is positive
and decreases to become negative above ca 150 MPa. These results
suggest that the phase separation is driven by the partial dehydration of OE groups of surfactant in the monomeric and micellar
states and that the structure of the liquid surfactant phase is
stabilized by the hydrophobic bonding of surfactant. The contribution of hydrophobic bonding to the phase separation, the clouding
phenomenon, is also clear from the fact that polyoxyethylene–type
nonionic surfactant with longer alkyl groups exhibit lower CT[20].
The structure of the liquid surfactant phase seems to resemble that
of gel swollen with water, in which the network of gel is built up
by the hydrophobic bonding of the alkyl groups of the surfactant.

In Figure 15 are shown the composition–pressure phase diagrams
close to the boundary between the micellar solution and the hydrated
solid + water phase for the $C_{12}E_5$–water systems at constant temperatures, 10, 20, and 30°C. It can be seen from Figure 15 that the

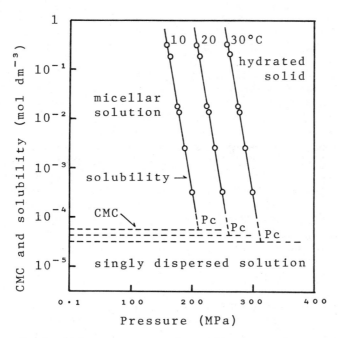

Figure 15. Composition–pressure phase diagrams close to the
boundary of regions of the micellar solution and the hydrated solid
+ water phase of the $C_{12}E_5$–water systems at various temperatures.

solubility of surfactant increases suddenly at a certain pressure
Pc (CSP)[2] with decreasing pressure owing to the effective disolution of surfactant as micellar form in water. This phenomenon of
critical disolution corresponds to the Krafft phenomenon and has
been already observed for the effect of pressure on the solubility
of ionic surfactant in water, as described in 1.1.

2.2 Effect of Pressure on the Apparent Molal Volumes of Nonionic Surfactants in Aqueous Solutions[2.1]

The partial or apparent molal volume has generally proved to
be a very useful tool in elucidating the interactions occuring in
solutions. Neal and Goring[37] have shown that the derivative of the
apparent specific volume of solute with respect to temperature,
d ϕ_{sv}/dT, is a sensitive measure of the effect of solute on the
structure of water, and concluded (for a variety of small, nonionic
solutes) that hydrophobic compounds, which promote water structure,
have lower values of d ϕ_{sv}/dT than hydrophilic compounds. On the
other hand, the partial or apparent molal compressibility is also
expected to be a measure of the effect of solute on water structure.

The hydrophilic property of $C_{12}E_n$ can be varied by changing
the OE chain length. The apparent molal volumes of $C_{12}E_n$ (n=6,
9.0, 14.8, 19.2 and 23.9) were determined as a function of pressure
on the basis of the density and compression data measured. Furthermore, for comparing with the hydrophilic parts of $C_{12}E_n$, the
apparent molal volumes of polyethlene glycol (PEG) oligomers with
various degrees of polymerization were also determined. Then, the
isothermal apparent molal compressibility, $K_\phi = -(\partial V_\phi/\partial P)_{T' \to T}$ for
these surfactants was correlated to the hydrophobicity of surfactant
molecules in connection with the interaction of the OE chain with
water. Finally, a micellar structure is disscussed in view of the
partial molal compressibility of micellar surfactant. Densities
of aqueous $C_{12}E_n$ and PEG solutions were measured using a digital
densimeter (Anton Paar, Model DMA 02C) at 298.15k. The compressions
were determined by the use of the electric contact method at 298.15K.
In these measurements, the concentration $C_{12}E_n$ was kept constant
at about 0.02 in molality, at which most of the surfactant molecules
(>99%) are dissolved in the micellar state since the CMC's of
$C_{12}E_n$ are in the range 6 x 10^{-5} to 2 x 10^{-4} in molality. The weight
fraction of PEG remains constant at 0.02.

The values of the apparent specific volume ϕ_{sv} for $C_{12}E_n$ and
PEG determined by the density measurements are given in Table IV.

Apparent molal volumes, V_ϕ, can be easily determined by the
expression $V_\phi = M \phi_{sv}$, where M is the average molecular weight.

Table IV.

	ϕ_{sv} (cm^3 g^{-1})	K_ϕ (cm^3 mole^{-1} MPa^{-1})
$C_{12}E_6$	1.00300	0.172
$C_{12}E_{9.0}$	0.95701	0.153
$C_{12}E_{14.8}$	0.92018	0.140
$C_{12}E_{19.3}$	0.90793	0.132
$C_{12}E_{23.9}$	0.89162	0.117
PEG(4.1)	0.85630	0.029
PEG(6.4)	0.85445	0.030
PEG(8.7)	0.84830	0.016
PEG(13.2)	0.84457	0.011
PEG(22.3)	0.84124	0.004

The slope of a linear plot of V_ϕ vs OE chain length gives the apparent molal volume assigned to one OE group, V_ϕ(OE). The values of V_ϕ(OE) for $C_{12}E_n$ and PEG are 36.5 and 36.8cm^3 mol^{-1}, respectively, in good agreement with literature values. Note that V_ϕ(OE) assigned to the hydrophilic group of micellar surfactant is identical to that for PEG. The volumetric behavior of OE chain in water cannot be distinguished between the micellar surfactant and PEG oligomers.

The apparent molal volume V_ϕ for $C_{12}E_n$ and PEG gave the almost linear tendency with increased pressure[21]. The slopes of these curves at atmospheric pressure, $K_\phi = -(\partial V_\phi/\partial P)_{T \to T'}$, are given in Table IV. The isothermal apparent molal compressibility decreases with an increase in OE chain length. The hydrophilic property of surfactant molecule increases with increased OE chain lenth. Therefore, it may be concluded that the decreasing tendency of K_ϕ corresponds to a relative reduction of the hydrophobic fraction in the surfactant molecule. In PEG, K_ϕ decreases also with an increase in the degree of polymerization. Sandell and Goring[39] studied the correlation between $d\phi_{sv}/dT$ and the conformation of PEG oligomers in aqueous solution. According to them, the intramolecular hydrophobic interactions could take place between backbone ($-CH_2CH_2-$) groups, resulting in a reduction in the hydrophobic character of the oligomer when compared to an equivalent, fully extended PEG chain. The ease of forming hydrophobic contacts between ($-CH_2CH_2-$) groups greatly increases with increasing chain length, especially in the range of low degree of polymerization. In both systems of aqueous surfactant and PEG solutions, therefore, the decreasing values of K_ϕ are attributable to a relative reduction in the hydrophobicity of the solute. K_ϕ, as well as $d\phi_{sv}/dT$, is available for a sensitive measure of the effect of homologous solute molecules on the structure of water.

We now consider the contributions of alkyl and OE groups to the
isothermal apparent molal compressibility. A linear relationship
between V_ϕ and OE chain length was confirmed at various pressures.
The values of $V_\phi(OE)$ were determined at various pressures from the
slopes of lines and are shown as a function of pressure in Figure
16, in which the values of $V_\phi(OE)$ for PEG oligomers are also
included. As is seen from Figure 16, the values of $V_\phi(OE)$ for both
surfactant and PEG are almost constant or increase slightly with
increasing pressure in the range studied. It is likely that the
interactions between OE chain and water are similar in both systems,
and that the solute and water molecules pack together closely.
Consequently, the hydrophilic shell of a micelle is considerably
resistant to compression.

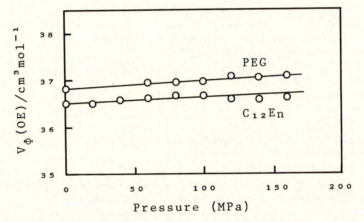

Figure 16. Apparent molal volume assigned for one OE group $C_{12}E_n$
and PEG as a function of pressure.

The contribution of the alkyl group in a micellar surfactant
to V_ϕ may be represented by $V_\phi - nV_\phi(OE)$, and is shown in Figure 17
as a function of pressure. The apparent molal volume assigned for
the hydrophobic core of a micelle decreases monotonically with increasing pressure. Consequently, the decreasing V_ϕ of micellar surfactant with pressure is attributable to the contraction of the hydrophobic core of the micelle. The isothermal apparent molal compressibility assigned for the micellar core is taken as the slope
of the curve in Figure 17, and is found to be $0.18 cm^3 mole^{-1} MPa^{-1}$
which is comparable to the compressibilities of liquid hydrocarbons.
From this fact, the micelle may be reasonably regarded as liquid in
its interior.

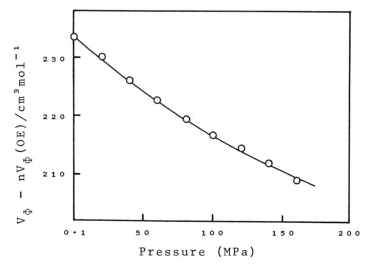

Figure 17. Apparent molal volume assigned for the alkyl group in a micellar surfactant as a function of pressure.

3. Effect of Pressure on Micelle Size

It has been found that the CMC vs pressure curve for ionic surfactants in aqueous solutions exhibits the maximum at the pressure near 100 MPa. We have already proposed an interpretation of this phenomenon according to the Le Chatelier's principle[6] as follows. The dissociation of micelles into monomers is caused by the compression up to the maximum pressure, ca 100 MPa, resulting in the increase in the number of smaller micelles. Whereas the association of monomers into micelles becomes promoted by the successive compression over the maximum pressure, resulting in the decrease in the number of larger micelles. However, we have not found experimental studies which deal with the direct observation of the variation of micellar aggregation number with pressure. We assembled a laser light-scattering apparatus designed for measurement under high pressure[22], and pursued the pressure dependence of micellar aggregation number, charge and concentration of representative ionic surfactant, sodium dodecyl sulfate (SDS) in the aqueous solution. In addition, we studied the aggregation number and concentration of micelle of a nonionic surfactant, hexaoxyethylene dodecyl ether ($C_{12}E_6$), under pressure.

The laser light-scattering apparatus permits the deduction of
the ratios of the intensity of the scattered light to the intensity
of the incident light at the scattering angles 45, 90, and 135°
simultaneously. These intensity ratios are plotted as a function
of time using an X-Y recorder, and time average intensity ratios
are obtained using a computer. From these time-averaged intensity
ratios, the Rayleigh ratio R_{90}, the dissymmetry coefficients Z_{45},
and the depolarization ratios ρ_v may be obtained for detergent
solutions at various detergent and salt concentrations and pressures. The aggregation number and charge of SDS micelles may be
estimated from the measured Rayleigh ratios by means of the Prins-
Hermans-Mysels-Princen theory (PHMP theory)[40]. In this estimation
we found that for pressures less than 200 MPa, sufficient accuracy
could be obtained by using the value of the refractive index increment for atmospheric pressure in the optical constant. In
Figure 18 we present a plot of aggregation number j and concentration C_m of SDS micelles versus pressure at constant total detergent
concentration C = 3.3 x 10^{-2} mole dm^{-3}. The concentration of
micelles C_m was determined using the equation C_m = (C-cmc)/j. In
Figure 18, the aggregation number vs pressure curve has a minimum

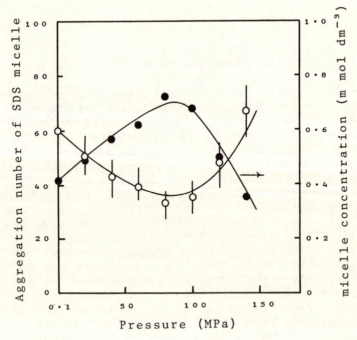

Figure 18. Aggregation number and concentration (at the total
SDS concentration, 3.3 x 10^{-2} mole dm^{-3}) of SDS micelles as a
function of pressure at 303 K.

near 100 MPa and the micelle concentration vs pressure curve has a
maximum near 100 MPa. These extrema correspond to the maximum in
the CMC vs pressure curve which is corroborating evidence for our
interpretation about the effect of pressure on micelle formation
of ionic surfactants in aqueous solutions discussed above in
Section 1.2.

    In Figure 19, we represent a plot of the effective charge,
z/j, of SDS micelle versus pressure. From Figure 19, it is
evident that pressure has little, if any, effect on the micellar
charge. Vikingstad and his associates have reached similar conclusions from their studies[12].

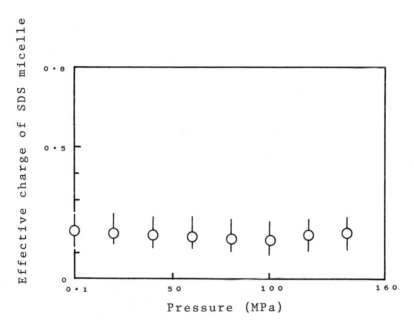

Figure 19. Effective charge, z/j, of SDS micelles as a function
of pressure at 303 K.

    The aggregation number for $C_{12}E_6$ micelles can be estimated by
the well-known Debye method which is correct for uncharged particles. In the construction of the Debye plots, we neglected the
variation of the CMC with pressure because the total surfactant
concentration $\gg$ CMC. The estimated aggregation numbers are shown
as a function of pressure in Figure 20. The aggregation number
for $C_{12}E_6$ micelles decreases from 330 at atmospheric pressure and
its rate of decrease becomes smaller with increasing pressure,

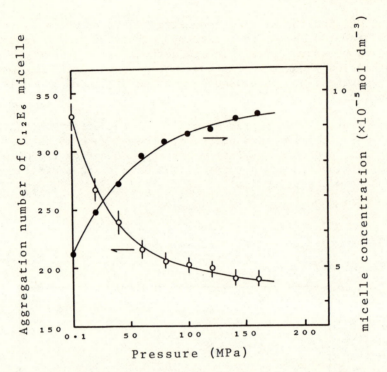

Figure 20. Aggregation number and concentration (at the total $C_{12}E_6$ concentration, 1.78×10^{-2} mole dm^{-3}) of $C_{12}E_6$ micelles as a function of pressure at 298 K.

whereas, the concentration of micelles increases and its rate of increase becomes smaller with pressure. This observation that there are no extrema in the curves, different from that found for SDS, is explained as follows. Similar to the effect of pressure on SDS micelles, the decrease in aggregation number and increase in concentration of micelles as shown in Figure 20 seems to indicate that the application of pressures up to 160 MPa causes dissociation of $C_{12}E_6$ micelles into monomers. We may seek to understand the lack of extrema by considering the balance of opposing forces in the formation of micelles by nonionic surfactants. The driving force for the association of nonionic amphiphiles into micelles is hydrophobic bonding, just as for the ionic surfactants. As described in Section 2.1, hydrophobic bonding is weakened by compression up to 100–150 MPa, whereas it is promoted for pressures greater than this (except at higher temperature)[22, 26, 35]. If hydrophobic bonding, the driving force for aggregation, passes through a minimum at a given pressure, we would expect the dissociation of micelles into monomers to also pass through a minimum at the same pressure. We must, however, also consider the effect of pressure on the force opposing the formation of micelles from nonionic amphiphiles, which is hydrogen bonding of the hydrophilic moiety with water. For polyoxyethylene-type nonionic surfactants, it has been suggested that the OE groups near the hydrocarbon core of the micelle lose some of their hydration water because of the requirement of close packing of the nonpolar tails[41, 42]. As described here in Section 2.2, compression enhances the hydration of the OE group, at least up to 400 MPa. Upon compression, the enhanced hydration of the six OE groups in $C_{12}E_6$ results in an unfavorable situation for the micellized state due to the steric requirement mentioned above, whereas compression creates a favorable situation for the unaggregated state due to an increase in the solubility of monomeric $C_{12}E_6$. Thus, the application of pressures beyond 150 MPa continues to drive the system towards the dissociation of micelles due to enhanced hydration of the OE groups. No distinct minimum can be found in the aggregation number versus pressure curve.

REFERENCES

1. S. D. Hamann, J. Phys. Chem., 67, 2072 (1963).
2. M. Tanaka, S. Kaneshina, T. Tomida, K. Nōda and K. Aoki, J. Colloid Interface Sci., 44, 525 (1973).
3. S. D. Hamann, J. Phys. Chem., 66, 1539 (1962).
4. R. f. Tudenham and A. E. Alexander, J. Phys. Chem., 66, 1839 (1962).
5. J. Osugi, M. Sato and N. Ifuku, Nippon Kagaku Zasshi, 87, 329 (1966); Rev. Phys. Chem. Japan, 35, 32 (1965).
6. S. Kaneshina, M. Tanaka, T. Tomida and R. Matuura, J. Colloid Interface Sci., 48, 450 (1974).
7. M. Tanaka, S. Kaneshina and G. Sugihara in "Proceedings of 7th International Congress on Surface Active Substances", Moscow (1977).
8. T. S. Brun, H. Høiland and E. Vikingstad, J. Colloid Interface Sci., 63, 89 (1978).
9. S. Rodriguez and Ho. Offen, J. Phys. Chem., 81, 47 (1977).
10. N. Nishikido, N. Yoshimura and M. Tanaka, J. Phys. Chem., 84, 558 (1980).
11. I. Satake, T. Tahara and R. Matuura, Bull. Chem. Soc. Jpn., 42, 319 (1969).
12. T. S. Brun, H. Høiland and E. Vikingstad, J. Colloid Interface Sci., 63, 590 (1978).
13. H. Høiland and E. Vikingstad, J. Colloid Interface Sci., 64, 126 (1978).
14. M. Tanaka, S. Kaneshina, K. Shin-no, T. Okajima and T. Tomida, J. Colloid Interface Sci., 46, 132 (1974).

15. K. Shinoda, T. Nakagawa, B. Tamamushi and T. Isemura, "Colloidal Surfactants," p.42, Academic Press, New York, 1963.

16. J. M. Corkill, J. F. Goodman and T. Walker, Trans. Faraday Soc., 63, 768 (1967).

17. E. Vikinagstad, A. Skauge and H. Høiland, J. Colloid Interface Sci., 72, 59 (1979).

18. W. L. Masterton, J. Chem. Phys., 22, 1830 (1954).

19. G. Nemethy and H. A. Scheraga, J. Chem. Phys., 36, 340 (1962).

20. N. Nishikido, N. Yoshimura, M. Tanaka and S. Kaneshina, J. Colloid Interface Sci., in press.

21. S. Kaneshina, M. Toshimoto, H. Kobayashi, N. Nishikido, G Sugihara and M. Tanaka, J. Colloid Interface Sci., 73, 124 (1980).

22. N. Nishikido, M. Shinozaki, G. Sugihara, M. Tanaka and S. Kaneshina, J. Colloid Interface Sci., 74, 474 (1980).

23. R. R. Balmbra, J. S. Clunie, J. M. Corkilland J. F. Goodman, Trans. Faraday Soc., 58, 1661 (1962).

24. J. S. Clunie, J. F. Goodman and P. C. Symons, Trans. Faraday Soc., 65, 287 (1969).

25. J. M. Corkill and J. F. Goodman, Advan. Colloid Interface Sci., 2, 297 (1969).

26. K. Shinoda, in "Solvent Properties of Surfactant Solutions," K. Shinoda, Editor, Chap. 1, Marcel Dekker, New York, 1967.

27. H. Saito, Nippon Kagaku Zasshi, 92, 223 (1971).

28. T. Tsumori, N. Nishikido, Y. Moroi and R. Matuura, Mem. Fac. Sci. Kyushu Univ., C9, 57 (1974).

29. F. Harusawa, S. Nakamura and T. Mitsui, Colloid & Polymer Sci., 252, 613 (1974).

30. H. Nakajima and S. Fukushima, The 29th Symposium of Colloid and Surface Chemistry (Japan Chem. Soc.), Matsumoto, 1976.

31. T. Sugano, M. Tsuchiya and K. Suzuki, The 21th Symposium of Colloid and Surface Chemistry, Kyoto, 1968.

32. K. Suzuki and M. Tsuchiya, Bull. Inst. Chem. Res., Kyoto Univ., 47, 270 (1969).

33. S. D. Hamann, in "High Pressure Physics and Chemistry," R S. Bradley, Editor, Vol. 2, p.144, Academic Press, New York, 1963.

34. K. E. Weale, "Chemical Reactions at High Pressures," Chap. 5, E & F. N. Spon Ltd., London, 1967.

35. K. Suzuki and Y. Taniguchi, Symp. Soc. Exp. Biol., 26, 103 (1972).

36. K. Suzuki and Y. Taniguchi, in "High-Pressure Science and Technology," K. D. Timmechaus and M. S. Barber, Editors, Vol.1, p.548, Plenum, New York, 1979.

37. J. L. Neal and D. A. Goring, J. Phys. Chem, 74, 658 (1970).

38. E. H. Amagat, Ann. Chim., 29, 68 (1893).

39. L. S. Sandell and D. A. I Goring, J. Polymer Sci., A 2, 9, 115 (1971).

40. E. W. Anacker, in "Cationic Surfactants," E. Jungermann,
     Editor, p.203, Marcel Dekker, New York, 1970.
41. E. H. Crook, G. F. Trobbi and D. B. Fordyce, J. Phys. Chem.,
     $\underline{68}$, 3592 (1964).
42. N. Nishikido, Y. Moroi and R. Matuura, Bull. Chem. Soc. Jpn.,
     $\underline{48}$, 1387 (1975); N. Nishikido, J. Colloid Interface Sci., $\underline{60}$,
     242 (1977).

FLUORESCENCE PROBES OF MICELLAR SYSTEMS—AN OVERVIEW

Lawrence A. Singer
Department of Chemistry
University of Southern California
University Park
Los Angeles, California 90007

The photophysical background of luminescence probes io described. In general, abrupt changes in the fluorescence spectrum or yield of polar probes with added surfactant lead to estimates of the critical micelle concentration (CMC) of micelles. However, such studies are complicated by the often encountered polar probe-surfactant interactions below the CMC's. Non-polar arenes tend to partition almost completely into micelles with exit rates smaller ($<10^6$ s^{-1}) than their fluorescence decay rates (10^7 - 10^9 s^{-1}). The fluorescence decay of naphthalene is a composite of fluorescences from probes solubilized in both aqueous and micellar microenvironments. The fluorescence decay from nonpolar arenes in ionic micelles is sensitive to molecular oxygen and counterion quenching. In general, the attractive and repulsive interactions between ionic micelles and charged quenchers strongly mediate the fluorescence quenching of micelle-solubilized probes. The exact location of the latter within the micelle structure is still not resolved. Fluorescence de-polarization experiments with arene probes in common ionic micelles indicate micellar microviscosities of 20-30 cp (ambient temperature) in agreement with more recent estimates from intramolecular excimer-forming probes. A statistical model for intramicellar bi-molecular reactions is described which has been success-fully applied to both steady-state and transient experiments. The parameters derivable from this

73

methodology include k_q (the rate constant for intramicellar reaction) and $[M_T]$ (the concentration of the
host micelle present during the reaction).

INTRODUCTION

Molecules introduced into chemical or biological systems
for the purpose of elucidating the chemical and/or physical properties of the host system are molecular probes. This approach
requires that some readily observable property of the probe molecule respond in a regular manner to changes in its microenvironment. Probes based on spectroscopic methodologies are very popular since they are (i) nondestructive to probe and host, (ii)
generally sensitive, and (iii) relatively easy to use. However,
a spectroscopic probe is a reliable and interpretable sensor only
to the extent that its local environment in the host is describ-
able in terms of well-defined reference systems. Menger[1] recently
expressed this point well when he wrote in regard to the use of
benzene as a spectroscopic probe of micelles that "this procedure
presupposes that solvents or solvent mixtures can simulate a
micellar environment. Unfortunately, no solvent system yet developed solvates a benzene ring on one side with water and on
the other side with hydrocarbon (as might occur in a micelle)".
In addition, the spectroscopic probe technique necessarily assumes
that the probe molecule does not perturb the local environment
(or structure). On balance, it seems that this methodology does
provide useful information on complex macrosystems that is not
readily available by other means.

The luminescence probe approach (Figure 1) utilizes changes
in the emission (fluorescence or phosphorescence) of the electronically excited probe molecule (P*) to elucidate specific
properties of the host system. Although this overview concen-
trates on fluorescence probes of micellar systems, it should be
noted that fluorescence techniques have been used extensively
for over 25 years in the study and assay of biological systems
(proteins, liposomes, membranes).[2,3,4] Any attempt to dis-
tinquish between these two topics is almost arbitary, and
methodologies pioneered in one area are usually applicable to
the other.

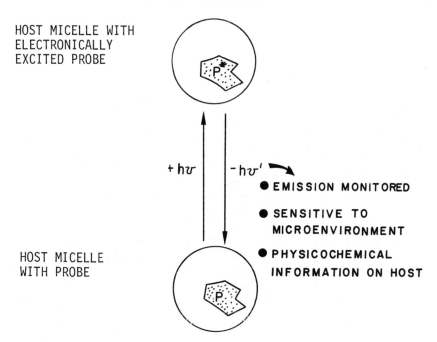

HOST MICELLE WITH
ELECTRONICALLY
EXCITED PROBE

$+ h\nu$ $- h\nu'$

● EMISSION MONITORED

● SENSITIVE TO
  MICROENVIRONMENT

● PHYSICOCHEMICAL
  INFORMATION ON HOST

HOST MICELLE
WITH PROBE

Figure 1.   Luminescence Probe as Sensor of Microenvironment.

THE PHOTOPHYSICS OF LUMINESCENCE PROBES

Electronic States of Organic Molecules

The more complex organic molecules typically absorb and emit
radiation in the spectral range 2500-6500 A which corresponds to
electronic transitions with energy changes of 2-5 eV or 45-115
kcal/mole.   Excitation may be by either continuous or pulsed
sources, with the latter now being generally commercially available following the proliferation of high intensity lasers in the
last 10 years.[5]

The state diagram in Figure 2 summarizes the common photophysical events that occur after electronic excitation of a ground
state molecule (S_o) into either its first (S_1) or second (S_2)
excited signlet state.   Internal conversion (a radiationless
transition between states of the same multiplicity) from
$S_2 \rightsquigarrow S_1$ is extremely fast ($k_{ic} \approx 10^{12}$ s^{-1}), and dominates over
all other pathways.   Thus, irrespective of which state is popu-
lated initially, the meaningful flow diagram for the excited
state molecules begins in S_1 (Kasha's rule[6]).

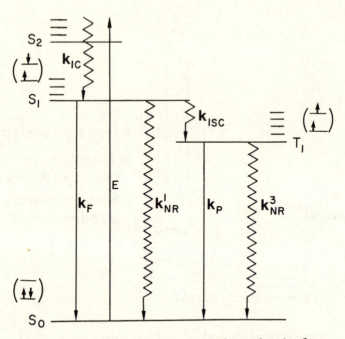

Figure 2.   State diagram and important photophysical processes
following excitation (E) of typical organic probe.

The unimolecular pathways of S_1 include radiative (<u>fluorescence</u>,
k_f) and nonradiative (internal conversion to S_o, k_{nr}^1)   decays and
<u>intersystem crossing</u> (an internal conversion between states of
different multiplicities) of $S_1 \rightsquigarrow T_1$ (k_{isc}).   Similarly, the T_1
returns to S_o by radiative (phosphorescence, k_p) and nonradiative
(k_{nr}^3) paths.

In the presence of a quencher, Q, of the S_1 (k_q^1) or T_1 (k_q^3)
states, additional radiationless decays operate which typically
follow pseudo-first-order kinetics.   A variety of mechanisms have
been elucidated for effective quenching at, or near, the diffusion
limit in fluid media ($k_q \lesssim k_{diff}$).[7] Note, that singlet-singlet
energy transfer by dipole-dipole coupling may occur over greater
than collisional distances in which case $k_q^1 > k_{diff}$.

Luminescence Yields. The Steady-State Experiment.

According to the above scheme, in the presence of Q, the quantum yield of fluorescence, <u>the number of photons emitted by S_1 per unit time/the number of photons absorbed by S_o per unit time</u>, is given by

$$\Phi_f = k_f/(k_f + k_{isc} + k_{nr}^1 + k_q^1[Q]) = k_f\tau_f \qquad (1)$$

where τ_f is the <u>fluorescence lifetime</u>. The <u>limiting fluorescence lifetime</u>, $\tau_f^L = (k_f + k_{isc} + k_{nr}^1)^{-1}$, is the lifetime observed in the absence of Q. The quantum yield of phosphorescence, <u>the number of photons emitted by T_1 per unit time/the number of photons absorbed by S_o per unit time</u>, is given by

$$\Phi_p = [k_{isc}/(k_f + k_{isc} + k_q^1[Q])][k_p/(k_p + k_{nr}^3 + k_q^3[Q])] =$$
$$k_{isc}\tau_f k_p\tau_p = \Phi_{isc}k_p\tau_p \qquad (2)$$

where Φ_{isc} is the quantum yield of intersystem crossing, <u>the number of S_1 molecules transforming into T_1 molecules per unit time/the number of photons absorbed by S_o per unit time</u>, and τ_p is the <u>phosphorescence lifetime</u>. Again $\tau_p^L = (k_p + k_{nr}^3)^{-1}$.

Typically, an emission quantum yield (Φ_f or Φ_p) is measured under the steady-state condition (continuous irradiation) by comparing the area under the emission curve with the area under the emission curve of a reference compound. The proper procedures for such measurements have been described in detail.[8,9]

Note that when Φ_f or Φ_p is measured in the absence (Φ_o) and presence (Φ) of Q, the quenching efficiency is conveniently presented in the Stern-Volmer manner which for fluorescence quenching is

$$(\Phi_f^o/\Phi_f) = (k_f\tau_f^L)/(k_f\tau_f) = 1 + \tau_f^L k_q^1[Q] = 1 + K_{sv}[Q] \qquad (3)$$

where the Stern-Volmer slope (K_{sv}) is the product of the limiting fluorescence lifetime and the bimolecular rate constant for quenching.

Luminescence Lifetimes. The Transient Experiment

Emission lifetimes (τ_f and τ_p) are directly measured in a transient experiment employing a pulsed excitation source. For the scheme in Figure 2, both the fluorescence and phosphorescence emissions will decay according to the simple exponential function

$$I_{(t)} = I_{(o)} e^{-(t/\tau)} \qquad\qquad (4)$$

where τ is either the fluorescence or phosphorescence lifetime. Since the excitation pulse width ideally should be narrower in time than the decay to be measured, nanosecond pulsed sources are required in order to measure fluorescence lifetimes which typically are on the submicrosecond time scale. However, deconvolution techniques can be used to extract the lifetime out of the more complicated decay curve that arises when the width of the exciting pulse is comparable to, or larger than, the emission lifetime.[10]

Exponential decays of decreasing lifetimes will be observed as the concentration of a diffusional quencher is increased. Since the fluorescence and phosphorescence lifetimes are given by $\tau_f = (k_f + k_{nr}^1 + k_{isc} + k_q^1[Q])^{-1}$ and $\tau_p = (k_p + k_{nr}^3 + k_q^3[Q])^{-1}$, the linear plots of τ_p^{-1} vs $[Q]$ will have intercepts of $(\tau_f^L)^{-1}$ and $(\tau_p^L)^{-1}$ and slopes of k_q^1 and k_q^3, respectively. Thus, for diffusional quenching of S_1 or T_1 by Q, measurable parameters from the transient experiment can predict the Stern-Volmer slope of the steady-state experiment ($K_{sv} = \tau_L k_q$).

When Q is within interaction distance of S_o, perhaps as a ground state complex, excitation yields S_1 (or T_1) subject to immediate ($\leq 10^{-9}$ s) and exclusive <u>static</u> quenching. Static quenching does not lead to a decrease in the observed emission lifetime, which typically measures events on a ns or longer time scale. However, it does decrease the emission <u>yield</u> measured in the steady-state experiment. Diffusional and static quenching can be distinguished by comparing the parameters of the transient experiment with the steady-state K_{sv}. For a more complete discussion of diffusional vs static quenching, see the recent review by Badley.[4]

Typical Values of Luminescence Yields and Lifetimes.

The generally observed range of values for Φ_f and Φ_p directly follow from the magnitudes of the k's in Figure 2. For many organic probes, typical values for the radiative rate constants are $10^6 \leq k_f \leq 10^{10}$ s-1 and $10^{-1} \leq k_p \leq 10^2$ s-1, with the latter reflecting the spin forbiddeness in the transition $T_1 \longrightarrow S_o$. Intersystem crossing rates range between $10^6 \leq k_{isc} \leq 10^{10}$ s-1, while the radiationless transition $S_1 \rightsquigarrow S_o$ is usually $k_{nr}^1 \leq 10^7$ s-1. Accordingly, k_f and k_{isc} often dominate the photophysics of the S_1 state meaning that $\Phi_f \approx k_f/(k_f + k_{isc})$ and $\tau_f \approx (k_f + k_{isc})^{-1}$. Because of a small activation energy often associated with intersystem crossing ($E_a \leq 3$ kcal/mole), Φ_f and τ_f may show a small temperature dependence. The above analysis leads to estimates of $10^{-4} \lesssim \Phi_f \lesssim 1$ and $10^{-10} \lesssim \tau_f \lesssim 10^{-6}$ s with the more commonly observed values being $0.05 \lesssim \Phi_f \lesssim 0.5$ and $10^{-9} \lesssim \tau_f \lesssim 10^{-7}$ s.

It has been known for many years that phosphorescence quantum yields typically are $\lesssim 10^{-4}$ in fluid media at room temperature (almost too low to measure), but orders of magnitude larger at 77°K in a rigid glass. This temperature dependence of Φ_p is related to the dramatic change in τ_p, and specifically the changing competition between k_p and k_{nr}^3 with change in temperature. The latter often decreases in magnitude from ~10^6 s^{-1} in fluid media at room temperature (where diffusional quenching operates effectively) to $10^{-1} - 10$ s^{-1} at 77° in a rigid glass.

Several recent studies have shown that phosphorescence probes are practical under micellar conditions in the presence of heavy atom perturbation [11,12] (which increases the magnitudes of k_{isc} and k_p and thus enhances Φ_p). With these longer-lived probes, the dynamic range of the luminescence probe experiment is extended to the millisecond time scale . Table I summarizes the key photophysical characteristics of fluorescence and phosphorescence probes.

Table I.   Comparative Characteristics of Fluorescence and
           Phosphorescence Emissions.

Process	Defined By	Typical Observations		Lifetimes, s
		Quantum Ylds.	Temp. Depend.	
Fluorescence	$\Phi_f = k_f \tau_f$	$(0.05 - 0.50)$	N.I.[a]	$(10^{-10} - 10^{-7})$
Phosphorescence	$\Phi_p = \Phi_{isc} k_p \tau_p$	$(\lesssim 10^{-4} - 0.1)$[b]	V.D.[c]	$(10^{-6} - 10)$[d]

[a] Nearly independent.

[b] Lower values generally observed at room temperatures in fluid media.

[c] Very dependent.

[d] Longer lifetimes generally observed for π,π^* triplets in rigid glass at low temperatures.

The linear dependence of Φ_o/Φ on [Q], predicted by eduation 3, and the exponential decays of the emissions (Equation 4), that are typically observed under homogeneous solution conditions, often are not realized with probes in micelles. The often observed nonlinear Stern-Volmer plots of the steady-state data, and the nonexponential decays in the transient experiments, result from a statistical distribution of the substrates among the available micelles. Accordingly, an ensemble of systems exists that requires special analytical methodologies as described later in this overview.

MICROENVIRONMENTAL EFFECTS

Influence of Polarity of Microenvironment

The local environment influences several luminescent parameters of the probe including spectral distribution, emission yield and lifetime, and degree of emission polarization.

Pioneering experiments designed to exploit the changes in these parameters with change in microenvironment were carried out by Weber and others in the 1950's on biomacromolecular systems.[3] The probes in these studies usually show a dramatic enhancement in Φ_f and a blue shift in the wavelength maximum of the fluorescence as the microenvironment changes from hydrophilic to hydrophobic. Typically these probes are almost nonfluorescent in water but strongly fluorescent in a protein microenvironment. Although Φ_f also tends to increase with increasing viscosity of the microenvironment, the polarity change seems to be of greater importance and Edelman and McClure[3] refer to these sensors as <u>hydrophobic probes</u>. Several examples of such probes are shown below.

HYDROPHOBIC PROBES

1 (ANS)   2 (DNS)   3 (ArMA)

ANS = 1- ANILINONAPHTHALENE-4-SULFONATE

DNS = 1- DIMETHYLAMINONAPHTHALENE-5-SULFONATE

ArMA = 5-(4'-ARSONOANILINO)-2-CHLORO-7-METHOXYACRIDINE

Dyes and Polar Probes in Micelles.   Complications

Due to Probe-Surfactant Interactions.

   In principle, any spectroscopic parameter that changes
abruptly as the microenvironment of the probe changes from aqueous
to micellar can be used as a CMC indicator as shown in Figure 3.
Unfortunately, complications are frequently encountered with dyes
and polar probes due to probe-surfactant interactions below the
CMC.

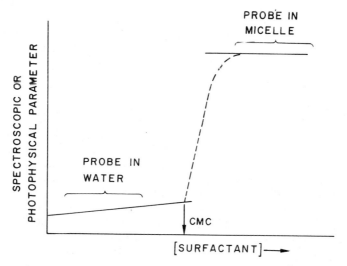

Figure 3.   Idealized probe response to change in microenvironment.

   The determination of CMC's by absorption spectral changes in
dyes has been used for over 30 years. Mukerjee and Mysels[13] noted
the potential errors in this method due to formation of dye-sur-
factant salts and mixed micelles at concentrations well below the
CMC of the pure surfactant. More recently, Robinson and coworkers[14]
studied the interaction of cationic acridine-type dyes with sodium
dodecyl sulfate (SDS) by both absorption and fluorescence techniques and detected two clearly different spectroscopic regions.
At concentrations below the surfactant CMC, the dyes displayed
blue-shifted spectra, decreased intensities at the absorption

wavelength maxima (possibly due to peak broadening), and decreased
fluorescences. At and above the CMC, slightly red-shifted spectra,
sharply increased intensities at the absorption wavelength maxima
(possibly due to peak narrowing), and increased fluorescence intensities were noted. It was suggested that the acridine-type dye
molecules assume a stacked aggregate structure with the anionic
surfactant below the CMC, but incorporate monomerically into SDS
micelles above the CMC.

Davis[15] reported that the fluorescence from 1-dimethyl-
aminonaphthalene-5-sulfonylglycine (4) was gradually enhanced and
blue-shifted (30-35 nm) with addition of cetyltrimethylammonium
bromide (CTAB) below and up to the CMC of the latter. No further
changes were noted with added CTAB above its CMC. In contrast,
the fluorescence yield of ammonium anilinonaphthalenesulfonate
(5) (positional isomer not indicated) is unchanged by added SDS
below the CMC, but is abruptly enhanced upon the formation of
micelles, and accordingly gives an estimate the CMC in excellent
agreement with other methods[16]. An earlier study[17] using the
magnesium salt of 8-anilinonaphthalene-1-sulfonate gave an
erroneously low estimate of the CMC of SDS, possibly because of
metal promoted probe-surfactant interaction.

Other environmentally sensitive polar fluorophors proposed
as micellar probes are indoles such as 6 (in water, λ_m = 371 nm;
in the CTAB micelle, λ_m = 355 nm)[18,19] and pyrene-3-carboxaldehyde
(7) (in methanol, λ_m = 450 nm with Φ_f = 0.15; in hexane, λ_m = 410 nm
with Φ_f < 0.001)[20]. However, a recent reexamination [21] suggests
that changes in the intensity and wavelength maximum of 7 are dependent on the protic or aprotic character, as well as the polarity,
of the medium. Further, nonexponential decays were noted in
ethanol-water solvent mixtures. The authors[21] point out that the
behavior of polarity probes such as 7 may be difficult to interpret
in the complicated microenvironment of a micelle.

Probe-surfactant interactions have been shown to increase with increasing hydrophobic structure in the probe. Minch and Shah[22] recently noted that uncharged merocyanine dyes (8-n) with alkyl groups longer than n-butyl show appreciable changes in their absorption spectra with added SDS below its CMC. From a study in our laboratory of the quenching of the fluorescence from a series of cationic pyrene derivatives (9-n) by the surfactant nitroxyl radical 10 (CMC = 4.6×10^{-4} $\underline{M}$), Atik[23] concluded that 9-11 (but not 9-1 or 9-5) associates with 10 at concentrations of the latter below its CMC. Finally, we recently reported electronic and esr spectral evidence for the formation of mixed aggregates of 10 and sodium 5-(1-pyrenyl) pentanoate (11-4) in dilute ($\sim 10^{-5}$ $\underline{M}$) aqueous solutions in the mole ration of 2:3.[24].

The above observations suggest that charged dyes and other polar molecules should be cautiously used as micelle probes because of (i) probe-surfactant interactions well below the CMC as well as (ii) a potentially complex dependence of the probe fluorescence spectrum and yield on the microenvironment.

Nonpolar Arenes in Micelles.

Distribution Between Aqueous Phase and Micelle. The above problem of probe-surfactant interactions below the CMC generally is not encountered with nonpolar arenes. Recent work by Almgren, Grieser and Thomas[25] shows that above the CMC, the association constants, K, of these probes with ionic micelles increase with increasing size of the arene (increasing hydrophobicity), and that for any single arene, K increases with increasing chain length of the surfactant constituting the micelle. Selected data is shown in Table II.

The exit rates of the nonpolar arenes typically fall into the range $k_{ex} \approx 10^3 - 10^6$ s^{-1}.[25] Accordingly, these micelle-solubilized arenes are expected to remain with their hosts during a single fluorescence experiment ($< 10^{-6}$ s), but should exit at rates comparable to, or faster than, their phosphorescence decays. Figure 4 correlates the time scales of these emission experiments with the time scale of micellar structural changes.

Smaller Arenes. Two-component decays. Smaller arenes, such as naphthalene, will distribute between the micelles and the water depending on the surfactant concentration. Hautala, Schore and Turro[26] demonstrated that the fluorescence decay from naphthalene in the presence of cetyltrimethylammonium chloride (CTAC) or CTAB micelles was a composite of emissions from probes residing in micellar and aqueous environments (Equation 5), and site exchange was slower than the time scale of the fluorescence experiment ($\lesssim 10^{-7}$ s).

Table II. Association Constants and Dissociation Rate Constants
           of Selected Arene Probes in the CTAB Micelle.[a]

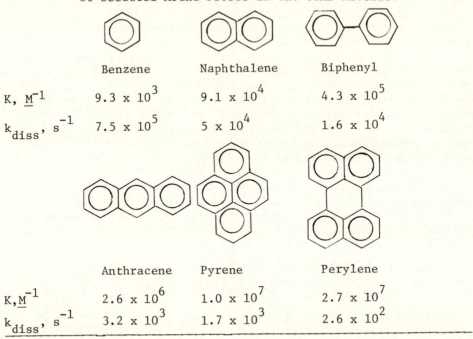

	Benzene	Naphthalene	Biphenyl
K, $\underline{M}^{-1}$	9.3×10^{3}	9.1×10^{4}	4.3×10^{5}
k_{diss}, s^{-1}	7.5×10^{5}	5×10^{4}	1.6×10^{4}

	Anthracene	Pyrene	Perylene
K, $\underline{M}^{-1}$	2.6×10^{6}	1.0×10^{7}	2.7×10^{7}
k_{diss}, s^{-1}	3.2×10^{3}	1.7×10^{3}	2.6×10^{2}

[a] From reference 25.

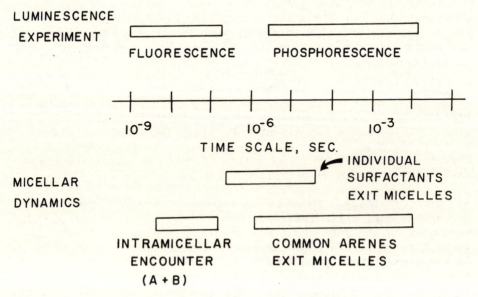

Figure 4. Correlation of luminescence probe experiments with
           time scale for micellar dynamics.

$$I_{(t)} = A_m \exp(-t/\tau_m) + A_w \exp(-t/\tau_w) \qquad (5)$$

A more recent reexamination[27] shows that composite fluorescences are observed in SDS also, but the shorter-lived ($\tau_w \approx 30$ ns) and weaker (A_w close to 0) fluorescence from naphthalene in the aqueous phase is often masked by the more intense ($A_m \approx 1$) and longer-lived fluorescence ($\tau_m \approx 50$ ns) from naphthalene in the micelle phase. The latter authors cleverly employed quenching counterions (see later discussion)(Br^- with CTAC, Cu^{2+} with SDS) to selectively reduce the contribution of the more intense fluorescence ($\tau_m < 10$ ns, $A_m \approx 0.9$) and reveal the weaker aqueous phase fluorescence component.

The Larger Arenes. The magnitude of the K's for the larger, commonly used, arenes (pyrene, perylene, anthracene) means that essentially all of these probes will reside in the micelles when the concentration of the latter is $[M_T] \gtrsim 10^{-4}$ M. The fluorescence lifetimes of these probes, which respond strongly to the microenvironment, can be exploited as monitors of micellization in the manner proposed in Figure 3.

Geiger and Turro[28] observed the fluorescence lifetime of pyrene in water (aerated, 126 ns; N_2-saturated, 226 ns) to be invariant with added CTAC or SDS up to their respective CMC's. At the CMC, the lifetimes abruptly increase as indicated in Table III as the probe microenvironment changes from aqueous to micellar.

Table III. Typical Fluorescence Lifetimes For Pyrene In Aqueous and Micellar Environments in the Presence and Absence of O_2. (Reference 28)

	Water	τ_f in		
		CTAC Micelle	SDS Micelle	CTAB Micelle
		(ns)		
Aerated	126	156	158	122
N_2-Saturated	226	281	314	165

Kalyanasundaram and Thomas[29] noted changes in the vibronic band intensities in the pyrene fluorescence spectrum as well as changes in fluorescence lifetime upon incorporation of pyrene in typical ionic micelles. They suggest analysis of the former as an additional methodology for measuring CMC's.

Intramicellar Quenching by O_2. The lengthening of the fluorescence lifetime upon incorporation of pyrene in CTAC or SDS micelles apparently results from localization of the probe in a microenvironment less favorable for encounter with potential quenchers in the system. The dynamics of intramicellar O_2 quenching has been clarified by the recent work of Turro, Aikawa and Yekta on 1,5-dimethylnaphthalene in the presence of CTAC and SDS micelles.[30]

In their scheme, (Figure 5) the probe resides exclusively in the micelles where it is subject to "static" (reaction with O_2 already present in the micelle at the time of excitation) and "dynamic" (reaction with O_2 that diffuses into the micelle subsequent to excitation) quenching. Using earlier data to determine the concentration of micelle-solubilized O_2,[31] and Poisson statistics (see later discussion) to determine the average occupancy number of O_2 per micelle, they analyzed the nonexponential fluorescence decays observed at $P_{O_2} > 1$ atm. The results indicate that $K_{eq} = 3 \times 10^2$ $\underline{M}^{-1}$ for O_2 incorporation into these ionic micelles which is consistent with the generally greater solubility of O_2 in organic solvents compared with water. The "static", intramicellar, quenching rate constant of $k_r \lesssim 5 \times 10^7$ s^{-1} demonstrates that quenching of this probe by O_2 in a micelle environment occurs at, or close to, the encounter limit as it does in bulk water, $k_q = 1.43 \times 10^{10}$ $\underline{M}^{-1}$ s^{-1}, and as was demonstrated previously with other probes in bulk organic solvents.[32]

The increase in fluorescence lifetime when a probe is incorporated into a micelle under normal aerated conditions (1 atm) is due to its concentration in a microenvironment relatively free of O_2, since the average number of O_2 molecules per micelle is only ~ 0.1 under ordinary atmospheric conditions.

Counterion Quenching. Fluorescence lifetimes do not necessarily lengthen upon incorporation of the arenes into micelles (see Table 4). Probes solubilized in ionic micelles with counterions capable of fluorescence quenching often show a decrease in lifetime (and fluorescence yield) as the microenvironment changes from aqueous to micellar.

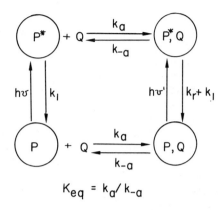

$$K_{eq} = k_a / k_{-a}$$

Figure 5.   Schematized "static" and dynamic quenching
            by O_2 of micelle-solubilized probe.   (Reference 30)

Table IV.   Influence of Counterions on the Fluorescence Lifetimes
            of Arenes Solubilized in Micelles.

Arene	Micelle	τ_f (ns)	Reference
Pyrene	CTAC	156	28
	CTAB	118	28, 41
	CTAB + Br$^-$ (0.1 $\underline{M}$)	90	41
	CTAB + I$^-$ (0.001 $\underline{M}$)	13	42
Naphthalene	CTAC	55	
	CTAB	7	27
	SDS	53	
	SDS + CuCl$_2$ (0.01 $\underline{M}$)	1.8	
Perylene	CTAC	5.0	
	CTAB	5.0	43
Anthracene	CTAC	2.2	
	CTAB	1.0	43

   The role of the micelle surface charge in counterion quenching
has been demonstrated in a number of experiments. Hautala, Schore
and Turro observed that the fluorescence lifetime of naphthalene
in the CTAC micelle is shortened, but in the SDS micelle is unchanged, upon addition of KBr.[26] Pownall and Smith[33] reported
that I⁻ is an effective quencher of the anthracene fluorescence
in the presence of CTAC micelles, while pyridinium ion is equally
as effective in the presence of SDS micelles, but neither is effective in the presence of the other micelle. These experiments and
others [34,35] reflect the attractive and repulsive interactions
between ionic micelles and charged quenchers of opposite and
similar charges that mediate encounters of the latter with micelle-
solubilized arenes (Figure 6). For a more detailed discussion
of this topic and the related observations on the reaction of the
hydrated electron with micelle-solubilized arenes, see the recent
excellent review by Thomas.[36]

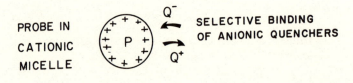

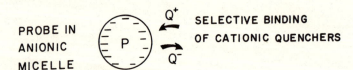

   Figure 6.   Micelle-mediated encounters between probes
               and ionic quenchers.

   Photoinduced Electron Transfer to Metal Counterions. Several
recent studies on photoinduced electron transfer between micelle-
solubilized probes and metal counterions further demonstrate the
significance of the electrostatic factors. Photoexcitation of
N-methylphenothiazine (MPTH) solubilized in copper dodecylsulfate
micelles leads to rapid (ns) and efficient (ϕ = 0.93) electron
transfer yielding MPTH⁺ and Cu⁺.[37] The energetically favorable

back electron transfer is inhibited by rapid escape of
Cu^+ ($\sim10^8$ s^{-1})[38] from the host micelle and separation from the
micelle-solubilized $MPTH^+$. The latter persists until random
reencounter and reaction with an aqueous phase Cu^+.

Very efficient photoinduced electron transfer occurs between
MPTH and Eu^{3+} cations under similar conditions.[38] In this system,
back electron transfer appears to compete with the slower escape
of Eu^{2+} ($\sim10^6$ s^{-1}) from the host micelle. Evidence was also
obtained for escape by direct transfer of Eu^{2+} from its host
micelle to a randomly encountered second micelle.

Brugger and Gratzel[39] reported a rather subtle, but potentially important, micelle-mediated charge separation reaction.
Photoexcitation of ruthenium (II) trisbipyridine ($Ru(bpy)_3^{2+}$) leads
to electron transfer reaction A with tetradecylmethylviologen
($C_{14}MV^{2+}$) (12) (k_{et} = 8 x 10^8 $\underline{M}^{-1}$ s^{-1} in the absence or presence
of CTAC micelles.

$$CH_3\overset{+}{N}\langle O \rangle\text{---}\langle O \rangle\overset{+}{N}\text{---}(CH_2)_{13}CH_3 \quad 2\,Cl^-$$

12

12

$$[Ru(bpy)_3^{2+}]^* + C_{14}MV^{2+} \xrightarrow{\quad k_{et} \quad} Ru(bpy)_3^{3+} + C_{14}MV^+ \quad (A)$$

$$Ru(bpy)_3^{3+} + C_{14}MV^+ \xrightarrow{\quad k'_{et} \quad} Ru(bpy)_3^{2+} + C_{14}MV^{2+} \quad (B)$$

The normally fast back reaction (B) was shown to be retarded
by a factor of at least 100 in the presence of the CTAC micelles.
It is suggested that $C_{14}MV^+$ incorporates into the CTAC micelle
which slows down (B) because of the repulsive interaction between
$Ru(bpy)_3^{3+}$ and the cationic micelle. The prolonged lifetime of
the transients produced by reaction (A) is significant because
these species are energetically capable of producing O_2 and H_2
from water at electrode surfaces.[40]

Intramicellar Quenching by Halide Counterions. The data in
Table 4 show that fluorescence lifetimes often are shorter for
arenes solubilized in the CTAB micelle compared with the CTAC
micelle.[27,28,41,43] This fluorescence lifetime difference is
ascribed to fluorescence quenching by the counterion Br^- in the
former micelles (Cl^- does not seem to quench arene fluorescence).
Iodide ion is an even more effective counterion quencher as shown
by the dramatic shortening of the fluorescence lifetime of pyrene
solubilized in the CTAB micelle from 118 to 13 ns by addition of
10^{-3} $\underline{M}$ I^-.[42] Qualitatively, the relative efficiencies of fluorescence quenching by halide ion are: I^- >> Br^- >> Cl^-.

If the fluorescence lifetime of the arene in the CTAC micelle
is used as an indication of the fluorescence lifetime in the
CTAB micelle in the absence of counterion quenching, then (according to a kinetic scheme for intramicellar quenching described later)

$$\tau^{-1}_{CTAB} = k_1 + \bar{n}k_q \approx \tau^{-1}_{CTAC} + \bar{n}k_q \qquad (6)$$

where k_q is the rate constant for intramicellar fluorescence
quenching by Br^- and $\bar{n}$ is the average number of counterions associated with a CTAB micelle. Using $\bar{n} \approx 50$,[44] the lifetime data in
Table 4 leads to estimates of k_q: anthracene, 1.1×10^7 s^{-1},
naphthalene, 2.5×10^6 s^{-1}; pyrene, 4.4×10^4 s^{-1}; perylene, no
difference in lifetime noted which leads to estimate of
$k_q \lesssim 4 \times 10^5$ s^{-1} (assuming that a 10% difference between τ_{CTAC} and
τ_{CTAB} would have been measureable). This analysis reveals orders
of magnitude differences in k_q which may be due to (i) real
differences in the rates of the fluorescence quenching reaction
after encounter of the excited arene and Br^- and/or (ii) differences in the intramicellar encounter frequencies of the reactants.
The latter could arise from different solubilization sites for the
arenes,[43] or from specific structural perturbations of the host
micelle by the different arenes that lead to different barriers
to intramicellar mobility.

Solubilization Sites of the Nonpolar Arenes. In general, the
detailed solubilization sites of the nonpolar arenes within ionic
micelles have not been elucidated. The similarity of the electronic absorption spectral data of benzene (at 0.7 mole fraction)
in the CTAB micelle with benzene in hexane was interpreted as
indicating a hydrocarbon-like environment for the probe in the
former.[45] However, Fendler and Patterson[46] point out the importance of the benzene/micelle mole ratio in such studies.
Earlier nmr studies by Ericksson and Gillberg[47] on benzene in
the CTAB micelle seem to indicate that the probe is solubilized at

the water-micelle interface at low benzene content, and that
additional benzene is solubilized nearby with displacement of water
from the interior. Overall, increasing the benzene content in the
micelle leads to a decrease in the polarity of the environment
sensed by the probe. Fendler and Patterson[46] propose that their
earlier observations on the reaction of benzene with the hydrated
electron[48] supports different solubilization sites for benzene in
the CTAB and SDS micelles, and propose solubilization at the
water-micelle interface in the former.

Mukerjee and coworkers[49] have examined the "solvent-induced"
bands in the electronic absorption spectra of benzenes and naptha-
lene which suggests that these probes are primarily located at
the water-micelle interface. Their conclusion was based on a
micelle structural model that excludes water from the micelle
interior.

Thomas and coworkers[36] have examined the chemical shifts in
the proton nmr spectra of CTAB in the presence of solubilized
pyrene probes and conclude that those with hydrophilic groups
(pyrenesulfonic acid, pyrenebutyrate) tend to locate towards, or
on, the surface while pyrene is solubilized more towards the
interior. Kalyanasundaram and Thomas[29] examined the vibrational
structure in the fluorescence spectrum of micelle-solubilized
pyrene (which is sensitive to solvent polarity) and also concluded that pyrene is solubilized away from the polar surface,
and that the polarity of the probe's microenvironment is determined by the degree of water penetration into the interior.
Micelles with larger head groups (such as CTAB) are subject to
greater water penetration than those with smaller head groups
(such as dodecylammonium chloride).[29] Rodgers and de Silva e
Wheeler[42] propose that intramicellar fluorescence quenching of
interior-solubilized pyrene (in CTAB) by Br^- occurs by way of
"water channels" that allows penetration by ionic quenchers. The
different degrees of anthracene and perylene fluorescence quenching by Br^- (discussed above) was ascribed by Patterson and Vieil[43]
to solubilization of the former at the micelle surface and the
latter in the micelle interior. More recently, Almgren, Grieser,
and Thomas[25] noted that arenes tend to be twice as soluble in
micelles composed of trimethylammonium surfactants compared with
micelles composed of alkylsulfate surfactants of the same hydrophobicity. They suggest that this difference may reflect solubilization of the arenes nearer the surface in the cationic micelles
where there is a specific interaction with the quaternary ammonium
group.

At this time, there seems to be general agreement that
the hydrophilic probes are located at, or very near, the water-
micelle interfacial region. However, while there are various
opinions about the binding sites of the nonpolar probes, the

consensus seems to be that these probes are solubilized in the <u>outer</u>
rather than the <u>inner</u> hydrophobic core. To a certain extent, this
uncertainty in probe binding reflects the overly simplified structural models of the ionic micelle that have prevailed for the past
thirty years. As newer and more detailed structural models are
presented[1], the key features of nonpolar arene binding in ionic
micelles should emerge.

MICELLE MICROVISCOSITY

One of the first attempts to measure micelle microviscosity
utilized fluorescence depolarization[50] which is based on the
competing rates of rotational diffusion and fluorescence decay in
the probe molecule.

Irradiation of a group of randomly oriented molecules with
plane-polarized light (Figure 7) results in selected excitation of
those molecules that have the direction of their absorption
oscillator parallel to the polarization plane of the exciting
beam. In fluid media, molecular rotation will further randomize
the excited molecules and the degree of polarization in the
emission is defined as

$$P = (I_{\parallel} - I_{\perp})/(I_{\parallel} + I_{\perp}) \qquad (7)$$

where $I_{\parallel}$ and $I_{\perp}$ are the fluorescence intensities observed through
polarizers oriented parallel and perpendicular to the plane of
polarization of the exciting beam.

The polarization, P, depends on the competition between the
rates of emission and rotational diffusion expressed in the Perrin
equation as

$$[(1/P) - (1/3)]/[(1/P_o) - (1/3)] = 1 + \tau \underline{k}T/(\eta V) \qquad (8)$$

where P_o is the observed polarization in a medium of high viscosity
at low temperature (where there is minimal reorientation of the
excited molecule prior to emission), τ_f is the average emission
lifetime, V is the effective volume of the probe molecule in cc
(assumed to be a sphere), η is the viscosity (poise), $\underline{k}$ is
Boltzman's constant, and T is the absolute temperature.

Shinitzky and coworkers,[50] in their classical study almost
10 years ago, presented a series of modifications applicable to
the commonly used planar arene probes. They show that when the
absorption and emission oscillators of the arene probe are parallel,

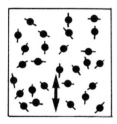 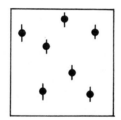 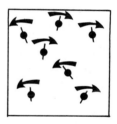

PLANE-POLARIZED
LIGHT(↕) IRRAD-
IATION OF RAND-
OMLY ORIENTED
PROBE MIXTURE

SELECTIVE EXCI-
TATION OF PROP-
ERLY ORIENTED
PROBES

ROTATIONAL
DIFFUSION
DEPOLARIZES
PROBES

Figure 7.   Fluorescence depolarization experiment.

Table V.   Micelle Microviscosities at Ambient Temperatures as
Measured by Fluorescence Depolarization Experiments.

Micelle	Arene Probe	$\bar{\eta}$, cp (°C)	Ea[a](kcal/mole)	Ref.[d]
DTAB[b]	2-Methylanthracene	26 (27)	7.2	50
	Perylene	17 (27)	9.6	50
CTAB	2-Methylanthracene	30 (27)	6.2	50
	Perylene	19 (27)	9.6	50
SDS	2-Methylanthracene	15	–	41
	2-Methylanthracene	36[c]	–	41
SDS	A Cyanine Dye	30 (25)	–	51

[a]Activation energy for rotational diffusion.

[b]Dodecyltrimethylammonium bromide.

[c]For an "aged" micelle.

[d]Reference.

as generally occurs in the longest wavelength abosrption band,
an equation identical to (8) obtains with the exception that η is
replaced by $\bar{\eta}$, with the latter being the "microviscosity" of the
system (the harmonic mean of the effective viscosities opposing the
in- and out-of-plane rotations of the planar arene). Experiments
of this type lead to estimates of $\bar{\eta}$ shown in Table 5.

The lower estimates of $\bar{\eta}$ obtained with perylene (τ_f = 5-6 ns)
compared with 2-methylanthracene (τ_f = 1-2 ns) may arise from
contributions to depolarization from rotation of the host micelle.
In general, the ideal probes for fluorescence depolarization
studies should (i) be rigid structures to avoid depolarization
arising from side group rotations, (ii) show high and constant P_o
values in the longest wavelength absorption band to eliminate
errors due to slight shifts in the absorption spectrum,(iii) have
τ_f's of 1-8 ns which will lead to measureable degrees of depolarization in media with viscosities of 1 - 100 cp (the range apparently
applicable to micelle interiors), and (iv) have intrinsically
large values for their extinction coefficients and Φ_f's which
means high sensitivity in fluorescence measurements.

The microviscosities measured in the fluorescence depolarization experiments (15-30 cp) indicate that the solubilization
sites of the probes are somewhat less fluid than hydrocarbon
solvents of similar chain lengths (1-2 cp), but still liquid-like.

The activation energies for rotational diffusion of perylene
in DTAB and CTAB were carefully remeasured as 8.4 and 8.6 kcal/mole,
respectively.[52] Dorrance, Hunter, and Philp point out the almost
exact correspondence of these values for the rotational activation
energy of perylene with the previously measured values of the
activation energy for intramicellar pyrene excimer formation in
the same cationic micelles.[53,54] This latter reaction
($^1Py^* + Py \longrightarrow {}^1Py^*$) is a diffusion-limited reaction[55] so that the
measured E_a presumably is the activation energy for translational
diffusion through the medium. The authors believe it is significant that these two separate experiments, proceeding on very
different time scales (a few ns for fluorescence depolarization
vs ~10^{-7} s for excimer formation), sense a similar activation
barrier. They suggest that the mobility of the pyrene molecules
in the micelle is very nearly two-dimensional (i.e. parallel-like
to the surface), and does not involve movement of the probe through
the center of the micelle.

Several recent reports have utilized intramolecular excimer
formation to study micelle microsviscosity. In this approach,
the excimer to monomer fluorescence ratio (I_E/I_M) from micelle-
solubilized probes is compared with the ratios obtained in a
series of suitable reference solvents of varying macroscopic
viscosities.[56-58] This ratio decreases with increasing η because

of the viscosity-dependent reorganizational activation energy (of
the probe geometry and the alkane chains in the host micelle)
associated with achieving the excimer conformation.   Turro and
coworkers[58] point out that the increasing ratio of I_E/I_M with
increasing temperature for <u>intramolecular</u> excimer formation (in
contrast to the inverse temperature effect on <u>intermolecular</u>
excimer formation) is "consistent with viscosity as the kinetically
limiting feature for achievement of the proper geometry for excimer
formation".   Zachariasse comments that the intramolecular probes
have the intrinsic advantage of requiring no more than a single
probe molecule per micelle, thereby minimizing structural perturbations of the host.[56]

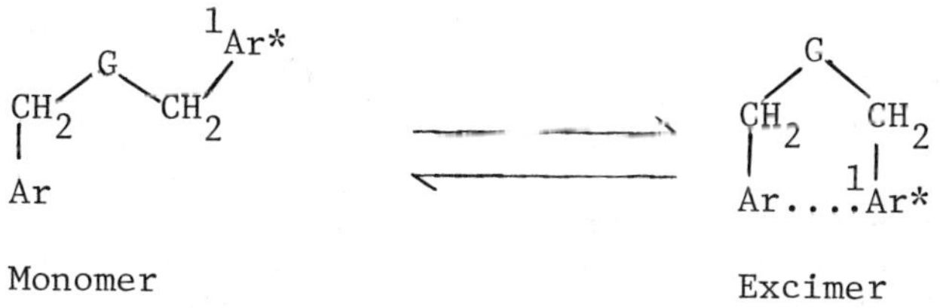

Monomer   Excimer

13, G = CH_2, Ar = 1-pyrenyl

14, G = CH_2, Ar = phenyl

15, G = O, Ar = 4-biphenyl

16, G = CH_2, Ar = 1-naphthyl

        Table 6 summarizes the recent results obtained with these
probes.   In general, the results show good internal agreement
and also agree with the microviscosities measured by the fluorescence depolarization experiments.   An interesting observation
requiring further clarification is the apparent dependence of the
measured microviscosity (or "microfluidity" as the term preferred
by the author) on probe size (13 vs 14).[56]

Table VI. Micelle Microviscosities as Measured by the Intramolecular
Excimer-Forming Probes.

Probe	Micelle	$\bar{\eta}$ (20°), cp	Reference
13	SDS	19	56
14	SDS	4	56
15	SDS	10	57
	CTAC	20	57
	CTAB	42	57
16	SDS	9	58
	CTAC	31	58
	CTAB	39	58

STATISTICAL MODEL FOR INTRAMICELLAR KINETICS

There has been notable success in using statistical models to
analyze the photophysical data from both steady-state and transient
experiments.[25,53,59-69] In this approach, the micelles are viewed
as fixed sites (on the time scale of the experiment) for complete
or partial incorporation of the reactants, with the distribution
of the latter among the micelles described by some distribution
function. (Figure 8)

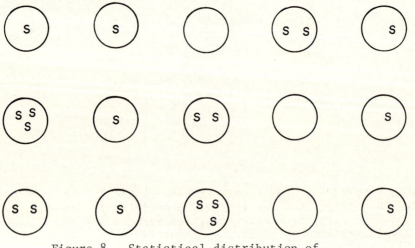

Figure 8. Statistical distribution of
substrate (S) among micelles
leads to ensemble of systems.

Poisson Distribution Model. Multistep Equilibrium

Model for Substrate Binding.

   In their pioneering work on intramicellar pyrene excimer formation, Dorrance and Hunter[53] analyzed the monomer and excimer
fluorescence quantum yields in terms of the ensemble $\sum\limits_{n=0}^{\infty} M.P_n$

(a micelle containing n probe molecules) described by the function

$$\alpha_n = (\bar{n})^n / (1 + \bar{n})^{n+1} \tag{9}$$

where α_n is the fraction of micelles that contain n pyrene molecules
and $\bar{n}$ is the average number of probe molecules per micelle. More
recent work on this and other intramicellar reactions indicates
that both steady-state and transient photophysical data are consistent with the standard Poisson distribution of the reactants
among the micelles (Equation 10).

$$\alpha_n = (\bar{n})^n \exp(-\bar{n}) / n! \tag{10}$$

   A Poisson distribution of the reactants among the micelles
directly follows from a multistep equilibrium model for association
of a substrate (S) with the same forward rate constant for binding
(k_b), but a linearly increasing dissociation rate constant (nk_{-b})
at each step (where n is the number of bound substrate molecules).

Scheme 1. Multistep Equilibrium Model for Binding

$$M + S \underset{k_{-b}}{\overset{k_b}{\rightleftharpoons}} M.S \qquad K_1 = k_b/k_{-b} = K_b$$

$$M.S + S \underset{2k_{-b}}{\overset{k_b}{\rightleftharpoons}} M.S_2 \qquad K_2 = K_b/2$$

$$M.S_{n-1} + S \underset{nk_{-b}}{\overset{k_b}{\rightleftharpoons}} M.S_n \qquad K_n = K_b/n$$

   In this scheme, the association constant at each step is
given by $K_b/n = [M.S_n] / \left\{ [M.S_{n-1}][S] \right\}$ and by successive

substitution

$$[M.S_n] = [M](K_b[S])^n/n! \tag{11}$$

so that

$$\sum_{n=0}^{\infty} [M.S_n] = [M]\left\{1 + K_b[S] + (K_b[S])^2/2 \cdots\cdots\cdots\right.$$

$$\left.\cdots(K_b[S])^n/n!\right\} = [M]\exp(K[S]). \tag{12}$$

Thus,

$$\alpha_n = (K_b[S])^n\exp(-K_b[S])/n! \tag{13}$$

and, if the substrate S is completely incorporated into the micelles,

$$K_b[S] = [S_T]/[M_T] = \bar{n} \tag{14}$$

where $[S_T]$ and $[M_T]$ refer to the <u>total</u> concentrations of substrate and micelle. The Poisson distribution function follows directly from equations 13 and 14.

Intramicellar Reactions

Intramicellar reactions are often designed so that there is single occupancy by the probe (P) molecule in order to simplify the mathematical and chemical schemes. This condition is satisfied when $[P_T]/[M_T] = \bar{n} \lesssim 0.1$ which means that most of the micelles do not contain any P ($\alpha_o \gtrsim 0.9$), but among the occupied micelles, single occupancy dominates. Co-reactants, such as quenchers (Q), added to this system will partition between the aqueous phase and the micelles, and the distribution among the latter will follow Poisson statistics to give an ensemble of micelles containing one probe molecule and n quencher molecules, $\sum_{n=o}^{\infty}$ M.P.Q$_n$.

The equations describing the results from steady-state and transient experiments have been reported for kinetics models where

(i)   Q is completely incorporated into the micelles with no intermicellar transfer occurring during the time of the experiment[62,64,66]

(ii) Q resides in both the aqueous phase and the micelles,
      but the time for site exchange is long compared to the
      time of the experiment[62,67], and

(iii) Q resides in both the aqueous phase and the micelles and the
      time for site exchange is comparable to, or shorter than,
      the time of the experiment[65,66].

    Some recent results from our laboratory using pyrene as the
probe are elaborated below as case (i) examples.

Intramicellar Fluorescence Quenching

    The kinetic scheme for case (i) fluorescence quenching is

Scheme 2.   Intramicellar Quenching

$$M.P.Q_n \xrightarrow{\alpha_n I_a} M.P^*.Q_n \qquad \text{Excitation of ensemble}$$

$$M.P^*.Q_n \xrightarrow{k_1} M.P.Q_n \qquad \text{All first-order decays of excited probe}$$

$$M.P^*.Q_n \xrightarrow{nk_q} M.P.Q_n \qquad \text{Intramicellar quenching}$$

where α_n is the fraction of total probes in the micelle $M.P.Q_n$
and $k_1 = \tau_f^{-1}$ (reciprocal of fluorescence lifetime measured in
the absence of Q). The intramicellar quenching is a first-order
rate (unit of s^{-1}) and linearly increases with the number of
quencher molecules in the micelle. For diffusion-limited reactions,
k_q measures the intramicellar encounter frequency of P* with Q.
Note that in this scheme (case i), each micelle in the ensemble
retains its integrity during the time duration of the experiment.

    For each micelle in the ensemble, a partial fluorescence
quantum yield is defined as

$$\phi_n = k_f/(k_1 + nk_q) = k_f \tau_f (1 + nA)^{-1} \qquad (15)$$

where $A = k_q/k_1$. The total fluorescence quantum yield is

$$\Phi_f = \sum_{n=o}^{\infty} \alpha_n \phi_n = \alpha_o \phi_o + \alpha_1 \phi_1 \cdots\cdots\cdots \alpha_n \phi_n \qquad (16)$$

and the quantum yield in the absence of quencher is

$$\Phi_f^o = k_f \tau_f \tag{17}$$

so that

$$\Phi_f / \Phi_f^o = \sum_{n=o}^{\infty} \alpha_n (1 + nA)^{-1} = \alpha_o + \alpha_1 (1 + A)^{-1} +$$

$$\alpha_2 (1 + 2A)^{-1} \ldots \alpha_n (1 + nA)^{-1} \tag{18}$$

where α_n is the Poisson weighting factor for the micelle containing n quencher molecules. Note that the quantum yield ratio in (18) is the inverse of the conventional Stern-Volmer format. In practice, the experimental data is simulated by equation 18 using the calculated α_n's with variable values for the A parameter until a best-fit is found. In our own work, contributions from succeeding terms in the ensemble are included until $[\alpha_n (1 + nA)^{-1}]/\sum_{n=o}^{\infty} [\alpha_n (1 + nA)^{-1}] \leq 0.01$. Figure 9 shows this approach for the fluorescence quenching of a series of cationic pyrene derivatives (9-1, 9-5, 9-11) by the surfactant nitroxyl radical 10 in the SDS micelle (where both reactants are completely incorporated).[68] Note the nonlinear form of the Stern-Volmer plot which is typical of such systems.

The fluorescence quenching data is simulated nearly as well (Figure 9, dotted lines) by the approximation

$$\Phi_f / \Phi_f^o = \alpha_o + (1 - \alpha_o)(1 + \bar{n}A)^{-1} \tag{19}$$

where α_o is the fraction of micelles that contain no Q (as calculated by equation 10). At higher concentrations of Q, as $\alpha_o \longrightarrow 0$, a linear Stern-Volmer plot is predicted. Estimates of k_q by (19) often are within 10% of values determined by the exact method. A comparison of Stern-Volmer factors calculated by the approximate and exact methods for values of A and $\bar{n}$ appears in Table 7. The results show that serious divergence between the two calculations is expected at larger $\bar{n}$ values (≥ 4) for systems with values of A ≥ 1.

Table VII. A Comparison of Calculated Partial Stern-Volmer Factors. (Reference 68)

$A^{c)}$	$\Phi_o/\Phi^{a,b)}$					
	$\bar{n} = 0.5$	1.0	2.0	3.0	4.0	5.0
0.1	1.03/1.05	1.08/1.10	1.17/1.19	1.28/1.28	1.42/1.39	1.50/1.46
0.5	1.09/1.18	1.28/1.37	1.77/1.76	2.33/2.19	2.93/2.67	3.44/3.10
1.0	1.16/1.27	1.48/1.59	2.36/2.31	3.29/3.16	5.09/4.34	6/07/5.10
2.0	1.25/1.38	1.74/1.84	3.26/3.13	5.41/4.73	8.01/6.65	10.1/8.56
5.0	1.40/1.50	2.12/2.22	4.73/4.54	9.15/8.10	15.6/13.0	22.1/18.1
10.0	1.49/1.57	2.36/2.42	5.68/5.51	12.4/11.3	23.3/21.0	38.6/31.5

a)Calculated by Equation (19)/calculated by Equation (18).

b)---- values that differ by $\geq$ 100%. ——— values that differ by $\geq$ 20%.

c)$A = k_q/k_1$.

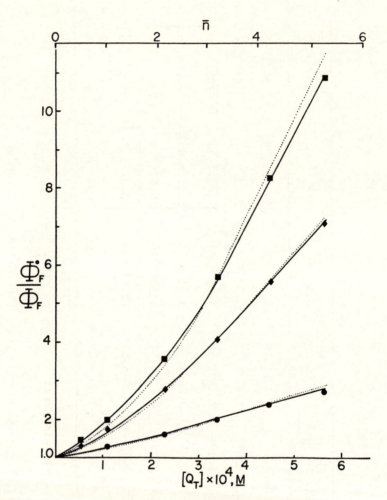

Figure 9.   Simulations of the steady-state fluorescence
            quenching data by Equation 18 _____ and
            Equation 19 ...... Best-fit values of A.
            Upper curves for 9-11: by (18), A = 2.76;
            by (19), A = 2.25.   Middle curves for
            9-5: by (18), A = 1.58; by (19), A = 1.32.
            Lower curves for 9-1: by (18), A = 0.42;
            by (19), A = 0.40.   Reproduced from
            reference 68 with permission of North–Holland
            Publishing Co.

The biexponential function describing the time dependence of the probe emission based on Scheme 2 is[62]

$$I_{(t)} = I_{(o)} \exp\left\{\bar{n}[\exp(-k_q t) - 1] - k_1 t\right\} \tag{20}$$

with the more convenient logarithmic form being

$$\ln(I/I_o) = \bar{n}[\exp(-k_q t) - 1] - k_1 t. \tag{21}$$

Note that in the absence of Q ($\bar{n} = 0$), the decay is a simple exponential function as expected. At sufficiently short t, where the approximation $\exp(-X) \approx (1 - X)$ is valid, equation 21 simplifies to the exponential function

$$\ln(I/I_o) \approx -(\bar{n}k_q + k_1)t. \tag{22}$$

At large t, the function approaches another exponential approximation

$$\ln(I/I_o) \approx -(\bar{n} + k_1 t). \tag{23}$$

Both of these limiting cases are useful as shown below.

Figure 10 is a semilogarithmic plot of the pyrene fluorescence decay in the SDS micelle in the presence of added surfactant nitroxyl radical 10 as quencher. Both fluorophor and quencher are completely incorporated into the SDS micelle. In the absence of Q, the fluorescence follows a simple exponential as expected. As [Q_T] is increased (higher $\bar{n}$ values), a second exponential segment at short t assumes greater importance with a slope that increases in magnitude according to equation 22. Analysis of these early exponential segments leads to $k_q = (1.4 \pm 0.1) \times 10^7 s^{-1}$.

In cases where the limiting slope at large t is realized, a second methodology can be used. According to equation 23, the limiting slope at large t is k_1, and the extrapolated intercept is $\bar{n}$. These graphically determined values can be used in equation 21, with k_q as a variable, to simulate the complete decay curve and so obtain a best-fit value of k_q.

Figure 11 illustrates this approach for the fluorescence quenching of the anionic pyrene derivative 11-4 by the surfactant nitroxyl radical 10 in the CTAC micelle.[70] The limiting slopes in

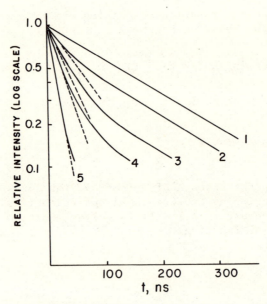

Figure 10.   Semi-logarithmic plot of the pyrene
fluorescence decay in the presence of
the SDS micelle in the absence (curve 1)
and presence of surfactant nitroxyl radical
10 as follows: curve 2, $\bar{n}$ = 1.0; curve 3,
$\bar{n}$ = 2.0; curve 4, $\bar{n}$ = 3.0; curve 5, $\bar{n}$ = 5.0.
Reproduced from reference 62 with permission
of North-Holland Publishing Co.

curves 2 ($\bar{n}$ = 0.75) and 3 ($\bar{n}$ = 1.50) agree with the limiting slope
in the absence of Q (k_1 = 7.6 x 10^6 s^{-1}), and the extrapolated
intercepts give $\bar{n}$ values indistinquishable from the expected
values based on $\bar{n}$ = $[Q_T]/[M_T]$. Significantly, $[M_T]$ is calculated
from the standard values of the key parameters for the CTAC
micelle (CMC = 4.0 x 10^{-3} $\underline{M}$, aggregation number = 59 $\pm$ 7)[71].
The best-fit simulations give k_q = 1.5 x 10^7 s^{-1}, in excellent agreement with the magnitude of k_q = 1.6 x 10^7 s^{-1} derived from simulation of the steady-state data using equation 18 (Figure 11-right).

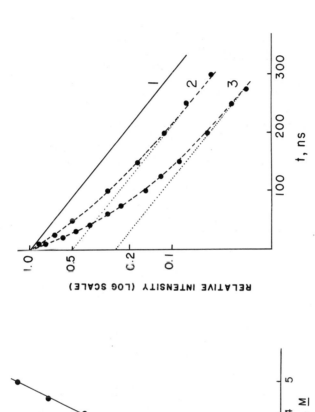

Figure 11. Left. Semilogarithmic plot of the fluorescence decay of sodium pyrene pentanoate (11-4) in the presence of the CTAC micelle in the absence (curve 1) and presence of surfactant nitroxyl radical 10 as follows: curve 2, $\bar{n}$ = 0.75; curve 3, $\bar{n}$ = 1.50. Right. Simulation of the steady-state data for the fluorescence quenching of 11-4 by 10 in the CTAC micelle using equation 18 with A = 2.1. (From reference 70)

Table 8 summarizes and compares the results of steady-state and transient fluorescence quenching experiments of pyrene and derivatives with 10 as quencher. In general, good agreement is found in the derived values of k_q from the two independent experiments. Further, the experimentally determined $\bar{n}$ values from the transient experiments are consistent with calculated values based on the expected $[M_T]$. The conclusion is that the key parameters of CMC and aggregation number for the host micelle (CTAC or SDS) are not seriously changed by the presence of several probes (fluorophor and quenchers).

The above methodology can be used to specifically examine the integrity of the host micelle in the presence of the probe molecules

Table VIII. Intramicellar Fluorescence Quenching by the Surfactant Nitroxyl Radical 10.

Fluorophor	Micelle	Transient Expt. $\times\ 10^{-7}\ s^{-1}$			Steady-State Expt.		Ref.
		$\bar{n}$	k_1	k_q	k_q	A	
Pyrene	CTAC	1–5	0.59	1.1	1.0	a	62
	SDS	1–5	0.55	1.4	1.5	a	62
Cationic Derivatives in SDS							
9–1		1–6	1.9	0.75	0.78	0.42	68
9–5		0.4–6	0.76	1.0	1.2	1.58	68
9–11		0.4–6	0.85	1.8	2.3	2.76	68
Anionic Derivatives in CTAC							
11–0		0.5–5	~20	b	3.5	0.18	70
11–4		0.5–5	0.76	1.5	1.6	2.1	70
11–11		0.5–5	0.76	1.5	1.8	2.3	70

----

[a]Approximate equation.

[b]Lifetime too short for accurate measurement with nitrogen laser apparatus.

and other additives, which is a major concern in all molecular
probe experiments. We studied the intramicellar excimer formation
reaction of pyrene (^{1}Py* + Py $\longrightarrow$ ^{1}Py*) in the CTAC micelle to
explore this point.[69] Intramicellar excimer formation follows a
scheme similar to Scheme 2 except that Q is replaced by Py, and $\bar{n}$
is defined as $[Py_T]/[M_T]$ which is the average number of pyrenes
per micelle. The time dependence of the pyrene monomer (^{1}Py*)
decay is described by the function in equation 20 with k_E (rate
constant for intramicellar excimer formation, an encounter-limited
reaction) replacing k_q.

Figure 12 shows the results of the transient experiment for
pyrene under conditions where $\bar{n}$ = 0.5 (α_2 = 0.076, α_3 = 0.013),
1.0 (α = 0.18, α_3 = 0.060, α_4 = 0.020), and 2.0 (α_2 = 0.27,
α_3 = 0.18, α_4 = 0.090, α_5 = 0.030).[69] In all 3 cases, the
graphically derived values for $\bar{n}$ are within experimental error of
the expected values for an invariant host micelle (i.e. $[M_T]_{exp}$ =
$[M_T]_{calc}$, from known parameters[71]). Further, the derived
value of k_E (by best-fit simulation of the decays) does not vary
with $\bar{n}$ even though at $\bar{n}$ = 0.5 essentially all excimer formation
occurs from doubly occupied micelles, while at $\bar{n}$ = 2.0, somewhat
more than 50% of the excimer formation occurs from micelles
containing 3 or more pyrene molecules. These results suggest that
there is no significant perturbation of the CTAC micelle by the
presence of several pyrene molecules.

Even more dramatic was the finding that sodium hexanoate added
to the above system had no effect on the experimentally derived
parameters (k_E and $\bar{n}$) up to a total additive concentration of
1.0 x 10^{-3} $\underline{M}$.[69] If the additive is completely incorporated into
the cationic micelles, this concentration corresponds to an
average of 10 hexanoates per micelle. Above this additive
concentration, the experimentally derived values of $\bar{n}$ significantly
decrease, while k_E slightly decreases indicating changes in the
host micelle.

Infelta and Gratzel recently described a similar study of
pyrene in the sodium cetyltrioxyethylene sulfate micelle (CTOES).[64]
Their results indicate k_E = 9 x 10^6 s^{-1} in that micelle. They
elucidate $[M_T]$ as described above, and subsequently an aggregation
number of 96 for the CTOES micelle (using a CMC = 1.0 x 10^{-4} $\underline{M}$
as determined from changes in the pyrene fluorescence upon incorporation in the micelle).

Table 9 summarizes recent examples of rates of intramicellar
reactions as elucidated by the statistical model approach. The
tabulated rate constants for fluorescence quenching, pyrene excimer
formation, and irreversible triplet energy transfer
(k's $\approx$ (1-2) x 10^7 s^{-1}) may represent the encounter frequencies of

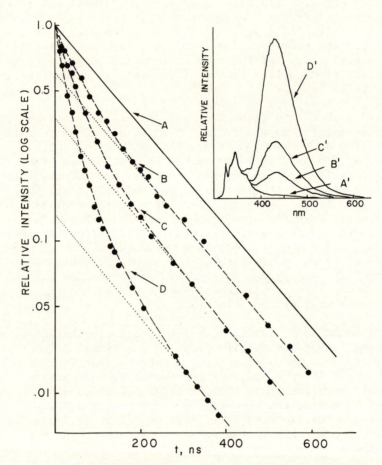

Figure 12.   Semilogarithmic plot of the fluorescence decay
from pyrene in the CTAC micelle. Curve A at
$\bar{n} = 0.075$ (no excimer formation). Curve B at
$\bar{n} = 0.50$. Curve C at $\bar{n} = 1.0$. Curve D at
$\bar{n} = 2.0$. ------Simulations based on equation
20 give $k_E = 1.2 \times 10^7$ s^{-1}. Inset. Steady-state
experiment showing monomer and excimer fluorescence normalized to monomer fluorescence in A'.
Reproduced from reference 69 with permission
of North-Holland Publishing Co.

Table IX. Selected Recent Determinations of Intramicellar Reaction Rates Based on the Statistical Model Approach.

Reaction Type	Reactants[a]	Micelle	k, x 10^{-7} s^{-1}	Reference
Fluorescence Quenching	^{1}Py* + surfactant nitroxyl radical 10	CTAC SDS	1.0 ± 0.1 1.5 ± 0.1	} 62
	^{1}Py* + Cu^{2+}	SDS	1.0	
	^{1}Py* + V^{2+}	SDS	1.1	} 60
	^{1}Py* + P^{+}	SDS	1.1	
Excimer Formation	^{1}Py* + Py	CTAC SDS	1.2 1.7	} 69
		CTOES[b]	0.9 ± 0.1	64
Triplet Energy Transfer	^{3}(1-BN)* + Tb^{3+}	SDS	6.2×10^{-5}	} 25
	^{3}(1-BN)* + Eu^{3+}	SDS	1.8×10^{-4}	
	^{3}MPTH* + t-Stilbene[c]	CTAB	1.5 ± 0.2	
	^{3}MPTH* + Naphthalene[d]	CTAB	2.8 ± 0.4 (3.3 ± 0.5)[c]	} 67
Electron Transfer	^{1}BT* + DQ	SDS	35	63

[a] Py = pyrene, V^{2+} = dimethylviologen, P$^+$ = cetylpyridinium , 1-BN = 1-bromonaphthalene, MPTH = N-methylphenothiazine, BT = 2-(4-aminophenyl) 6-methylbenzothiazol, DQ = duroquinone.

[b] Sodium cetyltrioxyethylene sulfate.

[c] Irreversible energy transfer.

[d] Reversible energy transfer.

[e] Back transfer rate.

those substrates solubilized in the indicated micelles since the same, or similar, reactions proceed at, or near, the diffusion-limit in homogeneous solutions. However, caution should be exercised in interpreting small differences among the apparently encounter-limited intramicellar reaction rates since the derived k's reflect the <u>intramicellar</u> <u>mobility</u> of the substrates as well as <u>effective</u> <u>micelle</u> <u>volume</u>. The latter refers to that volume of the micelle available for solubilization of the substrates. This type of reaction rate data should nicely complement other techniques in the continuing development of a more detailed picture of micelle dynamics and structure.

REFERENCES

1.   F. M. Menger, Accounts Chem. Res., $\underline{12}$, 111 (1979).
2.   S. Udenfriend, "Fluorescence Assay in Biology and Medicine", Academic Press, New York, N.Y., 1962.
3.   G. M. Edelman and W. O. McClure, Accounts Chem. Res., $\underline{1}$, 65 (1968) and references therein.
4.   R. A. Badley in "Modern Fluorescence Spectroscopy", E. L. Wehry, ed., Plenum Press, New York, N.Y., 1976.
5.   "1980 Laser Focus Buyers' Guide, 15th Edition", Advanced Technology Publications, Inc., Newton, MA, 1980.
6.   M. Kasha, Disc. Faraday Soc., $\underline{9}$, 14 (1950).
7.   N. J. Turro, "Modern Molecular Photochemistry", Benjamin/ Cummins Publishing Co., Menlo Park, CA, 1978, p. 296.
8.   C. A. Parker, "Photoluminescense of Solutions", Elsevier, New York, N.Y., 1968.
9.   J. N. Demas and G. A. Crosby, J. Phys. Chem., $\underline{75}$, 991 (1971).
10. J. N. Demas, J. Chem. Ed., $\underline{53}$, 657 (1976) and references therein.
11. K. Kalyanasundaram, F. Grieser, and J. K. Thomas, Chem. Phys. Letters, $\underline{51}$, 501 (1977).
12. R. Humphry-Baker, Y. Moroi, and M. Gratzel, Chem. Phys. Letters, $\underline{58}$, 207 (1978).
13. P. Mukerjee and K. J. Mysels, J. Am. Chem. Soc., $\underline{77}$, 2937 (1955).
14. B. H. Robinson, N. C. White, C. Mateo, K. J. Timmins, and A. James in "Chemical and Biological Applications of Relaxation Spectrometry", Wyn-Jones, Editor, D. Reidel Publishing Co., Dordrecht, Holland, 1975, p 201.
15. G. A. Davis, J. Am. Chem. Soc., $\underline{94}$, 5098 (1972).
16. K. S. Birdi, T. Krag, and J. Klausen, J. Colloid Interface Sci., $\underline{62}$, 562 (1977).
17. R. C. Mast and L. V. Haynes, J. Colloid Interface Sci., $\underline{53}$, 35 (1975).
18. N. E. Schore and N. J. Turro, J. Am. Chem. Soc., $\underline{96}$, 306 (1974).
19. N. E. Schore and N. J. Turro, J. Am. Chem. Soc., $\underline{97}$, 2488 (1975).

20. K. Kalyanasundaram and J. K. Thomas, J. Phys. Chem., <u>81</u>, 2176 (1977).
21. J. C. Dederen, L. Coosemans, F. C. De Schryver, and A. Van Dormael, Photochem. Photobiol., <u>30</u>, 443 (1979).
22. M. J. Minch and S. Sadiq Shah, J. Org. Chem., <u>44</u>, 3252 (1979).
23. S. S. Atik and L. A. Singer, J. Am. Chem. Soc., <u>101</u>, 5696 (1979).
24. S. S. Atik and L. A. Singer, J. Am. Chem. Soc., <u>101</u>, 6759 (1979).
25. M. Almgren, F. Grieser, and J. K. Thomas, J. Am. Chem. Soc., <u>101</u>, 279 (1979).
26. R. R. Hautala, N. E. Schore, and N. J. Turro, J. Am. Chem. Soc., <u>95</u>, 5508 (1973).
27. M. Van Bockstaele, J. Gelan, H. Martens, J. Put., J. C. Dederen, N. Boens, and F. C. De Schryver, Chem. Phys. Letters, <u>58</u>, 211 (1978).
28. M. W. Geiger and N. J. Turro, Photochem. and Photobiol., <u>22</u>, 273 (1975).
29. K. Kalyanasundaram and J. K. Thomas, J. Am. Chem. Soc., <u>99</u>, 2039 (1977).
30. N. J. Turro, M. Aikawa, and A. Yelta, Chem. Phys. Letters, <u>64</u>, 473 (1979).
31. F. B. Matheson and A. D. King, J. Colloid Interface Sci., <u>66</u>, 46 (1978).
32. W. R. Ware, J. Phys. Chem., <u>66</u>, 455 (1962).
33. H. J. Pownall and L. C. Smith, Biochemistry, <u>13</u>, 2594 (1974).
34. F. H. Quina and V. G. Toscano, J. Phys. Chem., <u>81</u>, 1750 (1977).
35. S. S. Atik and L. A. Singer, J. Am. Chem. Soc., <u>100</u>, 3234 (1978).
36. J. K. Thomas, Accounts Chem. Res., <u>10</u>, 133 (1977) and references therein.
37. Y. Moroi, A. M. Braun, and M. Gratzel, J. Am. Chem. Soc., <u>101</u>, 567 (1979).
38. Y. Moroi, P. P. Infelta, and M. Gratzel, J. Am. Chem. Soc., 101, 573 (1979).
39. P.-A. Brugger and M. Gratzel, J. Am. Chem. Soc., <u>102</u>, 2461 (1980).
40. K. Kalyanasundaram and M. Gratzel, Angew. Chemie, <u>41</u>, 759 (1979).
41. M. Gratzel and J. K. Thomas, J. Am. Chem. Soc., <u>95</u>, 6885 (1973).
42. M. A. J. Rodgers and M. E. Da Silva e Wheeler, Chem. Phys. Letters, <u>43</u>, 587 (1976).
43. L. K. Patterson and E. Vicil, J. Phys. Chem., <u>77</u>, 1191 (1973).
44. M. N. Jones and D. A. Reed, Kolloid-Z., <u>235</u>, 1196 (1970).
45. S. J. Rehfield, J. Phys. Chem., <u>75</u>, 3905 (1971).
46. J. H. Fendler and L. K. Patterson, J. Phys. Chem., <u>75</u>, 3907 (1971).
47. J. C. Ericksson and G. Gillberg, Acta. Chem. Scand., <u>20</u>, 2019 (1966).

48. J. H. Fendler and L. K. Patterson, J. Phys. Chem., 74, 4608 (1970).

49. P. Mukerjee, J. R. Cardinal, and N. R. Desai in "Micellization, Solubilization, and Microemulsions", K. L. Mittal, Editor, Plenum Press, New York, N.Y., 1977, p. 241.

50. M. Shinitzky, A.-C. Dianoux, C. Gitler, and G. Weber, Biochemistry, 10, 2106 (1971).

51. R. Humphry-Baker, M. Gratzel, and R. Steiger, J. Am. Chem. Soc., 102, 847 (1980).

52. R. C. Dorrance, T. F. Hunter, and J. Philp, J.C.S. Faraday II, 73, 89 (1977).

53. R. C. Dorrance and T. F. Hunter, J.C.S. Faraday I, 68, 1312 (1972).

54. R. C. Dorrance and R. F. Hunter, J.C.S. Faraday I, 70, 1572 (1974).

55. J. B. Birks, "Photophysics of Aromatic Molecules", Wiley-Interscience, New York, N.Y., 1970, p. 301.

56. K. A. Zachariasse, Chem. Phys. Letters, 57, 429 (1978).

57. J. Emert, C. Behrens, and M. Goldenberg, J. Am. Chem. Soc., 101, 771 (1979).

58. N. J. Turro, M. Aikawa, and A. Yekta, J. Am. Chem. Soc., 101, 772 (1979).

59. M. Tachiya, Chem. Phys. Letters, 33, 289 (1975).

60. M. A. J. Rogers and M. E. Da Silva e Wheeler, Chem. Phys. Letters, 53, 165 (1978).

61. B. K. Selinger and A. R. Watkins, Chem. Phys. Letters, 56, 99 (1978).

62. S. S. Atik and L. A. Singer, Chem. Phys. Letters, 59, 519 (1978).

63. A. Henglein and R. Scheerer, Ber. Bunsenges. Physik. Chem., 82, 1107 (1978).

64. P. P. Infelta and M. Gratzel, J. Chem. Phys., 70, 179 (1979).

65. P. P. Infelta, Chem. Phys. Letters, 61, 88 (1979).

66. A. Yekta, M. Aikawa, and N. J. Turro, Chem. Phys. Letters, 63, 543 (1979).

67. G. Rothenberger, P. P. Infelta, and M. Gratzel, J. Phys. Chem., 83, 1871 (1979).

68. S. S. Atik, and L. A. Singer, Chem. Phys. Letters, 66, 234 (1979).

69. S. S. Atik, M. Nam, and L. A. Singer, Chem. Phys. Letters, 67, 75 (1979).

70. S. S. Atik, Unpublished results.

71. C. L. Kwan, S. Atik, and L. A. Singer, J. Am. Chem. Soc., 100, 4783 (1978).

HISTORICAL ASPECTS OF SURFACTANT ADSORPTION AT LIQUID SURFACES

Charles H. Giles

University of Strathclyde

Glasgow, U.K.

The concept of the oriented monolayer is the foundation stone of modern colloid and interface science. It has universal importance in Nature, in biology, and in very many industrial and also domestic operations. We usually regard Langmuir as its discoverer, knowing that he received the Nobel Prize in 1932 for his work in this field. But he acknowledged his debt to his forerunners, especially Rayleigh. Here we briefly review their work and attempt to sort out the threads which make up the story of the discovery of the monolayer. The evidence on which the statements below are based is given in detail in earlier papers.[1-4]

Benjamin Franklin started it all. His often-quoted and picturesque account[1,5] has been shown to be the first serious attempt to study oil-on-water behavior scientifically. It was used many times in the 19th century as a basis for research. It reads thus: "In 1757, being at sea in a fleet of 96 sail bound against Louisburg, I observed the wakes of two of the ships to be remarkably smooth, while all the others were ruffled by the wind, which blew fresh. Being puzzled with the differing appearance, I at last pointed it out to our captain, and asked him the meaning of it? 'The cooks,' says he, 'have I suppose, been just emptying greasy water throught the scuppers, which has greased the sides of those ships a little,' and this answer he gave me with an air of some little comtempt as to a person ignorant of what everybody else knew. In my own mind I at first slighted his solution, tho' I was not able to think of another. But recollecting what I had formerly read in Pliny, I resolved to make some experiment of the effect of oil on water, when I should have opportunity...
"At length being at Clapham where there is, on the common, a large pond, which I observed to be one day very rough with the

wind, I fetched out a cruet of oil, and dropt a little of it on
the water. I saw it spread itself with surprising swiftness upon
the surface...

"I then went to the windward side, where (the waves) began to
form; and there the oil, though not more than a teaspoonful, produced an instant calm over a space several yards square, which
spread amazingly, and extended itself gradually till it reached
the lee side, making all that quarter of the pond, perhaps half an
acre, as smooth as a looking glass.

"After this, I contrived to take with me, whenever I went into
the country, a little oil in the upper hollow joint of my bamboo
cane, with which I might repeat the experiment as opportunity
should offer; and I found it constantly to succeed.

"In these experiments, one circumstance struck me with particular surprise. This was the sudden, wide and forcible spreading of
a drop of oil on the face of the water, which I do not know that
anybody has hitherto considered. If a drop of oil is put on a
polished marble table, or on a looking-glass that lies horizontally;
the drop remains in its place spreading very little. But when put
on water it spreads instantly many feet around, becoming so thin as
to produce the prismatic colours, for a considerable space, and
beyond them so much thinner as to be invisible, except in its effect of smoothing the waves at a much greater distance. It seems
as if a mutual repulsion between its particles took place as soon
as it touched the water, and a repulsion so strong as to act on
other bodies swimming on the surface, as straws, leaves, ships,
etc., forcing them to recede every way from the drop, as from a
center, leaving a large clear space. The quantity of this force
and the distance to which it will operate, I have not yet ascer-
tained; but I think it a curious enquiry, and I wish to understand
whence it arises...."

It appears that it was only later, in 1762, that this original
observation was brought back to Franklin's mind, and developed into
the above publication, which had so many years later repercussions.
In that year Franklin returned from London to Philadelphia for a
period, and on the voyage he happened to notice some curious effects of vibration at the interface between oil and water in a lamp
hanging in his cabin. After writing about this, in a letter to a
scientific friend, he made his Clapham experiment, probably some
time in 1770 or 1771.

The natural location of the Clapham pond has been identified[1]
and Franklin's experiment has recently been repeated by the author,
and thanks to the Yale University Library, the location and owner
of the house where he was staying at the time are now known[1].

The stimulus of Franklin's publication lasted throughout the
19th century and was a constant source of comment in the literature[1].
But then three new series of discoveries were developed independently, and led eventually to Langmuir's discovery. These were
made by Shields, Rayleigh, and Pockels respectively, and we may
also add Aitken.

Shields   John Shields, an enterprising textile manufacturer of
Perth, Scotland, noticed the calming effect of oil on water in a
pond at his works, just as Franklin had done. In due course he
initiated large-scale trials of wave-calming in rough seas at har-
bours in the East coast of Scotland. These trials were discussed
in the British Parliament, and indeed caused worldwide interest.[2]
A long account of Shields' experiments and their possibilities in
saving life at sea, including extended reports from the British
press, was compiled by the United States Life-Saving Service and
published in their Annual Report for 1883, from which the following
extracts are taken.[6]

"Mr. William D. Baker, Rockland, Massachusetts...offered for
experiment projectiles filled with oil and thrown from a gun or
mortar.... On January 5, 1883, the invertor made a trial...near
the mouth of Nauset Harbor."

Fourteen trial shots were made, but all failed in one way
or another; e.g., with the seventh shot, "The whole oily contents
of the projectile appeared to blow backwards over the gunner, who
was covered with oil."

Later at the same location the committee made a test by
spreading oil from a leaky dipper. "Thirty minutes and three pints
of oil sufficed to cover the whole area selected (forty-four thou-
sand yards)." Presumably this means square yards, which gives a
film thickness of about 460A, about 50 times as much as required
to form a monolayer. Much of it must therefore have been lost.

The wind blew at 20 m.p.h., and the oil obliterated the "white
caps" over the whole area covered. Oil was found to spread much
more rapidly in the direction of the wind than perpendicular to
it.

"It has been observed that cod-liver oil spreads over a larger
surface and holds together more tenaciously than either raw linseed
oil or refined petroleum. The latter is found to soon break up and
resolve itself into veins or streaks, between which the white caps
will appear as before..."

"The committee is of the opinion that the plan of Mr. Shields
can never be available for the purpose of the Life Saving Service,
but that it will be expedient to provide such boats as have to operate at a distance from land with the means of dispensing oil when
invention shall have perfected the most efficient device... The
conclusion is that oil exerts no influence upon a sea that breaks
on the shore... It would be as reasonable to suppose that a man
who entangles his feet when running rapidly will not fall because
his hair is oiled as that a wave will not break when its base is
impeded because its crest is oiled... The...printed statements
herewith...furnish conclusive evidence that in deep water oil has
a calming effect upon a rough sea..." Singed, B. C. Sparrow, Supt.,
Second L.S. District Committee.

Shields lodged British and American patents on the subject,[7]
and issued a prospectus of a company to exploit them, but nothing
further seems to have been done to develop these ideas.

One may speculate on the reasons for this: possibly the expense of the large amounts of oil needed, its ineffectiveness in extremely rough seas, and contamination of the coast line.

Aitken[2] The scientific aspect of the subject, however, seems to have attracted the notice of John Aitken, who lived in Falkirk, only about 40 miles from Shields' home town, and who must have read the extensive accounts of Shields' experiments in the Scottish press.

Aitken, a bachelor of independent means, did not take up paid employment after graduation in engineering at Glasgow, because of ill-health. Instead, he fitted out part of his home as a workshop and laboratory and made classical observations of natural phenomena with apparatus which he designed and made himself.

He devised and constructed apparatus to test theories of the calming action of oil, and found that it is not due to any reduction of friction between moving air and the water surface. His work was published in 1882-1883.[8]

Rayleigh[9,10] Aitken's work in turn may have been the stimulus to Rayleigh's renewed interest in surface films on water, described below. They were acquainted with each other, and were both Fellows of the Royal Society.[2]

Rayleigh was a physicist whose wide interests covered especially all types of wave motion, e.g., sound, and electric current phenomena. After publishing his classic work, "The Theory of Sound" in 1877-1878, his interest turned to wave motions in jets of water, and the effect on it of contamination of the water surface, with, e.g., soap.[4] His papers on the subject cover the period up to 1882, but then he turned his mind to other subjects, and only renewed his interest in 1890, when four papers under his name appeared,[3,4,11] in which it is clear that he was seeking a means of direct measurements of molecular sizes, and believed that the maximum extension of an oil film on water represented a layer one molecule thick. The difficulty he found was in determining this maximum extension precisely, but the solution to this problem was to hand, and was to be brought to his attention in a dramatic fashion.[3]

On January 12, 1891 Rayleigh received a long letter,* in German, from an unknown lady, Agnes Pockels, in Brunswick, Germany. In this letter the writer describes simple apparatus whereby she had measured the lowering of surface tension of a water surface as an oil film was progressively expanded on it:[12] "A rectangular trough, 70 cm long, 5 cm wide, 2 cm high, is filled with water to the brim, and a strip of tin about 1-1/2 cm wide laid across it perpendicular to its length... By shifting this partition...the

---

*This letter, including even the original envelope, still survives. It was delivered in rural England two days after posting in mid-Germany, a shorter time than is normally now taken by air-mail letters.

surface on either side can be lengthened or shortened in any proportion, and the amount of the displacement can be read off on a
scale held along the front of the trough." She measured the surface
tension at any part of the trough by a disc (a button!) suspended
from a balance. When a minute amount of oil was placed on the
surface, compression of the latter progressively reduced the surface tension.

This apparatus later became the model for the famous Langmuir
trough; but not only did Agnes Pockels invent this model, she described a number of experimental requirements now accepted by all
surface chemists.

The astonishing facts are that Agnes Pockels did all her work
in the kitchen of her home, in between domestic duties, and that
she had no scientific training or advice; moreover, she was only
18 years old when she began this work, ten years before writing to
Rayleigh. A relative of hers recollected that she became interested
in the subject by observation of the behavior of grease on water in
the sink when she was dish-washing. Equally remarkable was Rayleigh's response. Following a letter from him to clarify some
points ("With regard to your curiosity about my personal status, I
am indeed a lady."),[3] Rayleigh, realising the importance of her
method, which solved the problem he faced, with characteristic
magnaminity sent the letter in full to the Journal "Nature", with
a covering note recommending it to the editor. Both were published.[12]
We suspect that the editor included the covering note to forestall
any possible criticism for publishing a communication from an aca-
demically unqualified and hitherto unknown lady. Shortly after
this, Rayleigh became involved in other demanding work, especially
the discovery of argon, and only returned to this subject in
1899.[13] He then used the Pockels method to determine precisely
the minimum thickness of a layer of castor oil on water, which he
rightly believed to be one molecule deep, and found it to be 10A.
This is the first definite mention of the idea of a monomolecular
film.

The whole story surely forms one of the most remarkable in the
history of science.

It was the work of Rayleigh and Pockels which interested Langmuir and led to his development of the Langmuir trough and to the
basis of modern colloid and interface science - the oriented
monolayer.[14]

ACKNOWLEDGEMENT

We are indebted to Dr. J. C. Scott for drawing our attention
to the United States Life-Saving Service Report.[15]

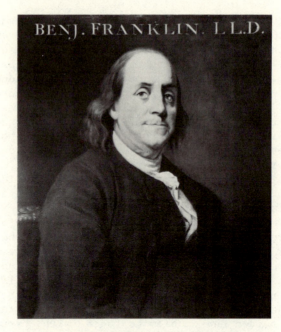

Benjamin Franklin (1706–1790)

John Shields (1822–1890)

Agnes Pockels   (1862–1935)

Lord Rayleigh   (1842–1919)

The house at Kasernenstrasse 7, Brunswick, Lower Saxony, where the Pockels family resided and where Anges Pockels made her historic experiments.

Sketch (made from memory by a member of the Pockels family) of the kitchen sink where Agnes Pockels made her original observations on the behavior of oil on water, leading to the design of her trough.

A recent repetition of the first scientific experiment
in surface chemistry, as made by Franklin in ca. 1770,
on the Mount Pond, Clapham, London. The spreading and
calming effect of one teaspoonful of olive oil on the
wind-agitated surface of the Mount Pond is shown, a few
minutes after the oil was placed on the surface.

View over the ha-ha and terrace garden at Terling Place,
Essex, Rayleigh's country seat. The view shows the West
wing of the house, where Rayleigh established his laboratories and workshops. It is said that he was in the
habit of promenading the walks shown here, when pondering
his scientific problems.

REFERENCES

1. C. H. Giles, Chem. and Ind., 1616 (1969).
2. C. H. Giles and S. D. Forrester, ibid., 80 (1970).
3. C. H. Giles and S. D. Forrester, ibid., 42 (1971).
4. S. D. Forrester and C. H. Giles, ibid., 469 (1971).
5. B. Franklin, Phil. Trans. Roy. Soc., 64, 445 (1774).
6. B. C. Sparrow, "Use of oil in calming rough seas," Ann. Rep.
    U.S. Life-Saving Service, pp. 427–487 (1883).
7. J. Shields, B.P. 3490 (1879); U.S.P. 289720 (4 December 1883);
    U.S.P. 334295 (January 12, 1886).
8. J. Aitken, Proc. Roy. Soc. Edinburgh, 12, 56 (1882–1883);
    Collected Papers, Cambridge: University Press, 1923, p. 75.
9. R. B. Lindsay, "Lord Rayleigh - the man and his work," Oxford:
    Pergamon, 1970.
10. R. J. Strutt, "John William Strutt, Third Baron Rayleigh, OM,
    FRS," London: Ed. Arnold, 1924: R. J. Strutt, Fourth Baron
    Rayleigh, FRS, "Life of John William Strutt, Third Baron Ray-
    leigh, OM, FRS. An augmented edition with annotations by the
    author and foreword by John N. Howard." Madison Milwaukee:
    University of Wisconsin Press, 1968.
11. J. W. Strutt, "Scientific Papers," Cambridge: University Press,
    Vols. I-VI, 1899–1920.
12. A. Pockels, Nature, London, 43, 437 (1891).
13. Lord Rayleigh, Phil. Mag., 48, 321 (1899).
14. I. Langmuir, J. Amer. Chem. Soc., 39, 1848 (1917).
15. For an account of the historical development of theories of
    wave-calming using oil, see: J. C. Scott, in A. R. Hall and
    N. Smith (eds), "History of Technology," third annual volume,
    163–186 (1978).

FORCES OPERATING IN ADSORPTION OF SURFACTANTS AND OTHER SOLUTES
AT SOLID SURFACES: A SURVEY

Charles H. Giles

Department of Pure and Applied Chemistry
University of Strathclyde
Glasgow, G1 1XL   U.K.

Outline of early work and ideas on adsorption
of solutes. The wide range of adsorption phenomena
and their importance in scientific, industrial,
domestic, and biological fields. The types of
force involved, and some methods used for their
identification. The theoretical basis and usefulness of the adsorption isotherm. State of
solute in the solid after adsorption and its investigation.

INTRODUCTION

No reader needs reminding of the general nature of absorption.
He may however profitably ponder the range of situations in which
it is important. Life itself depends on adsorption in many ways,
and a host of industrial, laboratory and domestic processes equally
do so. Its mechanisms are therefore of great interest.[1] Here we
shall consider how it depends on the more familiar types of chemical
bond, as well as on the structure of the adsorbing solid.

This brief review describes concepts and methods applicable to
all forms of adsorption of solutes by solids, though it reflects
the author's particular interests in aromatic solutes, especially
dyes.

Consider the behavior of a solute molecule in its rapid kinetic
motion in a solvent in contact with a solid surface; it moves around

123

surrounded by a constantly changing atmosphere of solvent molecules, which hold it in solution. There are however other forces
which attract it to the solid surface whenever it approaches closely,
and if these are strong enough they overcome those of the solvent
atmosphere. The result is that the solute may be held at the surface, either permanently, by a covalent bond, or for a limited time,
by weaker forces. If the solute has penetrated into micro-pores in
the solid and then becomes self-associated, it may be held there
because its particles are then too large to move freely.

THE GIBBS CONCEPT

The fundamental action in adsorption may be considered an
escape mechamism - in the case of solute adsorption, the solute
(the adsorbate) tends to escape from solution to the interface with
the solid (the adsorbent). This was first treated rigorously by
Gibbs, more than a century ago, in his well-known adsorption equation -

$$\Gamma = -\frac{1}{RT}\frac{\partial\gamma}{\partial\ln a}$$

where Γ is the surface excess of solute, i.e., the increased concentration in a layer next to the solid, a is the activity in solution, and γ the interfacial tension. If tension falls with increase
in activity (or concentration) of solute, it is an indication that
the solute is concentrating at the liquid/vapor interface. If the
tension rises with concentration, as it does at the air/water interface with some inorganic salts and some simple carbohydrate molecules in solution in water, that is an indication that the solute
is so strongly solvated that it is more concentrated in the bulk of
the solution than at the interface.

Few attempts have been made to check the relation experimentally. It has been confirmed for surface-active solutes at the
air/water interface,[2,3] but some attempts to confirm it for oil/
water interfaces have given indecisive results.[4,5] Experiments
with monolayers of fiber-forming polymers spread on water solutions
of dyes, show that the interfacial tension between the monolayer
and the dye solution decreases with rise in solution concentration.[6]
The dye is therefore concentrating at the interface..

These tests were made with anionic dyes and mono-layers of
protein and of cellulose. Measurement of air/water surface tension of dye solutions show that they also decrease in tension with
increase in concentration, even with very highly sulfonated and
therefore highly soluble dyes.[7,8] It seems a reasonable conclusion
that almost all aromatic solutes will tend to concentrate, i.e.,
adsorb, from solution at a water/solid interface, but whether they
actually do so, and to what extent, depends on extra-thermodynamic

factors. Thus adsorption will be prevented if the solute is ionized and the solid surface holds an electrostatic charge of the
same sign; or it will be assisted if the charge on the surface is
of opposite sign, or if there are strong attractions of other type
between solute molecule and solid surface. The same considerations
hold for aliphatic solutes and indeed for all surfactants, which of
course by definition concentrate at interfaces with water.

The nature of the forces which assist the interfacial concentration, and methods for their diagnosis, are the subject of the
present review, and are discussed in outline below.

NATURE OF FORCES RESPONSIBLE FOR SOLUTE ADSORPTION

These may be classified thus:

Chemical or physico-chemical forces,

      Covalent bonds
      Hydrogen bonds and other polar forces
      Ion exchange attraction
      van der Waals forces
      Hydrophobic attraction

Physical or mechanical forces

      Restriction of movement of solute aggregates in
        micro-pores
      Facilitation of entry of solute by progressive
        breakdown of substrate structure

METHODS OF IDENTIFICATION OF FORCES OPERATING IN SOLUTE ADSORPTION

A variety of methods can be used, including the following:

Use of monolayers, with measurement of pressure/area and surface
    viscosity;[9]
measurement of thermodynamic parameters;[10-12]
study of type of the adsorption isotherm;[13-15]
measurement of refractive index of solutions of model compounds,
    by the method of continuous variations;[16-18]
measurement of effect of variation of pH on adsorption, or of
    presence of other solutes;[12,19,20]
measurement of specific surface of the adsorbed species,[21-23]
measurement of extent of coverage of adsorbent surface.[15]

COVALENT BONDS

When a reactive dye with two reactive groups is applied to
cellulose, the fiber is rendered virtually insoluble in solvents,

e.g. cuprammonium hydroxide, which readily dissolve undyed cellulose. This is the result of cross-linking of the polymer structure
which is rendered more rigid and difficult to break up. A similar
effect can be seen in the action of this type of dye, in alkaline
solution on cellulose monolayers[24] (Figure 1). The pressure/area
curve increases in steepness with time until it ultimately is vertical, representing a quite incompressible film. A parallel effect
is also shown when the surface film viscosity is measured: this
parameter increases until when the condition of the vertical pres-
sure/area curve is reached, it is infinite.

Irreversibility of adsorption, on non-porous solids, is an
indication of covalent bonding between solute and solid. Thus
inorganic oxides in some cases adsorb phenols from water solution
and only a proportion of the solute can be desorbed by water; the
remainder is probably covalently bound.

ION EXCHANGE ATTRACTION

This is evident in adsorption of ionic solutes by ionogenic
substrates, particularly proteins, micro-organisms and some inorganic oxides. The evidence is shown in the influence of the pH
of the solution on the amount of solute adsorbed.

Anionic solutes are adsorbed on wool and nylon best at low
pH, whereby free basic groups, mainly - NH_2 (but also at very low
pH, - CONH-) are positively charged by attachment of a proton.
(Figure 2).

Cationic solutes show the opposite behavior. Cationic dyes
on acrylic fibers, and quaternary ammonium surfactants on micro-
organisms, are adsorbed best at high pH, when acidic groups, e.g.
carboxyl groups, are ionised. (Figures 3,4).

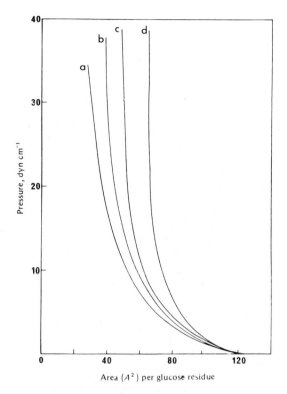

Figure 1. Effect of a dichlorotriazinyl reactive dye for cellulose, on a monolayer of cellulose:[24]

a, control, cellulose on pure water;
b, cellulose on 10^{-4}M dye solution, at pH 9.5, after standing 3h;
c, the same, after 10h.
d, the same, after 24 and 36h.

The surface viscosity of the monolayer increases from a to d,
becoming infinite for d, because of covalent bonds linking the
cellulose chains.

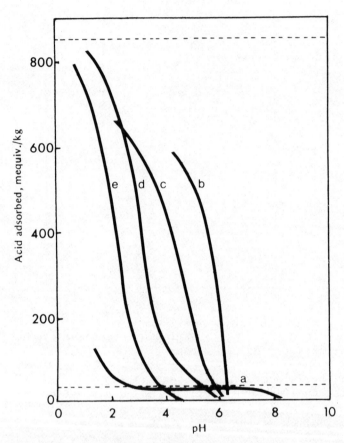

Figure 2. Acid titration curves of (a), nylon with dye C.I. 18050 (di-sulfonated), and (b-e), wool, with mono-basic free acids; b, dye C.I. 26660; c, C.I. 15510; d, naphthalene 2-sulfonic acid; e, hydrochloric acid.[19]

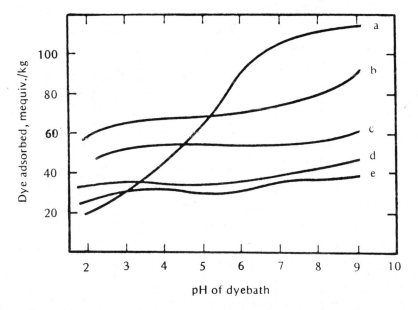

Figure 3. Alkali titration curves of various polyacrylonitrile fibers with dye C.I. Basic Blue 22, at the boil, for 16h in 1:40 w/w bath; a, Courtelle E; b, Beslon; c, Orlon 42; d, Acrilan 16; e Acribal.[25]

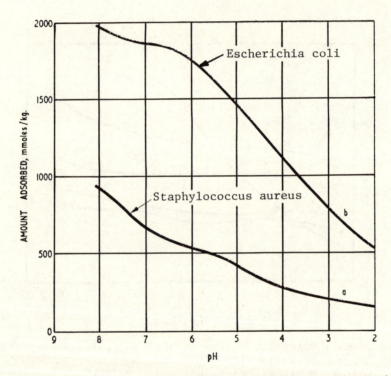

Figure 4. Alkali titration curves of micro-organisms with
cetyltrimethyl ammonium bromide; a, Staphylococcus aureus;
b, Escherichia coli.[26]

Table 1 Hydrogen Bond and Other Polar Complexes Detected Between Model Compounds[1,2].

Type of bond	Solutes		Solvent	Mol. ratio of complex a:b
	a	b		
Alk-OH + ArOH	D-Glucose	Phenol	W	0
			EG	1:6
C=O + ArOH	Acetone	Phenol	W	0
	Di-isobutyl ketone		D	1:2
	Ethyl methyl ketone		CCl$_4$	1:1,1:2
-N=N- + ArOH	Azobenzene	Benzyl alcohol	CCl$_4$	1:1
		Phenol	B	1:1,1:2
-COOR + ArCl	Ethyl acetate	Chlorobenzene	CCl$_4$	1:1
	Phenyl acetate		B	1:1

B = benzene; D = dioxan; EG = ethylene glycol; W = water
All tests at room temperature and in total mol. concn. 0.1 or 0.25

HYDROGEN BONDS AND OTHER POLAR FORCES

Figure 5 illustrates one direct method of revealing the probable operation of hydrogen bond forces in adsorption of non-ionic dyes by a polymer. The greater the number of bonding centers in the dye molecule, the more dye is adsorbed. These dyes give the 'C' type isotherm, which is discussed below, and therefore the present increases represent deepening penetration into the substrate structure.

Similar results follow the examination of the adsorption of organic solutes by nylon or wool. Solutes with free hydroxy-groups, e.g. phenols and aliphatic alcohols, are adsorbed to a much greater extent than those without such groups, many of which are not adsorbed at all. Water is also strongly adsorbed from non-aqueous solution.[28] These observations suggest hydrogen bonding.

The method of continuous variations also gives useful guidelines to an interpretation of adsorption forces, when used with solutions of model compounds for fibers. Some typical results are given in Table 1. One fact which emerges from these and other related data is that hydroxy-groups in carbohydrates are strongly protected by water and do not form intermolecular hydrogen bonds with phenals in an aqueous environment. The same conclusion was reached by a test with an anionic dye (Colour Index 24340) having free hydroxy-groups in its molecule, using solutions of cellulose and the dye in Cadoxen solvent.

The interpretation of these results is that cellulose adsorbs dyes from water by van der Waals polar and non-polar forces supplemented by weak acid-base attraction between hydroxy-groups in the fiber and any basic groups present in the dye.

By determination of thermodynamic parameters of reaction between model compounds representing dyes and cellulose, it has been found that carbohydrates in water form a bond with certain aromatic water-soluble solutes, e.g. naphthalene sulfonates and anthraquinone dyes, but no bond is formed with an azo-dye. It was suggested that the attraction is a form of π-bond between the aromatic nucleus and the multiple hydroxy-groups of the carbohydrate, which is not prevented by water. Possibly the aromatic π-electron structure is basic in character, except when an azo-group is present.

An examination of affinity values for a series of dyes on cellulose [12,19] shows that the presence of basic groups in the dye, especially unsubstituted amino-groups, raises these values.

The method of continuous variations has been used to differentiate between ion-exchange and hydrogen-bond forces acting with cellulose. Figure 6 shows that of the two direct cotton dyes used with cellulose solution, refractive index measurement reveals that

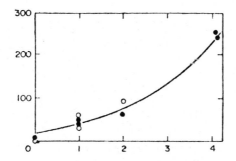

Figure 5. Relation between number of available hydrogen atoms
in multifunctional azobenzene non-ionic dyes (without 2- or
2'-substituents) and their maximum adsorption by (sec.) cellulose acetate.[27]

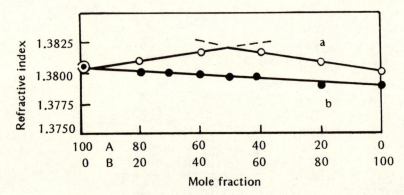

Figure 6. Refractive index measurement, by method of continuous variations, to study complex formation of direct cotton dyes with cellulose.[17] A, cellulose (calculated as cellobiose residues); B, (a) C.I. 24410, with free $-NH_2$ groups; (b) C.I. 24340, without free NH_2 groups. Solvent, Cadoxen; concentration, 0.1M.

the one (C.I. 24410) without free amino-groups forms no complex
with cellulose as mentioned above, but C.I. 24340, with similar
structure but with free amino-groups, does form a complex, in 1:1
ratio, dye molecule:cellobiose residue. Tests with monolayers
however, and measurement of the monolayer surface film viscosity,
give no evidence of bonding between cellulose and C.I. 24340,
suggesting that the bond is a weak acid-base type one, i.e. ion
exchange (the cellulose in this alkaline solution is rather more
anionic than in neutral solution). Confirming this interpretation,
there is no evidence of viscosity change with cellulose solution
and a cationic dye (Methylene Blue), though this dye does markedly
affect the pressure/area curve of the cellulose monolayer (Figure 7).
Hydrogen bonding with a <u>non-ionic</u> dye and cellulose acetate monolayer, which is unlike cellulose, not protected by water, is however clearly revealed by these surface viscosity tests.

VAN DER WAALS FORCES

These of course operate to varying degrees in all adsorptions,
but become most important with solutes of high molecular weight.
The forces are of two types: polarisation forces acting between
polar molecules, and non-polar or London forces. Both types
attenuate with the sixth power of the distance between the interacting molecules. Clearly then they are most effective when both
substrate and solute molecules are planar, so that there can be
the largest area in mutual contact, and also when the molecules
are polar. This explains why adsorption of dyes by cellulose or
cellulose acetate is favored by planarity in the dye molecule. In
the case of cellulose also, aggregation of the dye in the substrate
pores is favoured by a planar dye molecule, and so can favour high
adsorption.

Additional effects are also introduced by solute-solute van
der Waals forces, i.e. those which promote association in the
solution, with formation of micelles above the c.m.c. The increased
molecular weight then enhances the non-polar van der Waals forces
between surface and solute.

Indirect evidence can often be used to show the effect of
these forces on adsorption. The curves in Figure 2 show that the
anionic compounds are more readily adsorbed, i.e. they have higher
affinity, the higher the molecular weight, an effect that is undoubtedly due to increased non-polar forces acting between fiber
and anion of the solute.

HYDROPHOBIC ATTRACTION

A term often used to describe the tendency of hydrophobic
groups, especially alkyl chains, to associate together and escape
from an aqueous environment. Its first description is commonly

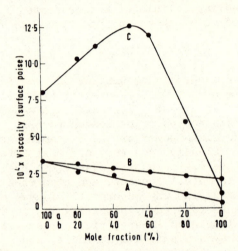

Figure 7. Surface film viscosity measurement, by method of continuous variation, of monolayers.   A, cellulose + Methylene
Blue on water; B, cellulose + direct cotton dye C.I. 14410 on
0.01M-NaCl (these combinations give weak ion-exchange or acid-
base bonding); C, mixed film of cellulose triacetate + a nonionic dye on water,[17] showing hydrogen bonding.

attributed to Kauzmann et al, in connection with protein reactions,[29] but Meggy had previously [30] made a similar suggestion to account for adsorption of dyes by wool. The effect is due to two causes acting together: Hydrogen bonds draw together water molecules and so tend to 'squeeze out' the hydrocarbon groups, which are then held together by their mutual non-polar van der Waals force. Thus each set of forces causes the respective assemblages of molecules or groups to associate together and to exclude the other. Hydrophobic attraction offers a useful concept to unify and illuminate known diverse phenomena, but it is not strictly a new type of bond. It is of course of importance in the formation of micelles of surfactants in water, and in their adsorption at hydrophobic surfaces.

DIAGNOSIS OF ADSORPTION MECHANISM FROM ISOTHERM SHAPE

Solute adsorption isotherms can be divided into four principal classes shown in Figure 8 and then into a number of sub-groups. The shape is determined e.g. by the relative orientation of the adsorbed solute and the substrate molecules, and this can often greatly assist in identification of the nature of the forces responsible for adsorption.[13-15]

SOME EFFECTS OF SUBSTRATE MICRO-POROSITY ON ADSORPTION

This should be recognised as a type of adsorption force. There is much evidence, especially from electron microscope studies, that many dyes are present in fibers in the form of large aggregated particles, e.g. in cellulose, and in several man-made fibers. Spectral examination shows that aggregates are present, at least small ones, even in the undried substrate, and are not an artifact produced in drying. The explanation has been given that the surface excess of dye, at the fiber-dye solution interface, forms an increasingly high proportion of the total amount of dye dissolved in the solution filling the pore, as the pore diameter decreases, and that this promotes the dye association.

Figure 9 shows the difference in amount adsorbed by cellulose of two dyes, of similar azo structure. One is the well-known Congo Red, benzidine $\rightarrow$ (naphthionic acid) and the other its 'half molecule', aniline $\rightarrow$ naphthionic acid,[2] both in the form of sodium salt. It is clear that the larger is adsorbed to a far greater extent than the smaller. The explanation appears to be that the larger molecule is much more highly aggregated in the pores of cellulose and once having formed aggregates is unable to escape.

SPECIFIC SURFACE MEASUREMENT AS AN AID TO INTERPRETATION OF ADSORPTION MECHANISM

Adsorption on an already adsorbed dye has been used to

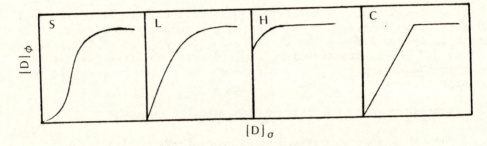

Figure 8.   The four classes of solute adsorption isotherm, S, given by solutes having strong intermolecular attraction parallel to the surface, and/or strong competition from a second solute; L, given by solutes with weak intermolecular attraction; H, given by solutes with very high attraction for the surface, e.g. by covalent bonding, or when their molecular weight is high; C, given by solutes which penetrate the solid preferentially to the solvent. S type curves often indicate solute molecule orientation perpendicular to the surface; L type may indicate flatwise adsorption to the surface.

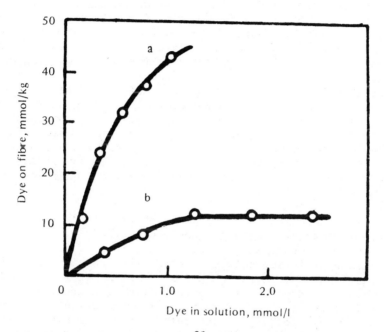

Figure 9. Adsorption isotherms[31] of a, Congo Red and b, its 'half-molecule', aniline ⟶ naphthionic acid (sodium salt), in buffer solution at pH9, on regenerated cellulose fiber at 50°C.

interpret the adsorption of the latter. This was done by adsorbing
p-nitrophenol (PNP) from water onto ghe dye in already dyed
fiber.[21-23] This solute is readily adsorbed on dye particles but
hardly at all on cellulose itself. From the difference in amount
of PNP adsorbed by dyed and undyed cellulose. The specific surface of the dye in the cellulose can readily be calculated
(Figure 10), and the results give interesting information regarding its physical state therein. Figure 11 shows that a high lightfastness direct dye in cellulose builds up quite large aggregated
particles, the size of the largest thus detected is of the same
order as the largest shown in electron micrographs of cellulose
film dyed with this type of dye. Similar examination with PNP of
cellulose film dyed with a direct dye of low lightfastness gave
the results shown in Figure 12, which indicate that with increasing concentration adsorption takes place in three distinct stages:
at first a monolayer forms over a very limited proportion of the
internal surface, then on this multilayers deposit, and finally
these break up into discrete three-dimensional aggregates, as
detected with the first mentioned dye. These stages are paralleled
well by the heat of dyeing and specific gravity measurements made
independently by other authors. (ref. 2) The decrease of sp. gr.
at higher dye concentrations can be explained by the blockage of
internal pores in the cellulose by the large dye particles, which
produces voids not penetrated by the flotation liquid used in the
measurement.

The same technique has been used by Blair and McElroy[33] with
cellulose acetate dyed with non-ionic disperse dye. In this case
the substrate adsorbs PNP markedly, but allowance for this gives
an interesting relation between dye adsorbed and its specific surface, which shows at first the formation of a monolayer of dye,
followed by slow deposit of a further layer (Figure 13). The
large surface covered by PNP with the substrate containing very
small amounts of dye, can be accounted for by a rapid initial
penetration of semi-crystalline regions of the substrate in the
earliest stages of dyeing, which exposes new internal surface in
voids which are then blocked by dye adsorbed subsequently.

THE EFFECTS OF ADSORPTION MECHANISM ON SUBSTRATE STRUCTURE

Adsorption forces cannot be considered without consideration
of their effect on the physical structure of certain micro-porous
substrates. This is an important aspect of adsorption studies,
though not always recognised as such. It is encountered where
the adsorption isotherm is linear ('C' type), sometimes with two
branches, both linear; the upper one may have a slope that is
positive, zero, or negative.[14,15] The cause is penetration of
the substrate structure by the solute, in regions not penetrated
by the solvent, whereby the structure is opened up and more internal surface exposed as adsorption proceeds. A theoretical

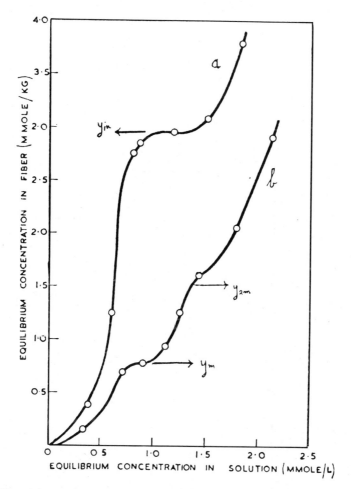

Figure 10. Adsorption isotherms for p-nitrophenol (PNP) on regenerated cellulose film. a, dyed with a direct cotton dye producing large aggregated particles in the substrate (see Figure 11 below) (C.I. 34045) (1.22 per cent on weight of film); b, undyed film.

The inflections at y_m represent the completion of the first condensed monolayer of adsorbed PNP; that at y_{2m} in curve b represents the completion of a second layer, and the subsequent rise shows that further layers then build up.

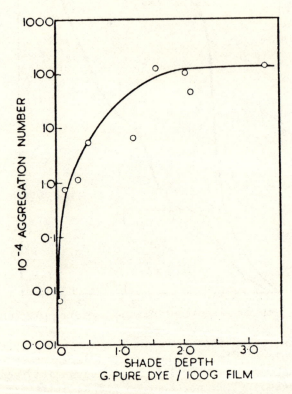

Figure 11.   Increase in aggregation number of adsorbed dye
(C.I. 34045) in regenerated cellulose film, with increase in
depth of shade of dye in film.[22]

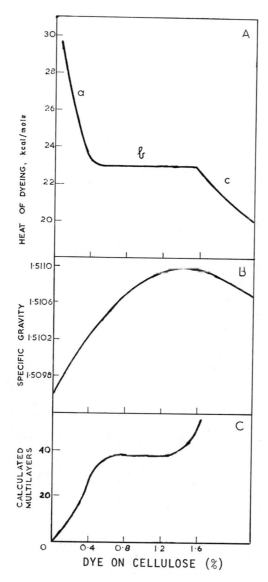

Figure 12.   Relations between amount of direct cotton dye
(C.I. 24410) on regenerated cellulose film, and various
measured parameters.[23] The tests showing heat of dyeing and
specific gravity are from ref.[32]

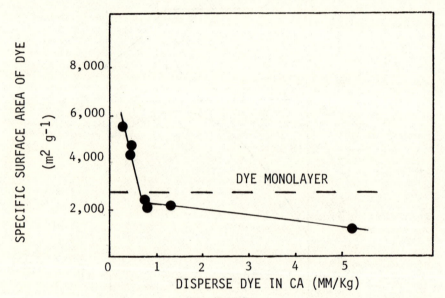

Figure 13. Relation between amount of non-ionic dye in cellulose acetate, and its specific surface area.[33]

treatment of the process is as follows. (Another treatment is given in ref.[14]). The amount of solute adsorbed (y) is expressed by the Langmuir equation -

$$y = \frac{by_m c}{1 + bc}$$

where y_m is the amount adsorbed when the first monolayer is complete, c is the concentration of solute in solution, and b is a constant, a function of temperature. If the internal surface of the adsorbent increases with amount of solute entering, then we may suppose that y_m increases proportionately with c. Therefore $y_m = k(1+\alpha c)$, where k is a constant and α is a coefficient of expansion of the surface. We may write $y = \beta c$, where β is another constant, and thus

$$b = \frac{\beta}{k + k\alpha c - \beta c}$$

This equation is valid only up to a critical value c = c = k/ $(\beta - k\alpha)$, i.e. $k + k\alpha c - \beta c = 0$ because if c is greater than c $b = \infty$ that is, the rate of escape of adsorbate is zero. Therefore, when the concentration c is reached the value of y remains fixed, provided no fresh internal surface is formed. The curve then becomes a horizontal straight line. This is the more usual condition found, but if a whole new region of internal structure is broken into at a given solute concentration, then the process is repeated and the second linear branch of the curve has a positive slope, or in rare cases it may have a negative slope.

The last-named situation gives the 'Z' type curve, with a re-entrant angle. When the fresh breakdown of structure occurs the new internal surface exposed may be so large that the resulting adsorption reduces the external solution concentration below that previously required for a larger adsorption, and the curve turns back towards the y-axis.[14,15,34]

This Z type curve has been detected for short term adsorption of PNP from a non-aqueous solvent on cellulose,[34] and recently, by Gilbert et al, for membrane-active drugs adsorbed from aqueous media on to bacteria and yeast.[35] These authors found that some of the systems gave Z curves, and some, the normal linear ('C') curve with a second branch of positive slope greater than that of the initial branch (Figure 14). In all these cases however severe disorganization of the cytoplasmic membrane of the cells was detected, both by electron microscopy, and by evidence of liberation of large quantities of cell constituents into the suspending fluid, occurring with drug concentrations only above that at the point of inflexion of the isotherm.

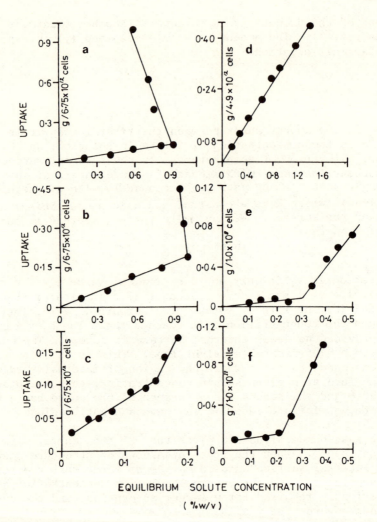

Figure 14. Adsorption isotherms for some surface-active antimi-
crobial agents, by thick washed suspension of micro-organisms.
a, 2-phenoxyethanol on E.coli NCTC 5933; b, 2-phenoxypropanol
on the same; c, 4-chloro-2-phenoxyethanol on the same; d,
2-phenoxyethanol on Ps.aeruginosa NCTC 6750; e, 3-(2-methyl-
phenoxy)-propane-1,2-diol on C.lipolytica NCTC 376; f, the same
on E.coli NCTC 5933.

At adsorptions above the inflection points there was gross
damage to the cytoplasmic membrane, with leakage of cell constituents; with Ps.aeruginosa (curve d) there is no inflection, and
no cell damage was observed.[35]

Systems giving 'C' type isotherms include synthetic polymers, e.g. polyester or nylon, adsorbing non-ionic solutes, and clays adsorbing amino-acids. In the latter systems the increase of internal surface with increase in adsorption is detected by x-ray meausrement.[36]

REFERENCES

1. For description of some of the types of adsorption important in everyday life and in Nature, see e.g. C.H. Giles, Chem. and Ind., 724, 770 (1964).
2. J.W. McBain and C.W. Humphreys, J. Phys. Chem., 36, 300 (1932); J.W. McBain and R.C. Swain, Proc. Roy. Soc. Ser. A, 154, 608 (1936).
3. E.S. Snavely, G.M. Schmid and R.M. Hurd, Nature (London), 194 439 (1962).
4. W.C.M. Lewis, Phil. Mag., 15, 499 (1908); 17, 466 (1909); Z. Phys. Chem., 73, 129 (1910).
5. C.W. Gibby and C.C. Addison, J. Chem. Soc. London, 119, 1306, (1936).
6. C.H. Giles and N. McIver, J. Colloid Interfac. Sci., 62, 329 (1977).
7. B. Milicevic, IVe Cong. Intern. de la Detergence, Sec. B, IV, 12 (1964).
8. C.H. Giles and A.H. Soutar, J. Soc. Dyers Col., 87, 301 (1971).
9. C.H. Giles, J. Soc. Dyers Col., 94, 4 (1978), and references cited therein.
10. Z. Yoshida, E. Osawa and R. Oda, J. Phys. Chem., 68, 2895 (1964).
11. C.H. Giles and A. McIntosh, Text. Res. J., 43, 489 (1973).
12. C.H. Giles, in "The Theory of Coloration of Textiles", C.K. Bird and W.S. Boston, Editors, Chap. 2, Dyers Co. Publications Trust, Bradford, England, (1975).
13. C.H. Giles, T.H. MacEwan, S.N. Nakhwa and D. Smith, J. Chem. Soc., London, 786, 3973 (1960).
14. C.H. Giles, D. Smith and A. Huitson, J. Colloid, Interface Sci., 47, 755 (1974).
15. C.H. Giles, A.P. D'Silva and I.A. Easton, J. Colloid Interface Sci., 47, 766 (1974).
16. See e.g. C.H. Giles, R.B. McKay and W. Good, J. Chem. Soc. London, 5434 (1961), and references cited therein.
17. V.G. Agnihotri and C.H. Giles, J. Chem. Soc., London, Perkin Trans. II, 2241 (1972).
18. C.H. Giles, V.G. Agnihotri and A.S. Trivedi, J. Soc. Dyers Col., 86, 451 (1970).
19. T. Vickerstaff, "The Physical Chemistry of Dyeing", 2nd Edn. Oliver and Boyd, London, 1954.
20. C.H. Giles and K.V. Datye, Trans. Inst. Metal Finishing, 40, 113 (1963).
21. C.H. Giles, R. Haslam, A.R. Hill and A.S. Trivedi, J. Appl. Chem. Biotechnol., 21, 5 (1971).

22. C.H. Giles and R. Haslam. Text. Res. J., $\underline{47}$, 348 (1977).
23. Idem., ibid., $\underline{48}$, 490 (1978).
24. C.H. Giles and N. McIver, J. Soc. Dyers Col., $\underline{90}$, 93 (1974).
25. D. Balmforth, C.A. Bowers and T.H. Guion, J. Soc. Dyers Col., $\underline{80}$, 577 (1964).
26. M.R.J. Salton, in "Proc. 2nd Internat. Congress Surface Activity", London, $\underline{4}$, 245 (1957).
27. C.H. Giles, Text. Res. J., $\underline{31}$, 141 (1961).
28. H.R. Chipalkatti, C.H. Giles and D.G.M. Vallance, J. Chem. Soc. London, 4375 (1954).
29. W. Kauzmann, Adv. Protein Chem., $\underline{14}$, 1 (1959); G. Nemethy and H.A. Scheraga, J. Chem. Phys., $\underline{36}$, 3382, 3401 (1962); J. Phys. Chem., $\underline{66}$, 1773 (1962).
30. A.B. Meggy, J. Soc. Dyers Col., $\underline{66}$, 510 (1950).
31. C.H. Giles and A.S.A. Hassan, J. Soc. Dyers Col., $\underline{74}$, 846 (1958).
32. E.H. Daruwalla and A.P. D'Silva, Text. Res. J., $\underline{33}$ 40 (1963).
33. H.S. Blair and M.J. McElroy, J. Appl. Polymer Sci., $\underline{19}$, 3161 (1975).
34. C.H. Giles and A.H. Tolia, J. Appl. Chem., $\underline{14}$, 186 (1964).
35. P. Gilbert, E.G. Beveridge and T. Sissons, J. Colloid Interface Sci., $\underline{64}$, 377 (1978).
36. D.J. Greenland, R.H. Laby and J.P. Quirk, Trans. Faraday Soc., $\underline{58}$, 829 (1962).

SURFACTANTS AND THE ENVIRONMENT: BIODEGRADATION ASPECTS

R. D. Swisher
Chemical & Environmental Consultant
Kirkwood, Mo. 63122

Surfactant biodegradation research is surveyed briefly from its beginnings in the early 1950s when incidents of environmental foaming began to draw attention. Topics include development of test methods, correlations between surfactant structure and biodegradability, biodegradation metabolic pathways, development of commercially feasible biodegradable surfactants and the current environmental situation.

INTRODUCTION

In the early 1950s a revolution occurred in the household detergent industry. New, more efficient formulations took over the market, displacing soap almost completely from two of its major uses, household laundering and dishwashing. The new formulations were based on synthetic surfactants and chelants; in large part these were, respectively, higher alkylbenzene sulfonates and sodium tripolyphosphate. The alkylbenzene mainly involved was TBS, in which the alkyl group was derived from tetrapropylene, a rather complex mixture of branched olefins derived in turn from propylene and averaging about twelve carbon atoms per molecule.

But TBS proved to be environmentally unsatisfactory because it was associated with increased foaming in sewage treatment plants and receiving waters wherever sewage entered the environment. While soap precipitated as non-foaming calcium and magnesium salts in natural waters, the TBS remained in solution. After all, that was why TBS was so successful as a cleanser in the first place -- it did not precipitate with calcium and magnesium ions.

149

Confronted with the environmental foaming problem in the mid-fifties, the detergent industry of the United States undertook to correct it. They soon reached a consensus that the preferable solution would be to redesign the surfactant's molecular structure to make it biodegradable -- in other words, to make it acceptable to bacteria as a food and energy source. If this could be achieved, once the surfactant had served its detergent purpose in the household it would then be destroyed by the bacteria in the sewage and receiving environment.

Please note: that was around 1955, about 25 years ago, 6 or 7 years before Silent Spring. If you used the word "ecology" back then, all you were likely to get in return would be a blank look.

The detergent industry solution was brought to a successful conclusion in the mid-sixties, with the introduction of the new product, linear alkylbenzene sulfonate, otherwise known as LAS. Much of the intervening time was spent in laboratory research on such things as development of biodegradation test methods, correlation of molecular structure with biodegradability, selection of likely surfactant structures for investigation, development of raw materials, products, processes and so on. Concurrent with the later stages of the laboratory work, manufacturing facilities had to be designed, constructed and brought into smooth operation in volumes of half a billion pounds per year or more. As it turned out, these facilities were not so much for the LAS itself, but rather to make the raw materials for the LAS. And also to make the raw materials for the raw materials for the LAS.

BIODEGRADATION TEST METHODS

Testing for biodegradability is in principle quite simple -- you just expose the compound to some bacteria and see what happens to it. But if the test procedure is to be meaningful for extrapolation to the real outside world there are at least three important prerequisites. First, it must provide easy and continuing access for all sorts of environmental bacteria, because bacteria differ in their capabilities for attacking different molecular structures. Second, it must provide physical and chemical conditions suitable for growth and propagation of those various bacteria, including any necessary macronutrients, micronutrients, vitamins, minerals and whatever. Since many of these necessities are unknown as yet, the best course at present is to use the natural medium appropriate to the bacteria being used -- river water for river bacteria, sewage for sewage bacteria, soil for soil bacteria and so on.

The third and most important requirement in a test procedure is time; time must be allowed for full acclimation of the bacterial test system to the test compound. Although only a few hours or a few days should be sufficient for a given bacterial species to mobilize its

full armament of constitutive and inducible enzymes, much more time
than that may be required. If only a few bacterial species are capable of degrading the test compound, and if the test system includes
only a few or none of those particular capable organisms, weeks or
months may be needed for those capable species to find their way into
the test system and multiply sufficiently to become a significant
fraction of the bacterial community. Once this has been accomplished,
biodegradation of the compound may then proceed just as speedily and
just as completely as that of any more popular compound.

Obviously the rarer are the capable species in the environment
and the longer is the acclimation time required in the test, the
greater is our uncertainty about how effective will be the biodegradation in the real world. Field tests in a variety of real environmental situations then become increasingly important. In the words
of the Biodegradation Master, Martin Alexander, "Biodegradation is
simply a matter of Faith, Hope and Acclimation; and the greatest of
these is Acclimation."

To get down to specifics, a biodegradation test system may be
quite complex, for example a fairly close modeling of a continuous
flow activated sludge sewage treatment process. Or it may be as
simple as a river-blivet, which is just a two quart bottle containing one quart of river water. You put in a little of the test compound and analyze from time to time by as many suitable means as you
can muster. This can be an exceedingly effective test method, depending almost entirely upon your own analytical competence. The
river bacteria carry out their share of the procedure, namely the
biochemical part, in a highly responsible manner provided you don't
swamp them with too much test compound.

SURFACTANT STRUCTURE AND BIODEGRADABILITY

Surfactants can differ one from another in the nature of the
hydrophobic group, the nature of the hydrophilic group and the nature
of the linkage between them. For the most part the biodegradability
of the surfactant is governed only by the molecular structure of the
hydrophobe. But before proceeding with that, there are two exceptions
I would like to mention briefly.

The first exception is the polyglycol hydrophile used in the
ethoxylate nonionic surfactants,

$$R-(OCH_2CH_2)_nOH$$

This particular hydrophile does influence biodegradability. Generally
for a given R, the smaller the number of glycol units, n (i.e., the
shorter the polyglycol chain), the easier the biodegradation.

The second exception is a case where the linkage affects the
biodegradation. This involves the oxygen atom linking the hydrophobe
and hydrophile in the linear primary alkyl sulfates,

$$CH_3(CH_2)_n CH_2-O-SO_3Na$$

Biodegradation of such compounds is perhaps twice as fast as that
of other surfactants, even those with otherwise identical structure
where the sulfur is joined directly to the terminal carbon instead
of through an oxygen atom. This facile hydrolysis of the alkyl sulfate is the result of sulfatase enzymes, which seem to be ubiquitous
in the environment.

But these sulfatase enzymes do not help very much with other
alkyl sulfates of non-linear structure. These are sometimes very
reluctant to degrade, for example this trimethylhexyl sulfate

$$C\overset{|}{\underset{|}{C}}C\overset{|}{C}CC-O-SO_3Na$$

pointed out by Hammerton.[1] This branched primary alkyl sulfate and
the linear primary mentioned above together provide a good demonstration of a basic principle first advanced by Hammerton[1,2] and by Sawyer[3,4]: surfactants with branched hydrophobes are generally more
resistant than are linear ones. Hammerton further concluded from his
studies that the chemical nature of the hydrophile and the mode of
linkage do not affect biodegradability very much, as already stated
above.

An instructive example is provided by tetrapropylene, the olefin used to manufacture TBS. Formed from propylene under rather
drastic conditions, tetrapropylene is a mixture of several dozen
isomers and close homologs, and the alkylbenzene made from it consists of a hundred or more components. I doubt whether the molecular
structure of even one of those components has ever been determined,
but in any case there are no linear ones among them -- all are highly
branched. A series of twenty different surfactants was synthesized
(listed in reference 5), all with a tetrapropylene type hydrophobe
but each having a different hydrophilic group or a different linkage. Every one of the twenty showed more or less resistance to
biodegradation, and it gradually became evident that tetrapropylene
was less than ideal as a hydrophobe for a biodegradable surfactant.
So tetrapropylene was abandoned despite its ready availability, low
cost and outstanding detergent performance.

The replacement product, LAS, was manufactured by alkylation
of benzene with linear olefins or chloroparaffins, followed by sulfonation of the resulting alkylbenzene. A general redistribution
occurs during the alkylation so that in the product the benzene
ring is found attached to the alkyl group at any of the positions

along the chain except little or none at the two end carbons. Alkyl chain lengths from ten to fourteen carbons are most effective; the exact chain length distribution in a given product is adjusted to suit the desired properties and uses of the product. The composition with regard to individual homologs and isomers is relatively easy to determine by gas chromatography after removal of the sulfonate group to restore volatility.

A mixture of equal parts of C_{12} and C_{14}LAS is shown in the upper chromatogram of Figure 1; the peaks denote the five C_{12} and the six C_{14} alkylbenzene isomers liberated by the desulfonation. This chromatogram was made from a river water solution of the two, sampled immediately after dissolving. The bottom chromatogram shows that same solution fifteen days later, at which time the methylene blue analysis for LAS had dropped to half the original value because of biodegradation by the bacteria in the river water. Here we see two characteristic features of LAS biodegradation.

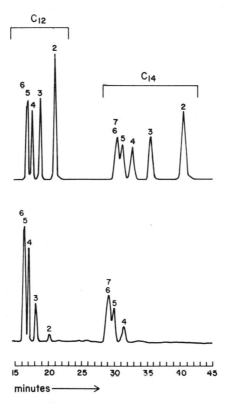

Figure 1. Biodegradation of C_{12} + C_{14} LAS mixture in river water, detected by desulfonation-gas chromatography (Swisher[6]).
Upper: Day zero, methylene blue analysis 5 mg/L.
Lower: Day 15, methylene blue analysis 2.5 mg/L.

First, the 2-phenyl isomers (those with the ring attached to the second carbon atom of the chain) have substantially disappeared. The 3-phenyls have not progressed quite so far, and the 5-, 6- and 7-isomers are mostly untouched at this state. They disappear within a few more days.

The second feature becomes evident upon measuring the peak areas in the chromatograms. Each C_{14} isomer has degraded a little faster than the corresponding C_{12}. Adding the individual isomers together, we find that about 60% of the C_{14}s are gone at this halfway point compared to about 40% of the C_{12}s. This more rapid biodegradation with increased homolog length was first pointed out for LAS by Huddleston & Allred[7] and has been observed to occur quite generally from C_6 to C_{16} at least.[8]

A single principle correlates these two effects: increased distance between the sulfonate group and the far end of the alkyl chain increases the speed of the primary biodegradation. This undoubtedly reflects the relationship between the surfactant structure and the geometry of the oxygenase enzyme molecule which catalyzes the attack at the end of the alkyl chain, initiating biodegradation.

LAS BIODEGRADATION PATHWAYS

Now let us turn to Figure 2, which shows chromatograms obtained during river water biodegradation of 5 mg/L of C_{12} LAS. The top chromatogram shows the state at the beginning. Four days later the methylene blue analysis was down to 2 mg/L, and the second chromatogram shows that the 2-, 3- and 4-isomers had already degraded. The three prominent new peaks show the presence of biodegradation intermediates from those three isomers as identified by the numbering. The two bottom chromatograms show that both the original LAS and the intermediates progressively disappear and that all were substantially gone within fifteen days in this particular experiment.

The new peaks were identified by infrared and mass spectroscopy, leading to a map of the earlier stages of the biodegradation pathway as shown in Figure 3. For simplicity the diagram is confined to the 2-phenyl components of the even chain lengths, the C_{10}, C_{12} and C_{14} homologs, at the left.

The first phase of the biodegradation is conversion of the terminal methyl group by ω-oxidation to the carboxylate at the right. This is analogous to the way bacteria attack linear hydrocarbons in the environment. One pathway begins under the catalysis of an oxygenase enzyme with the addition of a molecule of oxygen to the terminal methyl group, converting it to a primary hydroperoxide. This is then reduced to the alcohol, oxidized to the aldehyde and then to the carboxylate at the right. At this point primary biodegradation is

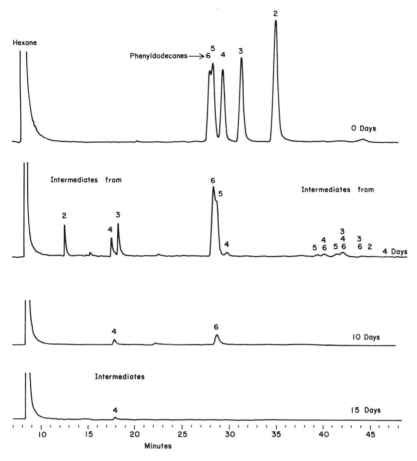

Figure 2. Biodegradation of C_{12} LAS in river water, detected by
desulfonation-gas chromatography (Swisher[9]).
Methylene blue analyses: Day zero, 5 mg/L; day 4, 2 mg/L.

near completion; even the longest chain carboxylates respond only
feebly in the methylene blue analysis and show only minimal foaming
and aquatic toxicity.

The next phase of the biodegradation, shortening of the chain,
is very rapid. Just about all living organisms, from bacteria to
people, have enzymes for metabolizing longer chain fatty acids by
the process known as β-oxidation. This is a sequence of several reactions which leads to the splitting off of the first two carbon
atoms from the chain in the form of an acetate group, leaving a
carboxylate two carbons shorter than the original. This process can
be repeated again and again, shortening the chain two carbons at a

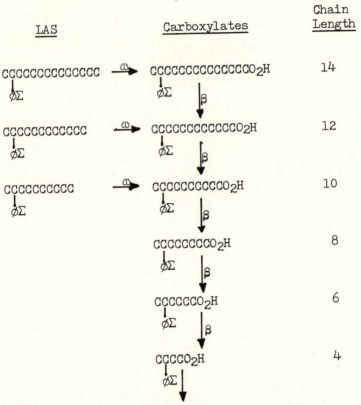

Figure 3. Earlier stages in biodegradation of 2-phenyl even LAS.
ϕ = benzene ring; Σ = SO$_3$Na group.

time. In our case in Figure 3 the β-oxidation enzymes evidently fit
the linear carboxylate portion of the molecule at the upper right
very well, because it degrades so fast that no significant amount is
detectable.[10] The next several steps of β-oxidation are likewise very
rapid, progressing downward toward the 3-sulfophenylbutyrate at the
lower right.

But by now the alkyl carboxylate chain is apparently so short
that the sulfophenyl group interferes with the proper fitting of its
molecule into the topography of the ordinary β-oxidation enzymes. As
a result this carboxylate remains unattacked, leading to the prominent intermediate peak in the chromatogram (Figure 2). However, soon
acclimation again occurs, and the degradation again proceeds. Observation of the ultraviolet spectrum shows that the benzene ring disappears, while the sulfonate sulfur is simultaneously liberated to
appear as inorganic sulfate.[11] The benzene ring biodegradation probably follows one or more of the catechol pathways available to many

bacteria, as Cain has demonstrated for the related 1-phenylalkane sulfonates.[12]

As Figure 3 shows, the C_{10}, C_{12} and C_{14} LAS homologs with 2-phenyl attachment all go through exactly the same series of shorter chain carboxylates if they follow this ω-, β-oxidation pathway. The corresponding 3-phenyl isomers give a slightly different series, all linked at the 3 position, and similarly for the 4-, 5-, 6-, and 7-phenyl isomers. Likewise with the odd chain length homologs -- the C_{11} and C_{13} LAS. Here the six isomers generate six more series, a total of twelve different sets of intermediates for the total LAS complex, each similar to the set in Figure 3. Several dozen different sulfophenylalkanoates are thus involved.

And that isn't the whole story -- other pathways are available and are used to some extent. For instance, α-oxidation may occasionally occur instead of β-oxidation, removing only one carbon instead of two, with resulting switching from an odd series to an even one or vice versa. And oxidation may also occur at the other end of the chain, generating sets of dicarboxylates. But all these dozens of intermediates are for the most part degraded almost as soon as they are formed. Only in a few cases of the shorter chain intermediates is much reacclimation necessary before biodegradation proceeds.

High pressure liquid chromatography (HPLC) is even better suited to detection of these intermediates than is desulfonation-gas chromatography. Using HPLC similar patterns of certain intermediates accumulating and then degrading have been observed in river water[13] and in pond water microcosms.[14]

Biodegradation of other surfactants generally seems to follow pathways much the same as those of LAS, at least if linear hydrophobes are involved. With linear primary ethoxylate nonionics, for example, oxidation of the hydrophobe chain is rapid, liberating the hydrophilic group in the form of free polyglycols which in turn degrade a little more slowly.[15]

CURRENT ENVIRONMENTAL STATUS

The conversion of the US household detergent industry to bio-degradable surfactants involved only one new product, LAS, which replaced the highly branched TBS. Among the nonionics no new product was necessary since a highly biodegradable material was already in use, linear primary alcohol ethoxylate. Here the industry conversion was achieved simply by eliminating the use of branched alcohol and alkylphenol ethoxylates.

The objective of the industry conversion was correction of surfactant-related foaming in sewage treatment plants and streams

and rivers and other environmental waters. I am happy to report that
this objective has been met eminently well.

But foaming is by no means the entire concern. By the time LAS
was commercialized in 1965 it had already been thoroughly tested not
only as a cleansing agent with ready biodegradability, but in its
environmental and human safety aspects as well. Although its toxicity to aquatic life was found to be somewhat greater than that of
TBS, it was expected that this difference would be more than offset
by the much lower environmental concentrations anticipated because
of its much better biodegradation. Finally, the mammalian toxicity
of LAS was found to be quite low, in the same range as other surfactants suitable for use in detergents.

On the basis of such information it was the judgment of the
detergent industry in 1965 that LAS was a safe and desirable material. Since that time the techniques of analytical and biological
chemistry and toxicology have continued to advance in sophistica-
tion and power. They have been and are being adapted to answer more
and more subtle questions regarding LAS and the environment -- questions quite unanswerable at the time LAS was being developed, questions which could not even have been formulated. These newer answers
have continued to support the initial judgment as to the safety of
LAS.[13] Development of new evaluation and monitoring capabilities will
continue on into the future, by the detergent industry and by other
champions of the environment. Although it seems unlikely that LAS
can threaten us with any environmental disaster at this late date,
eternal vigilance is the price of safety.

Communication is a continuing problem. For example, the information on the existence of the short chain carboxylate intermediates
was first published in 1963. Yet from time to time people continue
to rediscover them and to call for abandonment of LAS on that
account, as outlined for example in a recent review.[16] An alternate,
as yet unpublished evaluation[17] emphasizes two points. First, these
intermediates are themselves biodegradable if proper care is taken
:o see that the test conditions approach those met in the real world.
Second, their aquatic and mammalian toxicities are orders of magnitude below the toxicities of LAS and other surfactants, and their
maximum environmental concentrations, even assuming no biodegradation at all, are orders of magnitude below their toxic thresholds.

As pointed out earlier, laboratory test procedures using
synthetic media or other unnatural conditions may restrict the diversity and capability of their microbial populations compared to
those in the real world. On the other hand, measures taken in other
test procedures to eliminate such restrictions may possibly enhance
the biodegradation activity to exceed that of the real world. Once
this fundamental problem is recognized, little can be gained from

arguing about the relative merits of synthetic versus natural type laboratory tests. The question of environmental acceptability must ultimately be answered in terms of the real world -- what concentrations are actually met in the waters there, and what hazards do they impose? Judging from the experience gained in the past fifteen years of full scale use of LAS, I believe these hazards are small indeed.

REFERENCES

1. C. Hammerton, Proc. Soc. Water Treat. Exam., 5, 145(1956). reprinted in Inst. Sewage Purif. J. & Proc., 1957, 280
2. C. Hammerton, J. Appl. Chem. (London), 5, 517 (1955).
3. R. H. Bogan and C. N. Sawyer, Sewage Ind. Wastes, 27, 917 (1955).
4. C. N. Sawyer, R. H. Bogan and J. R. Simpson, Ind. Eng. Chem., 48, 236 (1956).
5. R. D. Swisher, in "Proc. Int. Biodegradation Symp., 3rd, 1975", J. M. Sharpley and A. M. Kaplan, Editors, pp. 853-865, Applied Science Publishers, London, 1976.
6. R. D. Swisher, J. Water Poll. Control Fed., 35, 877 (1963).
7. R. L. Huddleston and R. C. Allred, Develop. Ind. Microbiol., 4, 24 (1963).
8. R. D. Swisher, "Surfactant Biodegradation," Marcel Dekker, New York, 1970.
9. R. D. Swisher, J. Water Poll. Control Fed., 35, 1557 (1963).
10. R. D. Swisher, Chem. Eng. Progr., 60(12), 41 (1964).
11. R. D. Swisher, Yukagaku, 21, 130 (1972).
12. R. B. Cain, in "Treatment of Industrial Effluents," A.G. Callely, C. F. Forster and D. A. Stafford, Editors, pp. 283-327, Wiley, New York, 1976.
13. R. D. Swisher, W. E. Gledhill, R. A. Kimerle and T. A. Taulli, in "Proc. Int. Cong. Surface Active Substances, 7th, 1976," Vol. 4, pp 218-230, Moscow, 1978.
14. C. R. Eggert, R. G. Kaley and W. E. Gledhill, in "Proc. Workshop: Microbial Degradation of Pollutants in Marine Environments, 1978," A. W. Bourquin and P. H. Pritchard, Editors, pp 451-461, U. S. EPA Report 600/9-79-012, Gulf Breeze, 1979.
15. S. J. Patterson, C. C. Scott and K. B. E. Tucker, J. Am. Oil Chemists' Soc., 44, 407 (1967).
16. P. Pitter and T. Fuka, Tenside, 16, 298 (1979).
17. R. D. Swisher, (1980), Tenside, submitted for publication.

ENVIRONMENTAL AND HUMAN HEALTH ASPECTS OF

COMMERCIALLY IMPORTANT SURFACTANTS

Andrew Sivak, Muriel Goyer, Joanne Perwak,
and Philip Thayer
Arthur D. Little, Inc.
Acorn Park, Cambridge, MA. 02140

Seven types of surfactants comprise the majority of those presently used in commercial detergent formulations. These are linear alkylbenzene sulfonates (LAS), alkyl sulfates (AS), alcohol ethoxylates (AE), alkyl phenol ethoxylates (APE), alcohol ethoxy sulfates (AES), alpha olefin sulfonates (AOS) and secondary alkane sulfonates (SAS). LAS surfactants, the mainstay of detergent components, have been in use the longest and their paths of biodegradation are relatively well understood. Environmental levels of methylene blue active substances, the most commonly employed but non-specific measure of anionic surfactant concentration, indicate that LAS are readily biodegradable. Nonionic (AE and APE) and the anionic AES and AS surfactants are also biodegradable with APE degrading somewhat more slowly than the others. Acute toxic effects to aquatic life forms generally occur in adult vertebrates and invertebrates at surfactant concentrations from 1 to 20 mg/L; juvenile and developmental stages show effects at somewhat lower concentrations. Studies with mammalian species have shown acute oral toxicity to occur at doses of 650 to > 25,000 mg/kg. No evidence for carcinogenic, mutagenic or teratogenic effects has been noted. The present domestic and commercial use of these surfactants appears to present no problems with respect to human health and the aquatic environment.

INTRODUCTION

Five billion pounds of surface-active agents are produced
in the United States annually. Sixty-five percent of this volume is of the anionic type; an additional twenty-eight percent
is in the nonionic category.[1] Three anionic surfactants are
prime components of almost all types of household detergent
products, and as such, these surfactants find their way into
the environment with the resulting possibility of environmental
and human exposure. These three anionic surfactants are the
linear alkylbenzene sulfonates, alkyl sulfates and alpha olefin
sulfonates (Figure 1).

The linear alkylbenzene sulfonates (LAS) represent a
substantial portion of today's surfactant market; approximately
640 million pounds were produced in the United States in 1978.[1]
First introduced in 1965 to replace the more slowly biodegradable
tetrapropylene-derived alkylbenzene sulfonates (ABS), LAS are a
complex mixture of isomers and homologues whose proportions
are dependent on starting materials and reaction conditions.
The LAS in commercial use contain linear alkyl chains ranging
from 10 to 14 carbons in length with phenyl groups placed at
various internal carbon positions in the alkyl chain.[2]

The alkyl sulfates (AS) are widely used in specialty
products such as shampoos, cosmetics, toothpastes, etc., and
are also extensively utilized as wool-washing agents. The bulk
of AS in use are linear, primary AS, but some linear and branched
secondary AS are also utilized.[2] Primary AS are typically
prepared by conventional sulfation of the parent alcohol with
either sulfur trioxide or chlorosulfonic acid; secondary AS are
more readily prepared by reacting the parent alkene with
sulfuric acid.

Alpha olefin sulfonates (AOS) are relative newcomers to
the domestic synthetic detergent industry. However, recent
development of continuous, short contact sulfur trioxide sulfonation processes and increased availability of high purity
alpha olefin feedstock have made AOS surfactants competitive
with other surfactants presently on the market. The highly
exothermic, direct sulfonation of linear α-olefins with a
dilute stream of vaporized sulfur trioxide can follow several
paths, leading to a variety of reaction products.[2] Commercial
AOS formulations contain a mixture of alkene sulfonates and
hydroxyalkane sulfonates. In addition, trace amounts of
alkene disulfonates, hydroxyalkane disulfonates, saturated
sultones and unreacted α-olefins may also be present.[2] AOS
possess good detergency and foaming characteristics in hard
water and are utilized in heavy duty powder detergents of low
phosphate content.

A fourth type of anionic surfactant, the secondary alkane sulfonates (SAS), is largely limited to the European continent at this time. SAS are predominantly linear with the sulfonate group attached to a secondary carbon and randomly positioned along the carbon chain. They are produced commercially via a sulfoxidation reaction with n-paraffins in the $C_{14}-C_{18}$ range.[2] SAS have a good detergency and foaming properties as well as high water solubility characteristics and are principally used as components of liquid detergent formulations.

In addition to these four types of anionic surfactants, the balance of the household surfactant market is composed of two nonionic surfactants, the alcohol ethoxylates and alkylphenol ethoxylates and an anionic-nonionic hybrid, the alkylethoxy sulfates which are anionic in character. The nonionic surfactants, particularly the alcohol ethoxylates, have found wide use in newer detergent formulations due to their superior cleaning of man-made fibers, their tolerance of water hardness and their low foaming properties. Prepared commercially by reaction of an alcohol and ethylene oxide, some 476 million pounds of mixed linear alcohol ethoxylates (AE) are produced annually in the United States.[1]

The second category of nonionics, the alkylphenol ethoxylates (APE) have been largely replaced in domestic household products by the more rapidly biodegradable AE although they still find considerable use in industrial and agricultural applications.[2] Commercially, alkylphenols are manufactured by the addition of phenol to the double bond of an olefin in the presence of a catalyst such as boron trifluoride; the alkylphenol is purified by distillation, then reacted with several moles of ethylene oxide to produce APE.

Perhaps the fastest growing volume usage of the surfactant market are the alkyl ethoxy sulfates (AES).[1] They are known for their reduced sensitivity to water hardness, and their high foaming capabilities and are used primarily as components of liquid dishwashing products, shampoos and other household specialty products.[2] They are prepared commercially by ethoxylation of a fatty alcohol followed by sulfation with sulfur trioxide or chlorosulfonic acid. A total of 285 million pounds of AES were produced in 1978.[1]

ANALYTICAL PROCEDURES

The data presently available on the very low residual concentrations of surfactants and their biodegradation products in the environment suggest that their use poses no threat to

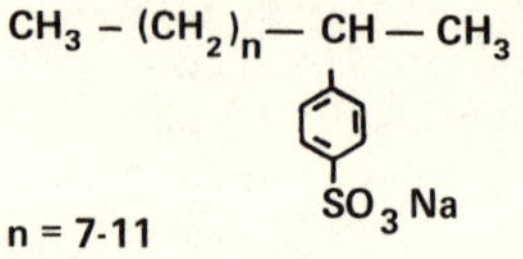

$CH_3 - (CH_2)_n - CH - CH_3$

$SO_3 Na$

n = 7-11

LINEAR ALKYLBENZENE SULFONATES
(LAS)

$CH_3 - (CH_2)_n - CH_2 - OSO_3 Na$

n = 10-16

ALKYL SULFATES
(AS)

$CH_3 - (CH_2)_n - CH = CH - CH_2 SO_3 Na$

65-65% Alkene Sulfonate

$CH_3 - (CH_2)_n - CH - CH_2 CH_2 SO_3 Na$
OH

35-40% Hydroxyalkane Sulfonate

n = 12-16

ALPHA OLEFIN SULFONATES
(AOS)

$C_n H_{2n+1} SO_3 Na$

n = 14-18

SECONDARY ALKANE SULFONATES
(SAS)

$CH_3 - (CH_2)_n - CH_2 - (O-CH_2)_x OSO_3 Na$

n = 8-16

x = 2-4

ALCOHOL ETHOXY SULFATES
(AES)

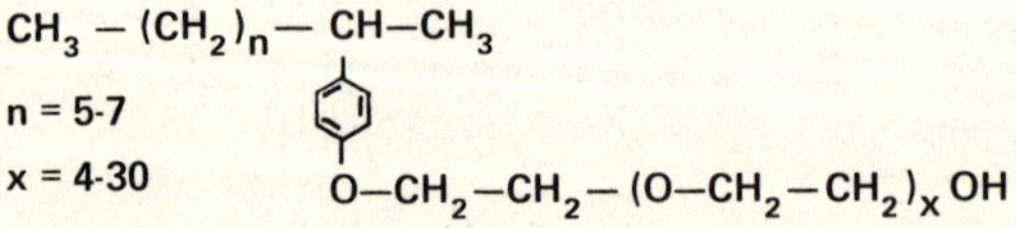

$CH_3 - (CH_2)_n - CH-CH_3$

n = 5-7

x = 4-30

$O-CH_2-CH_2-(O-CH_2-CH_2)_x OH$

ALKYLPHENOL ETHOXYLATES
(APE)

$CH_3 - (CH_2)_n - CH_2 - (O-CH_2-CH_2)_x OH$

n = 6-16

x = 3-20

ALCOHOL ETHOXYLATES
(AE)

Figure 1. Name and structure of representative surfactants.[2]

environmental quality.[2] Several analytical procedures are
available for the determination of surfactant concentrations
in the environment. They can be categorized into three major
areas: physical methods, chemical techniques and physicochemical analyses.

Two physical methods of analysis utilized to assess
presumptive levels of both anionic and nonionic surfactants in
the environment are foaming potential and surface tension.
Although the residual foaming potential of a partially degraded
surfactant can be used as a measure of biodegradation, the
usefulness of this method is limited. A transient phenomenon,
foaming can be affected by a wide variety of factors such as
temperature, humidity, size of test container, etc.; furthermore, foaming often is not a linear function of surfactant
concentration.[2,3]

Changes in surface tension can also be used as a measure
of biodegradation. This procedure is based upon the fact that
the presence of a few parts per million of a surfactant significantly lowers the surface tension of water. The magnitude
of this change increases (although not in a linear fashion)
with an increase in the concentration of surfactant until a
critical micelle concentration is reached; above this concentration, further increases in surfactant concentration produce
little or no change in surface tension.[3] Measurement of surface tension is quick and qualitative in that each surfactant
has a characteristic ability to lower surface tension. The
major drawbacks of the method are the lack of specificity,
insufficient sensitivity to distinguish minute changes in
surfactant concentration as biodegradation proceeds and the
ease with which foreign substances can distort results.[4]

By far, the most widely used method for the determination of anionic surfactants in environmental samples, is the
methylene blue method.[2] Methylene blue is a cationic dye
which, in the presence of anionic materials, forms a salt which
is readily extractable into organic solvents. Measurement of
the intensity of the blue color in the solvent provides a
measure of the amount of anionic material present. Because of
its simplicity and high degree of sensitivity (0.1 ppm), the
methylene blue reaction has become the standard method of
testing for anionic surfactants in water.[3,5,6] The methylene blue reaction, however, lacks specificity and cannot
distinguish among anionic materials.[3,7] Additionally, the
reaction is so responsive that it is prone to multiple positive
and negative interferences including many naturally occurring
materials.[3,8] Thus, the materials detected with this procedure
are referred to as methylene blue active substances (MBAS),

rather than as specific surfactants or their residues and cannot be considered necessarily to represent total anionic surfactants. The methylene blue procedure will not detect some intermediate degradation products of anionic surfactants and therefore, can be used only to measure intact surfactants.[9,10]

A considerable data base of MBAS levels for different bodies of water in the United States indicates MBAS levels generally well below 0.5 mg/L.[11-15] Where levels higher than 0.5 mg MBAS/L are found, these waterways usually receive untreated or inadequately treated sewage.[2] The actual level of anionic surfactants in natural water bodies is probably considerably less than the level of MBAS owing to the nonspecific nature of the MBAS method. There are currently no national water quality standards for MBAS in the United States but the U.S. Public Health Service has set a maximum permissible level of 0.5 mg MBAS/L for drinking water involved in interstate commerce and a number of states have also set 0.5 mg MBAS/L as the maximum permitted level in all waters within their boundaries.[2,5]

Two procedures employed in the determination of presumptive levels of nonionic surfactants in the environment are the measurement of either bismuth iodide active substances (BIAS) or cobalt thiocyanate active substances (CTAS). Both of these techniques are based on the reaction of the polyethoxylate chain of the surfactant molecule to form complexes with bismuth or cobalt and, like MBAS, are nonspecific.

The determination of bismuth iodide active substances (also commonly referred to as Wickbold's procedure) is applicable to both APE and AE with hydrophilic chains of between 6 and 30 ethylene oxide (EO) units.[16] After sublation (isolation by foaming) and several intermediate steps, the nonionic surfactant is precipitated with a modified Dragendorff reagent ($KBiI_4$ + $BaCl_2$ + glacial acetic acid), the complex formed is redissolved and the bismuth in solution titrated potentiometrically. The method has a sensitivity of 0.01 mg/L and is capable of detecting unchanged nonionic surfactants without interference from biodegradation products. The major disadvantages of the procedure are the necessity of multiplying the titration results by an empirical factor which varies according to the length of the ethoxylate chain, which may be unknown, as well as the lack of specificity. The method is also subject to interference by cationic substances which combine with the precipitating mixture and thus add to the apparent nonionic detergent content.[17]

The cobalt thiocyanate procedure is based on the formation of a blue complex between the ammonium cobaltothiocyanate reagent and the hydrophilic polyethoxylate chain of the nonionic surfactant. The complex is extracted into an organic solvent and the nonionic content determined spectrophotometrically. The method has a sensitivity of 0.1 mg/L.[18,19] Among several drawbacks of this procedure are its lack of sensitivity above 15 and below 3 EO units, the large differences in molar absorptivity depending on EO content, the large number of chemical interferences (e.g., strongly acidic or basic solutions, cationic surfactants, solid particles), and the lack of specificity.[3,18,20]

As with the anionic surfactants, there are presently no national criteria specifically limiting nonionic surfactants in waters of the United States.[2] Since in most instances, analytical methods do not distinguish between specific classes of nonionics and/or their degradation product, it is not possible to ascertain which type of surfactant contributes to levels of nonionics in waterways. Levels of AE and APE are not routinely monitored, as such, in the United States but when assays for both types of surfactants have been performed in European rivers, levels of nonionics are almost always lower than anionics at the same sampling point.[21,22]

Physicochemical methods of analysis have also been utilized to some extent in the study of surfactant biodegradation. Thin-layer, paper and gas chromatography have provided vital information on intermediate products as well as the metabolic routes of degradation.[3] However, these procedures are complicated, require relatively expensive equipment, may contain an element of subjective analysis in the use of paper as thin-layer chromatographs, are time-consuming and therefore not applicable for routine environmental analyses.[10] Infrared and ultraviolet spectroscopy have also been applied to the study of surfactant biodegradation but they are subject to many interfering substances and their reliability in undefined systems is uncertain.[3] High-performance liquid chromatography may provide a suitable new tool; it has recently been used to separate materials removed from an MBAS complex by cation exchange chromatography. Detection of 0.1 µg LAS was reported.[25]

Another analytical technique which has been applied particularly to the study of LAS biodegradation is the use of radioactively-labeled surfactants. The most commonly used label has been ^{35}S in the sulfonate group, but ^{14}C and ^{3}H have also been used.[3] This method is extremely sensitive and free from interferences. However, using the disappearance of ^{35}S-sulfonate as an indication of complete biodegradation may be uncertain in that, reportedly, the sulfonate group has been removed from the benzene ring both prior to and at the same time as ring cleavage.[23,24]

BIODEGRADATION

The biodegradability of a surfactant (i.e., the relative
ease with which microorganisms, mostly bacteria, can attack the
molecular structure of a surfactant) is a major consideration in
the evaluation of the environmental acceptability of a surfactant.
Biodegradation can be subdivided into primary and ultimate
biodegradation. Primary degradation relates to the minimum extent
of degradation needed to change the identity of a compound while
ultimate biodegradation involves the complete conversion of a
compound to carbon dioxide and water. Four laboratory tests
frequently used in the study of biodegradation are: biochemical
oxygen demand, evolution of carbon dioxide, die-away tests and
simulated sewage treatment processes.[2] Basically, all of these
tests involve addition of the surfactant to the test system containing nutrients and bacteria under appropriate conditions and
measurement of change of an appropriate indicator with time; this
is often the MBAS or nonionic titration procedures.

Studies carried out on biodegradation of LAS indicate rapid
and extensive biodegradability of this class of surfactants in
both laboratory and field situations (Table I).[2] Certain chemical
characteristics of LAS (alkyl chain length, phenyl group position)
can influence the rate of biodegradation to some degree.[3] However, all forms of LAS now commercially used are highly biodegradable.[2]

Of the other types of surfactants commonly employed in
household detergent products, perhaps the most rapidly degraded
are the linear alkyl sulfates which are readily hydrolyzed by
the ubiquitous sulfatase enzymes to inorganic sulfate and the
corresponding alcohol which eventually undergoes β-oxidation.[26]
However, if these are highly branched, they are degraded at a
considerably slower rate.[27] Linear AS are readily biodegraded in
standard BOD tests and CO_2 evolution procedures. Neither slight
branching nor increments in the length of the carbon chain appear
to exert a significant effect on the rate of degradation. Die-
away tests and simulated sewage treatment processes indicate
complete primary biodegradation of linear AS (as MBAS) within 1
to 3 days, even under anaerobic conditions.[2]

Information on biodegradation studies with the other anionic
surfactants is somewhat limited but the available data indicate
that they are quickly and readily biodegraded under both field
and laboratory conditions.[2] AOS in the C_{12} to C_{18} range possess
BOD values greater than 50% at 5 days with approximately 65% CO_2
evolved.[32] Similarly, BOD values for SAS with 13 to 18 carbon
atoms range from 20 to 56%; evolved CO_2 for these surfactants
range from 63-77% at 20 days.[32] AES surfactants are also substantially biodegraded as determined by BOD (35-68% at 5 days)

Table I. Biodegradation of Representative Surfactants in the Laboratory.[2,3]

Laboratory Test	Test Sample					
	C_{12} LAS	C_{12} AS	C_{12} AOS	C_{12} AES	C_{12} AE	Glucose
• *Biochemical Oxygen Demand*						
Estimates Extent of Biodegradation by Comparison with the Theoretical Amount of Oxygen Required to Completely Oxidize the Surfactant in a Given Time, e.g., 5 Days.	55%	63%	>51%	58%	91%	65–70%
• *CO_2 Evolution*						
Assesses Ultimate Biodegradation of a Surfactant by Bacteria to CO_2 and H_2O at a Given Time, e.g., 20 Days.	72%	85%	>65%	81%	>65%	70–87%
• *Die-Away Tests*						
Monitors Decreasing Surfactant Concentrations as the Surfactant Content Drops with the Passage of Time. The Most Common of These Tests are the River Water and Shake Culture Tests.	100% 3 Days MBAS	>95% 1 Day MBAS	100% <10 Days MBAS	100% 2-3 Days MBAS	100% <3 Days CTAS	– –
• *Simulated Treatment Processes*						
Involves Addition of Surfactant to Sewage Microorganisms. The Most Common Methods Include Batch, Semi-Continuous and Continuous Activated Sludge Processes, Trickling Filter and Anaerobic (e.g., Cesspool, Septic Tank) Systems	>97% 24 Hr. MBAS Activ. Sludge	>99% 24 Hr. MBAS Activ. Sludge	99% 24 Hr. MBAS Activ. Sludge	>98% 24 Hr. MBAS Activ. Sludge	100% 24 Hr. CTAS Activ. Sludge	– –

and evolved CO_2 data (71-100% at 20 days).[32] Neither the length
of the alkyl chain nor the length of the ethoxylate portion of
the molecule, at least in the range normally used in detergent
formulations (i.e., 2 to 4 EO units/mole) appears to significantly
influence the rate of AES biodegradation.

AOS, AES and SAS are completely degraded (as MBAS) in die-
away tests, generally within a few days. Some anaerobic degradation also occurs.[2] Field studies with these surfactants in
municipal sewage treatment plants indicate AOS, AES and SAS
surfactants are extensively removed during passage through the
plant.[28]

With respect to the nonionic surfactants, AE undergo extensive, relatively rapid primary biodegradation. Neither variations in the alkyl chain length nor increments in the length of
the ethoxylate portion of the molecule (within the range utilized
in detergent formulations) affect the rate of primary degradation.[29,30] Recent studies indicate that the alkyl chain is degraded more rapidly than the EO chain with little dependence on
the degree of branching but the primary branched chain ethoxylates are degraded more rapidly than 100% linear secondary AE.
The EO chain is extensively mineralized (80 - >95%) with only a
slight decrease in ultimate biodegradation up to 30 EO units.[31-33]
The major degradative pathway of AE thus appears to be oxidation
of the alkyl chain and hydrolysis of the ether linkage. The polyethoxylate moiety of the AE molecule readily degrades to form
lower molecular weight polyethylene glycols and ultimately, to
CO_2 and water.[2]

It is generally accepted that APE surfactants undergo primary biodegradation in a variety of test systems and in the field,
provided sufficient acclimation time is allowed.[35,36] The rate
of degradation of APE is influenced by the degree of branching,
the number of ethylene oxide units/mole and the position of
attachment of the benzene ring to alkyl chain. Less branching
results in a faster rate of degradation; an increase in the number
of EO units slows degradation; and attachment of the benzene ring
to a primary carbon in the alkyl chain results in a faster rate
of biodegradation.[2] The major degradative pathway of APE appears
to be shortening of the ethoxylate chain, perhaps by ω-oxidation.[3]
The extent of further degradation of either the alkyl chain or
the benzene ring is unknown.

ENVIRONMENTAL ASPECTS

The detection of low levels, in the range of 0.1 to 0.5 mg/L,
of MBAS in waterways has led to some concern for the effects of
surfactants on aquatic organisms. In the last 5-10 years, much

progress has been made in assessing environmental effects of surfactants and their degradation products, although most work has focused on LAS.

Acute toxicity to aquatic life forms generally occur in adult vertebrate and invertebrate species at surfactant concentrations between 1 and 20 mg/L; juvenile and developmental stages of these species show effects at somewhat lower concentrations.[2] A summary of LC50 values for the various surfactants is presented in Table II. Among these surfactants, one does not stand out as being considerably more toxic than the others. Invertebrates appear to be generally susceptible to these compounds in the same range as vertebrates, although toxicity to some marine bivalves and crustaceans occurs at concentrations greater than 100 mg/L.[2]

Table II. Acute Toxicity of Intact Surfactants to Aquatic Organisms.[2]

Surfactant	Range of Most Frequently Reported 24-96 hr LC50 Values (mg/L)	
	Fish	Invertebrates
LAS	1-10	1-100
AS	5-20	2->200
AOS	1-15	2-?
SAS	1-50	9-300
AES	1-10	5-20
AE	1-6	1-100
APE	4-12	1-100

The length of the carbon chain of surfactants appears to have a dramatic effect on toxicity. For LAS, an increase in the toxicity to various aquatic species has been associated with an increase in the length of the carbon chain up to 16 carbon units (Figure 2);[37] a decrease in toxicity is observed with chain lengths longer than 16 carbon units.[9,38] Toxicity also appears to increase as the position of the phenyl group occurs closer to the end of the alkyl chain.[2] Minor side products from LAS manufacture such as dialkyltetralines, dialkylindanes, and alkylnaphthalenes appear to be considerably less toxic than LAS isomers of comparable chain length.[2] Similar trends of increasing toxicity with increasing alkyl chain length have been observed for all anionic surfactants but this effect is paralleled by increased removal during sewage treatment so that exposure to aquatic organisms by the more toxic isomers is low.[2]

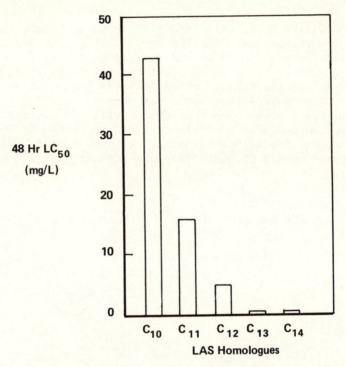

Figure 2. Effect of carbon chain length on the toxicity of LAS to the fathead minnow.[37]

The length of the ethoxylate chain among nonionics is also an important determinant of aquatic toxicity. Toxicity generally increases with decreasing ethoxylate chain length.[39-41] However, the effect of ethoxylate chain length is also a function of the alkyl chain length (Figure 3).[42] These results suggest that toxicity decreases with increasing ethoxylate chain length for C_{14}AES and increases with increasing ethoxylate chain length for C_{18}AES. Little change in toxicity with ethoxylate chain length was observed for C_{16}AES.

Sub-lethal effects of surfactants on aquatic organisms have been observed at somewhat lower concentrations than acute lethality. In fish, these effects commonly include such reactions as impaired swimming activity and altered breathing rate and opercular movement.[43] Such effects may occur at levels of 0.5 mg/L for LAS and AE.[2] Recovery from these effects can occur upon cessation of exposure. Other sublethal effects on fish have also been observed, for example, damage to chemoreceptors of the taste-buds in yellow bullhead and depressed olfactory bulbar response upon exposure to 0.1 mg/L $C_{12}AS$ in whitefish.[44,45] This effect might be of significance since it could impair feeding and migratory behavior.

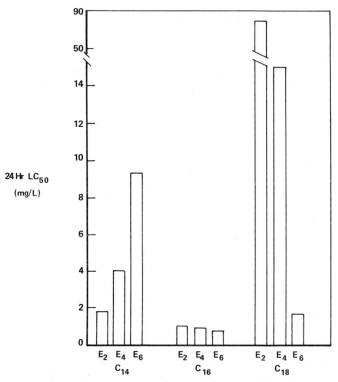

Figure 3. Effect of alkyl and ethoxylate chain length on the toxicity of AES to the fathead minnow.[42]

Sub-lethal effects such as reduced swimming activity, reduced heart rate, inhibition of siphon retraction, reduced burrowing activity, inhibition of formation of byssal threads, and intestinal damage have been noted in different species of aquatic invertebrates.[46] Most of these effects have been observed at concentrations of surfactants greater than 1 mg/L.[2]

Chronic toxicity has not been studied in depth. Where it has been evaluated, life cycle tests or toxicity tests on embryo and larvae have been used. No observed effect concentrations (NOEC) in long term tests on survival, total young production, mean brood size and frequency of reproduction have been determined for some surfactants (Table III).[47,48] These results indicate that chronic toxicity values for LAS, AE, and AES, may be as low as

0.1 mg/L for fathead minnow whereas LC_{50} values are commonly an order of magnitude higher than this. Results for the invertebrate <u>Daphnia magna</u> show chronic effects at similar levels (0.2 mg/L).[46,47,49]

Table III. Toxicity of Some Surfactants to Fathead Minnow.[2,47,48]

Surfactant	Acute 96 hr LC_{50} (mg/L)	Chronic NOEC (mg/L)
LAS		
$C_{11.2}$	12.3	5.1 - 8.4
$C_{11.7}$	4.1	0.48
$C_{13.3}$	0.86	0.11 - 0.25
AE		
$C_{12.5}$	-	0.32
$C_{14.5}$	∿ 1.2	0.18
AES		
$C_{13.7}$	∿ 1.3	0.1

Many surfactants are rapidly biodegraded, both in treatment facilities and in ambient waters. Reductions of up to about 95% for LAS have been observed upon treatment in activated sludge, thus reducing levels in sewage effluents significantly. In addition, LAS in the effluent (as measured by MBAS) is less toxic than intact LAS by a factor of 3-10. Presumptive biodegradation intermediates of LAS are considerably less toxic to both <u>Daphnia</u> and fathead minnow than intact LAS (Table IV).[37] The effects of biodegradation on the toxicity of two nonionic types are shown in Table V. These results suggest that APE are not biodegraded as rapidly as some other surfactants.[50] The degradation of AS may result in increased toxicity, since dodecanoic acid is more toxic than $C_{12}AS$; however, this product is very short-lived in solution.[49] On the other hand, the toxicity of AES and AOS has been shown to decrease steadily as a result of biodegradation.[2]

Numerous other factors affect the toxicity of surfactants to aquatic organisms. Increasing temperature appears to increase the toxicity of LAS, as does the stress caused by decreasing dissolved oxygen. Aquatic organisms may also be more sensitive to LAS in hard water than in soft, and the hardness of the culture water is known to affect the results of toxicity

Table IV. Acute Toxicity of LAS and Presumptive Biodegradation Intermediates.[37]

	48-Hr LC_{50} (mg/L)	
	Daphnia magna	Pimephales promelas
Intact LAS-C_{11}	5.7	16
Sulfophenylundecanoic acid, disodium salt (mixed isomers, 6- through 10-phenyl)	208	76.6
3-(Sulfophenyl) butyric acid, disodium salt	~ 6,000	~ 10,000
4-(Sulfophenyl)valeric acid, disodium salt	~ 5,000	~ 10,000

Table V. Toxicity of AE and APE to Goldfish after Biodegradation.[2,50]

	48-Hr LC_{50} (mg/L)	
Surfactant	Initial	After 4 Days in River Water[a]
$C_{12-14}AE_9$	5.1	91
$C_{12}AE_9$	1.9	> 20
$C_{12-15}AE_9$	1.4	91
C_9APE_{10}	5.4	3.7[b]

[a]Based on initial concentration.

[b]This value is within the reproducibility of the test system, indicating little or no biodegradation at 4 days.

tests.[51,52] The presence of suspended solids mitigates the effects of LAS, while previous exposures to LAS do not appear to affect toxicity.[52] Some of these results have been observed for other surfactants. However, little information is available on the effects of environmental conditions on the toxicity of AES, APE, and SAS.

The presence of other chemicals may also affect the toxicity of surfactants to aquatic organisms, although these interactions have not been extensively studied. LAS has been examined for its effects in combinations with some other chemicals, especially metals and pesticides. Additive effects have been observed with zinc, and apparent synergistic effects with copper and mercury.[2,53] Synergism has been reported with parathion, methyl parathion, ronnel, trithion and trichloronat.[2] No synergism, however, was found with dicapthon, guthion, EPN, or dieldrin.[2] LAS has also been shown to increase the toxicity of petroleum products to aquatic organisms.[54,55] However, no synergistic effects on toxicity have been observed for LAS in combination with other surfactants.[51]

LAS are rapidly taken up by fish and concentrated in tissues and organs. High levels are observed initially in the gills, whereas after a longer exposure, LAS and/or metabolites of LAS are concentrated in the gall bladder. Clearance is rapid, with a half-life of 2-3 days. Bioconcentration factors of 1000-9000 are reported based on the radioactivity associated with the radio-labeled LAS in the test water.[56-58] It is likely that LAS is extensively metabolized by fish and the eliminated products may well include some secondary products.

Several theories have been advanced to explain the effects of LAS, as well as other surfactants, on aquatic organisms. Some authors suggest that the toxicity of LAS is due to the formation of a complex with gill protein.[59] Other work in this area has pointed to an effect of LAS on the permeability of the cell mem-brane, either through polarization effects, or the loss of mucus as a diffusion barrier.[60,61] In any case, the selectivity of the gill cell membranes appear to be impaired upon exposure to LAS. Similar damage to the gills has been observed for other sur-factants.[2]

Some work has been devoted to the determination of the effect of surfactants on higher plants.[2,62-64] Effects of LAS, even when the plants are grown in solution, appear to occur at con-centrations greater than 50 mg/L,[62,63] although a 10 mg/L solu-tion of APE reduced growth in sorghum.[64]

An effect on birds has been reported with some surfactants, specifically AS and AE at high concentrations (several orders of magnitude above environmental levels).[65,66] Generally, the oil in the feathers is broken down removing their natural water-proofing. If feathers become soaked, lethal hypothermia results.

HUMAN SAFETY

Present day use of the major surfactants does not appear to represent a hazard to human health. The primary support for this view comes from the low order of acute mammalian toxicity and the general absence of chronic effects in mammalian test systems. Acute oral LD_{50} values in rodents generally range from 650 mg/kg to greater than 3000 mg/kg -- equivalent to the ingestion of approximately 1/4 pound of material by a human adult.[2] With chronic exposure, no-observed-effect-levels from 0.1% to 1.4% of the diet or 0.01% in drinking water have been reported (Table VI).[34,67-72]

Table VI. Oral Toxicity of a Series of Surfactants in the Rat.[2,34,67-72]

Surfactant	Acute Oral LD$_{50}$ (mg/kg)	Route	Chronic No-Observed-Effect Level Concentration	Duration
LAS	650 – 2480	Diet	0.5%	2 Yr
AS	1000 – 15000	Diet	1.0%	1 Yr
AOS	1300 – 2400	Diet	0.5%	2 Yr
SAS	1000 – 3000	Drinking Water	0.01%	1 Yr
AES	1700 – >5000	Diet	0.5%	2 Yr
AE	870 – >25000	Diet	0.1%	2 Yr
APE	1000 – 30000	Diet	1.4%	2 Yr

In rats, long-term feeding studies with LAS at levels up to 0.5% of the diet (which exceed estimated human consumption by over a thousand-fold) suggest no indications of any deleterious effects.[67] Subchronic (6 mo.) dietary exposure of rats to 1.8% LAS resulted in glomerular atrophy and destruction of urinary tubules, tissue damage in the liver and cecum and decreased body weight gain.[73] Simultaneous oral (300 mg/kg) and subcutaneous (1 mg/kg) administration of LAS to rhesus monkeys for 28 days produced no noteworthy effects other than reduced body weight gain and increased frequency of liquid feces.[74]

Addition of 1% AS to the diet of rats for one year produced no significant pathology.[68] Subchronic oral exposure of dogs to

200 mg AS/dog/day for 10 months was without effect[75] and the addition of up to 4% AS to the diet of rats for 16 weeks resulted in reduced body weight gain but no other indications of toxicity.[68]

No deleterious effects associated with AOS exposure were reported for rats fed either 1000 mg/kg/day in the diet for 90 days[2] or given 0.5% AOS in the diet for two years (mean daily intake: 195 mg/kg males; 259 mg/kg females).[69] Rats also appeared to tolerate well both repeated dermal and inhalation exposure to AOS.[2]

Little information is available on the effects of long-term exposure to SAS. No adverse effects were seen in rats fed 300 mg/kg/day for 45 days[76] or given 0.01% SAS in their drinking water for one year.[70]

Ingestion of AES surfactants in the diet (0.5%) or in drinking water (0.1%) for two years produced no deleterious effects in rats.[71]

With respect to the nonionic surfactants, two separate chronic studies with rats indicated no significant treatment-related effects resulted from ingestion of up to 1% AE in the diet for two years.[34] The only pathology finding of note was a focal myocarditis that increased in frequency as the dose increased in males. However, when the severity of the lesions was taken into account, no treatment-related effect was evident. Focal myocarditis is a common spontaneous type of lesion found in relatively high frequency in aging populations of rats and the incidence noted in the 0.5% and 1.0% AE treated males were comparable to reported background incidences of focal myocarditis in rats of this age. With respect to dermal exposure, repeated percutaneous application of up to 5% AE to the backs of Swiss mice 3 times per week for 18 months produced no neoplastic or pre-neoplastic lesions in these animals.[34]

A low order of chronic oral toxicity is also noted in experimental animals with most APE surfactants. Chronic feeding studies with rats fed 1.4% APE in the diet for 2 years[72] and rats and dogs administered 1000 mg/kg/day for two years gave no indications of significant toxicity associated with APE ingestion.[77] An area of uncertainty exists, however, with respect to APE in a narrow molecular weight range (APE_{15}-APE_{25}); this latter group of compounds, which are not normally used in detergent formulations, has been linked to an increased incidence of cardiotoxicity in dogs and guinea pigs following dietary exposures of relatively short intervals.[77] Focal cardiac necrosis was reported in dogs fed 40 mg/kg/day C_9APE_{20} for 90 days with lesions evident within five days at higher doses (1000 mg/kg). Rats, however, fed 5000 mg/kg/day under the same treatment regimen exhibited no cardiac pathology.[77]

Of the anionic type, a 1% concentration of LAS, which is above normal domestic use levels, is non-irritating to rabbit skin.[2] The same concentration of AS produced minimal skin irritation but no effects were seen at a concentration of 0.1% AS.[2] The data for AOS are inconsistent, probably due to such factors as sample purity, method of production, etc. For the most part, minimal to no irritation is seen with 1% concentrations of AOS.[2] Skin studies with the AES surfactants indicate mild to moderate irritation with 10% samples, with only minimal irritation seen at the 1% level.[2]

With the nonionic AE, acute skin irritation studies with undiluted samples produced slight to extreme irritation reactions in rabbits but these exposures are considerably greater than exposure under normal use conditions. In contrast, repeated application of 10% AE to the skin of rabbits produced minimal to mild irritancy; no irritation was noted with a 1% concentration.[2]

Table VII. Results of Skin Irritation Tests in Rabbits.[2]

Surfactant	Concentration	Result[a]
LAS	Undiluted	+++++
	1.0%	0
AS	> 10%	++++
	2%	+++
	1%	±
AOS	10%	± to +++++
	1%	±
SAS	> 20%	++++
AES	Undiluted	++++ to +++++
	10%	++ to +++
	1%	±
AE	Undiluted	+ to +++++
	15%	+
APE	25%	++

[a]Scale:
Nonirritating	0
Minimally Irritating	±
Slightly Irritating	+
Mildly Irritating	++
Moderately Irritating	+++
Severely Irritating	++++
Extremely Irritating	+++++

There is no evidence of skin sensitization in laboratory animals following exposure to domestic surfactants.[2] Skin sensitization studies with AOS indicate AOS surfactants are generally non-sensitizers; the few positive responses reported were either

irreproducible or subsequently attributed to incomplete hydrolysis of the products.[2] Processing conditions for commercial AOS
samples, if not adequately regulated, can result in the formation
of sultones during bleaching processes if the pH is less than 9.5.
Sultones have been shown to induce skin sensitization in guinea
pigs.[2] Thus, precise control of manufacturing conditions must be
maintained to ensure the elimination of these biologically reactive species.

Results of eye irritation tests in rabbits also show exposure
to surfactant concentrations higher than 1% produce moderate to
severe eye irritation according to the Draize procedure (Table
VIII). Instillation of LAS into the rabbit eye at concentrations
of 0.5% and 1.0%, LAS can induce immediate but reversible ocular
congestion and edema in rabbits while at, or below 0.1% LAS, mild
irritancy or no reaction is seen.[2] One percent concentrations of
AS and AOS produced little or no ocular irritation in rabbits
while studies with concentrated SAS materials (20-60% active)
suggest SAS are positive eye irritants; tests with more typical
use levels have not been reported for SAS.[2] Undiluted samples of
AES surfactants are positive eye irritants and are classified as
corrosive according to the Draize procedure. Moderate irritation
is seen with 10% solutions while 1-2% concentrations produce only
minimal conjunctival irritation.[2]

Eye irritation studies with the nonionic AE indicate that
concentrations greater than 10% produce varying degrees of irritation, but only transient irritation is noted with 1% concentrations.[2]

It should be noted, however, that comparisons of the effects
of instillation of a wide variety of substances into the eyes of
rabbits and monkeys consistently indicate more severe effects in
rabbits than in primates after identical treatment. This difference in response may be due to a number of factors. Most notably,
rabbits lack the fluid tears of monkeys and humans and they also
have a slower blinking reflex than primates.[78] Thus, removal of
foreign substances from the rabbit eye may be delayed, allowing
greater time for contact and injury to occur.

A vital component of any evaluation of human safety is the
potential of the substance in question to produce irreparable
harm through induction of a carcinogenic response, production of
mutational changes that may result in genetic damage or by exerting a teratogenic effect.

There are no indications of a direct carcinogenic response
associated with exposure of laboratory animals to any of the surfactants of present commercial importance (Table IX). Ingestion of

Table VIII. Results of Eye Irritation Tests in Rabbits.[2]

Surfactant	Concentration	Result[a]
LAS	Undiluted	+++++
	1.0%	+++
	0.1%	±
AS	> 20%	+++++
	10%	+++
	2%	++
	1%	±
AOS	> 10%	++++
	5%	+++
	1%	0
SAS	> 20%	++++
AES	Undiluted	+++++
	10%	+++
	2%	±
AE	Undiluted	+++++
	1%	0
APE	25%	++++

[a]Scale:	
Nonirritating	0
Practically Nonirritating	±
Minimally Irritating	+
Mildly Irritating	++
Moderately Irritating	+++
Severely Irritating	++++
Extremely Irritating	+++++

up to 0.5% LAS, AOS or AES, 1% AE and 1.4% APE for 2 yrs. have produced no indications of carcinogenicity in the rat.[34,67,69,71,72] Similarly, ingestion of 0.01% SAS in drinking water or 1% AS in the diet of rats for 1 yr. gave no indications of carcinogenic response.[68,70] Weekly percutaneous exposures of rodents to 10% AES or 5% AE for their life-time were also without effect.[34,71,79]

Repeated oral co-administration of some surfactants with known carcinogens, however, has been shown to enhance gastrointestinal tumor induction in rats.[82-86] Repeated concomitant administration of LAS (80 mg/rat orally 3 times/wk for 18 wk) with the carcinogen 4-nitroquinoline-N-oxide (NQO) (1 mg/rat orally 3xwk/18 wk) enhanced gastric tumor induction in rats (1.12 tumors/rat vs 1.00 tumors/rat with carcinogen treatment alone).[83] No co-carcinogenic effect was found, however, for LAS with another potent carcinogen, N-methyl-N'-nitro-N-nitrosoguanidine (MNNG).[86] Enhancement of MNNG tumor response has been demonstrated, however, by co-administration of either 2.5 mg/L C_{12}AS with 50 mg/L MNNG to rats in drinking water for 26-30 weeks[86] or 2000 mg/L APE with 100 mg/L MNNG to rats in drinking water for 63 weeks.[85] The incidences of tumors/rat in the above treated groups were 1.1 MNNG plus AS versus 0.5 for MNNG alone and 1.27 for MNNG plus APE compared to

0.6 tumors/rat for carcinogen alone. It is unclear, however, whether this enhanced gastrointestinal tumor induction in rats is due to enhanced carcinogen absorption or some other physiological mechanisms.

Table IX. Summary of Negative Carcinogenicity Findings for a Series of Surfactants.

Surfactant	Species	Route	Chronic Dose
LAS	Rat	Diet	0.5% x 2 Yr[67]
	Rat	Drinking Water	0.1% x 2 Yr[80]
AS	Rat	Diet	1.0% x 1 Yr[68]
AOS	Rat	Diet	0.5% x 2 Yr[69]
	Rat	Skin	10% 2 x Wk x 2 Yr[79]
	Mouse	Skin	5.0% 2 x Wk x 2 Yr[81]
SAS	Rat	Drinking Water	0.01% x 1 Yr[70]
AES	Rat	Diet	0.5% x 2 Yr[71]
	Rat	Drinking Water	0.1% x 2 Yr[34]
	Mouse	Skin	5.0% 2 x Wk x 2 Yr[71]
AE	Rat	Diet	1% x 2 Yr[34]
	Mouse	Skin	5% 3 x Wk x 18 Mo.[34]
APE	Rat	Diet	1.4% x 2 Yr[72]
	Dog	Diet	0.27% x 2 Yr[77]

Mutagenicity tests with surfactants of present commercial importance suggest no indications of mutagenic activity (Table X).[2] No cytogenetic lesions were observed in human leukocytes treated with LAS in vitro and chromosome studies with rodent bone marrow cells following 9 months dietary administration of 0.9% LAS or 3 months exposure to 1.1% LAS showed no induction of chromosome abnormalities.[2,87,88] A host-mediated assay with rats and dominant lethal studies conducted with mice also showed no increase in mutagenic index in LAS treated animals.[2,87]

A number of in vitro and host-mediated mutagenicity tests with AOS surfactants have produced negative results.[2] A single set of experiments did show a positive response in a host-mediated assay with rats; however, chemical fractionation studies suggest that this response may be due to materials having no direct relationship to the surfactant.[2]

Table X. Summary of Negative Mutagenicity Findings for a Series of Surfactants.[2,87-89]

Surfactant

	LAS	AS	AOS	SAS	AES	AE	APE
Cytogenetic Analysis							
Human in Vitro	•				•	•	
Rodent in Vivo	•	•			•	•	
Host-Mediated Assay	•		•				
Dominant Lethal Test	•				•	•	
Mutations in Microorganisms							
Bacteria			•		•		
Yeast			•		•		
DNA Repair Studies			•				

• Represents mutagenicity tests conducted; all were negative.

No indications of mutagenicity were noted in a dominant lethal study or in vivo or in vitro cytogenetic studies with a 55% AES:45% LAS mixture.[2] AES alone in the diet of rats for 90 days had no effect on chromosomes in bone marrow cells[88] and bacterial assays with Salmonella typhimurium and Escherichia coli as well as studies with the yeast, Saccharomyces cerevisiae, were negative.[89]

A cytogenetic study with AS showed no effect on rat marrow cells following 90 days exposure to AS in the diet.[88] Cytogenetic analysis of human leukocytes exposed to AE in vitro or hamster chromosomes following oral administration of 800 mg AE/kg were negative as were host-mediated tests conducted with AE.[2] There are no mutagenicity data available for SAS and APE surfactants.

The potential of these surfactants to exert a teratogenic effect or to impact adversely on reproductive capabilities have also been evaluated in some detail.

Two separate three-generation-studies in rats following 84 days exposure to 0.5% LAS in the diet[67] or 0.1% LAS in drinking water for 26 weeks gave no indications of adverse effects.[90] With respect to teratogenicity, other than earlier reports of irreproducible teratogenic effects of LAS emanating from the laboratories of Mikami at Mie University in Japan,[91] which have subsequently been discredited,[92] there is no evidence that LAS induced birth malformations in experimental animals.[2] Ingestion of 300 mg/kg/day by mice[93] and 780 mg/kg/day by rats[94] during early gestation resulted in no increased incidence of teratogenic anomalies. Similar negative results have been noted following percutaneous application of LAS to pregnant rats (60 mg/kg), rabbits (90 mg/kg) and mice (500 mg/kg).[95]

There are no indications of AE-related teratogenesis or adverse reproductive effects associated with the oral administration of up to 0.5% AE in the diet of either rats or rabbits.[34] Similarly, no evidence of terata or detrimental effects on litter parameters were attributable to the ingestion of up to 300 mg/kg AS by laboratory animals during organogenesis.[93] Reduced litter size and fetal loss were seen in mice but not rats or rabbits at doses that were severely toxic to the dams. Percutaneous treatment of pregnant mice with high concentrations (10-20%) of AS during early gestation appears to result in either death or normal survival.[96]

There are no data available on the effects of AOS on reproductive performance in laboratory animals. With respect to teratogenic potential, an increase in cleft palates was found in offspring of mice given 300 mg/kg of AOS by gavage on days 6-15 of pregnancy as well as an increased incidence of minor skeletal anomalies in both mice and rabbits at this dosage level.[97] These responses generally occurred in groups in which the dams exhibited toxic responses. No adverse effects were noted, however, in pregnant rats or their offspring following administration of 600 mg/kg AOS on days 6-15 of gestation.[97]

No data are available on the teratogenic effects of AES administered alone. However, oral administration of a commercial mixture of AES and LAS gave no indications of any embryotoxic or teratogenic effects in mice, rats or rabbits.[93] In addition, no adverse effects on fertility, lactation, litter size, survival or growth of offspring were seen in rats fed diets containing 0.1% AES for two generations.[34]

There is no information available to assess the potential for induction of teratogenic lesions in experimental animals with either APE or SAS surfactants.

SUMMARY

In summation, the information presented in this overview of the environmental and human health aspects of seven commercially important surfactants supports the view that as a class, these surfactants pose no threat to either human health or to the environment. The low levels present in U.S. waterways, their facile biodegradation, their low order of acute aquatic and mammalian toxicity and the general absence of chronic effects in mammalian test systems testify to the human safety and environmental acceptability of these materials.

ACKNOWLEDGEMENTS

This work was supported by the Soap and Detergent Association, 475 Park Avenue, New York, New York 10022. We are grateful to the members of the Surfactant Safety Subcommittee of the Soap and Detergent Association for their suggestions and assistance in obtaining information for our consideration, and to Ms. Margaret Miller who conducted an extensive search of the scientific literature.

REFERENCES

1. U.S. International Trade Commission, "Synthetic Organic Chemicals, United States Production and Sales of Surface-Active Agents," 1979.
2. Arthur D. Little, Inc., "Human Safety and Environmental Aspects of Major Surfactants," National Technical Information Service, Document PB 301 193/9ST, Springfield, Virginia, 1977; and references cited therein.
3. R.D. Swisher, "Surfactant Biodegradation," Marcel Dekker, Inc., New York, 1970; and references cited therein.
4. Organization for Economic Cooperation and Development, "The Pollution of Water by Detergents," Paris, 1964.
5. American Public Health Association, "Standard Method for the Examination of Water and Wastewater," New York, 1960.
6. American Society for Testing Materials, Annual Book of ASTM Standards, 32, 494 (1974).
7. R.D. Swisher, J. Am. Oil Chemist's Soc., 43, 137 (1966).
8. L.K. Wang, S.F. Kao, M.H. Wang, J.F. Kao and A.L. Loshin, Pro. Ind. Waste Conf., 33, 918 (1978).
9. C. Borstlap, Surf. Cong. No. 4, 3, 891 (1967).
10. W.E. Gledhill, Adv. Appl. Microbiol., 17, 265 (1974).
11. U.S. Environmental Protection Agency, "Quality Criteria for Water," EPA-44d9-76-023, Washington, D.C., 1976.

12. W.T. Sullivan and R.D. Swisher, Environ. Sci. Technol., 3, 481 (1969).
13. T.E. Brenner, J. Am. Chem. Soc., 45 433 (1968).
14. U.S. Geological Survey, New York MBAS Study, November 1970-April, 1972.
15. U.S. Environmental Protection Agency, STORET Data, 1980.
16. R. Wickbold, Int. Kongr. Grenzflachenaktive Stoffe, 6th, 1A, 373-380 (1973).
17. Organization for Economic Cooperation and Development. "The Determination of the Biodegradability of Surfactants Used in Synthetic Detergents," Paris, 1975.
18. N.T. Crabb and H.E. Persinger. J. Am. Chem. Soc., 41 752 (1964).
19. S.L. Boyer, Environ. Sci. Technol., 11 1167 (1977).
20. E. Heinerth, Tenside, 3, 1 (1966).
21. S.J. Patterson, C.C. Scott and K.B.E. Tucker, Water Pollut. Control, 3, 3 (1967).
22. P. Gericke and R. Schmid, Tenside, 10, 186 (1973).
23. R.B. Cain, A.J. Willets and J.A. Bird, "Biodeterioration of Materials," Vol. 2, Halstead Press Div., John Wiley and Sons, Inc., New York, 1971.
24. K. Oba, Jap. J. Hyg., 25, 494 (1971).
25. S. Hashimoto, K. Sakurai and T. Nagai, Bunseki Kaguku, 25, 639 (1976).
26. I.J. Higgins and R. B. Burns, "The Chemistry and Microbiology of Pollution," Academic Press, New York, 1975.
27. H.W. Huyser, Int. Kongr. Grenzflachenaktive Stoffe, 3rd, 3, 295 (1961).
28. K. Oba, K. Miura, H. Sekiguchi, R. Yagi and A. Mori, Water Res., 10, 149 (1976).
29. R.N. Sturm, J. Am. Chem. Soc., 50, 159 (1973).
30. W.E. Gledhill, Appl. Microbiol., 30, 922 (1975).
31. L. Kravetz, H. Chung, J.D. Rapean, K.F. Guin and W.T. Shebs, Water Res., in press (1980).
32. L. Kravetz, H. Chung, K.F. Guin, W.T. Shebs, Water Res., in press (1980).
33. D.H. Scharer, L. Kravetz and J.B. Carr, Tappi, 62, 75 (1979).
34. W.D. Hopping, Procter and Gamble Co., Cincinnati, Ohio, personal communication, 1979.
35. E.S. Lashen and K.A. Booman, Water & Sewage Works, 114, R155 (1967).
36. R.C. Allred and R.L. Huddleston, Southwest Water Works, J., 49, 26 (1967).
37. R.A. Kimmerle and R.D. Swisher, Water Res., 2, 31 (1977).
38. E. Hirsch, Vom Wasser, 30, 249 (1963).
39. K.J. Macek and S.F. Krzeminski, Bull. Environ. Contam. Toxicol., 13, 377 (1975).
40. A.W. Maki and W.E. Bishop, Arch. Environ. Contam. Toxicol., 8, 599 (1979).
41. N. Kurata, K. Koshida and T. Fujii, Yukagaku, 26, 115 (1977).
42. W.E. Gledhill, Monsanto Company, St. Louis, Missouri, personal communication, 1979.

43. A.W. Maki, "Special Technical Publ. 667," ASTM, Philadelphia, 1979.
44. J.E. Bardach, M. Fujiya and A. Hall, Science, 140, 1605 (1965).
45. T.J. Hara and B.E. Thompson, Water Res., 12, 893 (1978).
46. A. W. Maki, Pro. Int. Mar. Biolog. Symp. 14th., in press (1979).
47. A.W. Maki, J. Fish Res. Board Can., 36, 411 (1979).
48. W.F. Holman and K.J. Macek, Trans. Am. Fish Soc., 109, 122 (1980).
49. P. Lundahl and R. Cabridenc, J. Fr. Hydrol., 7, 143 (1976).
50. N. Kurata, K. Koshida and T. Fujii, Yukagaku, 26, 115 (1977).
51. M.A. Lewis and R.L. Perry, Pro. Symp. Am. Soc. Test. Mater. - Aquatic Toxicol., 4th., Chicago (in press).
52. A.W. Maki and W.E. Bishop, Arch. Environ. Contam. Toxicol., 8, 599 (1979).
53. C.-f. Tsai, and J.A. McKee, Water Res. Center, University of Maryland, Technical Report 44, PB 280-554 (1978).
54. R. Rehwoldt, L. Lasko, C. Shaw and E. Wirhowski, Bull. Environ. Contam. Toxicol., 11, 159 (1974).
55. K.E.F. Hokanson and L.L. Smith, Jr., Trans. Am. Fish Soc., 100, 1 (1971).
56. R.A. Kimerle, K.J. Macek, B.H. Sleight, III, and M.E. Barrows, Water Res., in press, (1980).
57. W.E. Bishop and A.W. Maki, Pro. Symp. Am. Soc. Test. Mater. - Aquatic Toxicol., 3rd, New Orleans (in press).
58. M. Kikuchi, M. Wakabayashi, H. Kojima and T. Yoshida, Ecotoxicol. Environ. Safety, 2, 115 (1978).
59. S.I. Tomiyama, Bull. Japan Soc. Sci. Fish., 40, 1291 (1974).
60. W.F. Jackson and P.O. Fromm., Comp. Biochem. Physiol., 58c, 167 (1977).
61. H.W. Manner and C. Muehleman, Env. Biol. Fish., 1, 81 (1976).
62. T. Taniyama, Mi Daigaku Kan kyo Kagaku Kenkyu Kiyo., 3, 93 (1978).
63. H.G.M. Dowden, M.K. Lambert and R. Truman, Aust. J. Plant Physiol., 5, 387 (1979).
64. M. Horowitz and A. Givelberg, Pest. Sci., 10, 547 (1979).
65. U.S. Department of the Interior, Fish and Wildlife Serv., "Final Environmental Statement: The Use of Compound PA-14 Avian Stressing Agent for Control of Blackbirds and Starlings at Winter Roosts," Washington, 1976.
66. G.L. Choules, W.C. Russel and D.A. Gauthier, J. Wildl. Manage., 42, 410 (1978).
67. E.V. Buehler, E.A. Newman and W.R. King, Toxicol. Appl. Pharmacol., 18, 83 (1971).
68. O.G. Fitzhugh and A.A. Nelson, J. Am. Pharm. Assoc., 37, 29 (1948).
69. B. Hunter and H.G. Benson, Toxicology, 5, 359 (1976).
70. J.M. Quack and A.K. Reng, Fette, Seifen, Anstrichm., 78, 200 (1976).
71. T.W. Tusing, O.E. Paynter, D.L. Opdyke and F.H. Synder, Toxicol. Appl. Parmacol., 4, 402 (1962).

72. P.S. Larson, J.F. Borzelleca, E.R. Bowman, E.M. Crawford, R.B. Smith, Jr., and G.R. Hennigar, Toxicol. Appl. Pharmacol., 5, 782 (1963).

73. M. Yoneyama, T. Fujii, M. Ikawa, H. Shiba, Y. Sakamoto, N. Yano, H. Kobayashi, H. Ichikawa, and K. Hiraga, Tokyo Toritsu Eisei Kenkyusho Nempo, 24, 409 (1973).

74. R. Heywood, R.W. James and R.J. Sortwell, Toxicology, 11, 245 (1978).

75. S.J. Fogelson and D.E. Shoch, Arch. Intern. Med., 73, 212 (1944).

76. G. Schneider, Soap Chem. Spec., Nv., 56 (1970).

77. J.F. Smyth and J.C. Calandra, Toxicol. Appl. Pharmacol., 14, 315 (1969).

78. W.R. Green, J.B. Sullivan, R.M. Hehir, L.G. Scharpf and A.W. Dickinson, "A Systematic Comparison of Chemically Induced Eye Injury in the Albino Rabbit and Rhesus Monkey," The Soap and Detergent Assoc., New York, 1978.

79. K. Booman, Soap and Detergent Association, New York, N.Y., personal communication, 1979.

80. S. Tiba, Shokuhim Eiseigaku Zasshi, 13, 509 (1972).

81. K. Booman, Soap and Detergent Association, New York, N.Y., personal communication, 1976.

82. M. Takahashi and H. Sato, Gann, 8, 241 (1969).

83. M. Takahashi, Gann, 17, 255 (1970).

84. M. Takahashi, S. Fukushima and H. Sato, Gann, 64, 211 (1973).

85. M. Takahashi, S. Fukushima and M. Hananouchi, Gann, 17, 255 (1975).

86. S. Fukushima, M. Tatematsu and M. Takahashi, Gann, 65, 371 (1974).

87. M. Masabuchi, A. Takahashi, O. Takahashi and K. Hiraga, Tokyo Toritsu Eisei Kenkyusho Kenkyusho Kenkyu Nempo, 27, 100 (1976).

88. J. Hope, Mutat. Res., 56, 47 (1977).

89. H. Stupel, Shell Chemical Co., Houston, Texas, personal communication, 1979.

90. G. Bornmann, A. Loeser and M. Stanisic, Fette, Seifen Anstrichm., 63, 938 (1961).

91. Y. Mikami, Y. Sakai, I. Miyamoto, S. Kitamura, H. Hujishima, Y. Wakai, S. Akiyoshi, H. Sediguchi, I. Agata, et. al., Mie Kaibo Gyoseki-shu, 21, 1 (1973).

92. H. Nichimura, Congenital Anomalies, 16, 175 (1976).

93. A.K. Palmer, M.A. Readshaw and A.M. Neuff, Toxicology, 3, 9 (1975).

94. S. Chiba, S. Shiobara, A. Imahori and T. Kitagawa, J. Food Sanitation, 17, 66 (1976).

95. A.K. Palmer, M.A. Readshaw and A.M. Neuff, Toxicology, 4, 171 (1975).

96. T. Nomura, S. Kimura, S. Hata, T. Kanzaki and H. Tanaka, Life Sci., 26, 49 (1980).

97. A.K. Palmer, M.A. Readshaw and A.M. Neuff, Toxicology, 3, 107 (1975).

ZEOLITE MATRICES AS SOLID SOLVENTS : ADSORPTION PROCESSES AND

TRANSITION METAL COMPLEXES. RELATIONSHIP TO SURFACTANT

Michel Che   Younès Ben Taârit

Université de Paris VI   Institut de Recherches sur la
                                    Catalyse - C.N.R.S.
75230 Paris Cédex 05 France   69626 Villeurbanne Cédex France

INTRODUCTION

This review is not intended to provide an exhaustive report on the structure and properties of zeolites, it is rather meant to emphasize the similarities between a number of features which appear to be common to both zeolites and micelles. Analogies exist in both the structure and dynamics of both classes as well as in their chemical behavior and catalytic properties. In particular *the solution* behavior of zeolites would examplify the strong link between these crystalline materials to surfactants.

THE STRUCTURE OF ZEOLITES

Zeolites whether natural or synthetic are crystalline alumino silicates[1]. The basic structure is made of a tridimensionnal array of SiO_4 and AlO_4 tetrahedra linked by their vertex oxide ions. Depending on the experimental conditions of crystallization : Silicon/ Aluminium ratio, temperature, pH, pressure ... a variety of zeolites characterized by typical arrangements of the tetrahedra can be formed. The tridimensionnal array of the $Si(Al)O_4$ tetrahedra, usually noted (TO_4) determines the formation of cavities, tunnels, channels of various shapes and sizes. Also lamellar and fibrous structures and weakly crosslinked chains may be encountered.

The substitution of Si^{4+} by Al^{3+} in the tetrahedra units generates a charge imbalance in the framework, where contrary to SiO_4 tetrahedra, AlO_4 tetrahedra bear a net negative charge. The charge balance could then only be achieved upon incorporation of cations into the framework structure of the zeolite. Sodium ions are usual-

189

ly the charge balancing cations. However, as in micelles, Na^+ could be exchanged by other alkali, alkaline-earth, ammonium, alkyl-ammonium, rare-earth or transition metal cations.

The structural formula of zeolites is therefore expressed as :

$$M_{x/n} \ (AlO_2)_x \ (SiO_2)_y \ mH_2O$$

for a crystallographic unit. n is the valence of the exchangeable cation M, x+y is the total number of tetrahedra per unit cell. These tetrahedra are arranged in various ways, thus generating various subunits and more specifically various polyhedra, which, in turn, are connected in various fashions resulting in various architectural types of zeolites with different porous structures. Essentially truncated cuboctahedra, known as α cages, truncated octahedra (β cages), 11-hedra (ϵ cages), 18-hedra (γ cages) are the principal cavities which are encountered in various types of zeolites. These polyhedra could be connected by various types of prisms depending on the faces involved : hexagonal prisms (double 6-rings or D6R) or octogonal prisms (double 8-rings D8R) or cubes. Table I lists the most frequently encountered zeolites and their basic building polyhedra together with the size of the main apertures.

As an example, in Faujasite or type X and Y zeolites two hexagonal faces of two β cages are connected by a hexagonal prism and each β cage is tetrahedrally linked to similar β cages by D6R's. This architecture results in larger voids than the β cages known as the supercages (α cages) which are interconnected through large apertures : 12 O rings. On the contrary in the case of A zeolites the β cages (also sodalite units or cavities) are interconnected tetrahedrally but through cubes linking the square faces of the sodalite units. Here, again, large cavities with, however, smaller size are formed, also interconnected through 8 O rings. Other structures such as mordenites are essentially made up with interconnected or parallel channels running along one or more of the crystallographic axes. Figure 1 shows some schematic structures of a number of zeolites.

Both the cage and channel-structured zeolites have an open enough structure to accomodate not only the extra-framework cations (countercations) which ensure the crystal charge balance, but also other molecules : N_2, O_2, H_2, CO, CO_2, CH_4, H_2O, NH_3 and eventually larger molecules depending on the size of the apertures.

Table I. Building Units and Apertures Sizes of Various Zeolites.

Zeolite	Unit Cell Formula	Type of Polyhedra	Si/Al	Main Aperture
Erionite	$Na_9(AlO_2)_9(SiO_2)_{27} \cdot 27\ H_2O$	ε, 23-hedron	3	3.6 x 5.2
Offretite	$K_{5.4}(AlO_2)_{5.4}(SiO_2)_{12.6} \cdot 15\ H_2O$	ε, 14-hedron	2.33	3.6 x 5.2//a
Levynite	$Ca_3(AlO_2)_6(SiO_2)_{12} \cdot 18\ H_2O$	Ellipsoidal 17-hedron	2	3.2 x 5.1
Omega	$Na_{6.8}TMA_{16}(AlO_2)_8(SiO_2)_{28} \cdot 21\ H_2O$	14-hedron	3.5	7.5
Sodalite	$Na_6(AlO_2)_6(SiO_2)_6 \cdot 7.5\ H_2O$	β	1	2.2
A	$Na_{12}(AlO_2)_{12}(SiO_2)_{12} \cdot 27\ H_2O$	α, β	1	4.2
N-A	$Na_4TMA_3(AlO_2)_7(SiO_2)_{17} \cdot 21\ H_2O$	α, β	2.43	4.2
ZK-A	$Na_8TMA(AlO_2)_9(SiO_2)_{15} \cdot 28\ H_2O$	α, β	1.67	4.2
Faujasite	$\|Na_{59}$ or K_{59} or $Mg_{29.5}$ or $Ca_{29.5}\|\ (AlO_2)_{59}(SiO_2)_{133} \cdot 235\ H_2O$	β, 26-hedron	2.25	7.4
X	$Na_{86}(AlO_2)_{86}(SiO_2)_{106} \cdot 264\ H_2O$	β, 26-hedron	1.23	7.4
Y	$Na_{56}(AlO_2)_{56}(SiO_2)_{136} \cdot 250\ H_2O$	β, 26-hedron	2.42	7.4
Chabazite	$Ca_2(AlO_2)_4(SiO_2)_8 \cdot 13\ H_2O$	20-hedron	2	3.7 x 4.2
Gmelinite	$Na_8(AlO_2)_8(SiO_2)_{16} \cdot 24\ H_2O$	14-hedron	2	3.6 x 3.9//a 7.0//c
Natrolite	$Na_{16}(AlO_2)_{16}(SiO_2)_{24} \cdot 16\ H_2O$		1.5	2.6 x 3.9
Thomsonite	$\|Na_4Ca_8(AlO_2)_{20}(SiO_2)_{20} \cdot 24\ H_2O$		1	2.6 x 3.9 6.7 x 7.0//c
Mordenite	$Na_8(AlO_2)_8(SiO_2)_{40} \cdot 24\ H_2O$		5	2.9 x 5.7//b

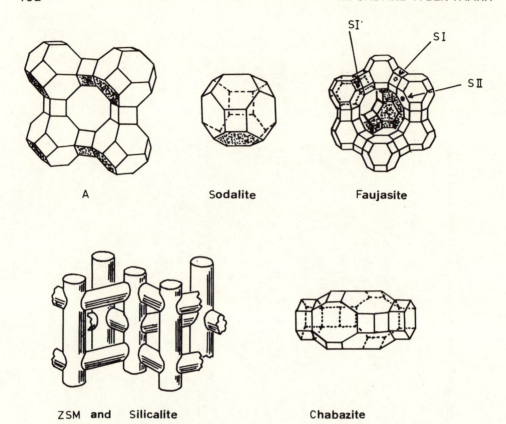

Figure 1. Schematic structures of some zeolites.

Cation Distribution Within the Network

A schematic representation of the zeolite lattice would be a simple linkage of SiO_4 and AlO_4 tetrahedra pictured as follows :

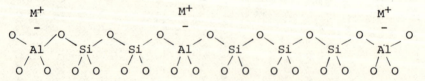

The AlO_4 tetrahedra bearing a negative charge, the countercation would then lie close to such centers. This linkage is comparable to surfactants with the silica-like part as the *hydrophobic* linkage and the $M^+ AlO_4^-$ duality as the hydrophilic *head group*. Thus the zeolite structure is in fact similar to that of any *amphiphile* of the anionic type. The zeolite crystallization might well be consi-sered as a micellization process starting from such units to build up a large crystalline micelle, with the polar *head groups* being

disseminated within the framework and few of them at the external
geometrical surface, though a large number must be located at the
accessible internal surface i.e. the supercages and their windows.
The closest analogue would be a reversed micelle to a certain extent.
Yet this comparison is not quite satisfactory due to the location of
a large number of these *head groups* in the accessible internal
surface, *"mixed or dual"* micelles should they exist would be a better
approach to zeolites.

In this zeolite open structure, cations occupy sites where the
electron density is expected to be maximum that is in the neighbour-
hood of *head group clusters*. In general the negative charge distribution is not a point charge distribution, the charge is rather
delocalized over the network oxide ions. Yet, in spite of the prevailing delocalization, specific crystallographic sites do exist
where the charge density is superior to the mean charge all over the
lattice presumably due to the presence of *head group assemblies*.
As an example in the faujasite type structure, essentially three
types of sites exist where cations preferentially sit : (i) the
centers of the hexagonal prisms connecting two sodalite cages or
sites S_I, the cations are then surrounded by 6 lattice oxide ions
thus experiencing an octahedral coordination. Among the surrounding
oxide ions, there must be a number of *head groups* since these sites
appear to have the highest occupancy factor with most cations.
(ii) Sites $S_{I'}$ are located against the internal hexagonal face of
the sodalite cages adjacent to sites S_I. The cations are there
surrounded by three lattice oxide ions and usually an extraframework
atom. (iii) Sites S_{II} are located within the supercages at the
entrance of the sodalite cages, again three lattice oxide ions are
coordinated to the *countercation* filling such sites, usually other
molecules would bind to these cations. These sites are the external
ones and are usually accessible to a wide range of molecules. Sites
I, I' and II are schematically pictured in figure 2. This distribution of the *countercation* sites is also indicative of the rather
"mixed" micelle character of zeolites. Moreover, in micelles, the
actual distribution of the cations among these various sites is
strongly dependent on the nature of the cation, its valency, its
radius, on the hydration state of the zeolite and on the presence of
various adsorbates (or solubilizates) within the porous structure.
Also, as expected within the same structure, this distribution varies
with the ratio of AlO_4 to SiO_4 tetrahedra which presumably affects
the distribution of the *head groups* within the network, thus
modifying the charge density distribution at specific sites. However
as in micelles this distribution of cations should not be viewed as
a rigid equilibrium. It has been shown that it must be considered as
a dynamic phenomenon. On the other hand the techniques used to
localize the cations and investigate their motion were very much the
same as those used in the case of micelles (X-rays, EPR, NMR, UV, IR
etc ...). Results provided by these techniques will be discussed in
detail in the case of transition metal ions. The main conclusion,

however is that *countercations*, as well as part of the network atoms
might move reversibly without any significant damage to the crystal
structure.

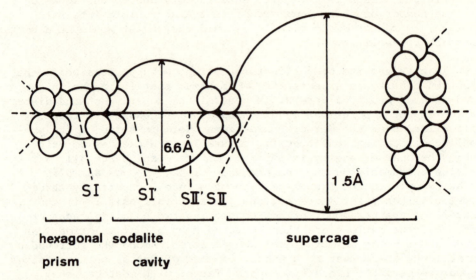

Figure 2. Schematic representation of cationic sites at the three-
fold axis of faujasite type zeolites.

ADSORPTION PROPERTIES

The adsorption properties of zeolites depend on the polar or
apolar nature of the sorbed compounds. The nature of the association
as well as the nature of the interacting sites are bound to vary
according to the nature of the adsorbate. The adsorption of polar
molecules is examplified by water adsorption and to a lesser extent
by ammonia adsorption which is however more characteristic of acid
base interactions between zeolites and sorbed molecules.

Water Adsorption

Quantitatively the volume of adsorbed water can be predicted to
depend on the volume of accessible cavities and also on the number
of available *hydrophilic* sites. In fact a plot of adsorbed water
per cc of zeolite void volume against the Si/Al ratio which expresses
the relative concentration of *hydrophobic/hydrophilic* units shows
that a limiting factor at high Al/Si ratios is the intracrystalline
available space, while at high Si/Al ratios, in spite of rather

important available space, water adsorption is relatively low, indicating that the limiting factor is the availability of *hydrophilic
sites* as shown by figure 3. Recently scientists from Mobil[2] on the

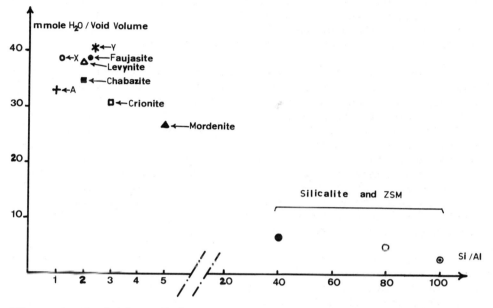

Figure 3. Variation of the number of moles of adsorbed water per void
volume unit as a function of the Si/Al ratio.

one hand and Union Carbide[3] on the other hand synthetized a new class
of zeolites with almost no aluminium, with silicon to aluminum ratios
which are in the 30-100 range. These materials known as the ZSM and
silicalite respectively are claimed to be rather hydrophobic[4].

    <u>Structure of adsorbed water</u>. A number of techniques including
NMR and Infrared spectroscopy were used to investigate the structure,
mobility and location of adsorbed water molecules in zeolites. Monovalent cation-exchanged zeolites were shown to adsorb water molecules
at essentially the cation – AlO_4^- duality. H bonding was shown by IR
spectroscopy to be the prevailing interaction between water and the
hydrophilic site. Two IR bands, a sharp one at 3690 cm^{-1} and a broad
one centred around 3550-3520 cm^{-1} [5] characterized adsorbed water. The
frequency of the former increased with the cation electrostatic field
in the series Li^+, Na^+, K^+, Cs^+ [6]. The following interaction scheme
was deduced from these observations :

The high frequency adsorption was assigned to the free OH vibration, while the low frequency one was attributed to the H bonded OH. Other water layers based on the water layer interacting with the hydrophilic sites as well as water aggregates based on a hydrophilic site are then formed. The differential heat of adsorption due to the weaker interaction decreases significantly with increasing coverage the limiting value being the heat of water condensation[7].

^{1}H NMR spectroscopy showed a fast exchange between water molecules in the large cavities with water in the β cages which was characterized by an independent usually broader signal indicating a slower molecular reorientation[8]. Thus again the location and mobility of water in zeolites closely paralleled the location and extent of interaction of water with micelles as well as the penetration depth in micelles[9]. Sodium or potassium of the zeolite could be easily exchanged to multi-valent cations using aqueous solutions of the desired cation. Therefore the cation is usually introduced in its hydrated form (there are cases, however, where ammine complexes rather than aquo complexes are introduced within the zeolite porous structure).

In the case of multi-valent countercation, two or more negative charges associated with two or more AlO_4 tetrahedra are to be neutralized by the same cation. Therefore, the charge balance could not be so well achieved as in the case of monovalent countercations since Loewenstein Law[10] precluded, in principle the existence of AlO_4 adjacent tetrahedra. Consequently a strong electric field develops between these unbalanced opposite charges. The primary effect of this field is to ionize water from the cation coordination into H^+ and OH^- moieties. While the hydroxide ion would bind directly to the cation, the proton would strongly interact with the negatively charged AlO_4 tetrahedra resulting in the formation of structural hydroxyl groups with a pronounced acidic character. The overall process would occur according to the following scheme :

$$n \; \underset{O}{\overset{O}{\text{Al}}} \diagdown \underset{}{\overset{}{\text{Si}}} + M^{n+}(H_2O)_x \rightleftharpoons \left| M(OH)_{n-1}(H_2O)_{x-n-1} \right|^+ + (n-1) \; \underset{O}{\overset{O}{\text{Al}}} \diagdown \overset{\overset{H}{|}}{\underset{}{\text{O}}} \text{Si}$$

Protons could be presumably *solvated* by excess water though no reliable evidence for the formation of H_3O^+ was ever reported. This is certainly a too short lived step to be detectable to any degree of certainty

$$\underset{\text{Al}}{\overset{O^- \quad O}{}} \text{Si} \; (H^+OH_2) \longrightarrow H_2O + \; \underset{\text{Al}}{\overset{O}{}} \text{Si}$$

would be a too fast process.

$$\begin{array}{c} H \\ | \\ O \\ {\diagup}^{\cdots} \end{array}$$

Both the metal hydroxide species and the silanol group (Si$\diagup$) were detected and characterized by infrared spectroscopy. The silanol groups in faujasite gave rise to absorptions at 3640 and 3550 cm^{-1}, depending on the location of the hydroxyl group : the former in the supercages, the latter in the sodalite units[11]. In the case of other zeolites, variations in the frequency of the vibration absorption were observed which are characteristic of the zeolite type. The hydroxide type hydroxyls were characterized by IR absorption at frequencies which depend on the nature of the cation in the 3620-3520 cm^{-1} range[12, 13].

In this interaction of water and zeolites the overall transformation is water splitting into H$^+$ and OH$^-$, each of the species being further *coordinated* by the *hydrophilic* duality (the structural head groups and the extraframework cations). This interaction is by all means comparable to salt dissolution in water, when both ions of the electrolyte are coordinated by the solvent molecules.

A particular class of zeolites is obtained by ammonium or alkyl-ammonium exchange of sodium ions. Thermal treatment of these zeolites removes the amine and *decationated zeolites* are formed, where only structural hydroxyl groups generated by the attack of the ammonium protons of structural *head groups* as well as those generated upon water splitting by the cation electric field show a strong acidic behavior towards a number of organic N bases as well as other hydrocarbons such as cumene, olefins, etc ... These zeolites appeared to be active catalysts in typical acid catalyzed reactions. Among these reactions, isomerisation[14], alkylation[15], hydration[16], dehydration[17], Prins reaction[18], amination of phenol or chlorobenzene[19], disproportionation of substituted benzene, carbonylation of olefins[20], condensation of aldehydes with esters[21] are often carried out on these zeolites. A reaction similar to the nucleophilic substitution of the sulfate group of the 2,4 dinitrophenyl sulfate by RNH-groups reported by Fendler and Fendler[22]. Cannizaro reaction[23], Beckman rearrangement of ketoximes[24], trimerisation of cyanogen[25], hydrogen transfer between alcohols and carbonyl compounds[15], transformation of benzyl mercaptan into stilbene[26] are also catalyzed by the decationated zeolite and other cation exchanged zeolites.

Hydrocarbon Adsorption

Paraffins. The adsorption of hydrocarbons can only occur provided the critical diameter is within the diameter of the apertures of zeolite cavities. This is known as the molecular sieve effect. Hence linear alkanes adsorption is favoured compared to that of branched paraffins. Among the molecules which do enter the zeolite porous system, diffusion effects depending on the size and shape of these molecules are at the origin of many processes of product separation. (See Tables II and III).

Table II. Critical Diameter of Some Hydrocarbons.

H.C.	C_2H_4	CH_4	C_2H_6	C_3H_6	$1-C_4H_8$	C_4H_8 cis	trans	C_3H_8	nC_4H_{10}	C_3H_6 (Δ)
C.D.$\overset{\circ}{A}$	4.07	4.08	4.36	4.95	4.95	5.58	4.95	5.1	5.1	5.2

Table III. Occluded and Excluded Molecules by Various Calibrated Zeolites

Zeolite classes	Cross section diameter $\overset{\circ}{A}$	Occluded molecules	Excluded molecules
chabazite gmelinite $Ba(AlO_2)_2(SiO_2)_4$	4.89 - 5.58	n-paraffins CH_4, C_2H_6 and smaller molecules N_2, O_2 ...	iso-paraffins aromatics
Na-Mordenite	4.0 - 4.89	CH_4, C_2H_6 N_2, O_2 ...	n-paraffins iso-paraffins
Ca-, Ba-Mordenite	3.84 - 4.0	Ar, N_2 and smaller molecules	all hydrocarbons

The driving force of adsorption of these non polar molecules is not quite clear : it was shown on the one hand that the heat of adsorption of ethane increased with the cation radius[27] at low coverage and that the heat of adsorption of propane increases with increasing coverage, thus indicating a stronger intermolecular interaction than the zeolite-alkane interaction[28]. However at low coverage it seems that interactions between the cations and paraffins are detectable though far from being overwhelming.

The general feature based on IR, NMR and neutron scattering for methane is the retention of a slightly hindered rotational freedom, around the molecule itself and circulation along the cavity walls with however short residence times at definite sites against the sodalite walls[29-30]. For larger normal paraffins and cyclohexane, it was shown that the self diffusion of paraffins decreases with increasing concentration and that at high loadings they behave as *intracrystalline liquids*.

These results tend to point to the absence of any strong

interaction between the zeolite and paraffins with, on the contrary,
dominant intermolecular interactions similar to those prevailing
in liquid phase hydrocarbons.

   Aromatics and olefins. The adsorption of benzene has been the
subject of numerous IR, UV and NMR investigations. Specific interactions with the cations were unveiled. Though the bond did not
appear to be a strong one, significant alterations of the UV spectrum
of benzene, together with shifts in the ring deformation absorptions
in the IR spectrum were interpreted as the result of a slight depar-
ture of the aromatic ring from planarity towards a near-chair
conformation[31]. Three meta-carbons of the aromatic ring were tilted
towards the cation located at site II while the remaining three were
slightly titled off the previous plane. Lechert and coworkers[32] used
^{1}H NMR to investigate the location and mobility of benzene at higher
coverages (4 or more benzene molecules per faujasite supercage). The
benzene rings were shown to be rotating around their sixfold axis
at S_{II} sites at temperatures as low as 150 K. Additional benzene
molecules were thought to sit at the opening of the large cavities
with the ring plane parallel to the window plane. At higher temperatures translational motion dominates. The initially slight tipping
at moderate temperatures amplifies to finally achieve isotropic
reorientation when benzene molecules come closer to each other i.e.
when intermolecular interactions prevail. Similar findings describing the motion of benzene were reported by Resing and Coworkers[33].
On the whole these hydrocarbons again behave as in *dilute* then
progressively *concentrated solutions* or in micellar media where the
relaxation mechanisms are quite similar to those observed in zeolites.
However there are instances where aromatics of low enough ionisation
potential and even benzene are ionized by suitably activated zeolites
with the appropriate Si/Al ratio which determines the electron affinity of the ionizing sites[34]. Then a charge transfer complex is
formed similar to those formed between perylene and sulfuric acid or
perylene and an iodine solution or to those formed in micelles[35].

   The interaction of olefins and zeolites appears to be more
specific and seems to involve the *hydrophilic* acid centers, rather
than related to the hydrophobic properties of zeolites. Indeed the
base characther of the double bond results usually in acid-base
interactions of the olefins with the appropriate acid sites of the
zeolite, be they protons, Lewis centers or cations located within
the zeolite network.

   Olefins react with acidic OH groups, however the nature of the
resulting complex was not elucidated, though zeolite protons were
shown to exchange with those of the olefin probably indicating a
short lived carbonium ion formation[36].

   Acid-base interactions dominate the nature of the complex formed
between olefins and alkali or alkaline-earth *countercations* as shown

from the ^{13}C chemical shift variations of adsorbed olefins[37,38].
The transition metal ion-olefin complex is somewhat different : it
is rather similar to those known in solution as Zeiss salts. In
particular Ag^+, Pt^{2+}, Cu^+ Y zeolites form complexes with propylene
characterized by the same structure as their solution analogues :
^{13}C NMR spectroscopy showed that the methylene carbon bond to the
transition metal ions was priviledged with respect to that between
the transition metal ion and the methyne carbon. Thus an assymmetric
Π bonding is suggested with perhaps a partial σ bond character
involving the *countercation* and the methylene carbon[38]. Such bonding
would favour a hydride abstraction from the methyl group leading
subsequently to the formation of a symmetric Π allylic complex which
is a serious candidate for catalytic oxidation, ammoxidation, etc...
which are indeed observed under proper conditions[38-40].

Dissolution of Solid Lattices

Zeolites, due to their multiple centers behave as *solid solvents*
for a variety of polar as well as non polar molecules. The *dissolved*
molecules were either split or simply *solvated* by a *functional group*
of zeolites. However solid lattices could also be *dissolved* in the
same manner as liquids or gases[29, 41].

Hence chromium and molybdenum hexacarbonyl crystals were shown
to *dissolve* within the zeolite cavities. IR studies showed that
$Mo(CO)_6$, $Re_2(CO)_{10}$, $Ru_3(CO)_{12}$ were adsorbed onto the zeolite without
any loss of carbonyl groups. However slight changes in CO vibration
frequencies indicated that probably the carbonyl groups were engaged
in an H bonding scheme with zeolite protons resulting in the
lowering of the initial symmetry of the $Mo(CO)_6$ molecule[42]. The
structures of both $Re_2(CO)_{10}$ and $Ru_3(CO)_{12}$ were shown to be preserved.
NMR spectroscopy showed that the ^{13}C shift was within the value
observed in $CDCl_3$ and other solvents suggesting (i) that the $Mo(CO)_6$
lattice has been *dissolved* since a narrow isotropic line was observed (ii) the molecules are isolated and freely tumbling (iii) no
appreciable change in the carbon electronic environment[43]. X-rays
determination showed that the location of individual metal carbonyl
molecules depended on the size of the molecule. $Mo(CO)_6$ was found
to be located at the center of the 12 membered rings of the supercages while $Re_2(CO)_{10}$ stretched between two such rings[42]. All data
prove that the carbonyl crystal lattice has been *dissolved* and that
H bonding was possibly the main prevailing interaction between the
zeolite lattice and the individual molecules.

These examples pinpoint the *solvent* role of the zeolite where
no strong interaction occurs between the *solvent* and the *solubili -
zate*, contrary to the strong interaction observed in the case of
water dissolution.

Another example demonstrates the unique character of zeolites as a solvent compared to liquid matrices : $Ir_4(CO)_{12}$ is a well known carbonyl where the iridium atoms form a regular tetrahedron each atom is surrounded by three carbon monoxide ligands arranged in a C_{3v} symmetry. This compound is hardly soluble in anay usual solvent under the most drastic conditions. However this carbonyl could be sublimed into the zeolite or could be formed in situ i.e. in zeo-zeolite upon carbonylation of Ir_{III} exchanged Y and X zeolites. Each carbonyl molecule remained isolated within the supercage with no formation of polymeric species nor a carbonyl crystalline lattice. Evidence for this behavior was provided by ^{13}C NMR and IR spectros-copy[44]. Interestingly enough while, all carbonyls in $Ir_4(CO)_{12}$ are linear, $Ir_4(CO)_{12}$ *solvated* in zeolites shows bridged carbonyls probably interacting with lattice protons. This interaction between the zeolite and the $Ir_4(CO)_{12}$ guest is strong enough to prevent the formation of the $Ir_4(CO)_{12}$ lattice. A high energy is needed to severe the carbonyl to zeolite interaction and form the crystal lattice. In fact $Ir_4(CO)_{12}$ could be extracted in refluxing toluene. In absence of toluene $Ir_4(CO)_{12}$ would rather decompose than escape to form a segregated crystal. This example bears very close resem-blance to what is reported on drug solubilization upon micelle formation[45].

Covalent lattices are not the only compounds which are *dissolved* by zeolites. Ionic lattices are even more easily *dissolved* by the *electrolyte type solvent* that zeolites proved to be. Halide salts especially the alkali salts could be dissolved within the zeolite network and the molecule totally ionized. Sodium nitrate, for instance, is dissolved in the intracrystalline cavities. Amazingly, the nitrate anion which is rather bulky with regard to the entry port of the sodalite cages (2.4 Å) finds its way into this cavity. Such salts (nitrates, perchlorates) when occluded exhibit enhanced stability, as if the ionic character has increased at the expense of the covalent character. Conversely, the stability of the zeolite itself is also enhanced[46, 47, 48]. Other molecules or atoms could also be solvated and strongly held to specific sites of the lattice by the ionizing virtue of these matrices. Hence sodium atoms were *captured* within the supercages and thermally stable Na_5^{4+} and Na_4^{3+} complexes were formed in NaX and NaY zeolites respectively[49]. Neutral molecules are also ionized when introduced together onto the zeolite : $NO + NO_2$ mixture is ionized into NO^+ NO_3^- salt-like complex also tightly occluded within the zeolite cavities[47].

CATION LOCATION AND MOTION

As already outlined the arrangement of AlO_4 tetrahedra leads, depending on the structure of the zeolite to sites with high local electron density. The symmetry of such sites would depend on the structure of the zeolite. Thus cations would sit close to such highly charged locations in order to achieve the best charge balance possible, yet depending on the valency of the cation, on its electronic structure, on the availability of other ligands within the zeolite, the occupancy of the available sites would vary considerably. Hence in the case of X and Y zeolites, while dehydrated Copper II ions occupy preferentially $S_{I'}$ to S_I sites[50] experiencing a distorted tetrahedral symmetry, in dehydrated NiII zeolites Ni^{2+} ions rather occupy S_I sites with an octahedral symmetry[51]. The presence of a potential ligand within the zeolite considerably modifies the prevailing equilibrium and back migration from internal locations to external sites where enough space is available so as to ensure the formation of typical transition metal ion complexes with the appropriate ligand is often observed[50, 52, 53]. This mobility seems to depend on the nature both of the cation, and the ligand : in fact it merely depends on the mutual affinity of the cation and the ligand and also on the initial location of the cation and indeed on the temperature (in other words on the potential barrier that the cation has to overcome). Other parameters might influence the cation motion as well, these include the presence of another type of cations, the presence of hydroxyl groups which may modify the charge distribution at various sites etc ... Table IV gives examples of the cation location dependence on various parameters.

Table IV. Cation Distribution. Influence of the Electronic Structure and Adsorbed Molecules.

Sites		S_I	$S_{I'}$	$S_{II'}$	S_{II}
Zeolites					
$Cu_{16}Na_{24}Y$	dehydrated	3.2 Cu^{2+}	11.4 Cu^{2+}		21 Na^+
	+ NH_3	2.1 Cu^{2+}	12.1 Cu^{2+}	9.4 NH_3	17.8 Na^+
	+ pyridine or C_5H_5N	1.9 Cu^{2+}	2.3 Cu^{2+}		26 Na^+
	+ naphtalene or $C_{10}H_8$	2.3 Cu^{2+}	3.5 Cu^{2+}		22 Na^+
$Ni_{14}Na_{23}HY$	dehydrated	12 Ni^{2+}	1.1 Ni^{2+}		21.3 Na^+
	+ NH_3	2.9 Ni^{2+}	4.0 Ni^{2+}	11 NH_3	19 Na^+
	+ pyridine	9.0 Ni^{2+}	2.5 Ni^{2+}		17 Na^+
	+ NO	3.3 Ni^{2+}	2.5 +5.2 Ni^{2+}	NO	24 Na^+

Besides this motion which is induced by the addition or removal of appropriate ligands (chemically induced motion), the cations were shown to undergo a dynamic motion within the lattice as ions do in

solution. For example Li^+ or Tl^+ *counterions* were observed to jump
from site to site, using NMR spectroscopy. Two kinds of jumps were
distinguished : jumps which occur with the cation adhering permanently to the zeolite walls (in plane) and others which take place
away from the windows and walls (out-of-plane jumps). The frequency
of these jumps which is already high is of course increased when
potential ligands (H_2O, NH_3 hydrocarbons etc...) were present or
with increased temperature. Nevertheless the intrinsic motion,
regardless of the chemically induced motion was shown to be quite
high[54,55].

REDOX REACTIONS

Transition metal ions are known to undergo Redox processes in
solution. Similar properties held when these ions are exchanged into
the zeolite. Rabo and coworkers[56] were first to show that Nickel II
ions were reduced to Nickel I ions using sodium metal according to
the following scheme :

$$Ni^{2+} + Na \longrightarrow Na^+ + Ni^+$$

Later it was demonstrated that less powerful reducing agents could
also result in the reduction of transition metal ions. Cu^{2+}, particularly suitable to EPR studies, was shown to be reduced at fairly
moderate temperatures into Copper I either by hydrogen or carbon
monoxide or ammonia[57, 58]. The resulting cupreous ions were still
distributed among the crystallographic sites as *counterions*. The
overall reduction scheme carried out in hydrogen atmosphere is the
following[57].

$$2\ Cu^{2+} + 2\ \left[Al\!\!\stackrel{O}{\diagdown\!\!\diagup}\!\!Si\right]^{-} + H_2 \longrightarrow 2\ Cu^+ + 2\ \left[Al\!\!\stackrel{\overset{H}{|}\,O}{\diagdown}\!\!Si\right]$$

in the case of ammonia a similar scheme holds with N_2 production and,
with carbon monoxide, the reaction was thought to proceed as follows :

$$2\ Cu^{2+} + 2\ \left[Al\!\!\stackrel{O}{\diagdown\!\!\diagup}\!\!Si\right]^{-} + CO \longrightarrow 2\ Cu^+ + CO_2 + \left[Al\quad\overset{+}{Si}\right]$$

$$+ \left[Al\!\!\stackrel{O}{\diagdown\!\!\diagup}\!\!Si\right]^{-}$$

Other transition metal ions Fe^{3+}, Ni^{2+}, Pd^{2+}, Pd^{3+}, Cr^{3+} could be
reduced according to a similar mechanism[59-63] which in most cases
would imply the formation of acidic hydroxyl groups or tricoordinated
aluminum sites adjacent to a positively charged silicon ion. This
latter moiety exhibited a Lewis type acidity.

Further reduction to the metallic state could be achieved as well, upon using hydrogen or other reducing agents including alkali metals. As in micelles, the size of the obtained crystallite varies depending both on the nature of the cation (Redox potential) on the zeolite type which determines the ionic/covalent character of the cation bond to the framework and of course the net charge at the cation. It also depends on the presence of other species, protons, other cations, on the nature of the reducing agent and on the reduction temperature. Traces of water, NH_3 or other compounds may dramatically modify the size of these crystallites most often through water or ammonia-assisted sintering. Hence Pd^{2+} was easily reduced to isolated atoms within the sodalite cages of a Y zeolite upon adding H_2 at room temperature, by contrast Ni^{2+} ions are reduced to larger crystals at much higher temperatures[64]. Yet reduction of this same Ni^{2+} zeolite with *hydrogen atoms* readily yields small clusters[65].

Pecular Redox reactions have been reported. Copper II ions were reduced by HI to produce Copper I ions and presumably Iodine according to Kasai[66]. On the other hand it was claimed that water could be split into H_2 and O_2 by transition metal ions hosted in zeolites. For instance CuIIY would react with water to yield oxygen and cupreous ions at high temperature. These would be reoxidized by water at moderate temperatures and hydrogen would evolve[67, 68]. Similar behavior was reported for silver Y zeolites[69]. TiIIIA zeolites split water under sunlight into H_2 and O_2 at room temperature catalytically[70] in a very similar way to water splitting exerted in solution by Ruthenium bipyridyl complexes under visible light assistance[71].

TRANSITION METAL COMPLEXES

As transition metal cations are located in various sites where obviously they must be coordinatively unsaturated (in the absence of other ligands than framework oxide ions) and as they are mobile enough to leave hidden sites to those accessible to a wide range of compounds, they were bound to coordinate appropriate ligands depending on the mutual affinity. The nature of the resulting complexes varies depending on whether or not the central ion is attached to the zeolite lattice, on whether or not charge transfer occurs between the ligand and the central cation.

Complexes Held by Electrostatic Forces

A number of complexes of transition metal ions were identified which principal characteristic was the absence of a binding link between the central ion and the zeolite lattice. Such type of complexes is examplified by Copper II tetrapyridine : $\left| Cu(NC_5H_5)_4 \right|^{2+}$

which is simply formed by treating Copper II-exchanged Y or X
zeolites with excess pyridine and subsequent heating at $\sim$ 100°C.
EPR analysis showed that the structure of the complex and the electron distribution within the central ion and its N-atom ligands was
identical to that observed for the same complex in pyridine or
ethanol or methanol solution. Therefore the lattice does not seem
to exert any electronic constraint on such type of complexes, as it
did not appear to exert any change in the case of neutral metal
carbonyls ; these charged complexes appear to be simply coulombically
held to the surrounding lattice which is to be considered as both
the *counteranion* and the *solvent*.

Similar complexes involving only complex-to lattice coulombic
interactions are the copper ammines complexes $|Cu(NH_3)_5|^{2+}$ and
$|Cu(NH_3)_4|^{2+}$[52, 72] and rhodium ammine $|Rh(NH_3)_5|^{2+}$[73]. Copper hexaquo
complex $|Cu(H_2O)_6|^{2+}$[52] as well as organometallic cobalt II isocyanate
complexes. In particular the methyl isocyanate low spin Cobalt II
was reported to form upon reacting methyl isocyanate : $CNCH_3$ and
Cobalt II zeolite activated in vacuo. Both octahedral and square
pyramidal complexes were obtained and identified using EPR spectroscopy[74].

Most of these complexes are allowed some motional freedom either
translational or rotational or both depending on the size of the
complex. They quite often undergo easy *ligand exchange* and the
central ion appeared to be exclusively subjected to its own ligand
field regardless of the zeolite field as essentially inferred from
identical EPR parameters of several of these paramagnetic complexes
when formed within different zeolite types. For example $|Cu(NC_5H_5)_4|^{2+}$
in X and Y type synthetic faujasite has identical parameters[52,75].
Similarly $|Cu(en)_2|^{2+}$ also has the same parameters in different
zeolites[76] thus indicating that the central ions were shielded by
their own ligands from the host lattice effects. Therefore the
zeolite lattice behaves both as an *anion* and as a *solid matrix*.

Complexes Linked to the Network

Usually upon activation of the zeolite the exchanged cation is
progressively stripped of its ligands and simultaneously binds to
the network oxide ions. Upon adsorption of a potential ligand,
depending on the experimental conditions this ligand would compete
with lattice oxide ions more or less effectively. In many cases the
ligand would not be effective to the extent of severing the lattice
to cation link and the latter remains bonded through at least a
Metal-$O_{lattice}$ bond to the zeolite network. On the other hand coordinated ligands may or may not transfer to or accept from the transition metal ion an integer number of electrons which would result in
an overall change of the oxidation state of the transition metal ion.

Among the ligands which usually compete effectively with oxide ions are base type ligands such as ammonia, pyridine, ethylenediamine (en) and other organic Lewis type bases. Olefins also behave as Lewis bases towards the Lewis acids that transition metal ions are. Hence complexes involving acid-base interactions are expected to form.

Other usual ligands to transition metal ions include hydrogen to form hydrides, carbon monoxide (carbonyls), nitric oxide (nitrosyls) etc... In this latter case the odd electron of NO may be transferred to the zeolite hosted transition metal ion, the complex formation then results in the reduction of the transition metal ion. Oxygen adducts implying oxidation of the transition metal ions are also expected to form with suitable transition metal complexes containing donor ligands.

A variety of techniques were used to identify this myriad of complexes. EPR proved to be one of the most powerful tools since in many cases paramagnetic species were formed or experienced a symmetry change or else disappeared. IR spectroscopy provided a wealth of information on the structure of the ligands and the various electronic changes within the ligand. UV spectroscopy complemented the EPR observations and X-rays diffraction also provided information on the structure and location of the complexes. NMR more recently provided evidence for the formation of olefinic and carbonyl complexes of transition metal ions in zeolites.

Ammine complexes. Besides those coulombically interacting with the lattice such as $|Cu(NH_3)_{4-5}|^{2+}$ etc... tetrahedral Cu(II) ammine were detected also using EPR spectroscopy[52]. Indeed when CuII pentammine was heated in vacuo most of the NH_3 ligands were removed thus resulting in free coordination sites around the cupric ions which would then bind to the lattice oxide ions to achieve a more favourable coordination state. Typically a tetrahedral Copper II complex is constituted by three lattice oxide ions ($O_{(3)}$) at S_I, sites and N-atom of an ammonia molecule. The Cu-O and Cu-N bond lengths and the geometry have been determined by X-rays diffraction studies[50]. Similarly octahedral Cobalt II triammine complexes were identified on the basis of quantitative adsorption of NH_3, IR and UV studies[77]. Square planar Cu(II) complexes $|(O_L)_2-Cu \, en|^{2+}$ were reported[75]. In all these cases the zeolite network behaves as a *solid solvent* and more interestingly as a *macro polydentate ligand* thus markedly influencing the electronic and chemical properties of the coordinated central ion.

Carbonyl complexes. A number of these complexes have been observed upon merely adsorbing carbon monoxide and/or heating in the presence of CO or CO + H_2 mixture or CO + H_2O mixture. Although carbon monoxide would rather bind to low oxidation state transition metal ions because of the stronger metal-carbon bond due to the

back donation from the cation (or metal) d orbitals to the carbon
monoxide Π^{*} orbital as rationalized by the Dewar Chatt Duncanson
(DCD) model[78], high oxidation cation could still coordinate CO
reversibly[79]. Platinum II, Pd(II), Rh(III), Ir(II) as well as Ag(I),
Cu(I) Y samples formed carbonyl complexes analyzed by IR and
^{13}C NMR[79]. The carbon of these cationic carbonyls proved to be electron defficient due to the poor back donating abilities of the cation.
However this electrophilic character was decreased upon insertion
into the coordination sphere of donor molecules : NH_3, NC_5H_5, en,
C_2H_4[83] which increase the back donating potentialities of the cation.
As expected the metal-carbon bond then gained strength[83].

   Paramagnetic transition metal carbonyls were first identified
using EPR and IR techniques : $(O_L)_3Pd(CO)_2$ was identified the number
of carbonyl ligands was confirmed using [13]CO labelling[60-61], Ni(I)
mono-, di- and tricarbonyls were identified on the basis of EPR and
IR analysis of [13]CO labelled materials[84]. The nature of the carbonyl
was predominantly determined by the pressure of CO admitted onto the
zeolite and by the sample temperature which is an important parameter
as far as the stability of these carbonyls is concerned[84, 85].
Hydrido-carbonyl complexes were identified using both the EPR and
ENDOR techniques[86]. Mixed ethylene-carbonyls were also formed upon
varying the CO/C_2H_4 partial pressure in the gas phase. For example
$(O_L)_3Ni(CO)_2C_2H_4$ and $-(O_L-)_3Ni(CO)(C_2H_4)_2$ were identified while the
former was a stable and inactive complex, the latter gave rise to
ethylene dimerisation presumably through an intramolecular rearrangement[87].

   More stable carbonyls were formed upon reacting Rhodium III or
Iridium III-exchanged X and Y zeolites. These *countercations* are
reduced in the presence of carbon monoxide under mild temperature
and pressure conditions to Rhodium I dicarbonyl and Iridium I
tricarbonyl similar in their structure and behavior to their solution
analogues[88, 89]. As their solution analogues, they catalyze the
carbonylation of methanol to acetic acid[90]. Moreover the same kinetics
and the same reaction intermediates were observed indicating that
the same reaction pathways are valid in the case of the soluble
complexes or hosted in zeolite matrices underlining the *solvent role*
of the zeolite lattice not only towards the precursor complexes but
also towards all the catalytic reaction steps.

   Nitrosyl complexes. Nitric oxide is a natural free radical which
can be involved in a number of complexes either as NO^+ species upon
transfer of its odd electron to an acceptor, or as NO^- upon capture
of an electron. Mono and dinitrosyl complexes of various transition
metal ions hosted in zeolites have been evidenced usually by IR, UV,
EPR and X-rays diffraction studies. In particular the full structure
of Co_4NO_4A zeolite has been determined by Seff[91].

   In X and Y zeolites dinitrosyl and mononitrosyl complexes are

formed depending on the experimental conditions. NiIIY were shown
to form mononitrosyl complexes as $Ni^{2+}(d^8)$ were reduced to $Ni^+(d^9)$
by the transfer of the NO odd electron to the cation d orbital thus
forming a NO^+ species. The Ni^+NO^+ complex however is not a pure ionic
species since the bonding scheme is similar to that prevailing in
carbonyls i.e. an important back donation from the cation d orbitals
to the Π^* orbital of NO according to the D.C.D. scheme. The formation
of the nitrosyl was observed not only by the appearance of d^9 EPR
signal but also by the shift of the NO vibration evidenced by IR
spectroscopy[63]. Further X-rays diffraction studies confirmed the
T geometry of the Ni-NO bond[52] expected when an NO^+ ligand binds to
a transition metal ion. Other ligands such as OH, H_2O, NH_3, NC_5H_5
and CO could be present in the coordination sphere of the nitrosyl[63].
Chromium nitrosyl has been detected either as a tetrahedral paramagnetic mononitrosyl

$$- O_L$$
$$- O_L \underset{}{\longrightarrow} Cr^+ - NO^+$$
$$- O_L$$

or a diamagnetic dinitrosyl

$$
\begin{array}{ccc}
- O_L & NO & NO \\
\diagdown & \diagdown \cdots & \diagup \\
Cr & & Cr \\
\diagup & \diagdown & \diagdown \\
ON & NO \cdots & O_L
\end{array}
$$

similar to chromium dinitrosyl known in inorganic chemistry. A
peculiar nitrosyl which does not seem to have a solution analogue is
the Cobalt(O) dinitrosyl obtained by the substitution of two H_2O
molecules by two NO molecules. EPR, UV and IR spectroscopies assigned
an octahedral structure to this Cobalt(O) dinitrosyl[92].

Mixed complexes. Mixed complexes such as carbonyl-nitrosyls
ammine nitrosyls hydrido-carbonyls or dinitrosyls are of a great
catalytic importance in many depoluting processes. Mixed CO, NO
complexes were shown to yield CO_2 + N_2 catalytically from exhaust
mixtures[94, 95]. Ammine nitrosyl complexes yield H_2O + N_2[94] and
dinitrosyls would convert NO catalytically to N_2 + O_2 through an
intramolecular coupling reaction.

The interest of the hydrido-carbonyl complexes in the conversion
of syn-gas is nowadays of the utmost topicality. These hydrido-
carbonyls were converted readily into hydrocarbons as well as CO + H_2
mixtures, also converted catalytically. Cobalt zeolite reduced by
Cadmium metal then reacted with CO + H_2 mixture gave olefins selectively[97]. It is postulated that probably cobalt carbonyls were formed
then reacted with hydrogen to give ultimately olefins. It is also
possible that the zeolite cavities stabilize small cobalt carbonyl
clusters which probably accounts for the high selectivity to low
olefins.

Oxo-complexes. As in solution, transition metal ions in zeolites, when suitably activated either by a preliminar partial reduction or by coordination of appropriate donor ligands, form various oxygen adducts. In particular by analogy to cobalt schiff bases, square pyramidal Cobalt II ammine complexes formed in zeolites do add molecular oxygen to form three different oxo complexes namely $\left| (NH_3)_5 CoIIIO_2^- \right|^{2+}$, $\left| (NH_3)_5 Co(III) \overset{O}{\frown} \underset{O}{\frown} CoIII(NH_3)_5 \right|^{4+}$ and $\left| (NH_3)_5 CoIIIO_2^- CoIII(NH_3)_5 \right|^{5+98}$. Cobalt II en complex also gives rise to an oxygen adduct of the form[98]

Pd(II)Y when heated in oxygen and in vacuo also gives rise upon addition of oxygen to $\left| Pd(II)-O_2 \right|^-$ or $\left| PdII-O_2^{3-} \right|$ complexes which are extremely reactive towards hydrocarbons and hydrogen[99]. Similarly $\left| NiO_2 \right|^+$ has been reported[100]. RhIII exchanged zeolites also give µ peroxo species which seem to be very active and selective in catalytic oxidation of olefins[38].

CONCLUSIONS

Transition metal ion exchanged in zeolites behave in a very similar way to what is usual in solution and their zeolite chemistry closely parallels their solution chemistry. Yet zeolites appeared to exert specific effects due to their porous system linking isolated large cavities. While in solution transition metal complexes might dimerize or further associate, the zeolite cavities due to their limited size do not usually accomodate so bulky complexes and preclude the association of individual complexes. Furthermore, besides the similarity of transition metal ions chemistry in zeolites and in solution, their complexes exhibit comparable catalytic properties.

Zeolites, therefore, appear to behave as *solid solvents* or as *mono- to polydentate ligands* and in some cases exhibit a restrictive effect on the nature of possible reaction intermediates or reaction products thus exerting what is termed the *shape selectivity effect*. Much to the resemblance to micelles, while polar molecules interact with *hydrophilic head groups and counterions*, paraffins and related molecules seem to be characterized by an important degree of motion within the zeolite as is experienced in micelles : the *solvent role* of zeolites closely resembles that of micelles. Further similarities appear in the distribution of *countercations* which in general outline the large analogy between inverse micelles and zeolites. However in many cases where cations sit within the large cavities which could be considered as the outer surface of this rigid micelle, the similarity is greater with normal micelles. Yet the quasi general availability of at least one coordination site at the *countercation* again relates zeolites to inverse micelles, though certain cations seem to be definitely inaccessible.

Last, zeolites as a rigid medium for homogeneous catalysis or metal catalysis is again a recollection of what is often observed in the case of micelles although the flexibility of micelles appear to be at variance with the rigidity of zeolites.

REFERENCES

1. D.W. Breck in "Zeolite Molecular sieves structure chemistry and use", J. Wiley & Sons, New York, 1974 and references cited therein.
2. E.M. Flanigen, J.M. Bennett, R.W. Grose, J.P. Cohen, R.L. Patton, R.M. Kirchner, J.V. Smith, Nature, 271, 512 (1978).
3. G.T. Kokotailo, S.L. Lawton, D.H. Olson, W.M. Meir, Nature, 272, 437 (1978).
4. W. Haiwald, W.D. Basler and H.T. Lechert, Proceedings of the Fifth International Conference on Zeolites, Heyden & Son Ltd., 562 (1980).
5. J.W. Ward, J. Catal., 11, 238 (1968).
6. J.W. Ward, J. Catal., 10, 34 (1968).
7. A.V. Kiselev in Molecular Sieve Zeolites-II, Advances in Chem. Series, 102, 37 (1971).
8. H. Pfeifer, Surf. Sci., 52, 434 (1975).
9. J.H. Fendler and E.J. Fendler, "Catalysis in Micellar and Macromolecular Systems", Academic Press, New York, 31 (1975).
10. W. Loewenstein, Amer. Mineral., 39, 92 (1942).
11. P. Gallezot and B. Imelik, C.R. Acad. Sci. Paris, B, 912 (1970).
12. J.W. Ward, J. Phys. Chem., 72, 4211 (1968).
13. J.W. Ward, "Zeolite Chemistry and Catalysis", J.A. Rabo Editor, A.C.S. Monograph, 171, 118 (1976) and references cited therein.
14. J.A. Rabo, P.E. Pickert, R.L. Mays, Ind. Eng. Chem., 53, 733 (1961).
15. W.E. Garwood and P.B. Venuto, J. Catal., 11, 175 (1968).
16. M. Nitta, H. Hattori, G. Natsudzaki, K. Tanabe, Shokubai Catalyst, 13, 103 (1971).
17. I.A. Bogod, V.R. Gurevitch and L.E. Meilumyan, Khim. prom., 657 (1972).

18. P.B. Venuto and P.S. Landis, Adv. Catal., 18, 259 (1968).
19. M. Yamamoto, N. Takamiya and S. Murai, J. Chem. Soc. Jap.,
     Chem. Ind. Chem., 2135 (1974).
20. P.S. Landis, U.S. Patent 3,334,132 ; R. Zh. Khim., 17N32P (1968)
21. Jap. Patent 4523 ; R3 Khim. 17H22IP (1973).
22. J.H. Fendler and E.J. Fendler "Catalysis in Micellar and
     Macromolecular systems". Academic Press, New York, p. 144
     (1975).
23. S. Trigerman, E. Biron and A.H. Weiss, Fourth Intern. Confe-
     rence on Molecular Sieves, April 18-22, 1977, Chicago.
     Recent Research Reports 107 (1977).
24. P.S. Landis and P.B. Venuto, J. Catal., 6, 245 (1966).
25. F. Wolf and P. Renger, Z. Chem., 12, 293 (1972).
26. P.S. Landis and P.B. Venuto, J. Catal., 21, 330 (1971).
27. N.N. Avgul, A.G. Bezus and O.M. Dzhigit, Adv. Chem. Ser.,
     102, 184 (1971).
28. M. Dubinin in discussion of A.V. Kiselev, Adv. Chem. Ser.,
     102, 64 (1971).
29. E. Cohen de Lara "Proceedings of the Fifth International
     Conference on Zeolites" Heyden & Son Ltd., 414 (1980).
30. D. Denny, V.M. Mastilhin, S. Namba and J. Turkevich, J. Phys.
     Chem., 82, 1752 (1978).
31. E. Garbowski, M. Primet, M.V. Mathieu and B. Imelik, Procee-
     dings of Workshop on adsorption of hydrocarbons in zeolites,
     Berlin, DDR, Nov. 19-22 (1979), p. 10.
32. H. Lechert, W. Schweitzer and H. Hacirek, ibid, p. 23.
33. H.A. Resing and J.S. Murday, Adv. Chem. Ser., 121, 414 (1973).
34. P. Wierzchowski, E. Garbowski and J.C. Vedrine, J. Chim. Phys.,
     (1980), submitted for publication.
35. J.H. Fendler and E.J. Fendler, "Catalysis in Micellar and
     Macromolecular Systems", Academic Press, New York, 255 (1975).
36. C.S. John and H.F. Leach, J.C.S. Faraday Trans., 73, 1595
     (1977).
37. D. Michel, W. Meiler and H. Pfeifer, J. Mol. Cat., 1, 85
     (1975/76).
38. Y. Ben Taârit and M. Che, "Catalysis by Zeolites", Elsevier
     Scientific publishing Co, Amsterdam, 187 (1980).
39. H. Arai and H. Tominaga, Asahi Garasu, Ind. Prom. Res. Reports,
     27, 93 (1975).
40. L.V. Skalbina, I.E. Kolchin, L. Ya Margolis, N.F. Ermolenko,
     S.A. Levina and L.N. Malashevich, Kinet. i. Katal., 12, 242
     (1971).
41. E. Cohen de Lara, Mol. Phys., 23, 555 (1972).
42. P. Gallezot, G. Coudurier, M. Primet and B. Imelik, ACS Symp.
     Ser., 40, 144 (1977).
43. Y. Ben Taârit, G. Wicker and C. Naccache, 2nd Intern. Symposium
     Magnetic Resonance in Colloid and Interface Science, Menton,
     France, July (1979).
44. P. Gelin et al., (1980), J. Mol. Cat., submitted for publication

45. J.H. Fendler and E.J. Fendler, "Catalysis in Micellar and Macromolecular Systems", Academic Press, New York, 43-43 (1975).

46. J.A. Rabo "Zeolite Chemistry and Catalysis", ACS Monograph, 171, 332 (1976) and references cited therein.

47. P.H. Kasai and R.J. Bishop Jr., "Zeolite Chemistry and Catalysis", ACS Monograph 171, 350 (1976).

48. R.M. Barrer and J.F. Cole, J. Chem. Soc. A, 1516 (1970).

49. P.H. Kasai and R.J. Bishop, Jr., J. Phys. Chem., 77, 2308 (1973).

50. P. Gallezot, Y. Ben Taârit and B. Imelik, J. Catal., 26, 295 (1972).

51. P. Gallezot, Y. Ben Taârit and B. Imelik, J. Catal., 26, 481 (1972).

52. C. Naccache and Y. Ben Taârit, Chem. Phys. Letters, 11, 11 (1971).

53. P. Gallezot, Y. Ben Taârit and B. Imelik, J. Phys. Chem., 77, 2556 (1973).

54. D. Freude, A. Prybilov and H. Schmiedel, Phys. Stat. Sol.(b), 57, K73 (1973).

55. D. Freude, U. Lohse, H. Pfeifer, W. Schirmer, H. Schmiedel and H. Stach, Z. Phys. Chem. (Leipzig), 255, 443 (1974).

56. J.A. Rabo, C.L. Angell, P.H. Kasai and V. Schomaker, Dis. Far. Soc., 41, 328 (1966).

57. C.M. Naccache and Y. Ben Taârit, J. Catal., 22, 171 (1971).

58. I.E. Maxwell, R.S. Downing and S.A.J. Van Langen, J. Catal., 61, 485 (1980).

59. R.L. Garten, W.N. Delgass and M. Boudart, J. Catal., 18, 90 (1970).

60. C. Naccache, J.F. Dutel and M. Che, J. Catal., 29, 179 (1973).

61. M. Che, J.F. Dutel, P. Gallezot and M. Primet, J. Phys. Chem., 80, 2371 (1976).

62. E. Garbowski, M. Primet and M.V. Mathieu, ACS Symposium ser., 40, 281 (1977).

63. C. Naccache and Y. Ben Taârit, J.C.S. Faraday Trans. I, 69, 1475 (1973).

64. D. Delafosse, "Catalysis by Zeolites", p. 235, Elsevier Scientific Publishing Co, Amsterdam 1980.

65. M. Che, M. Richard and D. Olivier, J.C.S. Faraday Trans. I, 76, 1526 (1980).

66. P.H. Kasai, (1980), personal communication.

67. P.H. Kasai and R.J. Bishop, Jr., J. Phys. Chem., 81, 1527 (1977).

68. D. Mikheikin, V.A. Shwets and V.B. Kazanskii, Kinetica i Kataliz, 11, 747 (1970).

69. P.A. Jacobs, J.B. Uytterhoeven and H.K. Beyer, J.C.S. Chem. Commun., 128 (1977).

70. S.M. Kuznicki and E.M. Eyring, J.A.C.S., 100, 6790 (1978).

71. J.M. Lehn and J.P. Sauvage, Nouv. J. Chim., 1, 449 (1977).

72. D.R. Flentge, J.H. Lunsford, P.A. Jacobs and J.B. Uytterhoeven, J. Phys. Chem., 79, 354 (1975).

73. C. Naccache, Y. Ben Taârit and M. Boudart, ACS Symposium ser., 40, 156 (1977).
74. E.F. Vansant and J.H. Lunsford, J.C.S. Chem. Commun., 830, 1972, J.CS. Faraday Trans. II, 69, 1028 (1973).
75. I.R. Leath and H.F. Leach, Proc. Roy. Soc. London A, 330, 242 (1972).
76. P. Peigneur, J.H. Lunsford, W. de Wilde and R.A. Schoonheydt, J. Phys. Chem., 81, 1179 (1977).
77. H. Praliaud and G. Coudurier, J.C.S. Faraday Trans I., 75, 2601 (1979).
78. M.J.S. Dewar, Bull. Soc. Chim. France C17 (1951). J. Chatt and L.A. Duncanson, J. Chem. Soc., 2939 (1953).
79. Y. Ben Taârit, Chem. Phys. Letters, 62, 211 (1979).
80. P. Gelin, (1980), unpublished data.
81. Y.Y. Huang, J. Am. Chem. Soc., 95, 6636 (1973).
82. K.G. Ione, P.N. Kuznetsov and V.N. Romannikov, Application of Zeolites in Catalysis, Publishing House of the Hungarian Academy of Sciences, Budapest, 87 (1979).
83. Y. Ben Taârit, H. Tzehoval, C. Naccache and B. Imelik, Proceedings of the Fifth Intern. Conf. on Zeolites, Heyden, 723 (1980).
84. D. Olivier, M. Richard and M. Che, Chem. Phys. Letters, 60, 77 (1978).
85. F. Bozon-Verduraz, D. Olivier, M. Richard, M. Kermarec and M. Che (1980), J. Phys. Chem., submitted for publication.
86. D. Olivier, M. Richard, M. Che, F. Bozon-Verduraz and R.B. Clarkson, J. Phys. Chem., 84, 423 (1980).
87. L. Bonneviot, D. Olivier, M. Che and M. Cottin (1980), J.C.S. Faraday I, submitted for publication.
88. M. Primet, J.C. Vedrine and C. Naccache, J. Mol. Cat., 4, 411 (1978).
89. P. Gelin, G. Coudurier, Y. Ben Taârit and C. Naccache, (1980), J. Catal., submitted for publication.
90. P. Gelin, Y. Ben Taârit and C. Naccache, Proceedings of the 7th Intern. Congress on Catalysis, Tokyo, July 1980, paper B15.
91. K. Seff, Accts. Chem. Res., 9, 121 (1976).
92. Y. Ben Taârit, H. Praliaud and G. Coudurier, J.C.S. Faraday Trans I, 74, 3000 (1978).
93. E. Garbowski, M. Primet, (1980), unpublished data.
94. W.B. Williamson and J.H. Lunsford, J. Phys. Chem., 80, 2664 (1976).
95. P.H. Kasai, R.J. Bishop and B. Mc Leod, J. Phys. Chem., 82, 279 (1978).
96. K.A. Windhorst and J.H. Lunsford, J. Am. Chem. Soc., 97, 1407 (1975).
97. D. Fraenkel and B.C. Gates, J. Am. Chem. Soc., 102, 2478 (1980)
98. R.F. Howe and J.H. Lunsford, J. Am. Chem. Soc., 97, 5156 (1975)
99. Y. Ben Taârit, J.C. Vedrine, J.F. Dutel and C. Naccache, J. Magn. Reson., 31, 251 (1978).
100. D. Olivier, M. Richard and M. Che, Chem. Phys. Letters, 60, 77 (1978).

AN ELECTRODIC APPROACH TO BIOELECTROCHEMISTRY

J. O'M. Bockris

Department of Chemistry
Texas A&M University
College Station, Texas   77843

This paper is a general one and meant to be a source of research concepts, rather than a description of research carried out. It is speculative and based upon bits of evidence which have come, in large during the last ten to fifteen years.[1] It suggests, in a sketchy kind of way, that much of the field of electrical potential in biology has been misunderstood, and that, for the most part, they are not "membrane potentials" but potentials which can be described as "fuel cell potentials."[2] This term will be duly explained.

It is not part of the case being made here that "membrane potentials"[3] (Donnan ones) do not exist in biology, or that the interpretations which involve them are in general wrong. They may play some part in the phenomenon of p.d.'s in biology. However, it seems that, at least in those situations where the processes of metabolism is occurring, the Nernst-Donnan membrane potential model is not an appropriate one for interpreting the potential differences observed.

Lastly, I would like to explain my title. I wish to explain two terms. Electrochemistry as a word to describe a field is unsatisfactory, because, in fact, the field consists of two very disparate parts. The first one usually dealt with in books concerns ionic solution, a homogeneous phase subject, which is not worth having as a separate subject from the general one of solutions. The second part of the subject concerns the heterogeneous system electronic conductor/ionic conductor and is more related to the field of catalysis than to the homogeneous field of solutions. For this reason two new terms seem desirable. The first part of the electrochemical field -solutions- is called "ionics," the second part is called "electrodics."[4]

CLASSICAL VIEW OF POTENTIAL DIFFERENCES IN BIOLOGY

This material which is in every textbook, and only one or two points will be made. The ideas go back to Nernst and the 19th century (Figure 1). It was taken up by Donnan, with whose name it is generally associated in textbooks of biology, and he added aspects of selective permeation and the separation of alkali metal cations into different concentrations on alternative sides of the membrane. The other two famous names associated with membrane potentials are by virtue of an application: I refer to the work of Hodgkin and Huxley,[3] who received a Nobel prize for their application of the ideas of Donnan to explain the spike potential and movement of electric currents down nerves.

Opposition to this classical view of potential differences in biology has been spreading for some 20 years. There is the philosophical difficulty[5] that electrical potential differences are universal at biological interfaces and that it is difficult to see how they can be associated with an equilibrium, when they take part in, and probably control, the rate of net forward reactions.

Another difficulty has been the fact that, although 50 to 100 millivolts[6] is the usual membrane potential, and easily rationalized in terms of the Nernst equations, there may be sometimes ovserved potential differences which are five times that, and these are difficult to rationalize, because of the fact that they suggest ratios of alkali metal cations on the two sides of the membrane in the region of 10^{-6}.

Such ratios are by no means impossible, but on the side where the concentration would have to be so low, it seems likely another reaction would be potential determining. The reactions which beg for consideration are the reduction of oxygen and the oxidation of organic materials to CO_2.

The response to light[7] of some fo the membranes indicates that a mechanism other than the Donnan one exists, and this objection has become stronger in the last few years when contrived electrosynthesizers have been made from semiconducting oxides and where it is clear that the process which causes the potential difference to occur is not remotely connected with those which cause membrane potentials.

The deepest blow to the classical theory has been given from experiments[8] done with a squid axon in which injections have been made which radically change the sodium or the potassium concentration without corresponding effect on the so-called membrane potential.

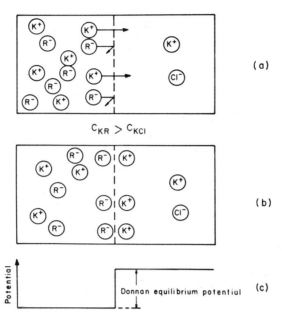

$$C_{KR} > C_{KCl}$$

Figure 1. Concentration difference across a boundary: The origin of the Donnan membrane potential, which is based upon thermodynamic concepts related to the Nernst Equation.

AN ELECTROCHEMIST'S INTERPRETATION OF SOME POTENTIAL DIFFERENCES IN BIOLOGICAL SYSTEMS

In Figure 2, we show the usual type of arrangement for measuring a membrane potential. The two references electrodes should be at the same potential as the react to the same chloride ion concentration. If they are not, this must clearly be due to the fact that the membrane interposes a potential difference, so that it is measured.

A solid state electrochemist looks at the system shown in Figure 2 with a different attitude.[9] Instead of seeing it as a site at which ions of different concentration levels are separated by different degrees of permeability, he invokes the idea that semiconductors and insulators form electrode/solution systems at which electron transfer reactions occur. These charge transfer reactions could be, for example, the reduction of oxygen, and, for example, the oxidation of glucose. The former would be a cathodic reaction in which electrons would have to trnasfer themselves from the semiconductor to the oxygen; whereas, with the oxidation of glucose, holes would be transferred from the membrane to the glucose.

At first sight, if one assumes that these reactions occur exclusively on each side of the membrane, respectively, then one

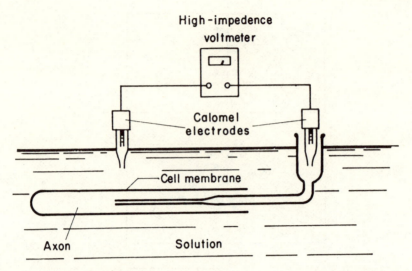

Figure 2.   An arrangement for measuring a membrane potential: The
two reference electrodes are in the same solution, and hence, the
only potential difference would be that caused by the membrane.
However, the two electrodes would sum the p.d.'s at the two interfaces and any IR drop between.

would at first expect a larger potential difference than one observes, one of several hundred millivolts (and indeed such potentials are occasionally observed in membrane potential measurements).
However, in practice, the fuel cell bielectrode which we are hypo-
thesizing would have at least two further potentials to subtract
from the two reversible thermodynamic potentials, which would, on
a zeroth approximation view, make up the potential difference
across the cell.   Thus, one would have to subtract the overpotential
due to each of the charge transfer reacitons and the IR drop which,
with normal rates of metabolism, may be high.[10]

In this model, the so-called membrane is a bielectrode.   The
electrons or holes are transferred across it by solid state processes, and the ions get "between the electrodes" (i.e., they get
across the membrane) by means of passage through the channels in
the membrane.

The idea of insulator/solution interfaces being regarded in
an electrodic way has been current since the late 1960's.[11]   The

polarization of duel cell potentials of 0.1 - 0.2 volts is familiar
to fuel cell researchers. That the membrane has sufficient electronic conductivity is more surprising. Let us discuss this in the
next section.

ELECTRONIC CONDUCTIVITY OF WET BIOLOGICAL MATERIALS

For some time, it was thought unlikely for biological materials
to have sufficient electronic conductivity to be of interest to
electrochemists and indeed St. Gyorgy--who for long has been keen
upon discussing the electronic/interface reaction aspects of biological phenomena--has always had to face the question of an apparent lack of conductivity.[12]

It is the more interesting, then, to refer to the work of
Rosenberg who was the first to show that conductivity was a function
of the wetness of the membrane.[13] Earlier researchers had worked
with membranes which were dry. There are great difficulties in
making measurements of electronic conductivity when the solutions
are wet and set up parallel paths of ionic conductivity. However,
Rosenberg managed to separate the two, and a diagram for his work
is shown in Figure 3. He found that the electronic conductivity of
a nember of biological membranes was large and big enough to--given
the thinness of the membrane--be consistent with the idea of a net
current pushing through the membrane of 100 mV.

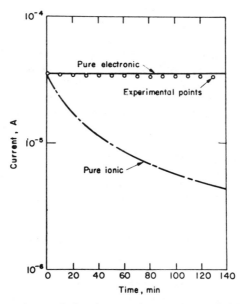

Figure 3. Electronic and ionic conductivity of biological materials.

THE HISTORY OF THE ELECTRODIC VIEW IN BIOLOGY

Cope was the first to make a suggestion which was near the suggestion which we are presenting now, and a diagram of his work is shown in Figure 4, where the concept is applied to an enzyme.[14]

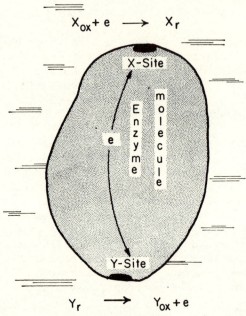

Figure 4. Cope's idea of cathode and anode sites in enzymes.[15]

Correspondingly, Del Ducca and Fucsoe presented, independently, a view which was not unlike that of Cpoe's in essence, but put quite differently, as is shown in Figure 5, where both the protein-containing membrane and the corresponding analogue of the fuel cell is shown in detail.[15] This paper was the first to bring out the fuel cell point of view.

Correspondingly to these contributions, some workers[16] have been interested in showing that a series of redox processes could mediate the potential difference which is needed to derive certain metabolic processes. Some of these would include interfaces.

THE ELECTROCHEMICAL ASPECTS

In 1969, the idea of electron transfer at interfaces as an important step in biological processes was described.[17] However, a number of aspects were not explained there, and it is appropriate to bring them into focus here.

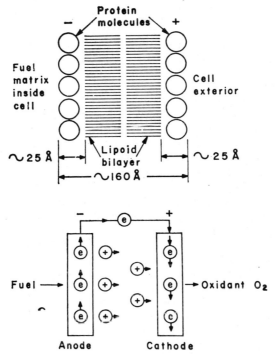

Figure 5.   Del Ducca and Fucsoe's version of the biological cell
as a fuel cell.[16]

We have to go back to Wagner and Traud in 1939 to find the
origin of the concepts which seem useful in biological systems.[18]
Developing an idea, which had been first suggested even earlier by
Evans and Hoar,[19] Wagner and Traud suggested that when a metal cor-
rodes, there are two current potential curves--at least as far as
a thought process is concerned. Thus, there is a driving force
which is equal to the thermodynamic potential differences between,
say, the elcetrode potential due to the dissolution of zinc and
the electrode potential due to the evolution of hydrogen at the pH
concerned. When the current begins to flow, the charge transfer
reaction of the zinc begins to take place and that for hydrogen as
well. Then, significant current densities develop at the interface
and--prior to them--significant overpotentials. The potential of
the surface remains the same but the important element is overpotential, the bias which differentiates the actual potential of
functioning of the couple from the reversible thermodynamic potentials of the two driving reactions.

Eventually, in the thought experiment, the cathodic reaction
rate of hydrogen evolution becomes equal in magnitude to the anodic
reaction rate of the anodic dissolution and the two reactions feed
on each other to the destruction of the material.

There are several things that one can point out about this hypothesis of Wagner and Traud which is the basic theorem of all degradation and probably has, consequently, one of the greater realms
of applicability of all scientific hypotheses (it is surely much
wider and more economically important than Faraday's concept of
electromagnetism).

One thing to point out is that if a situation is occurring
due to the Wagner-Traud mechanism, then it is not occurring at a
thermodynamic potential, in equilibrium, but in a steady state removed from equilibrium. This is helpful to thinking about biological
systems, because there can be progress in a reaction, although no
electrons cross the barrier. Thus, the number of electrons pumped
into the metal--or the number of holes leaving the membrane--is
equal to the number of electrons ejected form the metal, or the
number of holes transferred to it, so that there is no net reaction
rate. In the original Wagner and Traud hypothesis, there was a net
rate of corrosion, and in the application of this hypothesis to a
biology, there would be a net metabolic rate associated with the
net "cell potential."

The well-known electrodic law of Tafel should come in at this
point.[20] In Tafel's law (an electrochemical analogue of the Arrhenius law in chemical kinetics), one should observe a logarithmic
dependence of the magnitude of the electric current upon potential,
just as in normal kinetics one observes a logarithmic dependence of
the rate upon the reciprocal of the temperature. If one biased a
biological membrane system off its steady state potential and put
it into a biased potential, say, 0.1 or 0.2 volts away, that is,
with overpotential of 0.1 or 0.2 volts, one should observe a linear
logarithmic dependence of the current density upon potential, and
it one does this, it would give rise to a degree of verification of
the hypothesis which is being but forward.

It would not, however, mean the elimination of the hypothesis
if we did not observe the logarithmic current/potential relation,
because there could be a rate derterminging step, not only at
either one of the interfaces, but also in some solid state internal
processes, for example, hole/electron pair recombination or simple
in respect to charge transfer or holes or electrons through the
membrane.

LAZARO MANDEL

Mandel was the first to try out the Tafel line test.[21] Here,
what is happening is that a membrane has been clamped between two
flanges, and Luggin cappilaries have been utilized to measure the
potential on either side of the membrane, each side reacting to
auxiliary electrodes which are put into the two different compart-

ments of the cell. Thus, by biasing the central membrane off its
normal potential, one can examine the reaction rate/potential re-
lantionship at Side 1 and Side 2 of the cell. What one observes,
in the cases chosen by Mandel, is indeed the logarithmic dependence
of the current density on the overpotential.

Here, then, is evidence, slight and limited, but evidence for
the applicaiton of the hypothesis.

MITCHELL

The chemiosmotic theory of Mitchell (the recipient of another
Nobel Award) is shown in Figure 6.[22] It is a Nernstian concept, and
what is meant to happen is that on the one side protons are to
discharge and form hydrogen atoms which then are carried across by
some unknown process to the other side where they form protons once
more. This process happens several times, until a sufficient proton
gradient has been built up across the membrane so that the desired
potential difference can be accounted for in a Nernstian manner.
After that, the protons come back through channels in the membrane
and when they do, they cause the equilibrium of ADP with ATP to
change in favor the the ATP. This is because the left-hand side
of this reaction contains a proton so that if we increase the number of protons in the interface on the right in Figure 6, we shall
cause the transition of ADP to ATP, and hence store energy.

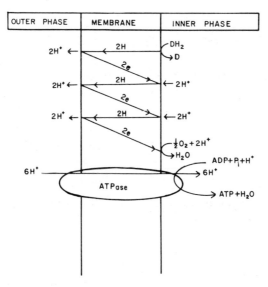

Figure 6. Mitchell's[23] model of the storage of energy by the ADP
and ATP system. Note that the model is basically electrochemical
but involves a Nernstian viewpoint.

Mitchell's theory contains the difficulties which inhabit
classical theories of membrane potentials. The essentail one is
the absence of a convincing identity of the driving force of the
overall reaction. In other models, this is avoided by having a net
chemical reaction occurring so that there is a ΔG to drive the reaction. But in the Mitchell hypothesis, there is no reason why the
proton should build up this gradient spontaneously. It is not un-
fair to call the theory ad hoc, apart from the fact that it is
clearly invalid to use an equilibrium thermodynamic mode of discussion in the dynamic situation portrayed.

BOCKRIS AND TUNULI

Bockris and Tunuli have attempted to make an analogue of the
Mitchell phosphorylation theory in terms of electrodics (Figure 7).[23]
It is hypothesized that, on the right-hand side, an electrodic
reaction occurs which may be, essentially, the oxidation of glucose.
Such reactions produce protons and so the change of the ADP to ATP
reaction--and the storage of energy--will be explained by the continuing oxidation of the glucose to CO_2. In the Bockris and Tunuli
electrodic view, electrons would pass through the membrane from
right to left (solid state conductivity of an insulator) and serve
to make the oxygen reduction reaction go on the left. Thus, with
the reduction of oxygen there comes a need for portons. These
are produced by the channeling of protons arising in the glucose
reaction.

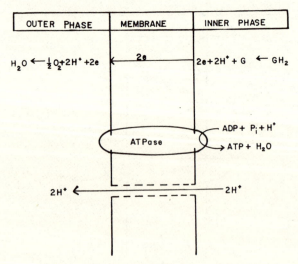

Figure 7. Bockris and Tunuli's view of the ADP – ATP storage. Electron transfer replaces proton transfer through the solid. The situation is no longer a Nernstian thermodynamic one, where equilibrium
is assumed, but it occurs at steady state, probably far from the
equilibrium potential values.

One advantage of this model is that one can see a driving force at work. (It is that of the oxidation of glucose.) There is no need for any analogue of the sodium pump to get hydrogen atoms through the membrane. Protons pass through because they are carrying a current between "the two electrodes" (it is other smaller cations would pass through, depending upon the concentration of the solution). Transfer of porotns from one side to the other could be accompanied by the transfer of other ions, depending on the composition of the solution.

BOCKRIS AND TUNULI'S EVIDENCE

Bockris and Tunuli have made an attempt to examine the hypothesis of electrodically functioning biological situations in terms of light-active ones, analogues of photosynthesis.[23] They took a platinized platinum electrode in aqueous solution and shone a light upon it, finding very small effects. They then extracted from spinnage a fraction containing photosystem I and one containing photosystem II.

In separate experimento, these were adsorbed from the solution onto the electrode surface, and the electrode again irratiated. A very important result which results is that with photosystem II, the currents were anodic but with photosystemI, cathodic. The current/potential lines reacted exactly the same way as those which come with photoelectrical work at classical semiconductors such as titanium dioxide or gallium phosphide, and it is clear that what has happened is that ceratin parts of the chlorophyll, the light active ones, have adsorbed upon the platinum electrode surface and acted as light receptors, stimulating electron transfer processes, one of which is oxygen evolution, and the other one, the cathodic one, may be hydrogen evolution.

It is important for the Bockris and Tunuli work to be continued and for us to find out whether it is possible to evolve hydrogen in this manner without the presence of an enzyme favorable to the evolution of hydrogen which hydrogenate, or a substance such as methyl viologen.

MORE SPECULATIVE MATTERS

Certain other matters may be referred to briefly here. One of them is the macroversion of what is being said, namely, making actual fuel cells, measuring the efficiency within the body and to power body mechanisms. Thus, it would be possible to make a fuel cell model which would drive an electric motor to power a pump in place of the heart.[24] One could have one electrode in part of the body fluids containing glucose and another in the parts con-

taining oxygen. The 10 watts necessary to run an electric motor
having the same power as the heart and pump blood around the body,
could be developed in the sufficient space.

At present, such attempts have been limited to the making of
fuel cells which may replace heart pacer batteries.

Correspondingly, electrochemical bone growth has become a well-
known surgical procedure, and one can point out that the mechanism
by which it occurs is as yet little understood.[25] As a hypothesis,
it is suggested that electrophoresis is involved. It may be that
substances such as appatite are electrophoresized onto whichever
of the bone surfaces is appropriate in its sign to attract the necessary material, and it is the formation of this at the interface
which accelerates the rate of growth and repair.

Lastly, it has been something of a mystery that magnetic effects
are observed upon biological entities.[26] However, it only in principle, directly one admits that metabolic processes are being carried
out by a series of electric current producing processes involving
potential differences, then the effect of a magnetic field becomes
at once understandable. This statement does not yet give a model
for the effect of magnetic fields upon biological organisms, but
coupling magnetic field effects with interfacial electron transfer
processes is perhaps an early step.

As biosystems on the earth are always under a mangnetic field,
but htis magnetic field changes with time, it is possible to speculate that the magnetic field/electrodic interaction possibility
has implications for the variation of biological development with
time and place.

SUMMARY

It is important to keep in formt of us what is essential in
the present paper and what is applicatory or speculative. The
essential is that it is unlikely that interfacial systems in biology are at equilibrium; that they are, therefore, rather in steady
state, and that it is possible that the steady state reactions include charge transfer reactions at interfaces.

If these propositions are accepted, it is a matter of finding
out how often a charge transfer reaction is rate determining the
functioning of processes at biological interfaces, and, of course,
later to assess what electrode reactions are occurring there.

REFERENCES

1. J. O'M. Bockris and S. Srinivasan. Nature, 215, 197 (1967).
2. B. V. Tilak, R. S. Yeo and S. Srinivasan. "Comprehensive
    Treatise of Electrochemistry," Vol. II, Ch. 2, eds., J. O'M.
    Bockris, B. E. Conway and E. Yeager (in press).
3. A. L. Hodgkin and A. F. Huxley. J. Physiol., 117, 500 (1952).
4. J. O'M. Bockris and B. E. Conway. Record Chem. Prog., 25(1),
    31 (1964).
5. J. O'M. Bockris and D. Drazic. "Electrochemical Science,"
    Taylor and Francis, London (1972).
6. L. R. Blinks. "Electrochemistry in Biology and Medicine,"
    eds., T. Shedlovsky, Ch. 10, Wiley, New York (1955).
7. G. Neil, D. J. D. Nicholas, J. O'M. Bockris and J. F. McCann.
    Heliotech. and Dev., 1, 481 (1976).
8. J. O'M. Bockris, D. Drazic and A. R. Despic. Electrochem.
    Acta, 4, 325 (1961).
9. J. O'M. Bockris. Joint U.S.-Australian Symp. on Bioelectro-
    chem., Pasadena, CA, July, 1979, Plenum Press, New York (1980).
10. J. O'M. Bockris and A. K. N. Reddy. "Modern Electrochemistry,"
    Vol. II, Rosetta Edition, Plenum Press, New York (1973).
11. L. I. Boguslavsky. "Comprehensive Treatise of Electrochem-
    istry," Vol. I, eds., J. O'M. Bockris, B. E. Conway and E.
    Yeager, Ch. 7, Plenum Press, New York (1980).
12. St. Syorgy. "Electronic Theory of Biology," Methuen, London
    (1948).
13. B. Rosenberg. Nature, 193 (1962).
14. F. W. Cope. Arch. Biochem. Biophys., 103, 352 (1963).
15. M. Del Ducca and Fucsoe. Int. J. Sci. Tech., 212 (1965).
16. J. O'M. Bockris and S. Srinivasan. "Fuel Cells: Their Elec-
    trochemistry," McGraw-Hill, New York, (1970).
17. J. O'M. Bockris. Nature, 224, 775 (1969).
18. C. Wagner and W. Traud. Z. Electrokhim., 44, 391 (1938).
19. U. R. Evans. "Introduction to Metallic Corrosion," Arnold,
    London (1963).
20. J. Tafel. Z. Phys. Chem. (Leipzig), 50, 641 (1905).
21. L. J. Mandel. "Modern Aspects of Electrochemistry," Vol. 8,
    eds., J. O'M. Bockris and B. E. Conway, Plenum Press, New
    York (1973).
22. P. Mitchell. Nature, 191, 144 (1961); FEBS Letts., 78, 1 (1977).
23. J. O'M. Bockris. Energy Res., 2, 9 (1978); J. O'M. Bockris
    and M. S. Tunuli. J. Electroanal. Chem., 100, 7 (1979).
24. J. Appleby, D. Y. C. Ng and H. Winestein. J. Appl. Electro-
    chem., 1, 79 (1971).
25. A. Pilla. Clinical Ortho., 124, 117 (1977).
26. A. Pressman. "Electromagnetic Field Effects on Biological
    Entities," Plenum Press, New York (1971).

SEMICONDUCTING PHOTOACTIVE BILAYER LIPID MEMBRANES

H. Ti Tien
Department of Biophysics
Michigan State University
East Lansing, Michigan 48824

One approach to the problem of understanding photo-synthesis quantum conversion is to investigate the manner in which the thylakoid membrane of chloroplasts achieves many of its physicochemical processes. Ideally, a great deal of information may be obtained from electrical measurements by placing of electrodes across the membrane. However, such an approach is not yet feasible for the thylakoid membrane owing to its small size. Alternatively, pigmented lipid membranes (BLMs and liposomes) are very suited for studying light transduction. This paper is concerned with certain photoeffects observed in pigmented membranes. The results are discussed in terms similar to those that occur at semiconductor/metal interfaces (Schottky barriers). General principles for electron transfer processes across the BLM are discussed. The conversion of light into electrical energy by pigmented BLM are demonstrated, and proposed schemes for the understanding of green plant photosynthesis via the thylakoid membrane are described.

INTRODUCTION

Photosynthesis can be viewed as coupled redox reactions in which water is oxidized and carbon dioxide is reduced. The driving force for the reactions is,

of course, solar radiation mediated by chlorophyll. Van Niel[1]
first proposed this idea in terms of the oxidant (OH) and
reductant (H). In terms of solid-state physics, these entities
are positive holes and negative electrons.[2] If one assumes that
chlorophylls are in an ultrathin liquid-crystalline-like lipid
bilayer,[3,4] absorption of light excites an electron to the conduction band and leaves a hole in the valence band. According to E.
Katz,[5] electrons and holes are free to move around to effect reduction and oxidation, respectively. In other words, chlorophyll
aggregate or chlorophyll dispersed in a lipid bilayer acts as a
semiconductor. The photogenerated electron can be transferred to
an electron acceptor. Similarly, the photogenerated hole can be
combined with an electron donor. That chlorophylls and their host,
the chloroplast, behave as a semiconductor has long been suggested
by many authors including Arnold and others.[4,6,7] To date the
main evidence that semiconduction is relevant to photosynthesis
come from the following sources:

(a) In dried plant chloroplasts and chromatophores
     of bacteria, the dark conductivity varies with
     the absolute temperature,

(b) The dried sample are photoconductive,

(c) The photoconductivity excitation spectra of
     dried materials are very similar to the absorption
     spectra of the chloroplasts,

(d) The photocurrent is dependent on the light intensity
     and

(e) A reconstituted bilayer lipid membrane (BLM)
     using chloroplast extract exhibits both the
     photovoltaic effect and photoconductivity.

Recently, owing to the interest in semiconductor electrochemical photocells for solar energy conversion parallels between
natural photosynthesis and semiconductor photoelectrolysis have
been noted.[8-11] In this paper the focus is on pigmented bilayer
lipid membranes(BLM). In particular experimental data on pigmented
BLM are presented and discussed in terms of the electronic energy
bands of semiconductor/metal (Schottky barrier) contacts.

QUANTUM CONVERSION IN PHOTOSYNTHESIS

As far as the primary events in photosynthesis are concerned,
it seems probable that an electron given up by the chlorophyll to
the electron acceptor on one side and recovered by the chlorophyll
from the donor on the other side of the thylakoid membrane is
moved by an "electron-pump" made of lipoprotein-pigmented complexes. The driving force of the "electron-pump" is provided of course
by the solar energy of light. However, the exact nature of the
primary process by which light is transduced into electrical and/or
chemical energy in green plants remains unclear. What seems clear
at present is the involvement of two primary photoreactions
mediated by chlorophylls.[12,13] The initial quantum conversion
steps are known to be not affected by temperature and have electrochemical characteristics in that chlorophyll-sensitized redox
reactions across the thylakoid membranes are involved. According
to current hypotheses the initial steps in photosynthesis are:
(i) photooxidation of a chlorophyll, (ii) charge separation and
transport of electrons, and (iii) formation of a membrane potential
and a gradient of hydrogen ions, which drive the synthesis of ATP.
All these primary reactions are assumed to take place in some
fashion in PS-I and PS-II which are thought to be spatially
separated in the thylakoid membrane.[12,13] Photons absorbed by
chlorophylls and accessory pigments drive electrons against the
gradient of electrochemical potential from a redox potential of
the H_2O/O_2 couple of about 0.8 volt to that of "X" at about -0.6
volt, resulting ultimately in the reduction of $NADP^+$ to NADPH
(Figure 1).

As already mentioned, Van Niel first proposed the idea of
photosynthetic redox reactions in terms of an oxidant and a
reductant. These entities are positive holes and negative
electrons in terms of solid-state physics.[2] If one assumes that
chlorophyll-protein aggregates in a lipid bilayer act as semi-
conductors, the photogenerated electron can be transferred to an
electron acceptor. Similarly, the photogenerated hole can be
combined with an electron donor. It seems that in natural photosynthesis the advantage of having a membrane separating two
aqueous solutions is twofold: (i) the membrane, besides providing
appropriate environment for the pigments, serves as a barrier to
prevent the occurrence of back reactions of the photoproducts, and
(ii) with the pigments (or photo-systems) located in different
parts of the membrane, the absorption of two photons for each
electron/hole pair generated is possible, thereby providing a
mechanism by which the energy of photons can be upgraded. Figure
1 shows a highly schematic view of the thylakoid membrane in terms
of the two photosystems, redox reactions, and electron transfer.
In this model it is assumed that one side of the thylakoid

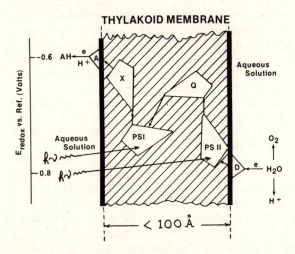

Figure 1.   A highly simplified diagram of Photosystems I and II
in the thylakoid membrane of the chloroplast. PS-I and and PS-II
are the two photosystems located on opposite sides of membrane/sol-
ution interfaces. Also shown is a simplified electron transfer
pathway, where an electron is donated by water to D (probably a
manganese-containing protein). The entire process probably starts
upon absorption of photons by PS-I and PS-II ending with the reduction of NADP+ to NADPH (AH). Q and X are still the unidentified
electron acceptors associated with PS-II and PS-I, respectively.
Note the scheme permits the absorption of two photons per electron
transported across the membrane. The scale on the left indicates
the relative redox potentials of the components of the electron
transfer chain.

membrane functions as a cathode (stroma side) and the other side
as an anode (intrathylakoid side). The photolysis of water by
holes is implicated in the scheme, in which an electrochemical
gradient of hydrogen ions is generated for driving the synthesis
of ATP.[4,14]

If the semiconductor model of photosynthesis outlined above
is of any relevance to the conversion of sunlight into electrical/
chemical energy by green plants, experimental tests are obviously
in order. There are at least two approaches. First, the most
direct kind of experiments would be by placing a pair of micro-
electrodes across the thylakoid membrane and measuring its
electrical properties both in the dark and under illumination.
Indeed, the minuteness and complexity of the thylakoid notwithstanding, Bulychev and colleagues[15] have performed just such an
experiment on giant chloroplasts of Peperomia metallica and
detected a light-induced potential difference. The second approach
to studies of chloroplast photosyntheses is to investigate "reconstituted" model systems. These include various solutions of
chlorophylls[16] pigment-coated electrodes,[17-19] chlorophyll monolayers,[20,21] micelles,[22,23] pigmented bilayer lipid membranes of
both planar and spherical configuration,[4,24,25] and related
membrane systems.[26,27]

In light of what we know about the photosynthetic thylakoid
membrane,[12,28] it is evident that planar bilayer lipid membranes
(BLM) and spherical bilayer lipid membranes (liposomes) are the
nearest model systems with which to investigate energy conversion
processes and redox reactions. In the following, pigmented liposomes and BLM will be described under separate headings.

ARTIFICIAL LIPID BILAYERS

Photoactive Liposomes

Liposomes are lipid microvesicles suspended in an aqueous
medium.[29,30] In this system a bilayer lipid membrane of spherical
configuration encloses a volume of aqueous solution. The literature up to 1978 on photoactive liposomes has been comprehensively
summarized,[4,31,32] so that only recent work directly related to
the topic under consideration will be discussed here.

To mimic light-induced reactions in the thylakoids of chloroplasts, we have formed chlorophyll-containing liposomes separating
two aqueous solutions in the presence of redox agents, as has been
done with the BLM. The experiments were designed to test the
photoassisted decomposition of water. A Clark-type electrode was
used for detecting oxygen. No oxygen evolution was observed after

numerous attempts, however.[33]   In view of these experiments with
negative results we tried a different approach by incorporating
oxygen evolving complexes (OEC) into liposomes.[34]   The OEC used,
which are assumed to be pigment-protein complexes, were obtained
from spinach chloroplasts. Our experience with pigmented BLM has
shown that an intact membrane system of high electrical resistance
is necessary for the generation and separation of charges by light.
Therefore it would also be of interest to demonstrate that a
sealed thylakoid is necessary for oxygen evolution. For these
purposes, two kinds of experiments were carried out: (i) the OEC
were incorporated directly into the lipid bilayer in the process
of liposome formation, and (ii) the OEC were added to preformed
liposomes.[34]   Indeed, we have found that broken thylakoids that
contain OEC, when fused with phosphatidyl choline liposomes,
evolved oxygen profusely. Also, incorporation of OEC into liposomes apparently stabilized the OEC and prolonged the system to
generate oxygen. Along these lines, Spector and Winget[35] have
recently shown that incorporation of a manganese-containing protein
into preformed liposomes can also evolve oxygen.

Photoelectric Bilayer Lipid Membranes

Bilayer lipid membranes(BLMs) of planar configuration are ultrathin structures of molecular dimensions and are usually formed by
spreading a droplet of lipid solution over a small hole in the
wall of a Teflon cup immersed in aqueous solution.[36]   The chlorophyll-containing BLM forming solution is prepared using the standard procedure and the BLM is formed in the usual manner.[4]   A
light intensity of 100-200 mW/cm^2 can be projected onto the BLM
from a tungsten-halogen lamp. A heat filter and a 8-cm water bath
are usually inserted between the light source and the BLM, and the
experimental area is shielded from spurious light. Aqueous solutions containing various compounds are used in different experiments. Many investigators have been able to modify their passive
characteristics by adding substances which endow BLMs with dynamic
properties (for reviews, see references 4, 31, 37). For example,
BLMs containing pigments are photosensitive and have been used as
models for the thylakoid membrane of chloroplasts and the visual
receptor membrane of the eye.[36,38]   These pigmented BLMs are photoelectric in that they are capable of transducing light to elec-
tricity. Here we will discuss only the results of photoelectric
chlorophyll-containing BLMs in terms of a semiconductor model.

Theoretical Considerations

   The BLM formed from chloroplast extracts is pictured as similar to that of a liquid crystal in two dimensions[3] and behaves as
an organic semiconductor. If these assumptions are granted, the

observed photoelectric effects of pigmented BLM are most easily[35] explained in terms of the band theory of semiconductors,[39] with particular reference to the junctions between metals and semi-conductors (SC). These junctions are known as Schottky barriers.[39] Such a Schottky barrier is illustrated in Fig. 2 (left). Since most interfaces are electrified, BLM/H_2O interfaces therefore are expected to possess similar characteristics. The space charge in a Schottky barrier is built up only in the semiconductor (SC) owing to the fact that the metal has a far greater density of charge carriers. Also, in a Schottky barrier, the conduction is electronic and probably takes place by electrons and holes tunnel-ed through the barrier. The potential of electrons (holes) is given by the Fermi level in the SC. In the case of pigmented BLM/H_2O interface, the aqueous solution plays the role of the metal, because it has a much higher density of charge carriers than the BLM. The result is a formation of a space charge region in the BLM at each interface of the membrane. Since the aqueous solution is not an electronic conductor, redox reactions involving ionic species must take place across each BLM/H_2O interface, if an electric current is to flow across the BLM (Fig. 2, right). How-ever, the current within the lipid bilayer may be electronic. For all practical purposes, an unmodified lipid bilayer behaves essentially as an organic SC. Thus, we can also use the Fermi level to describe the electron potential in the BLM. For aqueous solutions bathing the membrane, the chemical potential of electrons (holes) is most naturally described by the redox potentials of the electron acceptors and donors present in the solution. Fig. 3 shows a pigmented BLM separating two aqueous solutions. One of the most important features shown in Fig. 3 is that an ultrathin pigmented lipid bilayer (semiconducting) separates two aqueous solutions (highly conducting). Across the interfaces of such an ultrathin structure, a field of more than 100,000 volts per cm can be easily developed.[40]

Before considering what happens at the two interfaces of a pigmented BLM under illumination, let us complete the band theory of semiconductors as applied to the BLM system. We have already mentioned that a BLM is similar to a two-dimensional liquid cryst-al.[3] Into this array of lipids, two different pigments (or dyes) may be incorporated at opposite sides of the membrane. If these pigments (and/or dyes) were so chosen, one BLM/H_2O interface could be made to behave as a p-type SC in contact with a redox couple and the other interface acted as an n-type SC in contact with a different redox couple. Such a system is shown in Fig. 3, in which the energy levels of conduction band (CB) and valence band (VB) as well as the Fermi level (E_f) for the p-type BLM are indi-cated. E_g stands for the energy gap between the two bands. Illu-mination of such BLM/H_2O interfaces with light of energy greater

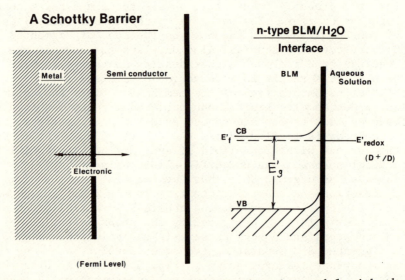

Figure 2.   Comparison of the Schottky barrier model with that
proposed for pigmented BLM/H_2O interfaces. <u>Left</u>: A Schottky
barrier is a junction between a semiconductor and a metal (or an
electrolyte), where space charge is built up only in the semiconductor and no electrochemical reactions take place across the
barrier. Right: Formation of space charge at n-type BLM/H_2O
interface. Aqueous solution contains redox couple D^+/D, CB =
conduction band. VB = valence band, E_g = energy gap, E_f = Fermi
level in the dark, which is the same as E_{redox}. A similar figure
can be drawn for an p-type BLM/H_2O interface (see text).

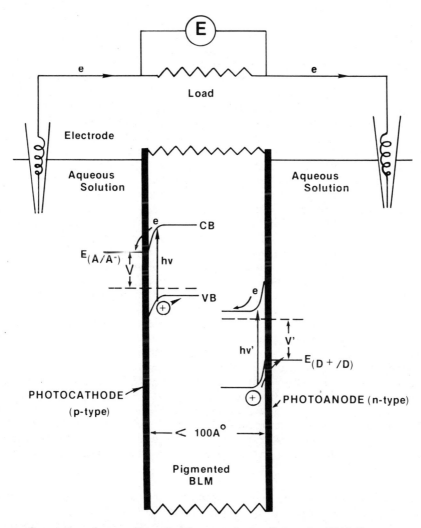

Figure 3.   Complete circuit for a photoelectric BLM for transducing light into electrochemical energy.   The diagram shows the
energy levels for a double Schottky-type BLM.   Charge generation
separation and transfer as well as redox reactions at the interfaces are also indicated (see Fig. 2 for notations).

than E_g (or E_g' for the interface at right) can result in the generation of electron-hole pairs in the space charge regions (depletion layers) where the band bendings have taken place (Fig. 3).
At each BLM/H_2O interface of the space charge region, these pairs are separated by the electric field. At the left region the minority charge carrier (i.e. electron) comes to the BLM/H_2O interface and is available for a reduction reaction, for example,
$A + e \rightarrow A^-$. Thus, the left side of the BLM interface acts as a photocathode, whereas the right BLM/H_2O interface, in which minority carriers for n-type BLM are holes, is the site for oxidation and therefore functions as a photoanode. It should be mentioned that the scheme illustrated, in a sense is analogous to the p-n junction in a photovoltaic cell. One major difference is that, in a solid-state p-n junction device, the majority carriers generated in the bulk of the SC are involved. Of importance to note in Fig. 3 are the relative positions of the conduction band(CB) and the valence band(VB) with respect to the redox level (E_{A/A^-} and $E_{D+/D}$). When the appropriate band overlaps the redox level of the solution, fast electronic transfer across the interface is expected. The maximum output photovoltage, as can be seen in Fig. 3, is the sum of $V + V'$, which is determined by the properties of pigmented BLM and redox couples present in the bathing solutions. At present one can list the factors that govern the photoredox reactions across such a system. These are: (i) the position of conduction band of the p-type BLM (ii) the energy of photogenerated electrons, (iii) the position of valence band of the n-type BLM, (iv) the energy of photogenerated holes, and (v) kinetics of minority charge carrier transfer across the two interfaces. For a double Schottky barrier type BLM, the conduction band of the p-type must be above E_{A/A^-} and the valence band of the n-type must be below the $E_{D+/D}$ as shown in Fig. 3. The depth of band bending region (so-called depletion layer) depends on the density of charge carriers and the magnitude of band bending as in metal/semi-conductor contacts. Efficient separation of electron-hole pairs is believed to take place when the excitons are created in the depletion layer under large field, so that the minor carrier can jump across the interface for a redox reaction.

Finally, insofar as charge separation is concerned, an excited Chl by visible light containing about 2eV of energy presents no difficulty. The difficulty appears to lie in the prevention of the back reaction, which under almost all circumstances is a thermodynamically favored reaction. Nature apparently has solved this problem by evolving an ultrathin, asymmetrical membrane separating two aqueous solutions. Thus, it makes possible, not only the physical separation of products but also at the same time provides two interfaces for carrying out redox reactions in a vectorial manner against the gradient of electrochemical potential.

Further, a membrane system (aqueous solution/lipid bilayer phase/
aqueous solution) possesses two distinct types of microenvironment,
one being the hydrophilic interface and the other hydrophobic lipid
bilayer core, for anchoring the light-absorbing pigment complexes.
It is tempting to speculate that the two photosystems are located
in different regions of the thylakoid membrane. One of the consequences of such a pigmented membrane system with two interfaces
permits the two photoevents operating in concert for upgrading
solar energy. Whether this is the mechanism employed by nature is
not absolutely certain. However, the constructing of an artificial
system based on the Chl-BLM experiments that mimic the ability of
plant chloroplast to transduce solar energy is definitely a project
worth pursuing.

ACKNOWLEDGEMENTS

This work was supported by USPHS Grant BM-14971.

REFERENCES

1.   C. B. Van Niel, Adv. Ezymol., 1, 263 (1941).
2.   R. K. Clayton, "Molecular Physics in Photosynthesis," Blaisdell
     Publishing Co., N.Y. (1965).
3.   H. T. Tien, J. Theoret. Biol., 16, 97 (1967).
4.   H. T. Tine, in " Photosynthesis in Relation of Model Systems"
     (J. Barber, ed.) Vol. 3, 116 (1979).
5.   E. Katz, in "Photosynthesis in Plants "Iowa State College
     Press, Ames, 1949, p. 287.
6.   W. Arnold, J. Phys. Chem., 69, 788 (1965).
7.   G. Tollin, Adv. Rad. Bio., 1, 70 (1964).
8.   G. Porter and M. D. Archer, Interdisciplinary Sci. Rev., 1,
     119 (1976).
9.   H. Gerischer, in "Solar Energy Conversion" (B.O. Seraphin, ed.)
     Topics in Applied Physics, 31, 115 (1979).
10. J. R. Bolton and D. O. Hall, Ann. Rev. Energy, 4, 353 (1979).
11. N. N. Lichtin, Chemtech., 10, 254 (1980).
12. J. Barber, Editor,"Topics in Photosynthesis," 3 vols., Elsevier,
     Amsterdam, 1976-1979.
13. Govindjee and R. Govindjee. J. Sci. Indust. Res., 36, 662
     (1977).
14. G. Hauska and G. Orlich, J. Memb. Sci., 6, 7 (1980).
15. A. A. Bulychev, V. K. Andrianov, G. A. Kurella, and F. F.
     Litvin, Biochim. Biophys. Acta, 420, 336 (1976).
16. G. R. Seely, in "Topics in Photosynthesis, Vol. 2" J. Barber,
     Editor, pp. 1-53, Elsevier, Amsterdam, (1977).
17. W. Haehnel and H. J. Hochheimer, Bioelectrochem. Bioenerget-
     ics, 6, 563 (1979).

18. J. Holoyda, C. R. Kannewuri and J. W. Kauffman, Thin Solid Films, 68, 205 (1980).

19. B. Schreiber and M. Dupeyrat, Bioelectrochem. Bioenergetics, 6, 427 (1979).

20. E. Chifu, M. Tomoaia, Z. Andrei and E. Conciu, Gazz. Chim. Ital., 109, 365 (1979).

21. A. F. Jansen, J. R. Bolton and M. J. Stillman, J. Am. Chem. Soc., 101, 6337 (1979).

22. R. Humphrybe, Y. Moroi, M. Gratzel, E. Pellizzetre, and P. Tundo, J. Am. Chem. Soc., 102, 3689 (1980).

23. M. Almgren and J. K. Thomas, Photochem. Photobiol., 31, 329 (1980).

24. Y. Sudo, T. Kawashima and F. Toad, Chem. Lett., 3, 355 (1980).

25. K. Kano, Y. Tanaka, T. Ogawa, M. Shimomura, Y. Okahata and T. Kunitake, Chem. Lett., 4, 421 (1980).

26. L. M. Loew, S. Scully, L. Simpson and A. S. Waggoner, Nature, 281, 497 (1979).

27. T. S. Snyder, S. H. Chiang and G. E. Klinzing, Solar Energy Materials, 2, 254 (1980).

28. J. T. Duniec and S. W. Thorne, J. Theoret. Bio., 85, 691 (1980).

29. D. Papahadjopoulos, in "Biological Horizons in Surface Science" L. M. Prince and D. F. Sears, Editors, pp. 159-225, Academic Press, N.Y., 1973.

30. A. D. Bangham, M. W. Hill and N. G. A. Miller, in "Methods in Membrane Biology" (E. D. Korn, ed.) Vol. 1, Plenum Press, New York, 1974, pp. 1-68.

31. D. S. Berns, Photochem. Photobiol., 24, 117 (1976).

32. J. H. Fendler, J. Phys. Chem., 84, 1485 (1980); Membrane Mimetic Chemistry, Wiley-Interscience, in press.

33. W. Stillwell and H. T. Tien, Nature, 273, 406 (1978).

34. W. Stillwell and H. T. Tien, Biochem. Biophys. Res. Commun., 81, 212 (1978).

35. M. Spector and G. D. Winget, Proc. Natl. Acad. Sci., 77, 957-959.

36. H. T. Tien, "Bilayer Lipid Membranes(BLM): Theory & Practice," Marcel Dekker, Inc., N.Y. (1974).

37. D. Mauzerall, in "Light-induced Charge Separation in Biology and Chemistry" (H. Gerischer and J. J. Katz, eds.) Dahlem Konferenzen, Verlag Chemie, Berlin, 1979, pp. 241-257; D. Mauzerall and F. T. Hong in "Porphyrin and Metalloporphyrins" K.M. Smith, Editor, Elsevier, Amsterdam, 1975. Chapter 17.

38. F. Gambale, A. Gliozzi, I. M. Pepe, M. Robello, and R. Rolandi, Gaz. Chim. Ital., 109, 441 (1980).

39. V. A. Myamlin and Yu V. Pleskov, Electrochemistry of Semi-conductors, Plenum Press, New York (1967); E. H. Rhoderick, "Metal-semiconductor Contacts," Clarendon Press, Oxford, 1980.

40. H. T. Tien, in "The Chemistry of Biosurfaces", M. L. Hair Editor, pp. 233-348, Marcel Dekker, Inc., New York, 1971.

CHEMISTS AND CARCINOGENS -- EXOGENOUS AND ENDOGENOUS

E. K. Weisburger and T. V. Reddy

Laboratory of Carcinogen Metabolism
National Cancer Institute
Bethesda, Maryland 20205

Reports from several countries indicate that
chemists have an increased risk of developing
neoplasms of the pancreas or lymphatic system.
Laboratory chemists are usually exposed to small
amounts of numerous substances, a condition which
obscures pinpointing the compounds responsible.
However, epidemiologic studies on production workers
in chemical, mining, and allied industries have
indicated that approximately 30 compounds or processes
are carcinogenic in humans. The great majority of
these 30 compounds are metabolized in the body by
enzymes of the P-450 system to activated electrophilic forms which in turn react with cellular
nucleophiles such as proteins, DNA, RNA, lipids, or
other constituents. During the process of carcinogenesis, there may be substantial changes in P-450
levels, as well as in components of the P-450 system
such as phospholipids. Control of cholesterol
synthesis may also be diminished, leading to an
increase in bile acid production, which in turn may
enhance the action of exogenous carcinogens. The
current investigation showed that feeding the nephrotoxic hepatocarcinogen 2-aminoanthraquinone to rats
led to increases in cholesterol and triglyceride
levels in liver, kidney and plasma of male rats.
Female rats showed a similar trend, except for kidney
values. In both sexes total and individual phospholipid levels of hepatic mitochondrial and microsomal
fractions increased. In males total and individual
phospholipids, namely phosphatidyl ethanolamine and

241

phosphatidyl choline, of kidney mitochondrial and
microsomal fractions increased. In females, which are
more susceptible to the nephrotoxic effect, the total
and individual phospholipid values tended to decrease.
N-Butylnitrosourea, a carcinogen with markedly
different structure, causes intestinal tumors in mice.
However, it also led to increases in cholesterol and
triglycerides of liver, kidney, spleen and plasma from
male mice. Total phospholipids and the individual
phospholipids increased, as did total microsomal and
mitochondrial phospholipids of liver and kidney. Thus,
despite their variant sites of action, the two
carcinogens had a similar effect on triglyceride,
cholesterol and phospholipid levels.

INTRODUCTION

In 1969 there was an initial report of a higher than expected
incidence of malignant neoplasms of the pancreas and lymphatic system
among chemists, members of the American Chemical Society.[1] Within
the past several years there have been confirmatory reports from
Sweden[2] and Great Britain,[3] all serving as warning signals to
chemists to evaluate carefully their working habits and possible
exposure to toxic materials. The identification of the responsible
substances is complicated since laboratory chemists usually work
with numerous compounds in the course of a day.

However, production workers in chemical and allied industries
are more likely to be exposed to larger total amounts of single
chemicals, as are persons using certain drugs on a chronic basis.
These populations are more suitable for epidemiological studies
which evaluate on a retrospective basis the possible long-term
toxic effects of such exposures. Such endeavors have shown that
approximately 30 substances or processes are associated with a
carcinogenic effect in humans (Tables I & II). Most, but not all,
of these substances also are carcinogenic in properly conducted
animal tests.[4] Nevertheless, occupational carcinogenesis due to
exposure to chemicals is not a recent development. Highly publicized
is the fact that in 1775 Sir Percivall Pott ascribed scrotal cancer
in chimney sweeps to their occupational exposure to soot. However,
in 1700 Bernardino Ramazzini, the author of "De Morbis Artificium"
attributed the high incidence of breast cancer in nuns to their
celibate life, inherent to their occupation. Current epidemiological
studies concur in the higher risk of this cancer among nuns.[5]
Moreover in 1531 Paracelsus and later Agricola described a disease
among miners in the Schneeberg region of Germany. The ailment,
thought to be tuberculosis of the lung, was later recognized as
carcinoma of the lung.[6] Bladder cancers due to exposure to aromatic

Table I. Chemicals and Industrial Processes Which Are Carcinogenic for Humans.

Substance or Process	Site Affected and Type of Neoplasm	Confirming Animal Tests
4-Aminobiphenyl	Bladder – carcinoma	+
Arsenic and certain compounds	Skin, lung, liver – carcinoma	–
Asbestos	Respiratory tract – carcinoma	+
	Pleura & peritoneum – mesothelioma	
	Gastrointestinal tract – carcinoma	
Auramine manufacture	Bladder – carcinoma	Not applicable
Benzene	Blood – leukemia	–
Benzidine	Bladder – carcinoma	+
Bis(chloromethyl)ether and technical grade chloromethyl ether	Lung – carcinoma	+
Chlornaphazine	Bladder – carcinoma	±
Chromium & certain compounds	Lung – carcinoma	+
Diethylstilbestrol	Female genital tract – carcinoma (transplacental)	+
Hematite mining (underground)	Lung – carcinoma	Not applicable
Isopropanol manufacture (strong acid process)	Respiratory tract – carcinoma	Not applicable
Melphalan	Blood – leukemia	+
Mustard gas	Respiratory tract – carcinoma	+
2-Naphthylamine	Bladder – carcinoma	+
Nickel refining	Respiratory tract – carcinoma	Not applicable
Soots, tars, & mineral oils	Skin, lung, bladder – carcinoma	+
Vinyl chloride	Liver – angiosarcoma Brain Lung – carcinoma Lymphatic system – lymphoma	+

Table II.   Chemicals Which Probably are Carcinogenic in Humans.

Substance	Site Affected (Human)	Confirming animal tests
Acrylonitrile	Colon, lung	+
Aflatoxins	Liver	+
Amitrole	Various sites	+
Auramine	Bladder	+
Beryllium & certain compounds	Bone, lung	+
Cadmium & certain compounds	Kidney, prostate, lung	+
Carbon tetrachloride	Liver	+
Chlorambucil	Blood	+
Cyclophosphamide	Bladder, blood	+
Dimethylcarbamoyl chloride	?	+
Dimethyl sulfate	Lung	+
Ethylene oxide	Gastrointestinal tract, blood	±
Iron dextran	Connective tissue	±
Nickel & certain compounds	Respiratory tract	+
Oxymetholone	Liver	−
Phenacetin	Kidney, bladder	±
Polychlorinated biphenyls	Skin, various sites	+
Thiotepa	Blood	+

amines were reported in 1895 by a surgeon from Frankfurt, approximately 35 years after factories for synthetic dyestuffs had been established. Therefore, the problem has existed for hundreds of years.[6]

However, to be cognizant of the effects of cancer, one has to consider the cell which is the building block for all tissue. When a cell attains a neoplastic or cancerous state, there is a relatively autonomous growth of the cell or the corresponding tissue and lack of the usual regulatory processes which normally govern cell division or function. One example is a pheochromocytoma, a tumor of the adrenal, which instead of producing adrenalin only when needed, produces this hormone continuously. This leads to elevation of blood pressure with concomitant harmful effects. Removal of the tumor usually reverses the symptoms.

The actual growth of a neoplasm, as evidenced by the rate of cell division, may sometimes be very slow, or it may be rapid, approaching that of embryonic tissue. Benign neoplasms or tumors are generally encapsulated and grow slowly. Although they do not metastasize to other organs or invade surrounding tissue, they may compress surrounding tissue by their expansion. Cells in benign tumors usually have relatively normal chromosomes, they are differentiated, that is they maintain relatively normal function, and they divide very little. Malignant neoplasms show abnormal chromosomes, poor differentiation, and frequent division. Furthermore, the neoplasm is not encapsulated, actively invades surrounding tissue and metastasizes to other organs. In this process, individual cells detach and move by the lymphatic or circulatory system to other sites in the organism.[7] The lack of growth control in neoplastic cells may lead to changes in the biochemical components of the cell -- enzymes, lipids and associated substances, DNA, RNA, and proteins, for example.[7] A great deal of effort has gone into determining the normal levels of cell or tissue constituents and comparing those with levels in preneoplastic or neoplastic tissues, in hopes of finding specific markers for a neoplastic condition. Unfortunately, exceptions have appeared which diminish the specificity of determining such values. However, observing the same trend with several indicators increases the probability that a neoplastic condition exists.

To avoid introducing new carcinogens into the environment, several regulations now require testing before a new chemical is distributed commercially. Government agencies, including Health & Welfare of Canada[8] or the Environmental Protection Agency[9] have published guidelines and protocols for the conduct of various short- and long-term tests on such compounds.[9] The cost of conducting these tests, mainly the long-term ones, is high. Nevertheless, it is better to test a new compound, before initiating widespread production and use, than to introduce a new toxic or carcinogenic agent into the environment.

Currently, the EPA recommends that 8 different short-term studies be done which detect gene mutations, chromosomal aberrations, and DNA damage. For definitive animal studies acute, sub-chronic and chronic tests are required. An accepted protocol for a chronic study calls for 50 test animals of each sex and of each species at each of at least 2 dose levels, in addition to the appropriate number of controls.

Many factors must be taken into account when testing any compound for long-term toxicity or carcinogenicity. Compound-related factors are concerned with the stability of the test material, purity, physical state (gas, liquid, solid), reactivity, solubility, and chemical structure. Stability, reactivity, physical state, and solubility are important in selecting the route of administration for any test compound which should also simulate as closely as possible the mode by which the compound contacts any exposed population.[10,11]

Animal-related factors encompass the species and strain of animal used, sex, age, spontaneous tumor incidence, and diet. The importance of diet and its influence in any toxicity or carcinogenicity study cannot be ignored. Low calorie diets may actually decrease the effect of certain carcinogens while deficient diets may enhance carcinogenicity. Augmentation by certain vitamins or other essential factors may also alter any possible carcinogenic effect.[12,13]

Diets may also contain vegetable matter, some of which may induce metabolizing enzymes which decrease the effect of exogenous carcinogens. The cruciferous plants such as brussels sprouts, cabbage, and cauliflower are most effective in this manner.[14,15] Traces of pesticides or antioxidants act in a similar fashion and may also occur in diets.[15] On the other hand, traces of mycotoxins such as aflatoxin B_1, ochratoxin or others may enhance any carcinogenic effect since several of the mycotoxins are themselves carcinogenic. Endogenous formation of nitroso compounds from dietary nitrite or a precursor (nitrate) and secondary amines could also increase carcinogenicity. Many N-nitroso compounds (N-nitrosamines, -amides, or -ureas) are relatively potent carcinogens in all species tested.[16]

The relative amount of lipid in a diet also plays an important role. Excess lipid often leads to excretion of excess cholesterol or formation of bile acids in the gastrointestinal tract. Experimental data show that such components may have a promoting or enhancing action on chemical carcinogens.[17]

Model experiments with skin tumors have shown that promoters or enhancers of carcinogenesis often have a surfactant effect or are closely related to a lipid-like material. The most widely used promoter is tetradecanoylphorbol acetate or TPA, in which the long fatty acid chain, besides the phorbol moiety, probably contributes to its effect. Other surfactants such as some Tweens and Spans act similarly.[18] The function of these materials may be to increase transport of the carcinogen through cell membranes perhaps by enhancing solubility. Dimethyl sulfoxide, sometimes considered a "wonder drug," also increases the relative tumor incidence after painting a polycyclic aromatic hydrocarbon on the skin, probably by enhancing absorption. Since people are exposed to many different substances in the environment, the possible interactive effects of various chemicals in a fashion similar to those mentioned, should be considered to a greater extent than is now done.

Of the approximately 30 compounds or processes considered carcinogenic for humans, some are considered direct-acting or primary carcinogens. Several alkylating agents, often used in treatment of neoplastic diseases, belong to this class, as well as a few industrial intermediates. Such compounds are so reactive that they need no metabolic activation in order to interact with cellular target macromolecules, including RNA, DNA, protein, lipids, or others.

The remainder, which represent the larger portion of human carcinogens, require metabolic activation and are called secondary or procarcinogens. Current theory is that the activation process produces electrophilic moieties which then react with the cellular nucleophiles such as DNA, RNA, or proteins.[19] At present the interactions with nucleic acids are the subject of much interest because these carry the genetic information of the cell. Nevertheless the importance of reactions with proteins, lipids and other constituents should not be overlooked since all these components are necessary for proper cellular function.

The actual metabolic activation pathway for any one carcinogen differs, depending on its structure. Polycyclic aromatic hydrocarbons, typified by the environmental contaminant, benzo[a]pyrene, are first activated by a microsomal cytochrome P-450 monooxygenase system to an epoxide or arene oxide. The cytochrome P-450 system contains not only P-450, an iron-containing protein (hemoprotein),[20] but also NADPH-dependent cytochrome P-450 reductase and a phospholipid component. There are different forms of P-450 reflecting the various monooxygenase activities; estimates range from 6 to hundreds or thousands of such forms.[21-23]

The initial arene oxide formed from benzo[a]pyrene serves as a substrate for the enzyme epoxide hydrase which may convert it to a dihydrodiol. A glutathione conjugate may be produced by glutathione S-transferase. This step eventually leads to excretion as a mercapturic acid or derivative. Nonenzymatic rearrangement of the arene oxide affords phenolic products which are readily conjugated

and excreted. However, further reaction of the P-450 system on the
dihydrodiol from benzo[a]pyrene affords another epoxide which is the
presumed ultimate metabolite, the _anti_ form of the 7,8-dihydrodiol-
9,10-epoxide of benzo[a]pyrene (Figure 1). This compound shows
considerable activity in various short-term tests often employed
to predict possible carcinogenicity and forms an adduct with
nucleic acid (Figure 2).[24] Currently, immunoassays afford the
most sensitive means to determine the level of the adduct in an
animal.

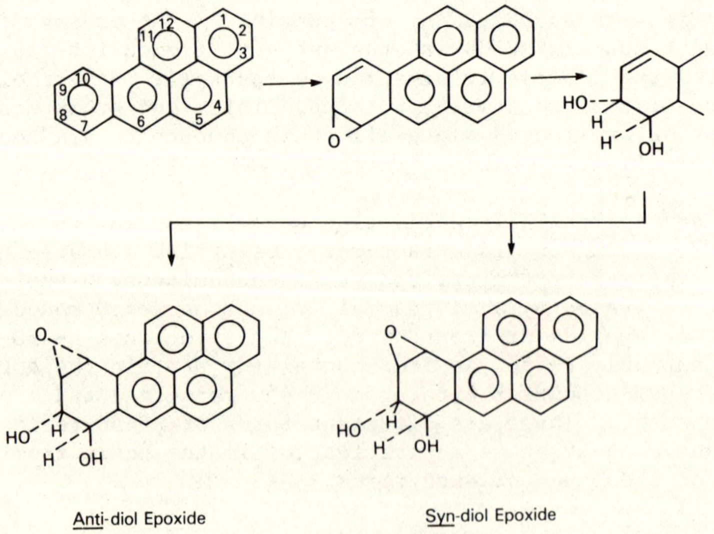

Anti-diol Epoxide   Syn-diol Epoxide

Figure 1.   Metabolism of benzo[a]pyrene to a diol epoxide .

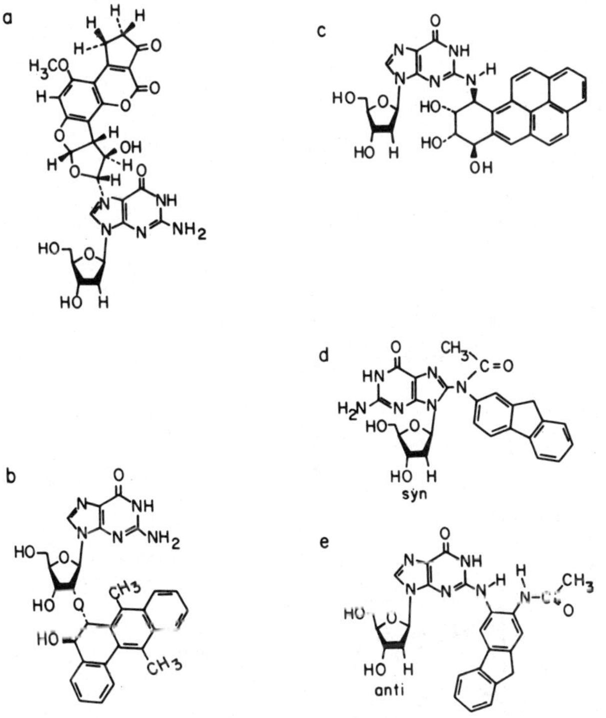

Figure 2. Adducts of activated carcinogens with guanosine of nucleic acids.

a. Adduct of aflatoxin B_1 to N-7 of guanosine
b. Adduct between 7,12-dimethylbenz[a]anthracene and guanosine at the 2'-O of the ribose moiety
c. Benzo[a]pyrene adduct to N^2 of guanosine
d. N-2-Fluorenylacetamide adduct to C-8 of guanosine
e. N-2-Fluorenylacetamide adduct with N^2 of guanosine

Aflatoxin B_1, the potent natural hepatocarcinogen produced by the fungus Aspergillus flavus, is also activated by an epoxide pathway (Figure 3). The epoxide system for activation also holds for some of the halogenated ethylenes, including vinyl chloride and trichloroethylene.

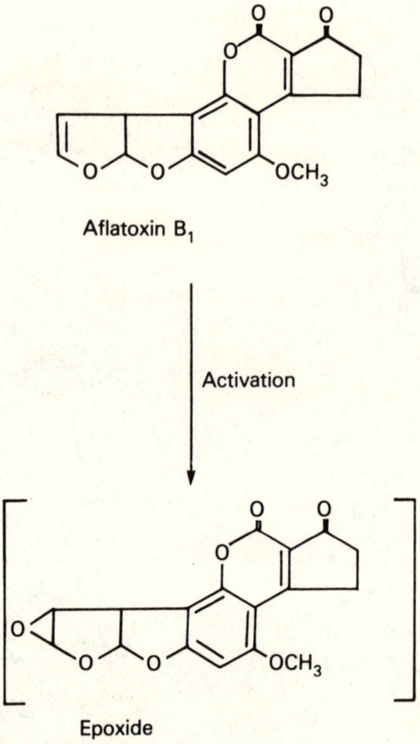

Aflatoxin B$_1$

Activation

Epoxide

Figure 3.   Activation pathway for aflatoxin B$_1$.

On the other hand, aromatic amines and amides, many of which are useful as intermediates in dyestuff and polymer production, are activated by a different mechanism.   The P-450 enzyme system is also involved, but the end results differ.   Ring hydroxylated derivatives of the amine or amide appear to be detoxification products since animal tests have shown no firm evidence of a carcinogenic effect.   However, hydroxylation of the nitrogen atom, also mediated by P-450, is a first step in the activation process (Figure 4).   For most carcinogenic amines or amides, N-hydroxylation is followed by any of several conjugation reactions which provide esters of the N-hydroxy derivative.   These esters such as the sulfate, acetyl ester, glucuronide, or phosphate react readily with proteins or nucleic acids in vitro and are implicated as well in the in vivo reactions.[25]

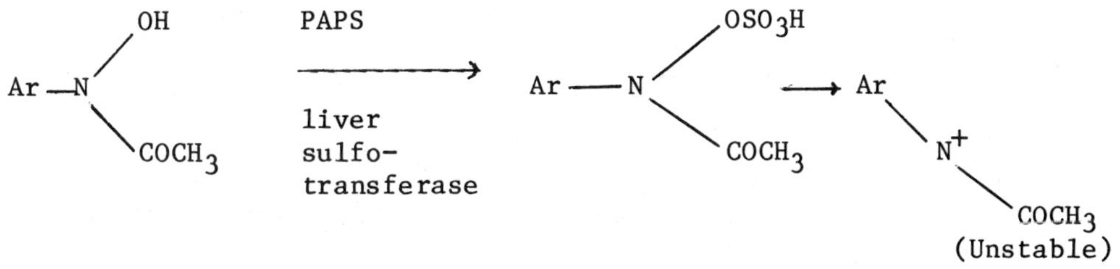

Ar = 2-Fluorenyl
PAPS = Adenosine-3'-phospho-5'-phosphosulfate

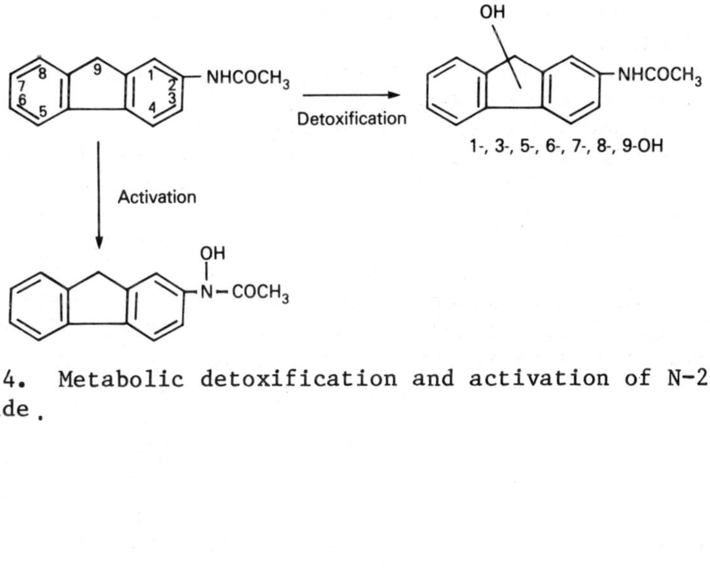

Figure 4.   Metabolic detoxification and activation of N-2-fluorenyl-
acetamide.

    Still another enzymic reaction may be involved in the activa-
tion of N-acetylarylhydroxylamines, namely an N-acyltransferase,
which transposes the acetyl group from the nitrogen to the oxygen
of the N-OH.[26]

$$Ar - N \begin{cases} OH \\ COCH_3 \end{cases} \xrightarrow{\underline{acyltransferase}} Ar - N \begin{cases} OCOCH_3 \\ H \end{cases}$$

                                                    unstable and reactive

The unstable N-acetoxyhydroxylamine reacts readily with transfer RNA, guanosine, and N-acetylmethionine. Such reactions may partially account for the finding that the aminoaryl and not the acetamidoaryl grouping is present to an appreciable extent in covalently bound DNA isolated from reactions of aromatic amines or amides in vivo.

N,N-Dialkylaminoazo dyes are presumably activated by a similar mechanism as the aromatic amides but after initial oxidative removal of one alkyl group by a tertiary amine oxidase.[19,26]

Another type of environmental carcinogen, dialkylnitrosamines and other N-nitroso compounds may also be activated through the P-450 enzyme system. It is envisaged that the initial step is α-hydroxylation of one carbon, yielding a very unstable intermediate. Spontaneous decomposition to a monoalkylnitrosamine occurs; the latter moiety collapses with loss of nitrogen to yield a carbonium ion which is the alkylating intermediate.[27] However, other mechanisms such as ω-oxidation may also be involved, depending on the structure of the nitroso compound. Furthermore many nitrosoureas are unstable under physiological conditions and yield a carbonium ion without the need for metabolic activation. Thus, the P-450 enzyme system is responsible for metabolic activation of diverse types of chemical carcinogens, as well as metabolic detoxification.

$$H_3C \atop H_3C \Big\rangle N - NO \longrightarrow \begin{array}{c} HOCH_2 \\ CH_3 \end{array} \Big\rangle N - NO \longrightarrow CH_3 - \underset{H}{N} - NO + H_2CO$$

                            unstable

$$\downarrow$$

$$CH_3{}^+ + N_2 + H_2O$$

Since phospholipids comprise part of the P-450 system, it was deemed of interest to study the effects certain compounds have on representative phospholipids and some related cell constituents.

The representative compounds were: 2-aminoanthraquinone (2-AAQ) which caused liver tumors;[28] 2,2'-diaminodiphenyldisulfide (DDDS) which led to acanthosis of the stomach;[29] and N-nitrosobutylurea (BNU) which led to intestinal tumors in mice.[30]

MATERIALS AND METHODS

Animals--Male and female 4-week-old Fischer strain rats and male C57Bl/6N mice (NIH animal facility) were used.

Diets--Animals were fed Wayne laboratory meal to which 2-AAQ was added at a level of 2%. Mice injected with BNU received a pellet diet (Wayne). The 2-AAQ diet was stored at 4°C until given to the animals. Controls received Wayne meal.

Preparation of plasma samples--Animals were anesthesized and blood was withdrawn into a heparin-treated syringe. The 3 to 4 ml samples were transferred to heparinized centrifuge tubes and recentrifuged at 2000 rpm at 0-4°C for 10 minutes. An aliquot of the plasma layer was aspirated and frozen at -20°C until used.

Aliquots of the liver, kidney and spleen were taken for the lipid extractions. The remaining tissue was used for subcellular fractionation. This procedure entailed initial preparation of 20% homogenates in phosphate buffered saline (pH 7.2) from each organ. The homogenates were spun at 700 x g for 15 minutes at 0-4°C. The supernatant layer was aspirated and spun at 9000 x g for 20 min. to afford a mitochondrial pellet. The resulting supernatant was spun at 105,000 x g at 0-4°C in a Beckman model L5 75B ultracentrifuge to yield the microsomal pellet. The mitochondrial and microsomal pellets were individually resuspended in phosphate buffered saline. Aliquots were used for the lipid extractions.

Lipid Studies

Plasma lipids--One volume of plasma was extracted 3 times in a 50 ml stoppered centrifuge tube with 10 volumes of a $CHCl_3$:MeOH (2:1 v/v) mixture. If necessary, the tubes were centrifuged at 2000 rpm for 10 minutes to settle any suspension. According to the method of Folch et al.[31] the supernatants were aspirated, combined and all was concentrated in vacuo at 40-50°. The residue was dissolved in $CHCl_3$:MeOH:H_2O (64:32:4, v/v/v) equal to 0.1 volume of the original lipid extract and concentrated twice; the final residue was dissolved in 10 ml $CHCl_3$:MeOH (2:1 v/v), filtered into a stoppered test tube and washed with 2 ml of saline solution to remove non-lipid impurities. After standing with 2 ml of saline overnight, the lower $CHCl_3$ layer was concentrated at 45-50° and made to a known volume with freshly distilled $CHCl_3$ for analysis or storage under nitrogen at -20° until analyses could be done.

Tissue lipids--An aliquot of each tissue was added to 10
volumes of CHCl$_3$:MeOH (2:1 v/v) and blended in a Polytron sonicator
for 2 minutes. The homogenate was allowed to settle overnight and
filtered. The residue was reextracted twice with CHCl$_3$:MeOH (2:1
v/v); the combined filtrates were evaporated in vacuo at 45-50° on
a rotary evaporator.

Analytical Methodology

The procedure of Bartlett[32] as modified by Marinetti[33] was
used for determination of phospholipid phosphorus in the various
lipid extracts and in phospholipid fractions from thin layer plates.

Total Phospholipids

Aliquots of lipid fractions and standard phosphate solutions
(20 ug/ml) were digested with 1 ml of 60% perchloric acid for 15
minutes. Blanks contained perchloric acid. Color was developed
by heating in a boiling water bath after addition of 7 ml distilled
water, 0.5 ml of 2.5% ammonium molybdate solution, and 0.2 ml of
aminonaphthol sulfonic acid reagent. The latter reagent was prepared by dissolving 0.5 g of 1-amino-2-naphthol-4-sulfonic acid
(Aldrich) and 1 g of sodium sulfite in 200 ml of 15% sodium bisul-
fite solution. It was stable for 1 week when stored at 4°C in a
brown bottle. The molybdenum blue formed was determined by reading the optical density at 830 nm (Bausch and Lomb Spectronic 20
colorimeter).

Separation of individual phospholipids: Phosphatidyl choline
(PC) and phosphatidyl ethanolamine (PE). The major individual
phospholipids were separated on thin layer plates (precoated
silica gel plates from E.M. Laboratories) by developing in one
dimension in CHCl$_3$:MeOH:7N NH$_4$OH (230:90:15 v/v)[34] to a distance
of 15 cm from the origin. The PC and PE were identified by comparing the mobilities with authentic standards. The spots were also
visualized by exposure to iodine vapor for 5 minutes in a sealed
chamber. The individual PC and PE bands were scrapped off and
analyzed for phospholipid phosphorus by digesting the gel with 60%
perchloric acid followed by color development as described earlier.
Silica gel digested with perchloric acid served as the blank.

Triglycerides: Glyceride glycerol from lipid extracts of
plasma and tissues was estimated by the method of Van Handel and
Zilversmit.[35] The lipid samples were first saponified with 0.5 ml
of 0.1 N ethanolic KOH at 70°C for 20 minutes. After addition of
0.2 ml of 0.4 N sulfuric acid to liberate the glycerol, 0.1 ml of
freshly prepared 0.05 M sodium metaperiodate solution was added,
and the mixture was allowed to stand at room temperature for 10
minutes. To stop the oxidation of glycerol to formaldehyde and
formic acid, 0.2 ml of freshly prepared 20% sodium sulfite solution

was added, followed by 8 ml of chromotropic acid reagent (0.5 g
4,5-dihydroxy-2,7-naphthalenedisulfonic acid in 10 ml water and
250 ml of 66% sulfuric acid) and all mixed well. The test tubes
were covered with marbles and placed in a boiling water bath for
30 minutes. After cooling the optical density was read at 570 nm.
A tripalmitin standard and a blank were run with each set of
analyses.

Cholesterol: Total cholesterol from the plasma and lipid
extracts was determined according to the method of Searcy and
Bergquist.[36] This involved adding an aliquot of the lipid extract
(50-100 μl) to 6 ml of reagent (filtered solution of saturated
ferrous sulfate in glacial acetic acid), filtering and acidifying
with 2 ml of concentrated sulfuric acid. After 10 minutes the
optical density was read at 490 nm against a blank of 50-100 μl of
$CHCl_3$. Appropriate standards were run for comparison.

RESULTS

2-AAQ - Feeding 2-AAQ in the diet for periods of 2 to 16 weeks
led to consistent increases in liver cholesterol and triglyceride
levels in both male and female rats (Table III). In males similar
results were noted for the kidney (Table IV). However, in females,
triglycerides and usually total cholesterol of the kidney were
decreased. In the plasma total phospholipids, total cholesterol,
and total triglycerides were all increased in both males and
females (Table V).

2-AAQ caused increases in total and individual phospholipids
(phosphatidyl ethanolamine and phosphatidyl choline) of liver and
kidney at all time periods in male rats; in females this trend also
held except that PC was decreased after 4 weeks of feeding and
remained so throughout the 16 week period of the experiment (Tables
VI and VII). In liver mitochondria and microsomes, total and
individual PL were increased in both males and females (Tables VIII
and IX). A similar pattern held for kidney fractions in males but
not in females (Tables X and XI).

DDDS is also an aromatic amine but it had a minimal effect in
animals, causing a hyperplastic reaction but no frank carcinomas.
The trend with this compound was similar -- a general increase in
phospholipid levels of kidney, spleen and liver. Although total
cholesterol levels increased, the triglyceride level per gram of
liver decreased after DDDS.[29]

The target and activation mechanism of N-butylnitrosourea are
different from that of 2-AAQ. Nevertheless, there were increases
in cholesterol, triglycerides, and total or individual phospholipids
in the plasma, kidney, spleen and liver of treated mice (Tables

Table III. Effect of 2-Aminoanthraquinone (AAQ) on Hepatic Cholesterol and Triglycerides of Male and Female Rats.

Feeding period (wk)	Group	Male		Female	
		Total Cholesterol mg/g wet weight	Total Triglycerides mg/g wet weight	Total Cholesterol mg/g wet weight	Total Triglycerides mg/g wet weight
2	CON	5.42 ± 0.22	10.72 ± 0.26	4.32 ± 0.18	9.71 ± 0.30
	AAQ	6.24 ± 0.20[a]	11.48 ± 0.32[b]	4.48 ± 0.16	9.81 ± 0.28
4	CON	5.12 ± 0.20	9.96 ± 0.28	4.45 ± 0.14	9.95 ± 0.32
	AAQ	6.96 ± 0.18[a]	12.14 ± 0.26[a]	5.29 ± 0.20[a]	10.72 ± 0.26[b]
8	CON	5.63 ± 0.16	10.16 ± 0.22	4.85 ± 0.12	10.02 ± 0.24
	AAQ	7.18 ± 0.16[a]	13.38 ± 0.24[a]	5.80 ± 0.16[a]	11.22 ± 0.30[a]
12	CON	5.85 ± 0.20	10.29 ± 0.18	4.79 ± 0.12	10.40 ± 0.36
	AAQ	7.88 ± 0.16[a]	13.97 ± 0.28[a]	6.03 ± 0.16[a]	12.75 ± 0.38[a]
16	CON	6.08 ± 0.15	10.58 ± 0.32	4.81 ± 0.11	11.28 ± 0.22
	AAQ	7.94 ± 0.22[a]	14.86 ± 0.36[a]	5.97 ± 0.14[a]	13.59 ± 0.26[a]

The values are the mean ± SD of 5 rats

[a]Different (p < 0.001) from control

[b]Different (p < 0.005) from control

Table IV. Effect of 2-Aminoanthraquinone (AAQ) on Kidney Cholesterol and Triglycerides of Male and Female Rats.

Feeding period (wk)	Group	Male		Female	
		Total Cholesterol mg/g wet weight	Total Triglycerides mg/g wet weight	Total Cholesterol mg/g wet weight	Total Triglycerides mg/g wet weight
2	CON	7.18 + 0.26	9.74 + 0.48	5.02 + 0.16	4.45 + 0.45
	AAQ	8.22 + 0.16[a]	10.85 + 0.20[a]	5.84 + 0.42[b]	3.95 + 0.14[c]
4	CON	7.46 + 0.18	10.42 + 0.28	5.28 + 0.14	4.62 + 0.18
	AAQ	9.46 + 0.24[a]	11.68 + 0.28[a]	5.74 + 0.26[d]	3.75 + 0.12[a]
8	CON	8.21 + 0.18	10.66 + 0.42	5.79 + 0.18	4.89 + 0.16
	AAQ	10.52 + 0.30[a]	12.48 + 0.18[a]	4.48 + 0.16[a]	3.62 + 0.10[a]
12	CON	8.68 + 0.26	10.82 + 0.18	5.68 + 0.17	4.90 + 0.12
	AAQ	9.78 + 0.28[a]	12.40 + 0.22[a]	4.28 + 0.16[a]	3.50 + 0.11[a]
16	CON	8.42 + 0.24	10.65 + 0.36	5.60 + 0.32	4.82 + 0.10
	AAQ	9.58 + 0.28[a]	12.62 + 0.52[a]	4.15 + 0.21[a]	3.50 + 0.11[a]

The values are the mean + SD of 5 rats

[a] Different ($p < 0.001$) from control

[b] Different ($p < 0.005$) from control

[c] Different ($p < 0.025$) from control

[d] Different ($p < 0.010$) from control

Table V. Effect of 2-Aminoanthraquinone (AAQ) on Plasma Lipids of Male and Female Rats.

Feeding period (wk)	Group	Male			Female		
		Total PL mg/100 ml	Total Cholesterol mg/100 ml	Total TG mg/100 ml	Total PL mg/100 ml	Total Cholesterol mg/100 ml	Total TG mg/100 ml
2	CON	121 ± 14.00	56.43 ± 2.80	246 ± 9.50	112 ± 6.50	53.46 ± 3.65	212 ± 12.00
	AAQ	146 ± 11.20[a]	65.61 ± 3.00[b]	269 ± 6.80[b]	137 ± 8.00[b]	60.28 ± 2.80[a]	244 ± 16.00[c]
4	CON	126 ± 10.80	58.26 ± 1.90	257 ± 10.50	116 ± 5.00	52.74 ± 3.00	210 ± 14.00
	AAQ	152 ± 11.60[c]	67.48 ± 2.60[b]	284 ± 12.00[b]	142 ± 6.00[b]	62.65 ± 4.00[d]	267 ± 10.00[b]
8	CON	129 ± 8.50	54.46 ± 2.40	238 ± 11.00	119 ± 7.20	50.36 ± 2.85	220 ± 16.00
	AAQ	160 ± 14.60[d]	68.12 ± 3.20[b]	276 ± 14.00[b]	149 ± 6.80[b]	61.75 ± 3.10[b]	260 ± 14.00[d]
12	CON	127 ± 8.60	53.56 ± 2.60	242 ± 11.00	122 ± 4.80	51.27 ± 2.60	216 ± 12.00
	AAQ	162 ± 10.80[b]	66.92 ± 2.50[b]	288 ± 15.00[b]	151 ± 5.20[b]	59.63 ± 2.20[b]	258 ± 16.00[d]
16	CON	126 ± 8.20	55.62 ± 3.00	236 ± 8.00	122 ± 6.40	51.85 ± 2.40	208 ± 10.00
	AAQ	160 ± 15.00[b]	67.48 ± 2.60[b]	269 ± 12.00[b]	152 ± 8.60[b]	60.56 ± 3.50[d]	256 ± 12.00[b]

The values are the mean $\pm$ SD of 5 rats

PL = Phospholipids; TG = Triglycerides

[a]Different ($p < 0.025$) from control

[b]Different ($p < 0.001$) from control

[c]Different ($p < 0.010$) from control

[d]Different ($p < 0.005$) from control

Table VI. Effect of 2-Aminoanthraquinone (AAQ) on Hepatic Lipids of Male and Female Rats.

Feeding period (wk)	Group	Male			Female		
		Total PL mg/g wet weight	Individual PL mg/g wet weight PE	PC	Total PL mg/g wet weight	Individual PL mg/g wet weight PE	PC
2	CON	33.28 ± 1.28	8.78 ± 0.42	14.96 ± 0.76	26.23 ± 1.02	7.93 ± 0.52	15.52 ± 0.66
	AAQ	36.47 ± 1.68[a]	10.24 ± 0.66[b]	18.66 ± 0.96[b]	29.58 ± 1.18[b]	9.24 ± 0.48[c]	15.72 ± 0.58
4	CON	32.96 ± 0.95	9.13 ± 0.58	15.24 ± 0.98	27.43 ± 1.16	8.12 ± 0.66	15.95 ± 0.96
	AAQ	38.35 ± 1.48[b]	10.96 ± 0.86[b]	18.42 ± 0.65[b]	31.09 ± 1.86[a]	10.48 ± 0.56[b]	14.55 ± 0.76
8	CON	33.95 ± 1.46	9.77 ± 0.74	15.60 ± 0.82	28.51 ± 1.42	7.92 ± 0.44	15.69 ± 0.92
	AAQ	39.18 ± 1.58[b]	11.48 ± 0.64[b]	19.69 ± 0.55[b]	32.94 ± 1.76[d]	10.52 ± 0.36[b]	13.99 ± 0.45
12	CON	31.68 ± 1.02	9.38 ± 0.56	15.92 ± 0.42	28.01 ± 1.65	8.19 ± 0.28	16.15 ± 0.62
	AAQ	40.83 ± 2.00[b]	11.69 ± 0.44[b]	19.56 ± 0.63[b]	35.25 ± 1.81[b]	10.91 ± 0.52[b]	14.09 ± 0.48
16	CON	31.91 ± 0.98	9.62 ± 0.36	16.28 ± 0.88	27.24 ± 1.92	8.02 ± 0.34	16.40 ± 0.56
	AAQ	40.62 ± 1.88[b]	12.25 ± 0.92[b]	20.04 ± 0.67[b]	35.72 ± 0.98[b]	11.25 ± 0.65[b]	13.98 ± 0.40

The values are the mean ± SD of 5 rats

PE = Phosphatidyl ethanolamine; PC = Phosphatidyl choline; PL = Phospholipids

[a]Different (p < 0.010) from control

[b]Different (p < 0.001) from control

[c]Different (p < 0.050) from control

[d]Different (p < 0.005) from control

Table VII. Effect of 2-Aminoanthraquinone (AAQ) on Kidney Lipids of Male and Female Rats.

Feeding period (wk)	Group	Male Total PL mg/g wet weight	Male Individual PL mg/g wet weight PE	Male Individual PL mg/g wet weight PC	Female Total PL mg/g wet weight	Female Individual PL mg/g wet weight PE	Female Individual PL mg/g wet weight PC
2	CON	31.42 + 1.20	9.02 + 0.26	12.55 + 0.55	29.85 + 1.42	8.42 + 0.43	11.58 + 0.86
	AAQ	34.08 + 1.42[a]	10.78 + 0.32[b]	13.22 + 0.46	30.24 + 1.02	10.78 + 0.58[b]	12.42 + 0.92
4	CON	31.68 + 1.02	9.42 + 0.38	13.02 + 0.48	30.12 + 0.61	9.42 + 0.61	12.16 + 0.68
	AAQ	34.95 + 1.16[c]	11.12 + 0.41[b]	13.85 + 0.66	30.62 + 0.98	10.15 + 0.45	13.18 + 1.00
8	CON	32.04 + 1.62	10.25 + 0.56	13.41 + 0.42	31.80 + 1.18	9.85 + 0.42	13.14 + 0.86
	AAQ	35.86 + 1.48[c]	12.46 + 0.44[b]	14.28 + 0.38[d]	24.54 + 0.85[b]	8.57 + 0.38[b]	10.62 + 0.62[b]
12	CON	33.02 + 1.50	10.18 + 0.48	13.89 + 0.52	32.00 + 1.30	10.10 + 0.68	13.84 + 0.68
	AAQ	36.82 + 1.46[b]	12.06 + 0.52[b]	14.98 + 0.46[d]	15.95 + 0.65[b]	5.85 + 0.32[b]	6.45 + 0.26[b]
16	CON	31.88 + 1.66	10.75 + 0.46	14.74 + 0.33	31.98 + 1.40	10.22 + 0.52	14.17 + 0.88
	AAQ	36.45 + 1.80[b]	12.81 + 0.30[b]	15.62 + 0.46[d]	15.48 + 0.75[b]	6.01 + 0.28[b]	6.47 + 0.32[b]

The values are the mean + SD of 5 rats

PE = Phosphatidyl ethanolamine;   PC = Phosphatidyl choline;   PL = Phospholipids

[a]Different ($p < 0.025$) from control

[b]Different ($p < 0.001$) from control

[c]Different ($p < 0.005$) from control

[d]Different ($p < 0.010$) from control

Table VIII. Effect of 2-Aminoanthraquinone (AAQ) on Hepatic Mitochondrial (9,000 x g pellet) Phospholipids (PL) of Male and Female Rats.

Feeding period (wk)	Group	Male			Female		
		Total PL mg/g wet liver	Individual PL mg/g wet liver PE	PC	Total PL mg/g wet liver	Individual PL mg/g wet liver PE	PC
2	CON	6.26 ± 0.32	1.70 ± 0.08	2.96 ± 0.2	5.98 ± 0.25	1.64 ± 0.09	2.72 ± 0.30
	AAQ	8.75 ± 0.42[a]	2.58 ± 0.12[a]	3.91 ± 0.23[a]	7.42 ± 0.31[a]	2.01 ± 0.10[a]	3.50 ± 0.19
4	CON	6.88 ± 0.28	1.85 ± 0.11	3.36 ± 0.21	6.25 ± 0.35	1.72 ± 0.06	2.98 ± 0.09
	AAQ	9.26 ± 0.52[a]	2.78 ± 0.16[a]	4.52 ± 0.18[a]	7.95 ± 0.24[a]	2.62 ± 0.08[a]	3.99 ± 0.13
8	CON	6.92 ± 0.42	2.15 ± 0.15	3.68 ± 0.24	6.90 ± 0.13	1.88 ± 0.07	3.41 ± 0.10
	AAQ	9.62 ± 0.62[a]	3.22 ± 0.08	5.45 ± 0.26[a]	8.53 ± 0.22[a]	2.85 ± 0.09[a]	4.11 ± 0.11[a]
12	CON	7.22 ± 0.68	2.36 ± 0.06	3.82 ± 0.16	7.02 ± 0.28	2.00 ± 0.11	3.74 ± 0.23
	AAQ	10.09 ± 0.82[a]	3.58 ± 0.08[a]	5.83 ± 0.20[a]	8.83 ± 0.22[a]	3.08 ± 0.13[a]	5.43 ± 0.16
16	CON	6.78 ± 0.65	2.31 ± 0.05	3.76 ± 0.16	7.18 ± 1.24	2.03 ± 0.17	3.82 ± 0.18
	AAQ	10.85 ± 0.78[a]	3.62 ± 0.07[a]	5.94 ± 0.26[a]	9.28 ± 0.35[a]	3.41 ± 0.15[a]	5.60 ± 0.16

The values are the mean ± SD of 5 rats

PE = Phosphatidyl ethanolamine; PC = Phosphatidyl choline; FL = Phospholipids

[a]Different (p < 0.001) from control

Table IX. Effect of 2-Aminoanthraquinone (AAQ) on Hepatic Microsomal (110,000 x g pellet) Phospholipids (PL) of Male and Female Rats.

Feeding period (wk)	Group	Male Total PL mg/g wet liver	Male Individual PL mg/g wet liver PE	Male Individual PL mg/g wet liver PC	Female Total PL mg/g wet liver	Female Individual PL mg/g wet liver PE	Female Individual PL mg/g wet liver PC
2	CON	11.88 ± 0.68	2.86 ± 0.16	5.97 ± 0.28	11.48 ± 0.70	2.88 ± 0.08	5.72 ± 0.26
	AAQ	13.26 ± 0.52^a	3.85 ± 0.18^b	6.64 ± 0.15^b	12.72 ± 0.58^a	3.28 ± 0.10^b	6.08 ± 0.18^c
4	CON	12.58 ± 0.70	3.22 ± 0.15	6.42 ± 0.16	11.81 ± 0.64	3.02 ± 0.10	6.18 ± 0.16
	AAQ	14.45 ± 0.60^d	4.12 ± 0.21^b	7.94 ± 0.19^b	13.26 ± 0.39^d	3.85 ± 0.13^b	6.27 ± 0.18
8	CON	12.69 ± 0.58	3.42 ± 0.16	6.75 ± 0.21	12.14 ± 0.47	3.19 ± 0.16	6.48 ± 0.12
	AAQ	15.27 ± 0.66^b	4.92 ± 0.14^b	8.46 ± 0.22^b	14.02 ± 0.72^b	4.35 ± 0.12^b	7.46 ± 0.09^b
12	CON	12.26 ± 0.48	3.16 ± 0.12	6.44 ± 0.17	12.58 ± 0.52	3.39 ± 0.11	6.52 ± 0.08
	AAQ	15.64 ± 0.88^b	5.22 ± 0.18^b	8.59 ± 0.18^b	14.88 ± 0.68^b	4.98 ± 0.09^b	7.89 ± 0.12^b
16	CON	13.12 ± 0.65	3.46 ± 0.20	6.62 ± 0.12	12.60 ± 0.62	3.40 ± 0.14	6.60 ± 0.11
	AAQ	16.38 ± 0.98^b	5.78 ± 0.16^b	8.82 ± 0.16^b	15.78 ± 0.71^b	5.12 ± 0.12^b	8.72 ± 0.14^b

The values are the mean $\pm$ SD of 5 rats

PE = Phosphatidyl ethanolamine;   PC = Phosphatidyl choline;   PL = Phospholipids

[a] Different ($p < 0.010$) from control

[b] Different ($p < 0.001$) from control

[c] Different ($p < 0.025$) from control

[d] Different ($p < 0.005$) from control

Table X. Effect of 2-Aminoanthraquinone (AAQ) on Kidney Mitochondrial (9,000 x g pellet) Phospholipids (PL) of Male and Female Rats.

Feeding period (wk)	Group	Male Total PL mg/g kidney	Male Individual PL mg/g kidney PE	Male Individual PL mg/g kidney PC	Female Total PL mg/g kidney	Female Individual PL mg/g kidney PE	Female Individual PL mg/g kidney PC
2	CON	6.85 + 0.62	1.62 + 0.08	2.74 + 0.06	6.38 + 0.21	1.55 + 0.06	2.48 + 0.12
	AAQ	7.69 + 0.58	1.98 + 0.11[a]	3.54 + 0.08[a]	6.78 + 0.20[b]	1.60 + 0.05	2.92 + 0.08[a]
4	CON	7.28 + 0.46	1.69 + 0.06	2.97 + 0.10	6.85 + 0.18	1.68 + 0.02	3.02 + 0.06
	AAQ	8.45 + 0.50[c]	2.15 + 0.12[a]	3.98 + 0.12[a]	6.29 + 0.25[d]	1.62 + 0.04	3.02 + 0.08
8	CON	7.85 + 0.30	1.73 + 0.08	2.95 + 0.12	6.87 + 0.24	1.71 + 0.05	2.95 + 0.12
	AAQ	8.92 + 0.36[d]	2.57 + 0.14[a]	5.06 + 0.14[a]	6.79 + 0.16	1.65 + 0.06	2.96 + 0.10
12	CON	7.66 + 0.28	1.98 + 0.11	3.31 + 0.16	7.23 + 0.26	1.82 + 0.08	3.12 + 0.14
	AAQ	9.43 + 0.35[a]	2.82 + 0.12[a]	5.62 + 0.08[a]	6.46 + 0.11[a]	1.45 + 0.06[a]	2.94 + 0.11
16	CON	7.72 + 0.26	1.86 + 0.08	3.42 + 0.11	7.32 + 0.15	1.78 + 0.05	3.30 + 0.16
	AAQ	9.14 + 0.33[a]	3.08 + 0.12[a]	5.96 + 0.16[a]	5.87 + 0.14[a]	1.42 + 0.06[a]	2.78 + 0.06

The values are the mean $\pm$ SD of 5 rats

PE = Phosphatidyl ethanolamine; PC = Phosphatidyl choline; PL = Phospholipids

[a]Different (p < 0.001) from control   [c]Different (p < 0.010) from control

[b]Different (p < 0.025) from control   [d]Different (p < 0.005) from control

Table Xl. Effect of 2-Aminoanthraquinone (AAQ) on Kidney Microsomal (110,000 x g pellet) Phospholipids (PL) of Male and Female Rats .

Feeding period (wk)	Group	Male			Female		
		Total PL mg/g kidney	Individual PL mg/g kidney PE	PC	Total PL mg/g kidney	Individual PL mg/g kidney PE	PC
2	CON	12.75 + 0.65	2.96 + 0.09	6.08 + 0.36	12.75 + 0.80	2.58 + 0.08	5.88 + 0.30
	AAQ	13.42 + 0.72	3.46 + 0.08[a]	7.01 + 0.26[b]	11.23 + 0.40[c]	2.48 + 0.09	5.90 + 0.22
4	CON	12.89 + 0.68	3.21 + 0.16	6.68 + 0.30	12.86 + 0.46	2.90 + 0.06	6.22 + 0.26
	AAQ	14.08 + 0.70[d]	4.18 + 0.12[a]	7.86 + 0.28[a]	10.86 + 0.52[a]	2.58 + 0.07[a]	5.78 + 0.18
8	CON	13.06 + 0.42	3.28 + 0.10	7.02 + 0.32	13.11 + 0.46	3.12 + 0.04	6.88 + 0.21
	AAQ	15.62 + 0.60[a]	4.62 + 0.18[a]	8.48 + 0.22[a]	10.87 + 0.38[a]	2.50 + 0.06[a]	6.02 + 0.20
12	CON	13.52 + 0.40	3.39 + 0.14	7.15 + 0.28	13.27 + 0.36	3.19 + 0.06	7.05 + 0.26
	AAQ	15.98 + 0.52[a]	4.98 + 0.16[a]	8.92 + 0.48[a]	10.80 + 0.28[a]	2.62 + 0.08[a]	5.42 + 0.18
16	CON	13.28 + 0.38	3.18 + 0.12	6.95 + 0.20	13.43 + 0.32	3.00 + 0.06	6.70 + 0.20
	AAQ	16.59 + 0.60[a]	5.26 + 0.18[a]	9.06 + 0.25[a]	10.56 + 0.34[a]	2.46 + 0.08[a]	5.52 + 0.16

The values are the mean + SD of 5 rats

PE = Phosphatidyl ethanolamine;   PC = Phosphatidyl choline;   PL = Phospholipids

[a]Different (p < 0.001) from control   [c]Different (p < 0.010) from control

[b]Different (p < 0.005) from control   [d]Different (p < 0.025) from control

XII-XV). With respect to mitochondrial and microsomal fractions
of the liver and kidney, the increase in phospholipid microsomal
fractions was somewhat higher than for mitochondrial fractions,
but not significantly (Tables XVI and XVII).

DISCUSSION

An extensive review on the role of lipids in cancer appeared
almost 25 years ago.[31] At that time it was known that the phospholipids were essential to the morphological structure of the cell.
The next few years brought the discovery of P-450,[20] its association
with and dependence on phosphatidylcholine for proper function.[38]
Therefore, besides a morphological function, phospholipids play a
role in the metabolism of both endogenous and exogenous substances.
They may also participate in the transport of various ionic or
uncharged molecules through biological membranes.[39] In addition,
receptors for some hormones or antigens may occupy space within the
lipid bilayer of the cell surface. Thus the response to hormones
or hormone-related events may be altered because of the type or
availability of lipids within the cell.[40,41] Phospholipid acts to
modify the physical state of cytochrome oxidase so that the enzyme
can function optimally; it also has a catalytic role in enzyme
activity.[42]

Furthermore, many xenobiotics tend to increase or "induce" the
levels of metabolizing enzymes.[43] Feeding rats with 2-AAQ, one of
the compounds under study, increased the levels of cytochrome P-450
and NADPH-cytochrome C reductase, both components of the P-450 system.
In addition cytochrome b_5, aryl hydrocarbon hydroxylase, epoxide
hydratase, as well as N-demethylases, azo dye reductase, and aniline
hydroxylase all increased.[44]

The increase in these various enzymes or proteins caused by
feeding 2-AAQ or other compounds would necessitate the formation or
construction of additional ribosomes. Concurrently, more lipid is
required, not only for the construction of the cellular membranes,
but also for the proper function of the induced P-450. Recent
studies have indicated the interrelationship between enzyme induction
and the turnover of phospholipids, proteins, and enzymes.[45]

Most of the studies on the changes in phospholipids during the
process of carcinogenesis have come from experiments with aminoazo
dyes (37,46) or with different types of transplanted hepatomas.[47]
However, studies on the laboratory carcinogen N-2-fluorenylacetamide
(FAA) have shown that feeding FAA to rats increased the liver phospholipid level.[48] Serum lipid levels also increased as did the
phospholipid:cholesterol ratio of the plasma membranes.[49]

Table XII. Effect of N-Butylnitrosourea (BNU) on Plasma Lipids of Male C57BL/6N Mice[a] .

Animals Killed at (wk)	Group	Total PL mg/100 ml	Total Cholesterol mg/100 ml	Total Triglycerides mg/100 ml
6	CON	116 + 6.0	48.5 + 1.8	217 + 10.0
	BNU	128 + 4.5[b]	52.8 + 1.4[b]	236 + 8.0[b]
12	CON	124 + 5.2	49.8 + 2.0	219 + 6.0
	BNU	136 + 6.0[c]	54.6 + 1.8[b]	240 + 12.0[b]
18	CON	128 + 7.0	48.8 + 1.5	216 + 9.0
	BNU	144 + 6.8[b]	55.8 + 2.1[c]	242 + 6.5[c]
30	CON	134 + 8.2	50.4 + 1.8	226 + 8.0
	BNU	156 + 7.6[c]	58.4 + 2.3[c]	251 + 6.8[b]

The values are the mean + SD of 6 mice

CON: Controls received only corn oil

PL = Phospholipids

[a]BNU (150 mg/kg) was administered in corn oil as 2 single (i.p.) doses once a week

[b]Different ($p < 0.005$) from controls

[c]Different ($p < 0.001$) from controls

Table XIII. Effect of N-Butylnitrosourea (BNU) on Kidney Lipids of Male C57BL/6N Mice[a].

Animals killed at (wk)	Group	Total PL mg/g kidney	Individual PL mg/g kidney		Total Cholesterol mg/g Kidney	Total Triglycerides mg/g Kidney
			PE	PC		
6	CON	20.65 ± 0.75	5.22 ± 0.28	9.62 ± 0.48	5.62 ± 0.22	7.16 ± 0.60
	BNU	22.98 ± 0.52[b]	6.82 ± 0.30[b]	12.82 ± 0.60[b]	6.28 ± 0.32[c]	8.65 ± 0.38[b]
12	CON	21.08 ± 0.66	5.46 ± 0.22	10.22 ± 0.62	6.08 ± 0.42	7.38 ± 0.52
	BNU	23.86 ± 0.64[b]	7.06 ± 0.42[b]	13.28 ± 0.78[b]	6.86 ± 0.30[c]	8.85 ± 0.46[b]
18	CON	21.68 ± 0.58	5.62 ± 0.26	10.88 ± 0.65	6.12 ± 0.52	7.22 ± 0.48
	BNU	24.62 ± 0.62[b]	7.28 ± 0.48[b]	13.66 ± 0.52[b]	7.42 ± 0.48[c]	9.29 ± 0.62[b]
30	CON	21.55 ± 0.85	5.48 ± 0.22	10.62 ± 0.54	6.26 ± 0.62	7.85 ± 0.64
	BNU	25.35 ± 0.66[b]	7.86 ± 0.36[b]	14.12 ± 0.92[b]	7.86 ± 0.64[c]	10.02 ± 0.72[b]

The values are the SD of 6 mice

PL = Phospholipids; PE = Phosphatidyl ethanolamine; PC = Phosphatidyl choline

CON: Controls received only corn oil

[a]BNU (150 mg/kg) was administered in corn oil as 2 single (i.p.) doses once a week

[b]Different (p < 0.001) from control

[c]Different (p < 0.005) from control

Table XIV. Effect of N-Butylnitrosourea (BNU) on Spleen Lipids of Male C57BL/6N Mice[a].

Animals killed at (wk)	Group	Total PL mg/g spleen	Individual PL mg/g spleen		Total Cholesterol mg/g spleen	Total Triglycerides mg/g spleen
			PE	PC		
6	CON	16.88 ± 0.82	4.01 ± 0.28	8.26 ± 0.46	3.82 ± 0.22	4.28 ± 0.26
	BNU	18.06 ± 0.65[b]	5.48 ± 0.22[c]	10.06 ± 0.38[c]	4.86 ± 0.26[c]	4.48 ± 0.02
12	CON	17.35 ± 0.90	4.38 ± 0.30	8.42 ± 0.39	3.90 ± 0.35	4.58 ± 0.30
	BNU	19.22 ± 0.75[d]	6.02 ± 0.26[c]	10.62 ± 0.40[c]	5.12 ± 0.46[c]	5.34 ± 0.24[c]
18	CON	17.50 ± 0.86	4.30 ± 0.32	8.82 ± 0.56	4.04 ± 0.40	4.96 ± 0.30
	BNU	19.28 ± 0.66[d]	6.32 ± 0.36[c]	10.88 ± 0.32[c]	5.32 ± 0.38[d]	5.56 ± 0.32[e]
30	CON	17.42 ± 0.68	4.52 ± 0.41	8.80 ± 0.50	4.12 ± 0.35	5.41 ± 0.32
	BNU	19.80 ± 0.58[c]	6.58 ± 0.38[c]	11.05 ± 0.58[c]	6.18 ± 0.46[c]	6.08 ± 0.40[e]

The values are the SD of 6 mice

PL = Phospholipids; PE = Phosphatidyl ethanolamine; PC = Phosphatidyl choline

CON: Controls received only corn oil

[a] BNU (150 mg/kg) was administered in corn oil as 2 single (i.p.) doses once a week

[b] Different ($p < 0.025$) from control

[c] Different ($p < 0.001$) from control

[d] Different ($p < 0.005$) from control

[e] Different ($p < 0.010$) from control

Table XV. Effect of N-Butylnitrosourea (BNU) on Hepatic Lipids of Male C57BL/6N Mice[a].

Animals killed at (wk)	Group	Total PL mg/g wet weight	Individual PL mg/g wet weight		Total Cholesterol mg/g wet weight	Total Triglycerides mg/g wet weight
			PE	PC		
6	CON	18.62 + 0.68	4.15 + 0.26	8.82 + 0.44	3.06 + 0.18	6.72 + 0.32
	BNU	23.48 + 0.72[b]	6.64 + 0.32[b]	12.98 + 0.62[b]	3.88 + 0.15[b]	7.86 + 0.35[c]
12	CON	19.58 + 0.70	4.48 + 0.18	9.52 + 0.50	3.42 + 0.20	6.84 + 0.42
	BNU	23.45 + 0.54[b]	7.38 + 0.38[b]	13.45 + 0.70[b]	4.60 + 0.20[b]	8.02 + 0.32[b]
18	CON	20.92 + 0.66	5.06 + 0.24	9.92 + 0.60	3.68 + 0.25	7.22 + 0.46
	BNU	24.28 + 0.82[b]	7.62 + 0.56[b]	13.91 + 0.48[b]	5.28 + 0.18[b]	8.65 + 0.42[b]
30	CON	21.45 + 0.88	5.08 + 0.35	10.02 + 0.53	4.02 + 0.28	7.48 + 0.52
	BNU	25.06 + 0.68[b]	7.60 + 0.52[b]	13.66 + 0.60[b]	5.69 + 0.22[b]	8.42 + 0.44[d]

The values are the SD of 6 mice

PL = Phospholipids; PE = Phosphatidyl ethanolamine; PC = Phosphatidyl choline

CON: Controls received only corn oil

[a]BNU (150 mg/kg) was administered in corn oil as 2 single (i.p.) doses once a week

[b]Different (p < 0.001) from control

[c]Different (p < 0.005) from control

[d]Different (p < 0.010) from control

Table XVI. Effect of N-Butylnitrosourea (BNU) on Liver Mitochondrial (9,000 x g pellet) and Microsomal (110,000 x g pellet)
Phospholipids (PL) of Male C57/BL/6N Mice[a] .

Animals Killed at (wk)	Groups	Total Mitochondria PL mg/g wet liver	Total Microsomal PL mg/g wet liver
6	CON	4.25 ± 0.25	8.08 ± 0.38
	BNU	$5.01 \pm 0..8^{b}$	9.72 ± 0.28^{b}
8	CON	4.45 ± 0.26	8.45 ± 0.30
	BNU	5.65 ± 0.22^{b}	9.88 ± 0.32^{b}
12	CON	4.80 ± 0.30	8.60 ± 0.22
	BNU	6.02 ± 0.28^{b}	10.22 ± 0.30^{b}
16	CON	4.78 ± 0.15	8.96 ± 0.24
	BNU	6.25 ± 0.20^{b}	10.85 ± 0.40^{b}

CON: Controls received only corn oil   PL = Phospholipids

The values are the mean $\pm$ S.D. of 6 mice

[a]BNU (150 mg/kg) was administered as 2 single (i.p.) doses once a
week.

[b]Different (p < 0.001) from controls

Table XVII. Effect of N-Butylnitrosourea (BNU) on Kidney Mitochondrial (9,000 x g pellet) and Microsomal (110,000 x g pellet)
Phospholipids (PL) of Male C57/BL/6N Mice[a].

Animals killed at (wk)	Groups	Total Mitochondrial[b] PL mg/g kidney	Total Microsomal[b] PL mg/g kidney
6	CON	4.58 + 0.22	8.46 + 0.36
	BNU	5.63 ∓ 0.16[c]	10.14 ∓ 0.28[c]
8	CON	4.72 ∓ 0.26	8.66 ∓ 0.41
	BNU	5.98 + 0.18[c]	10.48 + 0.38[c]
12	CON	4.88 + 0.15	8.92 ∓ 0.32
	BNU	6.26 + 0.20[c]	10.98 + 0.44[c]
16	CON	5.02 ∓ 0.14	9.62 ∓ 0.36
	BNU	6.68 ∓ 0.24[c]	11.64 ∓ 0.42[c]

The values are the mean $\pm$ S.D. from quadruplicate samples

CON: Controls received only corn oil   PL = Phosphilipids

[a]BNU (150 mg/kg) was administered as 2 single (i.p.) doses once a
week.

[b]Mitochondria and microsomal fractions were made from pooled kidney
samples from 6 mice

[c]Different ($p < 0.001$) from controls

Thus 2-AAQ fits into a pattern analogous to another hepato-carcinogen, FAA, in that phospholipid, required in the formation of metabolic enzyme systems is increased. This may be a relatively general type of response to toxic or foreign compounds; the relevance to and significance for chemical carcinogenesis still require investigation.

Additionally, the significance of increased cholesterol levels during the carcinogenic process needs further consideration. An increase in cholesterol uptake during feeding FAA,[50] and a rapid uptake of dietary cholesterol in precancerous and cancerous liver[51] were thought due to abnormal cholesterol storage.[52] The pattern for FAA was thus similar to that with the compounds we investigated in that an increase in cholesterol levels occurred.

Cholesterol itself is an intermediate in the synthesis of various steroid hormones and of certain bile acids. Whether the increase in cholesterol leads to greater excretion as such, greater hormone levels, or higher levels of bile acids was not determined. However, there are indications that certain bile acids have an enhancing or promoting action on chemical carcinogens, and not only on those affecting the intestinal tract.[17,53-55] Cholesterol alone has been implicated as a cocarcinogen in human colon.[56] Thus, there may be a cycle during which cholesterol is increased, in turn leading to even more harmful effects by enhancing the action of any carcinogen present. However, much additional research is required to delineate more specifically the role of cholesterol, and phospholipids in metabolic events and eventually in the processes leading to chemical carcinogenesis.

ACKNOWLEDGMENTS

The secretarial assistance of Frances M. Williams is greatly appreciated.

REFERENCES

1. F. P. Li, J. F. Fraumeni, Jr., N. Mantel, and R. W. Miller, J. Natl. Cancer Inst., 43, 1159 (1969).
2. G. R. Olin, Am. Ind. Hyg. Assoc. J., 39, 557 (1978).
3. C. E. Searle, J. A. H. Waterhouse, B. A. Henman, D. Bartlett, and S. McCombie, Brit. J. Cancer, 38, 192 (1978).
4. International Agency for Research on Cancer, "Monograph on the Evaluation of the Carcinogenic Risk of Chemicals to Humans - Chemicals and Industrial Processes Associated with Cancer in Humans," Lyon, France, 1979.
5. M. B. Shimkin, "Contrary to Nature," DHEW Publication No. (NIH) 76-720, U. S. Government Printing Office, Washington, D. C., 1977.

6. W. C. Hueper, "Occupational Tumors and Allied Diseases," Charles C Thomas, Springfield, 1942.
7. R. E. LaFond, Editor, "Cancer - The Outlaw Cell," American Chemical Society, Washington, D. C., 1978.
8. Health and Welfare Canada, The testing of chemicals for carcinogenicity, mutagenicity, and teratogenicity, 1973.
9. Environmental Protection Agency, Fed. Register 43 (no. 163) 37336, 1978.
10. N. P. Page, in "Environmental Cancer, Advances in Modern Technology," H. F. Kraybill and M. A. Mehlman, Editors, Vol. 3, pp. 87-171, Hemisphere, Washington, 1977.
11. E. K. Weisburger, J. Clin. Pharmac. New Drugs, 15, 5 (1975).
12. A. Tannenbaum, Cancer Res., 4, 673 (1944).
13. B. Lombardi and H. Shinozuka, Intern. J. Cancer, 23, 565 (1979).
14. W. D. Loub, L. W. Wattenberg, and D. W. Davis, J. Natl. Cancer Inst., 54, 985 (1975).
15. L. W. Wattenberg, Adv. Cancer Res., 26, 197 (1978).
16. P. N. Magee, Fd Cosmet. Toxicol., 9, 207 (1971).
17. B. S. Reddy and K. Watanabe, Cancer Res., 39, 1521 (1979).
18. T. J. Slaga, A. Sivak, and R. K. Boutwell, Editors, "Carcinogenesis -- A Comprehensive Survey," Vol. 2, "Mechanisms of Tumor Promotion and Cocarcinogenesis," Raven Press, New York, 1978.
19. E. C. Miller and J. A. Miller, in "Chemical Carcinogens," C. E. Searle, Editor, ACS Monograph 173, pp. 737-762, American Chemical Society, Washington, D. C., 1976.
20. R. Sato and T. Omura, "Cytochrome P-450," Kodansha Ltd., Tokyo, Japan and Academic Press, New York, 1978
21. D. W. Nebert, J. Natl. Cancer Inst., 64, 1279 (1980).
22. K. Kawajiri, H. Yonekawa, N. Harada, M. Noshiro, T. Omura, and Y. Tagashira, Cancer Res., 40, 1652 (1980).
23. K. Robie-Suh, R. Robinson, H. V. Gelboin and F. P. Guengerich, Science, 208, 1031 (1980).
24. B. Singer, J. Natl. Cancer Inst., 62, 1329 (1979).
25. C. C. Irving, in "Carcinogens: Identification and Mechanisms of Action," A. C. Griffin and C. R. Shaw, Editors, pp. 211-227, Raven Press, New York, 1979.
26. C. M. King, Cancer Res., 34, 1503 (1974).
27. G. P. Margison and P. J. O'Connor, in "Chemical Carcinogens and DNA," Philip L. Grover, Editor, Vol. 1, pp. 111-159, CRC Press, Boca Raton, Florida, 1979.
28. National Cancer Institute, "Bioassay of 2-Aminoanthraquinone for Possible Carcinogenicity," Carcinogenesis Technical Report Series No. 144, DHEW Publication No. (NIH) 78-1399, 1978.
29. T. Benjamin, R. P. Evarts, T. V. Reddy, and E. K. Weisburger, J. Toxicol. Environ. Health (in press).
30. J. M. Ward and E. K. Weisburger, Cancer Res., 35, 1938 (1975).
31. J. Folch, M. Lees, and G. H. Sloane-Stanley, J. Biol. Chem., 26, 497 (1957).
32. G. R. Bartlett, J. Biol. Chem., 234, 466 (1959).

33. G. V. Marinetti, J. Lipid Res., 3, 1 (1962).
34. D. Abramson and M. Blecher, J. Lipid Res., 5, 628 (1964).
35. E. Van Handel and D. B. Zilversmit, J. Lab. Clin. Med., 50, 152 (1957).
36. R. L. Searcy and L. M. Bergquist, Clin. Chim. Acta, 5, 192 (1960).
37. F. L. Haven and W. R. Bloor, Adv. Cancer Res., 4, 237 (1956).
38. H. W. Strobel, A. Y. H. Lu, J. Heidema, and M.J. Coon, J. Biol. Chem., 245, 4851 (1970).
39. D. E. Green, M. Fry, and G. A. Blondin, Proc. Natl. Acad. Sci. USA, 77, 257 (1980).
40. R. A. Knazek and S. C. Liu, Proc. Soc. Exp. Biol. Med., 162, 346 (1980).
41. C. R. Kahn, D. M. Neville, Jr., and J. Roth, J. Biol. Chem., 248, 244, 1973.
42. M. Fry and D. E. Green, Biochem. Biophys. Res. Commun., 93, 1238 (1980).
43. R. Kuntzman, Ann. Rev. Pharmacol., 9, 21 (1969).
44. R. Ramanathan, T. V. Reddy, and E. K. Weisburger, Fed. Proc., 38, 661, abstr. 2276 (1979).
45. T. Omura, Pharmacology & Therap., 8, 489 (1980).
46. W. J. P. Neish and A. Rylett, Brit. J. Cancer, 14, 737 (1960).
47. K. Y. Hostetler, B. D. Zenner and H. P. Morris, Cancer Res., 39, 2978 (1979).
48. K. R. Rees, G. F. Rowland, and H. F. Ross, Biochem. J., 82, 347 (1962).
49. N. Chandrasekhara and K. A. Narayan, Cancer Res., 30, 2876 (1970).
50. B. J. Horton and J. R. Sabine, Europ. J. Cancer, 7, 459 (1971).
51. B. J. Horton, G. E. Mott, H. C. Pitot, and S. Goldfarb, Cancer Res., 33, 460 (1973).
52. B. J. Horton, J. D. Horton, and H. C. Pitot, Cancer Res., 33, 1301 (1973).
53. Y. Hiasa, Y. Konishi, Y. Kammamoto, T. Watanabe, and N. Ito, Gann, 62, 239 (1971).
54. B. S. Reddy, Cancer, 36, 2401 (1975).
55. B. S. Reddy, T. Narasawa, J. H. Weisburger, and E. L. Wynder, J. Natl. Cancer Inst., 56, 441 (1976).
56. P. Cruse, M. Lewin, and C. G. Clark, Lancet, i, 752 (1979).

DISCUSSION

On the paper by B. Lindman

E. T. Reese, FSL WU.S.Army Lab, Natick, MA :
  1. I believe you said that the half-life of a surfactant molecule in a micelle is of the order 10^{-3} seconds. Is there a reference to how this was determined?
  2. Are there available comparable values for surfactant at water-air interface and phospholipid in biomembrane?

B. Lindman:
  1. The time is ca. 10^{-5} seconds for SDS micelles. The pioneering work on this is Ref. 4.
  2. Not that I know of.

D. Balasubramanian, University of Hyderabad, India:
  1. Are benzene, naphthalene, and pyrene surface-active? Mukerjee thinks the former two are, while Menger thinks water penetrates inside the micelle to regions near the solubilized hydrocarbon.
  2. Would the micelle microstructure be different for elaidate (9 trans) micelles from oleate (9 cis) micelles?
  3. Would someone comment on any recent work on the aggregation of surfactants as regular micelles (polar groups outside, alkyl groups as the core) in pure solvents other than water?
  4. Would you amplify on the results of volumetric studies on micelles that suggest that water does not penetrate into the body of the surfactants in micelles (Bergen work).

5. Do you think (or have evidence to think) that introduction of keto groups in the middle of a surfactant, e.g., a
keto hexadecyl trimethylammonium bromide, might lead to a bending
of the chain as a U, leading to the keto group in the interfacial
surface in contact with water?

B. Lindman:
1. Arguments against water penetration are given in the
paper as well as views on the site of solubilization of aromatic
compounds.
2. I have seen no information on this but there should be
moderate differences due to different packing conditions.
3. The strongly cooperative surfactant association should
be restricted to aqueous solutions but the behavior in non-
aqueous strongly polar solvents is of great interest.
4. Partial molar volumes of amphiphile alkyl chains and of
alkanes are closely the same in micelles and in pure alkanes, see
text.
5. The presence of a keto group certainly should influence
the micelle structure in some way. One possibility is what you
propose, another is that a keto group may permit water inside a
micelle; perhaps both effects are present. This would be interesting to study.

C. Jolicoeur, *University of Sherbrooke, Canada:*
1. Is it possible to determine, if any, the number of water
molecules involved in the hydration of α , β , ... etc., the
methylene groups in sodium carboxylate soap micelles?
2. Are the opposite effects of $RCOO$ and RSO_4 on the
chemical shift of ^{23}Na due to intrinsic properties of these
groups (e.g., polarizabilities) or to other phenomena (e.g.,
hydration)?

B. Lindman:
1. The question you raise is a very important one. We are
hoping to design an NMR experiment soon which can tell a little
about this, but maybe your own studies can provide the answer
before.
2. We would highly appreciate suggestions on this point! We
have suggested previously (J. Am. Chem. Soc. **97**, 3923 (1975))
that in the case of $- COO^-$ there is significant hydrogen-bonding
between head-group and water of counterion hydration while this
should be relatively unimportant for $- SO_4^-$. The very different
pKa values may be taken as some support for such a difference.
They hydrogen-bonding should be strengthened by the counterions
polarizing the water molecules; this effect should be larger for
a smaller "naked" ion. We think therefore that there is an
interplay between hydration and polarizability.

R. G. Laughlin, *Procter & Gamble Co., Cincinnati, OH*: There is an exceedingly large difference in the basicity of carboxylate vs. sulfite groups. Is there any direct evidence for hydrogen bonding to the sulfite group?

B. Lindman: I believe that this point is highly important and the different basicities would indicate the absence of a significant hydrogen-bonding for sulfonate end-groups. As far as I know there is no direct evidence for hydrogen-bonding to sulfonate either. This is in line with our interpretation of various counterion NMR studies.

C. H. Spink, *SUNY-CORTLAND, Cortland, NY* : Is there evidence that water penetration of the micellar core is increased when the micelles bind nonpolar solutes in solubilization reactions?

B. Lindman: The relation between solubilization and micelle hydration is a point that we certainly should study system-atically. We think there is evidence against a significant water penetration of the micellar core and certainly this should hold also in the presence of nonpolar solubilizates. The polar part of a surfactant is hydrated in micelles and this hydration can probably be very sensitive to solubilization in the outer parts of a micelle. It seem likely that this solubilization should reduce solubilization slightly but further experimental work is needed to clarify this.

On the paper by A. Ben-Naim

N. Mazer, *MIT* : Does your data and/or theoretical analysis suggest how the magnitude of the hydrophobic interaction, itself, varies as a function of pressure?

A. Ben-Naim: The answer is no. In order to study the pressure dependence of the hydrophobic interaction, one must examine the sign of the volume change which is associated with the process of the hydrophobic interaction, namely

$$\delta V^{HI} = \frac{\partial \delta G^{HI}}{\partial P}$$

278   DISCUSSION

C. A. Bunton, *University of California, Santa Barbara* : There
may be dipole interactions between vicinal alkoxy groups in the
1,2-dialkoxynaphthalenes. Will these interactions depend on the
solvent, e.g., on its dielectric constant? These interactions
would be essentially absent in the 1,7(?) isomer.

A. Ben-Naim: It is true that if the two isomers have different
dipole moments, that their interaction with the solvent will be
different. In our measure of the hydrophobic interactions, this
difference in the interaction energy is included in the quantity
that is referred to as the intramolecular hydrophobic interaction.

B. Yarar, *University of British Columbia, Canada*: Please comment
on (1) the nature of the forces leading to hydrophobic association and (2) the range of these forces.

A. Ben-Naim:
    1. The nature of the hydrophobic forces is not simple to
explain. It is still far from being understood. The reason is
that the origin of these forces comes from the organization of
the water molecules around the solute particles, and not from any
property of the solute themselves.
    2. There are some simulation studies of the hydrophobic
interaction, but these are still incomplete. There is, so far, no
experimental method that would tell us the range of these forces.
However, from the related information on the radial distribution
function of liquids (including water), one can expect that the
range of these forces does not extend beyond a few molecular
diameters.

On the paper by M. Tanaka, S. Kaneshina, G. Sugihara,
N. Nishikido and Y. Murata

N. Mazer, MIT : Does your data and/or theoretical analysis
suggest how the magnitude of the hydrophobic interaction, itself,
varies as a function of pressure?

M. Tanaka: The volume change on micellization, $\Delta \bar{V}_m$, decreases
with increasing pressure and changes from positive to negative

value through the pressure P_{max} where the c.m.c. is maximum. The $\Delta\bar{V}_c$, the amount of the contribution of hydrophobic group to $\Delta\bar{V}_m$, is the predominant contribution to $\Delta\bar{V}_m$ and shows the same pressure dependence as that of $\Delta\bar{V}_m$. The partial molal volume of the hydrophobic group is larger in the micelle than in the aqueous environment in the lower pressure region, and the situation reverses itself in the higher pressure region, because the compressibility of the hydrophobic group in the micelle, the interior of which is in liquid state, is larger than that in the aqueous environment. If the increase of the magnitude of the hydrophobic interaction is interpreted as the promotion of the aggregation of hydrophobic molecules in water, it might be said that the magnitude of the hydrophobic interaction decreases with increase of pressure in the lower pressure region, while it increases in the higher pressure region.

The amount of contribution of hydrophobic group to the partial molal volume of surfactant is water, $\bar{V}_c$, decreases monotonically with increasing pressure, and the partial molal entropy $\bar{S}_c$ can also be said to decrease, because ($\partial\bar{S}_c/\partial P)_T = -(\partial\bar{V}_c/\partial T)_P$ < 0. If the increase of the magnitude of the hydrophobic interaction implies an enhancement of the interaction between the hydrophobic molecule and water, the decrease of $\bar{V}_c$ and $\bar{S}_c$ with pressure is consistent with an increase of the magnitude of the hydrophobic interaction, such as the promotion of water structure (iceberg) in the immediate vicinity of the hydrophobic molecules.

R. Zana, CNRS, *Strasbourg, France*:

$$\Delta\bar{V}_m = (1 +\beta)RT(\frac{\partial\ln\ CMC}{\partial P})_T . \Delta\bar{G}_m$$

Equation (2), of your paper relating volume change upon micellization of the pressure dependency of CMC must satisfy the condition that the aggregation number is independent of pressure. Although you have shown that aggregation number changes with pressure, yet you have estimated $\Delta\bar{V}_m$ using Equation (2), that ignores this condition of constancy of aggregation number with pressure. Could you comment on this?

J. Desnoyers, *Universite de Sherbrooke* : As the direct measurement of $\Delta\bar{V}_m$ by compression study gives a fairly good agreement with that estimated from the above equation, especially in the case of SDeS. Neglect of the condition of constancy of aggregation number with pressure is not serious.

G. Sugihara: I and P. Mukerjee have recently estimated the contribution of aggregation number change with pressure to the volume change on micellization, and confirmed that this contribution is indeed negligible. Therefore the use of Equation (2) in the calculation of $\Delta\bar{V}_m$ seems to be justified.

On the paper by L. A. Singer

R. Zana, CNRS, Strasbourg, France : Could you comment further on
the site of solubilization of arenes and present the arguments
for and against their solubilization close to the polar head
groups?

I would like to point out that we have recently obtained
evidence in favor of a solubilization in the palisade layer, at
least of pyrene, from experiments involving the change of pyrene
fluorescence lifetime τ , upon addition of alcohols (butanol to
hexanol) to a micellar solution of tetradecyltrimethylammonium
bromide (TTAB). In the absence of alcohol, τ is small because of
the quenching of bromide ions. As alcohol is added and is incorporated in the palisade layer, with its OH group in contact with
water, bromide ions dissociate from the micelles and the lifetime
is sizeably increased. This, we believe, shows that pyrene is
dissolved close enough to the surface to be quenched by the
bromide ions which can never penetrate the micelles. Note that
the alcohols that we have used loosen up the micelle structure
and decrease the micelle aggregation number and one cannot argue
that their addition make the micelle more compact (R. Zana and P.
Lianos, unpublished results).

L.A. Singer: In my opinion, the weight of evidence indicates
solubilization of the nonpolar arenes at, or very near, the
surface of ionic micelles. Typical observations of spectroscopic
experiments (uv-vis, nmr) are reviewed in my manuscript. I
believe that such experiments must be carried out carefully with
consideration for the ratio of [probe]/[micelle]. (Fendler and
Patterson) An important conclusion from the experiments with
benzene is that the average microenvironment sensed by the probe
at a low [probe]/[micelle] is more polar than at a high [probe]/
[micelle]. As benzene is added, water appears to be displaced
from the micelle. (Ericksson and Gillberg) An earlier anomalous
result was the inability of Br$^-$ to quench the fluorescence of
perylene in the CTAB micelle which seems to indicate solubilization of this probe in the hydrophobic interior. (Patterson and
Vieil) I recently learned that this result is associated with an
intrinsically low rate of quenching for this system (Patterson,
private communication) and so does not require that perylene
reside far from the water-micelle interface.

J. B. Nagy, Facultes Universitaire de Namur, Namur, Belgium   :
You did not mention in your general scheme on ground and excited
states the possible presence of charge-transfer states. How do
these states influence the quantum yield or the fluorescence
lifetime of the molecules?

L. A. Singer: With many polar probes, a change in microenvironment from polar (aqueous) to less polar (micellar) leads to
a dedrease in the quantum yield and increase in lifetime of the
fluorescence. Such changes could occur if there is a closelying
charge-transfer state that mixes with the S_1 (π,π^*) state to
greater or lesser degrees in polar and nonpolar media, respectively. The rate of singlet to triplet intersystem crossing is
expected to increase with an increase in CT character of the
lowest excited singlet state. Therefore, as the polar probe
microenvironment is changed from aqueous to micellar, and as the
CT character of the lowest excited state decreases, the rate of
intersystem crossing decreases which directly leads to an increase in the fluorescence quantum yield and a longer fluorescence lifetime (assuming no change in the rate of radiative
decay of the S_1 state). Note that the influence of medium
polarity on fluorescence yield and lifetime in systems containing
carbonyl groups (such as pyrenecarboxaldehyde) is further complicated because of the opposite energetic responses of n, π^*
and π,π^* states to changes in medium polarity.

On the paper by C. H. Giles

D. Smialowicz, *American Cyanamid Corp.* : Can you provide the
source of data on the adsorption phenomena in the biological
field?

C. H. Giles: This is given in my manuscript.

On the paper by M. Che and Y. Ben Taarit

J. B. Nagy, *Facultés Universitaire de Namur, Namur, Belgium:*
     1. (Comment) I think it is important to underline here that
the resemblance between zeolites and reversed micelles is much
greater than with the normal micelles. This is due to the fact,
that in reversed micelles one can have a partially "naked" metal
ion (as in zeolite), while in normal micelles, the metal ions
remain always solvated.
     2. What is the influence of the electric field on the
surface acidity (geometry of distribution of the acidic sites)?
     3. How many water molecules can solvate a single acidic
site?
     4. I think evan Na^+ can interact specifically with olefins
or aromatic molecules, because of its partially solvated state.

Y. Ben Taarit:
1. I agree with the comment, yet the zeolite surface is a more complex concept than for nonporous solids, precisely because of a very limited external surface which is the geometrical surface and a rather <u>large</u> and <u>accessible internal</u> surface and an as large <u>internal hidden</u> surface. So that due to the distribution of cations among these two surfaces zeolites are rather thought of as a hybrid pertaining to both reversed and normal micelles.
2. The presence of a strong electric field is likely to increase the polarization of incoming molecules thus contributing to a higher mobility of the hydroxyl protons.
3. Few attempts were aimed at determining the number of water molecules solvating a single acidic (Brönsted) site. H_3O^+ was suggested but never seriously considered. H_9O^+ (H^+, $4H_2O$) was considered in the case of ZSM5 zeolites as the strong acid site which would convert methanol to hydrocarbons but was never characterized.
4. Na^+ ions should probably interact specifically with olefins but the interaction should be different and looser than with transition metal ions. Benzene interaction with Na^+ has been reported and actually seems to perturb significantly the aromaticity of the molecule.

On the paper by E. K. Weisburger and T. V. Reddy

V. K. Meyers, *Southern Illinois University* : Many Category I carcinogens which you mentioned -- such as antineoplastics which are alkylating agents, nitrosamines, some antibiotics produced by molds, and polynuclear hydrocarbons -- are also classified as suspected teratogens, namely compounds which cause birth defects when taken by pregnant animals or humans. As a matter of fact, about 30% of Category I carcinogens are also suspected teratogens. Also, out of 527 suspected teratogens (teratogenicity based on animal or human studies; source: "Registry of Toxic Effects of Chemical Substances", by Niosh) about 30% are Category I or suspected carcinogens. Can you comment on relationship between carcinogenicity and teratogenicity?

E. K. Weisburger: As far as I am aware there is no firm or well documented relationship between teratogens and carcinogens. The mechanisms of action, according to present concepts, are entirely different.

Part II

Thermodynamics and Kinetics
of Micellization in Aqueous Media

INVESTIGATION OF MICELLAR BEHAVIOR BY PULSE RADIOLYSIS

L.K. Patterson

Radiation Laboratory and Department of Chemistry
University of Notre Dame
Notre Dame, Indiana 46556

With pulse radiolysis techniques it is possible, on the nanosecond time scale, to generate a non-equilibrium distribution of transient species whose interactions with micellar media may be characterized in kinetic terms. Because of the wide variety of species that can be produced in this manner, such investigations have been shown useful in the study of (a) counterion-surface interactions, (b) monomer-micelle dynamics (c) substrate-micelle distributions. Further the effects of a heterogeneous environment on processes involving biologically important compounds have also been studied by pulse radiolysis in micelles. A brief review of this approach to micelle kinetics is given here.

INTRODUCTION

Over the past ten years, it has been shown that the techniques of radiation chemistry may be usefully applied to the study of micelle behavior. In particular, the use of pulse radiolysis allows interactions between transient species generated in the aqueous phase and components of the micellar pseudophase to be time resolved well into the nanosecond region. There are approximatly 50 published reports concerning application of this technique to the study of surfactant systems[1]. Such studies have proven useful in characterizing certain facets of micellar structure and dynamics as well as in exploring some radical processes of biochemical interest which show significant dependence on the microenvironment in which they occur. Additionally, it has been possible to investigate the kinetics of unstable intermediates which, due to hydrophobic character of the parent material, could not be generated in water radiolytically. The use of pulse radiolysis in studies of micelle phenomena is briefly reviewed here to illustrate the conditions under which the technique is applicable and the type of information that may be gleaned from it.

WATER RADIOLYSIS

Radiolysis of water generates several well characterized species of varying reactivity: e_{aq}^-, $\cdot OH$, $\cdot H$, H^+, H_2O_2.[2] Some of these may, in turn, react to produce secondary species with specific properties. The generation of a number of such secondary particles which have found utility in micelle studies is outlined in Figure 1. The assumption is inherent that these species are distributed homogeneously throughout the solution aqueous phase.

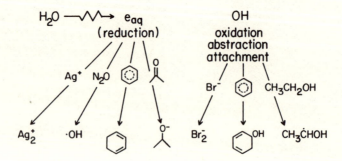

Figure 1. Outline for production of various secondary transient species from e_{aq}^- and $\cdot OH$ in pulse radiolysis.

The primary radicals e_{aq}^-, •OH, and •H are produced in dilute
solutions at relative concentrations of 1:1:∅.2; and the latter,
•H, has not been much utilized in such studies. It is possible,
by means of proper scavengers to eliminate either e_{aq}^- or •OH.
As evident from figure 1, e_{aq}^- may be replaced by an equivalent of
•OH in N_2O containing solutions. Hydroxyl radicals may be made to
react with various alcohols (e.g. t-BuOH) via hydrogen abstraction
to produce relatively stable alcohol radicals, hence effectively
removing •OH and leaving only e_{aq}^-. It can also react very efficiently with most surfactants. Such strategies provide the
experimentalist with considerable control over the initial radical
species present in solution.

    The pulse radiolysis technique itself involves use of a time
resolved spectrophotometer in whose sample chamber transients may
be produced by pulses of ionizing radiation. Opical changes in the
sample during the period following the radiolytic pulse may be

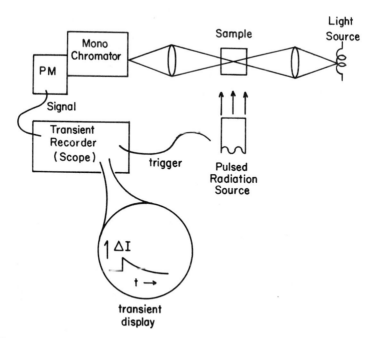

Figure 2. Schematic diagram for the pulse radiolysis apparatus.

monitored on an oscilloscope or, in more recent instruments, captured
on a transient recorder. An outline of the basic apparatus is given
in Figure 2 and detailed descriptions may be found in various texts.
Many such instruments are now highly automated, facilitating the
ease of data aquisition and providing great latitude in analysis.[3,4]

MICELLE INTERACTIONS WITH CHARGED RADICAL SPECIES

Hydrated Electrons

Because of the very high surface potentials exhibited by ionic
surfactant micelles, the reaction kinetics of charged radicals can
be markedly altered in micellar solutions. The initial pulse radiolysis measurements in surfactant systems were determinations of
e_{aq}^- reactions with benzene in the presence of sodium lauryl sulfate
(NaLS), cetyltrimethylammonium bromide (CTAB) and Igepal Co-730.[5,6]
These experiments clearly demonstrated the non-reactivity of e_{aq}^-
toward NaLS or CTAB and further, demonstrated the effects of
surfactants on e_{aq}^- capture by benzene, accelerating the rate in
CTAB and inhibiting it in NaLS. A number of similar measurements
were reported with hydrophobic aromatic hydrocarbons which partition
more strongly in the micellar pseudophase than does benzene.[7,8]
Such determinations confirmed the general trend of micellar effects
on e_{aq}^- reactions.

Simple negative repulsion of like charges was suggested for
NaLS and negatively charged intermediates.[9,10] Indeed this assumption was used by Infelta et. al.[10] to determine distribution constants in NaLS for substrates (CH_3NO_2, CH_3I) reactive with e_{aq}^-.
The assumption was made that only material in the aqueous phase
will encounter the electron. More recently a similar approach has
been taken to determine the partition coefficient for naphthalene[11]
in NaLS. It might be noted here that Henglein and co-workers have
suggested that some substrates in NaLS with sufficiently high
electron affinities may capture e_{aq}^- via a tunneling mechanism.[12]

Reaction of e_{aq}^- with substrates in positively charged micelles
such as CTAB is somewhat more complex. It is possible to concieve
of three types of interactions between electron (or any other anion)
and an oppositely charged micelle surface: a) surface capture of the
electron; b) lateral motion upon the micellar surface; c) intermicellar transfer by which the anion leaves the field of one
aggregate and enters another. These processes are illustrated in
Figure 3. A measure of e_{aq}^- capture at the micellar surface was
made with cetylpyridinium chloride micelles (CpyCl) in which e_{aq}^-
was found to be annihilated by pyridinium cation at diffusion con-
trolled rates. Measured rates of $k_{(e_{aq}^- + micelle)} = 5 \times 10^{12} M^{-1} sec^{-1}$
indicate the magnitude of surface electrostatic interaction with
e_{aq}^-.[13] Further, studies of CTAB -CpyCl mixed micelles demonstrated
that the e_{aq}^- once captured could move on the surface (Fig. 3b) to

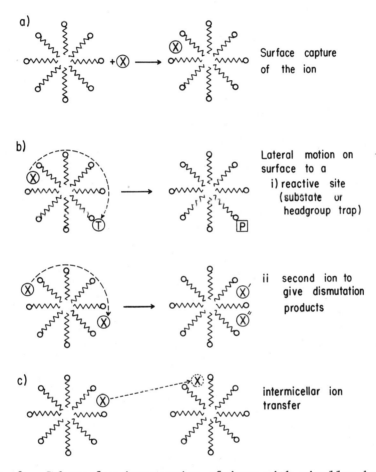

Fig. 3.   Scheme for interaction of ions with micelles having headgroups of opposite charge.

find a reaction site in very short time (c.a. t < 10 nsec.)[14] Further, it was found that electrons can indeed undergo intermicellar transfer (Fig. 3c) at rates dependent on CTAB concentration.   A parameter for characterizing movement among micelles to a reactive site (T) may be defined in terms of the fraction of micelles occupied by (T) which determines the average number of jumps required to find an occupied micelle, and in terms of the overall halflife for electron annihilation in the micelle system: $t_t = t_{1/2} (M_{oc}/M_{tot})$ where $t_{1/2}$ is the e_{aq}^- halflife, M_{oc} is the concentration of occupied micelles and M_{tot} is the total number of micelles.   Such halftimes for transfer determined from the CTAB-CPyCl system are given in Table I. These results strongly indicate that the residence time on the micelle ultimately limits the movement of electrons through solution. This may be illustrated by reconsidering the data from several determinations of rate constants for electron capture by arenes in CTAB micellar solution.[8,15]   In each case chosen, average occupancy of the micelles by arene was less than unity.   From the rate constant and the ratio of micelle to arene, intermicellar transfer or "hopping" half-times (t_t) were calculated on the assumption that e_{aq}^- trapped to occupied micelles always undergo reaction.   It may be seen from Table I that the values so calculated are in good agreement with those determined in mixed micelles.   The most significant variation appears in those arenes showing some water solubility where, especially at low concentrations, t_t will appear to be high.   In the case of naphthalene, correction could be made for this solubility using the partition coefficient of Evers et al.[11] Such correlation infers: a) rate constants for such systems calculated via pseudo first-order kinetics are predominantly governed by intermicellar electron transfer; b) reactions in the micelle with solubilized arenes are highly efficient.   The latter point is substantiated in the lack of dependence exhibited by such reaction on substrate electron affinities in cationic micelles compared to anionic cases.[15]

    Some measurements of e_{aq}^- reaction with sobulized substrates have been carried out in nonionic surfactant micelles where charge interaction is absent.[6,17,18]   In each case some inhibition to reaction was observed although varying from substrate to substrate. Such findings would indicate a limited barrier to the passage of electrons from the aqueous phase into the micelle or would indicate environmental changes altering the reactivity of e_{aq}^- toward substrate.

Secondary Radical Ions

    While the above studies provide some insight into the movement of ions among micelles, the time frame is such that little information may be obtained concerning behavior on the micelle surface. As seen above, the time for e_{aq} movement to an active site on CTAB is at the experimental limit.[14] However, several studies have been carried out with radical ions and micelle surfaces of opposite

Table I.   Intermicellar Transfer Times for e_{aq}^- in CTAB Micelles
Containing Electron Scavengers.

Scavenger	$[CTAB] \times 10^2 M$	Transfer time, nsec.	Ref.
Cetylpyridinium Chloride, conc varied.	1.0	40 ± 5	14
	5.0	23 ± 4	
	10.0	12 ± 2	
Pyrene, 5×10^{-5}M	1.0	38	15
	5.0	14	
	10	9	
Biphenyl 3.2×10^{-4}M	5.0	39	8*
$8. \times 10^{-4}$		27	
Naphthalene 5×10^{-5}M	5.0	31**	
5×10^{-4}		23	
Fluorene 2.7×10^{-4}	5.0	41	
Phenanthrene 5×10^{-4}	5.0	20	

---

* Because of high scavenger concentration in these systems the
fraction of occupied micelles was calculated from the Poission
distribution formula

$$f = \sum_{i=1}^{\infty} \frac{n^{-i} e^{-n}}{i!}$$

where n is the _average_ occupancy and i is the number of traps per
micelle.

** The concentration of naphthalene occupying the micelles was
determined assuming the partition coefficient of ref. (11).

charge[18,19,20]; understanding of the micelle surface as a vehicle for reducing the dimensionality of second order reactions has been gained.

In each case the disproportionation of radical ion, Ag_2^+ or Br_2^- was monitored as a function of surfactant concentration, and in each case a biphasic decay was observed. Whether the system was Ag_2^+ in NaLS or Br_2^- on CTAB the investigators attributed the slow decay to reactions in the bulk phase and the initial fast decay to reaction on the surface (fig. 3bii). Since in each case disappearance of the radical proceeds by second order processes, the proportion of radicals disappearing in different time ranges will depend on the proportion of micelles that are multiply occupied. This can be varied by both dose and surfactant concentration. Both systems gave results consistent with a Poisson distribution of radicals among micelles, a finding which provides considerable confirmation for the mechanism.

The data from the Br_2^- disproportionation in CTAB was modeled in terms of a two dimensional random walk on the unbound cationic amine head groups. Using Montroll calculations the authors were able to accurately predict Br_2^- behavior and provide values which suggest a movement from site-to-site on the surface of about 20 nsec,[18] significantly slower than the upper limit placed on comparable electron movement. In another study, a residence time of 15 μsec was derived for Br_2^- residence time on a singly occupied micelle,[20] a much smaller value than for Ag_2^+ in NaLS.[19]

These studies from several laboratories, taken together, may be seen to provide considerable insight into the influence of charged surfaces on ion movement and into the mechanism by which significant alteration in reaction kinetics may occur.

HYDROXYL RADICALS

By contrast with e_{aq}^-, hydroxyl radicals are highly reactive with most surfactants, the predominant reaction being a hydrogen abstraction from the hydrocarbon chain. It was established in early studies that above the CMC, reactivity of ·OH toward surfactant molecules decreases by an order of magnitude.[6,21] In part, this may be due to a drop in the number of targets as monomers aggregate into fewer large units. Additionally the head groups may form a barrier to passage of ·OH from the water phase to the hydrocarbon core.

The generation of such radicals and their subsequent kinetics has been usefully exploited to provide information on micellar dynamics. As these radicals differ from the parent surfactant monomers only by the removal of a single H atom (or by ·OH addition) they provide excellent probes with which to time resolve the behavior of individual surfactant monomers. Two studies have been carried out to determine entry and exit rates in the micellar equilibrium

$$Mo + M_n \overset{k^+}{\underset{k^-}{\rightleftharpoons}} M_{n+1} \tag{1}$$

where mo is monomer incorporated into a micelle of n units (M_n) to give a micelle of n+1 units (M_{n+1}). Henglein and Proske determined the monomer entry rate k^+ into micelles of sodium 1-(6'-dodecyl-benzene-sulfonate) by monitoring disappearance of the radical formed via OH reaction.[22] It was assumed that the radicals would only disproportionate in the aqueous phase (k_1) or by double occupancy of a micelle (k_2) the latter of which should be very efficient Here $R_{mi}^{\cdot}$ and $R_{mo}^{\cdot}$ are radicals in micellar and monomeric form.

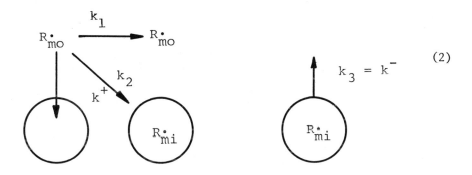

$$(2)$$

By varying the concentration of surfactant and developing an expression for the overall disappearance of R$\cdot$ by both rates they obtained $k^+ = 4 \times 10^8\ M^{-1}sec^{-1}$ and $k^- = 8 \times 10^{-5}\ sec^{-1}$. These were found to be in good agreement with values derived from relaxation measurements on the same system. This technique for obtaining k^+/k^- may be seen simple to apply and appears chiefly limited by the spectral accessibility of the radical absorption.

A second technique is that of Almgren et al.[23] in which surfactant radical may be oxidized by ferricyanide according to

$$R\cdot + Fe(CN)_6^{3-} \xrightarrow{\ H_2O\ } ROH + H^+ + Fe(CN)_6^{4-} \tag{3}$$

This reaction comes into competition with the monomer-micelle equilibrium of equation (1). In this system one may follow the bleaching of the ferricyanide to determine rates of reaction. Also, where the surfactant under study is anionic one may safely assume no association of ferricyanide and the micelle. From changes in the rate of reaction (3) with NaLS it was possible to extract values of k^- and k^+ in good agreement with literature values. The strength of this approach lies in not requiring radicals with intense optical absorption. Because of this the authors were able to successfully extend the technique to determine distribution constants for various alcohols between the aqueous and micellar phase.

MICELLES AS MODELS IN RADIATION BIOLOGY

Micellar effects on radiation induced reaction with various substrates of biological interest (pyrimidines,[24,25] purines,[26] violigen,[27] porphyrins,[28] and chlorophyll[29]) have been studied by pulse-radiolysis in a number of laboratories. Several of these involve reduction of the substrate by e_{aq}^- in a micelle either to (a) simulate to some degree a lipid-like environment (b) obtain sufficient concentration of a water insoluable substrate to make possible the study of radical reactions. As in the studies mentioned above, charge on the surfactant is a dominant factor in determining kinetics. Further, for some cases the water solubility of the substrate complicate the analysis of kinetic results. One system unrelated to e_{aq}^- processes but particularly suitable to pulse radiolysis measurements is the radiation induced peroxidation of poly-unsaturated lipids.

In biological systems significant damage to lipid components can occur by a radical induced mechanism. Although the process may be initiated in several ways, the use of ionizing radiation allows considerable control over the extent of reaction, and facilitates a more detailed study of the mechanism. The general scheme for such peroxidation is

$$RH \qquad R\cdot \qquad\qquad\qquad \text{initiation} \qquad\qquad\qquad (4a)$$

$$(R\cdot_p \qquad R\cdot_c)$$
$$R\cdot_c + O_2 \qquad R_cO_2\cdot$$

$$R_cO_2\cdot + RH \qquad R_cO_2H + R\cdot \qquad \text{propagation} \qquad\qquad (4b)$$

$$2R\cdot_c \qquad x \qquad\qquad\qquad \text{termination} \qquad\qquad\qquad (4c)$$
$$2RO_2\cdot \qquad x$$

where RH is a methylene-interrupted moiety of the form

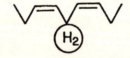

Upon loss of a hydrogen at the high liable doubly allylic site a conjugated radical   or

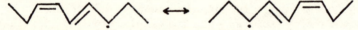

is formed ($R_c\cdot$). The absorption of this radical has been found to be very intense and hence is an excellent probe by which to time resolve various components of the chain mechanism given above.[30] The initiation step takes place by $\cdot$OH abstraction of a hydrogen from a site along the lipid chain though not necessarily at the doubly allylic site. This precursor radical may be labeled $R_p\cdot$. It has been found that the radical $R_c\cdot$ can be produced either by

intramolecular H transfer within $R_p^\cdot$ when the lipid is in monomeric
form or intermolecular •H, transfer when $R_p^\cdot$ is incorporated
into a micelle. The use of various radicals with different abilities
to abstract •H may be used to test selectivity of reaction at the
doubly allylic site. Values for the rate of radical peroxidation
have been measured in various fatty acids and the termination steps,
which depend highly on the radical environment, have been kinetically
characterized.[31] The method of Henglein and Proske, when applied
to the latter process, allows determination of entry and exit rates
for individual lipid molecules.[30]

Additionally, it has been possible to obtain information concerning processes of antioxidation by incorporating normally water
insoluble α-tocopherol into the micelle system. The α-tocopherol
blocks the lipid degradation by competition with the propagation step
via donation of an H• atom from a phenolic site.

$$AH + RO_2^\cdot \qquad A\cdot + RO_2H \qquad\qquad (5)$$

The subsequent α-tocopherol radical produces an intense transient
absorption easily monitored in the visible region and provides a
basis for determining rate constants for reaction 5 in different
lipid environments.

The rate constants obtained from this type of study are summarized in Figure 4. It should be pointed out that a limitation

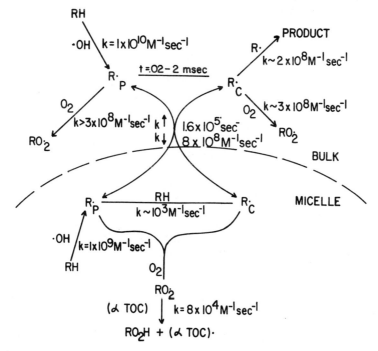

Figure 4. Kinetics for reactions in the lipid chain peroxidation
mechanism determined by pulse radiolysis.

of the pulse radiolysis technique-the necessity for fairly high
radical concentration-makes extremely difficult the study of the
propagation step (4b) in the peroxidation mechanism. At radical
concentrations required, the termination steps strongly influence
the behavior of the $RO_2^{\cdot}$ radical.

SUMMARY

The facility for producing non-equilibrium distributions of
easily monitored transient species by pulse radiolysis has provided
the micelle chemist with a variety of information concerning the
kinetics of charge interaction involving the micellar surface and
information concerning the movement of molecules across the micelle-
water boundary. Further, this technique has made it possible to
study transient behavior of biologically important species in a
heterogeneous environment. The information obtained by this technique and its generally applicability to micelle phenomena may be
seen to extend well beyond the limited regime of radiation chemistry.

ACKNOWLEDGMENT

The research described herein was supported by the Office of
Basic Energy Sciences of the Department of Energy. This is Document
No. NDRL-2111 from the Notre Dame Radiation Laboratory.

REFERENCES

1.   Numbers taken from the Notre Dame Data Center Computer files.
2.   M.S. Matheson and L.M. Dorfman, "Pulse Radiolysis", M.I.T. Press
      Massachusetts, 1969.
3.   L.K. Patterson and J. Lilie, Int. J. Radiat. Phys. Chem. 6,
      129 (1974).
4.   R.H. Schuler and G.K. Buzzard, Int. J. Radiat. Phys. Chem. 8,
      563 (1976).
5.   J.H. Fendler and L.K. Patterson, J. Phys. Chem. 74, 4608 (1970).
6.   K.M. Bansal, L.K. Patterson, E.J. Fendler and J.H. Fendler,
      Int. J. Radiat. Phys. Chem. 3, 321 (1971).
7.   S.C. Wallace and J.K. Thomas, Radiat. Res. 54, 49 (1973).
8.   J.H. Fendler, H.A. Gillis and N.V. Klassen, J. Chem. Soc.,
      Faraday Trans. I, 70, 145 (1974).
9.   L.K. Patterson, K.M. Bansal, G. Bogam, G.A. Infante, E.J.
      Fendler, J.H. Fendler, J. Am. Chem. Soc., 94, 9028 (1972).
10.   P.P. Infelta, M. Gratzel, and J.K. Thomas, J. Phys. Chem.
      78, 190 (1974).
11.   E.L. Evers, G.G. Jayson, I.D. Robb and A.J. Swallow J. Chem.
      Soc., Faraday Trans. I, 76, 528 (1980).
12.   M. Gratzel, A. Henglein and E. Janata, Ber. Bunsenges. Phys.
      Chem. 79, 475 (1975).

13. M. Gratzel, J.K. Thomas, and L.K. Patterson, Chem. Phys. Lett. 29, 393 (1974).
14. L.K. Patterson and M. Gratzel, J. Phys. Chem., 79, 956 (1975).
15. M. Gratzel, J.J. Kozak and J.K. Thomas, J. Chem. Phys. 62, 1632 (1975).
16. A.J. Frank, M. Gratzel, A. Henglein and E. Janata, Ber. Bunsenges. Phys. Chem. 80, 547 (1976).
17. T. Proske, Ch-H. Fisher, M. Gratzel and A. Henglein, Ber. Bunsenges. Phys. Chem., 81, 7711 (1977).
18. A.J. Frank, M. Gratzel, J.J. Kozak, J. Am. Chem. Soc. 98, 3317 (1976).
19. A. Henglein, and Th. Proske, Ber. Bunsenges. Phys. Chem., 82, 471 (1978).
20. Th. Proske and A. Henglein, Ber. Bunsenges. Phys. Chem. 82, 711 (1978).
21. L.K. Patterson, K.M. Bansal, and J.H. Fendler, Chem. Commun., 152 (1971).
22. A. Henglein and Th. Proske, J. Am. Chem. Soc. 100 3706 (1978).
23. M. Almgren, F. Grieser and J.K. Thomas, J. Chem. Soc. Faraday Trans. I, 75, 1674 (1979).
24. L.K. Patterson, K.M. Bansal, G. Bogan, G.A. Infante, E.J. Fendler and J.H. Fendler J. Am. Chem. Soc. 94, 9028 (1972).
25. J.H. Fendler, E.J. Fendler, G. Bogan, L.K. Patterson, K.M. Bansal, J. Chem. Soc. Chem. Commun. 14 (1972).
26. C.L. Greenstock, I. Dunlop, Int. J. Radiat. Phys. Chem. 5, 237 (1973).
27. M.A.J. Rodgers, D.C. Foyt, and Z.A. Zimek, Radiat. Res. 75, 296 (1978).
28. E.L. Evers, G.G. Jayson, and A.J. Swallow, J. Chem. Soc. Faraday Trans. 74, 418 (1978).
29. J.P. Chauvet, R. Viouy, E.J. Land, and R. Santus, C.R. Hebd. Seances Acad. Sci., Ser. D, 288 1423 (1979).
30. L.K. Patterson and K. Hasegawa, Ber. Bunsenges. Phys. Chem. 82, 951 (1978).
31. K. Hasegawa and L.K. Patterson, Photochem. Photobiol. 28, 817 (1978).
32. L.K. Patterson and K. Hasegawa, Radiat. Res. (In press).

FREQUENCY DISTRIBUTION SHIFTS IN MICELLAR KINETICS

Gerson Kegeles

Section of Biochemistry and Biophysics
The Biological Sciences Group
The University of Connecticut
Storrs, Connecticut   06268

A modified mass-action distribution model, the
so-called shell model for micellar systems, has been
recently published by the author. This model simu-
lates the critical micelle concentration behavior of
such systems. An internally self-consistent closed
form solution for the relaxation kinetics of the
initial process immediately following perturbation,
in micellar systems following this model, has been
published by the author during the year of this
Symposium. This has also for the first time fit the
relaxation time behavior down to infinite dilution.
With the aid of this equilibrium distribution and
application of the standard rate equations of chemical kinetics for the interaction of a monomer molecule with another monomer and each oligomer unit,
the instantaneous rate of change of the molar and
equivalent concentration of every oligomer throughout the distribution has been computed numerically
with a digital computer. This type of recursive
computation is similar to, but simpler than the
recursive calculations first published in 1961 by
J. L. Bethune and the author, for simulation of the
flow of reacting solutes in forced diffusion problems.
With these digital computer calculations, it has been
possible without further specialized assumptions to
predict the "overall" kinetics of such systems over a
long period of time, and to predict the local details
of frequency shifts in the micellar distribution as a
function of time.

INTRODUCTION

An early attempt to calculate the equilibrium distribution of
oligomers in a micellar system according to straightforward mass-
action law considerations was published by Meyer and van der Wyk[1].
Hoeve and Benson[2] used statistical mechanics to compute micellar
distributions which are not infinitely sharp. Mukerjee[3] has concerned himself in detail with equilibrium properties of micellar
systems, and criteria for a critical micelle concentration condition.
The relaxation kinetics of micellar systems were first studied[4,5]
experimentally in 1965 and 1966. Muller[6] first noted that a more
rapid process was measurable by nuclear magnetic resonance methods
than had yet been found by relaxation techniques. He explained
the rapid process as one of single monomer addition to or dissociation from micelles, and the slow process as one developing from
a large cascade of sequential applications of precisely the same
rate equations for such processes. He also characterized the slow
process as one in which a micelle would eventually dissociate completely into monomers. Nakagawa[7] and Lang et al.[8] further emphasized the importance of the equilibrium distribution of micelles in
the interpretation of their kinetic behavior. The latter authors
also pointed out that both the rapid process and the slow process
were measurable by relaxation techniques driven by pressure[9,10].
Sams, Wyn-Jones and Rassing[11] developed a theory for the rapid
process consistent with the picture that the ratio of forward to
reverse rate constants is the reciprocal of the free monomer concentration above the critical micelle concentration. They did not
treat the slow process in that study. While they predicted that a
plot of the reciprocal relaxation time for the fast process inter-
sects the concentration axis at the critical micelle concentration,
Nakagawa[7] reviews a number of computations in which such a plot
may extrapolate to positive, zero or negative values at infinite
dilution. In a series of recent papers, Aniansson et al.[12-16]
have treated both the fast and the slow processes in their theory
of relaxation kinetics of micellar systems. Their original starting
assumptions for the fast process were that the forward and reverse
rate constants for monomer-micelle interaction were approximately
independent of micelle size, instead of varying linearly according
to Sams et al.[11]. Aniansson et al.[12-14] also assumed a Gaussian
starting distribution of micelles, which would not be reached with
these assumed rate constants. In their more recent papers[15,16],
these authors develop the theory for both time domains from a
single set of rate constants consistent with the originally assumed
type of equilibrium distribution of micelles. This theory makes
use of the positive residual value for the reciprocal relaxation
time at the CMC to obtain information about the width of the micelle
distribution, and the most recent paper by Wall and Aniansson[16]
also predicts more details of the processes taking place, for a
number of cases, through computer simulations.

In a recent study[17], I have proposed a modified mass-action law model for the equilibrium distribution of micelles which predicts behavior consistent with the attributes of critical micelle concentration behavior. The initial kinetic consequences of such a shell model distribution have been examined[18] in a study which also provides a closed form solution versus concentration for the initial reciprocal relaxation time of the fast process. In the examples being presented below, the coupled kinetic rate equations for the elementary reaction steps involving all oligomers in such a starting distribution have been approximately linearized and solved numerically with a digital computer. The computation has been recycled by using as the new monomer concentration that produced by the entirety of monomer-micelle interactions occurring in a very short time in parallel, an approximate procedure permissible as long as the total relative shift of monomer concentration remains very small in each cycle. With the aid of this computational procedure, predictions are made for the overall kinetics as judged by following the monomer concentration, and for the local change and the rate of change, at each oligomer level, of the entire frequency distribution. This provides some insight, without any other prior assumptions, as to the detailed nature of the processes expected in both the early and the late phases of the kinetics, for numerous systems following this type of model.

COMPUTATIONAL PROCEDURE

The generalized rate of increase of concentration of an oligomer A_i is given by the standard kinetic equation

$$d[A_i]/dt = (k_{i-1,i}[A_o][A_{i-1}] - k_{i,i-1}[A_i])$$
$$+ (-k_{i,i+1}[A_o][A_i] + k_{i+1,i}[A_{i+1}]), \quad i=1, \cdots n-1 \quad (1)$$

Here $[A_o]$ represents the concentration of free monomer, and the subscript for the oligomer concentration $[A_i]$ represents the number of monomers added to one original monomer, the species A_i therefore ideality is made, thus providing that the individual rate constants for such elementary reaction steps are independent of time and concentration.

The starting conditions chosen for the digital computation are that the beginning equilibrium distribution is consistent with the modified shell model distribution function[17]:

$$[A_i]/[A_o] = f \frac{n!}{(n-i)!} \frac{1}{i+1} \left(\frac{K[A_o]}{n} \right)^i \quad (2)$$

Here f is the nucleation factor, a small number taken[2],[17] as
multiplying the intrinsic equilibrium constant, K, for the monomer-
monomer interaction only, so as to provide a small dimer concentration
acting as the nucleus for further polymerization. The quantity n+1
is taken as the maximum number of monomers which can be included in
a globular micelle.

In this model, the equilibrium formation constant for the
reaction step

$$A_o + A_i \xrightarrow{\rightarrow}{\leftarrow} A_{i+1} \tag{3}$$

is given by the expression

$$K_{i,i+1} = \frac{n-i}{n} \frac{i+1}{i+2} K \tag{4}$$

The rate constants consistent with this equilibrium formulation are
chosen for $i = 1, 2, \cdots n$ to be

$$k_{i,i+1} = \frac{n-i}{n}(i+1) k_f$$

$$k_{i+1,i} = (i+2) k_b \tag{5}$$

$$k_f/k_b = K$$

When the parameters in Equations (4) and (5) are taken to pertain
to the conditions immediately following the perturbation in a
relaxation process (i.e. at the new temperature or pressure), and
the concentrations in Equation (1) are selected to be consistent
with the original conditions of equilibrium (i.e. at the old temperature or pressure), substitution of Equations (4) and (5) into Equation (1) results in

$$d [A_i]/dt = k_b \{\frac{n-(i-1)}{n} i K[A_o][A_{i-1}] - (i+1)[A_i]$$

$$- \frac{n-i}{n}(i+1) K[A_o][A_i] + (i+2)[A_{i+1}]\}, i=2, \cdots n-1 \tag{6}$$

Additionally, for i=1, the first term on the right is multiplied
by f. For i=n, the last two terms do not exist.
Here, again, the starting concentrations $[A_o]$, $[A_i]$, $[A_{i-1}]$,
$[A_{i+1}]$ are calculated from Equation (2), with a different
value of K from that appearing in Equation (6). In the examples
presented, the numerical value for K in the starting equilibrium
distribution has been taken as 100 liters/mole, and that in Equation
(6) as 99 liters/mole. Numerical values for n,f, and the product
$K[A_o]$ in Equation (2) must also be supplied, which will differ from
case to case in the computations. Equation (6) has been integrated
as a simple first difference by taking the left hand side as

$\Delta[A_i]/\Delta t$, and assuming that during the very short time Δt all terms on the right hand side remain constant. The total equivalent concentration $C°$ is conserved and time-independent:

$$C° = \sum_{i=0}^{n} (i+1)[A_i] = \text{constant} \tag{7}$$

From this, the total rate of change of monomer concentration is given by

$$\Delta[A_o]/\Delta t \simeq d[A_o]/dt = - \sum_{i=1}^{n} (i+1)d[A_i]/dt \tag{8}$$

Once the time Δt and the intrinsic reverse rate constant k_b have been assigned numerical values, Equation (6) can be solved for the corresponding value of $\Delta[A_i]$. After this solution has been completed for all n oligomers and retained in memory, a new value of $[A_i]$ for $i=1,2\cdots n$ is computed, a value for $\Delta[A_o]$ is computed from Equation (8), and a new value for $[A_o]$ is obtained. These new values are now used to recycle the computation of Equation (6), and the whole recursive computation is repeated for as many cycles as desired. Many computations have been performed with a value of $k_b\Delta t = 10^{-2}$, corresponding, for example, to $\Delta t = 10^{-6}$sec. and $k_b = 10^4/$sec..

PREDICTIONS OF OVERALL KINETICS

For the purpose of portraying the overall kinetics as indicated by the time dependence of the monomer concentration, a logarithmic plot is used which is independent of the estimate for the infinite time value of the monomer concentration. If the difference between the monomer concentration at infinite time and at any time t is expressible by

$$[A_o]_\infty - [A_o]_t = \sum_i C_i e^{-t/\tau_i} \tag{9}$$

then the average value of τ at a given time can be obtained from the slope of a plot versus time of

$$\ln d[A_o]/dt = \ln \sum_i C_i e^{-t/\tau_i} (1/\tau_i) \tag{10}$$

The slope of this plot is

$$- \overline{(1/\tau)} = - \sum_i C_i e^{-t/\tau_i} (1/\tau_i^2) / \sum_i C_i e^{-t/\tau_i} (1/\tau_i) \tag{11}$$

It is evident that this slope is simply $-1/\tau$ for a process involving
only a single elementary reaction step. In the numerical predictions,
Equation (8) is used to plot directly the natural logarithm of
$\Delta[A_0]/\Delta t$. It is also seen that for a process involving a large
number of coupled reaction steps with different time constants,
Equation (11) predicts that even at zero time, the observed
relaxation time will be an average, and that as time goes on, the
faster processes for which $t >> \tau_i$ will damp out, weighting the average
toward longer relaxation times. Thus, it is to be expected that
for a micellar system above the critical micelle concentration,
the type of plot described will always tend to become more horizontal
as time progresses.

Shown in Figures 1-4 are a series of overall kinetics predictions
for the relaxation phenomena in four physically different systems,
for all of which the common parameter values have been chosen as
$f=10^{-4}$, K (original) = 100 liters/mole, K (new) = 99 liters/mole,
$\Delta t = 10^{-6}$ sec., $k_b = 10^4$/sec., n = 100. The systems are characterized in Figures 1-4, respectively, by starting values of the propagation coefficient $K[A_0]$ equal to 1.3, 1.4, 1.5 and 1.6. In each
successive system shown, the ratio of total equivalent concentration
to free monomer concentration has been increased, the ratio being
indicated in the legends below the Figures. Except for the case of
$K[A_0]$ = 1.6, Figure 4, all of the conditions might be practicable
experimentally, but this last case is probably at too high a concentration to represent a real experimental situation. It is seen
that as the concentration is raised above that at the critical
micelle condition, the curvature in the logarithmic plot of the rate
of change of monomer becomes more accentuated. Finally, at $K[A_0]$
values of 1.5 and 1.6, it is clear that simple recursive applications
of identical standard rate equations, Equation (6), with a single
set of rate constants consistent with the shell model distribution,
predict the development of a fast time and a slow time domain, with
approximately two orders of magnitude difference between them, for
the particular cases chosen. These examples would appear to be a
complete vindication of the original statements of Muller[6] concerning
the origin of the two time domains. Further light will be cast on
this when the detailed nature of the alterations of the entire
micelle distribution are examined below. Even for an experimental
case like that at $K[A_0]$=1.5, Figure 3, the experimentalist would
likely be unable to observe the predicted curvature in the transition region between the very fastest and the very slowest processes,
since the slopes of these Figures are second derivatives. From
data of attainable experimental accuracy, it would be easy to
interpret such a process as deriving from a simple intersection of
two straight lines.

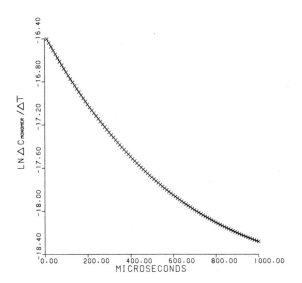

Figure 1. Logarithm of the rate of increase of monomer concentration with time, Equation (8), versus time after perturbation, in a net dissociation process. Assigned initial $K[A_0] = 1.3$, $C^o/[A_0] = 1.059$, $K = 100$ liters/mole. New $K = 99$ liters/mole, $f = 10^{-4}$, $k_b \Delta t = 10^{-2}$, $n = 100$.

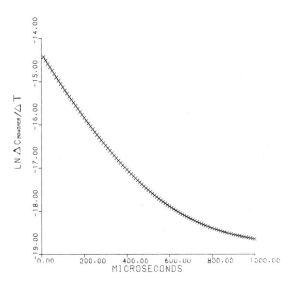

Figure 2. Logarithm of the rate of increase of monomer concentration with time, Equation (8), versus time after perturbation, in a net dissociation process. Assigned initial $K[A_0] = 1.4$, $C^o/[A_0] = 1.401$, $K = 100$ liters/mole. New $K = 99$ liters/mole, $f = 10^{-4}$, $k_b \Delta t = 10^{-2}$, $n = 100$.

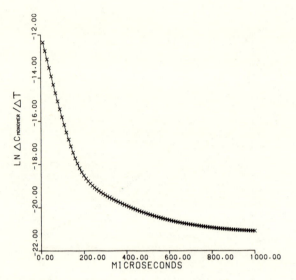

Figure 3. Logarithm of the rate of increase of monomer concentration with time, Equation (8), versus time after perturbation, in a net dissociation process. Assigned initial $K[A_0]=1.5, C^°/[A_0]=4.405$, $K=100$ liters/mole. New $K=99$ liters/mole, $f=10^{-4}$, $k_b\Delta t=10^{-2}$, $n=100$.

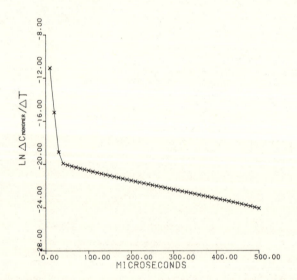

Figure 4. Logarithm of the rate of increase of monomer concentration with time, Equation (8), versus time after perturbation, in a net dissociation process. Assigned initial $K[A_0]=1.6$, $C^°/[A_0]=34.53$, $K=100$ liters/mole. New $K=99$ liters/mole, $f=10^{-4}$, $k_b\Delta t=10^{-2}$, $n=100$.

A validation of the linearization procedure, and an examination of other effects, such as the dependence of such predictions on the choice of the nucleation factor f and on the choice of the maximum micellar size n will be presented in a more complete discussion[19], together with an examination of systems closer to, and below their critical micelle concentration. The conclusion is that it is not necessary to make any special a priori assumptions about the nature of the kinetics in order to predict two time domains in the relaxation kinetics of micellar systems, as already stated earlier[18]. All of the requirements for the two time domains may be found in the equilibrium distribution and in standard rate equations. The examples just discussed above suggest as well that in some cases even the same micelle system in the same solvent may show only one time domain (the fast one) at low concentrations, but will show the slower time domain in addition, when the concentration is raised progressively above the critical micelle concentration. At extremely high concentrations, the slower time domain may seem to disappear again.

PREDICTIONS OF MICELLE REDISTRIBUTIONS

Since each $[A_i]$ value is stored for the duration of one cycle of the rate equation, Equation (6), in the computer memory, it is directly possible to reconstruct the time course of the frequency or molar distribution and the equivalent concentration or mass distribution of all oligomers. It is noted, however, that the present computations are restricted by their nature to typical relaxation kinetics cases of small perturbations, and it would not be possible to visualize directly the very tiny shifts in the absolute distributions occurring as the result of a single application (or cycle) of Equation (6). Therefore, instead of displaying the absolute molar and equivalent concentrations of each oligomer as a function of time, I have chosen to superpose upon the original distribution function the direct instantaneous rate of increase of oligomer molarity from Equation (6), or the derived rate of increase of equivalent concentration, $(i+1)(d[A_i]/dt)$. For the purpose of this exposition, it will suffice to present only plots of the original distribution of equivalent concentration of oligomers superposed upon their local rate of change with time, at various stages of the overall kinetic process. The ordinate in such a plot also represents the specific contribution of each individual oligomer to the rate of uptake or release of monomer. A series of plots on the molar scale will be presented in a more detailed account[19].

Shown in Figure 5 is a composite plot for the case $K[A_0]=1.3$, at a time 10 microseconds after perturbation, for the same process whose overall kinetics are shown in Figure 1. It is noted that the maximum rate of melting or disappearance of micelles (largest negative value of $d[A_i]/dt$) occurs at the higher molecular weight inflection point in the distribution curve, and the largest rate of production of micelles occurs at the lower molecular weight inflection point in the distribution curve, as previously pointed out in closed form in an earlier publication[18]. This is the detailed interpretation of the fast initial process according to the shell model distribution. It corresponds to the so-called exchange reaction[8], and to Muller's[6] description of the initial monomer-micelle interaction. An approximation to the effects shown in Figure 5 would be obtained by simple shearing of the entire distribution function downward in degree of polymerization, as suggested earlier[7,8,20]. The latter depictions are inexact for two reasons, however. First, a shift downward by a number of oligomer units greatly exaggerates the assumed nature of the fast relaxation process, in which only a few percent of the population in any single oligomer size is expected to lose one monomer. Second, the peak position in the original distribution has been shown [18] to be an invariant point in the period just following the perturbation: the initial rate of change of oligomer is directly proportional to the first derivative with respect to the degree of polymerization, of the starting mass distribution function, for the shell model. Such a result is not obtained by shifting the entire distribution downward by a number of oligomer units in degree of polymerization.

Figure 6 shows superposed on the same original equivalent concentration distribution function for $K[A_0]=1.3$, the rate of change of equivalent concentration for each oligomer at 100 microseconds after perturbation. This Figure shows that the position of maximum melting has moved downward in degree of polymerization compared to that shown in Figure 5, and that some appreciable melting is now occuring at the original peak position in the distribution.

Figure 7 shows superposed on the same original distribution function for $K[A_0]=1.3$, the rate of change of equivalent concentration for each oligomer at 1000 microseconds after perturbation. Although the maximum melting is now occurring at the original peak position, some melting is occurring, although at a much slower rate than earlier, across the whole micelle distribution. It is noted that there is now no position shown in which oligomers are being formed. All of the monomer which is being released, within the accuracy of the drawing, is being added to the pool of free monomer, which is not indicated on the graph.

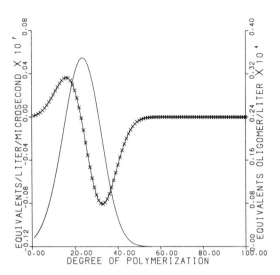

Figure 5.   Initial distribution, smooth curve and right hand axis, with instantaneous rate of increase of oligomers, curve with points and left hand axis, for $K[A_O]=1.3$, $k_b\Delta t=10^{-2}$, $f=10^{-4}$, original $K = 100$ liters/mole final $K = 99$ liters/mole, 10 microseconds after perturbation.

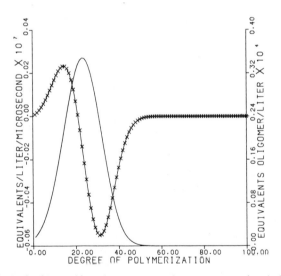

Figure 6.   Initial distribution, smooth curve and right hand axis, with instantaneous rate of increase of oligomers, curve with points and left hand axis, for $K[A_O]=1.3$, $k_b\Delta t=10^{-2}$, $f=10^{-4}$, original $K = 100$ liters/mole, final $K = 99$ liters/mole, 100 microseconds after perturbation.

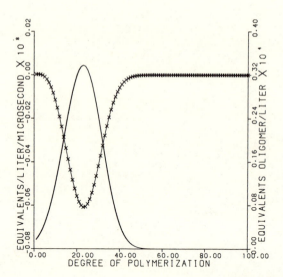

Figure 7. Initial distribution, smooth curve and right hand axis,
with instantaneous rate of increase of oligomers, curve with points
and left hand axis, for $K[A_o]=1.3$, $k_b\Delta t=10^{-2}$, $f=10^{-4}$, original $K = 100$
liters/mole, final $K = 99$ liters/mole, 1000 microseconds after
perturbation.

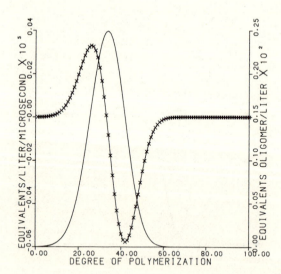

Figure 8. Initial distribution, smooth curve and right hand axis,
with instantaneous rate of increase of oligomers, curve with points
and left hand axis, for $K[A_o]=1.5$, $k_b\Delta t=10^{-2}$, $f=10^{-4}$, original $K = 100$
liters/mole, final $K = 99$ liters/mole, 10 microseconds after
perturbation.

This sequence of events agrees with Muller's[6] interpretation and with the predictions already made[18] for this same case, $K[A_0]=$ 1.3, where it was also stated that there was no indication of an overshoot effect during the fast process, and a return to higher degree of polymerization in subsequent slow processes, as variously predicted by numerous authors[7,8,20]. It is noted that Figure 1 for this case suggests only a gradual drift in relaxation time, rather than two distinct time domains. It is also noted that the time scale slows only by a factor of 10 between Figure 5, at 10 microseconds after perturbation, and Figure 7, at 1000 microseconds after perturbation.

In Figure 8 is shown, at 10 microseconds after perturbation, the rate of change of equivalent concentration of oligomer superposed on the original distribution function for the case $K[A_0]=1.5$, under the same conditions as those in Figure 3 for overall kinetics. Figure 8 may be compared with Figure 5 for the case $K[A_0]=1.3$, also at 10 microseconds after perturbation. Except for the large increase in rate noted on the left hand axis, the patterns look much the same, which is to be expected as long as the original mass or equivalent concentration functions have qualitatively the same shape. The values of $d[A_i]/dt$ at times shortly after perturbation are essentially the first derivative of the mass distribution function with respect to degree of polymerization. It is to be noted that with identical values for individual elementary reaction step rate constants, the rate of monomer release and uptake is approximately two orders of magnitude faster than at $K[A_0]=1.3$.

In Figure 9 is shown a similar superposition for the case $K[A_0]=1.5$, at 100 microseconds after perturbation, which, according to the overall kinetics shown in Figure 3, is still well within the time domain of the fast reaction period. However, examination of Figure 9 shows that a rather remarkable change has taken place from the situation shown in Figure 8, at 10 microseconds after perturbation. In Figure 9, not only is the position of maximum melting shifted downward in degree of polymerization to the original peak position, an effect already shown for $K[A_0]=1.3$ after 1000 microseconds in Figure 7, but for $K[A_0]=1.5$ at 100 microseconds, Figure 9, large micelles are being reformed simultaneously with micelles on the low molecular weight shoulder of the distribution plot. This effect would not have been predicted from Figure 3, which would suggest to the experimenter only one relaxation time at 100 microseconds, and would suggest to the theorist only one normal mode in the coupling of elementary reaction steps at this point in the kinetics.

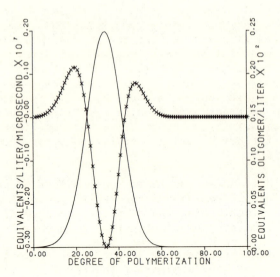

Figure 9. Initial distribution, smooth curve and right hand axis, with instantaneous rate of increase of oligomers, curve with points and left hand axis, for $K[A_o]=1.5$, $k_b \Delta t=10^{-2}$, $f=10^{-4}$, original K = 100 liters/mole, final K = 99 liters/mole, 100 microseconds after perturbation.

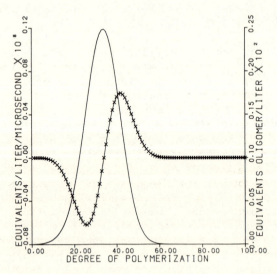

Figure 10. Initial distribution, smooth curve and right hand axis, with instantaneous rate of increase of oligomers, curve with points and left hand axis, for $K[A_o]=1.5$, $k_b \Delta t=10^{-2}$, $f=10^{-4}$, original K = 100 liters/mole, final K = 99 liters/mole, 1000 microseconds after perturbation.

In Figure 10 is shown, for $K[A_o]=1.5$, a superposition upon the original distribution during the slow reaction phase, 1000 microseconds after perturbation, of the rate of change of equivalent concentration of oligomers. At this point, the maximum rate of melting, although much slower than the original rate shown in Figure 8, is located near the lower molecular weight inflection point of the original distribution, while the maximum rate of growth is located in the micelle region near the inflection point at the higher molecular weight side of the peak. The region of the original peak concentration, at this stage of the kinetics, appears to be located near $d[A_i]/dt = 0$, i.e. this region is again roughly invariant. Detailed computer printout shows, in fact, that in all the cases studied thus far, the peak position rarely moves downward, and, if so, it moves only by one oligomer unit from the beginning of the computation to 1000 cycles of Equation (6). However, Figure 10 indicates that the kinetics at this stage, 1000 microseconds after perturbation, are slowly undoing what occurred rapidly during the very early stages of the kinetics shown in Figure 8. That this is rather precisely so can be seen by superposing the patterns shown in Figures 8 and 10.

Thus, the descriptions made by numerous authors in the earlier literature[7],[8],[20] of a downward shift of the entire distribution in the early stages, followed by a return, either partial or complete, to a peak position at higher degree of polymerization in a subsequent slow process, do not appear to be correct in detail. However, these authors have quite correctly stated the existence of a qualitative phenomenon, that of an overshoot of dissociation in the initial fast process, followed by a partial reassociation in a subsequent slow process. This phenomenon was missed in my earlier kinetic study[18] because I had not examined a sufficient variety of distributions, especially those for systems well above the critical micelle concentration. Rather similar details of this reassociation phenomenon have just been described for a different starting distribution[16].

DISCUSSION

The overshoot phenomenon appears to occur rather generally for all cases for which the overall kinetics, as judged by following monomer concentration, Figures 1-4, show two well-separated time domains. It seems characteristic that for such systems undergoing a net dissociation, the slow process involves a loss of excess small micelles and a rebuilding of a deficient population of large micelles, accompanied by a continual very small net release of free monomer. On the other hand, Figure 9 demonstrates that this rebuilding of large micelles begins even during the time period, characterized by following monomer concentration, of the fast process. At this writing, it also seems likely, as judged by computations with the

shell model, that only those systems which show simultaneous small
micelle buildup and large micelle buildup during part of the fast
process will also show two distinct time domains, such as those
displayed in Figures 3 and 4. Thus, except at very early times,
the fast process appears to be quite complex, and its very nature
changes distinctly with time, as shown in Figures 8 and 9.

With respect to the reversal of the overshoot, it is as if the
entire micelle distribution has a sort of buffering action. Having
been strained, or distorted, in the fast reaction period, it is
required to return to a distribution not far from that which it
had just prior to perturbation. If the strain consists of having
removed far too much material from the higher molecular weight
inflection point region and deposited it in the lower molecular
weight inflection point region, then this process will be slowly
reversed. Why this clearly happens for systems showing two time
domains in overall kinetics, but appears not to happen for systems
just above the critical micelle condition and not showing two
distinct time domains, is unclear. It is still conceivable that
the latter systems need only be studied by the present computational
procedure for 100 times as long (a rather impractical demand on
computer time), in order to bring out very minute, but qualitatively similar effects. That this probably would not be found
in the case of $K[A_O]=1.3$ treated above may be guessed from the
fact, already pointed out, that the process of transferring micelles
from one side of the distribution peak to the other at 10 microseconds after perturbation is occurring about 100 times as fast
in the case of $K[A_O]=1.5$ as in the case of $K[A_O]=1.3$. This introduces a large strain into the distribution at $K[A_O]=1.5$ which does
not occur to any comparable extent at $K[A_O]=1.3$. Consequently, the
undoing of an overshoot may not be needed for $K[A_O]=1.3$.

REFERENCES

1. K. H. Meyer and A. van der Wyk, Helv. Chim. Acta, 20, 1321 (1937).
2. C. A. Hoeve and G. C. Benson, J. Phys. Chem., 61, 1149 (1957).
3. P. Mukerjee, J. Phys. Chem., 76, 565 (1972).
4. P. J. Mijnlieff and R. Ditmarsch, Nature (London), 208, 899
    (1965).
5. G. C. Kresheck, E. Hamori, G. Davenport and H. A. Scheraga,
    J. Amer. Chem. Soc., 88, 246 (1966).
6. N. Muller, J. Phys. Chem. 76, 3017 (1972).
7. T. Nakagawa, Colloid Polymer Sci., 252, 56 (1974).
8. J. Lang, C. Tondre, R. Zana, R. Bauer, H. Hoffmann, and
    W. Ulbricht, J. Phys. Chem., 79, 276 (1975).
9. E. Graber, J. Lang and R. Zana, Kolloid-Z. u Z. Polym., 238,
    470 (1970).

10. R. Folger, H. Hoffmann and W. Ulbricht, Ber. Bunsenges. Phys.
     Chem., 78, 986 (1974).
11. P. J. Sams, E. Wyn-Jones and J. Rassing, Chem. Phys. Lett.,
     13, 233 (1972).
12. E. A. G. Aniansson and S. N. Wall, J. Phys. Chem., 78, 1024
     (1974).
13. E. A. G. Aniansson and S. N. Wall, J. Phys. Chem., 79, 857
     (1975).
14. E. A. G. Aniansson, S. N. Wall, M. Almgren, H. Hoffmann,
     I. Kielmann, W. Ulbricht, R. Zana, J. Lang and C. Tondre,
     J. Phys. Chem., 80, 905 (1976).
15. M. Almgren, E. A. G. Aniansson and K. Holmåker, Chem. Phys.,
     19, 1 (1977).
16. S. N. Wall and E. A. G. Aniansson, J. Phys. Chem., 84, 727
     (1980).
17. G. Kegeles, J. Phys. Chem., 83, 1728 (1979).
18. G. Kegeles, Arch. Biochem. Biophys., 200, 279 (1980).
19. G. Kegeles, to be published.
20. W. Baumüller, H. Hoffmann, W. Ulbricht, C. Tondre and R. Zana,
     J. Colloid Interface Sci., 64, 418 (1978).

THE ASSOCIATION OF IONIC SURFACTANTS TO MICELLES AND LIQUID CRYSTALLINE PHASES: A THERMODYNAMIC MODEL

Bengt Jönsson, Gudmundur Gunnarsson and Håkan Wennerström

Division of Physical Chemistry 2, Chemical Center

P.O.B. 740, S-220 07 LUND 7, Sweden

A model for the association behaviour of ionic surfactants is presented, in which it is emphasized that the formation of micelles in a dilute aqueous solution is but a first step in a continuing association process leading to liquid crystalline phases and also to reversed micellar solutions. Using an expression for the free energy, which contains contributions due to the hydrophobic effect and the electrostatic free energy, chemical potentials for all the components are derived. In particular the electrostatic contributions are treated in detail using the Poisson-Boltzmann equation and the cell model. Spherical, cylindrical, and planar aggregates are considered. The calculated chemical potentials are compared with experiments relating to monomer and counterion activities, phase equilibria and CMC values. In all cases it is found that there is good agreement between theory and experiment. It is particularily gratifying that the phase boundaries (including two phase regions) are predicted with good accuracy. In the last section of the paper the model is extended so that the micelle size distribution can be calculated allowing for all aggregation numbers. It is shown that the model gives reasonable agreement with characteristics of the size distribution that are determined from kinetic measurements.

317

INTRODUCTION

The association of amphiphilic molecules in an aqueous medium typically occurs in a stepwise manner as the amphiphile concentration is increased. In a sufficiently dilute solution there are only surfactant monomers. As the concentration is increased these often associate to form micellar aggregates. At still higher amphiphile concentrations lyotropic liquid crystalline phases are formed. For simple soaps the phase first formed is the normal hexagonal phase, consisting of cylindrical aggregates packed in an hexagonal array. At higher amphiphile concentrations a lamellar phase can appear as well as other phase structures. When a third weakly polar compound is added to the system the phase behaviour becomes even more complex. A typical three component phase diagram is shown in Figure 1. For a review of phase properties and micellar equilibria see refs. 1-4.

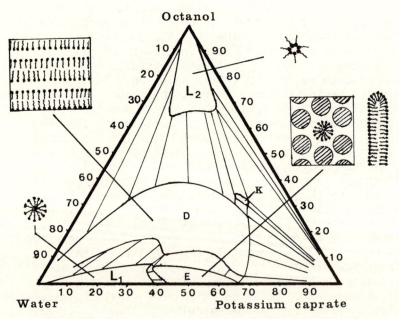

Figure 1. Phase diagram of the ternary system potassium caprate-octanol - water at 20°C as described by Ekwall and collaborators[5]. Inserted are schematic drawings of the structures of the aggregates. L$_1$ and L$_2$ denote isotropic solution phases and D (lamellar), E (hexagonal) and K (cubic) regions with liquid crystalline phases.

The formation of different aggregates can be seen as a compro-
mise between the hydrophobic interaction, which tends to remove the
apolar parts of the amphiphilic molecules from contact with the
water, and the energetically favourable interaction between the
polar groups and the water. The energy contributions due to the
hydrophobic effect have been rather well characterized from a semi-
empirical point of view[6], while the interactions involving the polar
groups have been less extensively studied. For ionic amphiphiles the
electrostatic interactions dominate but an explicit description of
the ion - ion and the ion - water interactions on a molecular level
is presently unfeasable. However, it is a general experience in
colloid chemistry that the electrostatic effects can be described
with reasonable accuracy on the basis of the Poisson-Boltzmann
equation.

In the present paper we address the problem: Is it possible to
describe, in a quantitative way, the association behaviour in ionic
amphiphile - water systems covering both the dilute aqueous solutions and the concentrated liquid crystalline phases within one and
the same model, where the essential free energy contributions are
due to the hydrophobic effect (conventionally described) and to the
electrostatic interactions, described using the non-linearized
Poisson-Boltzmann equation?

The present approach thus differs from previous models of micellar systems[7-10] and liquid crystalline phases[11,12] in that an attempt
is made to cover the whole concentration range. There are at least
two reasons for making such an attempt. First it is a common finding that aggregate or phase structure is remarkably insensitive
to molecular properties[13-16]. This also applies to some thermodynamic parameters such as partial molar enthalpies[17,18]. Second
micellar solutions and liquid crystalline phases are amenable to
different types of experimental studies. For micellar systems the
CMC is easily determined and this also applies to other thermodynamic[19,20] and kinetic parameters [21] while properties related to the
aggregate structure are rather difficult to determine. Structural
properties are much more easily determined in the ordered liquid
crystalline systems where X-ray diffraction methods can be used.
Thus it is possible to compare the theoretical predictions both
with thermodynamic and structural data.

BASIC MODEL

The total amphiphile-water system is described using the cell
model[22] where each cell contains an aggregate formed by the apolar
chains with the charges at the surface and an aqueous region. In the
first part of the article all cells are assumed equal, but in the
last section the theory is extended to include non-identical cells
in order to describe micellar size distributions. To be able to

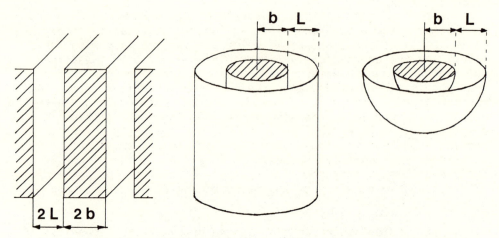

Figure 2. Schematic representation of three geometries, planar, cylindrical and spherical of the amphiphilic aggregates. /// represents the regions of nonpolar material with the aqueous medium outside.

calculate the electrostatic interactions a further simplification is made. The shapes of the cells are considered to be either spherical, cylindrical or planar as shown in Figure 2. It is also assumed that the water and the counterions reside entirely in the aqueous part[23], while the amphiphile can be both in the aqueous region and in the aggregate. Within this model the important contributions to the free energy are due to

i)   The electrostatic free energy, G_{el}

ii)   The free energy of ideal mixing of the components, G_{mix}

iii) The hydrophobic contribution to the free energy written as $\mu_{am}^{a} - \mu_{am}^{\theta,w}$

iv)   The constraint that the ionic groups of the aggregate are located at the aggregate surface, G_{c}.

The Van der Waals interactions can for typical ionic amphiphile-water systems be neglected since they are one to two order of magnitude smaller than the electrostatic interactions.

For each system the aggregate size can be characterized by one parameter, b (see Fig. 2), the optimal value of b is determined by requiring that the partial derivative of the free energy with respect to b is zero. In previous treatments of phase equilibria[11],[12] the free energies of different phases have been compared. This gives a measure of the relative stabilities of different structures but it does not describe the existence of two phase regions. To accomplish a full description of the phase equilibria it is necessary to calculate the chemical potential μ_i for all the components. One virtue of the description of the system in terms of the four free energy contributions listed above is that they can be quantified in such a way that it is possible to determine the chemical potentials by direct differentiation of G.

FREE ENERGY EXPRESSIONS

The lamellar and cylindrical aggregates are parts of liquid crystalline phases and they have, in principle, an infinite extension. The free energy, G, of such a system can thus be written as the free energy, G_0, of a single aggregate and its associated aqueous solution.

$$G = G_0 \tag{1}$$

In a solution of micelles the number of aggregates, N, is variable and there is also an entropic contribution G_{mix}^m, to G due to the mixing of the micelles. If we consider a single size one can write

$$G = N\, G_0 + G_{mix}^m \tag{2}$$

According to the basic model the different contributions to G_0 are

$$G_0 = n_{am}^a\, \mu_{am}^a + \Sigma n_i^w\, \mu_i^{\theta,w} + G_{el} + G_{mix} + G_c \tag{3}$$

Here n_{am}^a is the number of amphiphilic molecules in the aggregate and n_i^w the amount of component i in the aqueous region.

Since there will be for all aggregates a certain contact between the apolar core of the aggregates and the water the term μ_{am}^a will depend on the aggregate geometry. We assume that the geometry dependent term is proportional to the area of the aggregates with a proportionality constant γ. μ_{am}^a is then split as

$$\mu_{am}^a = \mu_{am}^{\theta,a} + \gamma \cdot A_{am} \tag{4}$$

where $\mu_{am}^{\theta,a}$ is constant independent of aggregate size and shape and A_{am} is the area per amphiphilic molecule calculated at the surface of the charges.

The electrostatic free energy G_{el} can be divided into two components, the energy in the ion - ion interactions E_{el} and the entropy decrease due to the induced inhomogeneous ion distribution S_{el}. The electrostatic effects are treated within the approximation of the Poisson-Boltzmann (PB) equation

$$-\varepsilon_0 \varepsilon_r \nabla^2 \phi = \rho = F \cdot \Sigma z_i c_{i0} \exp(-z_i e \phi/kT) \qquad (5)$$

where ε_0 is the permittivity of vacuum, ε_r the dielectric constant, ρ the charge distribution due to the ions in the solution, c_i the concentration, z_i the valency and c_{i0} the concentration at the surface of the cell for ion i, F is the Faraday constant, e the unit charge and kT the Boltzmann factor. Inherent in Equation (5) is the assumption that the electrostatic effects can be described using an average potential ϕ and an average charge distribution ρ.

In this approximation the energy, E_{el}, of the ion-ion interactions is

$$E_{el} = \tfrac{1}{2} \int \rho_T \cdot \phi \cdot dV = \tfrac{1}{2} z_{am} \cdot n_{am} \cdot e \cdot \phi_A + \tfrac{1}{2} \int \rho \cdot \phi \cdot dV = \tfrac{1}{2} \varepsilon_0 \varepsilon_r \int (\nabla \phi)^2 dV \qquad (6)$$

where ρ_T is the total charge distribution including the n_{am} charges $z_{am} \cdot e$ of the amphiphile in the aggregate surface where the potential is ϕ_A.

The entropy from the induced inhomogeneous ion distribution S_{el} and from G_{mix} can be written as

$$-T \cdot S_{el} + G_{mix} = RT \sum_i \int_{V_1} c_i \{\ln(c_i/c_0) - 1\} dV \qquad (7)$$

where the summation is over all ions and uncharged species except the water. The integral is over the aqueous part V_1 and in that region it is assumed water is present in excess and in that case the total concentration c_0 is approximately constant ($\cong 55$ M). In the micellar case there is an additional contribution to the entropy due to the entropy of mixing of the micellar aggregates. For simplicity we have chosen to neglect the effect of intermicellar interactions, in that case

$$G_{mix}^m = kT \cdot N \cdot (\ln c_m - 1) \qquad (8)$$

where c_m is the concentration of micelles in the solution.

The ionic groups are assumed to reside on the aggregate surface and this prevents the aggregates from growing without limit in all directions. The parameter b characterizing the aggregate size is thus limited to a maximum value b_{max} which is assumed to be the length of a fully extended amphiphile molecule. For systems of the reversed type on the other hand the minimum area per polar group A_{min} is the limiting value.

$$G_c = 0 \qquad\qquad b \leq b_{max} \qquad\qquad\qquad\qquad (9)$$

$$G_c = \infty \qquad\qquad b > b_{max}$$

and for reversed systems

$$G_c = 0 \qquad\qquad A \geq A_{min} \qquad\qquad\qquad\qquad (10)$$

$$G_c = \infty \qquad\qquad A < A_{min}$$

The assumption of a step-function behaviour of G_c is of course an idealization and the transition should be smooth in a more realistic model.

AGGREGATE SIZE

The optimal sizes of the aggregates are determined by the condition

$$\left(\frac{\partial G}{\partial b}\right)_n = 0 \qquad\qquad\qquad\qquad (11)$$

where G is the free energy expression from equations (1) - (3). The derivative $(\partial G/\partial b)_n$ can be determined in a closed form if the relation between the charge distribution and the electrostatic potential is written as an integral of a Greens function[25] and the evaluation results in a remarkably simple relation

$$\left(\frac{\partial G}{\partial b}\right)_n = (2 \cdot E_{el} - \gamma \cdot A)/b + \left(\frac{\partial G_c}{\partial b}\right)_n \qquad\qquad (12)$$

where A is the total area of the aggregates. For spherical aggregates there will be an extra term from G_{mix}^m.

$$\left(\frac{\partial G_{mix}^m}{\partial b}\right)_n = -\frac{3A}{4\pi b^3} \; kT \cdot \ln c_m \qquad\qquad (13)$$

Equations (11) and (12) state that for a lyotropic liquid crystal-line system where $b \leq b_{max}$ the aggregate size will adjust so that

$$2 E_{el}/A = \gamma \qquad\qquad\qquad (14)$$

Carboxylic soaps form at high concentrations and high temperatures lamellar liquid crystals, where the thickness of the lamellae vary with concentration showing that $b < b_{max}$. Thus for these phases the relation Equation (14) should be valid. Gallot and Skoulios[26] have determined the aggregate sizes for a series of potassium carboxylic soaps at 86°C by low angle X-ray diffraction. From the experimentally determined charge densities and thickness of the water layer the electrical energy E_{el} can be calculated from the PB Equation (5). Figure 3 shows the calculated value for $2 \cdot E_{el}/A$ for a series of potassium soaps, n=8 to n=22, at varying concentrations. In spite of the fact that there are substantial variations in A_{am} and L the quantity $2 \cdot E_{el}/A$ remains constant and one obtains the value 18.2 mN/m for γ, in accordance with a previous calculation by Parsegian[11]. The value of γ is considerably smaller than γ=51 mN/m found for interfaces between water and pure aliphatic hydrocarbons, but in good accordance with area energy relations for hydrocarbon-water contact estimated by Tanford[7] and by Missel et al.[27]

Experimental data for other temperatures and for other counter-ions show that the calculated value of γ is rather insensitive to temperature and that the variation with counterion in the alkali metal series is also insignificant as shown by data in Tables I and II. But when also an alcohol is added to a system the γ-value is no longer constant (Figure 4). The straight line in Figure 4 comes from the Equation

$$\gamma = X_{am} \cdot \gamma_{am} + X_{OH} \cdot \gamma_{OH} \qquad\qquad\qquad (15)$$

where X_{am} and X_{OH} are the mole fractions of amphiphile and alcohol in the aggregate. The values of γ_{am} and γ_{OH} are

$$\gamma_{am} = 18 \text{ mN/m} \quad \text{and} \quad \gamma_{OH} = 4 \text{ mN/M}$$

A clear demonstration of the effect of the constraint $b \leq b_{max}$ can be found for the surfactant Aerosol OT (di-2-ethyl-hexyl sodium sulphosuccinate) which forms a lamellar phase in the composition range 8 - 71 % w/w[28,29]. In this range $2 \cdot E_{el}/A$ varies between 12 and 8 mN/m but the lamellar thickness is constant at b = 9,8 Å corresponding to an extended chain. Thus in systems

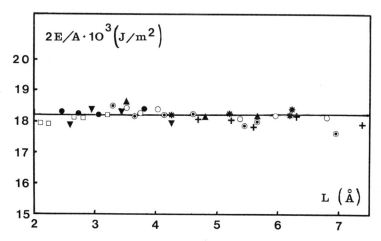

Figure 3. Two times the electrostatic energy per unit area, $2 \cdot E_{el}/A$, as a function of half the thickness of the water layer L for the lamellar mesophase of some potassium soaps at 86°C.

$\square = C_8K$, $\bullet = C_{10}K$, $\blacktriangledown = C_{12}K$, $\blacktriangle = C_{14}K$, $\odot = C_{16}K$,

$\bigcirc = C_{18}K$, $\ast = C_{20}K$ and $+ = C_{22}K$. The X-ray data are from Ref 26.

Table I. Two Times the Electrostatic Energy Per Unit Area for the Lamellar Mesophase of Potassium Soaps at Different Temperatures.

T (K)	$2 \cdot E_{el}/A$ (mN/m)
377	18.4 ± 0.1
359	18.2 ± 0.2
338	18.2 ± 0.1
318	17.8 ± 0.1

Table II.   Two Times the Electrostatic Energy Per Unit Area for
            the Lamellar Mesophase of Soaps with Different
            Counterions at 359 K.

counterion	$2 \cdot E_{el}/A$ (mN/m)
Na^+	17.9 ± 0.3
K^+	18.2 ± 0.2
Rb^+	18.8 ± 0.3
Cs^+	18.6 ± 0.2

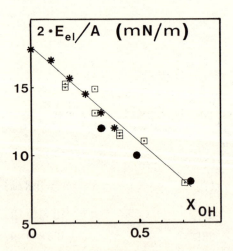

Figure 4. Two times the electrostatic energy per unit area,
          $2 \cdot E_{el}/A$, as a function of the mole fraction alcohol.
          $*$ = caprate, decanol at 55°C, $\boxdot$ = caprate, octanol at
          20°C and $\bullet$ = caprylate, decanol at 20°C.

where one has so called one dimensional swelling in a lamellar
phase, the thickness of the amphiphile lamellae are at their
maximum value according to the model.

In a three component system ionic amphiphile - alcohol - water
where there is often an extensive lamellar region at ambient temperature there can be both regions where $b = b_{max}$ and regions
where the lamellar thickness adjust according to Equation (14).
This is illustrated in Figure 5 which shows the calculated thickness for the system sodium caprate - octanol - water. Apart from
direct X-ray determinations of the thickness also deuterium NMR
measurements show that an all trans conformation of the chain is
approached as the alcohol content is increased as discussed by
Klasson et al. in this volume[30].

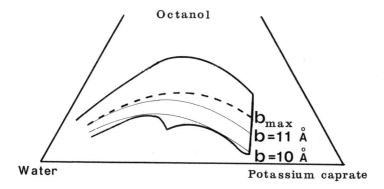

Figure 5. Calculated lines of constant and maximal aggregate
thickness plotted for the three component system potassium
caprate - octanol - water at 20°C.

CHEMICAL POTENTIALS

By taking the derivative of the free energy G in Equation (3) one obtains

$$\mu_j = \left(\frac{\partial G}{\partial n_j}\right) = \mu_j^\theta + \frac{\partial}{\partial n_j}(\gamma A) + \frac{\partial G_{el}}{\partial n_j} + \frac{\partial G_{mix}}{\partial n_j} \qquad (16)$$

The quantities G_{el} and G_{mix} depend on all the n_i and on first sight it seems an impossible task to determine $(\partial G/\partial n)$ in a closed form. However, Marcus[31] has shown that when the Poisson-Boltzmann equation is assumed valid several simplifications arises, and he determined the chemical potentials for the ions in the solution and the water for a polyelectrolyte system. In the present case the method due to Marcus can be generalized to account for the fact that the aggregate size is not constant and to include also the amphiphile. During the differentiation the amount of amphiphile in the aggregates, n_{am}^a, and in the aqueous region, n_{am}^w, will be assumed to be independent. At chemical equilibrium the chemical potentials μ_{am}^a and μ_{am}^w should be equal.

The calculations give the following expressions for the chemical potentials .

1. For the water

$$\mu_{H_2O} = \mu_{H_2O}^\theta - V_{H_2O} \cdot RT \cdot \Sigma c_{j0} \qquad (17)$$

The summation Σc_{j0} is over all components except water.

2. For all the other components in the aqueous region

$$\mu_i^w = \mu_i^{\theta w} + kT \cdot \ln c_{i0} \qquad (18)$$

3. For the components in the aggregate

$$\mu_i^a = \mu_i^{0a} + z_i \cdot e \cdot \Phi_A + kT \cdot \ln x_i + (\gamma_i A - E_{el} - kT \cdot \Sigma n_i^w +$$

$$+ RT \cdot V_1 \cdot \Sigma c_{i0}) \cdot A_i/A \qquad (19)$$

where x_i is the mole fraction of the component i in the aggregate and V_1 is the volume of the aqueous region.

For the micellar system there is an additional contribution to the chemical potential due to G^m_{mix}. For the water

$$\frac{\partial G^m_{mix}}{\partial n_{H_2O}} = - RT \cdot c_m \cdot V_{H_2O} \qquad (20)$$

For components in the aggregate

$$\frac{\partial G^m_{mix}}{\partial n_i} = \frac{kT}{n} \ln c_m \qquad (21)$$

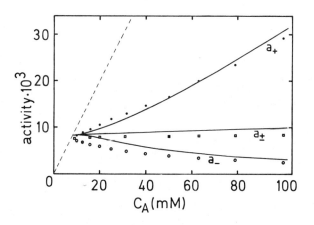

Figure 6. Single ion a_+(●), a_-(○) and mean ion $a_\pm$ (□) activities in sodium dodecyl sulfate solutions as a function of the total amphiphile concentration c_A. Experimental points from ref. 19.
    The solid lines are calculated from equations (18) and (19). (t = 25°C, ε_r = 78.3).

The most critical test of these expressions for the chemical
potentials is in the calculation of phase equilibria. However, an
indication of the accuracy of the expressions can be obtained by
comparing with experimentally determined activities of single
species. Mille and Vanderkooi[41] have shown that equation (17) for
the water chemical potential gives a good description of the osmotic
coefficient of micellar solutions. Counterion and amphiphile activities have been measured with ion selective electrodes in micellar
solutions[19,20]. Figure 6 shows a comparision between experimental
data and values calculated from equations (18) and (19) for sodium
dodecyl sulfate solutions. Also in this case there is a good agreement between theory and experiment and there are thus reasons to
believe that Equations (17-19) include the main contributions to
the chemical potentials.

PHASE EQUILIBRIA

The condition for equilibrium between two phases α and β is that
the chemical potentials of all species are equal in the two phases
i.e.

$$(\mu_i)_\alpha = (\mu_i)_\beta \tag{22}$$

for all i. For lamellar and hexagonal liquid crystalline phase and
for micellar solutions containing only spherical micelles of uniform size the Equations (17-21) contain explicit expressions for
the chemical potentials.

To calculate the electrical terms the solution to the PB Equa-
tion must be determined. From the Equations $(\partial G/\partial b)_n = 0$ or b =
= b_{max} the aggregate size is fixed, the surface charge density is
then determined from the known volume of the amphiphile. Then one
fixes the values of c_{+0} and c_{-0} and solves the PB Equation. The
chemical potentials for the amphiphile in the aggregate and in
the aqueous region are then checked if they are equal, if not a
new calculation with a new c_{-0} value is done. Except for the most
dilute systems, c_{-0} is small enough so that it does not influence
the solution of the PB Equation and a new iteration is only rarely
needed. The process is then repeated for a new value of c_{+0} relevant for another composition.

A convenient way of representing the calculations is to plot
the chemical potentials of the amphiphile versus the chemical potential of the water. For each type of phase a curve as shown in
Figure 7 is obtained.

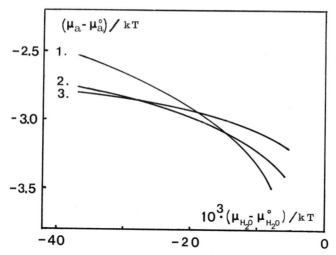

Figure 7. The chemical potential of amphiphile molecules μ_{am} as a function of the chemical potential of the water μ_{H_2O}.

1. is for a spherical, 2. is for a cylindrical and 3. is for a lamellar system.

At the intersections of these curves the two types of phases are at equilibrium. The stability regions for the different phases are then directly obtained by calculating the compositions of the phases at the intersection points.

Explicit calculations of phase equilibria have been performed for two types of systems: for a series of potassium carboxylate soaps at 86°C and for an Aerosol-OT water system. The calculations for the potassium carboxylate soaps have been performed in two different ways. The two calculations differ in that in the first series experimental values of b are used when available while in the second series b is calculated from Equation (14). The results summarized in Table III show that irrespective of the details of the calculations there is a remarkably good agreement with experimentally determined phase boundaries[26,32]. Particularly the extent of the two phase regions are accurately predicted.

Table III. Calculated and Experimental Phase Boundaries.

Phase boundaries in % w/w

soap	micellar	cylindrical	lamellar	
$C_{12}K$	- 29	40 - 62	68 -	a.
	- 35	43 - 58	66 -	b.
	- 36	44 - 59	66 -	exp.
$C_{14}K$	- 28	39 - 64	70 -	a.
	- 34	41 - 58	66 -	b.
	- 32	40 - 56	64 -	exp.
$C_{16}K$	- 27	38 - 66	71 -	a.
	- 31	39 - 58	66 -	b.
	- 27	34 - 55	63 -	exp.
$C_{18}K$	- 25	36 - 66	72 -	a.
	- 29	36 - 58	65 -	b.
	- 22	29 - 54	62 -	exp.

a: Phase boundaries calculated using a priori determined
   values for the aggregate dimension b.

b: Phase boundaries calculated using experimental values
   for the aggregate dimensions.

In the case Aerosol-OT water the model gives a good description
of the association behaviour over the entire concentration range
(except for the existence of a cubic phase which is not treated
in the model). At the maximum size, spherical AOT micelles contains six monomers and the cooperativity of the micelle formation
is rather weak. At 0.8 % a two phase region appears which extends
to 8 % AOT (experimental values 1.2 - 10 %)[33] where it is in
equilibrium with a lamellar phase (also found experimentally)
which extends up to 58 % (experimentally 71 %). At 78 % (experimentally 81 %) a reversed hexagonal phase appears.

THE CMC IN MICELLAR SYSTEMS

The association of monomeric amphiphiles to micellar aggregates is in the typical case cooperative enough to make it similar
to a phase transition and it can be characterized to a good approximation with a critical concentration, the CMC. For ionic amphiphiles the CMC is sensitive to the salt concentration and the value
of the CMC is strongly influenced by the electrostatic effects. The
theory presented in the previous sections should thus be able to
account for the variation of the CMC with amphiphile chain length,
with salt concentration and with counterion valency.

It is assumed that only micelles of aggregation number n exist
in the solution. The monomer micelle equilibrium can be described
by the equation

$$nA_1^- \rightleftarrows A_n^{n-} \tag{23}$$

The conditions for equilibrium are then

$$n\mu_{am}^a = n\mu_{am}^w = \mu_m \tag{24}$$

where μ_{am}^a, μ_{am}^w and μ_m are the chemical potentials of amphiphile in
the micelle, amphiphile in the water and of the micelle respecti-
vely. These can be written in terms of standard chemical potentials
as follows

$$\mu_m = n\mu_{am}^a = n\mu_{am}^{\theta,a} + kT \ln (f_n c_n) \tag{25}$$

$$\mu_{am}^w = \mu_{am}^{\theta,w} + kT \ln(f_1 c_1) \tag{26}$$

where f_1 and f_n are activity coefficients and where c_1 and c_n are
concentrations. It is assumed that the surface energy terms are
taken into $\mu^{\theta,a}$. Within the Poisson-Boltzmann equation it seems
most consistent to neglect the activity coefficient for the monomer[34]. Around the CMC the micelles occur at high dilution and one
can use the infinite dilution approximation. The electrostatic
contribution to the monomer activity in the micelle as in Equation
(12) then approaches G_{el}/n. If one considers only the electrostatic contribution to the activity factors one obtains

$$kT \ln f_n = G_{el} \tag{27}$$

where G_{el} is the electrostatic free energy per micelle.

Rearranging the above equations gives

$$\mu_{am}^{\theta,a} - \mu_{am}^{\theta,w} = kT \ln c_1 - \frac{1}{n} kT \ln c_n - \frac{1}{n} G_{el} \tag{28}$$

If it is assumed that 2 % of the amphiphile is in micellar form
at the CMC it is possible, from experimental CMC, data to calculate all terms on the right hand side of Equation (28). The result
for the alkyl sulfates are shown in Figure 8. In these calculations it is assumed the aggregation numbers and radii are that of
the maximum spherical micelles as calculated from Equations (9-2)
and (9-1) in ref. 6. The surface of charges is taken to be 3 Å
from the hydrocarbon core.

The points in Figure 8 fit a straight line with slope - 1.31 kT
which is in good agreement with results for nonionic amphiphiles
(The surface energy term A/n varies only slightly with the number
of carbon atoms in the chain). With values of the intercept and
slope in Figure 8 it is possible to calculate the effect of salt
on the CMC. Comparison between theory and experiment is shown in
Figure 9. The valency of the counterion has also a marked effect
on the CMC[36] which is also correctly predicted by the theory as
seen from Table IV.

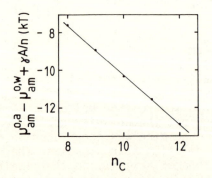

Figure 8. $\mu_{am}^{\theta,a} - \mu_{am}^{\theta,w} + \gamma A/n$ as calculated from Equation (31) and
experimental CMC values (from ref. 35) for n-alkyl sul-
fates plotted versus number of carbon atoms in the hydrocarbon chain, n_C. The straight line is a least square
fit to the calculated points with slope - 1.31 and the
intercept 2.87. For the micelle concentration mole fraction units have been used. (t = 21°C, ε_r = 79.7).

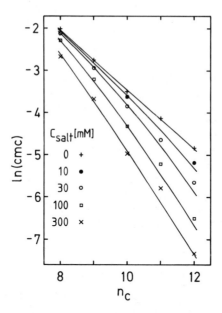

Figure 9. ln(CMC) versus alkyl chain length for n-alkyl sulfates
at different salt concentrations. The solid line are
calculated from Equation (28) and the experimental
points are from ref. 35 (t = 21°C, ε_r = 79.7).

Table IV. Comparison between Experimental and Theoretical CMC
Values for Dodecyl Sulfate with Monovalent and
Divalent Counterions.

(DS)

Compound	Experimental[a] t=25°C	Theoretical t=21°C
	CMC (mM)	
NaDs	7.4	7.83
$Mg(DS)_2$ $6H_2O$	0.88	
$Mn(DS)_2$	1.1	
$Co(DS)_2$ $6H_2O$	0.83	1.22
$Cu(DS)$ $4H_2O$	1.0	

a) From Reference 36.

MICELLAR SIZE DISTRIBUTIONS

In the previous section the effect of polydispersity in the micellar size distribution was neglected. In this section the treatment is extended to calculations of micellar size distributions. The goal is to explain the cooperativity in the micelle formation process as well as to explain that micelles are small nearly spherical over wide ranges of amphiphile and salt concentration and of temperature.

In order to obtain a micellar size distribution it is necessary to specify the geometries of micelles larger than the maximum spherical micells (c.f. Equation (9)). Experimental evidence indicates that micelles grow to be rodlike at high amphiphile and salt concentrations[27]. It is therefore assumed that micelles with aggregation numbers larger than that of the maximum spherical micelle are hemisphere capped cylinders[37] with the radius of the hydrocarbon core equal to the length of a fully extended hydrocarbon chain.

Aggregates of all sizes from dimers to infinite cylinders are allowed. To each aggregate we allot a volume V_n that depends on the aggregation number n. The free energy per cell can be written as previously and the free energy is summed over all cells. There is however an extra contribution to the free energy that comes from the mixing of the cells, G_{mix}^{cells}

$$G_{mix}^{cells} = \sum_n N_n kT \ln(n) \qquad (29)$$

where the sum is over all cells and where N_n is the number of cells with aggregation number n and Y_n their relative concentrations. Thus the quantities

$$Y_n = N_n / (\sum_n N_n) \qquad (30)$$

specify the size distribution.

As previously we can derive expressions for chemical potentials. The results are similar to the previous ones and are written here for the sake of completeness.

$$\mu_+^w = \mu_+^{\theta,w} + kT \ln c_{+o}^n \qquad (31)$$

$$\mu_-^w = \mu_-^{\theta,w} + kT \ln c_{-o}^n \qquad (32)$$

$$\mu_{H_2O} = \mu_{H_2O} - RT (c_{+o}^n + c_{-o}^n + c_m^n) \qquad (33)$$

$$\mu_{am}^a = \mu_{am}^{\theta,a} + G_s^n/n + \mu_{el}^n + kT/n \ln c_m^n + kT/n \ln Y_n \qquad (34)$$

where $c_m^n = 1/V_m^n$. μ_{el}^n is the electrostatic part of the chemical potential and G_s^n/n the surface energy term. All quantities with superscript n depend on n. The only difference from the previous formulas is the last term in Equation (34). By using the equilibrium condition

$$\mu_-^w = \mu_{am}^a \qquad (35)$$

we obtain

$$kT/n \ln Y_n = - (\mu_{am}^{\theta,a} - \mu_{am}^{\theta,w}) - G_s^n/n - \mu_{el}^n - kT/n \ln c_m^n + kT \ln c_{-o} \quad (36)$$

At not too high concentrations c_m^n can be neglected in Equation (33) and then are c_{+o}^n and c_{-o}^n independent of n.

The quantities μ_{el}^n, c_m^n and c_{-o}^n in Equation (36) are obtained from solution of the Poisson-Boltzmann equation, which is relatively straightforward to solve numerically for spheres and infinite cylinders but not for the hemisphere capped cylinders. It is therefore assumed that any quantity, F(n), that is needed for the hemisphere capped cylinders is obtained by interpolating between the spheres and the infinite cylinder in the following way

$$F(n) = F(\infty) + A_F/n + B_F/n^2 \qquad (37)$$

where the constants A_F and B_F are determined from $F(n_s)$ and $F(n_s-1)$. $F(\infty)$ is the value for an infinite cylinder and n_s is the aggregation number of the maximum spherical micelle.

As the aggregates get smaller it gets increasingly difficult to pack the hydrocarbon chains into spheres. The surface area per amphiphile in the small aggregates is therefore expected to be larger than predicted by the spherical model. This can be taken into account by including an extra term, $\Delta\mu_s^n$, in G_s^n/n. This term approaches zero as the aggregates get larger and we therefore assume that

$$\Delta\mu_s^n = 0 \quad \text{for } n \geq n_s \qquad (38)$$

for the smaller values of n we assume that the contribution is inversely proportional to the radius of the hydrocarbon core, b_h, so that

$$\Delta\mu_s^n = \alpha/b_h + \beta \qquad (39)$$

The values of the constants α and β are fixed from equation (38) and the requirement that the concentration at the minima in the micellar size distribution is correctly predicted. The reason for introducing this extra term into G_s^n/n is that it is necessary to do so to describe the cooperativity in the micelle formation process. The inclusion of the extra term as in Equation (39) is essentially an ad hoc assumption. When this extra term has been specified we can hope that the theory, at least qualitatively, predicts the behaviour of the micellar size distribution as the amphiphile concentration, salt concentration and temperature are varied. The term $(\mu_{am}^{\theta,a} - \mu_{am}^{\theta,W})$ in equation (36) is taken as a parameter which is adjusted so that the experimental value of the CMC is obtained.

Now that all terms in the right hand side in equation (36) have been described lets turn to a short description of the computational procedure.

i)   Values of c_{+0}^n and c_{-0}^n are guessed and assumed independent of n.
ii)   The Poisson-Boltzmann equation is solved for the spheres and the infinite cylinder.
iii) All necessary quantities for the hemisphere capped cylinders are interpolated.
iv) $\mu_{am}^{\theta,W} - \mu_{am}^{\theta,W}$ is guessed and values of all Y_n are calculated.
v)   It is checked whether $\Sigma_n Y_n = 1$. If not are steps iv and v repeated.
vi)   The above calculations are repeated until a micellar size distribution for several concentrations is obtained, all of which have the same value of $\mu_{am}^{\theta,a} - \mu_{am}^{\theta,W}$ and which give approximatly the correct value of the CMC.

The results of some calculations for dodecyl sulfate with monovalent and divalent counterions are shown in Table V and in Figure 10. The aggregation numbers are in reasonable agreement with experimental values which are of the order of 60 for monovalent counterions[38] and of the order of 90 - 100 for divalent counterions[39]. The σ values for the divalent counterions are in good agreement with experimental values[40] which are of the order of 11 - 13. The values for the monovalent counterions are however nearly a factor of two to low[21]. This probably reflects the fact that the parameters for the small micelles are poorly estimated.

CONCLUSION

A model expression for the free energy of ionic amphiphile water systems has been developed. The essential energy contributions are due to the hydrophobic effect, which is described through a term independent of aggregate structure and a term proportional

Table V.   Calculated Number Average Aggregation Numbers, n_n, and
           Values Where σ^2 is the Dispersion of the Distribution,
           for Dodecyl Sulfate (DS) with Monovalent and Divalent
           Counterions.

Concentration of DS (mM)	Valency of counterion	n_n	σ
10.21	1	64.8	7.0
12.98	1	65.5	6.0
15.67	1	65.8	5.8
21.29	1	66.4	5.7
43.42	1	68.3	5.8
4.26	2	96.3	10.8
5.37	2	97.0	11.0
10.58	2	98.6	11.0
18.78	2	100.2	11.3

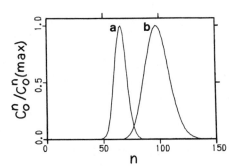

Figure 10. Concentration of amphiphile in micelle of aggregation
            number n, c_0^n, as function of the aggregation number n
            for dodecyl sulfate. The curves are normalised to the
            same maximum value. a) Monovalent counterions, c_A =
            10.21 mM, c_0^n(max) = 0.16 mM. b) Divalent counterions,
            c_A = 5.45 mM, c_0^n(max) = 0.12 mM. c_0^n(max is the con-
            centration at the maxima in the micellar size distri-
            bution and c_A the total amphiphile concentration.
            (t = 25°C, ε_r = 78.3).

to the aggregate - water contact area, and to electrostatic interactions, described using the Poisson-Boltzmann equation. The free
energy expression is simple enough to make it possible to evaluate
its derivatives to obtain chemical potentials and aggregate geometries. It has been shown that the model with good accuracy
describes the equilibrium properties of binary amphiphile - water
systems. This applies to monomer and counterion activities, to the
CMC values, to optimal aggregate geometries and to phase equilibria.
The calculations on the micelle size distributions show that the
simple model does not explain the cooperativity in the micelle
formation process and that an additional energy contribution has
to be added for the smaller aggregates, where apparently the semi-
microscopic description of the aggregates is no longer valid.
When such a correction term is added a good description of the
size distribution is obtained and one obtaines, for example, a
rationalization of the difference between systems with monovalent
and divalent counterions.

REFERENCES

1. P. Windsor, Chem.Rev. 68, 1, (1968).
2. P. Ekwall, in "Advances in Liquid Crystals", G. Brown, Editor,
    Vol 1, o. 1, Academic Press, New York, 1975.
3. G.J.T. Tiddy, Phys.Reports 57, 1, (1980).
4. B. Lindman and H. Wennerström, "Topics in Current Chemistry",
    Vol. 87, p. 1, Springer, Berlin, 1980.
5. P. Ekwall, L. Mandell and K. Fontell, J.Colloid Interface Sci.
    31, 508, (1969).
6. C. Tanford, "The Hydrophobic Effect", Wiley, New York, 1973.
7. C. Tanford, J.Phys.Chem. 84, 2469 (1974).
8. R. Nagarajan and E. Ruckenstein, J. Colloid Interface Sci.
    71, 580 (1979).
9. J.N. Israelachvili, D.J. Mitchell and B.N. Ninham, J.Chem.Soc.
    Faraday II 72, 1525,(1976).
10. N.A. Mazer, M.C. Carey and G.B. Benedek, in "Micellisation,
    Solubilisation and Microemulsions", K.L. Mittal, Editor, Vol, 1,
    p. 359, Plenum, New York, 1977.
11. V.A. Parsegian, Trans. Faraday Soc. 62, 848 (1966).
12. D.E. Mather, J. Colloid Interface Sci. 57, 240 (1976).
13. J. Charvolin and P. Rigny, J.Chem.Phys. 58, 3999 (1973).
14. J. Ulmius and H. Wennerström, J.Magn.Resonance, 28, 309 (1977).
15. G. Lindblom and H. Wennerström, Biophys.Chem. 6, 167 (1979).
16. H. Wennerström, B. Lindman, O. Söderman, T. Drakenberg and
    J.B. Rosenholm, J.Amer.Chem.Soc. 101, 6860 (1979).
17. J.B. Rosenholm, M.R. Hakala and P. Stenius, Mol. Cryst.Liq.
    Cryst. 45, 285 (1978).
18. I. Danielsson, J.B. Rosenholm, P. Stenius and S. Backlund,
    Progr. Colloid Polymer Sci. 61, 1 (1976).

19. S.G. Cutler, P. Mears and D.G. Hall, J.Chem.Soc. Faraday
    Trans. I, 74, 1758 (1978).
20. E. Vikingstad, J. Colloid Interface Sci. 72, 68 (1979).
21. E.A.G. Aniansson, S.N. Wall, M. Almgren, H. Hoffman, I. Kielman,
    W. Ulbricht, R. Zana, J. Lang and C. Tondre, J.Phys.Chem. 80,
    905 (1976).
22. T.L. Hill, "Statistical Mechanics", Addision-Wesley,Reading,
    Mass., 1960.
23. H. Wennerström and B. Lindman, Phys. Reports 52, 1 (1979).
24. H. Wennerström and B. Lindman, J. Phys. Chem. 83, 2931 (1979).
25. B. Jönsson and H. Wennerström, (1980), J. Colloid Interface
    Sci., in press.
26. B. Gallot and S.E. Skoulios, Kolloid-Z.Z. Polymere 208, 37
    (1966).
27. P.J. Missel, N.A. Mazer, G.B. Benedek and C.Y. Young, (1980),
    J. Phys. Chem., 84, 1044 (1980).
28. P. Ekwall, L. Mandell and K. Fontell, J. Colloid Interface
    Sci. 33, 215 (1970).
29. K. Fontell, J. Colloid Interface Sci. 44, 318 (1973).
30. T. Claesson and U. Henriksson, (1980), this volume.
31. R.A. Marcus, J.Chem.Phys. 23, 1057 (1955).
32. J.W. McBain and W.C. Sierichs, J.Amer.Oil.Chem.Soc. 25, 221
    (1948).
33. E.J. Staples and G.J.T. Tiddy, J. Chem. Soc. Faraday I, 74.
    2530 (1978).
34. G. Gunnarsson, B. Jönsson and H. Wennerström, J. Phys. Chem.,
    in press.
35. H.F. Huisman, Proc.Konc.Ned.Akad.Wetensch. B67, 367 (1964).
36. S. Miyamoto, Bull. Chem. Soc. Japan 33, 130 (1960).
37. J.E. Leibner and J. Jacobus, J. Phys. Chem. 81, 130 (1977).
38. K.J. Mysels and L.H. Princen, J. Phys. Chem. 63, 1696 (1959).
39. I. Satake, I. Iwamatsu, S. Hosokawa and R. Matuura, Bull.
    Chem. Soc. Japan 36, 204 (1963).
40. W. Baumüller, H. Hoffman, W. Ulbricht, C. Tondre and R. Zana,
    J. Colloid Interface Sci. 64, 418 (1978).
41. M. Mille and G. Vanderkooi, J. Colloid Interfac. Sci., 59,
    211, (1977).

THERMODYNAMICS OF MICELLAR SYSTEMS: VOLUMES AND HEAT CAPACITIES

OF ALKYLDIMETHYLAMINE OXIDES IN WATER

J. E. Desnoyers, D. Roberts, R. DeLisi[1] and
G. Perron
Department of Chemistry
Université de Sherbrooke
Sherbrooke, Québec, CANADA   J1K 2R1

As part of a general study of the thermodynamic properties of micellar systems, the apparent molal volumes
and heat capacities of the homologous alkyldimethylamine
oxides, $C_x DAO$, where x = 4,6,8 and 10, were measured with
a flow densimeter and a flow microcalorimeter. A wide
temperature range was covered with $C_8 DAO$, $C_6 DAO$ was
studied at 25 and $5°C$ and $C_4 DAO$ and $C_{10} DAO$ at $25°C$ only.
The changes in volume and heat capacity during micellization are reported. The present data are compared with
those of ionic surfactants and organic-aqueous mixed
solvents. As with many other hydrophobic solutes which
have strong acid-base interactions with water, the apparent and partial molal heat capacities of $C_8 DAO$ and
$C_{10} DAO$ pass through a sharp maximum region and then
level off to a constant value.
Since the thermodynamic functions are mostly sensitive
to the local environment of the molecules, no fundamental
differences are observed between the properties of organic-aqueous mixtures which show microheterogeneities
(amines, alcohols) and true micellar systems.

INTRODUCTION

This paper is part of a series on the thermodynamic of micellization. Our general aim is to measure directly all the main
thermodynamic properties of typical surfactants in the micellization
region in order to generate data that could be used to test quantitatively the main theories and models for micellization. Free
energies, enthalpies, heat capacities and volumes have already been

343

reported as a function of concentration and temperature for the
homologous series alkylammonium bromides[2-5], nonyl and decyltrimethylammonium bromides[6,7] and sodium decanoate[4,5,8]. In the case of
the two alykltrimethylammonium bromides, isentropic compressibilities
were also determined. We now wish to extend this study to non-ionic
surfactants.

The alkyldimethylamine oxides (C_xDAO) were chosen for the
following purpose. First of all, compared with most non-ionic
surfactants, their critical micelle concentrations (CMC) are reasonably high. This is important since, with the equipment we have on
hand, direct thermodynamic properties can be measured with reasonable
precision only if the concentration of the solute is above approximately 0.01 mol kg^{-1}. With C_xDAO we can investigate the pre-micellar
region for homologs up to C_{10}, since C_{10}DAO has a CMC at about
0.014 mol kg^{-1} at 25°C. Another reason for this choice comes from
our studies of organic-aqueous mixtures. It was found that systems
which are hydrophobic and at the same time have strong acid-base
type of interactions with water, namely amines[9], alcohols[9,10] and
alkoxyethanols[11], show microheterogeneities in the water-rich
region. Their observed thermodynamic changes are somewhat similar
to micellization. Since the amine oxides also have very strong
acid-base interactions with water, they can therefore be expected
to link our studies on organic-water mixtures with those on
surfactants.

A fair amount of studies have been made on C_xDAO in water. An
interesting feature is that, being weak bases, they behave as typical
non-ionic surfactants at pH above 7 and as typical ionic surfactants
at low pH[12-14]. Much of these studies have been directed towards
the determination of the size and shape of the micelles and in
particular of C_{12}DAO. In general, it seems that C_{12}DAO forms
small spherical micelles in the neutral form, but their size
increases significantly becoming cylindrical in the protonated
form and in the presence of added electrolyte. They readily form
mixed micelles with ionic surfactants[15].

Benjamin has investigated systematically the thermodynamic
properties of these surfactants in water. He measured the
enthalpies of solution[16] and C_xDAO in the neutral and protonated
form and found that the concentration dependence of the enthalpies
are much more regular when the surfactant is in the non-protonated
form. However, the enthalpies of micellization ΔH_m derived from
these data show an anomalous dependence on chain length. He also
determined the volumes of micellization through density measurements[17]; even if he did not make systematic measurements in the
transition area, he observed that ΔV_m was always positive,
increasing with chain length, as it is generally observed with
surfactants[18]. He extended some of these studies by investigating
the influence of urea[19].

In the present work, we will report precise apparent molal volumes and heat capacities of the homologs C_4DAO, C_6DAO, C_8DAO and $C_{10}DAO$. In some cases, especially with C_8DAO, the temperature dependence will also be examined. We will report elsewhere[20] data on enthalpies and activities. In all cases, the surfactants will be in the neutral form. We hope eventually to extent these studies for C_xDAO in the protonated form.

EXPERIMENTAL

Several different syntheses of amine oxides are reported in the literature[12,21,22]. These involve the oxidation of the alkyl-dimethylamines using various oxidizing agents. Of these methods, a modified version[14,15] of the synthesis described by Hermann[12] was found to be the most suitable for the preparation of C_4DAO, C_6DAO and C_8DAO.

To 1 mole of C_xDimethylamine (C_8 and C_6 from Ames Laboratories Inc., C_8 from ICN Pharmaceuticals Inc., C_4 from Chemicals Procurement Laboratories Inc.) was added an equal volume of methanol. Hydrogen peroxide solution (Fisher, 30%,) slightly less than the stoichio-metric amount, was added slowly to the cooled reaction flask. The clear solution was refluxed at $50^{\circ}C$[23] for approximately 6 hours after which the flask was left stirred at room temperature for a further 24 hours. During this time the solution had become viscous. A half-molar equivalent of sodium sulphite was added to destroy any unreacted H_2O_2. After filtration the solution was washed with petroleum ether (30-60°C) to remove unreacted amine. Previous reports[14,15] suggest that the aqueous solution of C_xDAO is best dried by freeze-drying. Since C_xDAO are very hygroscopic, this technique is both laborious and time-consuming. On the other hand, it was found that water could be removed efficiently by adding 2-propanol which forms an aqueous azeotrope. The azetrope was removed by distillation under vacuum (water-pump), and the process was repeated several times to yield the solid C_xDAO. The product was recrystallized twice from acetone previously dried with $CaSO_4$, and the crystals were kept over P_2O_5 under vacuum for several days prior to use. A sample of C_8DAO was also prepared by the method described by Craig and Purushothaman[21] and the same densities were observed for their aqueous solutions. $C_{10}DAO$ was obtained as the commercial product "Barlox 10S", a 30% solution supplied by Lonza Inc. The solid $C_{10}DAO$ was purified and isolated as described above.

The water content of the recrystallized products was determined by Karl Fischer titration. It was found to be typically of the order 3 to 5% water. Similar determinations were made by the conductimetric titration of the C_xDAO solution with hydrochloric acid. The two determinations agreed within the limits of experi-mental error, and the molalities were accordingly corrected for the

initial water content. The solutions for the measurement of density
and heat capacity were prepared by weight from the stock solution.
Where possible the same solution was used for the measurement of
the densities and heat capacities at several temperatures. The
solutions were kept in well-sealed bottles with minimum air-space
above the liquid. Some measurements were repeated on "old"
solutions and showed that there was no appreciable deterioration
in the quality of the solution with time.

The procedure used for the measurement of density and heat
capacity using the flow densimeter and microcalorimeter has been
previously described[6],[7]. In the present investigation, the two
flow instruments were placed in series. In the heat capacity
experiment the difference between the initial and final temperatures
is $0.76^{\circ}K$. As a consequence, the temperature of the density
measurements are systematically $0.38^{\circ}K$ lower than the mean temperature for the heat capacity data. Density data are required to
convert heat capacities per unit volume, the measured function, to
heat capacities per unit weight. It can readily be shown that a
difference of $0.38^{\circ}K$ between both sets of measurements makes a
negligible error on the heat capacity conversions.

RESULTS

The apparent molal volumes and isobaric heat capacities, ϕ_V
and ϕ_C, were derived from the differences in densities and heat
capacities per unit volume in the usual manner[11],[18]. These were
then plotted against the solute molality m. When additional
measurements were made with new stock solutions or with newly
purified products, a systematic shift (less than 0.2%) was observed
in the values of ϕ_V and ϕ_C. This shift can be attributed to the
differences in water content of $C_x DAO$, this most likely arising
from changes in atmospheric humidity. Even though the analyses
based on Karl Fischer and conductivity agreed inside their
respective expected uncertainty, neither of these techniques can be
considered highly reliable with the present system. The water
content is rather high for a Karl Fischer titration and the weak
basic character of $C_x DAO$ decreases the sharpness of the conductivity
changes. As a result, small differences in concentration at the
level of the experimental uncertainty can account for the shift in
ϕ_V and ϕ_C. In order to correct for this, the molality of the
stock solutions were adjusted so that their densities fell on the
curve of the density versus molality plot for those series of
measurements made when the relative humidity was at its minimum.
Then excellent agreement was obtained for different sets of
solution.

The corrected original volume and heat capacity data will be
reported at the same time as the enthalpies and activities[20]. At

low molalities in the pre-micellar region, ϕ_V and ϕ_C are linear functions of m. The infinite dilution standard values ϕ_Y^o are equal to the standard partial molal quantities $\overline{Y}_2^o$. These and the initial slopes A_V and A_C are summarized in Table I. The present ϕ_V^o for

Table I.   Volumes and Heat Capacities of Alkyldimethylamine Oxides in water.

Solute	T^a	ϕ_V^o	ϕ_C^o	A_V	A_C
	^oC	cm^3mol^{-1}	$JK^{-1}mol^{-1}$	$cm^3mol^{-2}kg$	$JK^{-1}mol^{-2}kg$
C_4DAO	25.0	119.60	445	– 1.75	– 11
C_6DAO	5.0	148.56	602	– 4.13	– 16.0
	25.0	151.52	620	– 3.25	– 6.0
C_8DAO	0.5	178.28	773	– 6.4	0
	2.0	178.48	776	– 5.8	0
	5.0	179.0	792	– 5.0	4.0
	15.0	181.04	798	– 4.3	10.0
	25.0	183.09	806	– 2.64	25
	35.0	184.80	785	– 1.4	33
	55.0	188.4	780		
$C_{10}DAO$	25.0	215.23	988	–76.8	267

^{a} Temperatures for ϕ_V = T – 0.38^oC except C_4DAO when both measurements are at 25^oC.

C_8DAO can be compared with that of Benjamin[17]; he obtained 183.9 cm^3mol^{-1} at 30^oC while the present value interpolated from the data at 25 and 35^oC is 184.0 cm^3mol^{-1}. Group additivity for ϕ_V^o and ϕ_C^o can also be used to estimate the accuracy of our data. The differences between $C_{10}DAO$, C_8DAO, C_6DAO and C_4DAO at 25^oC are respectively 32.14, 31.57 and 31.92 cm^3mol^{-1} and 182, 186 and 175 $JK^{-1}mol^{-1}$. The usual contributions of two CH_2 groups are for ϕ_V^o 32.0 cm^3mol^{-1} and for ϕ_C^o 176 $JK^{-1}mol^{-1}$. This therefore sets the accuracy of our data at approximately ± 0.3 cm^3mol^{-1} and ± 6 $JK^{-1}mol^{-1}$ for ϕ_V and ϕ_C. On the other hand, the relative precision as a function of concentration is better by about an order of magnitude.

The relative volumes, $\phi_V - \phi_V^o$, are shown as a function of m at 25°C in Figure 1. An expanded scale is shown for $C_{10}DAO$ at low concentration. Data from different stock solutions are shown by different symbols. The partial molal volumes $\bar{V}_2$ obtained from a plot of $\Delta(\phi_V m)/\Delta m$ against the mean molality are also shown. The initial decrease in volume followed by an increase is typical of the behavior of most organic solutes, including surfactants, in water. With surfactants, the increase in ϕ_V becomes very sharp and corresponds to the micellization region. The determination of the change in volume during micellization, ΔV_m, is obtained

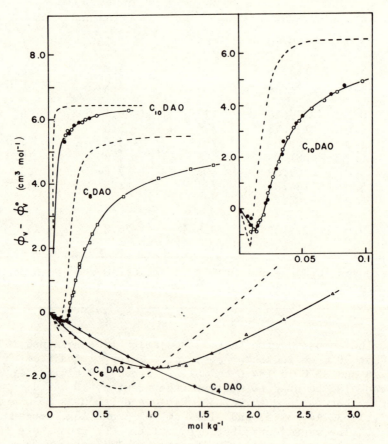

Figure 1. The relative apparent molal volumes of alkyldimethyl-amine oxides in water at 24.6°C. In the case of C_4DAO, the temperature was 25.0°C. The different symbols for the data of C_6DAO and $C_{10}DAO$ refer to different stock solutions that have been corrected as indicated in the EXPERIMENTAL section.

from a phase-separation model[8,18]; essentially $\bar{V}_2$ of C_xDAO in the pre- and post-micellar regions are extrapolated to the CMC. For this purpose, the CMC was taken as the initial break in $\bar{V}_2$. The ΔV_m obtained are all positive and increase the chain length, as previously observed by Benjamin[17]. These values are reported in Tabel II.

The corresponding data for heat capacities are shown in Figure 2. Again there is a close similarity between these results and those of hydrophobic solutes which can have acid-base type of interactions with water[9-11]. These include alcohols and amines and some surfactants[4]. With the lower homologs, ϕ_c is relatively constant at low molality but decreases at high molalities. For C_8DAO a large hump is observed with ϕ_c, and even more so with $\bar{C}_{P,2}$, in the micellization region. With C_{10}DAO, the hump region becomes very narrow and $\bar{C}_{P,2}$ can be considered discontinuous in the micellization region.

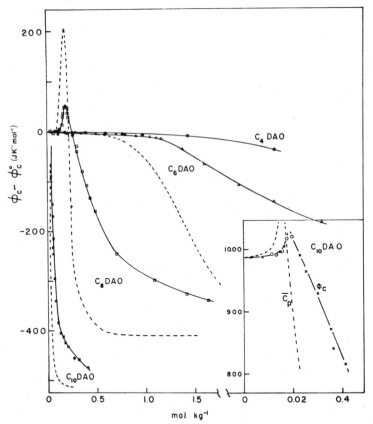

Figure 2. The apparent molal heat capacities of alkyldimethylamine oxides in water at 25°C. The different symbols with C_6DAO and C_{10}DAO refer to different stock solutions as in the case of volumes.

Table II. Functions of Micellization of Alkyldimethylamine Oxides in Water.

Solute	T^a / °C	ΔV / cm^3 mol^{-1}	ΔC_m / JK^{-1} mol^{-1}	$\Delta\phi_C$(hump)^b / JK^{-1} mol^{-1}	CMC / mol kg^{-1}		
					ϕ_V(min)	ϕ_C(break)	ϕ_C(max)
C$_4$DAO	25.0					1.43	
C$_6$DAO	5.0				1.45	1.45	
	25.0				0.84	1.13	
D$_8$DAO	0.5	8.62	− 625	297	0.31	0.28	0.38
	2.0	8.38	− 580	294	0.29	0.26	0.37
	5.0	7.87	− 520	243	0.27	0.23	0.33
	15.0	6.71	− 503	144	0.20	0.16	0.27
	25.0	6.17	− 410	58	0.19	0.13	0.19
	35.0	5.90	− 398	21	0.13	0.09	0.18
	55.0	∼ 5.0	− 290 ± 20		∼ 0.08		
C$_{10}$DAO	25.0	7.85	− 514	∼ 25	0.014	0.014	0.019

a Temperatures for ϕ_V = T − 0.38°C except C$_4$DAO when both measurements are at 25°C.

b $\Delta\phi_C$(hump) is the difference between the maximum in ϕ_C and the value of ϕ_C at the initial break.

The hump in ϕ_C is predicted from a phase transition model[8].
It corresponds to the relaxational part of the heat capacity, i.e.
it is related to the shift in CMC with temperature. As a first
approximation it is proportional to the square of the enthalpy of
micellization. At 25°C ΔH_m is large and positive for C_8DAO and
C_{10}DAO but close to zero for C_6DAO[20]. It is therefore normal that
no maximum in $\phi_C - \phi_C^{\circ}$ is observed with C_6DAO.

As with other surfactants[8,18], the change in heat capacity
during micellization, ΔC_m, is obtained by extrapolating $\overline{C}_{p,2}$ in
the pre- and post-micellar region to the CMC. Since these
$\overline{C}_{p,2}$ are relatively constant in these regions, the precise choice
of the CMC is not critical. The observed ΔC_m, reported in Table II,
are all negative as with other surfactants, and decrease in magnitude with chain length.

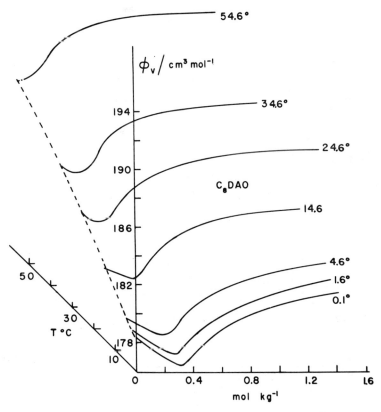

Figure 3.   The apparent molal volume of C_8DAO as a function of
temperature.

As in the case of ionic surfactants, micellization occurs over a range of concentration, and it is difficult to define a CMC from heat capacity data. For example, in the case of $C_{10}DAO$, the initial break in $\bar{C}_{p,2}$ is at 0.012 mol kg^{-1}, and $\bar{C}_{p,2}$ reaches a steady state at nearly an order of magnitude higher. With a phase transition model the initial break and the maximum in ϕ_c (see Table II) should occur at the same concentration[8]. An analysis of the temperature dependence of the CMC of C_8DAO, using ΔH_m and ΔC_m data, suggests that the most self-consistent CMC is in-between the initial break and the maximum[20].

The homolog C_8DAO was studied over a wide temperature range and C_6DAO at 25 and 5°C. The data for C_8DAO are summarized in Figures 3 to 5. With C_6DAO at 5°C the data (not shown) are

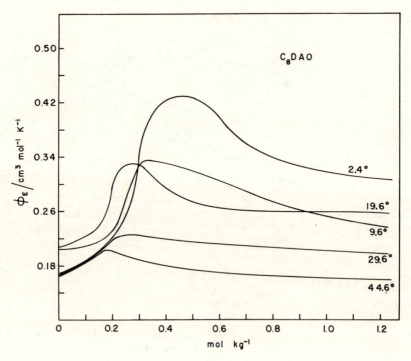

Figure 4.   The apparent molal expansibilities of C_8DAO as a function of temperature and molality.

similar to those at 25°C except that the changes in ϕ_C and ϕ_V [20] occur at higher molalities. Since at 5°C ΔH_m is not zero anymore a small hump or maximum would have been expected in the ϕ_C curve. This was not observed.

The changes in ϕ_V of C_8DAO are relatively sharp at low temperature and more ill-defined at high temperature (Figure 3). This is better seen in Figure 4 where the apparent molal expansibilities, $\phi_E \simeq \Delta\phi_V/\Delta T$, are shown. There is a large maximum in ϕ_E in the micellization region, which decreases with temperature. There seems to be some anomaly in the trends between 9.6 and 19.6°C, but the uncertainty on these ϕ_E obtained indirectly can possibly account for this. Similar maxima in ϕ_E are generally observed with micellar systems[4,7] and alcohol-aqueous mixtures[11] and are probably related to the relaxational contribution to expansibilities[4,8].

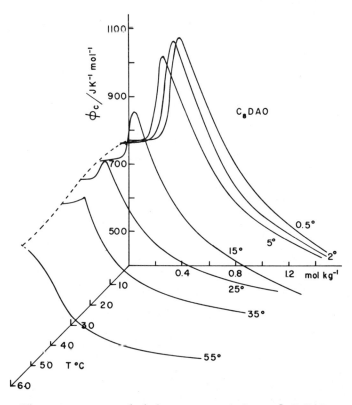

Figure 5.   The apparent molal heat capacities of C_8DAO as a function of temperature and molality.

The temperature dependence of ϕ_C of C_8DAO is also quite typical of hydrophobic solutes which can form hydrogen bonds with water[4,9-11]. In the pre-micellar region, ϕ_C and the concentration dependence of ϕ_C (i.e. A_V) do not change much with temperature. On the other hand, the transitions are nearly first order at low temperatures and practically non-existent at $55^{\circ}C$. This is even more evident if $\bar{C}_{P,2}$ are examined rather than ϕ_C, as shown in Figure 6 for three temperatures. At $35^{\circ}C$ there is only a small hump in $\bar{C}_{P,2}$ but at $0.5^{\circ}C$ the function becomes nearly discontinuous. It becomes difficult to determine ϕ_C accurately in the hump region if the hump is narrow. Since the magnitude varies to a large extent, and non-linearly, with temperature, ϕ_C now depends to some extent on the experimental change in temperature in the calorimetric measurement. The situation is especially bad with $C_{10}DAO$ where the transition region is very narrow.

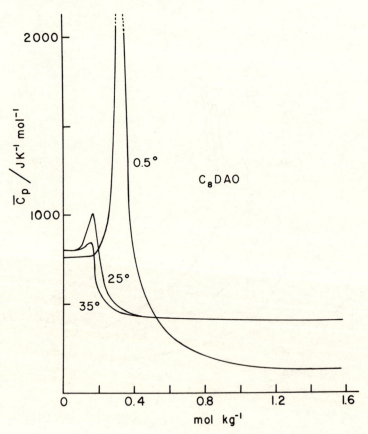

Figure 6.   The partial molal heat capacities of C_8DAO at various temperature.

The temperature dependence of ΔV_m and ΔC_m of C_8DAO_{18} (Table II) present no special problem. As with ionic surfactants, the magnitude of these functions decreases with temperature as we would expect if these functions are primarily reflecting the decrease in hydrophobic hydration of the dispersed monomers.

DISCUSSION

Our aim in this work was to compare aqueous-organic mixtures which show microheterogeneities with true micellar systems. For this purpose C_8DAO is compared in Figure 7 with an ionic surfactant, octylammonium bromide, and triethylamine, all at $5^{\circ}C$. All these solutes are chemically similar. The CMC of C_8DAO and C_8NH_3Br are

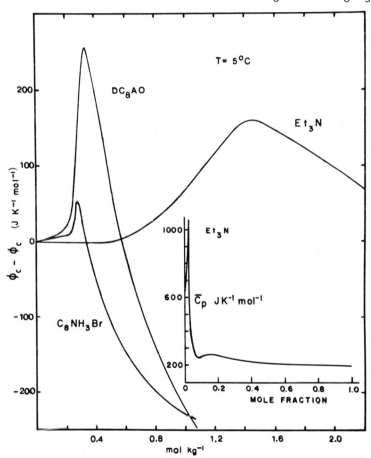

Figure 7. Comparison of the heat capacities of C_8DAO with those of octylamine hydrobromide and triethylamine at $5^{\circ}C$.

comparable, which suggests that the hydrophilic character of the polar and ionic heads are similar. The larger hump with C_8DAO reflects the larger ΔH_m of nonionic surfactants (the relaxational part of ϕ_C is proportional to ΔH_m^2). The transition with Et_3N corresponds approximately to that of C_6DAO, which is not unexpected; the strong hydrophilic character of the amine oxide neutralizes the effect of two CH_2 groups. The only major difference is that ϕ_C of C_6DAO shows no maximum or hump in the transition area, although at $5°C$ it has a positive, albeit small, ΔH_m. Solutes such as Et_3N, tert-butanol, n-butoxy-ethanol, are not usually considered surfactants although their $\bar{C}_{P,2}$, as exemplified in Figure 7, certainly show similar trends, especially if they are plotted on a mole fraction scale.

The similarity between the three systems in Figure 7 indicates that the thermodynamic functions are reflecting similar interactions or local environment. All these solutes are hydrophobic[25]. As a result, in all cases at infinite dilution, there is a positive contribution to $\bar{C}_{P,2}^o$ and negative contributions to $\bar{H}_2^o$, $\bar{V}_2^o$ and $\bar{K}_2^o$. At low concentrations, hydrophobic interactions will affect the thermodynamic functions in a linear fashion.

With some functions, e.g. $\bar{H}_2$, these initial slopes are large, while with others, e.g. $\bar{C}_{P,2}$, they are often small. These hydrophobic interactions may often lead to solvent-shared association complexes of small clusters as in clathrate hydrates[26]. It could well be that the hump region with ϕ_C corresponds to the relaxation of these smaller clusters[9,11]. Beyond this intermediate zone contact association begins, and this leads to fairly well-defined micelles with long-chain surfactants but to more ill-defined aggregates with solutes such as triethylamine. Still, the local environment of the solutes are the same. The hydrophobic part of the molecule, which affects mostly the thermodynamic functions, are in contact only with other hydrophobic groups. In other words, in all these systems at high concentration, the hydrophobic part of the solute will dissolve only into the oily microphases. In general, mixtures of surfactants and these other hydrophobic solutes which have strong acid-base character lead to mixed microstructures as evidenced by the changes in thermodynamic functions[27]. There is a mutual reinforcement which is largely responsible for the existence of micromulsions.

In all cases, at high temperatures (say above $50°C$), the changes in thermodynamic functions of hydrophobic solutes become very gradual, and it becomes difficult to speak of micellization anymore. Of course, these solutes are still surface active and will still interact preferentially with oils, but these interactions have now little to do with the existence of micelles and with the structure of water.

ACKNOWLEDGEMENT

We are grateful to Lonza Inc. for a sample of $C_{10}DAO$ supplied under the trade name of Barlox 10S. We also thank the Natural Science and Engineering Council of Canada for financial help.

REFERENCES

1. On leave of absence from Istituto di Chimica Fisica, Universita di Palermo, Palermo, Italy.
2. J. E. Desnoyers and M. Arel. Can. J. Chem. <u>45</u>, 359 (1967).
3. P. -A. Leduc, J. -L. Fortier and J. E. Desnoyers. J. Phys. Chem. <u>78</u>, 1217 (1974).
4. R. DeLisi, G. Perron and J. E. Desnoyers. Can. J. Chem. <u>58</u>, 959 (1980).
5. R. DeLisi, G. Perron, J. Paquette and J. E. Desnoyers. Can. J. Chem. (submitted).
6. G. M. Musbally, G. Perron and J. E. Desnoyers. J. Colloid Interface Sci. <u>54</u>, 80 (1976).
7. R. DeLisi, C. Ostiguy, G. Perron and J. E. Desnoyers. J. Colloid Interface Sci., <u>71</u>, 147 (1979).
8. J. E. Desnoyers, R. DeLisi and G. Perron. Pure Appl. Chem. <u>52</u>, 433 (1980).
9. G. Roux, D. Roberts, G. Perron and J. E. Desnoyers. J. Solution Chem. (in press).
10. C. de Visser, G. Perron and J. E. Desnoyers. Can. J. Chem. <u>55</u>, 856 (1977).
11. G. Roux, G. Perron and J. E. Desnoyers. J. Solution Chem. <u>7</u>, 639 (1978).
12. K. W. Herrmann. J. Phys. Chem. <u>66</u>, 295 (1962); <u>68</u>, 1540 (1964).
13. W. L. Courchene. J. Phys. Chem. <u>68</u>, 1870 (1964).
14. S. Ikeda, M. Tsunoda and H. Maeda. J. Colloid Interface Sci. <u>70</u>, 448 (1979); <u>67</u>, 336 (1978).
15. D. G. Kolp, R. G. Laughlin, F. P. Krause and R. E. Zimmerer. J. Phys. Chem. <u>67</u>, 51 (1963).
16. L. Benjamin. J. Phys. Chem. <u>68</u>, 3575 (1964).
17. L. Benjamin. J. Phys. Chem. <u>70</u>, 3790 (1966).
18. J. E. Desnoyers, R. DeLisi, C. Ostiguy and G. Perron in "Solution Chemistry of Surfactants", K. L. Mittal, Editor, Vol. 1, 221, Plenum Press, New York, 1979.
19. L. Benjamin. J. Coll. Sci. <u>22</u>, 389 (1966).
20. R. DeLisi, D. Roberts, G. Perron and J. E. Desnoyers (in preparation).
21. J. C. Craig and K. K. Purushothaman. J. Org. Chem. <u>35</u>, 1721 (1970).
22. M. Fieser and L. Fieser. "Reagents for Organic Synthesis" Wiley-Interscience, New York, (1969), Vol. 2.

23.   D. B. Lake and G. L. K. Hoh.   J. Amer. Oil Chem. Soc. $\underline{40}$, 628 (1963).

24.   C. Jolicoeur and G. Lacroix.   Can. J. Chem. $\underline{54}$, 624 (1976).

25.   F. Franks and D. S. Reid in "Water, A Comprehensive Treatise", F. Franks, Editor, Chap. 5, Vol. 2, Plenum Press, New York (1973).

26.   K. Iwasaki and T. Fujiyama.   J. Phys. Chem. $\underline{81}$, 1908 (1977).

27.   G. Perron, R. DeLisi, I. Davidson, S. Généreux and J. E. Desnoyers.   J. Colloid Interface Sci. (in press).

THERMODYNAMIC PROPERTIES OF BINARY AND TERNARY AQUEOUS SURFACTANT
SYSTEMS

Jarl B. Rosenholm, Reid B. Grigg and Loren G. Hepler
Department of Chemistry and Oil Sands Research
Laboratory
University of Lethbridge
Lethbridge, Alberta, Canada T1K 3M4

We have made measurements by flow calorimetry and
flow densimetry that have led to apparent and partial
molar heat capacities and also apparent and partial
molar volumes of aqueous solutions of surfactants
(cationic, anionic, and non-ionic) at concentrations
both smaller and larger than the critical micelle
concentrations. Results of these measurements lead to
independent determinations of the critical micelle
concentrations and also permit evaluations of ΔC_p and
ΔV values for micelle formation. All such ΔV values
are positive, while all ΔC_p values are negative. We
have also made similar measurements of heat capacities
and densities on solutions of p-xylene, octane, and
decanol in surfactant solutions in an effort to gather
information that will ultimately improve our understanding of solubilization. Some exploratory measurements of enthalpies of solution have also been made on
these same three component systems.

INTRODUCTION

Investigations of the thermodynamic properties of solutions
of surfactants (or any other solutions) have two general kinds of
values that are pertinent to our research to be described here.
First, thermodynamic data can be used in the various equations of
classical thermodynamics that permit one to use a certain number
of experimental data for calculation of a substantially larger
number of properties. For example, enthalpy data permit calculations of the variations of equilibrium properties over ranges of

359

temperatures; enthalpy and heat capacity data permit similar calculations that are applicable over wider ranges of temperatures. Similarly, volumetric data permit calculation of equilibrium properties
over ranges of pressures. The other kind of use of thermodynamic
data has to do with gaining improved microscopic or molecular understanding of solute-solute and solute-solvent interactions. Several
authors in two recent books[1,2] have described one or both of these
kinds of applications of thermodynamics to solutions of surfactants.
We also call attention to three other useful publications[3-5] that
deal with these same kinds of applications.

The publications[1-5] cited above provide a good general background for our thermodynamic investigations of surfactant solutions.
We now turn to consideration of some recent investigations that are
more explicitly related to our work.

Many earlier investigators have obtained information about enthalpies of micellization from the temperature dependence of the
critical micelle concentration. Unfortunately, this common approach
is subject to important disadvantages. First, differentiation as in
dln(CMC)/dT inevitably magnifies experimental errors and uncertainties.
Second, there are fundamental difficulties that are specific to surfactant systems as discussed previously by Muller[6] and by Rosenholm,
Burchfield, and Hepler.[7] All of these difficulties are compounded
further by the second differentiation involving $d\Delta H^o/dT$ that is required for evaluation of heat capacities of micellization from the
temperature dependence of the critical micelle concentration.

Various investigators have obtained information about the
enthalpy of micellization by way of calorimetric measurements of
heats of dilution. In general, heats of micellization obtained in
this way are likely to be more reliable and accurate than those
derived less directly from the temperature dependence of the critical micelle concentration. A few investigators[8-12] have made such
measurements at more than one temperature and have then obtained
information about the change in heat capacity associated with
micelle formation by way of $\Delta C_p = d\Delta H^o/dT$. Although this approach
does involve one differentiation and the associated magnification
of errors and uncertainties, it is generally better than the approach
described in the preceding paragraph, which involves two differen-
tiations and also other[6,7] difficulties.

Another approach to gaining information about the change in
heat capacity to be associated with micellization involves direct
calorimetric measurements of heat capacities of solutions of surfactants. Desnoyers and colleagues at Université de Sherbrooke
have reported[13-16] the results of many such measurements and have
also described[16] in considerable detail how these heat capacities
can be used in several thermodynamic calculations. We have chosen
to follow a similar calorimetric approach, with results that are
summarized later in this report.

Information about volume changes to be associated with micelle formation can be obtained from the pressure dependence of the critical micelle concentration. This approach involves the magnification of errors and uncertainties associated with the differentiation dln(CMC)/dP and also complications analogous to those previously investigated[6,7] in connection with the temperature dependence of the critical micelle concentration. In spite of these difficulties, several investigators[17-21] have obtained useful information about volume changes from the pressure dependence of the critical micelle concentration. Other investigators[13-16,22-25] have measured densities of surfactant solutions and then obtained information about volume changes associated with micellization by way of apparent and partial molar volumes; we have chosen to follow this approach, with results that are summarized later in this report.

It is well known that many substances (such as octane, decanol, etc.) that are nearly insoluble in water are much more soluble in micellar solutions. Thermodynamic investigations of solubilization of this kind are applicable to effects of temperature and pressure and also to improving our microscopic understanding, just as for the two component systems discussed earlier. There have been only a very few previous thermodynamic investigations directly related to our work on these ternary systems. We call particular attention to the work of Vikingstad and Høiland,[26-28] who have measured densities of three component solutions (water, relatively concentrated surfactant, relatively dilute organic solute) and calculated apparent molar volumes of the organic solutes. We have made similar density and also heat capacity measurements on various other three component (water, surfactant, organic solute) systems, leading to apparent molar volumes and apparent molar heat capacities of the organic solutes. Finally, we have also measured heats of solution of organic solutes in surfactant solutions.

EXPERIMENTAL

All of our heat capacity measurements have been made with a Picker flow calorimeter of the type that has been described in several publications[29-31] from the Université de Sherbrooke. Operation of the calorimeter has been checked as recently recommended.[32] Densities of solutions were measured with flow densimeters that have been described previously.[33] Heats of solution have been measured with a titration calorimeter[34] that permits injection of aliquots of organic solute into surfactant solution. The results of all measurements refer to 25.0°C.

Commercially available surfactants of the best available quality were purified by recrystallization from appropriate solvents, washed (usually with ether) and then dried in vacuum desiccators.

Octane, p-xylene, and decanol of high purity were used without further treatment.

RESULTS

Results of measurements of heat capacities and densities of solutions are usefully expressed in terms of apparent molar heat capacities and apparent molar volumes of solutes. The apparent molar property ϕ_Y is defined according to

$$\phi_Y = [Y(solution) - Y(solvent)]/n_s \qquad (1)$$

in which the symbols have the following meanings: ϕ_Y is the apparent molar property of the solute, Y(solution) is the extensive property (heat capacity or volume here) of a specified quantity of solution, Y(solvent) is the same property of the amount of pure solvent contained in the specified quantity of solution, and n_s is the amount (moles) of solute in the specified quantity of solution.

To obtain apparent molar heat capacities and apparent molar volumes of solutes at infinite dilution, where apparent molar properties become identical with corresponding partial molar properties, we have fitted our results for dilute solutions to equations of the following types. For non-ionic solutes we have used

$$\phi_Y = \phi_Y^o + B_Y m \qquad (2)$$

and for ionic solutes we have used

$$\phi_Y = \phi_Y^o + A_Y (d_1^o m)^{\frac{1}{2}} + B_Y m \qquad (3)$$

In these equations ϕ_Y^o represents the desired limiting value of ϕ_Y at infinite dilution, A_Y is a limiting slope derived from the Debye-Hückel theory, d_1^o is the density of pure solvent, m is the molality, and B_Y is an adjustable parameter. Millero[35] has thoroughly reviewed the applicability of the Debye-Hückel theory and Equation (3) to apparent molar volumes of electrolytes and also evaluated the limiting slope at 25°C as $A_V(d_1^o)^{\frac{1}{2}} = 1.865$ cm^3 mol$^{-3/2}$ kg$^{1/2}$ for electrolytes of 1:1 charge type. Most previous investigators of heat capacities of aqueous electrolytes have used $A_C(d_1^o)^{\frac{1}{2}} = 28.95$ J K^{-1} mol$^{-3/2}$ kg$^{1/2}$ for electrolytes of 1:1 charge type, as reported by Philip and Desnoyers[36] and Leduc, Fortier, and Desnoyers.[37] There is some recent evidence[38,39] that a slightly larger value is better. Because the best value is not quite certain and also because we want our derived values to be conveniently comparable to some earlier results, we use the $A_C(d_1^o)^{\frac{1}{2}}$ value quoted

above. The present small uncertainty in the best value of A_c is of
substantial importance for highly charged electrolytes, but it is of
little numerical importance with respect to our analyses of heat
capacities of dilute solutions of 1:1 electrolytes.

For some purposes it is useful to consider excess apparent
molar properties defined as

$$\phi_Y^{EX} = \phi_Y - \phi_Y^o - A_Y(d_1^o)^{\frac{1}{2}}m \tag{4}$$

for electrolytes and as

$$\phi_Y^{EX} = \phi_Y - \phi_Y^o \tag{5}$$

for non-electrolytes.

For many thermodynamic calculations it is necessary to derive
partial molar properties from the corresponding apparent molar
properties that we have represented by ϕ_Y. Such calculations are
conveniently done by way of

$$\overline{Y} = \phi_Y + m(d\phi_Y/dm) \tag{6}$$

It is also possible to do these calculations by way of procedures
summarized long ago by Young and Vogel.[40]

We now turn to presentation of some numerical results obtained
from our measurements on solutions of several surfactants and also
on sodium propionate. The first results to be considered are the
ϕ_V^o and ϕ_C^o values that are listed in Table I. These values for the
non-electrolyte DMDDAO were obtained by fitting Equation (2) to our
apparent molar volumes and heat capacities, while these values for
the various electrolytes were obtained by fitting Equation (3) to
our corresponding apparent molar volumes and heat capacities.

Next, we consider the determination of critical micelle concentrations from our apparent molar heat capacities and volumes.
These determinations have been based on graphs of excess apparent
molar heat capacities and volumes defined according to Equations
(4) and (5), in which ϕ_Y^{EX} values are plotted against corresponding
molalities as illustrated in Figures 1 and 2. We identify the
breaks in graphs of ϕ_Y^{EX} against m with the CMC, with results that
are summarized in Table II. In this connection we note that many
"simple" electrolytes investigated here and at the Université de
Sherbrooke and also sodium propionate investigated as part of this
work all have ϕ_Y^{EX} values that are considerably smaller than those
observed for surfactants above the CMC. Further, all graphs of ϕ_Y^{EX}
against m for these "simple" electrolytes yield smooth curves with
relatively small slopes. The breaks illustrated in Figures 1 and 2
are therefore properly associated with the onset of micelle formation

Table I. Apparent Molar Volumes and Heat Capacities at Infinite
Dilution.

Solute[*]	ϕ_V^o $cm^3\ mol^{-1}$	ϕ_C^o $J\ K^{-1}\ mol^{-1}$
Na^+P^-	53.5	146.2
Na^+Oc^-	132.8	574.8
Na^+L^-	195.0	920.2
Na^+DDS^-	247[**]	1040
DDA^+Cl^-	231.0	922
DMDDAO	237.2	1195

[*] Abbreviations used here and subsequently: Na^+P^- = sodium propionate, Na^+Oc^- = sodium octanoate, Na^+L^- = sodium laurate, Na^+DDS^- = sodium dodecyl sulfate, DDA^+Cl^- = dodecylammonium chloride, and DMDDAO = N,N-dimethyldodecylamine oxide.

[**] See discussion in the main text concerning the possibility that a lower value is better.

Table II. Critical Micelle Concentrations Determined from Graphs of ϕ_Y^{EX} (Equations 4 and 5) against m.

Surfactant	CMC from ϕ_V^{EX} $mol\ kg^{-1}$	CMC from ϕ_C^{EX} $mol\ kg^{-1}$
Na^+Oc^-	0.37	0.38
Na^+L^-	0.026	0.026
Na^+DDS^-	∿0.008	<0.01
DDA^+Cl^-	0.014	0.014
DMDDAO	∿0.0021	∿0.0022

rather than with "ordinary" solute-solute interactions.

It is possible to make several comparisons of our results in Tables I and II with results of earlier investigators as follows.

Our CMC values for aqueous sodium octanoate are in good agreement with values listed by Mukerjee and Mysels,[41] based on such "classical" methods as surface tensions, etc. Our CMC based on ϕ_V^{EX} is larger than that found similarly by Leduc and Desnoyers,[42] while our CMC based on ϕ_C^{EX} is smaller than their value obtained similarly. Both of our values are in good agreement with their average value. Our ϕ_V^o is in good agreement with the value reported by Leduc and Desnoyers,[42] while our ϕ_C^o is 19 J K^{-1} mol^{-1} smaller than the value Desnoyers and colleagues[32] have recalculated from their earlier[42] measurements. Although this difference is larger than both our estimates of likely uncertainties, it should also be noted that the general dependence of ϕ_C on concentration is the same in both investigations and that similar treatments of both sets of results lead to similar ΔC_p values for micellization.

Our ϕ_V^o for sodium laurate is in good agreement with the value reported by Brun, Høiland, and Vikingstad[23] and both our CMC values are in good agreement with values cited by Mukerjee and Mysels.[41]

For sodium dodecyl sulfate our CMC values are less certain than for several of the other surfactants we have investigated. The larger than usual uncertainty results from a larger than usual scatter in the experimental results and also from "breaks" in the graphs of ϕ_V^{EX} and ϕ_C^{EX} against m that are less sharp than for several other surfactants. In spite of these difficulties, our CMC is in reasonable agreement with values (mostly ranging from 0.0080 to 0.0084 molar) cited by Mukerjee and Mysels.[41]

Musbally, Perron, and Desnoyers[13] and Brun, Høiland, and Vikingstad[23] have made density measurements leading to ϕ_V and thence ϕ_V^o values for aqueous sodium dodecyl sulfate. Their results have led to ϕ_V^o = 238.0 and 237.2 cm^3 mol^{-1}, respectively, as compared with our (Table I) ϕ_V^o = 247 cm mol^{-1}. The lowest concentrations investigated by these earlier workers were 0.014 molal in Sherbrooke[13] and 0.007 molal in Bergen[23] as compared to our 0.0012 molal. If we consider only our results for m >0.007 mol kg^{-1}, we obtain a ϕ_V^o in general agreement with the earlier[13,23] values. Because our measurements extended to concentrations well below the CMC whereas the earlier measurements[13,23] stopped at concentrations near or above the CMC, there is no doubt that our ϕ_V^o is, at least in principle, better than either of the earlier values. Unfortunately, the uncertainties and potential errors in ϕ_V values increase substantially with decreasing concentrations so that it is possible that our ϕ_V^o really isn't better than the smaller values derived from the earlier investigations[13,23] and also from results of our measurements on

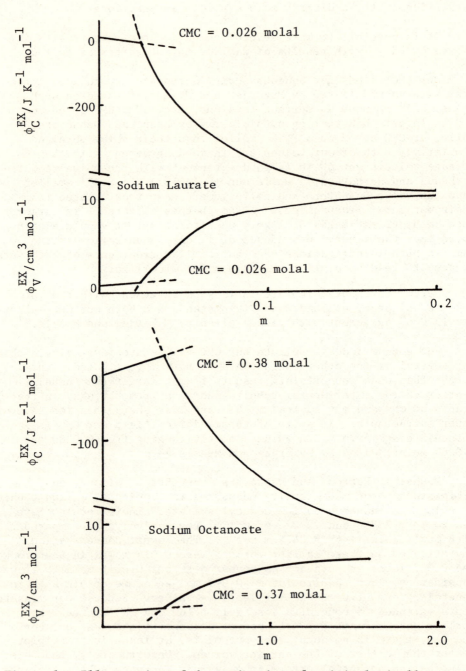

Figure 1.   Illustration of determination of critical micelle concentrations for anionic surfactants.   Measurements of ϕ_V and ϕ_C
were made at concentrations below and above the CMC.

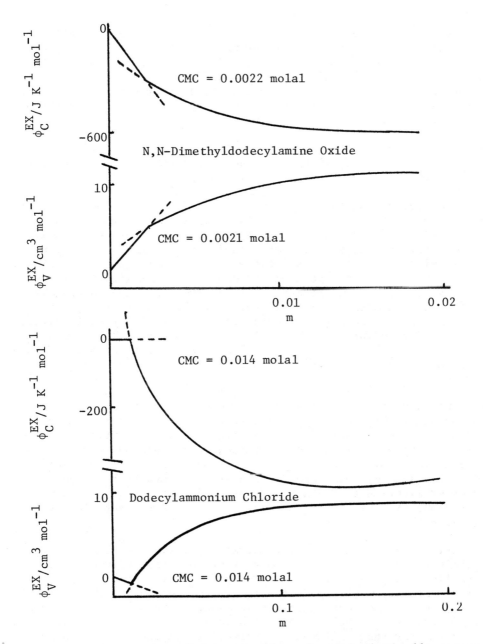

Figure 2. Illustration of determination of critical micelle concentration of a non-ionic and a cationic surfactant. Measurements of
ϕ_V and ϕ_C were made at concentrations below and above the CMC.

solutions with m >0.007 mol kg^{-1}.

Our ϕ_C^o for aqueous sodium dodecyl sulfate is in reasonable agreement with the value previously estimated by Musbally, Perron, and
Desnoyers.[13] Their values of ϕ_C at higher concentrations are in
only fair agreement with our values; differences between their
values and ours for sodium dodecyl sulfate solutions are larger than
for other substances that have been investigated in both Sherbrooke
and Lethbridge.

Our CMC values for dodecylammonium chloride and for N,N-
dimethyldodecylamine oxide are in good agreement with values that
have been cited by Mukerjee and Mysels.[41]

Several of the investigators[13,14,20,23,42] that we have already
cited have used results of their investigations to obtain ΔV and ΔC_p
for micellization of various surfactants. All of our results lead
to similarly positive values of ΔV and similarly negative values for
ΔC_p of micellization. In all cases where comparisons are possible,
we can obtain ΔV and ΔC_p values in good agreement with those previously reported. Unfortunately, there are sufficient uncertainties
in the various methods of data treatment that no ΔV or ΔC_p can yet
be considered to be uniquely determined. Some of the difficulties
in obtaining unambiguous ΔV and ΔC_p values are readily apparent on
inspection of the graphs of ϕ_Y^{EX} against concentration in our Figures
1 and 2 and in similar figures published by Desnoyers and colleagues.[13,14,42]

We have made heat capacity and density measurements on three
component systems consisting of water, relatively concentrated
surfactant, and relatively dilute organic solute. Surfactants used
have been dodecylammonium chloride and sodium dodecyl sulfate. Our
organic solutes, which are nearly insoluble in pure water, were
p-xylene, octane, and decanol. Analysis of results has been in
terms of Equation (1) in which Y(solvent) represents the volume or
heat capacity of a specified mass of the mixed solvent consisting
of water plus surfactant.

All of our apparent molar volumes, ϕ_V, for the three solutes in
both surfactants are nearly the same as the molar volumes of the
pure liquid solutes. Various group additivity methods[26-28,43]
permit estimation of apparent molar volumes of our three solutes in
pure water; all of our ϕ_V values for solutes in surfactants are
larger than the ϕ_V values for the same solutes in pure water. Our
ϕ_V values for these solutes in surfactants in relation to corresponding molar volumes for pure solutes and ϕ_V values for these same
solutes in pure water are in general agreement with earlier results
reported by Vikingstad and Høiland[26-28] for alkanes and alcohols in
sodium alkylcarboxylate surfactants.
It is also possible to use various group additivity methods[43]

for estimation of ϕ_C values for p-xylene, octane, and decanol in pure water; all of our experimental ϕ_C values for these solutes in surfactants are considerably less than the corresponding ϕ_C values for the same solutes in pure water.

Finally, we have made some exploratory measurements of enthalpies of solution of p-xylene, octane, and decanol in solutions of dodecylammonium chloride and of sodium dodecyl sulfate, partly because such enthalpies of solution are related to the variation of solubility of solute in surfactant solution. All of our enthalpies of solution have been exothermic, ranging from ΔH values of about -0.1 kJ mol^{-1} for octane and p-xylene in sodium dodecyl sulfate to -12.6 kJ mol^{-1} for decanol in dodecylammonium chloride.

ACKNOWLEDGMENTS

We are grateful to the Natural Sciences and Engineering Research Council of Canada and to the Alberta Oil Sands Technology and Research Authority for support of parts of our research on aqueous solutions of surfactants.

REFERENCES

1. K. L. Mittal, Editor, "Micellization, Solubilization, and Microemulsions," Vol. 1, Plenum Press, New York, 1977.
2. K. L. Mittal, Editor, "Solution Chemistry of Surfactants," Vol. 1, Plenum Press, New York, 1979.
3. P. Ekwall and P. Stenius, in "Surface Chemistry and Colloids," M. Kerker, Editor, International Review of Science, Physical Chemistry, Series 2, Vol. 7, p. 215, Butterworths, London, 1975.
4. C. Tanford, "The Hydrophobic Effect: Formation of Micelles and Biological Membranes," John Wiley & Sons, New York, 1973.
5. G. C. Kresheck, in "Water: A Comprehensive Treatise," F. Franks, Editor, Vol. 4, Chapter 2, Plenum Press, New York, 1975.
6. N. Muller, In ref. 1, pp. 229-239.
7. J. B. Rosenholm, T. E. Burchfield, and L. G. Hepler, J. Colloid Interface Sci. In press.
8. G. Pilcher, M. N. Jones, L. Espada, and H. A. Skinner, J. Chem. Thermodynamics, 1, 381 (1969).
9. L. Espada, M. N. Jones, and G. Pilcher, J. Chem. Thermodynamics, 2, 1 (1970).
10. M. N. Jones, G. Pilcher, and L. Espada, J. Chem. Thermodynamics, 2, 333 (1970).
11. H. Kishimoto and K. Sumida, Chem. Pharm. Bull., 22, 1108 (1974).
12. S. Paredes, M. Tribout, J. Ferreira, and J. Leonis, Colloid Polymer Sci., 254, 637 (1976).
13. G. M. Musbally, G. Perron, and J. E. Desnoyers, J.Colloid Interface Sci., 48, 494 (1974).

14. G. M. Musbally, G. Perron, and J. E. Desnoyers, J. Colloid Inter-
     face Sci., 54, 80 (1976).
15. R. De Lisi, C. Ostiguy, G. Perron, and J. E. Desnoyers, J.
     Colloid Interface Sci., 71, 147 (1979).
16. J. E. Desnoyers, R. De Lisi, C. Ostiguy, and G. Perron, In ref.
     2, pp. 221-245.
17. S. D. Hamann, J. Phys. Chem., 66, 1959 (1962).
18. M. Tanaka, S. Kaneshina, T. Tomida, K. Noda, and K. Aoki, J.
     Colloid Interface Sci., 44, 525 (1973).
19. M. Tanaka, S. Kaneshina, K. Shin-No, T. Akajima, and T. Tomida,
     J. Colloid Interface Sci., 46, 132 (1974).
20. S. Kaneschina, M. Tanaka, T. Tomida, and R. Matuura, J. Colloid
     Interface Sci., 48, 432 (1975).
21. M. Tanaka, S. Kaneshina, S. Kuramoto, and R. Matuura, Bull.
     Chem. Soc. Japan, 48, 432 (1975).
22. L. Benjamin, J. Phys. Chem., 70, 3790 (1966).
23. T. S. Brun, H. Høiland, and E. Vikingstad, J. Colloid Interface
     Sci., 63, 89 (1978).
24. E. Vikingstad, A. Skauge, and H. Høiland, J. Colloid Interface
     Sci., 72, 59 (1979).
25. S. Harada and T. Nakagawa, J. Solution Chem., 8, 267 (1979).
26. E. Vikingstad and H. Høiland, J. Colloid Interface Sci.,
     64, 510 (1978).
27. E. Vikingstad, J. Colloid Interface Scio, 68, 287 (1979).
28. E. Vikingstad, J. Colloid Interface Sci., 72, 75 (1979).
29. P. Picker, P.-A. Leduc, P. R. Philip, and J. E. Desnoyers, J.
     Chem. Thermodynamics, 3, 631 (1971).
30. J.-L. Fortier, P.-A. Leduc, and J. E. Desnoyers, J. Solution
     Chem., 3, 323 (1974).
31. G. Perron, J.-L. Fortier, and J. E. Desnoyers, J. Chem.
     Thermodynamics, 7, 1177 (1975).
32. J. E. Desnoyers, C. De Visser, G. Perron, and P. Picker, J.
     Solution Chem., 5, 605 (1976).
33. P. Picker, E. Tremblay, and C. Jolicoeur, J. Solution Chem.,
     3, 377 (1974).
34. G. J. Ewin, B. P. Erno, and L. G. Hepler, Manuscript in pre-
     paration.
35. F. J. Millero, in "Water and Aqueous Solutions: Structure,
     Thermodynamics, and Transport Processes," R. A. Horne, Editor,
     Chapter 13, Wiley-Interscience, New York, 1972.
36. P. R. Philip and J. E. Desnoyers, J. Solution Chem., 1, 353
     (1972).
37. P.-A. Leduc, J.-L. Fortier, and J. E. Desnoyers, J. Phys. Chem.,
     78, 1217 (1974).
38. J. J. Spitzer, I. V. Olofsson, P. P. Singh, and L. G. Hepler,
     Can. J. Chem., 57, 2798 (1979).
39. D. J. Bradley and K. S. Pitzer, J. Phys. Chem., 83, 1599 (1979).
40. T. F. Young and O. G. Vogel, J. Am. Chem. Soc., 54, 3025 (1932).
41. P. Mukerjee and K. J. Mysels, "Critical Micelle Concentrations
     of Aqueous Surfactant Systems," NSRDS-NBS 36, U. S. Gov't.

Printing Office, Washington, 1971.
42. P.-A. Leduc and J. E. Desnoyers, Can. J. Chem., 51, 2993 (1973).
43. O. Enea, C. Jolicoeur, and L. G. Hepler, Can. J. Chem., 58, 704 (1980).

ADDED NOTE: A very recent paper [R. De Lisi, G. Perron, and J. E. Desnoyers, Can. J. Chem., 58, 959 (1980)] provides new calorimetric and volumetric data for solutions of two surfactants together with detailed thermodynamic analysis of the phase separation model for micelle formation; this thermodynamic analysis is directly relevant to the use of our partial molar heat capacities and volumes.

THERMODYNAMICS OF THE SPHERE-TO-ROD TRANSITION

IN ALKYL SULFATE MICELLES

P.J. Missel, N.A. Mazer, M.C. Carey and G.B. Benedek
Department of Physics, 13-2018 M.I.T.
Cambridge, Massachusetts 02139
Department of Medicine, Harvard Medical School and
Peter Bent Brigham Hospital, Boston, Ma.   02115

          Above the CMC, alkyl sulfate micelles exhibit a
sphere-to-rod transitition which is dependent on
temperature, NaCl concentration and detergent
concentration. Using the techniques of quasielastic
light scattering we have studied this transition as a
function of these variables and have also investigated
the effects of alkyl chain length, counter-ion size and
urea concentration on micellar growth. These experimental data are interpreted using a quantitative model for
the sphere-to-rod transition in which a thermodynamic
parameter K, which measures the difference in chemical
potential for a detergent molecule in the spherical or
cylindrical micellar structure, is seen to play a
fundamental role. The contributions of electrostatic and
hydrophobic interactions to the value of K are discussed
using a theoretical equation and are assessed
quantitatively from the experimental deductions of K as
a function of NaCl concentration, temperature and the
other variables. The influence of alkyl chain length,
counter-ion size and urea concentration on K are found
to be quite large and provide new insights into the
thermodynamics of the sphere-to-rod transition.

INTRODUCTION

In the past, information on the size, shape and thermodynamics of ionic detergent micelles have been almost exclusively
derived from measurements of the CMC itself and of micellar
properties (i.e. sedimentation data, turbidities, diffusion
coefficients...) that have been extrapolated to the CMC.[1-6] More
recently, we[7-10] and other workers[11,12] have shown that such
information can likewise be obtained at detergent concentrations
much greater than the CMC, using the techniques of quasielastic
light scattering. In the case of Sodium Dodecyl Sulfate (SDS)
systems, our deductions of the mean hydrodynamic radius ($\overline{R}_h$) have
demonstrated a continuous transition in micellar size and shape
from spherical aggregates ($\overline{R}_h \sim 25 \text{Å}$) to polydisperse rod-like
structures whose mean size increases with increases in NaCl
concentration, decreases in temperature and increases in
detergent concentration. In conjunction with these results we
have developed a thermodynamic model for the sphere-to-rod
transition in which the detergent molecules are assumed to form a
distribution of micelles with aggregation number $n = n_o$, $n_o +1$,
..., $n_o + k$,... where n_o corresponds to the spherical micelle and
$n_o + k$ corresponds to a prolate sphero-cylindrical micelle with k
molecules in the cylindrical portion. The relative occupancies of
these micellar states, X_n, depend upon the corresponding standard
chemical potentials denoted by μ_n°. The choice of a linear dependence of μ_n° on n gives rise to varying occupancies, denoted by X_n,
that decrease exponentially with n at a rate dependent on the
detergent concentration X on a thermodynamic parameter K, which
reflects the difference in chemical potential between a molecule
in the spherical and cylindrical portions of the micelle
respectively. The theory predicts a transition from spheres to
polydisperse rods under conditions when the product K(X-CMC)
exceeds n_o^2 .

In the present paper, we present a summary of this theory and
compare its predictions with experimental data on the concentration dependence of $\overline{R}_h$ in SDS solutions containing high NaCl
concentrations (0.6-0.8M). By fitting theory to experiment,
deductions of the thermodynamic parameter K are obtained as
functions of temperature and NaCl concentration. We also present
in this paper an overview of our new experimental studies concerning the effects of: alkyl chain length, counter-ion size and
added urea concentration on the sphere-to-rod transition. The
influence of these variables on $\overline{R}_h$ is found to be quite marked
and can be analyzed in terms of the changes these variables
produce on the parameter K using our model. From such an analysis
we have obtained new insights into the thermodynamic factors
which govern the sphere-to-rod transition in alkyl sulfate
systems.

MATERIALS AND METHODS

Our earlier publications on SDS systems [7-10] fully document the materials and methods employed in the present studies. A brief discussion of the theory of quasielastic light scattering, the relevant equations and data analysis techniques employed in deducing the mean hydrodynamic radius, $\bar{R}_h$, have likewise been given in these papers. [7-8,10] The SDS was from the same lot of material procured from British Drug Houses (BDH, Poole, UK) as used in our previous study, [10] and was > 99.5% pure in terms of alkyl chain length and was free of dodecanol. The remaining detergents (the sodium salts of octyl, decyl, and undecyl sulfates and the lithium, potassium and cesium salts of dodecyl sulfate) were synthesized from alcohols of the highest purity (>99%) from Humphrey Chemical Company, (New Haven, Connecticut) according to a method communicated to us by Procter and Gamble laboratories (Cincinnati, Ohio, courtesy of Dr. Ronald Jandacek.) The various inorganic salts and urea employed were ACS certified reagent grade.

THERMODYNAMIC MODEL OF THE SPHERE-TO-ROD TRANSITION

On the basis of previous measurements of the mean hydrodynamic radius, $\bar{R}_h$, mean scattered intensity, $\bar{I}$, and mean radius of gyration, $\bar{R}_g$, obtained on SDS solutions we have presented evidence for a sphere-to-rod transition occurring at SDS concentrations above the CMC. [7-10] Within the limits of high temperature (>50°C), low NaCl concentration (<0.4M) or low detergent concentration (approaching the CMC), the SDS micelles attain a minimum $\bar{R}_h$ value of ∿25Å. This size is comparable to the length of an extended detergent monomer, and is compatible with the spherical micellar structure initially proposed by Hartley [13] for ionic detergent micelles. Conversely at lower temperatures, high NaCl concentrations and high SDS concentrations, the $\bar{R}_h$ values grow appreciably, exceeding 200Å . The corresponding variations in $\bar{I}$ and $\bar{R}_h$ suggest that such micellar growth is consistent with the formation of rod-like structures with aggregation numbers exceeding 1000. Additional information obtained from QLS measurements shows that the polydispersity of the rod-like micelles is exceedingly broad (+50-70%). [10]

From these observations we have concluded that the structure of SDS micelles is consistent with the sphero-cylindrical model originally proposed by Debye and Anacker for cationic micelles, [14] as shown in Figure 1. In this model, the smallest micelle is a sphere containing n_o molecules. (n_o is approximately 60 for the SDS micelle). [1] Micelles with larger aggregation numbers have n_o

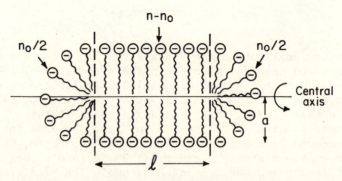

Figure 1. Prolate spherocylindrical model for extended alkyl sulfate micelle as proposed by Debye and Anacker.[14] There are n_o molecules in the endcaps, while the remaining molecules pack into a cylindrical region between these endcaps.

molecules in the spherical endcaps, but have the additional molecules incorporated into the cylindrical portion which extends between the endcaps. In this conceptualization there are two environments for the molecules within the micelle, one in the spherical endcaps, the other in the cylindrical interior. Due to differences in the surface area per head-group in these two environments, a molecule will experience different electrostatic interactions with its neighbors as well as hydrophobic inter-actions at the micelle/water interface depending upon its location in the micelle. Such factors result in different standard chemical potentials for molecules located in the spherical or cylindrical parts of the micelle. As will be shown below, the tendency for micelles to grow from spheres to rods is related to the difference between these two chemical potentials. In accordance with our previous experimental observations we have developed a simple thermodynamic model for the sphere-to-rod transition analogous to the theories proposed by Mukerjee, [15] Tausk et al.[16] and Israelachvili et al.[17] . This theory may be briefly summarized as follows. To represent the micellar size distribution we utilize a set of mole fractions X_n (moles of micelles/mole of solvent) where n is the aggregation number of the micellar species. We allow n to take values n_o, n_o+1, n_o+2, ..., consistent with our picture of the prolate spherocylindrical micelle. The condition of chemical equilibria between micelles and monomers requires that:

$$X_n = X_1^n \exp\left[- \left(\mu_n^\circ - n \mu_1^* \right) / RT \right] \qquad n \geq n_o \qquad (1)$$

where X_1 is the equilibrium mole fraction of monomers and $\mu_n^\circ - n\mu_1^\circ$ is the difference in standard chemical potential between a micelle of aggregation number n and n monomers in solution. This equation shows X_n is equal to the product of a statistical factor X_1^n, which gives the probability of localizing n monomers at one place in the solution, and a Boltzmann factor, which represents the thermodynamic advantage of associating the detergent monomers into the micelle. In this regard, the quantities $\mu_n^\circ - n\mu_1^\circ$, can be considered as energy levels for the different states of aggregation and it is their dependence on n which largely determines the micellar size distribution. In the present model, we assume that μ_n° depends on the number of molecules present in the spherical and cylindrical portions of the micelle in an additive way. Thus μ_n° is given by:

$$\mu_n^\circ = \mu_{n_o}^\circ + (n - n_o) \mu^\circ \tag{2}$$

where $\mu_{n_o}^\circ$ is the chemical potential of n_o monomers in the spherical micelle, and μ° is the chemical potential per monomer in cylindrical portion. Combining Equations (1) and (2) with the condition of material conservation:

$$X = X_1 + \sum_{n=n_o}^{\infty} n\, X_n \tag{3}$$

where X is the total detergent concentration (mole fraction units), we are then able to solve for X_1, and the set of X_n as functions of X and the thermodynamic parameters, μ_{n_o}, μ° and μ_1°. Before discussing the results it is helpful to define two new thermodynamic parameters:

$$X_B = \exp [(\mu^\circ - \mu_1^\circ) / RT] \tag{4a}$$

$$K = \exp [(\mu_{n_o}^\circ - n_o\mu^\circ) / RT] \tag{4b}$$

From Equation (4a) we see that X_B is a measure of the difference in chemical potential between a molecule located in the cylindrical part of the micelle and a molecule free in solution. Under conditions where cylindrical micelles exist in the system, X_B approximately corresponds to the CMC of the system, and conveys thermodynamic information deduced from the CMC values (i.e., the difference in free energy between a monomer in solution and that in a micelle). Conversely the thermodynamic parameter K is a measure of the difference in chemical potential between n_o molecules located in the spherical versus n_o molecules located in the cylindrical portions of the micelle. As will be demonstrated, K is an important quantity which determines the extent of micellar growth from spheres to rods, and its value can be deduced directly from measurements of $\bar{R}_h$. Returning to the problem of determining the X_n distribution, we find in the limit where $K(X-X_B) \gtrsim n_o^2$, a rather uncomplicated result for the micellar size distribution as a function of X:

$$X_n (X) = \frac{1}{K} \exp [- n / \sqrt{K(X - X_B)}] \qquad (5)$$

The mole fraction of micelles with n molecules decreases exponentially with n, where the rate of decrease is given by $[K(X - X_B)]^{½}$. Using Equation (5) in the proper weighted average over the hydrodynamic radii of the various micellar species, we may calculate $\bar{R}_h$ as a function of $K(X - X_B)$. This functional relationship shown in Figure 2 is the basis for our quantitative analysis

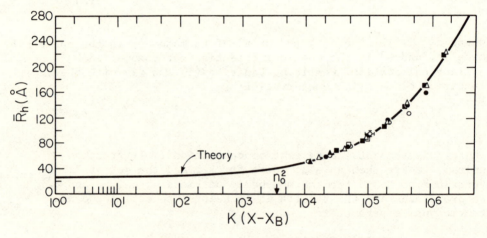

Figure 2. The theoretical functional dependence for $\bar{R}_h$ versus $K(X-X_B)$ (solid curve). Data is from our previous study in 0.8 M NaCl: (■) – 17°C, (△) – 20°C, (●) – 25°C, (o) – 30°C, (□) – 40°C, (▲) – 50°C.

of the experimental $\bar{R}_h$ values. We see from the figure that in the limit $K(X-X_B) \lesssim n_o^2$, $\bar{R}_h \to 25Å$, whereas for $K(X-X_B) > n_o^2$, $\bar{R}_h$ increases rapidly with $K(X-X_B)$. From the point of view of the experimentally adjustable variables, $\bar{R}_h$ will depend upon detergent concentration through the factor X, and will also depend upon temperature, counter-ion concentration, and other variables like alkyl chain length, through the parameter K. Thus the theory provides a direct prediction for the dependence of $\bar{R}_h$ on detergent concentration if K is held constant. In a recent series of experiments[10] we have carefully tested this prediction by

measuring the concentration dependence of $\bar{R}_h$ in 0.8M NaCl, at
various temperatures (17, 20, 25, 30°C). At each termperature we
have deduced the value of K by making one parameter fit to the
experimental concentration dependence of $\bar{R}_h$ using the theoretical
curve (Figure 2). We have plotted the experimental data in Figure 2
using the product of the deduced value of K and the appropriate
value of $(X-X_B)$ as the abscissa for each $\bar{R}_h$ value. (X_B is derived
from CMC values according to the procedure in Appendix III of
reference 4.) As seen in Figure 2, the agreement between theory and
experiment is excellent for all temperatures and for a range of
values which span 2 orders of magnitude.

Having seen that the theory can correctly predict the mean $\bar{R}_h$
of the system, we are able to determine, using the theory, how the
actual size distributions vary with concentration. In Figure 3, we
show the size distributions as they would occur for solutions of
0.8M NaCl at 25°C with detergent concentrations varying from 0.016
– 2 gm/dL. For all these distributions, $K = 6.64 \times 10^8$ and the
only parameter that changes is $(X-X_B)$. Each successive distribution represents a doubling of the detergent concentration. In the
upper panel of Figure 3 we present X_n as a function of aggregation
number. These exponential distributions decrease more and more
gradually with successive increments in detergent concentration. In
the lower panel, we have plotted nX_n as a function of aggregation
number. This represents the amount of detergent associated with
micelles of a given aggregation number. As the detergent concentration is doubled, the area under each curve is increased by a factor
of 2, and the mean aggregation number increases in aggregation
number, from close to 60 at detergent concentrations close to the
CMC to over 1000 at 2 gm/dL SDS. Note that the distributions shown
here are exceedingly broad. In fact the actual degree of polydispersity as reflected by the ratio of weight and number averaged
aggregation numbers $\bar{n}_w/\bar{n}_n$ approaches 2, as in Mukerjee's theory .
The large degree of polydispersity predicted here is comparable
with direct experimental estimates of the polydispersity from the
QLS measurements.

APPLICATION OF THEORY TO THE EFFECTS OF CHAIN LENGTH,
COUNTERION IDENTITY, AND THE ADDITION OF UREA

The ability of our theory to predict the concentration
dependence of $\bar{R}_h$ and the micellar polydispersity, provides strong
support for its validity. Hence, we can now exploit the theory to
study the dependence of the thermodynamic parameter K on additional
physical-chemical conditions. For this purpose it is convenient to
write log K as follows:

$$\log K = (\mu^\circ_{n_\circ} - n_\circ \mu^\circ) / RT$$

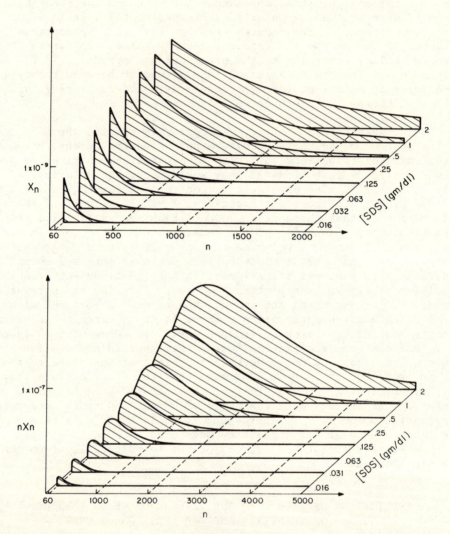

Figure 3. Distribution of micellar sizes as they would appear for
SDS in 0.8M NaCl at 25°C for $0.016 \leq X \leq 2$ gm/dL. a) (upper panel)
X_n versus n.   b) (lower panel) $n\overline{X_n}$ versus n.   The lower panel
represents the amount of detergent present in micelles of a given
aggregation number n.

$$= n_o (\mu^{\circ}_{n_o} / n_o - \mu^{\circ}) / RT \qquad (6)$$

From this equation we can appreciate that K is a measure of n_o multiplied by the difference in chemical potential between a molecule in the spherical and one in the cylindrical portion of a micelle. The factor n_o will depend on how many molecules can pack into the sphere, whereas the chemical potential difference per monomer ($\mu^{\circ}_{n_o}/n_o - \mu^{\circ}$) would be expected to reflect the difference in headgroup areas between the sphere and the cylinder, as suggested by Tanford's theoretical work.[18] Simple geometric considerations alone[19] suggest that n_o should vary as the square of chain length whereas the factor ($\mu^{\circ}_{n_o}/n_o - \mu^{\circ}$) should remain virtually independent of chain length. We may thus separate the effect of chain length on K from other effects by expressing the n_o factor in Equation (6) as αn_c^2 (where $\alpha \simeq 0.4$).[19] We may consider ($\mu^{\circ}_{n_o}/n_o - \mu^{\circ}$) as consisting of two contributions, electrostatic and hydrophobic, so that log K now becomes:

$$\log K = \alpha n_c^2 \ [\ \frac{\Delta Fel}{RT} + \gamma_{HI} \frac{(A_s - A_c)}{RT} \ ] \qquad (7)$$

The electrostatic contribution, ΔFel can be calculated using electrostatic theories of the double layer,[10] and is found to be unfavorable for the formation of rodlike micelles because of the increase in surface charge density in going from the sphere to the cylinder. Thus ΔFel is negative in sign, as more energy is required to form the cylindrical portions of the micelle than the spherical portions. However the magnitude of ΔFel is decreased by increasing the added NaCl concentration.[8,10] The theoretical calculations show $\Delta Fel/RT$ to very from $-.81$ in 0.3M NaCl to $-.68$ in 0.8M NaCl and to be nearly independent of temperature. These findings are consistent with experimental values of K at these NaCl concentrations.[8,10] In addition to its dependence on ionic strength, ΔFel can in principle be affected by the size and chemical properties of the particular counter-ions, as well as the nature of the head group.

In accordance with the theoretical work of Reynolds et al.,[20] we have written the hydrophobic contribution to log K (in Equation (7)) as a proportionality constant, γ_{HI} , for the hydrophobic interaction energy per unit area, times the difference in hydrocarbon/water contact area per monomer between the spherical

---

(1) In our previous paper, we outlined how we deduced the difference in surface area between n_o SDS molecules in the spherical and cylindrical configurations to be $\simeq 1500 Å^2$. Dividing this value by $n_o = 60$ yields $25 Å^2$.[10]

and cylindrical geometries (A_s - A_c). Using a value for γ_{HI} of 24 cal/mole-$Å^2$)[20] and an estimate of (A_s - A_c) of 25.2$Å^2$ (1) we calculate γ_{HI} (A_s - A_c)/RT to be 1.01 at 25°C. Thus this value shows that the negative electrostatic term is overcome by the hydrophobic term and favors the formation of rod-like micelles. Physically, this occurs because A_c < A_s and thus less water can penetrate between the head groups on the cylindrical compared with the spherical portion of the micelle. We expect that this term can be modified however by adding chemicals which affect the hydro-phobic interaction of the solvent, such as urea. Interestingly our theoretical calculation of ΔFel/RT and experimental deductions of log K suggest that the influence of temperature on K is a result of the temperature dependence of the hydrophobic term γ_{HI}(A_s - A_c)/RT. This conclusion further suggests that γ_{HI} contains a significant enthalpic term which contributes to the unfavorable in-teraction between hydrocarbon and water. In order to experimentally test the theoretical implications of Equation (7) we have recently begun a systematic study of the effects of detergent chain length, counterion size and added urea concentration on the size of the alkyl sulfate micelles. An overview of the results of these studies follows.

We consider first the effect of detergent chain length. In Figure 4 we show experimental measurements of the hydrodynamic radius as a function of temperature for sodium alkyl sulfates of various chain lengths in solutions of 1M NaCl (the C8, 10, 11, and 12 alkyl sulfates). At a detergent concentration of 2 gm/dL, there is virtually no micellar growth for the lower chain lengths (C_8 and C_{10}); R_h remains less than 30Å. But for the chain length C_{11} there is a dramatic growth to sizes over 200Å. Even at a lower concentration (1 gm/dL), the C_{12} micelles grow considerably larger than for the C_{11} detergent. From our previous discussion of Equations (5) and (7) we expect that such effects are the result of the influence of chain length on the parameter K, whose logarithm should vary with n_c^2. A quantitative analysis of this and other data at various NaCl concentrations shows that log K does vary approximately with n_c^2.[19]

Next, we consider the effect of various alkali counter-ions. In Figure 5 we present data showing the relative effects of the sodium, potassium and cesium chlorides at salt concentrations of 0.45M and lithium chloride at 1M on the temperature dependence of $\bar{R}_h$ for dodecyl sulfate micelles. In each case the detergent was synthesized using the particular alkali counter-ion and the chloride salt of the same alkali counter-ion was used as the added electrolyte. As is well known, the hydrated radii of the alkali ions vary inversely with their atomic number and ionic radius as shown in Table I.[21] From Table I we see that for any given temper-ature, the $\bar{R}_h$ value increases as the radius of the hydrated ion decreases. Thus using the cesium counter-ion, which has the

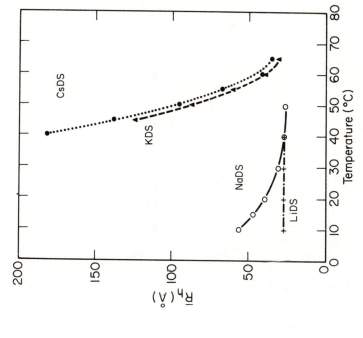

Figure 5. Effect of various alkali metal counter-ions on the $\underline{R}_h$ of dodecyl sulfate micelles in solutions of alkali chloride:

(●) – 0.5 gm/dL CsDS, 0.45M CsCL;
(▲) – 0.5 gm/dL KDS, 0.45M NaCl;
(○) – 2 gm/dL SDS, 0.45 M NaCl;
(+) – 2 gm/dL LiDs, 1M LiCl.

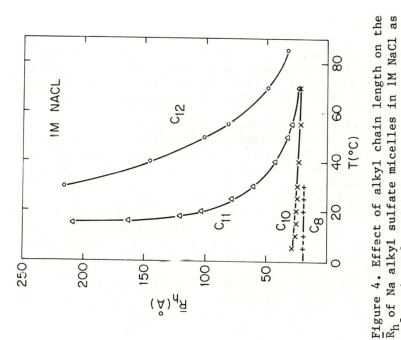

Figure 4. Effect of alkyl chain length on the $\underline{R}_h$ of Na alkyl sulfate micelles in 1M NaCl as a function of temperature:

(+) – 2 gm/dL Na octyl sulfate;
(x) – 2 gm/dL Na decyl sulfate;
(△) – 2 gm/dL Na undecyl sulfate;
(o) – 1 gm/dL Na do decyl sulfate.

Table I. Effect of Various Alkali Counter-ions on Dodecyl Sulfate
Micelles.

Ion	Li	Na	K	Cs
Atomic Number	3	11	19	55
Ionic[22] Radius (Å)	0.68	0.97	1.33	1.67
Hydrated[21] Radius of ion (Å)	2.37	1.84	1.23	1.16
K (40°C)	$\lesssim 10$ *	$\lesssim 3 \times 10^3$	2.03×10^9	4.05×10^9
(ΔFel/RT)	$\lesssim -.941$	$\lesssim -.843$	$-.619$	$-.607$

(*) Taken from the data point $\bar{R}_h$ (2 gm/dL, 0.45M LiClm 40°C) =
25/5Å.

smallest hydrated radius, for detergent concentration 0.5 gm/dL
CsDS the micellar size has a very marked temperature dependence
even at relatively high temperatures (40-65°C), forming micelles
which grow from $\sim$ 30Å to over 180Å. With the slightly larger
potassium ion, there is also a marked temperature dependence of
$\bar{R}_h$ but the micelles have radii about 10% lower than those formed
using cesium at the same detergent concentration over the temperature range $45°C \leq T \leq 65°C$. (2)   For the case of sodium, whose
hydrated radius is substantially larger than either the cesium or
potassium ions, the micelees experience only a moderate temperature dependence: the micellar size reaches a maximum value of only
a third of the maximum value for cesium, even after increasing the
detergent concentration four-fold to 2 gm/dL SDS, and moreover,
micellar growth begins to occur at a much lower temperature, i.e.
$\sim$30°C. Finally we note that for the largest alkali ion lithium,

(2) The CMT's of the detergents with these four counter-ions can
be arranged in ascending order as follows: LiDS, 0-5°C; NaDs,
$\sim$26°C; CsDS $\sim$ 38°C; and KDS, $\sim$ C. It was not possible to
supercool the solutions below the data points shown on account of
rapid detergent precipitation.

the $\bar{R}_h$ values show almost no micellar growth in solutions of 2 gm/dL LiDS and remain less than 27Å even when the ionic strength is increased to 1M LiCl. As anticipated earlier, a qualitative understanding of the effect of counter-ion size on $\bar{R}_h$ can be obtained by considering the parameter K in the context of Equation (7). Table I shows experimental deductions of log K for the different counter-ions obtained from the data of Figure 5. As expected, log K increases as the hydrated counter-ion size decreases. Assuming that the hydrophobic term in Equation (7), $\gamma_{HI}(A_s - A_c)/RT$, is independent of the counter-ion size and concentration, and estimating its value at 40°C to be ~ 0.98, we can estimate the value of the electrostatic term $\Delta Fel/RT$ as a function of counter-ion size. These deductions are likewise shown in Table I, and show that $\Delta Fel/RT$ is most negative for lithium, but decreases in magnitude as the hydrated counter-ion size decreases. This seems qualitatively reasonable in that the "smaller" counter-ions should be able to approach the sulfate head groups more closely and thus more effectively screen the negative electrostatic charge density at the micelle surface, which as previously noted is higher for the cylindrical region of the micelle than for the spherical region. These results are qualitatively consistent with the NMR studies of Lindman et al.[23] who have shown that the strength of interaction between alkali counter-ions and the sulfate head group also vary inversely with the hydrated counter-ion size. We are presently attempting to refine our electrostatic calculations of $\Delta Fel/RT$ so that we can quantitatively understand the origins of this effect.

Finally, we present in Figure 6 experimental data showing the effect of added urea on the $\bar{R}_h$ of 2 gm/dL SDS micelles for three temperatures, starting in 0.8M NaCl at 2 gm/dL SDS. The data show a marked decrease in $\bar{R}_h$ with added urea. At the urea concentration of 2M, the micelles at 20°C have decreased in size from their initial radius of ~ 220 Å to their minimum radius of 25 Å. Qualitatively, these results suggest that urea acts to decrease the magnitude of the hydrophobic term in Equation (7) so that now the electrostatic term ultimately dominates and forces the micelles back into the spherical state. In a manner similar to the previous analysis of the counter-ion effect, we can deduce the experimental dependence of log K on urea concentration, calculate the electrostatic term (which is only weakly affected by urea) and thereby estimate how the hydrophobic term decreases with urea concentration. Table II displays these calculations for the SDS system at

---

(3) The effect of urea on the dielectric constant of water was taken from reference 24 and was used to deduce the change in $\Delta Fel/RT$ with added urea, represented in the third row of Table II. (We assume in our calculations that the only effect of urea is to change the dielectric constant of the solvent.)

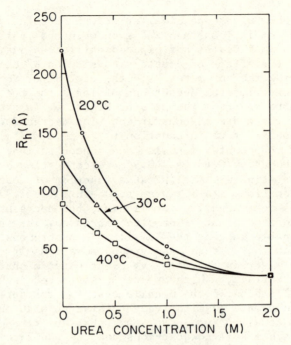

Figure 6. Effect of added urea on the $\bar{R}_h$ of SDS micelles at three temperatures (2 gm/dL SDS in 0.8M NaCl).

Table II. Effect of Urea on SDS Micelles in 0.8M NaCl at 20°C.

Urea (M)	ln K	$(\Delta Fel/RT)$	$\gamma_{HI}(A_s-A_c)/RT$	(cal/mole-Å^2)
0	21.05	-.681	1.034	23.82
0.2	19.76	-.679	1.010	23.26
0.33	19.08	-.678	0.998	22.99
0.5	18.34	-.677	0.985	22.69
1.0	16.05	-.675	0.944	21.74
2.0	7-11	-.670	.8-.86	18.4-19.8

20°C. (3) The data show an approximate linear decrease in the hydrophobic term by about 9% per mole of added urea. From this value we can deduce that the parameter γ_{HI} decreases from 23.8 cal/(mole-Å^2) in the absence of urea to 19.8 in 2M urea. The former value is in good agreement with the estimates of Reynolds et al.[20] from solubility data, and with the estimates of Wennerstrom[25] based on a thermodynamic analysis of counter-ion binding to liquid crystalline phases in detergent-water systems. The latter value is close to that deduced from studies of the effect of urea on the growth of bile salt micelles.[26]

CONCLUSION

We have used the techniques of quasielastic light scattering to demonstrate the existence of a sphere-to-rod transition occurring in alkyl sulfate micellar systems at concentrations above the CMC. In addition we have presented a quantitative thermodynamic model of this transition in which the parameter K, a measure of the difference in chemical potential between the spherical and cylindrical regions of the micelle, is shown to play an essential role in governing the growth of micelles above the CMC. The theory is shown to be in excellent agreement with experimental data on the concentration dependence of the micellar size distribution in SDS solutions at high NaCl concentrations. From experimental deductions of the parameter K as a function of temperature, alkyl chain length, counter-ion concentration and size and added urea concentration, new insights are obtained into the magnitudes and relative importances of the electrostatic and hydrophobic interactions which determine micellar size.

ACKNOWLEDGEMENTS

Dr. Mazer wishes to thank Professor Werner Kanzig and the department of Solid State Physics, E.T.H., Zurich, Switzerland for providing him a research fellowship during which time this manuscript was prepared. This research is supported in part by M.I.T. Center for Materials Science and Engineering, NSF Grant No. DMR 76-80895 and by NSF Grant No. CHE 77-07666 (G.B. Benedek); NIH Research Grant No. AM 18559 and Research Career Development Award AM 00195 (M.C. Carey).

REFERENCES

1. K. J. Mysels and L. H. Princen, J. Phys. Chem. 63, 1696 (1959).
2. E. Matijevic and B.A. Pethica Trans. Faraday Soc 54, 587 (1958).
3. M. F. Emerson and A. Holzter, J. Phys. Chem 71, 1898 (1967).
4. W. Prins and J. J. Hermans, Proc. Kon. Ned. Akad. Wet., Ser. B, 67, 298 (1964).

5. H. F. Huisman, Ibid 67, 367, 376, 388, 407 (1964).
6. M. F. Emerson and A. Holtzer, J. Phys. Chem. 71, 3320 (1967).
7. N. A. Mazer, G. B. Benedek, and M. C. Carey, J. Phys. Chem. 80, 1075 (1976).
8. N. A. Mazer, G. B. Benedek and M. C. Carey in "Micellization, Solubilization, and Microemulsions", Vol. 1, K. L. Mittal, Ed., Plenum Press, New York, 1977, P. 359.
9. C. Y. Young, P. J. Missel, N. A. Mazer, G. B. Benedek and M. C. Carey, J. Phys. Chem. 82, 1375 (1978).
10. P. J. Missel, N. A. Mazer, G. B. Benedek, C. Y. Young, and M. C. Carey, J. Phys. Chem. 84, 1044 (1980).
11. M. Corti and V. Degiorgio, Ann. Phys. 3, 303 (1978).
12. D. F. Nicoli, D. R. Dawson and H. W. Offen, Chem. Phys. Lett. 66, 291 (1979).
13. G. S. Hartley, "Aqueous Solutions of Paraffin-Chain Sales," Hermann and Cie., Paris, France, 1936, Chapter 7.
14. P. Debye and E. W. Anacker, J. Phys. Colloid Chem. 55, 644 (1951).
15. P. Mukerjee, J. Phys. Chem. 76, 565 (1972).
16. R. Tausk and J. Th. G. Overbeek, Colloid Interface Sci., 2, 379 (1976).
17. J. N. Israelachvili, D. J. Mitchell, and B. W. Ninham, J. Chem. Soc., Faraday Trans., 72, 1525 (1976).
18. C. Tanford, J. Phys. Chem. 78, 2469 (1974).
19. P. J. Missel, N. A. Mazer, G. B. Benedek, and M. C. Carey, to be published.
20. J. A. Reynolds, D. B. Gilbert, and C. Tanford, Proc. Natl. Acad. Sci. U. S.A., 71, 2925 (1974).
21. P. Mukerjee, K. J. Mysels, and P. Kapauan, J. Phys. Chem. 71, 4166 (1967).
22. R. C. Weast, Ed., "CRC Handbook of Chemistry and Physics," 58th edition, CRC Press, Inc., Cleveland, Ohio, 1977, p. F-213.
23. B. Lindman, G. Lindblom, H. Wennerstrom and H. Gustavsson, same as reference 8, page 195. See also reference 21.
24. E. H. Grant, S. E. Keefe, and R. Shack, Adv. in Mol. Relax. Proc. 4, 217 (1972).
25. H. Wennerstrom, (1980), personal communication. See his paper in this symposium.
26. N. A. Mazer, M. C. Carey, R. F. Kwasnick, and G. B. Benedek, Biochemistry 18, 3064 (1979).

THE INFLUENCE OF AMPHIPHILE STRUCTURE ON THE MICELLAR BEHAVIOR OF
POTASSIUM ALKYLCARBOXYLATES: A THERMODYNAMIC AND ULTRASONIC
RELAXATION STUDY

Carmel Jolicoeur, Jean Paquette and Yvan Lavigne
Department of Chemistry, Université de Sherbrooke
Sherbrooke, Quebec, Canada. J1K 2R1
and
Raoul Zana
Centre de Recherche sur les Macromolécules, C.N.R.S.
6, rue Boussingault, 67083 Strasbourg, Cedex, France

The micellar behavior of a series of alkyl- and aryl-
carboxylates has been investigated from the concentration
dependence of apparent molar volumes (ϕ_V) and heat capacities (ϕ_C), ultrasonic absorption (α/f^2) and relaxation
frequencies (f_1). Data were obtained for up to ten compounds of similar molar volumes having eight or more carbon
atoms and widely different shapes. All of the alkylcarboxylates examined were found to exhibit micellar aggregation from both the thermodynamic and the ultrasonic
absorption results. The critical micelle concentrations
derived from the different properties examined were in
mutual agreement, the CMC values for the various solutes
being in the range 0.3 to 0.7 mol ℓ^{-1}. The influence
of amphiphile structure on the CMC's, as well as on the
amphiphile exchange kinetics, were found well related to
the hydrophobic surface area of the hydrocarbon residue.
Some evidence of specific solute structural effects was
observed in the changes in surfactant ϕ_V and ϕ_C upon
micellization.

INTRODUCTION

The influence of solute structural factors on the excess
thermodynamic properties of solutions has been the subject of
numerous investigations in aqueous solutions [1-8] and in non
aqueous mixtures [9-10]. From studies on homologous series and
isomers, there often appeared a "solute shape" effect on the
thermodynamic properties of dilute aqueous solutes [1-5],

389

although the direct consequences of solute structural parameters could not be resolved satisfactorily from possible contributions due to variations in other solute properties, for example, solute polarizability, solute-solvent contact area, polar group solvation, etc. Further attempts to elucidate this question have been performed recently, based on the thermodynamic properties ($\bar{V}^o$, $\bar{C}_p^o$, ΔH_s^o in H_2O and D_2O) of a series of potassium carboxylates having large hydrocarbon groups of different shapes, though of closely similar intrinsic molar volumes [11]. Rather unexpectedly, the concentration dependence of the properties of bulky, near-spherical, solutes such as potassium-adamantane-1-carboxylate showed variations typical of micellar systems. Since there appeared little information available on the influence of surfactant shape in micellar behavior[7-9] a more detailed investigation of this aspect was undertaken, combining thermodynamic and rapid kinetic methods.

In the present report, we describe the concentration dependence of the apparent molar volumes, apparent molar heat capacities and ultrasonic absorption for the potassium aryl- and alkylcarboxylates illustrated in Figure 1. Numerous detailed studies using these methods have now been reported for many different types of micellar surfactants[12-14], so it may be expected that their combined application to the present systems can provide an accurate thermodynamic and kinetic description of the consequences of the structure of surfactants on their micellar properties.

EXPERIMENTAL

I- Methods

The experimental methods used in the measurement of solution densities and specific heats have been described with appropriate references by De Grandpré $et\ al.$[15]. The ultrasonic absorptions have been measured using standard methods, either interferometric techniques (1-10 MHz) or pulse techniques (5-150 MHz) as previously used by Graber $et\ al.$[16]. All measurements were performed at 25.0^oC.

II- Materials

The carboxylate salts investigated here were prepared by titration of the corresponding acids with KOH in alcohols or in alcohol-water mixtures. The acids were available commercially, except for c-octylcarboxylic acid which was prepared from dichromate oxidation of c-octylmethanol in aqueous media. These acids were purified by vacuum distillation, and their purity was verified by GC and TLC methods. The salts were recrystallized in alcohols, mostly iso-propanol, and dried in vacuo at 50^oC for 48 hrs or more. Samples of each compound were back titrated in water using HCl;

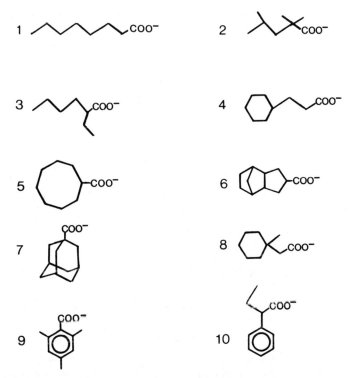

Figure 1. Chemical structures of the various potassium aryl-
and alkyl-carboxylates investigated; the corresponding
designations used here are: 1. n-Octanoate. 2. 2,2,4-
Trimethylpentanoate. 3. 2-Ethylhexanoate. 4. c-Hexylpro-
pionate. 5. c-Octylcarboxylate. 6. Tricyclo(5.2.1.0^{2,6})
decane-4-carboxylate. 7. 1-Adamantane carboxylate.
8. 2-(1-Methylcyclohexyl)acetate. 9. 2,4,6-Trimethylben-
zoate. 10. 2-Phenylbutyrate.

the titration data agreed with expected results within 0.1 to 0.5%
in all cases.

RESULTS

I- Apparent Molar Volumes and Heat Capacities

The calculation of apparent molar volumes (ϕ_V) and heat capacities (ϕ_C) were carried out as described by De Grandpré et $al.$[15]
or Rosenholm et $al.$[17]. The variation of ϕ_V and ϕ_C with molar
concentration is illustrated in Figures 2-5 after subtraction of
the Debye-Hückel limiting law ($Ac^{\frac{1}{2}}$); the infinite dilution values
(ϕ^0) (reported later in table II) were also subtracted from the
data for comparison at a common origin; the uncertainty on the
data shown are respectively $\pm$ 0.1 cm^3 mol^{-1} and $\pm$ 2JK^{-1} mol^{-1}. In
all cases where abrupt changes in slope occurred over the

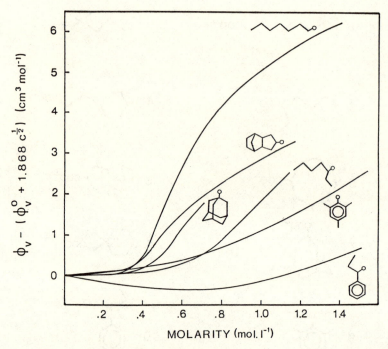

Figure 2. Concentration dependence of ϕ_V of various potassium alkyl-
and aryl-carboxylates at 25°C, after subtraction of the
Debye–Hückel limiting law (symbols refer to Figure 1).

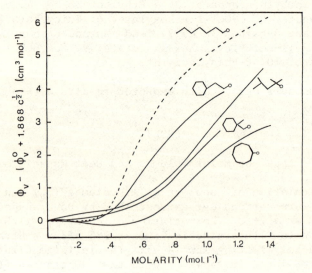

Figure 3. Same as Figure 2, with data for K–n–Octanoate shown as a
dashed curve (symbols refer to Figure 1).

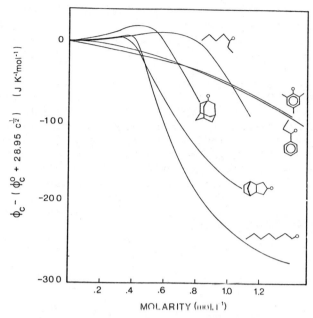

Figure 4. Variation of ϕ_C with molar concentration for several potassium alkyl- and aryl-carboxylates at 25°C, after subtraction of the Debye-Hückel limiting law (symbols refer to Figure 1).

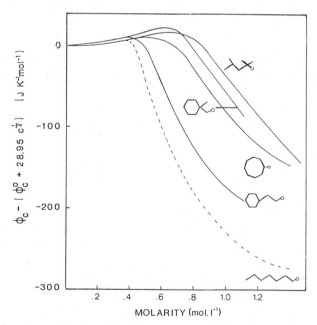

Figure 5. Same as Figure 4, with data for K-n-Octanoate shown as a dashed curve (symbols refer to Figure 1).

concentration range investigated, critical micelle concentrations were determined as the intersection of lines drawn through the data below and above this change in slope; the CMC values derived by this procedure are reported in Table I.

The changes in apparent (or partial) molar volumes (ΔV_m) and heat capacities (ΔC_m) upon micellization (defined for the transfer of 1 mole of solute from the bulk solution into the micelle at the CMC) were evaluated from the slopes of the ϕ_V and ϕ_C curves in the post-micellar region, following Musbally *et al.*[18]. These results are given in Table II, together with the ϕ_V^o and ϕ_C^o values of the various compounds, and ΔV_m^{us} data (ΔV_m^{us} from ultrasonic absorption) described below. Since variations in the apparent (or partial) molar quantities at the CMC are not as sharply defined as with longer n-alkyl surfactants[13,18], the uncertainties in ΔV_m and ΔC_m will be larger, of the order of 10%.

II- Ultrasonic Absorption

The ultrasonic absorption (α/f^2, α: absorption coefficient, f: frequency) were obtained as function of concentration up to near solubility limits, and as function of frequency between 1.67 and 115.4 MHz. Typical results at a fixed frequency (15.2 MHz) are plotted in Figure 6 as function of molal concentration; the horizontal dotted line shows the ultrasonic adsorption of water which remains invariant upon addition of surfactant up to the CMC. Several of the data obtained as function of frequency are illustrated in Figure 7 for *c*-OctCOOK as four concentrations above the CMC.

Table I.   CMC Values (mol ℓ^{-1}), Obtained from ϕ_V, ϕ_C and Ultrasonic Relaxation data.

Solutes[a]	CMC (ϕ_V)	CMC (ϕ_C)	CMC (us)	Average
2	0.56	0.65	0.59	0.61
5	0.54	0.55	0.51	0.53
7	0.46	0.46	0.45	0.46
4	0.35	0.40	0.38	0.38
6	0.35	0.35	0.30	0.33
n-Oct-K	0.36	0.37	0.35	0.36

[a]   Numbers refer to compounds shown in Figure 1.

Table II. ΔV_m and ΔC_m for Several K-Alkylcarboxylates.

Solutes[a]	ϕ_V^o	ϕ_C^o	ΔV_m	ΔV_m^{us}	ΔC_m
	$cm^3\ mol^{-1}$	$JK^{-1}\ mol^{-1}$	$cm^3\ mol^{-1}$	$cm^3\ mol^{-1}$	$JK^{-1}mol^{-1}$
2	135.7	546	10.0[b]	7.3[c]	420
5	137.0	474	6.7	3.5	282
7	144.1	477	6.7	---	310
4	142.9	504	7.5	4.5	360
6	146.3	499	5.0	2.8	308
n-Hept-K	---	---	---	5.4[d]	---
n-Oct-K	142.6	564	9.1	5.3	422

[a] numbers refer to Figure 1

[b] ΔV_m from ϕ_V data, $\pm 1\ cm^3\ mol^{-1}$

[c] ΔV_m^{us} from ultrasonic data, $\pm 1\ cm^3\ mol^{-1}$.

[d] data from reference 16.

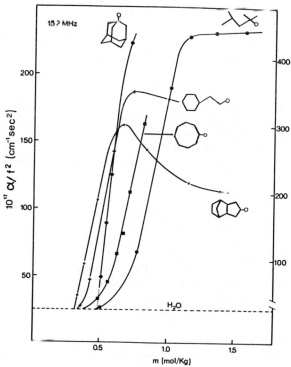

Figure 6. Variation of the ultrasonic adsorption (α/f^2) at fixed frequency and as function of concentration for several potassium alkylcarboxylates; $f = 15 \cdot 2 MHz$.

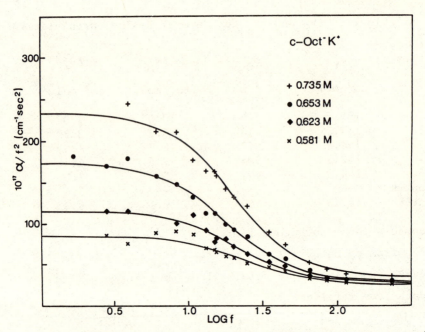

Figure 7. Frequency dependence of the ultrasonic absorption (α/f^2)
          in solutions of potassium c-octylcarboxylate at four
          different concentrations.

        The ultrasonic absorption data first allow accurate evaluation
of the CMC from the sharp increase in α/f^2 at the onset of micelle
formation[12]. The CMC values derived from these data are included
in Table I with CMC determinations from ϕ_V and ϕ_C. The variation
in α/f^2 for dilute micellar solutions is characteristic of a single
fast relaxation process and may be represented as:

$$\frac{\alpha}{f^2} = \frac{A}{(1 + f^2/f_1^2)} + B \qquad\qquad (1)$$

where f_1 is the relaxation frequency of the process leading to
absorption, B, a constant and A, the relaxation amplitude. It
has now been amply demonstrated that the fast relaxation process
observed is that involving the exchange of surfactant molecules
between the bulk of the solution and the micelle[12].

        The relaxation frequency (f_1) or relaxation time τ_1 ($\tau_1 =$
$(2\pi f_1)^{-1}$) has been related to the kinetic and physical parameters
of the micellar system as follows[19]:

$$2\pi f_1 = \frac{1}{\tau_1} = \frac{\overline{k}}{\sigma^2} + \frac{\overline{k}\,a}{n} \qquad\qquad (2)$$

where $\bar{k}$ is the rate constant for the dissociation of a surfactant monomer from a micelle having an average aggregation number n; σ^2, the variance corresponding to a Gaussian function taken to describe the distribution of micelle aggregation numbers; and a, the reduced concentration ((C-CMC /CMC) giving the ratio of micellar to monomeric surfactant. The absorption amplitude A is further related to several kinetic and equilibrium parameters of the micellar system through[20]

$$A = \frac{2\pi^2 \rho v}{10^3 RT} \left(\frac{\bar{k}}{n}\right) \tau_1^2 \left(\Delta V_m^{us} - \frac{\alpha \ \Delta H_m}{\rho \ c_p}\right)^2 \tag{3}$$

where ρ is the solution density, v the ultrasonic velocity, α the thermal expansion coefficient of the solution and c_p, its specific heat at constant pressure; ΔH_m represents the enthalpy of micellization defined for the same process as ΔV_m.

The relaxation time (τ_1) and absorption amplitude (A) derived from the ultrasonic data are given in Table III and the

Table III. Relaxation Times (τ_1) and Amplitudes Observed in Aqueous Solutions of Various Alkyl Carboxylates.

Solutes[a]	c	$\tau_1 = (2\pi f_1)^{-1}$	A
	(mol ℓ^{-1})	$(10^{-9}$ sec$)^b$	$(10^{17}$ cm^{-1} sec$^2)^b$
2	1.2906	2.07	210
	1.1234	2.18	225
	0.9902	2.45	215
	0.8850	2.56	167
	0.6994	2.61	142
5	0.7535	6.94	190
	0.6536	8.40	165
	0.6225	7.94	92
	0.5812	7.24	60
7	0.5438	12.2	191
	0.5082	10.0	108
	0.4748	7.25	49
4	0.7926	10.6	645
	0.6718	11.4	745
	0.5402	18.9	660
6	1.1454	6.13	115
	0.9006	7.09	157
	0.7522	10.6	275
	0.6114	13.3	335

[a] compound numbers refer to Figure 1. [b] ± 10%

relaxation frequencies (f_1) are plotted in Figure 8 as function of
a. Within experimental error, all solutes exhibit the linear behavior predicted by Equation (2), except for K-adamantane-1-carboxy-
late, for which f_1 appears to decrease with concentration[1]

    As indicated by Equation (2), the slope and intercept of the
curves in Figure 8 yield respectively k^-/n and k^-/σ^2 which are
listed in Table IV. The ratio of these quantities (σ^2/n) describes
the polydispersity of the micelles and are also given in Table IV.
The rate constants k^+ for the association of the surfactant molecule to the micelle have been evaluated from the relationship

$$K = \frac{k^+}{k^-} = \frac{1}{CMC} \qquad (4)$$

---

[1] Because of the limited solubility of this compound which pre-
    vented investigation over a sufficiently wide concentration
    range, only the intercept k^-/n may be considered meaningful.

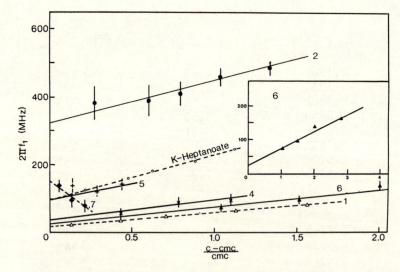

Figure 8. Change in the ultrasonic relaxation frequency (f_1) with
           solute concentration; the latter is given here as
           (C-CMC)/CMC, *i.e.* the ratio of solute concentrations
           respectively in the micellar and monomeric states. The
           numbers in the figure refer to compounds in Figure 1.

Table IV. Kinetic and Other Parameters from Ultrasonic Relaxation
Data for the Various Potassium Alkylcarboxylates.

Solutes[a]	CMC	k^-/n	k^-/σ^2	σ^2/n	k^+/n
	mol ℓ^{-1}	10^8 sec^{-1}	10^8 sec^{-1}		10^8 (M^{-1} sec^{-1})
2	0.59	1.2	3.4	0.35	2.0
5	0.51	0.98	1.0	1.0	1.9
7	0.45	---b			
4	0.38	0.59	0.46	1.3	1.6
6	0.30	0.50	0.25	2.0	1.7
n-Hept-K[c]	0.61	1.5	0.82	1.8	2.5
n-Oct-K[c]	0.35	0.46	1.1	4.0	1.3

a   numbers refer to formulae in Figure 1

b   the slope of $2\pi f_1$ vs c (Figure 8) is undetermined.

c   data from reference (16).

and are included as k^+/n in Table IV, *i.e.* since n is undetermined
for the systems studied here. Finally, having the kinetic parameters required in Equation (3), the volume change upon micellization could be calculated from the absorption amplitudes and the
results are given in Table II as ΔV_m^{us}. The latter results were
obtained under the assumption that the term ($\alpha \Delta H_m/\rho c_p$) in Equation
(3) is negligible compared to ΔV_m. This is sufficiently accurate
for the present purpose, since, for water at 25°C ($\alpha/\rho c_p$) ≈ 0.05
cm^3/kJ and ΔH_m is generally weak[21].

DISCUSSION

I- General Micellization Behavior.

As noted in the RESULT section, the concentration dependence
of ϕ_V and ϕ_C for most systems investigated here exhibits sharp
changes in slope at concentrations between 0.3 and 0.7 mol ℓ^{-1}
(Figures 2,3). The ϕ_V data, for all compounds, except for those
containing aryl groups, show the characteristic large volume increase of micellar aggregation. By comparison with the behavior
of K-octanoate for which micellar properties have been well documented[16], it is quite remarkable that the bulkier solutes (*e.g.*
the polycyclic compounds) exhibit volume changes which are closely
analogous to those observed for micellar aggregation; such changes
are much larger and of opposite sign compared to those for weak
solute-solute interactions in dilute solutions of low molecular
weight organic compounds[22].

Similar conclusions of the micellar behavior of the alkylcarboxylates studied here are also clearly inferred from the concentration dependence of ϕ_C (Figures 4,5). Again, a comparison of
the various results with those for K-octanoate shows closely related behaviors (except for compounds having aromatic groups), differing mainly by the concentration values for which the typical
drop in ϕ_C is observed[13,18]. It is also noteworthy that all systems giving evidence for micelle formation also exhibit a positive
initial concentration dependence of ϕ_C; the aryl substituted compounds do not form micellar aggregates and exhibit a negative initial slope. This observation adds further support to the assignment of the ϕ_C maxima to a contribution resulting from thermal
perturbation of the micellar association equilibria, as discussed
earlier with regards to other association processes[23].

The ultrasonic absorption data reported in Figure 6 provide
additional straightforward evidence of the micellar behavior of
the various alkylcarboxylates. The large increase in ultrasonic
absorption over a narrow range of concentration is typical of micellar aggregation, and is not observed in systems where progres-
sive or continuous association occurs as, for example, with bile
salts[24]. In the latter systems, the ultrasonic absorption increases with concentration, but no sharp break is observed in the concentration dependence curve. This is also the qualitative behavior
found with one of the arylsubstituted carboxylates: 2,4,6-trime-
thylbenzoate (#9 in Figure 1).

From these various observations, it can be concluded that all
of the potassium alkylcarboxylates investigated here can undergo
micellar type association, regardless of the shape of the alkyl
substituents. The variations in the structure of the alkyl substi-
tuent examined being fairly large, it can be expected that the
behavior found here will be generally true for all carboxylate
salts with alkyl groups of size comparable to $n\text{-}C_7H_{15}$.

II- Critical Micelle Concentrations

The CMC values derived from ϕ_V, ϕ_C and ultrasonic absorption
data (Table I) agree mutually within the experimental error involved in each determination; there are no systematic differences
suggesting that the thermodynamic and ultrasonic data reflect different aspects of the micellar association of these compounds.
Since the CMC is related to the free energy of micellization via:

$$\Delta G_m = RT \ln CMC \qquad (5)$$

(where the CMC is given in mole fraction units), we have sought to
relate the observed CMC values to various molecular parameters of
the amphiphiles. The latter having similar intrinsic and apparent
molar volumes at infinite dilution (Table II), various attempts

were carried out to correlate directly the CMC values with the
molecular parameters of the hydrocarbon groups, namely polarizabilities, effective lengths, effective cross sections and surface
areas. While the former three properties had to be estimated from
group contributions or scale molecular models, the surface area of
the hydrocarbon group could be computed accurately using a method
developed by Hermann[25]. The contact solvation area of the hydrophobic group (hydrophobic surface area) were thus obtained, and the
relationship between these surface areas and the CMC values is
illustrated in Figure 9. The observed general trend is far more
regular than that found in correlations with other parameters; the
CMC decreases with increasing hydrophobic surface area, as expected
from data on homologous series of n-alkylsubstituted surfactants[26].
There is apparently little specific influence of solute structural
factors, except in the case of 2-ethylhexanoate (or octane-3-car-
boxylate) which exhibits a much larger CMC than its isomer n-octa-
noate with a comparable hydrophobic surface area. However, it
seems quite clear that the data for this pair of compounds mainly
reflect the positional isomerization of the ionic group (changing
from C_1 to C_3), rather than structural modifications in the hydrocarbon chain. Changing the position of the hydrophilic group on
the alkyl chain is known to have a marked influence on the micellar

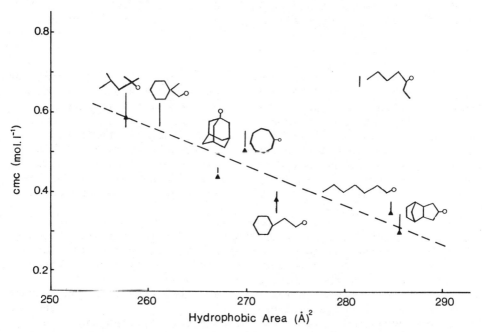

Figure 9. Variation of CMC for several potassium alkylcarboxylates
           as function of the hydrophobic area of the amphiphiles;
           ▲: CMC from ultrasonic adsorption; vertical bars:
           range of values obtained from ϕ_V and ϕ_C data.

behavior of surfactants[27]. Thus, although the CMC data are not
sufficiently numerous and accurate to decide wether the hydrophobic
surface areas are better related to the CMC or to ln CMC (i.e., ΔG_m)
there is strong indication that hydrophobic solvation area is a
main factor in determining the free energy of micellization.

III- ΔV_m and ΔC_m Values.

The series of ΔV_m values obtained from ϕ_V data and those calculated from the relaxation amplitudes (ΔV_m^{us}) differ by a substantial fraction, the ΔV_m^{us} values being systematically lower. This
type of discrepancy, although less important, had been reported
previously[16] and are likely to originate in the explicit assumptions
in the calculation of ΔV_m^{us} using Equation (3). Considering the
various quantities involved and the sign of the discrepancy, the
most likely cause of differences would appear to be in the use of
molar concentrations rather than the required activities, a problem
which is exacerbated in the concentrated solutions investigated
here. This aspect should thus be reexamined if, and when, activity data for these compounds become available. Attempts to corre-
late ΔV_m (or ΔV_m^{us}) with molecular parameters, as discussed earlier
in the interpretation of the CMC data, failed to provide indica-
tions that a single effect could be dominant. This is not really
surprising since ΔV_m may depend on subtle molecular packing and
hydration effects of the surfactant in both the monomeric and the
micellar states.

The heat capacity changes upon micellization of the surfactants
examined here (ΔC_m, Table II) are enormous, corresponding to more
than half of the ϕ_C^o values of the monomeric solutes in water.
Such behavior has now been observed with many ionic and nonionic
micellar surfactants[13,15,17,18] and can be largely attributed to
the loss of the hydration shell of the hydrophobic residue when
the amphiphile is transferred from water to the micelle. In the
latter state, surfactants generally appear to have ϕ_C (or $\bar{C}_p$) values close to those for pure organic substances of same molecular
weight.

As with the ΔV_m data, there is no simple relationship between
ΔC_m and surfactant molecular parameters such as hydrophobic surface
area. Again, this could reflect structure-specific interactions
occurring either in the hydration of the monomers, or in the solute-
solute interactions within the micellar aggregates. In the present
case, however, some distinction of effects seems possible; the
hydration contribution to ϕ_C^o of the alkylcarboxylates has been
shown to be dominated by the hydrophobic surface area[11] and,
consequently, a large part of the variations found in ΔC_m values
must result from ϕ_C differences in the micellar state.

IV- Kinetic Parameters and Polydispersity of Micelles.

The kinetic parameters relevant to the micellization behavior are the rate constant k^+ and k^- which respectively describe the rates of association and dissociation of a surfactant molecule to a micelle. Unfortunately the average aggregation number of the micelles examined here are not available from independent measurements, so the rate constants can only be discussed from the ratios k^+/n and k^-/n as reported in Table IV. Nonetheless, k^+/n and k^-/n are all close to 10^8 mol sec^{-1}, and, thus, even with aggregation numbers as low as 10, the k^+ values would lie close to 10^9 mol^{-1} sec^{-1} for every compound studied here. This clearly indicates that, for the surfactant molecules investigated here, as with more classical amphiphiles, the reaction by which a surfactant molecule associates with a micelle is close to being diffusion controlled. Moreover, the shape of the surfactant alkyl chain does not have a drastic influence on the rate at which a surfactant ion penetrates into a micelle; this may further suggest that the surfactant molecules in the micelles retain a translational mobility on the micellar surface which is also nearly diffusion controlled.

The k^-/n results may be better visualized and discussed as the inverse quantities n/k^- which represent the average residence time of a surfactant molecule in the micelle. For all compounds investigated here, these are extremely short, of the order of 10^{-8} sec. Interestingly, the residence time of the cyclic surfactants (#4 and 6) are very similar to that found with K-n-octanoate, in spite of the rather different shapes of these compounds. The relatively low value observed with 2,2,4-trimethylpentanoate (#2) could reflect a low aggregation number which we have estimated as $\sim$ 10 using the effective length calculations of Tartar[28]. The calculations assume a spherical micelle of radius equal to that of the extended chain of the surfactant, and a volume per surfactant equal to that calculated by an equation given by Tanford[26].

A relationship between the kinetics of micellar exchange processes and the shape of the amphiphile may be again found through hydrophobic surface areas. As a "first order" observation, it may be noted that the ultrasonic relaxation frequencies at the CMC ($f_1 = k^-/\sigma^2$, intercepts in Figure 8) vary regularly with the hydrophobic surface area of the surfactants; in fact, the more appropriate quantity log f_1 decreases quite linearly with hydrophobic surface area as illustrated in Figure 10. The basis of this correlation may be seen to originate in the residence time (n/k^-) which increases with increasing hydrophobic surface area. These observations being fully consistent with conclusions from CMC data, both the thermodynamic and the kinetic stability of the micelles thus appear related to the hydrophobic surface area of the surfactants.

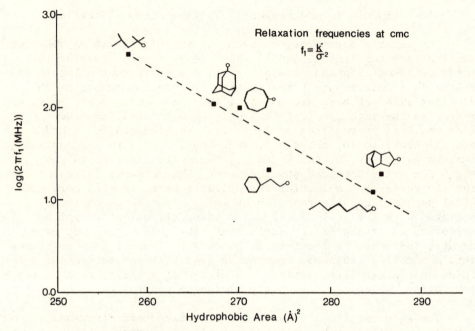

Figure 10. Relationship between relaxation frequencies and hydrophobic surface areas for several potassium alkylcarboxylates.

Finally, the polydispersity evidenced with these micelles (σ^2/n, Table IV) appear unusually low in most cases, but it is not clear whether the lower σ^2/n values are due to narrow distributions of micelle sizes, or to large aggregation numbers. It should also be mentioned that the distribution width concept which applies to large aggregation numbers (e.g. > 50) may not be applicable to systems with n ≃ 10.

CONCLUSION

The main conclusions derived from the present investigation are readily summarized as follows. The various potassium alkylcarboxylates with hydrocarbon groups of volume close to that of $n\text{-}C_7H_{15}$ all exhibit micellar-type aggregation in solution. The thermodynamic stability of these aggregates as defined by the CMC (or ln CMC), as well as the kinetic stability monitored by ultrasonic relaxation frequencies, appear to be mainly determined by the hydrophobic surface area of the alkyl groups. Specific effects related to the structure or rigidity of the surfactant molecules were observed only in ΔV_m and ΔC_m, (changes in the surfactant partial molar volume and heat capacity upon micellization), but these quantities are not yet amendable to unambiguous interpretation.

ACKNOWLEDGEMENTS

The authors gratefully acknowledge financial support from the Canadian "National Science and Engineering Research Council", the "Ministère de l'Education du Québec" and NATO (Grant No. 1382).

REFERENCES

1. F. Franks and H. T. Smith, J. Chem. Eng. Data 13, 538 (1968).
2. G. L. Amidon, S. H. Yalkowsky and S. Leung, J. Pharm. Sci. 63, 1858 (1971).
3. M. Sakurai, T. Komatsu and T. Nakagawa, J. Solution Chem. 4, 511 (1975).
4. M. Lucas and H. LeBail, J. Phys. Chem. 80, 2620 (1976).
5. C. Jolicoeur and G. Lacroix, Can. J. Chem. 54, 624 (1976); C. Jolicoeur, J. Boileau, S. Bazinet and P. Picker, Can. J. Chem. 53, 716 (1975); C. Jolicoeur and G. Lacroix, Can. J. Chem. 51, 3051 (1973).
6. P. Stenius, Acta Chem. Scand. 27, 3897 (1973).
7. D. Attwood, J. Phys. Chem. 80, 1984 (1976).
8. T. Hirota and M. Nakamura, J. Am. Oil. Chem. Soc. 48, 786 (1976).
9. J. T. Edward, P. G. Farrell and F. Shahidi, Can. J. Chem. 57, 2585 (1979); J. Phys. Chem. 82, 2310 (1978).
10. S. N. Bhattacharyya and D. Patterson, J. Solution Chem. 9, 247 (1980) and references cited therein.
11. Y. Lavigne, M.Sc. Thesis, Sherbrooke (1979).
12. R. Zana and J. Lang, Comp. Rend. Acad. Sci. Paris, Ser. C. 266, 893 (1968); J. Lang, G. Tondre, R. Zana, R. Bauer, H. Hoffman and W. Ulbright, J. Phys. Chem. 79, 276 (1975).
13. R. DeLisi, C. Ostiguy, G. Perron and J. E. Desnoyers, J. Colloid Interface Sci. 71, 147 (1979).
14. E. Vikingstad, A. Skauge and H. Hoiland, Acta Chem. Scand. A33, 235 (1979); J. Colloid Interface Sci. 72, 59 (1979)
15. Y. DeGrandpré, J. B. Rosenholm, L. L. Lemelin and C. Jolicoeur. (This proceedings volume.)
16. E. Graber, J. Lang and R. Zana, Koll. Z.Z. Polym. 233, 470 (1970); E. Graber and R. Zana, Koll. Z.Z. Polym. 233, 479 (1970).
17. J. B. Rosenholm, R. B. Grigg and L. Hepler (these Proceedings).
18. G. M. Musbally, G. Perron and J. E. Desnoyers, J. Coll. Interface Sci. 54, 80 (1976).
19. E.A.G. Aniansson and S. Wall, J. Phys. Chem. 78, 1024 (1974); ibid. 79, 857 (1975).
20. R. Zana and S. Yiv, Can. J. Chem. (in press).
21. K. Shinoda, T. Nakagawa, B. Tamamushi and T. Isemura, "Colloidal Surfactants," E. Hutchinson and P. Van Rysselberghe, Editors, pp. 31-32, Academic Press, New York (1963).
22. G. Roux, G. Perron and J. E. Desnoyers, Can. J. Chem. 56, 2808 (1978).

23. C. Jolicoeur, L. L. Lemelin and R. Lapalme. J. Phys. Chem. 83, 2806 (1979).
24. A. Djavanbakht, K. Kale and R. Zana, J. Colloid Interface Sci. 59, 139 (1977).
25. R. Hermann, J. Phys. Chem. 75, 363 (1971); ibid. 76, 2754 (1972).
26. C. Tanford, J. Phys. Chem. 78, 2469 (1974).
27. J. C. Evans, J. Chem. Soc. 579 (1956).
28. H. V. Tartar, J. Colloid Interface Sci. 14, 115 (1959).

FORMATION OF MICELLES OF CETYLTRIMETHYLAMMONIUM BROMIDE IN WATER-ACETONE SOLUTIONS

Lavinel G. Ionescu* and Valfredo Tadeu De Fávere
Laboratório de Química de Superfícies
Departamento de Química
Universidade Federal de Santa Catarina
Florianópolis, S.C.   88000   BRAZIL

The critical micellar concentration (CMC) of aqueous solutions of cetyltrimethylammonium bromide (CTAB) containing different amounts of acetone has been determined at 25° and 40° C by means of surface tensiometric measurements. Experimental parameters such as the standard free energy (ΔG_m^o), enthalpy (ΔH_m^o) and entropy of micellization (ΔS_m^o) were also determined. The experimental results indicate that: 1) micelle formation is somewhat enhanced by the rise in temperature and 2) acetone has inhibitory effect on the formation of micelles of CTAB. This inhibitory effect increases as a function of the acetone concentration and it becomes total as the mole fraction of acetone approaches 0.076 (25% by volume). The effect on micellization and the observed changes in ΔG_m^o, ΔH_m^o and ΔS_m^o can be explained in terms of interactions, such as hydrogen bonding, between water and acetone resulting in a decrease of hydrophobic forces in the ternary system. A comparison with micelle formation for CTAB in other aqueous solutions including cosolvents such as dimethylsulfoxide (DMSO), dimethylformamide, dimethylacetamide, dioxane, tetrahydrofuran, acetonitrile, methanol, ethanol, n-propanol and isopropanol shows that the effect of acetone represents an intermediate case between the highly polar DMSO and the short chain alcohols.

INTRODUCTION

As part of our study of the process of micellization in non-aqueous solvents and solutions of various solvents in water,[1-5] we have decided to analyze in some detail the effect of acetone on the formation of micelles of cetyltrimethylammonium bromide (CTAB) in aqueous solutions.

Acetone is a rather common organic solvent and is often used as a medium for many organic reactions. It belongs to the general group of aprotic dipolar solvents such as dimethylsulfoxide (DMSO); N,N'-dimethylformamide (DMF); N,N'-dimethylacetamide; tetrahydro-furan (THF), dioxane, acetonitrile, benzonitrile and others.[6-8]

The study of the effect of cosolvents on micellization in aqueous solutions and the formation of normal micelles in nonaqueous solvents is relatively new and no attempt will be made to discuss it here. This subject has originally been treated by Ray and Némethy[9,10] and it has been reviewed recently in the literature.[11]

There are not many reports of micelle formation in water-acetone solutions. Miyagishi[12] studied the effect of organic additives on the micellization of dodecylammonium halides in aqueous solutions of alcohols, urea, dioxane, acetone and formamide using conductivity methods and the emf cell: calomel/1M KCl/sample solution/AgCl,Ag. The critical micellar concentration (CMC) was found to increase in the presence of urea, dioxane, formamide and acetone and decrease in the presence of alcohols (C_2-C_4).

In subsequent papers,[13,14] Miyagishi reported the results of more detailed studies on the micellization of alkylammonium chlorides (C_{12}-C_{18}) in water-acetone and water-n-propanol solutions at dif-ferent temperatures. He determined the critical micellar concen-tration, the degree of dissociation of the micelle (α), the effec-tive coefficient of electrical energy (K_g) and thermodynamic para-meters such as the standard free energy of micellization (ΔG_m^o), enthalpy (ΔH_m^o) and entropy of micellization (ΔS_m^o). Both the CMC and α increased with additive concentration up to a maximum value and subsequently decreased. K_g varied between 0.6 and 0.8. The standard free energy of micellization at 35° C, ΔG_m^o, ranged between -6 and -9 kcal/mole for dodecylammonium chloride in various soultions of water-acetone and was divided into two terms, the hydrophobic component, ΔG_n^o, and the hydrophilic component, ΔG_p^o. The value of ΔG_p^o became more negative with the concentration of n-propanol and acetone and contributed to the stabilization of the micelle, while ΔG_n^o became less negative. It was concluded that the disruption of micelles in the presence of the cosolvent was due to an increase in the free energy of the hydrophobic group of the surfactant molecule.

Treiner and his associates have determined the standard free energy of transfer, ΔG^0_{transf}, of sodium decylsulfate (SDS) and decyltrimethylammonium bromide (DTAB) from pure water to water-acetone mixtures by means of vapor pressure measurements [15] and have also determined the degree of dissociation (α) and the apparent charge (Z) of micelles of the same surfactants in water-acetone and water-n-propanol solutions by means of electrical conductance.[16] ΔG^0_{transf} ranged from 0 to -8 kJ/mole. It went through a minimum and then increased for acetone rich solutions. The apparent charge (Z) of micelles of SDS and DTAB showed a small initial decrease as a function of acetone and n-propanol and subsequently remained constant. The constant value of Z was interpreted as the result of two concomitant phenomena: an increase in α caused by the preferential solvation of cations by the organic component and a decrease in the aggregation number of the micelles. Both of these processes are believed to take place while the highly ordered water structure is progressively destroyed by the cosolvent.

MATERIALS AND METHODS

The acetone used was analytical reagent grade supplied by Merck do Brasil, S.A.. It was employed without any additional treatment or purification. Cetyltrimethylammonium bromide, $CH_3(CH_2)_{15}\overset{+}{N}(CH_3)_3 Br^-$, (CTAB), was purchased from Aldrich Chemical Company, Milwaukee, Wisconsin, USA. It was recrystallized twice from ethyl alcohol and dried under vacuum for two days. Deionized distilled water was used for the preparation of all the solutions.

The solutions were prepared volumetrically at the following mole fractions (X) of acetone: 0.0, 0.005, 0.0127, 0.0414, 0.0577, 0.0755. 0.0949 and 0.140. All of them contained at least fifteen different concentrations of CTAB. The surface tension of the water-CTAB-acetone solutions was measured at 25^0 and 40^0 C by means of a Fisher Model 21 Semi-Automatic Tensiometer. Ten milliliter aliquots of the solutions were placed in a Petri dish with a diameter of 6 cm. The temperature of the solutions was brought to 25^0 or 40^0 C using a water bath and the Petri dish was kept at the desired temperature by placing it in a container through which water was circulated from a constant temperature bath. The tensiometer was set at a constant height. The final surface tension of any solution was the average of at least three independent measurements.

The CMC's were determined from plots of the surface tension of the solutions versus the concentration or the logarithm of the concentration of CTAB. The marked change in the plots was taken as an indication of micelle formation and the inflection point was considered to correspond to the CMC. Linear plots were taken as an indication that micelle formation does not occur. [2,4]

The thermodynamic parameters ΔG_m^o, ΔH_m^o and ΔS_m^o were determined using standard equations [17,18] derived on the basis of the assumption that the process of micellization involves formation of a distinct micellar phase at the CMC and that the concentration of monomers in solution is constant, once micelles are formed. The experimental accuracy in the values determined for ΔG_m^o is about ±500 J/mole . On the other hand, ΔH_m^o and ΔS_m^o are more approximate since they were calculated on the basis of measurements at two temperatures only.

RESULTS AND DISCUSSION

Some typical experimental results obtained for the surface tension of different CTAB solutions in various water-acetone mixtures at 25° C are given in Figure 1. Most plots of surface tension versus

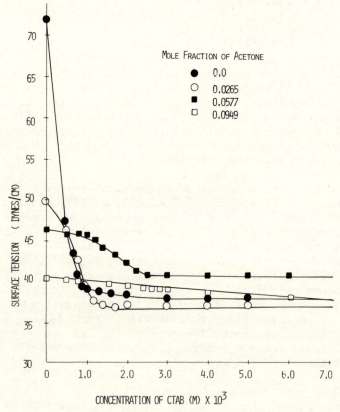

Figure 1. Dependence of surface tension on the concentration of cetyltrimethylammonium bromide for the water-CTAB-acetone system at 25° C.

the concentration of CTAB exhibit an initial marked drop and subsequently level off. The inflection point in the curve was taken as
the CMC. At times, plots of surface tension versus the logarithm of
the concentration of surfactant afforded a better determination of
the CMC. Results similar to those of Figure 1 have been obtained for
the same solutions at 40° C. A summary of the CMC's determined for
CTAB in various solutions of water and acetone is given in Table I.

Table I. Critical Micellar Concentration of Cetyltrimethylammonium
Bromide in Aqueous Solutions of Acetone.

Mole Fraction of Acetone	Critical Micellar Concentration at 25° C (M X 10³)	Critical Micellar Concentration at 40° C (M X 10³)
0.0	0.920	1.00
0.0050	1.00	1.10
0.0127	1.09	1.20
0.0265	1.31	1.45
0.0414	1.60	1.80
0.0577	2.20	2.81
0.0755	2.60	3.60
0.0949	-	-
0.140	-	-

The experimental values obtained for the thermodynamic functions
ΔG_m^o, ΔH_m^o and ΔS_m^o for the formation of CTAB micelles in water-acetone
solutions are given in Table II.

Table II. Some Thermodynamic Properties for the Formation of Micelles
of Cetyltrimethylammonium Bromide in Water-Acetone Solutions at 25° C.

Mole Fraction of Acetone	ΔG_m^o at 25°C (kJ/mole)	ΔH_m^o (kJ/mole)	ΔS_m^o at 25° C (J/mole-deg)
0.0	-17.3	-4.31	+43.5
0.0050	-17.1	-4.68	+41.0
0.0127	-16.9	-4.93	+40.2
0.0265	-16.4	-5.23	+37.7
0.0414	-15.9	-6.07	+33.1
0.0577	-15.1	-12.6	+ 8.37
0.0755	-14.7	-16.8	- 7.30
0.0949	-	-	-

The experimental results indicate that the CMC is increased by
the rise in temperature. A strict thermodynamic analysis shows,
however, that the free energy of micellization is slightly more
negative at 40° C, indicating that micelle formation in this case is
somewhat favored by the slight rise in temperature. The critical
micellar concentration is known to frequently depend on temperature,
but in many cases the dependence is highly irregular. The nature of
this effect is hard to predict because it depends on a series of
factors related to the restructuring of water and the interactions
between water and the surfactant. For example, for N-alkylbetaines
(C_{10} and C_{11}) the CMC decreases, reaches a minimum and then increases
as a function of temperature and for N-alkylbetaines (C_{12}) the CMC
increases as a function of temperature.[19,20] Our observation can
be explained in terms of the two interactions responsible for the
micellization, i.e., hydrophobic interactions and the break up of
the water structure. Higher temperatures, on one hand, enhance the
disruption of the water structure, and on the other hand, diminish
hydrophobic interactions. At lower temperatures, the effect is
exactly the contrary. The net result is a balancing of the two
effects in the temperature range studied.

The experimental results represented in Table I and in Figure 2
clearly indicate that the CMC also increases as a function of acetone
concentration. The effect of acetone is slightly more pronounced at
40° than at 25° C. It is relatively small at low cosolvent concentration, but it increases as the mole fraction of acetone approaches
0.0755. At mole fractions of acetone higher than 0.0949 we did not
observe micelle formation and the plots of surface tension versus
the concentration of CTAB were all linear. We have shown conclusively
for the H_2O-CTAB-DMSO system by means of proton spin lattice relaxation measurements that linearity in the surface tension plots corresponds to absence of micelle formation.[2-4]

The ΔG_m^o values determined for micellization in the water-CTAB-
acetone ternary system at 25° C increased almost linearly from -17.1
kJ/mole to -14.7 kJ/mole with increasing concentration of acetone and
were always less negative than the value determined for the formation
of CTAB micelles in pure water (Table II). The approximate enthalpy
of micellization calculated ΔH_m^o, is exothermic and almost constant
at mole fractions of acetone between 0.0050 and 0.0414. The corresponding values of the entropy of micellization, ΔS_m^o, decrease
gradually from +41.0 J/mole-deg to +33.1 J/mole-deg. This implies
that the negative free energy of micellization is principally the
result of the entropy term in the water-CTAB-acetone system at low
acetone concentrations. This conclusion is in agreement with the
general concept that micelle formation in aqueous solutions is   an

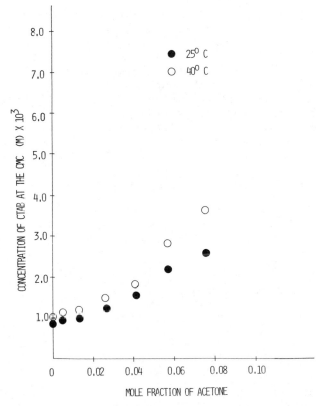

Figure 2. Dependence of the critical micellar concentration of cetyl-
          trimethylammonium bromide on the composition of water-
          acetone solutions.

entropy directed process and arises mainly from the break up of the
"Frank-Evans icebergs" or "microcrystals" of the ordered water structure, even though the formation of aggregates by the surfactant molecules is an entropy decreasing process.

    Since the ΔS_m^o values increase with the addition of acetone
(Table II), an increase in the orderliness of the water-CTAB-acetone
system takes place as the mole fraction of acetone is increased. This
is consistent with a strong interaction, such as hydrogen bonding,
between water and acetone. The formation of H-bonds between H_2O and
CH_3COCH_3 is a well established fact. It is also interesting to note
that acetone forms a clathrate of the stoichiometry $CH_3COCH_3 . 17H_2O$

and this molar ratio corresponds approximately to a mole fraction of 0.055, similar in concentration to the water-acetone solutions where micelle formation is highly inhibited.[21-23]

A further addition of acetone caused a significant change in the relative contributions from the enthalpy and entropy terms, i.e., at a mole fraction of acetone of 0.0755, ΔH_m^o and ΔS_m^o become -16.8 kJ/mole and -7.30 J/mole-deg, respectively. This type of change implies that the driving force for micellization in the water-CTAB-acetone system under these conditions must be attributed to the enthalpic term. We have observed similar behavior for CTAB in many of the other systems studied, including cosolvents such as DMSO, DMF, DMA, tetrahydrofuran, dioxane and acetonitrile.[1-5,24,25]

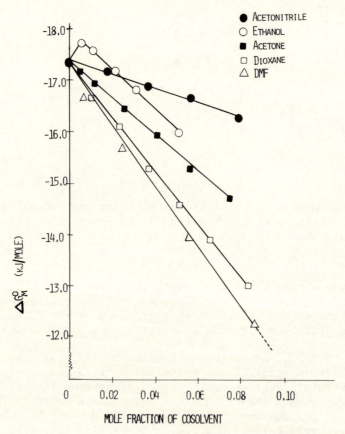

Figure 3. Dependence of the free energy of micellization on the mole fraction of cosolvent for aqueous solutions of cetyltrimethylammonium bromide at 25° C.

A comparison of values obtained for the CMC of CTAB in different aqueous solutions in previous studies may be useful. For example, for the ternary system H_2O-CTAB-DMSO at 25° C, the CMC varied from 9.20×10^{-4} M (pure water) to 14.0×10^{-3} M ($X_{DMSO} = 0.275$)[2] and for N,N'-dimethylformamide the CMC at 25° C varied up to 29.5×10^{-3} M ($X_{DMF} = 0.258$).[1] In these cases the inhibition of micelle formation took place at an approximate cosolvent mole fraction of 0.330 and the restructuring to the medium was attributed to the formation the stoichiometric hydrates $DMSO.2H_2O$ and $DMF.2H_2O$.

On the other hand, study of the formation of micelles in the system water-CTAB-ethanol at 25° C gave values of CMC between 7.50×10^{-4} M ($X_{Ethanol} = 0.0078$) and 1.70×10^{-3} M ($X_{Ethanol} = 0.0516$). At low concentrations, ethanol as well as methanol, n-propanol and isopropanol facilitate micelle formation and at higher concentrations they all inhibit it.[24] The values determined for the CMC of CTAB in aqueous solutions of tetrahydrofuran, dioxane and acetonitrile are similar to those obtained for acetone.[25] An analysis of all the CMC values available for CTAB in different mixed solvent systems indicates that acetone represents an intermediate case between the highly polar aprotic solvents such as DMSO and the short chain alcohols like methanol and ethanol.

A graphic representation of the standard free energy of micellization of CTAB at 25° C in some typical systems studied is given in Figure 3. As can be seen, for all of the cosolvents, with the exception of ethanol, ΔG_m^o becomes more positive with the addition of the cosolvent. The process of micellization appears to be least favored in DMF and most favored in ethanol for low concentrations of the cosolvent. Acetone represents an intermediate case.

ACKNOWLEDGMENTS

Financial support provided by CNPq-National Research Council of Brazil to LGI by Grants Nos. 1111.5713/78 and 40.2548/79 is gratefully acknowledged.

REFERENCES

1. L.G. Ionescu, T. Tokuhiro and B.J. Czerniawski, Bull. Chem. Soc. Japan, 52, 922 (1979).
2. L.G. Ionescu, T. Tokuhiro, B.J. Czerniawski and E.S. Smith, in "Solution Chemistry of Surfactants", K.L. Mittal, Editor, Vol. 1, pp. 487-496, Plenum Press, New York, 1979.

3. T. Tokuhiro and L.G. Ionescu, in "Solution Chemistry of Surfac-
    tants", K.L. Mittal, Editor, Vol. 1, pp. 497-506, Plenum Press,
    New York, 1979.
4. T. Tokuhiro, L.G. Ionescu and D.S. Fung, J. Chem. Soc. Faraday
    Trans. II, 75, 975 (1979).
5. D.S. Fung, "Molecular Interactions in Solutions of Surfactants
    and Micelles", Doctoral Dissertation, University of Detroit,
    1978.
6. A.J. Parker, Quart. Rev., 16, 163 (1962).
7. B. Tchoubar, Bull. Soc. Chim. France, 2069 (1964).
8. C. Agami, Bull. Soc. Chim. France, 1021 (1965).
9. A. Ray, Nature, 231, 313 (1971).
10. A. Ray and G. Némethy, J. Phys. Chem., 75, 809 (1971).
11. L. Magid, in "Solution Chemistry of Surfactants", K.L. Mittal,
    Editor, pp. 427-453, Plenum Press, New York, 1979.
12. S. Miyagishi, Bull. Chem. Soc. Japan, 47, 2972 (1974).
13. S. Miyagishi, Bull. Chem. Soc. Japan, 48, 2349 (1975).
14. S. Miyagishi, Bull. Chem. Soc. Japan, 49, 34 (1976).
15. C. Treiner and A. Le Besnerais, J. Chem. Soc. Faraday Trans. I,
    73, 44 (1977).
16. C. Treiner, A. Le Besnerais and C. Micheletti, in "Advances in
    Chemistry Series, No. 177 - Thermodynamic Behavior of Electro-
    lytes in Mixed Solvents - II", W.F. Furter, Editor, pp. 109-128,
    American Chemical Society, Washington, D.C., 1979.
17. N. Muller, in "Reaction Kinetics in Micelles", E.H. Cordes,
    Editor, pp. 1-23, Plenum Press, New York, 1973.
18. D.G. Hall, Trans. Faraday Soc., 66, 1351,1359 (1970).
19. J.H. Fendler and E.J. Fendler, "Catalysis in Micellar and Ma-
    cromolecular Systems", Academic Press, New York, 1975.
20. J. Swarbrick and J. Daruwala, J. Phys. Chem., 73, 2627 (1969).
21. M.J. Blandamer, Adv. Phys. Org. Chem., 14, 204 (1977).
22. F. Franks, Editor, "Water - A Comprehensive Treatise", Vols.
    1-6, Plenum Press, New York, 1979.
23. W.K. Khanzada and C.A. McDowell, J. Molec. Struct., 7, 241
    (1971).
24. L.G. Ionescu and F. de Paula Soares Mol Filho, Paper Presented
    at the 32nd Annual Meeting of the Brazilian Association for the
    Advancement of Science - SBPC, Rio de Janeiro, Brazil, July 6-12,
    1980, Abstract 57-D.2.4.
25. L.G. Ionescu and V.T. de Favere, Paper Presented at the 9th
    Annual Meeting of the Brazilian Biochemical Society - SBBq and
    Symposium on Biological Membranes, Caxambu, Minas Gerais, Bra-
    zil, April 24-28, 1980, Abstract F-17.

THE MOTIONAL STATE OF HYDROCARBON CHAINS IN THE TERNARY SYSTEM

SODIUM OCTANOATE - 1-DECANOL - WATER STUDIED BY DEUTERIUM NMR

Tomas Klason and Ulf Henriksson

Department of Physical Chemistry
The Royal Institute of Technology
S-100 44 STOCKHOLM 70, SWEDEN

The system Sodium Octanoate - 1-Decanol - Water
has been studied in the liquid crystalline phases by
means of quadrupole splittings in the ^{2}H NMR spectra
from deuterated octanoate and decanol. The mole ratio
decanol/octanoate is found to have a big influence on
the motional state of the hydrocarbon chains. For high
decanol content the chains are fairly ordered while at
lower decanol content the population of *gauche* conformations is increased. For compositions where there is a
large area per headgroup the probability of a *gauche*
conformation around the first C-C-bond is high. This can
be seen as a consequence of the tendency to minimize
energetically unfavourable hydrocarbon -water contact.
In the region of the lamellar phase that exhibits one-
dimensional swelling the state of the hydrocarbon chains
is independent of the water content while in the region
with two-dimensional swelling increased area per head-
group is accompanied by an increased disorder in the
hydrocarbon chains. For high decanol content the order
parameter profile for the decanol chain has a maximum.
This has been interpreted as a consequence of the
formation of hydrogen bonds between the alcohol and the
carboxylate groups.

INTRODUCTION

The ternary system sodium octanoate - 1-decanol - water
has been subject to a great number of investigations. One reason
is that it displays a variety of phase structures at various com-
postions as can be seen in the phase diagram reproduced in Figure 1.
Ekvall *et al.*[1] have proposed not less than five different mesophases (B, C, D, E and F) from X-ray data and partial molar volumes. Two isotropic solution phases, L_1 and L_2, containing normal
and reversed micelles also exist in this system. The D-phase has
lamellar structure with bilayers of amphiphilic molecules separated by water. There are two regions with rods arranged in a hexagonal structure. In the E-phase the aggregates are of normal type
and in the F-phase of the reversed type. The existence of a separate phase in the C-region has been questioned first by Tiddy,[2] and
successful separation of sampels from the C-region into L_1 and D-
phase has recently been reported by Danielsson, <u>et al.</u>[3] It has also
been reported that the D-phase region extends over parts of the
region B[3,4].

It has been found by calorimetry that the partial molar enthalpies depend more on composition than on the actual structure
formed[5]. ^{13}C-NMR and Raman studies[5] indicate that solubilization of
alcohol in normal micellar solutions tend to increase the probability of *trans* conformations in the hydrocarbon chains.

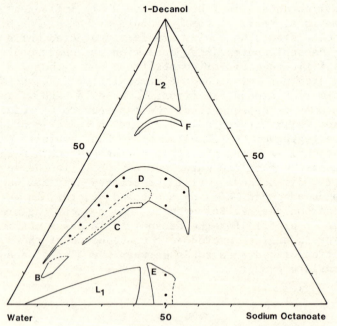

Figure 1.   Phase diagram in per cent by weight showing the one-phase
regions for the system Sodium Octanoate-Water-1-Decanol[1].   The
sample compositions, corrected for the difference in molar weights,
referred to in the text are marked with dots.

In this work we have studied the motional state of the hydrocarbon chain both for the octanoate and the decanol in the lyotropic
liquid crystalline phases in this system by means of static ^{2}H
quadrupole splittings from deuterated hydrocarbon chains. This
method has recently been widely used[6-10] both in surfactant-containing
liquid crystals and in phospholipid bilayers. Statistical-mechanical
models have also been used to describe the state of hydrocarbon
chains [11-12].

EXPERIMENTAL

The experiments were performed using sodium octanoate-d$_{15}$,
sodium octanoate -2,2-d$_2$, 1-decanol-d$_{21}$, 1-decanol-1,1-d$_2$ and
1-decanol -2,2-d$_2$ from Larodan AB and sodium octanoate and 1-decanol
from BDH. The water was double distilled and any traces of acid
were removed form the soap by extraction with ether. Homogeneity
of the samples was achieved by melting or at least heating them to
an easy-flowing state followed by vigorous shaking. Finally the
samples were left to cool slowly. During the cooling, they were
examined and shaken. They were then stored in a bath at 20°C.
During the investigation it was found that at some compositions
samples containing only perdeuterated soap, alcohol and water did
not get the structure indicated by the phase diagram. This was
most noticeable in the reversed hexagonal F-phase where the samples
contained two phases, liquid crystal and isotropic solution, instead of liquid crystal only. Replacing the soap with a mixture of
octanoate and octanoate-d$_{15}$ with a ratio of 3:1 removed the isotropic
solution. This indicates that the deuteration disturbs the phase
transitions as has been reported also for the phase transition temperature for phospholipids[13]. As a consequence all the deuterated
compounds have been diluted in this way before use.

The NMR experiments were performed at 20 ± 0.5° C on Bruker
CXP-100 and B-KR 322s spectrometers operating at 13.82 MHz. Both
normal Fourier transform techniques and the quadrupolar echo method
were employed[14].

In order to minimize the effects of acoustic ringings in the
NMR-probe, we have applied a scheme with 180° phase shifts on the
first 90° pulse in the quadrupole echo sequence combined with
successive addition and subtraction of the NMR-signal.

THEORY

Information about the average orientation of molecules in
liquid crystalline phases can be obtained from static NMR parameters such as dipole couplings, quadrupole couplings and chemical
shift anisotropies. The deuterium nucleus has spin quantum number

I = 1 and thus an electric quadrupole moment. The principal axis of the quadrupole coupling tensor for a ^{2}H-nucleus which is covalently bonded to a carbon atom is directed along the C-D bond. From the observed quadrupole splittings in the ^{2}H NMR-spectrum, order parameters characterizing the average orientation of the different segments in the hydrocarbon chain can be determined[6-10]. The order parameter S is given by the time average

$$S = \frac{1}{2} \cdot \overline{(3 \cos^2 \theta_{DM} - 1)} \tag{1}$$

where θ_{DM} is the time-dependent angle between a C-D bond and the symmetry axis of the liquid crystal (the "director").

In a lamellar phase the director coincides with the normal to the surface of the lamellae. In hexagonal phases the director is oriented along the axis of the cylindrical aggregates. Since the lateral diffusion of amphiphile molecules is rapid, this motion contributes to the averaging of the quadrupole interaction in the hexagonal phase. In order to compare the motional state of the hydrocarbon chains in the different phases it is necessary to re-late the order parameters in the hexagonal phase to a normal to the aggregate surface instead of the director. Due to the rapid la-teral diffusion the following relation is valid in the hexagonal phase[8,15]:

$$S_N = -2 \cdot S^{obs} \tag{2}$$

where S_N is the order parameter relative to the surface normal and S^{obs} is the value defined in Equation (1). In the lamellar phase:

$$S_N = S^{obs} \tag{3}$$

All order parameters for hexagonal phases reported in this work are given relative to a local normal according to Equation (2).

In the binary system potassium laurate-water Mely *et al.*[16] have found that S_{N_2} is only about 20 % lower in the hexagonal phase with the area 52Å^2/headgroup than in the lamellar phase with 36 Å^2/headgroup. That the order parameters do not change very much in spite of the considerable difference in area per headgroup was ex-plained as a consequence of the fact that only motions along the long axis of the cylinders contribute to the measured order para-meter. The interaction in the other directions is averaged to zero due to the rapid lateral diffusion.

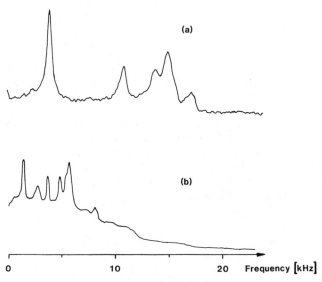

Figure 2. Fourier transforms of quadrupolar echoes from samples
containing octanoate-d_{15} with mole ratio water/octanoate = 9.3.
The quadrupolar echo method gives the two symmetric parts of the
spectrum folded onto each other. (a) refers to D-phase with 1.0
mole of decanol per octanoate and (b) refers to E-phase with 0.07
decanol per octanoate.

RESULTS AND DISCUSSION

Typical spectra from perdeuterated octanoate are shown in
Figure 2. Unambigous assignments can only be done using selectively deuterated compounds. These results are marked with a ● in all
figures. For the other segments in the octanoate molecule we have
assumed the order parameters to decrease or remain constant along
the chain implying an increased flexibility towards the end. On
this basis a tentative assignment of octanoate spectra in the hexagonal phase is relatively easy due to small splittings and few
overlapping peaks. In the lamellar phase the assignment is more
difficult, the spectra are broader, the peaks themselves are broader and the number of more or less overlapping peaks is high. The
decanol spectra are even more difficult to assign due to the longer
chain and the fact that the biggest order parameter usually does
not correspond to the initial segment. In the lamellar phase in the
system sodium decanoate-decanol-water Niederberger and Seelig[17]
have found that there is a maximum in the order parameter "profile"
around the fourth segment. In our tentative assignments we have
used this finding when it is clear from the spectra that the decanol order parameter profile has a maximum.

The measured order parameters reflect both molecular orientation and averaging of the angular dependent function in Equation (1)

due to molecular motions. The molecular motions that, more or less effectively, cause this averaging are lateral and rotational diffusion of the whole molecule and internal motions in the hydrocarbon chain (*trans-gauche* isomerizations). A *trans-gauche* isomerization requires about 10^{-10} s,[18] while the lateral diffusion constant for octanoate molecules in the lamellar phase in this system is $2.1 \cdot 10^{-10}$ m^2/s [19].

The effect on the order parameters of molecular orientation relative to the director is most important in the beginning of the alkyl chains since the amphiphile molecules are more or less anchored at the surface due to the possibilities of hydrogen bond formation. A few segments down the chain, however, rotational isomerization around the C-C bonds dominates.

Lamellar Phase with Mole Ratio Soap to Water = 1:9.3

Figures 3d, 3e, 4b and 4c show the order parameters along the chain for octanoate and decanol in lamellar phase with the water content of 9.3 moles of water per octanoate.

The order parameter profiles for octanoate and decanol in the lamellar phase changes drastically for both species when the mole ratio decanol/octanoate increases from 1.0 to 1.6. There is a

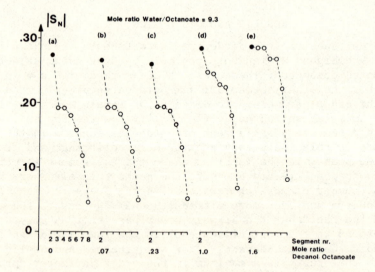

Figure 3. Order parameters for Sodium Octanoate relative to the surface normal of the aggregate as function of segment position for constant mole ratio water : octanoate = 9.3. (a) – (c) refer to the E-phase, (d) and (e) to the D-phase. ● refers to measurements with selectively deuterated compounds.

very pronounced increase of the order parameter especially in the middle of the chain. It must be noted, however, that the first segment in both cases have practically the same order parameter and its average orientation is thus not changed. The rather rapidly decreasing order parameters along the octanoate chains for decanol/octanoate = 1.0 show that at this composition there is a high degree of disorder in the hydrocarbon part with increasing probabilities of *gauche* conformations towards the end of the chain.

The general increase of S when the decanol content is increased reflects a decrease in conformational freedom for the chains, i.e., they have a higher population of trans conformations and are more straight. Increasing the amount of decanol results in a lowering of the electrostatic repulsion between the carboxylate head-groups due to the increased distance between the octanoate molecules. This makes a closer packing of the hydrocarbon chains possible. This effect is also seen in the X-ray data of Ekwall et al.[1] where the area per headgroup in the lamellae decreases from 27.2 to 24.7 Å^2 and the thickness of the lamellae increases from 20 to 23Å on this increase of the decanol content.

For the mole ratio decanol/octanoate = 1.0 the octanoate has a big difference between S_2^{oct} and S_3^{oct} which disappears when decanol is added as is seen in Figure 3. This indicates that there is a

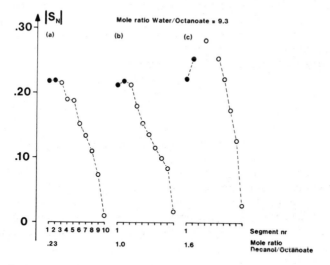

Figure 4. Order parameters for 1-decanol. Constant mole ratio water : octanoate = 9.3. (a) refers to the E-phase, (b) and (c) to the D-phase. For decanol/octanoate = 1.6 the spectrum from perdeuterated decanol clearly shows a peak giving the order parameter $S_N = 0.28$. In this case it is, however, impossible to estimate the number of segments represented by this peak.

high probability of *gauche* conformations around the C_2 - C_3 bond.
This point will be further discussed in connection with the results
from the hexagonal phase.

The order parameters for the decanol chain is for the higher
decanol content characterized by a maximum (Figure 4c). S_1^{dec} and
S_2^{dec} are also considerably smaller than S_2^{oct}. This can be explained
as a consequence of the formation of hydrogen bonds between decanol
and octanoate. The hydrocarbon chain of a decanol molecule that is
hydrogen bonded to the carboxylate group of an octanoate molecule
will, due to geometrical factors and the orientation of the lone
pairs on the carboxylate group, make a considerable angle with the
hydrocarbon chain of the octanoate if both chains are in the all-
trans state. In order to fill the volume of the lamellae the chains
will of course be more parallel on a time scale longer than the
trans-gauche isomerization time. The upper part of the decanol chain
can, by means of suitable rotational isomerization around the first
C-C-bonds, be bent with respect to the rest of the molecule. This
makes it possible to form a hydrogen bond between the hydroxyl group
and the lone pairs of the carboxylate and still keep the main part
of the hydrocarbon chain parallel to the octanoate chain. Furthermore, the terminal methylgroups in decanol and octanoate will then
be at approximately the same distance from the hydrocarbon-water
interface.

The maximum in the order parameter profile for decanol is
considerably less marked with 1.0 mole decanol per octanoate than
for 1.6. This can as discussed above be explained by the larger
area/polar group for low decanol content and the consequent more
disordered motional state of the hydrocarbon chains.

Hexagonal Phase with Mole Ratio Soap to Water 1:9.3

The effect on the octanoate upon decanol addition is, as can
be seen in Figures 3a-c and 4a, small within the E-phase. The
hexagonal phase cannot accomodate more than about 0.25 moles of
decanol per octanoate with this water content and such a small
amount of solubilizate does not affect the octanoate chains very
much.

The order parameters S_N for the octanoate are generally smaller than in the lamellar phase. Much of this must be attributed to
the packing problems in a cylinder. The diameter of the rods in
the hexagonal phase is close to the thickness of the bilayers in
the lamellar phase. However, in a cross section of a rod there is
only room for one methyle group in the center. This implies that

for most of the chains the probability of *gauche* conformations is
increased considerably.

In the hexagonal phase the difference between S_2^{oct} and S_3^{oct} is
even more marked than in the decanol-poor lamellar phase. This
shows, as mentioned above, that the probability of gauche conformations around the C_2-C_3 bond is high. The area per headgroup in the
hexagonal phase is about 48 $\overset{o}{A}{}^2$ without decanol and decreases to
around 40 $\overset{o}{A}{}^2$ with 0.23 moles of decanol per octanoate[1]. There seems
to be a correlation between the appearance of high population of
gauche conformations for the first two segments and larger areas
per headgroup. This means that energetically unfavourable contact
between hydrocarbon chains and water can be minimized if the chain
is bent in the upper part, since gauche arrangements can fill the
volume more effectively.

Lamellar Phase with Mole Ratio Decanol/Octanoate = 3.0

The order parameter profiles for decanol and octanoate from
samples with 3 moles of decanol per octanoate are found in Figures
5 and 6. Ekwall *et al.*[1] have from X-ray data found that in this
region the lamellar phase swells one-dimensionally i.e. when the
amount of water is increased the distance between the lamellae increases while the area/headgroup is constant.

The order parameters for the decanol do not change considerably
when the mole ratio water/octanoate increases from 25.7 to 79.3.
This is in good agreement with the concept of one-dimensional
swelling in this region. The order parameters for the octanoate,
however, show a significant monotonous decrease with increasing

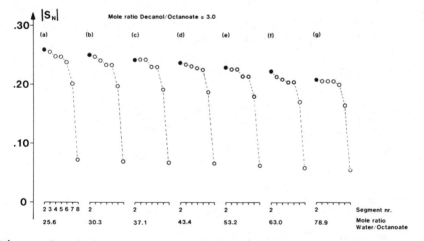

Figure 5. Order parameters for sodium octanoate. Constant mole
ratio decanol : octanoate = 3.0 in the D-phase.

water content. In Figure 7 S_2^{oct} and S_1^{dec} are plotted as functions of the water content.

The most evident explanation of the decrease in S^{oct} is that some fraction of the octanoate molecules are present in the inter-lamellar water layer. Due to rapid exchange with the octanoate molecules in the lamellae the observed order parameter is reduced. The measured order parameter is then given by

$$S^{oct,obs} = (1 - X) \cdot S^{oct,lam} \tag{4}$$

where X is the fraction of octanoate present in the water layers. The simplest model is that the amount of free octanoate is propor-

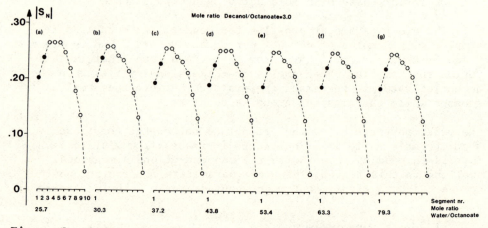

Figure 6.   Order parameters for 1-decanol. Constant mole ratio decanol : octanoate = 3.0 in the D-phase.

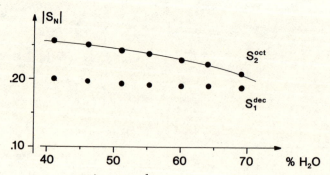

Figure 7.   Observed S_2^{oct} and S_2^{dec} as functions of water content in per cent by weight. The full line was obtained from a least squares fit to Equation (4).

tional to the amount of water present, i.e. $X = p \cdot n_{aq}$. A fit of
this model to the experimental data is also shown in Figure 7. The
obtained value of p is 1 molecule of octanoate per 300 water molecules, which corresponds to the concentration 180 mM. This is close
to what Ekwall *et al.*[1] call the lower association concentration
(l.a.c.). The isotropic water solutions of octanoate in the two-
phase region where lamellar phase is in equilibrium with L_1-solution
have octanoate concentrations near the l.a.c. and the obtained value
of p is thus quite reasonable. From the fit the value $S_2^{oct,lam}$ =
= 0.28 is also obtained.

Lamellar Phase with Decanol/Octanoate = 1.1

For this mole ratio, the lamellar phase shows two-dimensional
swelling[1] when the amount of water is increased. From Figure 8 it is
seen that the behaviour of the octanoate order parameters is
different compared to the region with one-dimensional swelling
(Figure 5).

For the sample with 6.3 water/octanoate the amount of water is
far from sufficient for complete hydration of both the polar groups
and the counterions. This forces the counterions closer to the
surface which reduces the lateral electrostatic repulsion between
the polar groups. The resulting smaller area per headgroup leaves
little room for chain isomerization as is evident from the order
parameter profile in Figure 6a.

When the mole ratio water/octanoate is increased to 9.3 the
counterions become more hydrated and less tightly bound to the
lamellae. The consequent increased lateral repulsion between the
headgroups leads to an increase in the area per headgroup and increased disorder in the hydrocarbon chains.

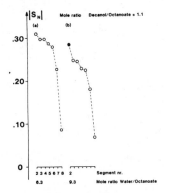

Figure 8. Order parameters for sodium octanoate. Constant mole
ratio decanol : octanoate = 1.1 in the D-phase.

leads to an increase in the area per headgroup and increased disorder in the hydrocarbon chains.

CONCLUDING REMARKS

The mole ratio decanol/octanoate is found to have a very big influence on the motional state of the hydrocarbon chains in the liquid crystalline phases. Ekwall *et al.*[1] found that there is a change from one- to two-dimensional swelling when the decanol content decreases below 2 moles decanol/octanoate. A comparison of the order parameter profiles for both decanol and octanoate shows that there are considerable changes in the hydrocarbon chain mobility up to 1.6 moles decanol/octanoate but only minor effects when the mole ratio is increased from 1.6 to 3.0.

The amount of water has considerable influence on the state of the hydrocarbon chains only in the decanol and water poor part of the lamellar phase region. This is a consequence of the two-dimensional swelling that occur upon increasing the amount of water in this region.

ACKNOWLEDGEMENTS

We wish to thank Drs. J.C. Eriksson and L. Ödberg for fruitful discussions in connection with this work. Financial support has been obtained from the Swedish Natural Science Research Council.

REFERENCES

1. P. Ekwall, L. Mandell, K. Fontell and H. Lehtinen, Acta Polytechnica Scand., 74, (1968) I - III.
2. G. J. T. Tiddy, J. Chem. Soc., Faraday Trans. I, 68, 369 (1972).
3. I. Danielsson, R. Friman and J. Sjoblom, paper presented at the "VIIth European Chemistry of Interfaces Conference", Turku 1980.
4. G. Lindblom, B. Lindman and G. J. T. Tiddy, J. Amer. Chem. Soc., 100, 2299 (1978).
5. J. B. Rosenholm, Thesis, Turku 1978.
6. J. Charvolin, P. Manneville and B. Deloche, Chem. Phys. Letters, 23, 345 (1973).
7. J. Seelig, Quart. Rev. Biophys., 10, 353 (1977), and references cited therein.
8. U. Henriksson, L. Odberg and J. C. Eriksson, Mol. Cryst. Liq. Cryst., 30, 73 (1975).
9. K. Abdolall, A. L. MacKay and M. Bloom, J. Magn. Res., 29,

309 (1978).
10. N. O. Petersen and S. I. Chan, Biochemistry, 16, 2657 (1977).
11. S. Marcelja, Biochem. dt Biophys. Acta, 367, 165 (1974).
12. D. W. R. Gruen, Biochem. et Biophys. Acta, 595 161 (1980).
13. N. O. Petersen, P. A. Kroon, M. Kainosho and S. I. Chan, Chem. Phys. Lipids, 14, 343 (1975).
14. J. H. Davis, K. R. Jeffrey, M. Bloom, M. I. Valic and T. P. Higgs, Chem. Phys. Letters, 42, 390 (1976).
15. J. Charvolin and P. Rigny, J. Chem. Phys., 58, 3999 (1973).
16. B. Mely, J. Charvolin and P. Keller, Chem. Phys. Lipids, 15, 161 (1975).
17. W. Niederberger and J. Seelig, Ber. Bunsenges. Physik. Chem., 78, 947 (1974).
18. R. E. London and J. Avitabile, J. Amer. Chem. Soc., 99, 7765 (1977).
19. G. Lindblom and H. Wennerstrom, Biophys. Chem., 6, 167 (1977).

NEAR-INFRARED AND HEAT CAPACITY INVESTIGATIONS OF THE STATE OF

WATER IN SURFACTANT AND ALCOHOL SOLUTIONS

Y. DeGrandpré, J.B. Rosenholm*, L.L. Lemelin and C.
Jolicoeur
Department of Chemistry, Faculté des Sciences, Uni-
versité de Sherbrooke, Sherbrooke, Qué. Canada. J1K 2R1
* Department of Physical Chemistry, Abo Akademi
Porthangatan 3-5 SF-20500 Abo 50, FINLAND

The state of water in surfactant solutions and in
various alcohol-water mixtures has been investigated using
near-infrared spectroscopy, flow densimetry and flow heat
capacity calorimetry. The surfactant systems studied thus
far comprise solutions of the anionic amphiphiles C_2H_5COONa,
$C_7H_{15}COONa$, $C_{11}H_{23}COONa$, $C_8H_{17}SO_4Na$ and $C_{12}H_{25}SO_4Na$ over
concentration ranges extending close to their solubility
limit. The properties of water solubilized in n-alkanols
were also examined over the miscibility ranges for the
following linear alcohols: CH_3OH, C_2H_5OH, C_3H_7OH, C_4H_9OH,
$C_5H_{11}OH$, $C_6H_{13}OH$, $C_8H_{17}OH$ and $C_{10}H_{21}OH$.

In surfactant solutions, the spectral data gives
evidence for differences in the hydration of alkylcarboxylate and alkylsulphate micelles. On the other hand, both
the spectral and thermodynamic data of dilute water in
n-alcohols indicate extensive hydrogen bonding, comparable
to, or greater than, that existing in liquid water.

INTRODUCTION

Since water is a key component of many colloid systems of
practical importance, there is a justified interest for monitoring
its thermodynamic and molecular properties in such systems. In
large excess as the solvent, or present as a minor component, the
state of water in aqueous mixtures has been the concern of numerous investigations in many areas of solution chemistry, biochemistry and biophysics. In spite of the involvement of many
powerful contemporary physical methods, many molecular aspects of

431

hydration phenomena remain highly elusive. This is due primarily
to fast exchange dynamics (molecule as well as proton exchange)
and, also, to sensitivity limits of the methods employed, especially in cases where water is the major solvent constituent. In
dilute aqueous systems, highly sensitive methods will be required
to monitor variations in the properties of a small fraction of the
water molecules which are perturbed by solute-solvent interactions.

Among the physical properties and methods which exhibit high
sensitivity towards molecular interactions in solution, heat capacity and infrared absorption in the overtone region have been
found useful in studies involving various ionic and non-ionic compounds in water[1-6]. The work described here was undertaken with
the aim of applying these methods to characterize the properties
of water in several binary mixtures of fundamental significance
in the chemistry of oil/water/surfactant systems. The investigation is concerned mainly with the thermodynamic and molecular
state of water in aqueous solutions of ionic surfactants and in
n-aliphatic alcohols, in relation to other investigations on ternary and higher order systems[7-12].

EXPERIMENTAL

I- Methods

a) <u>Infrared Spectra</u>. The differential near-infrared spectra
reported below were recorded on a Cary-14 spectrometer in the
region 800-1100nm, following a procedure described in several previous reports[3,13,14]. In this method, the influence of a solute
(or temperature) on the spectrum of the solvent (water or alcohol)
is recorded directly by varying the pathlength of the sample cell
to account for the solute excluded volume (or density changes with
temperature). The length of the reference cell (ℓ_R) is thus maintained at 10.00 cm (or 5.00 cm) while the length of the sample
cell (ℓ_S) is adjusted in such a way that the same number of moles
of solvent will be present in the sample and reference compartments. The sample cell pathlength is readily calculated from:

$$\ell_S = \ell_R \left[\frac{d_o}{d} \left(\frac{1000 + mM}{1000} \right) \right] \qquad (1)$$

where d and d_o are respectively the solution and solvent densities,
and m the molality of the solute having molecular weight M.

In the cases where the solute also exhibit IR absorption in
the region of interest (e.g. aqueous solutions of organic compounds which show C-H overtone absorption), the experimental differential spectrum may be further corrected using the spectrum of
the solute recorded under identical conditions in D_2O; the latter

exhibits only weak absorption in the region 800-1100nm.

b) <u>Density Measurements</u>. The density measurements were performed with a vibrating tube flow densimeter described by Picker
and co-workers[15];   the apparatus has a sensitivity of 1 x 10^{-6} g
cm^{-3}, and is capable of an accuracy between 2 to 5 x 10^{-6} g cm^{-3}
depending on the density increment between the reference liquid
(solvent) and the solution.

c) <u>Heat Capacity Measurements</u>. The heat capacity measurements
were carried out with a flow microcalorimeter designed by Picker
$et\ al.$[16].   The instrument operates in a differential mode (solution vs solvent) and yields the difference in the volumetric specific heats (σ, $JK^{-1}cm^{-3}$) of the liquids.   The differential resolution of the instrument used is $\Delta\sigma/\sigma$ = 1 x 10^{-5}, which, for
aqueous solutions of electrolytes will allow significant measurements at concentrations down to 10^{-2} mol 1^{-1}.   The volumetric
specific heats are converted to the weight specific heats c_p
($JK^{-1}g^{-1}$)using the measured densities

$$\frac{c_p}{c_p^o} = \frac{\sigma}{\sigma_o} \times \frac{d_o}{d} \qquad (2)$$

II- Materials

The alkylsulfate salts were obtained from Eastman Kodak and
purified by repeated recrystallization in alcohol-ether mixtures.
The carboxylate salts were prepared by neutralization of the corresponding acids with NaOH in dry ethanol;   these salts were also
recrystallized from ethanol-ether mixtures.

The n-aliphatic alcohols used in this work were distilled
over Mg or CaH_2 in an inert atmosphere and their final water content (0.01-0.05 wt %) was titrated using an automated Karl Fisher
analyser (Aquatest).

All solutions were prepared by weight in a dry nitrogen atmosphere.   The dilute solutions of water in alcohols were prepared
by weight dilution of a 1% water solution in the alcohol (stock
solution) with dry alcohol.

RESULTS

a) <u>Near-IR Spectra.</u>   The differential absorption spectra recorded for the various solutions as reported below were measured
at 6nm intervals and the data were stored on computer cards;   similar treatment of the data for solute absorption (when required)

allowed spectrum subtraction and normalization, as well as computer plotting of the resulting spectra. The overall uncertainty in the corrected differential spectra was usually inferior to 0.01 absorbance unit.

b) <u>Heat Capacity and Density Data.</u> From the measured densities and specific heats, the apparent molar volumes ϕ_V and heat capacities ϕ_C were calculated according to:

$$\phi_V = \frac{M}{d} - \frac{1000 \ (d-d_o)}{m \ dd_o} \tag{3}$$

$$\phi_C = Mc_p + 1000 \ \frac{(c_p - c_p^o)}{m} \tag{4}$$

where the various symbols have the significance given above. The uncertainty on these quantities depends on the system and the concentration range investigated. Usually, uncertainties on ϕ_V and ϕ_C will be or the order of 0.1 cm^3 mol^{-1} and 1 JK^{-1} mol^{-1}, respectively, for simple aqueous solutions. With dilute solutions of water in alcohols, the uncertainty on $\phi_V(H_2O)$ and $\phi_C(H_2O)$ will be several times larger.

DISCUSSION

I- Surfactant Solutions

a) ϕ_V and ϕ_C Results. Typical results of apparent molar volumes and heat capacities of surfactants in aqueous solutions are illustrated in Figures 1 and 2 with the data for sodium octanoate. In all the surfactant systems investigated here, as well as in many others[17,18], ϕ_V increases markedly upon formation of the micellar aggregates, usually, in a narrow range of concentration above the CMC. This effect has been discussed as resulting from two contributions: the dehydration of the monomeric amphiphile and, transfer of the latter into the micellar core which has a low packing density (e.g. comparable to packing densities of liquid hydrocarbons[19]). The sharpness of the ϕ_V change near the CMC increases with the surfactant hydrocarbon chain length, as may be expected from an enhanced degree of cooperativity of the micellization process.

The apparent molar heat capacity data of sodium octanoate illustrated in Figure 2 is, likewise, typical of ϕ_C behavior in micellar solutions. Up to the CMC, ϕ_C may increase slightly, but sharply decreases at concentrations exceeding the CMC. This

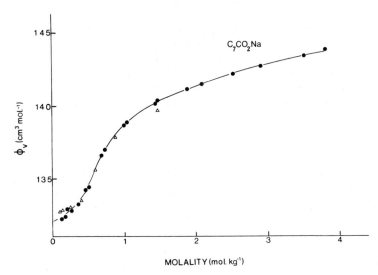

Figure 1. Apparent molar volume ϕ_V of Na-octanoate in water at $25^{\circ}C$;
Δ: data from reference 18a; $\bullet$: present results.

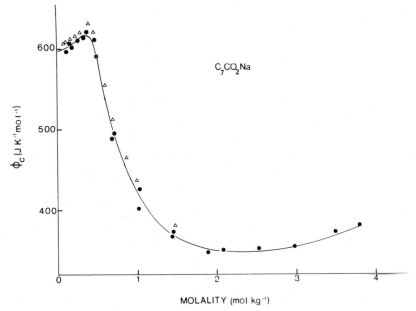

Figure 2. Apparent molar heat capacity ϕ_C of Na-octanoate in water
at $25^{\circ}C$; Δ: data from reference 18a; $\bullet$: present results.

marked drop in ϕ_C may be understood on the basis of monomer dehydration (loss of large positive C_P contribution due to hydration
effects associated with the alkyl group[20]) and, again, from the
analogy between the micellar core and liquid hydrocarbons[21]. On
the other hand, the ϕ_C maximum frequently observed with surfactants
near their CMC is qualitatively explained from a perturbation of
the micellar association equilibria[22]. Such "relaxational" heat
capacity effects can be accounted for quantitatively in other systems where well defined two-state equilibria can be specified.

From the data shown in Figures 1 and 2, the changes in volume
and heat capacity associated with the micellization process (ΔV_m,
ΔC_m) are readily obtained, usually, by transforming the apparent
quantities ϕ_V and ϕ_C into the corresponding partial molar quantities $\bar{V}$ and $\bar{C}_p$[21]. While detailed tabulations of results will be
reported elsewhere, two general observations are worth noting at
this point. Firstly, for the alkylsulfates and carboxylates
studied here, the variation of ϕ_V and ϕ_C at high concentrations
are weak and regular; thus, changes in the micelle structure or
size must occur either, over a broad concentration range, or, with
relatively little change in volume and heat capacity[1]. Secondly,
ΔV_m and ΔC_m values obtained for alkylsulfates and alkylcarboxylates
do not exhibit conclusive differences. This shows that such quantities are dominated by contributions from the alkyl groups; contributions arising from differences in ionic group hydration (monomer
or micelle) do not appear significant. These observations, the
latter especially, is of particular interest for comparison with
spectroscopic results.

b) <u>Near-Infrared Results</u>. 1. General basis. We illustrate
in Figure 3, the general basis of the near-infrared differential
method used here and in several previous studies[3,13,14,23,24].
The top curve in this figure shows the absorption spectrum of water (1.00 cm) in the second overtone region; the bottom curve
illustrates a differential spectrum obtained with water at different temperatures (reference cell: 25°C, sample cell, 18°C);
this and following differential spectra of aqueous solutions are
shown with positive absorbances towards the lower part of the figure, for consistency with previously published spectra. Such temperature difference spectra exhibit isosbestic behavior in the
temperature range (0-60°C) and least-squared deconvolution into
Gaussian components yields the two bands drawn as dashed lines[14].

---

[1] The behavior of C_8 surfactants is not ideally suited for investigation of such effects, but C_{12} amphiphiles also exhibit weak
variations in ϕ_V and ϕ_C in the post micellar region. A number
of other properties also exhibit rather weak changes upon
variation of micelle size or geometry, as discussed by Lindman
and Wennerström[11].

These have been assigned to two different categories of OH oscillators in water, separated by an average enthalpy of 10 kJ mol^{-1},
each category having a rather broad distribution of states as
indicated by the linewidths. For the discussion, these two types
of OH oscillators will be labelled "free OH" and "bonded OH" (or
OH$\cdots$O), though they are better described respectively as weakly
interacting, and hydrogen bonded, OH groups.

As illustrated in Figure 4, dilute solutions of polar aprotic
non electrolytes (1 molal) generally yield a differential hydration spectrum which is similar in shape and position to temperature
difference spectra (Figure 4A)[3]. In previous work, variations in

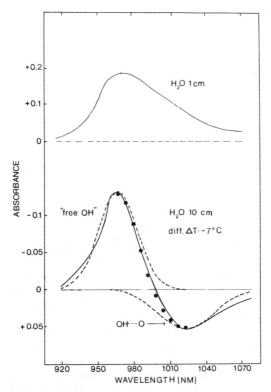

Figure 3. Upper curve: near-infrared spectrum of 1.00 cm of water
    at 25°C in the 2nd overtone region. Lower curve: diffe-
    rential near-infrared spectrum of water with reference
    cell at 25°C and sample cell at 18°C. (For comparisons
    with previously published spectra, the differential ab-
    sorption curves show negative absorbance above the X-axis).
    The dotted lines are computed assuming Gaussian linesha-
    pes; data from reference 14.

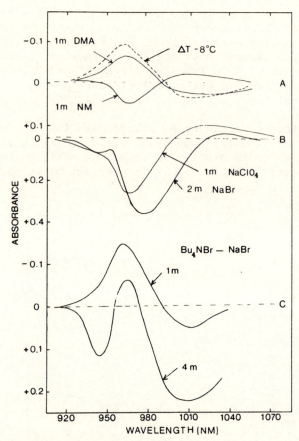

Figure 4. Differential hydration spectra observed with various
        nonelectrolytes and electrolytes at 25°C (after subtrac-
        tion of intrinsic solute absorption as necessary):
        A: DMA: dimethylacetamide; NM: nitromethane; the
        dotted line illustrates a temperature difference spectrum
        of water (reference 3).
        B: 1 m NaClO$_4$ and 2 m NaBr (reference 3 and 13).
        C: Different spectrum Bu$_4$NBr-NaBr at 1 m and 4 m (reference
            13 and 24).
the intensity of the high frequency component ("free OH") was interpreted in terms of hydration of the polar functional groups of
the solutes and pertubation of the hydrogen-bonding equilibrium
in water.[2]

---

[2] The use of the high frequency component is indicated, since
     the low frequency band may include significant intensity due
     to O-H···X modes, where X is any hydrogen-bonding acceptor
     site.

Inorganic electrolytes also yield differential S-shaped hydration spectra, although some ionic specificity in the lineshapes and absorption extrema are clearly observed (Figure 4B). In spite of these variations, the integrated absorption of the high frequency band (free OH) observed within a series of anions were shown well related to the structure disrupting influence of these ions and not to their primary hydration interactions.[3]

With dilute solutions of quaternary ammonium salts (R_4NX), the hydration spectra are similar to those encountered with non electrolytes, when comparing R_4NX salts (R = Me, Et, Pr, Bu) with alkali halides. The difference spectrum (Bu_4NBr – NaBr) obtained with 1 molal solutions is very closely related to a temperature difference spectrum, and this has been interpreted as a manifestation of a structure stabilizing influence of Bu_4N^+[13,14]. In concentrated solutions of the larger R_4NBr salts (Pr_4NBr and Bu_4NBr), an additional band was observed at $\sim$ 950nm, the intensity of which increased with concentration and temperature[24] (Figure 4C). From these observations, and based on the spectrum of dilute water in weakly interacting solvents, the 950nm band was attributed to OH oscillators free from interactions with neighboring water molecules for a time longer than the O-H vibration period, $i.e.$, O-H groups in a hydrocarbon-like environment provided by the alkyl groups of the large R_4N^+ cations.[3] The interactions to which such OH groups participate are weaker than those of the OH groups designated as "free" in water, near room temperature (970nm). However, judging from the 3rd O-H overtone of HOD in the dilute vapour (900nm)[25], the hydrocarbon environment still exerts considerable influence on the O-H oscillator; similar conclusions are also borne out from comparisons of fundamental infrared frequencies[25,26].

2. <u>Results for micellar solutions and related systems.</u> The differential hydration spectrum of Na octylsulfate is illustrated in Figure 5 as function of concentration; these spectra are similar in every respect, except in magnitude, to those recorded with Na dodecylsulfate. The spectrum at 0.90M is further compared with that obtained with Na_2SO_4 at a similar concentration. Because of the weak intensity of the bands at low surfactant concentrations, the method is not sufficiently sensitive to ascertain significant changes in lineshape before and after the CMC (for Na octylsulfate: $\sim$ 0.13m). However, the differential hydration spectra of micellar solutes are clearly different from that of the inorganic electrolyte Na_2SO_4 (a better comparison would be with $PrSO_4Na$ or $BuSO_4Na$ as done with alkyl carboxylates discussed below). The differential hydration spectra of alkylsulfate micelles exhibit a marked increase in the intensity of the "free-OH" absorption (970nm), of

---

[3] It is noteworthy that with Me_4NBr and Et_4NBr, the 950 nm band was absent even at the highest concentrations (4m) and temperatures (60°C).

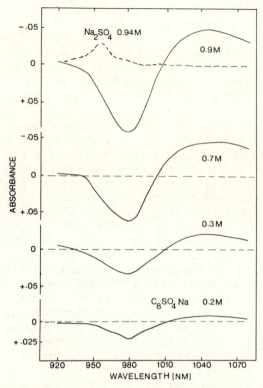

Figure 5. Differential hydration spectra of sodium octylsulfate as
        function of concentration; the spectrum obtained with
        Na_2SO_4 (0.94 molar) is illustrated as a dashed curve.

magnitude approximately twice that observed with NaBr (Figure 4B).
If the interpretation given earlier can be applied to micellar
systems as well (*i.e.* assuming no important changes in OH oscillator strength due to high electric fields near the micelles), then
the hydration of the micelles lead to an overall decrease of the
hydrogen-bonding interactions involving water molecules, compared
to pure liquid water. From the integrated intensity of the free
OH band and with reference to temperature difference spectra, it
may be estimated[14] that the effect involves, an average of 1.5 OH
groups per Na octylsulfate molecule.

    The above result appears in direct contradiction with a number
of other data (e.g., viscosity, diffusion[26]) which yield average
hydration numbers of ∿ 9 water molecules per molecule of micellar
surfactant. However, the near-IR data, as interpreted here, only
show the changes in the population of weakly interacting OH groups
(970nm) in water, and an overall increase of these "free OH"

groups does not preclude important hydration of the micelles. Several hydration effects can lead to a net increase of "free-OH" groups namely the structure-breaking effects (Frank and Wen[20]) or the "scavenging" of oxygen lone-pairs upon cation hydration (Symons *et al.*[28]).

The influence of surfactant concentration on the differential hydration spectrum of sodium propionate and octanoate is illustrated in Figures 6 and 7. In this case also, the hydration spectra of the micellar amphiphile is sharply different from the spectra recorded with the short chain carboxylate. The hydration spectrum of Na-propionate shows a marked reduction of the intensity associated to the free OH groups (970-980nm); this effect is approximately proportional to concentration, and can be mainly attributed to the hydrogen-bonding of water to the carboxylate headgroup. Through the procedure referred to above[14], the "free-OH" intensity change was estimated to correspond to one OH group per propionate

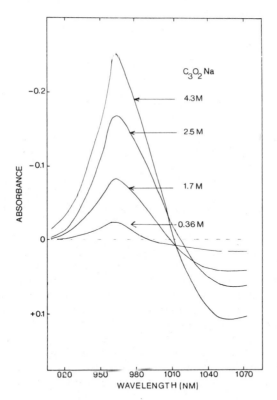

Figure 6. Differential hydration spectra of Na-propionate as function of concentration.

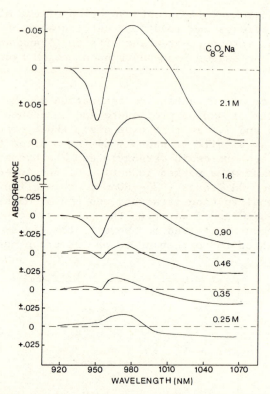

Figure 7. Concentration dependence of the differential hydration
          spectrum of Na-octanoate.

molecule at low concentrations ($\sim$ 0.5 M), decreasing to 0.5 OH
group at 5 M.

As with the sodium octylsulfate hydration spectra, the low
concentration data obtained for Na octanoate do not allow reliable
conclusions on the changes in lineshape occuring near the CMC, but
the spectral features above the CMC clearly show an additional
component in the region 950-960nm.[4] This behavior, also observed
with Na-dodecanoate, suggests a significant specificity in the
hydration of the anionic micelles, although no corresponding manifestation could be found in the thermodynamic properties discussed
earlier. In view of previous results with concentrated Pr_4NBr
and Bu_4NBr (Figure 4C), and with water diluted in weakly interacting

---

[4] In previous work[24], this feature was not fully explored in so-
     dium octanoate hydration spectra; it is interesting to recall
     however that this high frequency band ($\sim$ 950nm) was not observed
     in solutions of tetrabutylammonium octanoate.

solvents (tetrahydrofuran, nitromethane), this component can be
tentatively assigned to OH groups located in hydrocarbon-like
environments as further qualified below. Following recent discussions on the penetration of water in micelles[27,29,30], this would
seem rather straightforward evidence for such penetration (taken
simply as a water hydrocarbon contact). It is, however, difficult
to understand the different behaviors of RSO_4^- and $RCOO^-$ micelles
in this respect.

Among other investigations which have provided evidence of
specific behavior of RSO_4^- and $RCOO^-$ micelles, the work of Gustavsson et al.[31] on ^{23}Na NMR chemical shifts should be recalled. The
^{23}Na chemical shifts upon micelle formation were found of opposite
signs with RSO_4^- and $RCOO^-$ surfactants. This effect was interpreted
on the basis of differences in the induced polarization of the
hydration sphere of micelle-bound Na^+ ions, by the surfactant head
group. To explain the large paramagnetic shift observed with $-CO_2^-$,
it was suggested that the water molecules hydrating the sodium ion
can hydrogen-bond to the carboxylate group, i.e. $RCOO^- \cdots H-O \cdots Na^+$.
Similar evidence of head group specificity was also found from
^{23}Na relaxation rates[32] and quadrupolar splittings[33]. The latter
could be interpreted as due to differences in the binding geometry
of the Na^+ to the head groups. With RSO_4^- surfactants, the hydrated

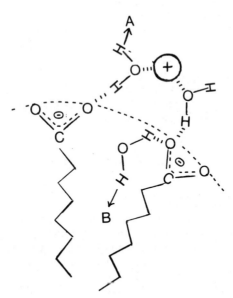

Figure 8. Schematic representation of partial hydration of a carbo-
          xylate micelle illustrating water molecules with "free-OH"
          groups. A: water molecule shared between cation and
          anion. B: water molecule with one OH group towards the
          interior of the micelle.

Na^+ ions are bound to the micelle, symmetrically with respect to the three oxygens of the OSO_3^- group and in line with the main axis of the alkyl chain. With $RCOO^-$ micelles, binding of the sodium ions would instead occur with an important angle relative to the main axis of the alkyl chain, possibly as shown in Figure 8.

The evidence derived from ^{23}Na NMR data offers some basis for interpretation of the near-IR hydration spectra of carboxylate micelles through interactions such as depicted in Figure 8. If a water molecule (labelled A in Figure 8) can be shared by an ion pair in such a way that one OH group remains free of interactions with other carboxylates or water molecules ($-COO^-\cdots H-O\cdots Na^+$), then electrostatic polarization of this free OH group could enhance its vibrational frequency[34]. The absence of such effects with RSO_4^- micelles would be the result of a lower hydrogen-bonding ability of the $-SO_4^-$ ion compared to $-CO_2^-$ (as indicated by the relative pKa's of the conjugate acids).

An alternate explanation which is simpler, and at present preferred, may be suggested as shown with the water molecule labelled B in Figure 8. A fraction of the water molecules solvating the $-COO^-$ groups can have one OH group momentarily decoupled from other molecules or ions, and pointing inwards to the interior of the micelle; this particular orientation would be assisted by electrostatic repulsion between the proton and the bound Na^+ ion. By analogy with other situations discussed above, these decoupled OH groups would be responsible for the 950-960nm band observed in carboxylate micelles. Considerations on the relative sizes of the $-CO_2^-$ and SO_4^- head groups would also favor this interpretation, the smaller CO_2^- group being (sterically) less efficient in shielding the hydrocarbon chains from water contact. Further work with other anionic surfactants (e.g. RSO_3Na) should help refine this aspect.

II- Alcohol Water Mixtures.

1. <u>Apparent Molar Volumes and Heat Capacities</u>. The apparent molar volume and heat capacity of water at infinite dilution (ϕ_V^o and ϕ_C^o) in various n-alkanols are reported in Figure 9, as function of the number of carbon atoms in the alcohols; the molar volume and heat capacity (V^o, C_p^o) for liquid water are also included as data for the "zero-carbon" homolog in this series. As is apparent from these data, ϕ_V^o of water diluted in the lower alcohols is considerably lower than V^o of liquid water; $\phi_V^o(H_2O)$ increases with the hydrocarbon chain length of the alcohols, and in n-OctOH, it reaches a value close to the molar volume of liquid water. On the other hand, the apparent molar heat capacity of water in the same alcohols is always found higher than the molar heat capacity of pure water. $\phi_C^o(H_2O)$ increases regularly with the chain length of the alkanols up to C_5, and decreases slightly in higher homologs.

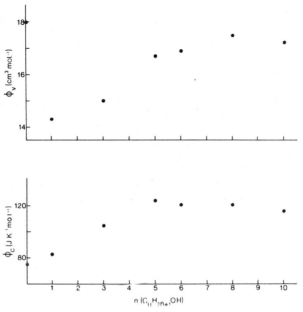

Figure 9. Limiting apparent molar volume and heat capacity of
water in various n-alkanols.

The magnitude of $\phi_C^o(H_2O)$ in these non aqueous solvents appears
intriguing, since the large molar heat capacity of liquid water
(relative to other simple fluids) is attributed to its exceptionally high degree of cooperative hydrogen-bonding interactions. It
would therefore be inferred from the C_p measurement that the extent
of hydrogen-bonding of water molecules in alcohol solutions can be
even greater than that in pure water. The remaining of this work
was thus concerned with attempts to assess the hydrogen-bonding
state of water in alcohol-water mixtures using, again, near-IR
spectroscopy in the second OH overtone region.

2. Near-IR spectra of Water in Alcohol-Water Mixtures. The
investigation of alcohol-water mixtures using infrared absorption
spectroscopy is faced with a number of intrinsic potential difficulties which may be summarized as follows. Although, on the time
scale of the IR measurement, the exchange of O-H protons and water
molecules may be considered slow (slow exchange limit), the OH
absorption bands are usually broad, so there are no obvious reasons
to expect the resolution of distinct bands corresponding to the
O-II groups of H_2O and ROH respectively. Dissolution of water molecules in alcohols will lead to new types of hydrogen-bonding
interactions in which the H_2O molecules act either as donors or
acceptors; consequently, the presence of water will perturb the
initial hydrogen-bonding equilibrium in the alcohols, and the IR
spectral features resulting from these various effects will be
difficult to unravel. In addition, the possible occurence of

combination bands involving the C–H and O–H modes[35], could further
obscure the spectral changes due to the water–alcohol interactions.
Such problems must therefore be identified and resolved before any
meaningful conclusion can be derived regarding the hydrogen–bonding
interactions of interest here.

a) OH absorption in pure alcohols. To characterize the intrinsic OH absorption in pure alcohols, we have recorded several
differential near-IR spectra of neat alcohols against their deuterated analogues. The results obtained are illustrated in Figure
10 for MeOH, EtOH and PrOH. These and following spectra are shown
with positive absorption upwards in contrast with spectra discussed
previously; the various spectra reported below differ also from
previous ones, in that they are differential only with respect to
one component.

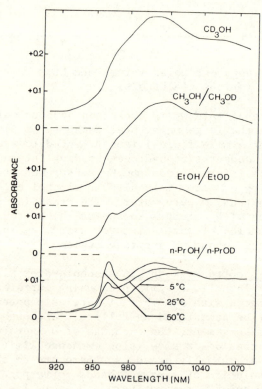

Figure 10.   OH absorption of 5.00 cm of various alcohols as neat li-
             quids at 25°C.   CD$_3$OH (sample); CH$_3$OH (sample) versus
             CH$_3$OD (reference); C$_2$H$_5$OH (sample versus C$_2$H$_5$OD (re-
             ference; C$_3$H7OH (sample) versus C$_3$H7OD (reference) at
             5, 25 and 50°C.

With MeOH, the absorption spectrum of CD_3OH (Figure 10, upper curve) should yield directly the OH absorption, since overtones of C-D modes are very weak in the region investigated here. The differential spectrum CH_3OH/CH_3OD should also yield the OH absorption, and the latter will be identical to the CD_3OH spectrum, provided C-H/O-H mixed combination modes do not contribute significantly[5]. As illustrated in Figure 10, the spectra are indeed identical within experimental error, so complications arising from C-H/O-H combinations can be disregarded, at least for MeOH.

The OH absorption observed from spectra recorded with the three pairs MeOH/MeOD, EtOH/EtOD and PrOH/PrOD all exhibit a broad band with a maximum near 1000nm and a narrow high frequency component centered at 965nm. The resolution of this high frequency band increases with the chain length of the alcohol and shows a marked temperature dependence in the case examined (PrOH). The increase in intensity with increasing temperature suggests a tentative assignment of the 965nm band to "free OH" groups in the neat alcohols in accordance with results of extensive studies by Luck on the temperature dependence of alcohol spectra[36].

b) OH absorption spectrum of water in alcohol-water mixtures. The near-IR absorption spectra of water in various n-alkanols were obtained as function of concentration over the miscibility ranges, and the data for 1.0 mol ℓ^{-1} solutions are given in Figure 11. As described earlier, in these experiments the reference cell (dry alcohol) is maintained at a fixed pathlength, while the length of the sample cell (water-alcohol) is varied to account for the apparent molar volume of the added water. Thus, differential spectra such as shown in Figure 11 reflect the OH absorption of water, plus any differences in the OH absorption of the alcohol in the neat liquid and in the solution. The influence of water concentration on these spectra may be seen in Figure 12 for an intermediate alcohol, n-BuOH

Returning to the data for 1 molar solutions of water in the various alcohols (Figure 11), it is readily noted that the spectral features (lineshapes, wavelengths and intensities) are strikingly similar in all systems, except for solutions in MeOH. In each case, the main absorption is a broad band centered at $\sim$ 980nm; the latter is markedly different from the OH absorption bands of pure alcohols (Figure 10), appearing more related to the OH absorption in liquid water (dashed curve). These general similarities in OH absorption bands are thus in qualitative agreement with

---

[5] Any combination modes involving the C-H and O-H modes would be strongly disturbed by isotopic substitution of the C-H hydrogens.

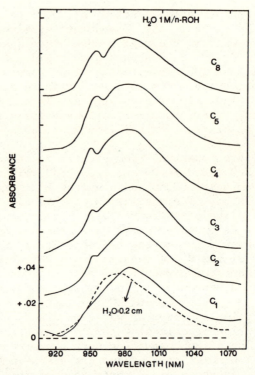

Figure 11. OH absorption spectrum of water at 1.0 Mℓ^{-1} in various
alcohols at 25°C; the reference cell pathlength was
10 cm and the length of the sample cell was adjusted
to cancel out absorption due to the alcohol.

expectations from C_p data discussed earlier.

A second feature common to the spectra of dilute water in
alkanols is the occurence of a narrow high frequency component
centered at an average wavelength of 950nm. The latter appears as
a shoulder for H_2O/MeOH solutions, but it is fairly well resolved
in the higher alcohols. Based on the similarities in the spectra
of Figure 11, and on previous observations on bands at 950nm, a
tentative interpretation of the dilute water spectra in alcohols
may be advanced as follows. The main absorption at 980nm originates from water OH groups having a distribution of hydrogen-bonding
energies comparable to that existing in liquid water; as in earlier assignments, the 950nm band may be attributed to water OH
groups in a hydrocarbon-like environment, $i.e.$ surrounded mainly
by alkyl residues. On the other hand, because subtraction of the
alcohol absorption is performed using the pure alcohol spectrum,

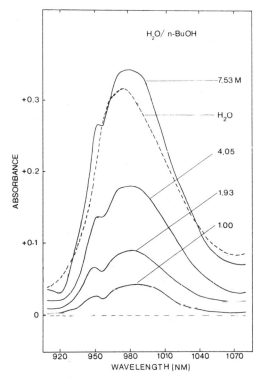

Figure 12. OH adsorption spectrum of water in n-BuOH at several
            concentrations and 25°C obtained as described in Figure
            11; dashed spectrum recorded for water with a 3 cm cell.

it must be acknowledged that changes in the population (or oscillator strength) of the alcohol "free" OH groups could also contribute
intensity changes in the 960-965nm region (Figure 10); this could
be responsible for the "dip" near 960nm. At present, there seems
little hope that the relative contributions from the two types of
"free" OH groups (HOH and ROH) can be evaluated quantitatively,
but the results obtained here provide good indications that these
may be distinguished in some cases. At a qualitative level, this
could still be very useful for investigations on complex mixtures
containing water and aliphatic alcohols.

     In spite of quantitative limitations in the interpretation of
the spectra, further information may be derived from a comparison
of the molar integrated intensities of H_2O in the H_2O–ROH mixtures
($I_{H_2O}^{ROH}$). These were obtained for pure water and for each of the
water-alcohol solutions, and are reported in Figure 13. The data
given for solutions are averages from at least four measurements

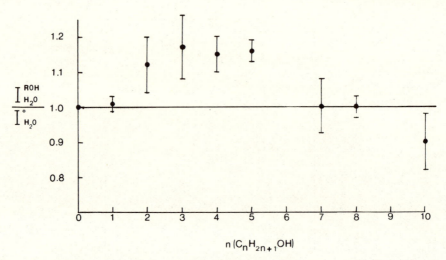

$$\frac{I_{H_2O}^{ROH}}{I_{H_2O}^{o}}$$

$n\,(C_nH_{2n+1}OH)$

Figure 13. Relative molar integrated intensities of water in various alcohols obtained by integration of the absorption in the interval 920 to 1070nm; the data are normalized to that of pure water; error bars indicate standard deviations with four or more spectra between 1 and 4 M (or saturation).

in the concentration range 1 to 4 mol ℓ^{-1} (or solubility limit)[6]; the molar integrated intensities measured in the interval 920-1070nm were all normalized to that of liquid water ($I_{H_2O}^{o}$).

The ratios $I_{H_2O}^{ROH}/I_{H_2O}^{o}$ plotted as function of alcohol chain length show increasing intensities of the water OH absorption, from MeOH to PenOH; in higher homologs the OH intensity decreases and becomes comparable to that of liquid water. Since the oscillator strength of overtones and combination modes of the OH groups are inversely related to the interaction energies of these OH groups, the intensity pattern should reflect, correspondingly, the relative extent of H_2O hydrogen-bonding in water and in the alcohols (the extent of hydrogen-bonding should be taken here as the product of the number of bonds times the bond energies). The overall intensity pattern is consistent with inferences from heat capacity results, in that the intensity ratios are constant within 25% for all systems studied here; however, more detailed comparisons would require an examination of the functional dependence of near-IR

---

[6] The data showed some concentration dependence, the magnitude of which is reflected in the standard deviations illustrated as error bars. At this point, however, no attempt was made to interpret such concentration dependences.

intensities and C_p values on the hydrogen-bonding equilibrium parameters.

The inverse relationship between the integrated intensity and hydrogen-bonding energies may be expressed to first order as:

$$I_{OH} = I_{OH}^o - AX_{OH\cdots O} \Delta H_{OH\cdots O} \qquad (5)$$

where I_{OH} is the observed integrated intensity, I_{OH}^o the integrated intensity of the unperturbed OH group, and $X_{OH\cdots O}$ the mole fraction of hydrogen-bonded OH groups. $\Delta H_{OH\cdots O}$ represents the hydrogen bonding enthalpy, and A is a constant (or a function) relating the oscillator strength to $\Delta H_{OH\cdots O}$. In the case of heat capacities, the contribution resulting from the hydrogen-bonding equilibrium (relaxational contribution, neglecting here differences in C_p of free and bonded states of the OH groups) can be given as[37]:

$$\varepsilon_p^{relax} = X_{OH} X_{OH\cdots O} \frac{(\Delta H_{OH\cdots O})^2}{RT^2} \qquad (6)$$

where X_{OH} and $X_{OH\cdots O}$ are the mole fractions of free and bonded OH groups respectively. The IR intensities and the heat capacities are thus both related to the hydrogen-bonding equilibrium constant (which determine X_{OH} and $X_{OH\cdots O}$) and enthalpy; hence, quantitative correlations of the two types of data should be possible if reliable estimates of K and $\Delta H_{OH\cdots O}$ can be obtained. While enthalpy data do not appear available for all systems examined here, the solubility of water in n-BuOH and higher homologs provides some interesting indications on hydrogen-bonding interactions in these systems. In all n-aliphatic alcohols between C_4 and C_{10} the alcohol/water ratio at water saturation is between 2 and 3 (increasing with alcohol chain length). This does not necessarily imply that each water molecule is hydrogen-bonded to 2 or 3 alcohols molecules, but, since solubility must be the result of interaction between OH groups it is well conceivable that water molecules in alcohols have an average number of hydrogen bonds comparable to that in liquid water. In the latter, this average number has, of course, a maximum value of 2.

It may therefore be concluded that the different types of data examined here are all consistent with the proposal that water molecules diluted in aliphatic alcohols are extensively hydrogen-bonded to the alcohol. The thermodynamic and spectroscopic results indicate that the state of such water molecules are comparable to that existing in liquid water, although nothing can be said on the structural aspects of the hydrogen-bonded complexes. Moreover, the state of the water molecule appears only weakly dependent on chain length of the alcohols, especially for alcohols larger than pentanol.

ACKNOWLEDGEMENTS

The authors are indebted to the Ministère de l'Education du
Québec and to the Natural Science and Engineering Research Council
of Canada for financial support of this work. Discussion of the
results with Prof. B. Lindman and H. Wennerström is also kindly
acknowledged.

REFERENCES

1. W.A.P. Luck in "Water, A Comprehensive Treatise", F. Franks,
    Editor, p. 235, Plenum Press, New York 1973.
2. J.E. Desnoyers and C. Jolicoeur, in "Modern Aspects of Electro-
    chemistry", J. O'M. Bockris and B.E. Conway, Editors, Plenum
    Press, Vol. 5, New York (1969).
3. J. Paquette and C. Jolicoeur, J. Solution Chem. 6, 403 (1977).
4. S. Cabani, S.T. Lobo and E. Matteoli, J. Solution Chem. 8, 5
    (1979).
5. G. Roux, G. Perron and J.E. Desnoyers, Can. J. Chem. 56, 2808
    (1978).
6. C. Jolicoeur and G.Lacroix, Can. J. Chem. 54, 624 (1976)
7. F. Franks, Editor, "Water, A Comprehensive Treatise",
    Vol. 5, Plenum Press, New York (1975).
8. P. Ekwall, Adv. Liquid Cryst. 1, 1 (1975).
9. J.B. Nagy, (these proceedings).
10. J.H. Fendler and E.J. Fendler, Catalysis in Micellar and Ma-
    cromolecular Systems, Academic Press, New York (1975).
11. B. Lindman and H. Wennerström. (these proceedings).
12. J.B. Rosenholm, K. Larsson and N. Dinh-Nguyen, Colloid Polymer
    Sci., 255, 1098 (1977).
13. C. Jolicoeur, N.D. The and A. Cabana. Can. J. Chem. 49, 2008
    (1971).
14. P. Philip and C. Jolicoeur, J. Phys. Chem. 77, 3071 (1973).
15. P. Picker, E. Tremblay and C. Jolicoeur, J. Solution Chem. 3,
    377 (1974).
16. P. Picker, P.A. Leduc, P.R. Philip and J.E. Desnoyers, J. Chem.
    Thermo. 3, 631 (1971).
17. E. Vikingstad, A. Skauge and H. Høiland, Acta Chem. Scand. A33,
    235 (1979); J. Colloid Interface Sci. 72, 59 (1979).
18. a) P.A. Leduc and J.E. Desnoyers, Can. J. Chem. 51, 2993
    (1973); b) R. DeLisi, C. Ostiguy, G. Perron and J.E. Des-
    noyers, J. Colloid Interface Sci. 71, 147 (1979).
19. T.S. Brun, H. Høiland and H. Vikingstad, J. Colloid Interface
    Sci, 63, 89 (1978); E. Vikingstad and H. Høiland, J. Colloid
    Interface Sci., 64, 510 (1978).
20. H.S. Frank and W.Y. Wen, Disc. Faraday Soc. 24, 133 (1957).
21. G.M. Musbally, G. Perron and J.E. Desnoyers, J. Colloid Inter-
    face Sci., 54, 80 (1976).
22. J.E. Desnoyers, R. DeLisi and G. Perron, Pure and Appl. Chem.
    52, 433 (1980).

23. C. Jolicoeur and P. Philip, J. Solution Chem. $\underline{4}$, 3 (1975).

24. C. Jolicoeur, J. Paquette and M. Lucas, J. Phys. Chem. $\underline{82}$, 1051 (1978).

25. D. Eisenberg and W. Kauzmann, "The Structure and Properties of Water", Oxford University Press, (1969).

26. I.D. Kuntz and C.J. Cheng, J. Am. Chem. Soc. $\underline{97}$, 4852 (1975).

27. B. Lindman, H. Wennerström, H. Gustavsson, N. Kamenka and B. Brun, Pure Appl. Chem., $\underline{52}$, 1307 (1980).

28. S.E. Jackson and M.C.R. Symons, Chem. Phys. Letters, $\underline{37}$, 551 (1976).

29. F.M. Menger, Acc. Chem. Res. $\underline{12}$, 111 (1979).

30. Bengt Svens and B. Rosenholm, J. Colloid Interface Sci. $\underline{44}$, 495 (1973).

31. H. Gustavsson and B. Lindman, J. Am. Chem. Soc. $\underline{100}$, 4647 (1978).

32. H. Gustavsson and B. Lindman, J. Am. Chem. Soc. $\underline{97}$, 3923 (1975).

33. G. Lindblom, B. Lindman and G.J.T. Tiddy, J. Am. Chem. Soc. $\underline{100}$, 2299 (1978).

34. R.D. Waldron, J. Chem. Phys. $\underline{26}$, 809 (1957).

35. W.A.P. Luck, ref. 1, p. 297.

36. W.A.P. Luck, in "Structure of Water and Aqueous Solutions", W. A. P. Luck, Editor, p. 248, Verlag Chemie, Weinheim (1974).

37. C. Jolicoeur, L.L. Lemelin and R. Lapalme, J. Phys. Chem. $\underline{83}$, 2806 (1979).

EFFECTS OF CHANGES IN THE HYDROPHILIC PORTION OF A HETEROPOLAR SURFACTANT ON MICELLIZATION

Israel J. Lin and Y. Zimmels

Mineral Engineering Research Center

Technion - IIT, Haifa, Israel

The critical micelle concentration (CMC) in aqueous solution, effective chain length (n_{eff}), and hydrophobicity of various straight chain ionic surfactants containing two or more polar functional groups at one end or at opposite ends of an amphiphile molecule - are considered.

The n_{eff} concept is used to quantify the hydrophobic-hydrophilic ratio of this type of surfactants. Several numerical examples are presented.

The physicochemical properties of the surfactant in solution are examined through the ratio between the heteropolar parts of the molecule. Shielding of the methylene groups close to the polar head groups by the ionic atmosphere in the micelle surface is evaluated. Possession of two or more hydrophilic groups protects the surfactant against total expulsion from the water.

Molecular models and application of the n_{eff} concept demonstrate the feasibility of packing surfactant monomers into micelles, with water penetration of the latter.

INTRODUCTION

Surfactants containing both hydrophilic and hydrophobic portions, namely amphiphile molecules (anionic, cationic, nonionic, amphoteric or ampholytic), aggregate and form micelles under the influence of hydrophobic interactions. In the process of micellization, the hydrocarbon (H.C.) or fluorocarbon (F.C) chains fall within the micelle core while the polar head groups remain in contact with the aqueous medium at the micelle-solution interface; in these circumstances energetically unfavourable exposure of the H.C. chains to the medium is minimized.

Effects of structural modifications on surface and colloidal properties were reported in numerous studies of surfactants possessing a single hydrophilic group[1]. By contrast, surfactants possessing two or more hydrophilic groups attached to the alkyl chain are more complex, and only a limited number of publications[2] deal with the relationship between the structure of these surfactants and their physicochemical properties.

The present study reports on the effects of changes in the hydrophilic portion of heteropolar surfactants, on micelle formation.

THERMODYNAMIC CONSIDERATIONS

The thermodynamics of micellization, in aqueous solution, of classical simple ionic surfactants consisting of a single H.C. chain with a terminal hydrophilic group, is well known. For complex surfactants, the relevant thermodynamic parameters are functions of structural modifications, such as the number and position of the polar groups, H.C. tails, branching, coiling, double and triple bonds (unsaturation), perfluoroalkyl and polysiloxane groups, E.O. and P.O. bridging groups, aromatic moieties, cis-trans configurations, etc.

Micellization consists in reversible aggregation of a given number of molecules or ions of an amphiphile, forming a body of colloidal dimensions. The main physical factors controlling micellization in aqueous media are the free-energy increments of the hydrophobic radicals (attractive) and polar parts (repulsive) of the molecules. With certain simplifications, for an amphiphile consisting of a single H.C. chain with a hydrophilic group at one end, the thermodynamic quantities associated with micellization are given by[3] :

$$\Delta G_m = (1 + K_g)RT\ln \text{CMC} \tag{1}$$

$$\Delta H_m = -(1 + K_g)RT^2(\partial \ln \text{CMC}/\partial T)_p \tag{2}$$

$$\Delta S_m = (\Delta H_m - \Delta G_m)/T \tag{3}$$

where ΔG_m, ΔH_m, and ΔS_m are the the Gibbs free energy, enthalpy and entropy of micellization, respectively, of the individual surfactant in solution, R is the universal gas constant, T absolute temperature and K_g the number ratio of counter ions to long-chain ions in the micelle (or the effective coefficient of electrical energy of micellization).

Resolving the overall values of the thermodynamic parameters into the contributions of the H.C. radical, the polar head group, and the micelle-solution interface, we have

$$\Delta G_m = \sum_j \Delta G_j = \Delta G_{H.C.} + \Delta G_p + \Delta G_W \tag{4}$$

or

$$\Delta G_m = n \times \Delta G_{CH_2} + \Delta G_p + \Delta G_W \tag{5}$$

where ΔG_{CH_2} (which is negative and represents the terminal CH_3, the $\alpha - CH_2$, and the remaining CH_2 groups) is the incremental free-energy change per added methylene group; ΔG_p (which is positive) is the increment per polar head group to the coulombic free-energy change associated with electrostatic charge repulsion (ion-ion interaction in the case of a ionic amphiphile, dipole-dipole interaction in that of a zwitterionic one); ΔG_W refers to hydration of the polar groups at the interface; n (which represents the H.C.- water contact area) is the number of CH_2 and CH_3 groups in the saturated H.C. tail

A linear incremental change in ΔG_m occurs when the chain is lengthened, except for very short chains (n < 6). Combining (1) and (5), we obtain:

$$(1 + K_g)RT\ln CMC = n \times \Delta G_{CH_2} + \Delta G_p + \Delta G_W \tag{6}$$

Hence for an homologous series of surfactants, a plot of $\ln CMC$ vs. n yields the increment for a methylene group from the slope, and the increment for the polar group (opposing forces) from the intercept on the ordinate ($\Delta G'_p = \lim_{n \to 0} \Delta G_m$, where $\Delta G'_p = \Delta G_p + \Delta G_W$ in the case of a 1:1-type surfactant). Based on the principle of linearity of free energies, Equation (6) describes the dependence of the CMC on the structural and chemical composition of the surfactant.

Combining (1), (3) and (5), we obtain:

$$(1 + K_g)RT\ln CMC = (\Delta H_{CH_2} - T\Delta S_{CH_2}) \times n + (\Delta H_p - T\Delta S_p) +$$

$$+ (\Delta H_W - T\Delta S_W) . \tag{7}$$

Both Equations (5) and (7) apply for simple chain amphiphiles. To generalize the dependence of micelle formation on structural modifications of the heteropolar portions, the concept of n_{eff} is introduced and Equations (6) and (7) become:

$$(1 + K_g)RT\ln CMC = n_{eff} \times \Delta G_{CH_2} + \Sigma p \times \Delta G_p + \Delta G_W \tag{8}$$

and

$$(1 + K_g)RT\ln CMC = (\Delta H_{CH_2} - T\Delta S_{CH_2}) \times n_{eff} + \Sigma (\Delta H_p - T\Delta S_p) \times p$$

$$+ (\Delta H_W - T\Delta S_W) \tag{9}$$

where p is the number of polar head groups. Accordingly, the CMC value for each individual surfactant is constant under given conditions $(P, T, \Delta G_i)$ and is determined by the composition and structure of its molecule.

CRITICAL MICELLE CONCENTRATION

Micelle formation can be inhibited (delayed to a higher concentration) by several means: (i) increased temperature, (ii) reduced chain length of the surfactant, (iii) incorporation of hydratable groups (such as ether linkages or other polar substitutions) in the H.C. chain, (iv) unsaturation in the H.C. tail (replacement of single bonds by double or triple ones), (v) branching in the hydrophobic group, (vi) increased number of polar heads, (vii) shifting of the head group from the terminal to the median position of the H.C. tail, and (viii) reduced number of hydrophobic functions, such as aromatic or heterocyclic centres.

It is well known that in homologous series of straight-chain surfactants, the CMC decreases approximately logarithmically as the number of methylene units in the tail increases, i.e.

$$\log CMC = A - B \times n \tag{10}$$

In water, the reduction in CMC per CH_2 group is almost the same for all ionic micellar systems of 1:1-type paraffin-chain salts[4] - namely, by a factor of about 3.2 for homologous nonionic surfactants, and by a factor of about 2 for ionic ones[5]. In the case of surfactants possessing more than one polar head group (with different gegenions), this reduction varies with the number and types of polar groups involved.

Equation (10) may also be written as:

$$\log CMC = A - B \times n_{eff} \tag{11}$$

where A and B are experimentally determinable empirical constants for a given temperature. The value of B is about 0.3 and may be interpreted as indicating that the standard free energy of micellization $- \Delta G_m$ increases by 1.08 kT/(CH$_2$) for a 1:1-type surfactant.

Lin et al.[6] derived expressions for the CMC of aqueous solutions of long-chain surfactants as function of n_{eff}. With no inorganic salt added, the relationship reads:

$$\log CMC = -\phi' n_{eff}/[2.303kT(1 + K_g)] + \text{const.} \tag{12}$$

where $\phi' n_{eff} = \Delta G_{CH_2} n_{eff}$ is the free energy change associated with transfer of the hydrophobic portion of the amphiphile molecule from the aqueous medium to the micelle interior and reflecting the hydrophobic interactions of methylene groups, and k is Boltzmann's constant. Equation (12) serves to estimate the effective chain length in long-chain surfactants. Other methods for n_{eff} evaluation are described and reported elsewhere[7-9].

The large CMC value in heteropolar surfactants possessing two or three ionic groups at the end of the H.C. tail results mainly from the stronger electric repulsive force. According to Shinoda, Equation (12) becomes:

$$\log CMC = -\phi' n_{eff}/[2.303kT(1 + iK_g)] + \text{const.} \tag{13}$$

where i is the number of ionic groups. Thus if log CMC is plotted against n_{eff}, a straight line results, the slope of which yields ϕ', the average hydrophobic contribution per CH$_2$ group to the total free energy of micellization. This is again the familiar "log (property) - vs. - chain length" linearity (Traube's rule), which yields the hydrophobic energy per CH$_2$ residue. The free energy of the aqueous system decreases when hydrophobic tails emerge from the water and penetrate the hydrophobic environment.

For a 1:1-type surfactant, we may assume the same order of electric work at micellization, so that the contribution of the head group to the CMC is approximately the same. For surfactants possessing two H.C. tails and a single head group, the contribution of the hydrophilic group is again almost the same (see Table 1) for a given chain length.

Table I.   Effect of Hydrophilic Group and Counterion on CMC of Ionic Surfactants with Almost the Same H.C. Tail (no supporting electrolyte).

Univalent H.C. compound	CMC, mol/lit	Univalent F.C. compound*,[27]	CMC	Bivalent H.C. compound[28]	CMC**
$R_{11}COONa$	0.015 (40°C)	$C_{10}F_{21}COOH$	0.00048	$(R_{12}SO_3)_2Mg$	0.002 (25°C)
$R_{12}COOK$	0.0125 (25)	$C_{10}F_{21}COOK$	0.00034	$(R_{12}SO_4)_2Mg$	0.0018 (25)
$R_{12}SO_3Na$	0.01 (20)	$C_{10}F_{21}COONa$	0.00043	$(R_{12}SO_4)_2Ca$	0.0012 (55)
$R_{10}COO(CH_2)_2SO_3Na$	0.011 (25)	$C_{10}F_{21}COOLi$	0.00039	$(R_{12}SO_4)_2Pb$	0.002 (54)
$R_9COO(CH_2)_3SO_3Na$	0.019 (25)			$(R_{12}SO_4)_2Zn$	0.0021 (60)
$R_{12}SO_4K$	0.0078 (40)				
$R_{12}SO_4Na$	0.0081 (25)			$(R_{12}SO_4)_2Cu$	0.0013 (30)
$R_{12}SO_4Li$	0.0089 (25)				
$R_{12}NH_3Cl$	0.013 (25)			$(R_{12}SO_4)_2Sr$	0.0011 (67)
$R_{12}N(CH_3)_3Cl$	0.017 (30)				
$R_{12}N(CH_3)_3Br$	0.016 (25)				
$R_{12}NC_5H_5Cl$	0.015 (30)				
$R_{12}NH_3NO_3$	0.011 (25)				
$C_{10}H_{21}CH(COO^-)N^+(CH_3)_3$	0.013 (27)				

* Note that the CMC for fluorinated surfactants of chainlength n is similar to the H.C. analogue of chainlength $1,5 \times n$.

** Since Krafft points of bivalent metal salts of ordinary ionic surfactants are generally higher than room temperature, therefore they are usually far less soluble than the corresponding univalent type and do not form micelles around room temperature.

The thermodynamic driving force for micelle formation (self aggregation) at constant P and T is the hydrophobic effect (see Table 1 and Equation (13)), whereby H.C. tails of amphiphile molecules are expelled from an aqueous medium to avoid H.C.-water contact.

STRUCTURAL ASPECTS

While micelles of ionic or zwitterionic surfactant are spherical, ellipsoidal or oblong culindrical aggregates and contain 20 to 120 molecules (the aggregation number), those of non-ionic surfactants may contain 100 to 1000. This is because electrostatic repulsion between ionic head-groups is a major factor and exceeds its steric counterpart between nonionic ones. Factors governing the size, shape and aggregation number of micelles include: concentration, temperature, pressure, ionic strength, H.C. chain length, nature of the head group, structural modifications, type of counterion, mode of intermolecular action and type of additives.

Formation of micelles (colloidal dimensions) creates local nonpolar environments within the aqueous phase. Micelles of simple amphiphiles with a single H.C. tail increaoe in size with the length of the alkyl tail in a homologous series, or with the ionic strength of the aqueous medium.

Amphiphile molecules may be said to build organized structures merely by raising the concentration of the surfactant in water at constant temperature. For example, transition to rod-shaped micelles (flat-based or hemisphere-capped cylinders) may occur at higher concentration, well above the regular CMC[10], thereby creating a new CMC level[11,12].

Figure 1 shows structures formed by simple amphiphiles (single head group jointed to a H.C. tail). Transition from one structure to another may be induced by changing the physicochemical conditions (cxternal variables) such as temperature or pH and by addition of a cosurfactant. Cylindrical (with hemispherical ends) and lamellar (bilayer form) micelles are unrestricted in their growth in length, and thus able to accommodate any number of amphiphile molecules.

The classical pattern of aggregation (Figure 2) consists of an internal H.C. core and a surface composed of polar groups. In Figure 2b, the aggregates of a nonfunctional surfactant are in the form of bilayers of amphiphiles with the H.C. tails in intimate contact inside, and the polar groups in contact with the aqueous medium outside. Proposed structures for surfactants with two ionic groups at one end of the H.C. are shown in Figure 2c, where the H.C. chains are fully extended and perpendicular to the bilayer surface. Systems with two ionic groups, one on each side of the linear H.C. chain, are shown in Figure 2d.

STRUCTURE FORMATION IN SURFACTANT SOLUTION

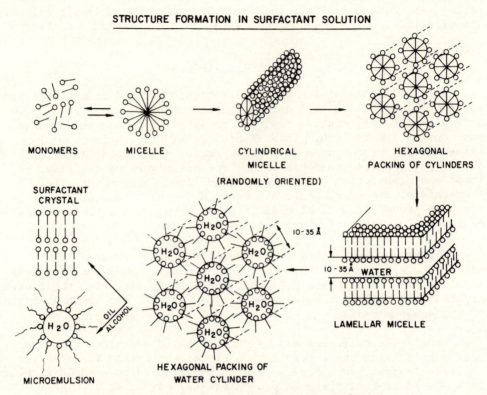

Figure 1. Structure formation in surfactant solution on increase of the surfactant concentration[14].

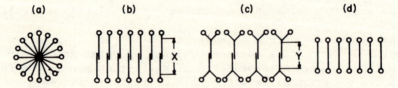

Figure 2. Proposed structures of different surfactant micelles (folded structures not shown).

There is no agreement as to the exact composition of the micelle interior: a purely H.C. core, or H.C. partially mixed with water. The thickness of the hydrophobic core, or x-dimension (see Figure 2b), clearly cannot exceed the length of two fully extended H.C. chains, since it has been assumed that the CH_2 group adjoining the polar head group falls within the hydration sphere of the latter, and thus does not have hydrophobic properties. Accordingly, we have $x \leq 2(n-1)$. In the system of Figure 2c, the number of CH_2 groups involved in formation of the micelle core is thus $n_{eff} < n$, hence $y < 2n_{eff}$. Generally, since $n_{eff} < n-1$, then $y < x$.

For the systems in Figures 2b and 2c we may predict, on the basis of thermodynamical considerations and comparing CMC values, that for linear surfactants with two polar heads, n_{eff} is always lower than for those with a single terminal polar head.

For the system in Figures 2c and 2d (sandwich-like structure) there is also incomplete emergence of the amphiphile tail from the aqueous environment, due to the positive contribution of ΔG_p and to the screening effect of the ionic atmosphere.

The micelle-solution interface (which comprises the innermost part of the electric double layer for ionic micelles, and the outer part of the diffuse double layer) is an important element, being often the site of interaction between micelle-solubilized species and hydrophilic solution components. For ionic micelles, roughly 70% of the counterions are sufficiently strongly attracted to the charged surface to become part of the kinetic micelle[13].

RESULTS AND DISCUSSION

Tables II and III, and Figure 3, summarize the CMC values of surfactants with two and more hydrophilic groups, located either at one end of the H.C. chain or one on each side of it (symmetrical and non-symmetrical systems). The values for long-chain electrolytes with two or more polar heads are larger than those for the corresponding 1:1-type surfactants (for example, potassium 9, 10-dihydroxystearate has been reported[15] to have a CMC value 15 to 20 times greater than the ordinary stearate) – possibly because the former have several dissociable groups at the end of the H.C. tail; the higher CMC values indicate a much weaker tendency to association. These surfactants are characterized by a lower B (see Table IV) and n_{eff} values, and a lower Krafft point, as well as higher solubility and hydrophile-lipophile balance (HLB) compared with corresponding 1:1-type paraffin chain salts.

Table II: CMC Values and Krafft Points of Surfactants Possessing Two and More Hydrophilic Groups.

Formula*	n	$T^\circ c$	CMC mol/lit	Krafft point, $^\circ c$	** $1,08 kT$	Ref
$R_n CH(COOK)_2$	8	25	0,35			30
	10	25	0,13		$A=1,54; B=0,221$	
Potassium Alkyl Malonate	12	25	0,048		$Kg=0,49; \phi'=1,08 kT$	
	14	25	0,017			
	16	25	0,0063			
	18	25	0,0023			
	6	25	0,79			
$R_n CH(COOK)CH(COOK)_2$	8	25	0,28		$A=1,7; B=0,226$	
	10	25	0,095		$Kg=0,37$	31
Potassium Alkane Tri-Carboxylates	12	25	0,034			
	14	25	0,012			
$R_n CH(SO_3Na)(COOH)$	12	28	0,0024			
	14	28	0,0006			
α-Sulphonated Fatty Acids	16	28	0,0001			2,32
$NaO_3SO(CH_2)_n OSO_3Na$	12	-		12,0		
	14	45	0,010	24,8		
	16	60	0,0045	39,1	***	33
Disodium α,ω - Sulphates	18	70	0,0028	44,9		
$NaO_3SC_6H_4O(CH_2)_n OC_6H_4SO_3Na$	4	25	>0,01	-		
	6	25	0,0043	< 20		
α,ω - Dibenzene Sulphonates	8	-	-	28	***	34
	10	60	0,002	59		
	12	70	0,001	70		
$R_n CH(SO_3Na)COO(CH_2)_2 SO_3Na$	14	25	0,008			2,32
disodium salts of 2-sulphoethyl esters	16	25	0,0025			
$NaO_3S(CH_2)_3 OOC(CH_2)_n COO(CH_2)_3 SO_3Na$	10	40	0,0305	< 0		
	12	40	0,0165	23,5	$A=2,92$	25
Disodium di-3-sulphopropyl α,ω-	14	40	0,0085	31,0	$B=0,142$	
Alkane Dicarboxylates	16	40	0,004	38,5		
$KOOC(CH_2)_n COOK$						
Dipotassium di-carboxylates	14	40	0,32			35
	16	25	0,011			

* R_n represents a fatty alkyl group, $C_n H_{2n+1}$

** $1,08 kT = 0,64$ Kcal/mol.

*** Since the temperatures at which the CMCs were determined vary with the compound, the values of A,B,Kg, and ϕ' are not determinable from the current data.

Table III. CMC of Na – Carboxylates[36] at 40°C.

Type	Formula	R	Symbol	Purity, %	CMC, M/1
Alkane monocarboxylic acids	R-COOH	$C_{11}H_{23}$	C_{11} —	98,1	$1,5 \times 10^{-2}$
		$C_{13}H_{27}$	C_{13} —	98,1	$2,0 \times 10^{-3}$
		$C_{15}H_{31}$	C_{15} —	98,2	$7,0 \times 10^{-4}$
Alkane dicarboxylic acids, (-1,1)	R-CH ⟨COOH / COOH⟩	$C_{10}H_{21}$	C_{11} Y	92,2	$2,8 \times 10^{-2}$
		$C_{12}H_{25}$	C_{13} Y	96,6	$4,8 \times 10^{-3}$
		$C_{14}H_{29}$	C_{15} Y	92,2	9×10^{-4}
		$C_{16}H_{33}$	C_{17} Y	93,4	$1,9 \times 10^{-4}$
		$C_{18}H_{37}$	C_{19} Y	85,0	$3,8 \times 10^{-5}$
Alkane dicarboxylic acids	R-CH-CH$_2$-COOH / COOH	$C_{10}H_{21}$	C_{12} T	93,2	$2,5 \times 10^{-2}$
		$C_{12}H_{25}$	C_{14} T	94,5	$3,5 \times 10^{-3}$
Alkane dicarboxylic acids (-1,3)	R-CH-(CH$_2$)$_2$-COOH / COOH	C_8H_{17}	C_{11} T	99,9	8×10^{-2}
		$C_{10}H_{21}$	C_{13} T	99,8	$1,2 \times 10^{-2}$
		$C_{12}H_{25}$	C_{15} T	96,0	$2,4 \times 10^{-3}$
Tetracecane tricarboxylic acid (-1,2,2)	R-C-CH$_2$-COOH (COOH / COOH)	$C_{12}H_{25}$	C_{14} +	97,2	5×10^{-2}
Pentadecane tricarboxylic acid (-1,3,3)	R-C-(CH$_2$)$_2$-COOH (COOH / COOH)	$C_{12}H_{25}$	C_{15} +	98,2	$3,6 \times 10^{-2}$
1-Br-Alkane carboxylic acids	R-CH-COOH / Br	$C_{10}H_{21}$	C_{11} Br	97,3	$2,2 \times 10^{-2}$
		$C_{12}H_{25}$	C_{13} Br	94,6	$4,5 \times 10^{-3}$
		$C_{14}H_{29}$	C_{15} Br	98,0	$1,5 \times 10^{-3}$

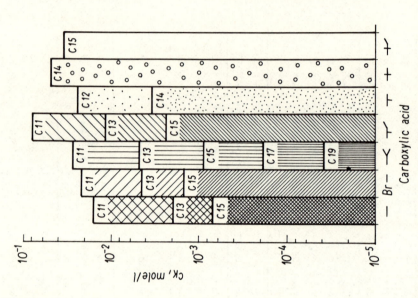

Figure 3. Critical micelle concentration of homologous series of Na carboxylates at 40°C. (After Table III.)

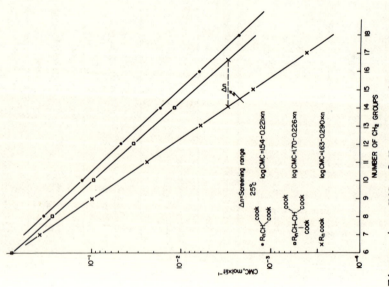

Figure 4. CMC of K mono-, di-, and tri-carboxylates as function of H.C. chain length.

Table IV. B Values for Homologous Series of H.C. and F.C. Surfactants Possessing One and Two Hydrophobic Tails and Single Chain Surfactants Possessing Double or Triple Polar Heads Groups.

Formula	B	Ref	Formula	B	Ref
$R_n COOK$	0.290	(28)	$R_n CH(COOK)_2$	0.221	28
$R_n SO_4 Na$	0.295	(28)	$R_n CH(COOK)CH(COOK)_2$	0.226	31
$R_n SO_3 Na$	0.294	(28)	$NaO_3 S(CH_2)_3 OOC(CH_2)_n$ $COO(CH_2)_3 SO_3 Na$	0.142	25
$R_n NH_3 Cl$	0.296	(28)	$R_n CH(PO_3 HNa)COONa$	0.166	37
$R_n N(CH_3)_3 Cl$	0.286	(28)	$R_n CH(PO_3 Na_2)COONa$	0.092	37
$R_n C_5 H_5 NBr$	0.295	(28)			
$C_n F_{2n+1} COOH$	0.444	(28)			
$C_n F_{2n+1} COOK$	0.572	(28)			
$C_n F_{2n+1} COONa$	0.647	(28)			
$(C_n F_{2n+1})_2 POONa$	0.462	(28)			
$(R_n SO_3)_2 Mg$	0.413	(28)			

Figure 4 shows the CMC values of potassium mono-, di- and tricarboxylates vs. H.C. chain length, in the absence of an added salt. The relationship is linear, as per Equation (10), indicating that each additional methylene group contributes an equal measure of hydrophobicity. 1:1-type surfactants (e.g. $R_n COOK$) served as calibration curve for the 2:1-type e.g. $R_n CH(COOK)_2$ for calculation of the effective length n_{eff}, and the screening range, Δn, of the polar head groups.

The CMC vs. alkyl-chain length relationship in homologous series was used to calculate the change in free energy associated with emergence of a methylene group from an aqueous into a micellar environment. By comparing the CMC values for compounds with the same alkyl chain but different head groups, relative differences in the thermodynamic parameters of micellization can be deduced.

The effect of a bi-polar head group in a symmetrical surfactant is shown in Figure 5. The corresponding spacings of the CMC of disodium α,ω-sulphates and sodium alkyl sulphates are used as measure of the difference in hydrophobicity.

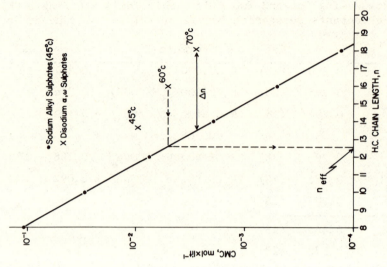

Figure 5.   CMC vs. n of sodium alkyl sulfates and disodium α, ω, − sulfates.

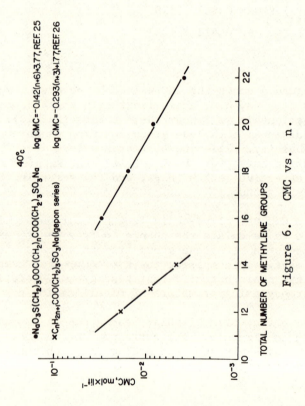

Figure 6.   CMC vs. n.

The structural parameter is presumed to manifest itself primarily through its influence on the distance between charged centres. This distance, together with the dielectric properties of the aqueous medium, affects the magnitude of the electrostatic field interaction between them; the stronger the interaction (in non-symmetrical versus symmetrical surfactants), the lower hydrophilicity of the polar heads. The number of methylene groups in the polymethylene bridging group — $(CH_2)_n$ — also affects hydrophilicity. Δn tends to zero as the group becomes shorter, and vanishes at $n_{eff} = n$ (see again Figure 5). For short surfactants, with $n_{eff} > n$, all methylene groups are completely screened by the two polar heads. Accordingly, when $n_{eff} < n$ the spacing of the charge centres becomes more or less structure-independent.

From the data in Figure 6 for ester-containing surfactants, it is seen that the CMC-reducing power of the CH_2 units (those in the alkyl chain and those situated between the ester and sulphonate groups) is approximately half that in the H.C. chain of a normal 1:1-type surfactant in its effect on the log CMC ($0.142/0.293 \simeq 0.5$). Both the ester- and polar-heads reduce the hydrophobicity of the H.C. chain. This is consistent with the recently published conclusion of Rosen and Nakamura[16], according to whom the cohesive energy per CH_2 group in symmetrical surfactants containing two arylsulfonate groups (α,ω-bis sodium p-sulfophenoxy alkanes) equals 0.55 kT as against the value of 0.95 kT found for monosulfonates from adsorption data on alumina.

The hydrophobic interactions in micelles are adequately treated in literature. It is well known that in many systems emergence of the alkyl chain from the water into the micelle phase is related to the chain length of the molecules in contact with the water[17]. There is good evidence[18-20] that one to five methylene groups (the exact number depends on the size, shape and orientation of the head group) immediately adjoining a polar head group are still in the aqueous environment (the hydration sphere of the head group) and contribute little to the hydrophobicity of an amphiphile, because of the screening effect of the head group of the latter[21]. Water-micelle interaction data are given in Table V, where the hydration numbers correspond approximately to the hydration of the polar head group and the counterions.

For surfactants containing more than one polar group, several more CH_2 groups are screened by the ionic atmosphere. In this type of amphiphiles, chain length decreases ($n_{eff} < n$) and the CMC increases, as a result of which only n_{eff} methylene groups are contained in the micelle core*.

---

* For the screening effect on surface-active anionic and cationic substances containing oxyethylene groups, see elsewhere[22].

Table V: Hydration Numbers of Micellar Aggregates
           Expressed as the Number of Water Molecules
           per Amphiphile Ion.

amphiphile^{a}	hydration no.
$C_{12}OSO_3Na$	9
$C_{12}OSO_3Na$	8
$C_{12}N(CH_3)_3Cl$	5
$C_{14}N(CH_3)_3Cl$	5
C_7CO_2Na	8.5-8.9
C_7CO_2Na	8.7
$C_8(C_6H_4)SO_3Na$	9

a C_n is a n-alkyl chain with n   carbon atoms.

     Further support for these considerations is found in the
following:
(i) The values of -1.04 to -1.08 kT obtained[4] for the free
energy change per CH_2 group involved in the transfer of alkyl chains
from the water to the micelle phase are less than the value -1.39 kT
for complete transfer from an aqueous to a hydrocarbon environment,
representing the maximal effect of hydrophobicity. Insofar as this
discrepancy is due to incomplete withdrawal of the micellized monomer
from contact with the water, it indicates that up to 25%, (1-1.06/
1.39) × n, of the CH_2 groups adjoining the polar group at the micellar
interface are probably exposed to water. In other words, micellization is not as effective in eliminating H.C. – water contact.

(ii) Available evidence[23,24] on water penetrating to the H.C. core,
to a depth of several methylene groups; in surfactants with two
functional head groups, penetration is deeper and the hydration
shell thicker.

     All these are plausible explanations for the reduction of n_{eff}.
We suggest that in structurally modified surfactants with two and
more polar head groups, n need not represent the entire hydrocarbon tail; in other words, $(n - n_{eff})$ CH_2 groups adjoining the
head group are excluded in the calculation of the chain length.
(Generally, the difference $(n - n_{eff})$ represents the solvent inter-
penetration distance.)

     Although minimization of the H.C. – aqueous solution interface is a major driving force for micellization, only n_{eff} CH_2 groups should occupy the core and water should be excluded to this extent. As a rule, a completely solvent-free core cannot be envisaged in structurally modified surfactants.

Thus, with n_{eff} groups taken into consideration in the core, solvation of the polar head is stronger in short-chain than in long-chain amphiphiles. For these, with $n = 4$ to 7 (depending on a variety of conditions, e.g. type of surfactant, supporting electrolyte, number of polar head groups, temperature, gegenions, etc.) the aggregation number should be almost zero, all CH_2 groups are screened, and no micelles are formed. Unfortunately, this assumption cannot be verified for compounds with two and more polar head groups, in the absence of sufficiently accurate data.

CONCLUDING REMARKS

In an attempt to clarify the relation between the structure of a surfactant and its physicochemical properties, it was established that the hydrophilic and hydrophobic functions can be separated. The polar head groups of the amphiphile inhibit micelle formation; for surfactants with a constant chain length the CMC value increases in the sequence: "non-ionic → ionic (single head) → ionic (two heads)". With two polar head groups, the inhibitory effect is stronger than with a single group. The small values of B (Equation 11) compared to similar monofunctional surfactants indicate much lower cohesive energy per CH_2 group.

The attractive factor derives from the hydrophobic effect (cohesive interaction) which seeks to minimize the H.C. - water contact. This factor is not independent of the nature of the head groups, since the screening action of the polar head reduces the number of CH_2 units in the lipophilic group contributing to the hydrophobic effect. Only the term n_{eff} × ϕ'_{CH_2} (Equation 12 or 13) represents the net free energy change in transition of the H.C. tail from an aqueous environment to the micelle core.

Introduction of a second ionic group, remote from the first, into the structure of a 1:1-type surfactant reinforces the hydrophilic character of the molecule and consequently reduces the size of the micelle (aggregation number). The two-head group molecule has a smaller number of effective CH_2 groups per head group, i.e. the cohesive energy is reduced. The increase in repulsion between the head groups in the micelles makes for increased solubilization of polar components (increased space available for water penetration); by contrast, the reduced aggregation number in the micelle makes for reduced solubilization of nonpolar components.

The hydrophobicity of the amphiphile molecule depends largely on its end state (number and position of polar heads). The hydrophobic moiety is strongly influenced by the ionic atmosphere of the polar head, to the extent that $n_{eff} < n$. In other words, increased hydrophilicity tends to shorten the paraffin chain. Part of the H.C. tail is already shielded from the aqueous environment in proportion to n_{eff}.

Molecular models and the n_{eff} concept demonstrate the feasibility of packing surfactant monomers into micelles with water penetration of the latter.

More research work is called for a complex surfactants such as aerosols and zwitterionics (ampholytic materials behaving like anionics at high pH and like cationics at low pH). It still remains to define the relative hydrophilicities of the relevant group of the surfactant, as well as classify the polar functional groups according to their hydration characteristics, and examine their influence on the lipophilic group.

ACKNOWLEDGMENTS

This work was sponsored by the Technion – V.P.R. Fund, Technion City, Haifa. The authors wish to thank the Mineral Engineering Research Center (MERC) for providing the necessary facilities and assistance.

REFERENCES

1. I.J. Lin, J.P. Friend, and Y. Zimmels, J. Colloid Interface Sci., 45, No. 2, 378 (1973).
2. K. Shinoda, T. Nakagawa, B. Tamamushi, and T. Isemura, "Colloidal Surfactants", Academic Press, New York, N.Y. (1963).
3. V.A. Volkov, Colloid J., USSR, 37, No. 5, 763 (1975).
4. I.J. Lin, and P. Somasundaran, J. Colloid Interface Sci., 37, 731 (1971).
5. P. Mukerjee, J. Phys. Chem., 66, 1375 (1962).
6. I.J. Lin, J. Phys. Chem., 76, 2019 (1972).
7. I.J. Lin, and A. Metzer, Ibid, 75, 3000 (1971).
8. I.J. Lin, and A. Metzer, Inter. J. Miner. Process., 1, 319, (1974).
9. I.J. Lin, B.M. Moudgil, and P. Somasundaran, Colloid and Polymer Sci., 252, No.5, 407 (1974).
10. B.A. Pethica, in "Proc. 3rd Inter. Cong. of Surface Activity" Cologne, Vol. I, 212 (1960).
11. Y. Zimmels and I.J. Lin, Colloid and Polymer Sci., 252, 594, (1974).

12. Y. Zimmels, I.J. Lin, and J.P. Friend, Ibid, $\underline{253}$, 404 (1975).
13. P. Mukerjee, Ber. Bunsenges. Phys. Chem., $\underline{82}$, 931 (1978).
14. D.O. Shah, Chem. Eng. Educ., 14, Winter (1977).
15. N.W. Gregory, and H.V. Tartar, J. Am. Soc., $\underline{70}$, 1992 (1948).
16. M.J. Rosen, and Y. Nakamura, J. Phys. Chem., $\underline{80}$, 873 (1977).
17. G.L. Amidon, et al. Ibid, $\underline{79}$, 2239 (1975).
18. J. Clifford, Trans. Faraday Soc., $\underline{61}$, 1276 (1965);
    Corkill, J.M., J.F. Goodman, and T. Walker, Ibid $\underline{63}$, 768 (1967).
19. C. Tanford, "The Hydrophobic Effect", John Wiley & Sons,
    New York, 12 and 54 (1973).
20. G.C. Kresheck, in "Water, A Comprehensive Treatise", Vol. 4,
    F. Franks, Ed., Plenum Press, New York, 95 (1975).
21. R. Nagarajan, and E. Ruckenstein, J. Colloid Interface Sci.,
    $\underline{71}$, No.3, 580 (1979).
22. I.J. Lin, and L. Marszall, Ibid, $\underline{57}$, No.1, 85 (1976);
    I.J. Lin, and L. Marszall, Tenside Detergents, $\underline{14}$, No. 3, 131,
    (1977).
23. T. Drakenberg, and B. Lindman, J. Colloid Interface Sci.,
    $\underline{44}$, 184 (1973).
24. D. Stigter, J. Phys. Chem., $\underline{78}$, 2480 (1974).
25. M. Ueno, et al., J. Am. Oil Chems' Soc., $\underline{49}$, 250 (1972).
26. I.J. Lin, in "Colloid & Interface Sci., Aerosols, Emulsions,
    and Surfactants", Vol. II, Academic Press, New York, 431 (1976).
27. I.J. Lin, and L. Marszall, Tenside Detergents, $\underline{15}$, No. 5, 243,
    (1978).
28. I.J. Lin, Ibid, $\underline{17}$ (1980).
29. K. Shinoda, J. Phys. Chem., $\underline{59}$, 432 (1955).
30. K. Shinoda, Ibid, $\underline{60}$, 1439 (1956).
31. J.K. Weil, and A.J. Stirton, Ibid, $\underline{60}$, 899 (1956).
32. M. Ueno, S. Yamamoto, and K. Meguro, J. Am. Oil Chems' Soc.,
    $\underline{51}$, 373 (1974).
33. M.J. Rosen, M. Baum, and F. Kasher, Ibid, $\underline{53}$, 742 (1976).
34. P.H. Elworthy, J. Pharm. Pharmcol., $\underline{11}$, 557 (1959).
35. A. Serrano, D. Bochnia, and H. Schubert, Tenside Detergents,
    $\underline{14}$, No.2, 67 (1977).
36. P. Mukerjee, and K. Mysels, "Critical Micelle Concentrations
    of Aqueous Surfactant Systems", Nat. Stand, Ref. Data Ser.,
    Nat. Bur. Stand. No. NSRDS-NBS 36, Washington, D.C., (1971).
37. H. Wennerstrom and B. Lindman, J. Phys. Chem., $\underline{83}$, 2931 (1979).

EPR OF SPIN PROBES IN AQUEOUS SOLUTIONS OF SURFACTANTS

M. Schara and D.D. Lasic

J. Stefan Institute, E. Kardelj University of
Ljubljana
61000 Ljubljana, Yugoslavia

Spin probes have been used to study the aggregation of potassium palmitate molecules.
The partitions of the spin probes between the
hydrophobic and hydrophilic environment, as
well as the possibility of hydrocarbon chain
ordering in the micellar interior are discussed.

INTRODUCTION

Electron paramagnetic resonance (EPR) has been applied to furnish
evidence of molecular aggregation and to evaluate the monomer –
aggregate exchange rate and dissociation constants.[1,2,3] The
importance of EPR in studies of catalysis in micellar systems
has been reviewed recently.[4] EPR has proved to be able to evaluate the degree of molecular ordering in lyotropic phases, where
large molecular aggregates are available.[5] It is also possible
to detect nonspherical shape of micelles.[6] Of special importance
are information concerning the distribution of molecules between
the solvent and aggregates,[7] especially as some substances can
be dissolved in water only via the incorporation into micelles.
Namely many substances of low solubility in water have to be
administered to living systems. Therefore knowledge of the
aggregate structure plays a vital role in the transfer of such
substances and the corresponding cellular incorporation process
studies.

EXPERIMENTAL

Purified potassium palmitate(K-P) was used. The spin probes were synthesized by Dr. Pečar from our laboratory. We used the fatty acid type spin probes

$$HOOC-(CH_2)_m-C-(CH_2)_n-CH_3$$

designated as HFASL(m,n) and their corresponding methyl esters MeFASL(m,n). The samples were placed in 1mm inner diameter glass capillaries, in different concentration ranges of the water dissolved surfactant, with an addition of the spin probe in the final concentration of about 10^{-4}M. The spectra were taken on a Varian E-9 X band EPR spectrometer.

RESULTS

A 10^{-4}M solution of MeFASL, where due to the molecular aggregation of the spin probe molecules only a spectrum of small intensity can be observed, was titrated by a K-P solution. The dilution of the MeFASL by K-P molecules increases the intensity of the spectrum as shown in Figure 1.

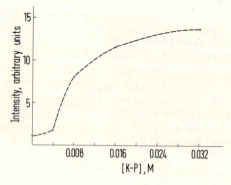

Figure 1. Peak to peak height of the first derivative EPR spectra of MeFASL(10,3) water solution as a function of the K-P concentration.

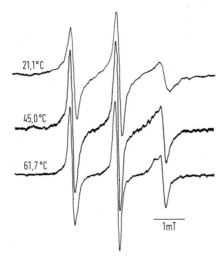

Figure 2. EPR spectra of HAFASL(10,3), 10^{-4}M, dissolved in 1% K-P water solution.

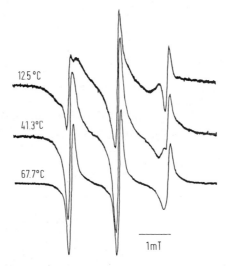

Figure 3. EPR spectra of MeFASL(10,3), 10^{-4}M, dissolved in 5% K-P water solution.

A step decrease in the isotropic hyperfine splitting from 1.57 to 1.47 mT coincides with the largest intensify increase. Figures 2 and 3 show the HFASL(10,3) and MeFASL(10,3) spectra in 1 and 5% K-P solutions respectively. It is important to stress the appearance of the anisotropic lines above the transition temperatures, which could be explained by an increased

partitioning of the spin probe into the interior of the micelle.
On the other hand in Figure 4, we can follow the distribution
of the spin probe and we find that the apparent relative intensity
increase above the transition temperature comes from the line
narrowing. It probably means a decrease in the correlation times.
Their change with temperature is characterized by the activation
energy 21.7 J/mole. The high field line m=-1 of HFASL(10,3)
splitting becomes observable in 12% K-P above the transition
temperature, like for the small spin probe HFASL(0,1) in the
lamellar phase of 70% K-P as shown in Figure 5.

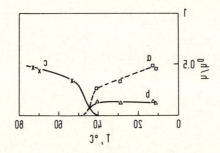

Figure 4. Temperature dependence of the peak to peak height of
the m=-1 first derivative EPR lines a) water dissolved HAFASL
(10,3) component, b) lipid dissolved component below T_c and
c) the micelle dissolved component above T_c.

In the same range we get a drop in the hyperfine splitting for
HFASL(0,1), which is proportional to the lipid to water concentration ratio, meaning that for these spin probes we observe
a fast exchange between the lipid and water compartment (Figure 6.).
Using solutions of the paramagnetic ion $Fe(CN)_6^{3-}$, we could show
that the spectrum above T_c in Figure 3, could not be changed.
Therefore the distinguished anisotropy of the high field hyperfine line can be inferred to pertain to the micellar hydrocarbon
chain ordering.

DISCUSSION

Ordered lipids with the hydrocarbon chains aligned and the
polar heads facing the water lipid interface can be characterized
by the chain segment order parameter[8] $S_i = < 3 \cos^2 0 - 1 >$ where

0 is the angle between the normal to the interface and a direction perpendicular to the CH_2 plane of a chain segment i. The
brackets denote thermal average over all configurations of the
hydrocarbon chain. The rate of these motions can be characterized by the rotational correlation time   i.

     EPR can furnish information on both the ordering and the
rates of motions.[9] The spin Hamiltonian can be divided into an
averaged time independent and a fluctuating time dependent term.

$$H(t) = \overline{H(t)} + H(t) - \overline{H(t)}$$

The properties of the spin probes - (paramagnetic molecules) in
their environment are best characterized by the values of the
second rank tensors $\underline{g}$ and $\underline{A}$, describing the interactions of the
spin probe free radical with the paramagnetic nuclei and their
influence on the EPR spectrum. The spin Hamiltonian can be
written

$$H = \beta \vec{S} \underline{g} B + \vec{S} \underline{A} \vec{I}$$

Here S and I mean the electron and nuclear spin, β the Bohr
magneton and B the magnetic field. The nuclear Zeeman term was
neglected. Both tensors can be represented as sums of an iso-
tronic and an anisotropic component $\underline{A} = \underline{a} + \underline{A}$. The effect of
these anisotropic components is used when calculating the aver-
aged Hamiltonian eigenvalues and the corresponding spectral
lines. The isotropic tensors which are sums of the diagonal
tensor elements $a = Tr\underline{A}/3$ are directly related to the free electron density at the nitrogen nucleus of the nitroxide group[10].
Therefore they are sensitive to the polarity of their environment.
Larger values of a are measured in polar environments[11] and we
can measure the distribution of the spin probe between the environments of different polarity. The measured spectra show that there
is an exchange between different environments of the spin probes
when they are in the micellar solutions. The exchange rate depends on the spin probe water solubility. Therefore, the averaging is more complete for HFASL(0,1) than for larger spin probes.
The partitioning into the micelles increases with temperature.
Very narrow lines are observed in the water solutions before the
onset of the micelle formation above T_c, when the hydrocarbon
chains get melted. We believe that these are small premicellar
aggregates, since at higher temperatures the splitting decreases,
meaning a more difficult access of water molecules to the nitroxide group. Either the molecules are present as monomers or in
small aggregates with K-P, which prevents the broadening interactions between the spin probe free radicals. Namely in the gel
phase below T_c we observed a broadened spectrum. Due to the
paramagnetic broadening and the subsequent broadening of the
micelle dissolved probe spectra , we could assume that the

nitroxide group is at least in the water micelle interface in a
state of exchange in addition to the spin probe spectra super-
imposed pertaining to the water dissolved probe. At higher temperatures the exchange rate is larger than $10^8 s-1$ leading to
averaged lines. Since the remaining spectrum shows symmetrical
lines, we believe that the hyperfine tensor anisotropy is averaged in the 1% K-P micelles.

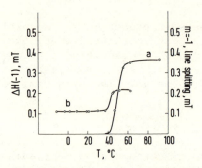

Figure 5. a) m=-1 line splitting of the HFASL(10,3) spin probe,
di-solved in 12% K-P as a function of temperature b) line width
variation for HFASL(0,1) dissolved in the lamellar 70% K-P
solution.

     There are several possibilities to prevent the observations
of the local chain ordering. The molecules are probably able
to rotate about their long axes, causing a change in conformation
which reorients a specified chain segment in space. The motions
are usually fast and can lead to partially narrowed spectra,
which reflect ordering and rates of motion. Finally there[12] is
the exchange of spin probe molecules between water and micellar
compartments or even a finite lifetime of whole micelle. We
would get a drop in the order parameter if the lifetime in both
compartments is short, namely the observed order parameter would
be $S = x_m S_m$ proportional to the mole fraction x_m of the spin
probe in the micelles. Water penetration into the micelle might
be important as well.[13] The molecules can move translationally
in the micelle[14,5] with their polar heads bound to the micelle
surface or the whole micelle may reorient in space ($\tau = 4 \ \Pi\eta R^3/3kt$)
randomly, thus eliminating the possibility to observe ordering if
the radius R is small and the viscosity η is low to allow short
reorientation times. Further, if it rotates, these rotations
could again produce partial averaging of the spectral line

splitting. If the micelle is spherical, the translational motion
of the molecule could produce a complete averaging assuming that
$\mathcal{P} \Delta B < (1^2/D_t)^{-1}$; i.e., the magnetic anisotropy $\mathcal{P} \Delta B$ of the spin
probe is smaller than the rate of molecular reorientation. Here
D_t is the translational diffusion constant of monomer in the micelle.

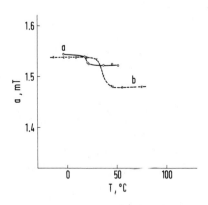

Figure 6. Temperature dependence of the isotropic hyperfine
splitting of HFASL(0,1) in 10% K-P solution (a), and in 70%
K-P lamellar phase (b).

For MeFASL(10,3) in 5% K-P the observed splitting shown in
Figure 3 could be explained by the anisotropy caused by an order
parameter of the hydrocarbon chains of about 0.2. The resonance
field B_r the extrema of the m=-1 line can be calculated from the
relation

$$B_r = (h\nu/\beta) \left\{ (\tilde{g}_{\parallel}^2 - \tilde{g}_{\perp}^2) \left[0.5\sin^2\!\mathcal{Y} \sin^2\!\Omega + \cos^2\!\mathcal{Y} \cos^2\!\Omega \right] + \tilde{g}_{\perp}^2 \right\}^{-1/2}$$

$$+ \left\{ \tilde{A}_{\parallel}^2 - \tilde{A}_{\perp}^2 \left[0.5\sin^2\!\mathcal{Y} \sin^2\!\Omega + \cos^2\!\mathcal{Y} \cos^2\!\Omega \right] + \tilde{A}_{\perp}^2 \right\}^{1/2}$$

here the hyperfine tensor components are averaged by the rapid
motions in an ordered environment

$$\tilde{A}_{\parallel} = a + (2/3) \ (\ A_{\parallel} - A_{\perp} \ ) S_3$$

$$\tilde{A}_{\perp} = a - (1/3) \ (\ A_{\parallel} - A_{\perp} \ ) S_3$$

and correspondingly for the $\tilde{g}$ values.

Now the external separation between the lines for a model of a spherical micelle rotating about an axis inclined by the angle Ω to B and $\mathcal{I}$ is the angle between the magnetic symmetry axis of the paramagnetic center and the axis of rotation. The difference ΔB is 0.43 mT if we took $S_3 = 0.2$. Since we have not observed such a distinguished splitting by HFASL(10,3) it might be that the less polar molecules of MeFASL can diffuse translationally more easily in the micellar interior with the polar heads bound to the surface of the micelle.

If rotation of the micelles is assumed to be slow, then we should introduce a special rotation of the spin probe, where finally the nitroxide should reorient about the axis perpendicular to the symmetry axis of the nitroxide free electron orbital. Finally if the micelles rotate like spherical tops with their axes changing orientation in the time intervals larger than the anisotropy, we could also observe for spherical micelles an anisotropic spectrum of the type shown in Figure 3. The liquid crystal type anisotropies might interfere in some with the solvent micelle distribution measurements for some substances.

CONCLUSION

The intensities of amphiphilic spin probes spectra in water solutions increase by the addition of nonparamagnetic amphiphiles, an effect very important in spin probe distribution research in living systems. Small aggregates have a good access for water molecules. In larger micelles we can observe anisotropy of the nitroxide spin probes, which could mean only an anisotropic environment in the micellar interior for such micelles in concentrations of five and more percent potassium palmitate in water.

REFERENCES

1. K. K. Fox, Trans. Frarday Soc. 67, 2802 (1971).
2. N. M. Aterton and S. Strach, J. Chem. Soc. Faraday Trans. 68, 374 (1972).
3. C. Jolicoeur and H. L. Friedman, J. Sol. Chem. 7, 813 (1977).
4. J. H. Fendler and E. J. Fendler, "Catalysis in Micellar and Macromolecular Systems", Academic Press, New York, 1975.
5. J. Seelig, in "Spin Labelling", Ed. L. J. Berliner, Academic Press, New York, 1976, p. 373.
6. M. Schara, F. Púsnik and M. Šentjurc, Croat, Chem. Acta 48, 147 (1976).
7. J. R. Ernandes, H. Chaimovich and S. Schreier, Chem. Phys. Lipids, 18, 304 (1977).
8. S. Marcélja, Biochim. Biophys, Acta 367, 165 (1974).

9.   H. M. McConnell, in "Spin Labelling", Ed. L. J. Berlinger,
     Academic Press, New York, p. 525.
10. A. Carrington and A. D. McLachlan, "Introduction to Magnetic
     Resonance", Harper and Row, New York, 1967.
11. O. H. Griffith and P. C. Jost in "Spin Labelling", Ed. L. J.
     Berlinger, Academic Press, New York, 1976, p. 525.
12. G. Amansson, J. Phys. Chem., $\underline{82}$, 2805 (1978).
13. H. Wennerstrom and B. Lindman, J. Phys. Chem., $\underline{83}$, 2931 (1979).
14. C. Fouchet, Thesis, Unviersity of Paris-Sid, Orsay Centre, 1972.

DIELECTRIC RELAXATION SPECTROSCOPY OF ZWITTERIONIC

SURFACTANTS IN AQUEOUS MICELLAR SOLUTIONS

S. C. Müller[*] and R. Pottel

Drittes Physikalisches Institut
Universität Göttingen, Bürgerstrasse 42-44
D3400 Göttingen, West Germany

The complex relative electric permittivity of
aqueous solutions of zwitterionic surfactants has been
measured in the range of 1 MHz to 40 GHz at various
concentrations and temperatures. The dipolar headgroups consist of the cationic ($-N^+(CH_3)_2-$), ($-NH_2^+-$),
($-N^+(CH_3)_3$) or ($-N^+(CH_3)_2H$) and the anionic ($-CO_2^-$),
($-SO_3^-$) or ($-PO_4^--$) group. An empirical relaxation
spectral function and a model spectral function
especially developed for solutions of spherical or
ellipsoidal micelles have been fitted to the experimental data. From the adjustable parameters the
following results have been derived: The ellipsoidal
axial ratios cover the range 1 to 5. The reorientation time of the hydration molecules is three times
larger than in bulk water. The values of a correlation number for the diffusive motion of the headgroup's
outer ion indicate that the coupling between adjacent
zwitterions is weak. The mobilities of the outer
ions are at least four times smaller than the mobilities of the corresponding unbound ions, their activation
enthalpies are found to be 5 kcal/mol. In solutions
of increased conductivity an additional dielectric
dispersion/absorption region has been observed below
50 MHz due to interfacial polarization effects at the
boundary between micelles and the conducting solvent.

[*]Present address: Department of Chemistry, Stanford University,
Stanford, CA 94305

INTRODUCTION

Dielectric relaxation spectroscopy has been frequently used as a tool to investigate molecular motions and structural properties of colloidal and biomolecular solutions[1-3]. But only rarely has this experimental technique been applied to micellar systems[4-7], although characteristic polarization phenomena have been predicted due to the electrical properties of the micellar surface[8]. For our dielectric measurements we have chosen aqueous micellar solutions of various amphiphiles whose hydrophilic parts consist of a positively and a negatively charged group bound together to form zwitterions. Thus, because of the permanent electric dipole moment of the headgroups, the dielectric permittivity spectra of the surfactant solutions contain information on the reorientational motion and the average arrangement not only of the moderately dipolar water molecules but also of the strongly dipolar zwitterionic groups. No artificial labels have to be introduced that might disturb the molecular structure of the micelles. The choice of our systems has also been motivated by the fact that amphiphilic molecules with similar zwitterionic headgroups and one or two hydrocarbon chains are important constituents of biomembranes. The mobility and arrangement of the hydrophilic groups may substantially influence the structure and function of membranes. From this point of view it appears interesting to investigate the behavior of zwitterions and their hydration water at a micellar surface, and to compare the results to data from similar experimental studies on double layers of zwitterionic phospholipids[9].

The measurements of the complex relative permittivity $\varepsilon(\nu) = \varepsilon'(\nu) - i\varepsilon''(\nu)$ reported in this Communication were performed over a wide frequency range (1 MHz $\leq \nu \leq$ 40 GHz) by applying weak alternating electrical fields $E = \hat{E} \exp(i2\pi\nu t)$, ($\hat{E} \leq 1$ V/cm), to the surfactant solutions and observing the relaxing dielectric polarization $P = \hat{P}(\nu) \exp(i2\pi\nu t) = [\varepsilon(\nu) - 1]E/4\pi$ set up in the systems. Micellar solutions of five different zwitterionic surfactants were investigated at various concentrations and temperatures. The low molecular weight electrolyte content was kept low enough to avoid exceedingly high conductivity losses at the lower limit of the frequency band of measurement. The $\varepsilon(\nu)$ spectra were evaluated in terms of a model spectral function providing information about the orientation correlation number and the mobility of the hydrophilic headgroups, the number and the relaxation time of the hydration water molecules, and the shape of the micelles.

MATERIALS AND METHODS

Aqueous Solutions

The surfactant molecules with their structural formulae are listed in Table I.   In the following they will be referred to by the shorthand notations indicated below their names. SPB and HB were obtained from Henkel (special synthesis), ABA from Hoechst (tradename: HoeS1564). PC and PDME were synthesized especially for our purposes[10]. Except for ABA all chains contain 16 C-atoms.

The investigated solutions (Table I) were prepared by adding doubly distilled, degassed and sterilized water to a preweighed amount of solute. The pH values were close to the isoelectric points. Consequently, the zwitterionic state of the ampholytic molecules predominated by far. The electric conductivity σ (measured at 10 kHz) of the original HB and ABA solutions, mainly due to NaCl retained during the synthesis, were too high for dielectric measurements to be extended to frequencies below 50 MHz and therefore were reduced by dialysis. This removal of small salt ions was effective until a limiting content of electrolyte was reached, probably determined by the binding of ions to the micelles. The final conductivities of all investigated systems as presented in Table I never exceeded 0.21 Ω^{-1} m^{-1} at 25°C and were frequently much lower. Taking pure aqueous NaCl solutions as a reference and neglecting a possible reduction of the electrolyte conductivity caused by ion-micelle interactions, the electrolyte content can be crudely estimated to be much lower than 0.02 mol/ℓ in most of the surfactant solutions.

The Krafft temperature of SPB and HB solutions was indicated by the onset of turbidity at approximately 18°C. Accordingly, the temperature range of our measurements was restricted to temperatures higher than 20°C. In addition to the systems already mentioned, we studied the effect of solubilization of n-decanol by HB micelles on the dielectric properties. The highest attainable mole ratio of the solubilisate to HB was 0.4.

Relatively high surfactant concentrations were necessary in order to obtain information on the dynamic behavior of the hydration water molecules. At solute concentrations below 0.05 mol/ℓ the amount of influenced water was too small to be separated from bulk water contributions in a significant way. The influence of monomers on the results of the measurements could always be neglected because the cmc of the investigated or of some comparable surfactants is very low: 5 x 10^{-5} mol/ℓ for SPB at 30°C[11], 2 x 10^{-5} mol/ℓ for HB at 20°C[12], 0.9 x 10^{-3} mol/ℓ for N-docecyl-β-alanine at 30°C[13], < 2 x 10^{-4} mol/ℓ for egg lysolecithin[14].

Table I. Names and Structural Formulae of the Zwitterionic Surfactants. Solute Concentrations c, Temperatures T, and Conductivities σ of the Investigated Solutions.

Solute	Structural Formula	c [mol/ℓ]	T [°C]	σ [$\Omega^{-1}m^{-1}$]
N-hexadecyl-(N,N-dimethyl)-3-ammonio-1-propane-sulfonate (N-hexadecyl-sulfopropyl-betaine) (SPB)	$CH_3-(CH_2)_{15}-\overset{\underset{\displaystyle CH_3}{|}}{N^+}-(CH_2)_3-SO_3^-$ (with a second CH_3 on N)	0.05 0.2 0.31 0.4 0.6	25 20 to 53 25 30 30	0.002 0.004 to 0.009 0.008 0.009 0.012
N-hexadecyl-betaine (HB)	$CH_3-(CH_2)_{15}-\overset{\underset{\displaystyle CH_3}{|}}{N^+}-CH_2-CO_2^-$ (with a second CH_3 on N)	0.2 0.4	25 20 to 50	0.03 0.042 to 0.075
N-alkyl-β-alanine (ABA)	$CH_3-(CH_2)_{n-1}-(NH_2)^+-(CH_2)_2-CO_2^-$ n: 8 10 12 14 16 18 %: 3 5 50 23 11 8	0.21 0.21	25 50	0.155 0.236
N-hexadecyl-phospho-choline (PC)	$CH_3-(CH_2)_{15}-O-\overset{\overset{\displaystyle O}{\|}}{\underset{\underset{\displaystyle O}{\|}}{P}}-O-(CH_2)_2-N^+-CH_3$ (with two CH_3 on N)	0.23	25	0.21
N-hexadecyl-phospho-(N,N-dimethyl)-ethanolamine (PDME)	$CH_3-(CH_2)_{15}-O-\overset{\overset{\displaystyle O}{\|}}{\underset{\underset{\displaystyle O}{\|}}{P}}-O-(CH_2)_2-N^+-CH_3$ (with H and CH_3 on N)	0.13	32	0.049

Experimental Techniques

The spectrum of the total complex permittivity $\varepsilon_{tot}(\nu) = \varepsilon'(\nu)$ $- i\varepsilon''_{tot}(\nu)$ of the surfactant solutions was determined by frequency domain measurements between 1 MHz and 40 GHz. $\varepsilon''_{tot}(\nu)$ includes dielectric and conductivity losses. Input impedance measurements were performed at about 20 frequencies on a special sample cell using a commercial admittance bridge (Boonton 33D/1) between 1 MHz and 100 MHz, and impedance bridge (Hewlett-Packard 803A) between 50 MHz and 800 MHz. The cell constructed for this purpose consists of a short piece of coaxial line which is terminated by an impedance matched teflon window and a circular stainless steel tube (diameter 7 mm) containing 1 to 2 ml of the solution. The tube acts as a waveguide that is excited far below its cut-off frequency[15]. Based on a thorough description of the electromagnetic field within the liquid-filled cell[16], we have proposed an equivalent circuit that represents the electrical properties of the cell with high accuracy[17]. Thus, by carefully calibrating the cell and reducing systematic errors of the bridges, ε' and ε'' can be determined with an accuracy better than ±1% down to 5 MHz. Electrode polarization effects, the magnitude of which depends on the nature and the concentration of ionic species in the solutions, may introduce larger errors for $\nu < 5$ MHz, especially in those cases where the sample conductivity exceeds 0.05 Ω^{-1} m^{-1}.

By the aid of five double beam interferometers, constructed with standard waveguide devices, a sensitive interferometric method was applied for frequencies between 1 GHz and 40 GHz to determine the wavelength and the attenuation per wavelength of a wave propagating through a circular waveguide filled with the liquid[15]. From these measurements the complex permittivity could be derived within an error $|\Delta\varepsilon'/\varepsilon'| \leqslant 1\%$ and $|\Delta\varepsilon''_{tot}/\varepsilon''_{tot}| \leqslant 2\%$. Errors in the determination of the frequency were neglibibly small.

RESULTS

As a typical example for the measured dielectric spectra the results for the real and imaginary part of the permittivity of a 0.2 molar SPB solution at 20°C and 45°C are plotted in Figure 1. Here and in the following figure the less interesting conductivity losses $2\sigma/\nu$ due to the drift of ionic impurities have been subtracted from the total losses $\varepsilon''_{tot}(\nu)$, according to

$$\varepsilon''(\nu) = \varepsilon''_{tot}(\nu) - 2\sigma/\nu, \tag{1}$$

in order to obtain the loss $\varepsilon''(\nu)$ originating from dielectric polarization phenomena only. The two distinct dispersion/absorption regions in Figure 1 are related to the restricted reorientational motions of the solvent water molecules ($\nu > 1$ GHz) and the solute zwitterions ($\nu < 1$ GHz).

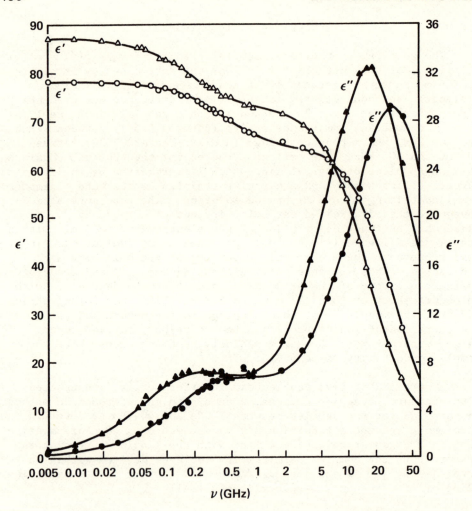

Figure 1. The measured complex permittivity spectrum of a 0.2 molar solution of SPB at 20°C (Δ,▲) and 45°C (O,●): The real part, $\varepsilon'(\nu)$, and the imaginary part excluding conductivity contributions, $\varepsilon''_{tot}(\nu) - 2\sigma/\nu$, are plotted versus the frequency, ν. The solid curves represent the fitted relaxation function R(ν) according to Equation (2).

In Figure 2 the permittivity spectrum of a 0.4 molar HB solution is shown. Clearly a third dispersion/absorption region appears at the low frequency limit of the spectrum (ν < 20 MHz). This additional relaxation process was observed in HB and ABA solutions. It is probably caused by conductivity contributions with relaxational

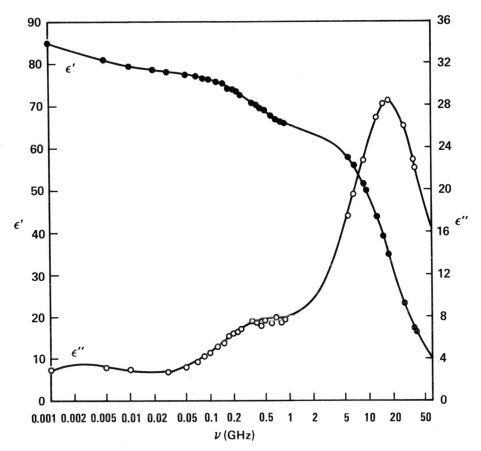

Figure 2. The measured complex permittivity spectrum of a 0.4 molar
solution of HB at 25°C. The symbols indicate the measured values of
the real part (●) and imaginary part (○) excluding conductivity
contributions. The solid curves represent the fitted relaxation
function R(ν).

behavior (Maxwell-Wagner effect or counterion relaxation). Since
in this Communication we are mainly concerned with the dielectric
properties of the dipolar molecules in the solutions, we will not
present a detailed description of the additional low frequency
relaxation, but only briefly return to the question of its origin
at the end of the discussion.

Within the limits of experimental error the measured spectra
can be analytically described by a linear superposition of Cole-
Cole relaxation terms. The resulting empirical relaxation spectral
function is

$$R(\nu) = \varepsilon_o + \sum_{k=1}^{3} \frac{\Delta\varepsilon_k}{1 + (i2\pi\nu\tau_k)^{1-h_k}} - i\frac{2\sigma}{\nu} \qquad (2)$$

The parameters $\Delta\varepsilon_k = \varepsilon_k - \varepsilon_{k-1}$ denote the relaxation strengths:
$k = 1$ refers to the water, $k = 2$ to the zwitterion contribution.
$\Delta\varepsilon_3$ is nonvanishing only for the spectra of HB and ABA solutions.
The widths of the continuous Cole-Cole type relaxation time
distributions, symmetric with respect to the principal relaxation
times τ_k, are determined by the parameters h_k ($0 \leqslant h_k < 1$).

The parameter values ε_o, ε_k, τ_k, h_k ($k = 1,2,3$) for each
solution were obtained by fitting $R(\nu)$ to the experimental data
$\varepsilon_{tot}(\nu_1),\ldots, \varepsilon_{tot}(\nu_J)$, measured at J different frequencies. A
nonlinear least-squares fitting procedure was used to determine the
absolute minimum of the variance

$$V = \frac{1}{J-1} \sum_{j=1}^{J} |R(\nu_j) - \varepsilon_{tot}(\nu_j)| . \qquad (3)$$

Examples of these fits are shown in Figure 1 and Figure 2. Because
of the distinct separation of the two or three relaxation regions,
all parameters could be calculated with satisfactory accuracy.
When the conductivity was treated as an adjustable parameter, its
value was found to be equal to the measured value within the
experimental error.

The results shall now be briefly summarized, as far as they
are necessary to support the discussion in terms of a model of
the surfactant solutions given in the next section. A detailed
compilation of the parameter values can be found elsewhere[17].

While the width of the relaxation time distribution is negligibly
small in pure water, the distribution parameter h_1 of the solvent
water in the micellar solutions is found to increase with the
volume fraction v of the solute ($h_1 = 0.04$ at $v = 0.16$), where v
is calculated from the water molarity in the solution c_w and the
pure water molarity c_{wo} according to

$$v = 1 - c_w/c_{wo} , \qquad (4)$$

and the apparent molar volume of the solvent water is assumed to be
c_{wo}^{-1} as in pure water.

The solvent water relaxation time τ_1 is increased with respect
to the relaxation time τ_w of pure water ($\tau_w = 8.25$ ps at $25°C$[18]).
The quantity $(\tau_1 - \tau_w)/\tau_w$ is approximately proportional to v within
the concentration range considered, and attains a value of about
0.04 for $v = 0.16$. Qualitatively we may conclude that the micellar

solutions contain hydration water molecules that can be distinguished
from water molecules in pure water by their increased reorientation
times.

   In Figure 3 some of the ε_1 values (error ±0.3), which according
to Equation (2) denote the part of the static permittivity $\varepsilon(\nu \to 0)$
due to the solvent diluted by the solute, are plotted versus v.
The dashed line represents an empirical relation

$$\varepsilon_{sw}^{emp}(v) = 78.5 - 1.7 \frac{vc_{wo}}{[\,mol/\ell\,]} \qquad (5)$$

that holds for the static permittivity ε_{sw} at 25°C of a large variety
of nondipolar, nearly spherical solute particles[19].

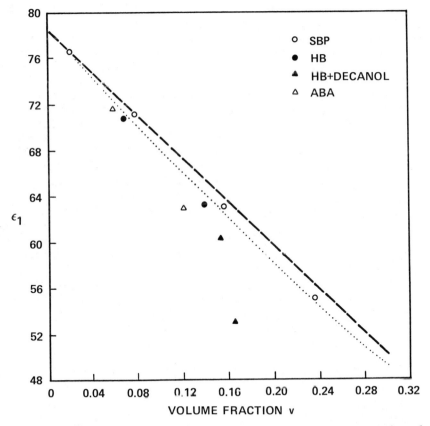

Figure 3.   Static permittivity ε_1 of the solvent water diluted by
the solute versus volume fraction v of the surfactant at 25°C.
The dashed and dotted lines are calculated according to Equations
(5) and (6), respectively.

The dotted line in Figure 3 was computed according to the Maxwell-Lewin formula[20]

$$\varepsilon_{sw}^{ML}(v) = \varepsilon_{ow} + v(\varepsilon_c - \varepsilon_{ow}) \frac{3\varepsilon_{ow}}{2\varepsilon_{ow} + \varepsilon_c - v(\varepsilon_c - \varepsilon_{ow})} \qquad (6)$$

with $\varepsilon_{ow} = 78.5$ (static permittivity of water at 25°C) and $\varepsilon_c = 2$ (permittivity of liquid paraffines). ε_{sw}^{ML} is the comprehensive permittivity of a heterogeneous mixture consisting of a continuous dielectric with permittivity ε_{ow} and spherical homogeneous dielectric particles with permittivity ε_c. The majority of the static permittivities predicted by Equations (5) and (6) clearly tend to be higher than the measured ε_1 values. A depression of this extent cannot be explained by dielectric saturation effects[7]. We attribute this excess decrement to the solvent depolarization enhancement caused by a non-spherical relative to a spherical particle, thus concluding that the zwitterionic surfactants in HB and ABA solutions form non-spherical micelles. In the following we preferentially assume these micelles to be oblate ellipsoids of revolution. However, from our data no distinction can be made between the oblate and the prolate micellar shape.

From the parameters describing the zwitterion contribution to the dielectric spectra we calculate the molal increments $\Delta\varepsilon_2/c$ at 25°C within an error of ±2 ℓ/mol to be 89 ℓ/mol for PC, 85 ℓ/mol for PDME, 72 ℓ/mol for SPB, 52 ℓ/mol for ABA, 36 ℓ/mol for HB. Apparently the differences in the $\Delta\varepsilon_2/c$ values correspond to the different dipole moments of the solutes. The product $\Delta\varepsilon_2 \times T_{abs}$ (T_{abs} = absolute temperature) is constant throughout the investigated temperature range. The relaxation times τ_2 at 25°C are 750 ps (0.2 molar SPB), 900 ps (0.23 molar PC), 1380 ps (0.13 molar PDME at 32°C), 430 ps (0.4 molar HB), 960 ps (0.21 molar ABA), the error amounts to 3%. All systems are characterized by a relaxation time distribution corresponding to h_3 values between 0.1 and 0.25.

The evaluation of the third distinct relaxation process observed for HB and ABA solutions results in parameter values 20 ns $\leqslant \tau_3$ $\leqslant$ 70 ns, 8 $\leqslant \Delta\varepsilon_3 \leqslant$ 12 and 0.1 $\leqslant h_3 \leqslant$ 0.26.

DISCUSSION ON THE BASIS OF A SOLUTION MODEL

Theoretical Model of the Zwitterionic Micellar Solutions

In order to establish direct relations between the molecular behavior of the solutions and the measured permittivity sepctra we present an evaluation of our experimental data in terms of a solution model for oblate ellipsoidal micelles. We restrict ourselves

to a rough outline of the main features and the essential parameters
of the model. A thorough description including different micellar
shapes and an examination of various approximations involved has
been published previously[7].

A sketch of a micelle and the adjacent water molecules is shown
in Figure 4a. The ellipsoidal axes are denoted by a and b (a < b).
The model is constructed by replacing the hydrocarbon core, the
zwitterions, the hydration region of the micelles and the bulk
water phase by continuous dielectrics with respective permittivities.
The matter of all the surfactant molecules (except for the outer
ionic charge) is treated as an ellipsoid consisting of a homogeneous
dielectric of real permittivity $\varepsilon_c \approx 2$. The volume fraction v of
these ellipsoids is given by Equation (4). The contribution arising
from the hydration molecules (those water molecules that are influenced by the solute with respect to their reorientation time τ_H) is
represented by a layer of a continuous dielectric medium with permittivity

$$\varepsilon_H(\nu) = \varepsilon_{\infty w} + \frac{\varepsilon_{ow} - \varepsilon_{\infty w}}{1 + i2\pi\nu\tau_H} , \qquad (7)$$

surrounding the core ellipsoid. $\varepsilon_{\infty w}$, ε_{ow} denote the limiting high-
and low-frequency values of the pure water permittivity and are
known from the literature[18]. The ε_H-layer extends the aggregates
to hydrated micelles the volume fraction v' of which is related to

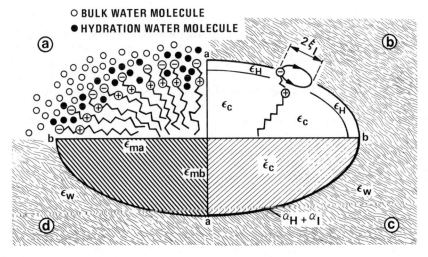

Figure 4.   Sketch of the model for aqueous solutions of ellipsoidal
zwitterionic micelles indicating the replacement of particular
molecular regions by continuous dielectrics.

the number Z_H of hydration molecules per solute molecule by the equation

$$Z_H = \frac{c_{wo}}{c_w} (v' - v).$$ (8)

The artificial separation of the headgroups from the interpenetrating hydration molecules does not seriously affect the dielectric properties[7].

Calculating the contribution to the dielectric polarization due to the zwitterionic headgroups we note that essentially the diffusive motion of the outer ion relative to the inner ion within a zwitterionic group is effective. Thus the motion of the inner ions is neglected, while the outer ions are assumed to perform restricted diffusive motions with mobility u_I along a circular path with radius ξ_I at the surface of the ellipsoid (Figure 4b), which with respect to a harmonically alternating local electrical field directed tangentially to the micellar surface provide the ellipsoidal particles with a surface polarizability density

$$\alpha_I(\nu) = \alpha_I(\infty) + \frac{\Delta\alpha_I}{1 + (2i\pi\nu\tau_I)^{1 - h_I}},$$ (9a)

where

$$\Delta\alpha_I = \frac{n_I g_I}{2kT} (\xi_I e_o)^2$$ (9b)

and

$$\tau_I = \frac{\xi_I^2}{u_I kT},$$ (9c)

k denoting Boltzmann's constant, T the absolute temperature, e_o the elemental charge, and n_I the local average number density of the outer ions. The parameter h_I is introduced in order to allow for a relaxation time distribution. A possible correlation in the orientation of neighboring zwitterions is expressed by the orientation correlation factor g_I. $\alpha_I(\infty)$ stands for very fast distortion polarization mechanisms not to be considered in further detail.

To a very good approximation the dielectric behavior of the thin hydration layer (thickness of the layer h << a) can be represented by a local surface polarizability density

$$\alpha_H(\nu) = h \frac{\varepsilon_H(\nu) - 1}{4\pi},$$ (10)

This procedure requires the core permittivity ε_c to be slightly reduced to[7]

$$\breve{\varepsilon}_c = 1 + \frac{v}{v'} (\varepsilon_c - 1).$$ (11)

The resulting ellipsoid with a volume polarizability density
$(\bar{\varepsilon}_c - 1)/4\pi$ and a surface polarizability density $(\alpha_I + \alpha_H)$, as
sketched in Figure 4c, can be converted into an exactly equivalent
ellipsoid that consists of a homogeneous anisotropic dielectric
medium with the permittivities ε_{ma}, ε_{mb} with respect to electric
fields parallel to the a- or b-axis (Figure 4d). The details of
this conversion are described elsewhere[7].

We now consider the micellar solutions as a dispersion of the
hydrated micelles of volume fraction v' in a homogeneous dielectric
medium with the permittivity of pure undisturbed water

$$\varepsilon_w(\nu) = \varepsilon_{\infty w} + \frac{\varepsilon_{ow} - \varepsilon_{\infty w}}{1 + i2\pi\nu\tau_w} \qquad , \qquad (12)$$

surrounding the micelles (Figure 4), where $\varepsilon_{\infty w}$, ε_{ow}, τ_w are known
quantities[18]. The formula for the comprehensive permittivity $\varepsilon_M(\nu)$
of such a heterogeneous system is a rather complicated function of
ε_w, ε_{ma}, ε_{mb}, v' and a/b[7]. In the limiting case of spherical
particles (a/b = 1, $\varepsilon_{ma} = \varepsilon_{mb} = \varepsilon_m$) it reduces to the much simpler
form of Equation (6), where ε_{sw}^{ML}, ε_{ow}, ε_c have to be replaced by
ε_M, ε_w, ε_m respectively. The relaxation spectral function of the
micellar solutions finally can be written as

$$R_M(\nu) = \varepsilon_M(\varepsilon_w(\nu), \varepsilon_{ma}(\nu), \varepsilon_{mb}(\nu), v', a/b) - i\frac{2\sigma}{\nu} \qquad . \qquad (13)$$

By fitting $R_M(\nu)$ to the measured spectra in the same manner as
described in the previous section optimal values for the following
quantities could be determined (approximate errors in brackets);
a/b($\pm$0.2, for a/b = 1: + 0.2), $Z_H(\pm1)$, $\tau_H(\pm3)$, g_I $\xi_I^2(\pm8\%)$, u_I/ξ_I^2
($\pm$6%) and $h_I(\pm15\%)$. Parameter values and some derived quantities
for approximately 0.2 molar solutions at 25°C are compiled in
Table II.

Axial Ratios

The axial ratios indicate that SPB-, PC- and PDME-micelles
appear to be spherical, while a non-spherical form prevails in HB-
and ABA-systems with (oblate) a/b values up to 3. The differences
in shape seem to be correlated with differences in the viscosity η
of the solutions ($\eta < 2.0$ cP for SPB, PC; $\eta > 50$ cP for HB, ABA
at 25°C[17]). For PDME, however, no viscosity data are available.

As mentioned above, our data only provide information about
deviations from the spherical shape. In addition to the model function
for oblate ellipsoids presented in the previous section we have
derived a similar function for the prolate ellipsoidal form[7] that
in most cases reproduces the measured spectra equally well, although
the prolate axial ratios can be computed with only low accuracy.

Table II. Results for the Parameters of the Model for Micellar Solutions with Surfactant Molarities c = 0.2 mol/ℓ at the Temperature T = 25°C (PDME: c = 0.1 mol/ℓ, T = 32°C).

	Zwitterion	b/a	z_H	τ_H/τ_w	$g_I \xi_I^2$ [Å²]	u_I/ξ_I^2 [$10^6 sg^{-1} Å^{-2}$]	h_I
SPB	$-N^+(CH_3)_2-(CH_2)_3-SO_3^-$	1	13	3.3	53	2.0	0.11
HB	$-N^+(CH_3)_2-CH_2-CO_2^-$	2.5	7	3.0	23	4.3	0.13
ABA	$-N^+H_2-(CH_2)_2-CO_2^-$	3.0	7	3.5	48	1.1	0.24
PC	$-PO_4^--(CH_2)_2-N^+(CH_3)_3$	1	8.5	3.1	47	2.2	0.14
PDME	$-PO_4^--(CH_2)_2-N^+(CH_3)_2 H$	1	5.5	4.0	55	0.84	0.14

	$g_I u_I$ [$10^7 sg^{-1}$]	ξ_I^{max} [Å]	g_I^{min}	u_I^{max} [$10^7 sg^{-1}$]	$u_I^{unbound}$ [$10^7 sg^{-1}$]
SPB	10.6	6	1.5	7.1	$C_3H_7SO_3^-$:24; HSO_3^-:32
HB	9.8	3.8	1.6	6.3	$CH_3CO_2^-$:27; HCO_3^-:36
ABA	5.3	4.6	2.2	2.3	
PC	10.3	5	1.9	5.5	$N^+(CH_3)_4$:29
PDME	4.6	5	2.2	2.1	$N^+(CH_3)_3$ H:30

They are found to be larger than the oblate a/b values. Thus, if
we assume the prolate form for the HB and ABA solutions, the large
axial ratios indicate that the aggregates form long rods. Unless
further data are available to characterize the size and shape of the
zwitterionic micelles at high concentrations, e.g. by using quasielastic light scattering spectroscopy in conjunction with measurements
of scattered light intensity as performed for SDS micellar systems[21],
we will not be able to distinguish between different possible non-
spherical shapes. Since all other parameter values in Table II,
except for a/b, are nearly independent of the assumptions for the
micellar shape, the following presentation will be confined to the
results obtained for oblate ellipsoids.

Hydration Water

In order to discuss the number Z_H of hydration molecules per
solute molecule we refer to experimental Z_H values for amino acids
in the zwitterionic state (Z_H = 10.8 for 4-amino butanoic acid[22])
which are nearly equal to the number of nearest neighboring water
molecules. By comparing the surface area of the surfactants'
zwitterionic headgroups with that of the non-aggregating amino acid
zwitterions, we roughly estimated Z_H values of 15 for PC, 14 for SPB,
10 for HB and 6 for ABA[7]. From this point of view the Z_H values
listed in Table II suggest the headgroups of SPB and ABA to be
nearly as extensively hydrated as if they were completely surrounded
by the solvent, while the hydration at the surface of PC, PDME and
HB micelles appears to be less pronounced as would be the case in
an unbound, non-aggregated state. A more detailed consideration
of the hydration properties of the phospholipids PC and PDME is
given elsewhere[10].

The increase of the reorientation time τ_H of the hydration
water molecules to values 3 to 4 times larger than the reorientation
time τ_w of molecules in pure water (τ_w = 8.25 ps at 25°C) is a common
feature for all investigated micellar systems, indicating that similar
changes of the water structure occur in the region of the zwitterionic
headgroups. An increase in τ_H is a typical characteristic for interaction of water with hydrophobic groups ($-CH_3$, $-CH_2-$[4,23]) and with
charged molecular groups that show tendency to strong hydrogen
bonding ($-CO_2^-$ [22,24]). For comparison we mention τ_H/τ_w values for
aqueous solutions of amino acids: 3.2 for 4-amino butanoic acid,
2.5 for 6-amino hexanoic acid[22].

Headgroups of the Surfactant Molecules

The properties of the headgroups' outer ions are characterized
by the quantities g_I ξ_I^2 and u_I/ξ_I^2 (Table II) involving the three

parameters g_I, u_I, ξ_I of Equation (9). We first look at the products
of these two quantities, $g_I u_I$, which are independent of the a
priori unknown diffusion path radius ξ_I. They fall into a very
narrow range for SPB, HB and PC (Table II). Considering the substantial differences in the chemical structure of the headgroups
this is a remarkable finding. In contrast to this surfactant group
$g_I u_I$ adopts values twice as small for PDME and ABA. The difference
with respect to SPB, HB and PC is probably related to the bonding
of hydrogen instead of methyl groups to the positively charged
nitrogen. Additional hydrogen bonding within the hydrophilic region
of the PDME and ABA micelles may influence the molecular interactions
in a way that leads to an increase of the orientational correlation
between adjacent groups coupled with a decrease of their mobilities.

In order to compute g_I and u_I separately an estimate for ξ_I has
to be introduced. By deriving the maximum anion-cation distance
from known bond lengths and assuming the zwitterions to be oriented
tangentially with respect to the micellar surface, we get maximum
values ξ_I^{max} (Table II). Accordingly a lower limit for the correlation number g_I^{min} and an upper limit for the mobility u_I^{max} can be
determined. From the results shown in Table II we conclude that the
coupling of the diffusive motion of the headgroups' outer ions is
fairly small. A more pronounced cooperativity ($10 \leqslant g_I^{min} \leqslant 100$)
has been reported for similar zwitterions in phospholipid bilayers
where the number density per unit area of headgroups at the (planar)
surfaces is expected to be higher than at the (curved) micellar surfaces

The maximum mobilities u_I^{max} of the outer ions in SPB, HB and PC
micelles are 4 to 6 times smaller than the mobilities of the corresponding unbound ions which were derived from limiting equivalent
conductivity data[26] and are listed in Table II. For ABA and PDME a
decrease in the mobilities by a factor of about 15 is observed.
These results clearly show that the diffusive motion is slowed
down by a considerable amount as soon as the molecular groups are
incorporated into a micellar surface region. If located at a bilayer
rather than a micellar surface, the mobility of the outer ions is
further reduced. For aqueous solutions of dimyristoyl phosphatidyl
choline u_I^{max} values of the order of 0.1×10^7 sg^{-1} are found[9].

Effects of Temperature, Concentration and Solubilization

The temperature dependence of the model parameters was investigated for a 0.2 molar SPB and a 0.4 molar HB solution. It turned
out that the parameters a/b, Z_H, τ_H/τ_w, $g_I \xi_I^2$ and h_I varied by
less than 10% when the temperature was raised from 20°C to 50°C[17].
Our further discussion will be confined to the mobility data. Holding
the ξ_I^{max} values constant we derived activation enthalpies
$\Delta H = 5.6 \pm 0.15$ kcal/mol for SPB and $\Delta H = 4.5 \pm 0.15$ kcal/mol for

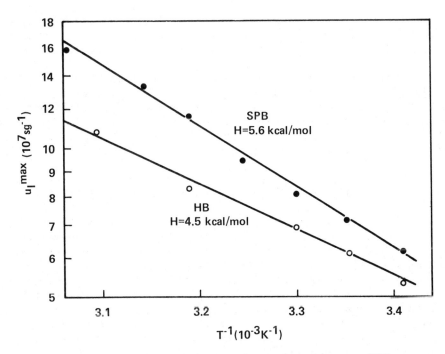

Figure 5. Arrhenius plot of the maximum mobilities u_I^{max} of the headgroups' outer ions in 0.2 molar SPB and 0.4 molar HB solutions.

HB headgroups from an Arrhenius-type plot of the maximal mobilities u_I^{max} (Figure 5). Possible changes of ξ_I with temperature may affect the accuracy of these data. Slightly lower ΔH values are found in the same temperature range for the mobilities of corresponding unbound ions (HSO_3^-:3.5 kcal/mol, $C_2H_5SO_3^-$:4.5 kcal/mol, HCO_2^-: 3.4 kcal/mol, $CH_3CO_2^-$:3.9 kcal/mol). Activation enthalpies of several comparable zwitterionic molecules in aqueous solution derived from relaxation-time measurements are 4.5 kcal/mol for 1 molar β-alanine and 4.0 kcal/mol for 1.5 molar glycine[25]. Apparently there is no substantial difference between the ΔH values of aggregated and non-aggregated zwitterions.

Only small changes occur in the parameter values when the solute concentrations of HB and SPB solutions are varied according to Table I. An increase of the SPB concentration from 0.05 mol/ℓ up to 0.6 mol/ℓ is accompanied by a 10% increase in g_I ξ_I^2, a 20% decrease in u_I/ξ_I^2 and a 20% increase in h_I. This could be explained by small conformational changes of the aggregates. However, within the limits of error no significant deviations from the spherical shape were observed. A decrease in Z_H from 14 for $c < 0.2$ mol/ℓ to 10 at the upper concentration limit is probably associated with

the overlapping of the hydration regions of neighboring micelles.
In fact, the average distance of micelles in the highly concentrated
0.6 molar SPB solution can be roughly estimated to be less than 20 Å.

The solubilization of decanol in the micelles of a 0.4 molar
HB solution results in a drastic growth of the axial ratios of the
(oblate) ellipsoids from a/b = 2.5 (HB without solubilisate) to
a/b = 5.0 (HB with a mole ratio 0.4 of solubilisate), in agreement
with similar observations about solubilization effects on micellar
size and shape in solutions of anionic[27] and cationic[28] surfactants.

Conductivity Contributions with Relaxational Behavior

In our presentation of the dielectric data on the basis of the
model spectral function $R_M(\nu)$ (Equation (13)) we have neglected
the additional relaxation process appearing in the dielectric spectra
of HB and ABA solutions for frequencies below 20 MHz (Figure 2).
In a qualitative way we had attributed this process to conductivity
influences with relaxational behavior. In fact, if the zwitterionic
micelles are considered as non-conducting particles in a conducting
solvent, a dielectric relaxation process referred to as Maxwell-
Wagner effect is to be expected, that reflects the polarization of
the interfacial boundaries in such a heterogeneous system[29]. This
dielectric effect may play an important role in any colloidal solution[1-3,29]. It can be included into our model of micellar solutions
by modifying the $R_M(\nu)$ function in Equation (13) according to

$$R_M(\nu) = \varepsilon_M(\varepsilon_w(\nu) - i\,\frac{2\sigma_w}{\nu}\,,\ \varepsilon_{ma}(\nu),\ \varepsilon_{mb}(\nu),\ v',\ a/b),\qquad (14)$$

where the solvent is characterized by the permittivity ε_w of pure
water and an appropriate conductivity term $2\sigma_w/\nu$ (σ_w = solvent
conductivity). Using this function we were able to describe some
of the low frequency data. However, the requirement that the
relaxation time of the Maxwell-Wagner process must be inversely
proportional to σ_w was not always fulfilled.

Provided that a certain amount of ions in the solution are
adsorbed at the micellar surface, the low frequency behavior can
also be affected by the diffusive motion of counterions within a
shell next to the surface of the aggregates. This motion should
give rise to an additional relaxation process which is suitable
to explain some of our low frequency data. In order
to elucidate the nature of the conductivity contributions several
studies were carried out by systematically varying the amount and
the type of added electrolyte[17]. In the evaluation of these studies
we neglected contributions caused by exchange processes between
monomers and micelles or by the reorientational motions of the

entire micelles which may slightly influence the dielectric properties
below 10 MHz. From the results, which will be published separately,
it appears to be likely that both relaxation mechanisms, the Maxwell-
Wagner effect and the counterion relaxation, contribute to the low
frequency part of our measurements. A similar conclusion was drawn
from dielectric studies of simpler types of colloidal systems, such
as aqueous polystyrene suspensions, where the existence of two
adjacent dispersion/absorption regions at low frequencies could be
verified[30].

The validity of the parameter values for the micellar shape,
the hydration water and the zwitterionic headgroups was not
reduced when the model spectral function $R_M(\nu)$ was modified to
represent the measured permittivity data in the entire frequency
range.

ACKNOWLEDGMENTS

We thank the Deutsche Forschungsgemeinschaft for financial
support. The donation of surfactant samples by Hoechst AG,
Frankfurt/Main, and by Henkel & Cie., Düsseldorf, is gratefully
acknowledged. The numerical calculations were performed on a
computer financed by the Stiftung Volkswagenwerk.

REFERENCES

1.   H. P. Schwan, Proc. IRE, 47, 1841 (1959).
2.   S. Takashima and A. Minakata, Dig. Lit. Dielectr. 1973, 37,
     602 (1975).
3.   G. Schwarz, in "Dielectric and Related Molecular Processes",
     M. Davies, Editor, Specialist Periodical Reports, Vol 1,
     pp. 163-191, The Chemical Society, London, 1972.
4.   U. Kaatze, C. Limberg and R. Pottel, Ber. Bunsenges. Phys.
     Chem., 78, 555 (1974); 78, 561 (1974).
5.   E. A. S. Cavell, J. Colloid Interface Sci., 62, 495 (1977).
6.   R. B. Beard, T. F. McMaster and S. Takashima, J. Colloid
     Interface Sci., 48, 92 (1974).
7.   R. Pottel, U. Kaatze and S. C. Müller, Ber. Bunsenges. Phys.
     Chem., 82, 1086 (1978).
8.   G. Schwarz, J. Phys. Chem. 66, 2636 (1962).
9.   U. Kaatze, R. Henze and R. Pottel, Chem. Phys. Lipids 25,
     149 (1979).
10. U. Kaatze, S. C. Müller and H. Eibl, (1980), Chem. Phys. Lipids,
     submitted for publication.
11. K. W. Hermann, J. Colloid Interface Sci., 22, 352 (1966).
12. P. Molyneux, C. T. Rhodes and J. Swarbrick, Trans. Faraday Soc.,
     61, 1043 (1965).

13. T. Okumura, K. Tajima and J. Sasaki, Bull. Chem. Soc. Jap.,
     47, 1067 (1974).
14. L. Saunders, Biochem. Biophys. Acta, 125, 70 (1966).
15. U. Kaatze, Adv. Molec. Relax. Processes, 7, 71 (1975).
16. K. Giese and O. Göttmann, (1978), unpublished data.
17. S. C. Müller, Doctoral Thesis, Math. Nat. Fak., Univ. Göttingen,
     1978.
18. U. Kaatze and R. Pottel, in "L'Eau et les Systèmes Biologiques",
     A. Alfsen and A. J. Berteaud, Editors, Colloqu. Intern. du
     C.N.R.S., 246, 111 (1976).
19. R. Pottel, K. Giese and U. Kaatze, in "Structure of Water and
     Aqueous Solutions", W. A. P. Luck, Editor, pp. 391-407,
     Verlag Chemie, Weinheim, 1974.
20. C. J. F. Böttcher and P. Bordewijk, "Theory of Electric
     Polarization", Vol. 2, Ch. 15, Elsevier Scient. Publ. Comp.,
     Amsterdam, 1978.
21. N. A. Mazer, M. C. Carey and G. B. Benedek, in "Micellization,
     Solubilization, and Microemulsions", K. L. Mittal, Ed., Vol. 1,
     pp. 359-381, Plenum Press, New York, 1977.
22. R. Pottel, D. Adolph and U. Kaatze, Ber. Bunsenges. Phys. Chem.,
     79, 278 (1975).
23. R. Pottel and U. Kaatze, Ber. Bunsenges. Phys. Chem., 73,
     437 (1969).
24. U. Kaatze, Ber. Bunsenges. Phys. Chem., 77, 447 (1973).
25. J. L. Salefran, Doctoral Thesis, Bordeaux, 1978.
26. Landolt-Börnstein, "Zahlenwerte und Funktionen", Vol. II, 7,
     p. 260, Springer, Berlin, 1960.
27. D. E. Clarke and D. G. Hall, Colloid Polymer Sci., 252,
     153 (1974).
28. N. Kamenka, H. Fabre, M. Chorro and B. Lindmann, J. Chim. Phys.,
     74, 510 (1977).
29. M. Davies, in "Dielectric Properties and Molecular Behaviour",
     N. E. Hill, W. E. Vaughan, A. H. Price, M. Davies, Eds., p. 282,
     Van Nostrand, London, 1969.
30. C. Ballario, A. Bonincontro and C. Cametti, J. Colloid Interface
     Sci., 54, 415 (1976).

MICELLE-MICELLE INTERACTION IN AQUEOUS MEDIA FROM THE SECOND VIRIAL COEFFICIENT

D.K. Chattoraj[1]   K.S.Birdi[2]   and S.U. Dalsager [2]
(1) Department of Biochemistry and Biophysics
Kalyani University, Kalyani, W. Bengal, India
(2) Fysisk-Kemisk Institut, Technical University
of Denmark, Building 206, DK 2800 Lyngby/Denmark

The aggregation of detergents to form micelles in aqueous systems has been of much current interest. However, in order to understand the solution properties one needs to know the solvent-micelle, micelle-micelle and micelle-electrolyte interactions, in systems consisting of water + micelles + electrolyte. A rigorous expression applicable to dilute macromolecule solutions, which takes into account all the factors which would be expected to influence the chemical potential of a solution of macro-ion (or ionic micelles) has been derived by Scatchard:

$$ B = (M_m)^{-2} \left[\frac{Z^2}{4 \cdot m} + \frac{\beta_{MM}}{2} - \frac{(\beta_{MS})^{2} \cdot m}{(4 + 2_{SS} \cdot m)} \right] $$

where B is the second virial coefficient (as determined from membrane osmometry), Z is the charge (equal to the aggregation number of the micelle); where β_{ij} are the derivatives of activity coefficients (f_i), $\beta_{MM}(= \partial \ln f_M / \partial M_m)$

is the micelle-micelle interaction term, $\beta_{SS} (= \partial \ln f_m / \partial m)$ is the electrolyte-solvent interaction term, $\beta_{MS} (= \partial \ln f_{M_m} / \partial m)$ is micelle-electrolyte (counter-ion binding term, m is the electrolyte concentration.

The variation of the second virial coefficient, B, for micellar systems of $C_{12}H_{25}SO_4Na$ and $C_{12}H_{25}N(CH_3)_3Br$,

as a function of added electrolyte has been analyzed in
order to estimate the various interactions in these micellar systems. The classical solution property, i.e., osmotic
pressure, is analyzed for two different ionic detergents
as a function of added electrolyte. The second virial coefficient is found to provide much useful information as
regards the differences between those two systems.

INTRODUCTION

The amphiphiles, such as sodium dodecyl sulphate (NaDDS), dodecyl trimethyl ammonium bromide (DDAB), etc., aggregate to form
micelles in aqueous phase when the concentration of amphiphiles is
over critical micelle concentration (CMC). In order to understand the
solution properties of micellar systems, it is obvious that the
weight average aggregation (N_w) and the number average aggregation
(N_n) need be measured. In current literature, even though a great
many studies on N_w have been reported, very few studies on N_n have
been documented. The light-scattering method has been used in most
cases to determine N_w, while membrane osmometry has been used for
the determination of N_n.[1,2] The second virial coefficient (B) for
the micellar systems, as determined from light-scattering and membrane osmometry has never been extensively analyzed in the current
literature.[2]

However, from the osmotic pressure and light-scattering
experiments, the second virial coefficients (B) of various proteins
and synthetic polymers[4] dissolved in aqueous and non-aqueous media,
have been calculated extensively by various workers. Physico-chemical theories have been developed to interpret the intra-chain, in-
ter-chain and solvent interactions of randomly coiled polymer[3,4,5]
and denatured protein[6] in the liquid medium.

The value of second virial coefficient of rigid and globular
native proteins[3,7] at isoionic pH have been examined in terms of the
excluded volume theory for a polymer. It has recently been shown
that both protein-protein attraction and repulsion effects arising
from the London-van der Waals interactions and the excluded volume
effects are involved in the experimentally evaluated values of the
second virial coefficient of a rigid protein having zero net charge.
At a pH different from the isoelectric point, the second virial
coefficient of the macro-ion is considerably high because of the
Donnan effect, protein-ion and protein-protein interaction effects.
Scatchard[9] has developed mathematical theories to include all these
interactions in the second virial coefficients.

The molecular weights (number average) and second virial coefficients of the ionic and non-ionic and charged micelles have been
recently evaluated from membrane osmometry measurements[2,10-12]. An
attempt will be made in the present paper to understand various types
of interactions which may occur in micellar systems, analogous to the
analysis reported on the data on the molecular weight and second
virial coefficient of a protein.

Second virial coefficient for the non-ionic micelle.

At higher, above CMC, concentrations of a detergent the neutral
amphipathic molecules such as polyoxyethylene nonyl phenol ethers
containing 10 (NPE $_{10}$), 13 (NPE $_{13}$) and 18 (NPE $_{18}$) moles of ethylene
oxide, respectively, are known to aggregate in large numbers and thus
form micelles[10,11]. CMC for these different solutes are closely
related with the chain length, nature of head group of the micelles
and other solution parameters. The (number average) molecular weights
(M_m) and second virial coefficients (B) of these micelles reported
earlier by Birdi[10,11] are quoted in Table I.

Table I. Theoretical Second Virial Coefficient of Non-ionic
         Micelles.[10,11]

Surfact-ant	R in A° (1)	M_m (1)	f/f_o (1)	a/b (oblate)	f_{IS} (2)	$B_e \cdot 10^4$ ml·mol gm^{-2}
NPE $_{10}$	39.5	100,000	1.19	4.0	1.6	1.0
NPE $_{13}$	36.0	69,000	1.20	4.5	1.8	1.8
NPE $_{18}$	38.2	55,000	1.42	7.0	3.0	5.6

(1) Ref. 10 and 11.
(2) Calculated from Equation (1). (Cf. below)

The hydrodynamic (Stokes) radius of each micelle, as determined
earlier from the gel-filtration retention time[10,11], have also been
included in this table along with the frictional ratio f/f_o. From the
values of these ratios, the axial ration a/b (for the oblate shaped)
micelles are calculated, neglecting the hydration effect[3]. These are
also given in Table I.

     Like protein, we shall assume here that the inner core of
the micelle is rigid to a reasonable extent and if the micelle is
spherical in shape with radius R, then the value of the second virial
coefficient (B_e) can be calculated purely on the basis of the
excluded volume effect[3] from Equation (1).

$$B_e = \frac{16 \, \Pi \, N \, R^3}{3 \, M_m^2} \tag{1}$$

Here N is the Avogadro number and M_m is the average molecular weight of the micelle. (Throughout this study we will denote $M_n = M_m$). From recent studies[1,13] it has been shown that like proteins, micelles are non-spherical ellipsoid in shape. The shape of the micelles is not free from controversy (that is prolate or oblate). Non-ionic micelles are recently shown to be oblate-shaped. We shall present our analysis for oblate-shaped micelles. It has been shown that for rigid ellipsoidal particles B_e may be calculated from the equation.[8]

$$B_e = \frac{16 \, \Pi \, N \, R^3}{3 M_m^2} \, f_{IS} \tag{2}$$

where f_{IS} is the correction factor for the non-spherical shape first derived by Isihara[14,15,16]. Isihara has described the mean radius, of the ellipsoidal molecule as:

$$\rho = 2 \, \Pi \, a \, \{ \sqrt{1-e^2} + (\frac{\sin^{-1} e}{e}) \}; \text{ oblate} \tag{3}$$

$$2 \, \Pi \, b \, \{ 1 + \frac{(1-e^2)}{2e} \log(\frac{1+e}{1-e}) \}; \text{ prolate} \tag{4}$$

where the eccentricity, e, is given as:

$$e = \frac{a^2 - b^2}{a^2}, \quad \text{oblate} \tag{5}$$

$$= \frac{b^2 - a^2}{b^2}, \quad \text{prolate} \tag{6}$$

The surface areas, s, of the ellipsoidal molecule is given as:

$$s = 2 \, \Pi \, a^2 \, \{ 1 + (\frac{1-e^2}{2e}) \, \log(\frac{1+e}{1-e}) \}; \text{ oblate} \tag{7}$$

$$= 2 \, \Pi \, ab \, \{ \sqrt{1-e^2} + \frac{\sin^{-1} e}{e} \} \, ; \text{ prolate} \tag{8}$$

The Isihara shape factor, f_{IS}, is equal to unity in the case of spherical molecules, but >1 for non-spherical (i.e. ellipsoidal or cylindrical) molecules. The expression for f_{IS} is thus as follows for ellipsoidal molecules:

$$f_{IS} = \frac{1}{4} + \frac{\rho s}{16 \, \Pi \, v}$$

$$\cong 1 + \frac{1}{15} e^4 + \frac{37}{60} e^6 + \ldots\ldots, \quad e \ll 1 \qquad (9)$$

Values of f_{IS} for oblate shaped micelles calculated for different values of a/b of the micelles have also been included in Table I, along with the theoretical values of B_e for oblate shaped particles calculated with the help of Equation (2).

In the case of several iosionic proteins of various shapes[8], B is found to be always significantly higher than the measured value of the second virial coefficient B. From thermodynamic and other considerations, it has also been shown,

$$B = B_e + B_a \qquad (10)$$

where B_a stands for contribution of the protein-protein attraction in the medium. A glance at Tables I and II will at once indicate that B is always less than B_e so that B_a for the non-ionic micelle is negative.

Table II. Second Virial Coefficients of Non-ionic Micelles (see Table I).[10,11]

Surfactant	$B \cdot 10^4$ (1) ml·mol/gm^2	$-B_a \cdot 10^4$ (= B - B_e)	$a_m \cdot 10^{33}$ $\frac{cm^3 ergs}{molecule^2}$
NPE_{10}	0.36	0.64	44
NPE_{13}	1.2	0.60	19.5
NPE_{18}	1.9	3.70	77

(1) Ref. 10 and 11.

These negative values are presented in Table II for oblate shaped particles. The moleclules of micelles thus formed in the aqueous medium above the CMC are also able to attract each other by net London-van der Waals attraction forces as a result of which B becomes less than B_e. In analogy with the Hamaker theory[17,18] for the attraction between the colloidal particles, we may write

$$B_a = B_a^{11} + B_a^{22} - B_a^{12} \tag{11}$$

where B_a^{11} and B_a^{22} are the micelle-micelle and solvent-solvent interactions; B_a^{12} is the micelle-solvent interaction which reduces the inter-micellar attraction. Our results indicate that $B_a^{11} + B_a^{22}$ is numerically greater than B_a^{12}. For a real gas, the virial equation may also be derived in which the second virial coefficient becomes equal to $(b_v - \frac{a_v}{RT})$ where a_v and b_v are van der Waals attraction and co-volume constants. Values of a_v for straight chain hydrocarbons C_3H_8 to $C_{26}H_{54}$ are $0.26 \cdot 10^{-34}$ to $7.3 \cdot 10^{-34}$ ergs-cm^3/molecule^2, respectively. It has already been shown from the thermodynamic standpoint[8] that B_a for isoionic protein may be taken to be equal to a_m/RT, where a_m is the attractive constant of the macromolecule (equal to RTB_a). Values of a_m for micelles, given in Table II, indicate that the order of the attraction constant for proteins and the micelles are of the same magnitude. In gases B_a^{22} and B_a^{12} terms are absent. Further, in the case of gases, a_v is equal to $\bar{V}^2(\partial E/\partial \bar{V})_T$, where E and $\bar{V}$ are the internal energies and volume per mole of gas. In the case of micelles and proteins[8], a_m is equal to $\bar{V}^2(\partial G/\partial \bar{V})_T$ so that a_m can only be compared with a_v after entropy correction. It is of considerable interest to note that a_m for a globular protein is of the same order of magnitude as that of micelles. Both proteins and micelles have comparable size and asymmetric shape. The thermodynamic treatment for such attraction has already been discussed.[8]

Donnan effect in the charged micelles.

In the case of the isoionic proteins and non-ionic micelles, we thus find that the experimentally determined second virial coefficient involves terms containing the respulsive and attractive effects between the colloidal particles as a result of the excluded volume and van der Waals cohesional interactions, respectively. When the pH has been shifted far from the iso-ionic pH, the protein molecule acquires positive or negative charge Z. The second virial coefficient of the charged protein as measured from the osmotic pressure has been found to be significantly higher than that measured at isoionic pH. Scatchard[9] has shown that this high value of B arises mostly from the Donnan effect as a result of the existence of net charge of the macromolecule of higher or lower pH. From theoretical analysis, it may be shown[9] that

$$B_{Don} = \frac{1000 \, v_1}{M_m^2} \frac{z^2}{4m} \tag{12}$$

where Z and M_m are the net charge and molecular weight of the macro-
ions, respectively. In the case of charged micelles, $Z=N_m$. The
partial specific volume, v_1, of the solvent may be taken as unity
($v_1 \sim 1$), and the molal concentration m of the neutral salt added
before the experiment may be taken to be equal to its molar concentration, since the concentration of the salt solution is not too
high.

From the osmotic pressure measurements, the molecular weights
(M_m), (number average) aggregation number (N_m) and second virial
coefficient (B) of micelles formed by cationic and anionic detergents
have been measured by Birdi and coworkers[2,12] quite recently. In
Tables III and IV, values of these measured parameters for DDAB and
NaDDS micelles for different salt concentrations m are given for
further analysis. The variation of B with added electrolyte (NaCl)
concentration for NaDDS (and preliminary data for $C_{11}H_{23}SO_4Na$) are
given in Figure I. It should be noted that M_m and N_m for DDAB (cationic) detergent do not change much with increase of m. On the other
hand, in the case of NaDDS (ionic) micelles, M_m and N_m increase
significantly with increase of the concentration of the neutral salt
of the medium.

It is to be noted that the values of B for the charged micelles
are relatively high in magnitude as compared to that of the non-ionic
micelles. We will now examine whether this high value of B arises
solely due to the Donnan effect arising from the excess of accumulation of inorganic ions in the chamber containing the macroions at
osmotic equilibrium. If a molecular unit of a micelle contains N_m
number of monomers each containing unit cationic or anionic head
group, then the net charge Z of the micelle will be equal to N_m.
Inserting the values of Z ($=N_m$), M_m and m in Equation (12), B_{Don} has
been calculated for each system. Values of B_{Don} thus given in Table
III are found to be higher than B by 30 to 100 fold, depending upon
the values of N_m and m. Donnan effect alone therefore is unable to
account for the measured value of B which in all probability contains
terms containing other types of micellar interactions.

Interactions between macro-ions and small ions.
From detailed mathematical analysis, Scatchard[9] has shown that
the inorganic ions accumulated near a charged macro-ion may form an
ion-atmosphere due to the electrostatic effect whose contribution to
the second virial coefficient may be calculated from the equation

Table III. Virial Coefficients of NaDDS Micelles at 40°C

Salt conc. (NaCl, mol/ℓ)	$B \cdot 10^4$ $\frac{ml \cdot mol}{gm^2}$	$B_{Don} \cdot 10^4$ $\frac{ml \cdot mol}{gm^2}$	$(B-B_{Don}) \cdot 10^4$ $\frac{ml \cdot mol}{gm^2}$	$B_{ms} \cdot 10^4$ $\frac{ml \cdot mol}{gm^2}$	$B_{ms}^c \cdot 10^4$ $\frac{ml \cdot mol}{gm^2}$	$B_{mm} \cdot 10^4$ $\frac{ml \cdot mol}{gm^2}$	N_m	M_m
0.10	4.82	301	−296	3480	16	−280	103	29800
0.20	2.92	150	−148	1510	7	−140	112	32200
0.30	1.85	100	−98	853	3.6	−95	117	33800
0.40	0.85	75	−74	66	2.5	−72	129	37400
0.50	0	60	−60	522	2.6	−58	138	39700
0.55	−0.53	55	−56	560	2.4	−53	152	43900
0.60	−0.96	50	−51	740	2.45	−49	183	52800
.65	−1.0	46			2.8	−44	256	
0.7	.56	43	−44	1220	3.1	−40	346	99800
0.75	−0.53	40	−39	2940	3.3	−37	425	122400
.8	0	38			4.4	−33	700	201600

Table IV. Second Virial Coefficients of DDAB Micelles at 40°C.

Salt conc. (KBr, mol/ℓ)	$B \cdot 10^4$ $\frac{ml \cdot mol}{gm^2}$	$B_{Don} \cdot 10^4$ $\frac{ml \cdot mol}{gm^2}$	$B_{ms} \cdot 10^4$ $\frac{ml \cdot mol}{gm^2}$	$B_{ms}^c \cdot 10^4$ $\frac{ml \cdot mol}{gm^2}$	$B_{mm} \cdot 10^4$ $\frac{ml \cdot mol}{gm^2}$	N_m	M_m
0.10	5.48	262	1940	14.8	−242	86	26500
0.30	2.15	87	312	2.94	−82.2	84	25900
0.50	1.56	52	132	1.4	−49.2	87	26800
0.90	1.07	29	41	0.56	−27.4	88	27200

$$B_{ms} = - \frac{1000 \ v_1 \ \beta^2_{ms} \ m}{M^2_m \ (4 + 2\beta_{ss} \ m)} \qquad (13)$$

Here β_{ss} stands for the rate of change of the activity coefficient (γ_s) with concentration of neutral salt in the medium.

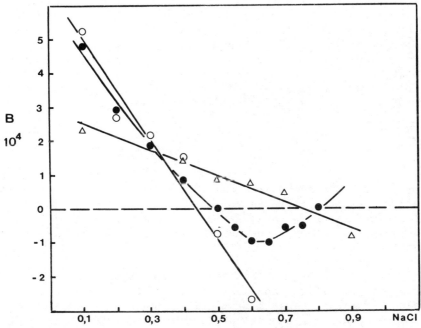

Figure 1. Plot of second virial coefficient, B, versus number average aggregation number, N_n, for various alkyl sulphates. Na; $C_{11}H_{23}SO_4Na$ at 40°C ($\triangle$); $C_{12}H_{25}SO_4Na$ (NaDDS) at 30°C ($\circ$) and 40°C ($\bullet$).

Using the Debye-Hückel theory of electrolytes, it may be shown that

$$\beta_{ss} = 2(\partial \ln\gamma_s/\partial m = - \frac{0.586}{\sqrt{m}(1+1.55\sqrt{m})^2} + 0.251 + 0.0424m \quad (14)$$

where $\ln\gamma_s = - \frac{1.172\sqrt{m}}{1+1.55\sqrt{m}} + 0.251 \ m + 0.212 \ m^2$. Scatchard[9] has defined

β_{ms} as coefficient related to the electrostatic interaction of inorganic ions with macro-ions of net change Z. Such interaction may

lead to the formation of the diffuse ion atmosphere around the
charged macro-ion and following the Debye-Huckel treatment, value
of β_{ms} has been calculated by Scatchard using Equation (15)

$$\beta_{ms} = - \frac{1.17(Z^2)}{\sqrt{m}(1=0.328R_m\sqrt{m})^2} \qquad (15)$$

Here R_m is the effective radius of the macro-ion with correction for
the asymmetry effect. In the case of micelles, the value of R_m is
calculated as follows. The interior volume, V_m (or the hydrophobic
core) of a micelle[13] may be taken to be equal to $(N (27.4+26.9n_c))$
where n_c stands for the number of carbon atoms in the alkyl chain of
the detergent molecule. The volume of each polar cationic or anionic
head group can be assumed as $50A°^3$. The radius R_m of the equivalent
sphere of a micelle may be calculated from the relation

$$R_m = [\frac{3\{(27.4+26.9n_c) + 50\}N_m}{4\Pi}]^{1/3} \qquad (A°) \qquad (16)$$

β_{ms} for NaDDS and DDAB micelles may be calculated by Equation
(15) and using appropriate values of Z, R_m and m. Using the
calculated values of β_{ms} and β_{ss} in Equation (13), B_{ms} for NaDDS and
DDAB micelles have been computed for several concentrations of the
neutral salts.

In calculating B_{ms}, it has been assumed that the electric
potential of the diffuse double layer at a given salt concentration
originates from the charge Z of micelle. However, it is well known
that the net charge of a micelle is considerably less than Z due to
the extensive binding of the counter-ions. If f_b stands for the
fraction of the charged sites remaining bound with counter-ions, then
the net charge Z_{net} responsible for the generation of potential in
the diffuse double layer is equal to $(1-f_b)Z$. For micelles, the
fractions of the charged sites bound with counter-ions vary between
0.7 to 0.8[2] irrespective of the concentration of the neutral salt of
the medium so that f_b may be take to be equal to 0.75 on the
average. We can, therefore, calculate Z_{net} for each value of Z (equal
to N_m). Replacing Z by Z_{net} in Equation (15), corrected values of B_{ms}^c
may be computed from Equation (13) with consideration of the ion
binding effect. A similar approach for the correction for the ion
binding effect has been used[20] in evaluating the electrical free
energy change for the charged monolayer forming Stern-Gouy type of
composite double layer. These values for NaDDS and DDAB micelles are
included in Tables III and IV.

From close examination of the data presented in Tables III and
IV, we note that values of $B_{Don}-B_{ms}^c$ are still considerably larger

than the measured value of B at a given salt concentration. This therefore points out that some other contributions must be included in the second virial coefficient besides those originating from the Donnan effect and electrostatic interaction between charged micelle and small inorganic ion.

Micelle-micelle interactions.

From the thermodynamic analysis of the second virial coefficient of a macro-ion, Scatchard[3,9] has shown that

$$B = \frac{1000 \, v_1 \, z^2}{M_m^2} \left[\frac{z^2}{4m} + \frac{\beta_{mm}}{2} - \frac{\beta_{ms}^2 \, m}{(4+2\beta_{ss} m)} \right]$$

$$= B_{Don} + B_{mm} - B_{ms} \qquad (17)$$

or $\quad B_{mm} = B - B_{Don} + B_{ms} \qquad (18)$

Here B_{mm} is the contribution of the macro-ion/macro-ion interaction to the second virial coefficient which is equal to half the coefficient β_{mm} considered by Scatchard[9]. Since B, B_{Don} and B_{ms} for NaDDS and DDAB micelles are known, values of B_{mm} may be computed with the help of Equation (18). These are included in Tables III and IV.

We may now analyze the second virial coefficient of the micelle more objectively in terms of various types of interactions occurring in the solution medium. If the micelle is non-ionic, then at infinite dilution (Π/c) of the micellar system will be equal to (RT/M_m) in agreement with van't Hoff law indicating ideal colligative properties of the macromolecules in solution. At higher concentrations, the micelles may repel each other due to the excluded volume effect and attract each other due to the cohesional effect. Experimental measured values of B include both these effects.

In the case of ionic micelles, the macro-ions are highly charged so that inorganic ions will be drawn in excess close to the micelles due to the Donnan effect. Even under this condition, (Π/c) becomes equal to (RT/M_m) at infinite dilution so that the molecular weight of the micelles may be calculated from the graphical extrapolation. The Donnan effect for the excess accumulation of the inorganic ions is included in the B_{Don} term of Equations (12) and (17). From relation (12) it is clear that the Donnan effect is low when X is low or m is high. Unlike proteins, Z for micelles are extremely large so that B_{Don} presented in Tables III and IV are not negligible even when m is close to one molar.

From both Tables III and IV, we note that B is considerably lower than B_{Don}. There are two reasons for such difference which have already been pointed out in earlier sections. The inorganic

counter-ions accumulated in excess around the charged macro-ions
may partly remain bound with the charged sites of the micelle forming
ion-pairs due to the strong electrostatic attraction whereby the
fixed part of the double layer is formed. The rest of the counterions along with co-ions around the charged micelles will form the
diffuse double layer following the Poisson-Boltzmann distribution
principle. All these ionic interactions are included in the B_{ms}
term in Equations (13) and (17). For DDAB micelle, B_{ms} is also
considerably less than B_{Don} which means that the Donnan effect to
the second virial coefficient is reduced only to a small extent
by the formation of the fixed and diffuse double layer surrounding
ionic micelle. It also appears from Table IV as well as from Equation
(18) that the charged micelles surrounded by the ion atmosphere may
interact with each other whereby the Donnan effect on the virial coefficient will be further reduced to a larger extent. B_{mm} thus consisting of micelle-micelle interaction is negative. The charged micelles may interact with each other due to the penetration of the
double layer. With increase of the salt concentration, the potential
of the electrical double layer is decreased. B_{mm} and B_{ms} for DDAB micelles also decrease with increase of the ionic strength of the medium as a result of the decrease of the potential in the diffuse double
layer. It also appears that besides electrostatic interactions, B_{mm}
also includes B_e and B_a terms discussed earler for non-ionic micelles.
These contributions may or may not be very significant. Further, this
term may also be related to the micellar hydration which is grossly
affected by the concentration of the neutral salt in the medium.

It should also be noted from the table that the aggregation
number (N_m) of DDAB micelles are more or less independent of the
ionic strength. We can then assume that the surface potential in the
diffuse double layer decreases with increase of ionic strength of the
medium during which the surface charge density depending on N_m
remains constant. Since ion/macro-ion and macro-ion/macro-ion
interactions under this situation depend on the diffuse double layer
potential, B_{mm} and B_{ms} are also found in Table IV to decrease with
increase of the ionic strength of the medium.

For NaDDS micelles, however, N_m increases continuously from 100
to 700 with increase of ionic strength from 0.1 to 0.8. From 0.1 to
0.2, such increase is small so that the surface potential and hence
B_{mm} and B_{ms} still decrease in this range of concentration with
increase of ionic strength of the medium. However, beyond m equal to
0.4, sharp increase of N_w and the charge density leads to the considerable increase in the surface potential. This increase may also
be enhanced further by the change of shape of the micelle from sphere
to ellipsoid. This increase of potential must be so high that it is
not compensated by the extent of its decrease due to the increase of
m. Beyond 0.4 value of m, therefore, the surface potential and hence
B_{mm} and B_{ms} increase because of the net increase of the surface

potential with increase of the salt concentration of the medium. We always find, Table III, $-(B_{mm}-B_{ms})$ to be slightly less in magnitude than B_{Don} so that B, according to Equation (17), is always small but positive. On the other hand, similar values of $B_{mm}-B_{ms}$ and B_{Don}, respectively, indicate that the magnitude of the former is greater than the latter when m is greater than 0.5 so that B becomes negative. The reason for this behaviour is related to the enormous increase of charge (or the aggregation number) for NaDDS micelle at salt concentrations higher than 0.5. Below m equal to 0.5, however, $B_{mm}-B_{ms}$ is lower than B_{Don} so that B remains positive. From all these, it appears that mignitude of B_{Don}, B_{mm} and B_{ms} are controlling factors in determining the sign and magnitude of B.

Second virial coefficient of micelles in n-Propanol-H_2O mixtures.

The value and sign of measured second virial coefficient B is determined by the magnitudes of B_{Don}, B_{mm} and B_{ms} (Equation (17)). The micellar systems of NaDDS, CTAB (cetyl trimethyl ammonium bromide) and NaL (sodium laurate) were studied in varying concentration of added n-propanol. The variation B versus added propanol concentration is given in Table V.

Table V. Second Virial Coefficients of NaDDS, CTAB and NaL as a Function of n-Propanol Concentration[12].

		n-Propanol (mol/kg)				
System		0	0.333	0.832	1.664	2.33
NaDDS	$B(\frac{ml\cdot mol}{gm^2})$	7.8	9.6	1.2	-1.9	-39.5
	$B_{Don}(\frac{ml\cdot mol}{gm^2})$	1005	1005	1005	1005	1005
CTAB	$B(\frac{ml\cdot mol}{gm^2})$	3.8	-	1.6	-7.3	-29.0
	$B_{Don}(\frac{ml\cdot mol}{gm^2})$	625	-	625	625	625
NaL	$B(\frac{ml\cdot mol}{gm^2})$	34.7	22.9	7.5	-43	-58
	$B_{Don}(\frac{ml\cdot mol}{gm^2})$	1691	1691	1691	1691	1691

It is seen that B is positive in low propanol concentration and
negative when propanol concentration is greater than about 0.9 mol/L.
This indicates that the values of the terms B_{Don}, B_{mm} and B_{ms} change
in magnitude, such that

$$B_{Don} + B_{mm} > B_{ms} \quad , \quad \text{at propanol concentration} < 0.9 \text{ mol/L}$$

$$B_{Don} + B_{mm} < B_{ms} \quad , \quad \text{at propanol concentration} > 0.9 \text{ mol/L}$$

Since the propanol concentration at which $B \sim 0$ is the same in all the
different systems, it indicates that the effect of added propanol on
the terms B_{mm} and B_{ms} arises from similar interactions.

The data of Table V are clearly showing that the term B_{Don}, even
though it remains large in value, is compensated by B_{ms} and B_{mm}. The
reason B_{Don} is constant for constant salt concentration (m = 0.03
mol/L) arises from the fact that area/charge on the surface of
micelle is constant.

However, it is worth noticing that the magnitudes of negative B
values are very large at high propanol concentrations. Further,
studies of micellar systems are needed before these data can be extensively analyzed.

Comparison of second virial coefficient and instrinsic viscosity of ionic micelles.

In the following, we will give some preliminary data on NaDDS
micelles, which allow a description of the second virial coefficient
and the hydrodynamic properties of the micellar systems. It has been
shown that in good solvents for sufficiently large macro-molecules
the ratio: $\dfrac{B \, M_m}{|\eta|} \to 1.6$. This relation has been found to be valid for
various polymer systems (such as polystyrene, poly(vinyl acetate)
etc.). However, the NaDDS data for $\dfrac{B \, M_m}{|\eta|}$ versus M_m (plots not given)
indicate that in systems of charged macromolecules this relation is
not valid. Further data are necessary before a more thorough analysis
can be given about the relation between B and $|\eta|$. The plots of B and
$|\eta|$ versus added electrolyte concentration, m, as given in Figure 2
indicate that the region where both B and $|\eta|$ begin to deviate from
one kind of interaction to another occurs around m$\sim$0.5 mol/L. This
region, we will suggest, is where spherical micelles (i.e. m<0.5
mol/L) are being transformed into ellipsoidal micelles (i.e. m>0.5
mol/L). Since both B and $|\eta|$ are independently determined experimental
quantities it is obvious that such correlation as given in Figure 2
confirms the discussion given on the analysis of B in the earlier
sections of this report.

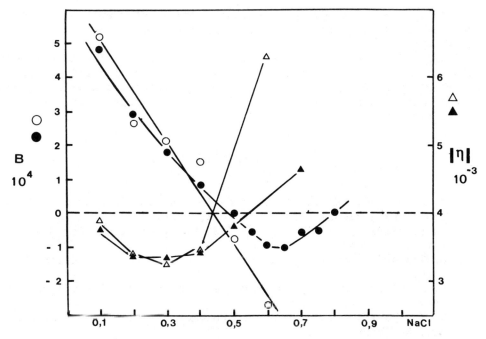

Figure 2. Variation of second virial coefficient, B, and intrinsic viscosity, $|\eta|$, as a function of added electrolyte (NaCl) concentration: B at 30°C (○); at 40°C (●): $|\eta|$ at 30°C (△); at 40° C (▲).

CONCLUSION

The purpose of this study was to analyze the second virial coefficient, B, as determined from osmotic pressure measurement of NaDDS and DDAB. The magnitude and sign of B is determined by various interactions as given in Equation (17)

$$B = B_{Don} + B_{mm} - B_{ms} \qquad (17)$$

It is obvious that it is not easy to analyze such expression which contains contributions from different parameters. However, the systematic research, which is being undertaken in this laboratory, is planned in such a way that the magnitudes of individual contributions can be estimated quantitatively. The data analyzed above show that: (i) in systems where addition of electrolytes gives rise to an appreciable increase in aggregation number, the value of B becomes negative (i.e. for NaDDS).

(ii) in systems where aggregation number does not change with the addition of electrolyte (i.e. for DDAB) the value of B decreases to almost zero.

(iii) B_{Don} is much larger than B for ionic micelles. The calculated value of B_{ms} is approximately of the same 'absolute' magnitude as B. In other words, $B_{Don} \sim B_{mm}$. However, before further analysis can be given, more data are needed, and this is under progress in this laboratory.

REFERENCES

1. K. L. Mittal, Editor, "Micellization, Solubilization and Micro-emulsions", Plenum Press, New York, 1977.
2. K. S. Birdi, S. U. Dalsager and S. Backlund, Trans Faraday Soc., (1980) in press.
3. C. Tanford, "Physical Chemistry of Macromolecules", Wiley, New York, 1961.
4. P. J. Flory, "Principles of Polymer Chemistry", Cornell University Press, Ithaca, 1953.
5. H. Yamakaya, "Modern Theory of Polymer Solutions", Harper and Row, New York, 1971.
6. S. Lapanje and C. Tanford, J. Amer. Chem. Soc., 89, 5030 (1967).
7. H. B. Bull and K. Breese, Arch. Biochem. Biophys., 149, 164 (1972).
8. D. K. Chattoraj and R. Chatterjee, J. Colloid Interface Sci., 54, 364 (1976).
9. G. Scatchard, J. Amer. Soc., 68, 2315 (1946).
10. K. S. Birdi, Koll. Z. u. Z. Polymere, 250, 731 (1972).
11. K. S. Birdi, Koll. Z. u. Z. Polymere, 252, 551 (1974).
12. K. S. Birdi, S. Backlund, K. Sørensen, T. Krag and S. U. Dalsager, J. Colloid Interface Sci., 66, 118 (1978).
13. C. Tanford, J. Phys. Chem., 76, 3020 (1972).
14. A. Isihara, J. Chem. Phys., 18, 1446 (1950).
15. A. Isihara and T. Hayashida, J. Phys. Soc., Japan 6, 40 (1951).
16. A. Isihara and T. Hayashida, J. Phys. Soc., Japan 6, 46 (1951).
17. H. C. Hamakar, Physica 4, 1058 (1937).
18. E. J. Verwey and J. Th. G. Overbeek, "Theory of the Stability of Lyophobic Colloids", p. 103, Elsevier, Amsterdam, 1948.
19. D. K. Chattoraj and A. K. Chatterjee, J. Colloid Interface Sci., 21, 159 (1966).
20. R. P. Pal and D. K. Chattoraj, J. Colloid Interface Sci., 58, 46 (1975).
21. S. U. Dalsager, (Licentiat) Thesis, 1980, Technical University of Denmark, Denmark.

INTERACTION OF CETYLTRIMETHYLAMMONIUM BROMIDE WITH SODIUM DODECYLSULFATE IN ELECTROLYTE AND NONELECTROLYTE ENVIRONMENTS

A. B. Mandal and S. P. Moulik

Department of Chemistry, Jadavpur University

Calcutta 700032, India

Results of interaction between cetyltrimethyl-ammonium bromide(CTAB) and sodium dodecylsulfate(SDS) at levels below and above their critical micelle concentrations(CMCs) in aqueous medium and in the presence of additives like NaCl, glucose, urea, p-tert-alkyl-phenoxypolyoxyethyleneether(Triton X 100), polyoxy-ethylenesorbitanmonolaurate(Tween 20), polyoxyethyl-enesorbitanmonooleate(Tween 80) and polyethyleneglycol (M.W. 600, PEG 600) are presented. Above certain con-centrations, the product of formation (the complex, $CTA^{+}...DS^{-}$) became insoluble. The formation of the precipitate could be greatly influenced by the additives. Both NaCl and urea decreased the solu-bility, whereas glucose increased it. The effects of the nonionic surfactants TX 100, Tween 20 and Tween 80 showed some peculiarities when SDS was taken below and above its CMC in solutions containing both CTAB and nonionics above their CMCs. Below the CMC of SDS, TX 100 decreased the solubility while Tweens and PEG increased it. Above the CMCs of all the surfactants, TX 100 showed more stabilization of the complex than the Tweens and PEG. The solubility products, activity coefficients, thermodynamic parameters of the complex and the ternary phase diagrams of CTAB-SDS-Tweens are presented. These are expected to offer a greater per-spective of the physicochemical aspects of interactions of large oppositely charged ions in the nonmicellar and micellar states in electrolyte and nonelectrolyte environ-ments.

521

INTRODUCTION

In aqueous solutions, two or more surfactants under suitable conditions may form mixed micelles. The formation of mixed micelle is easier when the surfactant ions bear similar charges or they are either mixtures of ionic and nonionic types or of only nonionic types. When two oppositely charged surfactant ions interact, normally precipitation takes place at more or less equal proportions of the two; when any one of them is in excess, solubilization in the micelles of the prevailing component may prevent the formation of a separate phase or precipitate[1]. This may also be true for a mixture of several surfactants when one of them is in large excess. While investigations on mixed micelles constituted of surfactants having the same ionic charge types and on mixtures of ionics and nonionics have been the interests of surface chemists[2-5], interactions of oppositely charged compounds have been rarely studied[6,7]. Such a study with large ions of opposite charges have considerable promise in the field of coacervation[8].

Our recent interests have been in the properties of nonionic surfactants like Triton X 100 (TX100), Tween 20 and Tween 80. TX 100 is widely used in biological work, e.g., separation of proteins from cell membranes[9,10], enzyme substitute for phospholipid metabolism[11,12], solubilization of erythrocytes, mitochondria, viruses and liposomes, etc.[13-18]. An extraction procedure based on solubilization in TX 100 has been proposed for the estimation of vitamin A in natural products[19]. The nonionic surfactants, Tween 20 and Tween 80 are extensively used for the enhancement of the gastrointestinal absorption of steroids[20,21a]. The use of different Tweens in the same prescription increases the total solubilization power owing to the formation of mixed micelles[21b]. In a recent publication[22], we have characterized the TX 100 micelles in aqueous medium in the absence and presence of different additives. We have also studied[23] the interactions of a cationic detergent (CTAB) and an anionic detergent (SDS) with TX 100 and have concluded that mixed micelles are formed preferably through the intake of the ionic detergents by the TX 100 micelles; the reverse process is not thermodynamically favored.

In the present paper, results of the interaction of two oppositely charged surfactants, CTAB and SDS, below and above their critical micelle concentrations are presented. Effects of different environments on the solubility of the product resulting from the addition of NaCl, glucose, urea, polyethyleneglycol, TX 100, Tween 20 and Tween 80 will be described. This will help explain the features of interactions of large oppositely charged ions and the versatile actions of TX 100 and the Tweens to induce solubilization through mixed micelle formation, a phenomenon important in chemical, industrial, biochemical and pharmaceutical areas[24,25].

EXPERIMENTAL

Materials and Method

For the grade, purity and characteristics of the surfactants, we refer to our earlier works[26,27]. The polyethylene glycol was a pure grade material of BDH (British Drug House) with an average molecular weight 600 and an average number of ethyleneoxide groups of 13. The head group of TX 100 on the average contained 9.5 oxyethylene units. Tween 20 and Tween 80 were also pure grade materials of BDH, each containing 20 oxyethylene units. The critical micelle concentrations of these matereals were checked by surface tension method (CMC Tween 20 = 0.05 mM; CMC Tween 80 = 0.01 mM) and agreed closely with literature value[28]. NaCl, urea and glucose were BDH analar grade compounds. Doubly distilled conductivity water of specific conductance, 1.5×10^{-6} mho cm^{-1} at 25°C, was used as the solvent.

Conductance measurements were taken in an ELICO conductivity bridge made in Hyderabad, India. A dip type cell of cell constant 1.0 cm^{-1} was used. The uncertainty in the conductance measurements was within ± 0.5%. Measurements were made at 30 ± 0.02°C if not otherwise stated.

Absorbance measurements were taken in a Perkin Elmer digital uv-visible spectrophotometer in cuvetts of 1 cm path length.

Solutions having different concentrations of CTAB and mixtures of CTAB and the nonionic surfactants or the additives were prepared and thermostated for 30 mins. Thermostated solution of SDS (taken in the same media as for CTAB) were progressively added. After each addition of SDS, solutions were mixed thoroughly with a magnetic stirrer placed inside the container. After thermal equilibrium had been regained, the conductance or absorbance of the mixture was measured. The effect of dilution was avoided by using SDS at a concentration nearly 100 times that of CTAB and by adding the former to the latter dropwise from a micro burette. The concentration of SDS at the point of maximum solubility (the turbidity point) was determined by plotting conductance against concentration of SDS. There always was a distinct break at the point of phase separation. The same course was followed in measuring the absorbance at a visible wavelength (430 nm). A similar break in the absorbance-concentration curve was noticed at the same stage of addition. In most of the cases, the conductance method was used. In a few cases, where considerable salt was added, this method was insensitive and the optical method was followed.

RESULTS

The essential part of the experimentation was to register the turbidity point when SDS was added to a fixed concentration of CTAB in the absence and presence of various additives. Some typical results are shown in the Figures 1 and 2.

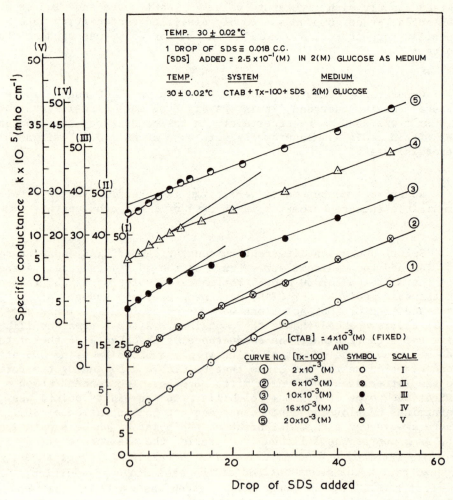

Figure 1. Conductometric determination of the solubility points of the complex in presence of changing TX 100 in 2M glucose medium.

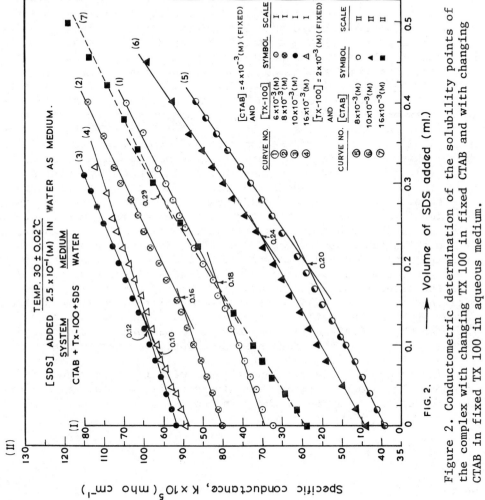

FIG. 2.

Figure 2. Conductometric determination of the solubility points of the complex with changing TX 100 in fixed CTAB and with changing CTAB in fixed TX 100 in aqueous medium.

Distinct breaks were observed when conductance was followed with the addition of SDS. A 1:1 complex salt of CTAB and SDS was considered on the basis of the interactions of large oppositely charged ions reported earlier[6],[ ].

The formation of turbidity in a CTAB solution below its CMC with the addition of SDS (also below its CMC) can be visualized as a solubility product exceeding phenomenon[6]. Such a point would obviously depend on the environments prevailing. Addition of salts and other additives should have significant effects. In Figure 3, turbidity points of such a titration run at different levels of CTAB has yielded a break at a concentration 70 mM, almost the CMC of the compound. The log SDS (log C_i) plot against square root of the ionic strength (II) of the system also yielded a straight line showing a break at 90mM close to the CMC (the reported literature values range between 60 - 100 mM). Regression analysis of the first linear portion of the plot gave an intercept -4.5 ± 0.03. The thermodynamic solubility product of the complex $CTA^+...DS^-$ was thus 1×10^{-9}. The breaking point signified that the interaction between the two oppositely charged surfactant ions has a different complexation above the CMC. It also suggested that SDS could be used to measure the CMC of CTAB. Fixing the concentration of CTAB at its CMC, the addition of SDS caused initial turbidity due to the formation of the complex, which increased in quantity and subsequently got dissolved at concentration close to the CMC of SDS. Since the complex phase (precipitate) could not be destroyed by the low dilution occured in the system, the disappearance of it indicates dissolution of CTAB into the micelles of SDS (the CMC of SDS is approximately 10 times more than the CMC of CTAB; besides, premicellar association of the former may start solubilizing the latter at lower concentrations than the CMC). CTAB could thus be used to measure the CMC of SDS. A detailed study of the above phenomena would be instructive.

In Figure 3, the variation of log C_i with $1^{\frac{1}{2}}$ of the added NaCl has been also shown. For an uni-univalent electrolyte, the solubility product, L_s is given by the relation,

$$L_s = (C_i^\pm)^2 (\gamma_i^\pm)^2 = (C_o^\pm)^2 (\gamma_o^\pm)^2 \qquad (1),$$

where $C_o^\pm$, $C_i^\pm$, $\gamma_o^\pm$ and $\gamma_i^\pm$ are the mean ionic concentrations and the mean ionic activity coefficients without and with the addition of salt respectively.

Equation (1) can be transformed into

$$\log C_i = \log (C_o^\pm \gamma_o^\pm) - \log \gamma_i^\pm \qquad (2).$$

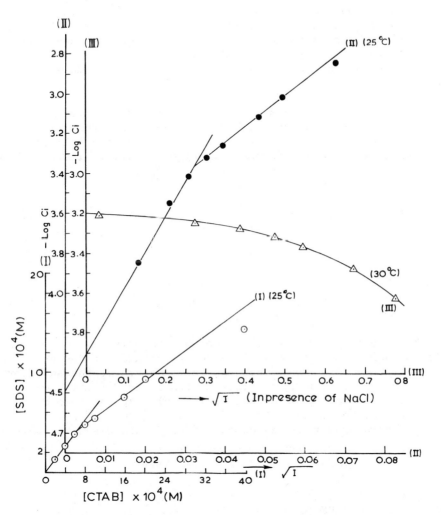

Figure 3. Results of titration of CTAB with SDS in the absence and presence of external salt. Scale I: Concentration of SDS required to generate turbidity points at various concentrations of CTAB. Scale II: Plot of -log C_i versus $I^{\frac{1}{2}}$ in the absence of external electrolyte. Scale III: Plot of -log C_i versus $I^{\frac{1}{2}}$ in the presence of NaCl

Since $\gamma_i^{\pm}$ is a function of the ionic strength(I), a plot of $\log C_i$ versus $I^{\frac{1}{2}}$ should be linear at low ionic strengths. Where no external salt was added, the ionic strength was contributed by the ions of the CTAB and SDS in the solution. At relatively large addition of NaCl, contributions of CTAB and SDS were neglected. It is interesting to note that the addition of NaCl decreased the solubility of the complex which is abnormal. Though the ionic strength was too large for the Debye Hückel limiting law to be valid, yet the decrease was unexpected. Comments on this will be made in the next section.

The effects of various substances on the solubility of the complex at a fixed concentration of CTAB were also remarkable. These are depicted in Figure 4. While both urea and NaCl diminished the solubility, glucose increased it significantly. The curves are strikingly linear. The least square fitting equations for them are

$$\text{Urea} \quad : \quad \log C_i = -3.123 - \log \gamma_i^{\pm} \tag{3}.$$

$$\text{NaCl} \quad : \quad \log C_i = -3.20 - \log \gamma_i^{\pm} \tag{4}.$$

$$\text{Glucose:} \quad \log C_i = -3.60 - \log \gamma_i^{\pm} \tag{5}.$$

The solubility of a slightly soluble material can be a measure of the standard thermodynamic free energy change for the process. Its temperature dependence then can be a measure of the enthalpy change. Plots of both L_s and $\log L_s$ with T and T^{-1} are shown in Figure 5. From the slope of the reciprocal temperature plot, ΔH_s^o was calculated to be 28.72 kJ mol^{-1}. The ΔG_s^o and ΔS_s^o for the process at temperatures ranging between 15°–55^oC are given in Table 1.

Table I. Thermodynamic Parameters for the Solubility of the $CTA^+...DS^-$ Complex at different Temperatures. $\Delta H_s^o = 28.72$ kJ mol^{-1}.

Temp(^oK)	$-\log L_s$	$-\Delta G_s^o$ (kJ mol^{-1})	ΔS_s^o (kJ mol^{-1} K^{-1})
288	7.14	39.37	0.1961
298	6.94	39.60	0.2036
303	6.80	39.45	0.2066
313	6.72	40.27	0.2159
323	6.59	40.76	0.2244
328	6.49	40.77	0.2279

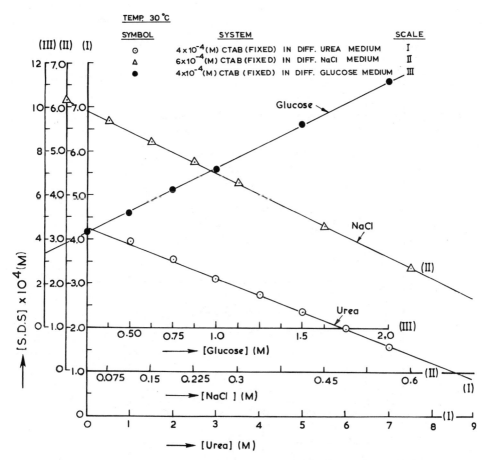

Figure 4. Dependence of the turbidity point at fixed CTAB concentration when NaCl, glucose and urea were progressively added to the medium.

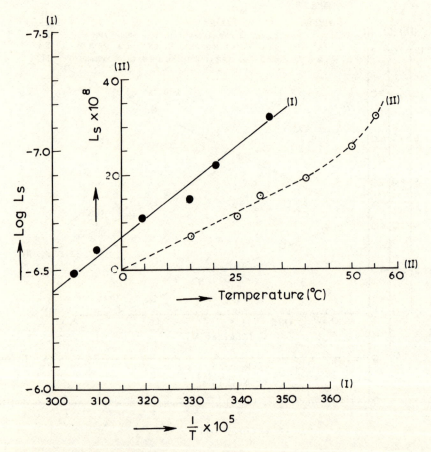

Figure 5. Plots of L_s versus temperature, and log L_s versus reciprocal temperature.

The effects of nonionic surfactants, TX 100, Tween 20 and Tween 80 and a water soluble polymer PEG 600 are presented in Figure 6. Both increase and decrease in the solubility are observed. The plots describe the concentration of SDS required to reach the solubility limit at a fixed concentration of CTAB(4.0 mM) well above its CMC in the presence of various concentrations of the additives. The nonionic surfactants were also kept above their CMCs. Earlier results were presented for the interaction of SDS (concentration below CMC) with CTAB when the latter was present in the mixed micellar[23] state with the nonionics. Here also the variations are remarkably linear whose least square analyses yield the following equations.

TX 100 (IA) : $\log C_i = -1.86 - \log \gamma_i^{\pm}$ (6)

TX 100 (IB) : $\log C_i = -2.21 - \log \gamma_i^{\pm}$ (7)

Tween 80(IIA) : $\log C_i = -3.16 + \log \gamma_i^{\pm}$ (8)

Tween 20(IIB) : $\log C_i = -3.16 + \log \gamma_i^{\pm}$ (9)

Only TX 100 had a diminishing effect on the solubility of the system; other agents showed increased solubility.

The boundary of micelles and precipitate was also studied in presence of different additives. In fact, CTAB + SDS + Nonionic + Water + Additive meant a five component system. Since, the solvent medium was always in large excess and therefore constant and the additive concentration was kept nonvariant, the system practically reduced to a three component one. The results were thus conveniently analyzed on a triangular co-ordinated system. The phase diagrams are illustrated in Figures 7 - 9. The micellar–non micellar boundary in the presence of PEG 600 was significantly lower than in the presence of TX 100. Both urea and NaCl lowered the boundary while glucose increased it. Similar trends were observed for Tween 80 combinations in the presence of the additives. Tween 20 also corresponded fairly with these findings. The compositions at the peak points and the plait points designated as X's and K's are given in Table II. From the plait points consideration, the order of the effectivities of the additives in the system SDS–CTAB–TX 100 is glucose > water > NaCl > urea. For SDS–CTAB–Tween 20 and SDS–CTAB–Tween 80 systems, the orders are glucose ~ NaCl > water > urea and glucose > water > urea > NaCl respectively. The orders of the maxima of the boundaries for these systems are glucose > water > NaCl > urea, glucose ~ NaCl > water > urea and glucose > water > urea > NaCl respectively. The agreements between the X points and K points are thus exact. In aqueous medium, the plait points compositions showed that mixtures

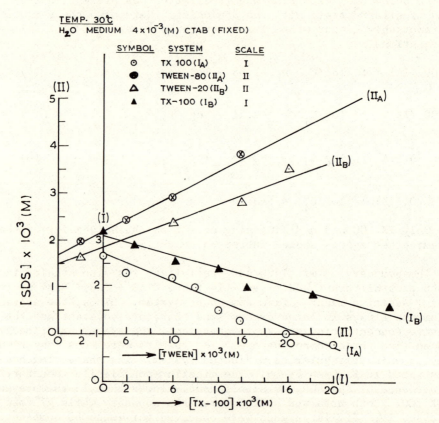

Figure 6. Effects of TX 100 and Tweens (both above CMC) on the turbidity points when SDS (below CMC) was added to a constant concentration of CTAB (above CMC) at 30°C.

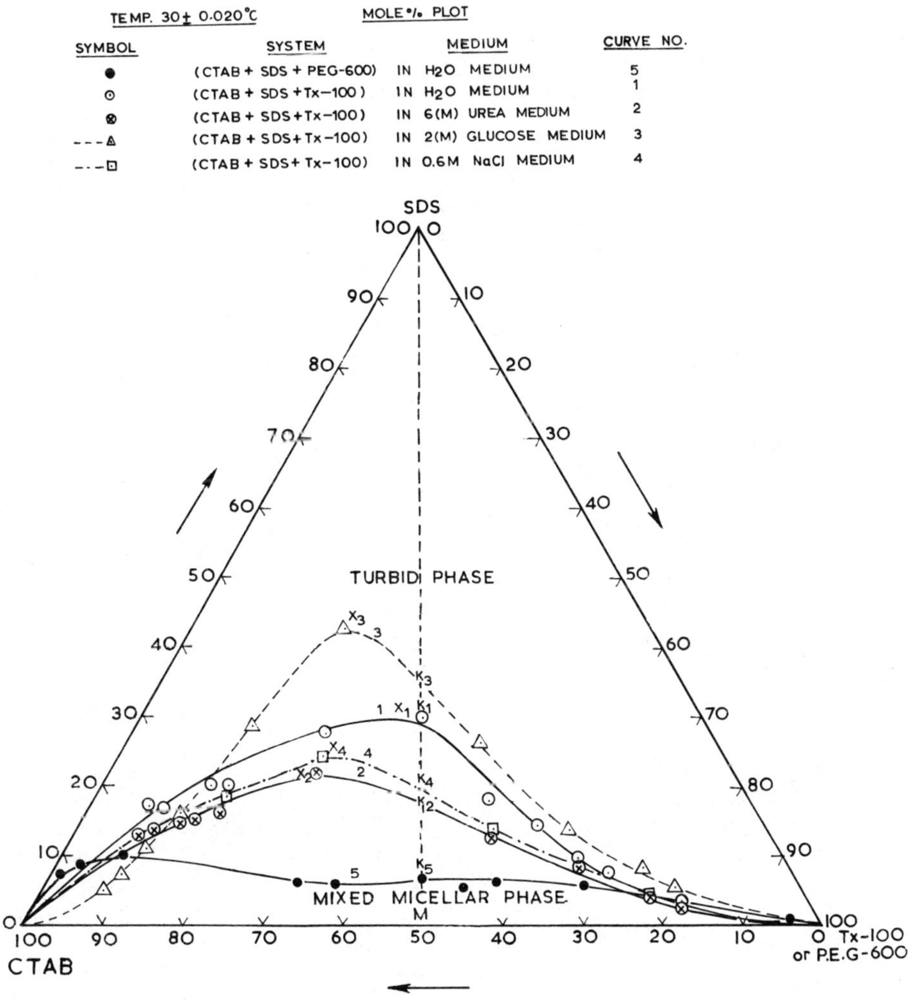

Figure 7. Ternary phase diagram of TX 100 (or PEC 600)–CTAB–SDS in aqueous, 6M urea, 2M glucose and 0.6M NaCl media.

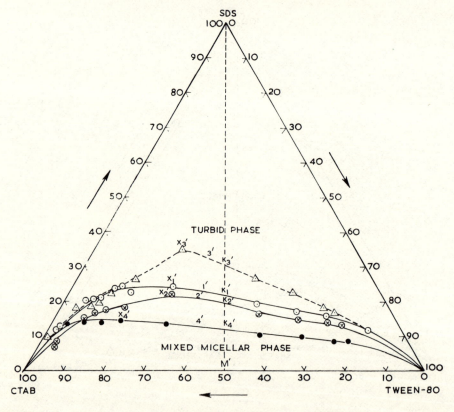

Figure 8. Ternary phase diagram of Tween 20–CTAB–SDS in aqueous, 6M urea, 2M glucose and 0.6M NaCl media.

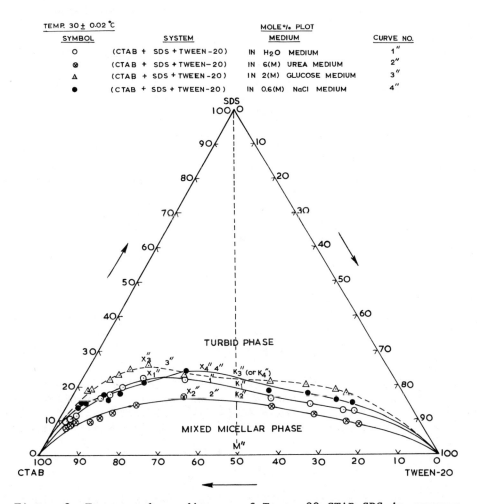

Figure 9. Ternary phase diagram of Tween 80–CTAB–SDS in aqueous, 6M urea, 2M glucose and 0.6M NaCl media.

of CTAB and TX 100 at 70% level was necessary for the dissolution
of 30% SDS; a mixture of 80% was required to dissolve 20% SDS when
TX 100 was replaced by the Tweens, and when the nonionic was PEG 600,
the mixed level became as high as 92% to solubilize only 8% of SDS.
Thus, the uptake was maximum when TX 100 was the nonionic.

Table II. Compositions of the X and K points in Mole Percent[a].

Combinations	Water	Urea(6M)	Glucose(2M)	NaCl(0.6M)
			Media	
SDS	30(30)	22(18)	43(35)	25(20)
CTAB	37(35)	52(41)	37(33)	48(40)
TX 100	33(35)	26(41)	20(32)	27(40)
SDS	22(20)	17(16)	26(22)	24(22)
CTAB	60(40)	53(42)	59(39)	46(39)
Tween 20	18(40)	30(42)	15(39)	30(39)
SDS	25(22)	21(20)	35(31)	15(12)
CTAB	50(39)	52(40)	42(35)	68(44)
Tween 80	25(39)	27(40)	23(34)	17(44)
SDS	10(8)			
CTAB	82(46)			
PEG 600	8(46)			

a: K point values in parentheses.

In 0.6M NaCl environment, the maximum SDS solubilization was observed with both Tween 20 and TX 100. 2M glucose and 6M urea evidenced this in TX 100 and Tween 80 cases. The activities of TX 100
and Tween 20 were remarkably close to Tween 80 in 6M urea environment.

DISCUSSION

The interaction between CTAB and SDS depends on various factors.
Below the CMC, it is primarily affected by the electrostatic factor,
the hydrophobic interaction is considered secondary and co-opera-
tive[29]. The overall solvent structure also has an influence on the
interaction. This is substantiated by the relatively low enthalpy
and large entropy values given in Table 1. The nonelectrolytes,
urea and glucose have opposite effects on the solubility or the
activity. The increased activity coefficient of the complex CTA^+...
DS^- (solubility decrease compensated by activity coefficient increase
to keep the thermodynamic solubility product constant) in urea

solution could be rationalized from solvent structural consideration. The iceberg surrounding the non polar part of the interacting species[30] melts in presence of urea[31] generating kinetically more labile entities with increased activities prone to form products at comparatively low concentrations. Only electrostatic factor is responsible for the complexation, because urea simultaneously destroys hydrophobic effect, if any. Glucose, on the other hand, organizes water structure[32] which acts like a barrier to the interacting species. The activity coefficient is decreased and more SDS is needed to reach the solubility limit, i.e., the solubility product increases in the process. The effect of NaCl on the reaction is striking. The salt acts like urea decreasing the solubility of the complex. This is contrary to the effects normally observed for electrolytes' solubility in added salt environments. A salt having uncommon ions should not behave likewise. The curve on scale II in Figure 3, depicts the expected decrease of the activity coefficient with increasing ionic strength (such ionic strengths were low and imparted by the ions of CTAB and SDS). At high ionic strengths offered by NaCl, a salting out type phenomenon was anticipated. The Debye Hückel type activity effect was overriden by the salting out effect thus enforcing complexation through the hydrophobic effect.

From the thermodynamic solubility product, the mean ionic activity coefficients of the complex salt in different environments were computed. These are presented in Tables III – V. The solubility product in true sense deals with the ionized forms of the species. The large hydrophobic type ions of CTAB and SDS might also form ion pairs[33]. The corrected solubility product, L_a will then be

$$L_a = (C_i \, \alpha \gamma_i^{/\pm})^2 \qquad (10),$$

where α is the degree of dissociation of the ion pair, and $\gamma_i^{/\pm}$ is the corrected mean ionic activity coefficient.

Combining Equations (1) and (10) we have,

$$L_a = L_s \, \alpha^2 \, (\gamma_i^{/\pm} / \gamma_i^{\pm})^2 \qquad (11).$$

The coefficient ratio may be taken equal to unity for most of the practical situations, thus

$$L_a \approx L_s \, \alpha^2 \qquad (12)$$

For 1% ion pairing, L_a is 0.98 part of L_s, and for 10% ion pairing it is 0.81 part of L_s. Since the concentrations of the large interacting ions were well below CMCs, more than 1% ion pairing was not anticipated. For large hydrophobic ions, Mukhayer and Davis[7] reported α as high as 0.96. The solubility product reported here is then fairly close to the thermodynamic value.

Table III. Activity Coefficients of the Complex in Self Induced Environments.

Ionic strength[a] x 10^4	- Log C_i	$\gamma_i^\pm$
3.43	3.845	0.2211
6.85	3.545	0.1110
9.80	3.420	0.0832
12.75	3.323	0.0666
15.47	3.262	0.0578
23.60	3.119	0.0416
29.50	3.022	0.0333
54.26	2.846	0.0222

a: Reported ionic strengths are the combined contributions of CTAB and SDS.

Table IV. Activity Coefficients of the Complex in NaCl Environment.

Ionic strength[b]	- Log C_i	$\gamma_i^\pm$
0.075	3.244	1.106
0.150	3.282	1.207
0.225	3.323	1.328
0.300	3.369	1.475
0.450	3.478	1.897
0.600	3.624	2.656

b: Contributions due to ions of CTAB and SDS were neglected.

Table V. Activity Coefficients of the Complex in Glucose and Urea Environments.

Conc.(M)	- Log C_i		$\gamma_i^\pm$	
	Glucose	Urea	Glucose	Urea
0.25	3.361		0.579	
0.50	3.288		0.490	
0.75	3.212		0.411	
1.00	3.147	3.402	0.354	1.902
1.50	3.041		0.277	
2.00	2.955	3.448	0.228	2.114
3.00		3.497		2.378
4.00		3.557		2.718
5.00		3.624		3.171
6.00		3.703		3.805
7.00		3.800		4.756

The interaction of CTAB at a concentration above its CMC, and SDS below its CMC have special features compared to the state where both of them are below their CMCs. Solubilization of the latter into the micelles of the former was expected. Experimental results show that precipitation at concentrations of SDS approximately 2 mM (at least one fourth of the CMC) takes place. The concentration of CTAB was 4 mM (five times its CMC). The vitality of the electrostatic interaction through deorganization of the CTAB micelles is thus realized. The limiting solubility point is increased by the Tweens and decreased by TX 100. Solubilization in TX 100 and Tweens of both CTAB and SDS was expected[23]. This would expectedly increase the solubility limit which was observed only for the Tweens. Similar is the case with PEG 600 which solubilized by way of increased nonpolar environment and partly through complexation with the polyethyleneoxide chain. Such complexation is maximum for the Tweens (having 20 polyethylenexide residue) and minimum for TX 100 having only 9.5 units of such residue in its head group. The SDS interacted product of the released CTAB monomers by the actions of the nonionics was thus less stabilized in TX 100, and being at concentrations greater than the solubility limit became progressively out of phase. Of the Tweens, the head groups are the same; the hydrophobic tail of Tween 80 is larger than Tween 20. Hydrophobic solubilization and stabilization is therefore more in the former than in the latter.

The interaction of CTAB and SDS both above their CMCs is complex itself and becomes more so in the presence of the nonionics added at levels greater than their respective CMCs. In the first place, micelles of opposite charges are supposed to break down and form ion pairs or precipitate, if one of the two is not in large excess to solubilize the other to form mixed micelles. The phase diagrams obtained represent the pattern of mutual solubility for the three surfactant components all above their CMCs in aqueous and other modified environments. The phase boundary line is higher in TX 100 than in Tweens indicating solubilization of more SDS in the form of soluble complex in TX 100+CTAB combinations. The reverse behaviors of TX 100 with SDS above its CMC than at below (discussed above) is difficult to reconcile in a straight forward way. Further work in this direction is wanted. Glucose, urea and NaCl demonstrated similar behaviors at concentrations of CTAB and SDS below and above their CMCs. PEG 600 was again the exception showing lowest phase boundary curve in the series. For stabilization of oppositely charged surfactant mixtures at concentrations above their CMCs, TX 100 would be a better choice than Tweens. Addition of sufficient glucose could further enhance the stabilization in certain range of composition of the cationic plus anionic plus nonionic surfactant systems.

ACKNOWLEDGEMENTS

One of us (ABM) expresses his thankfulness to the CSIR, Govt. of India for awarding him a junior research fellowship during the tenure of which the work was initiated.

REFERENCES

1. C. Tanford, "The Hydrophobic Effect: Formation of Micelles and Biological Membranes", Wiley Interscience, New York, 1973.
2. K. Schinoda, T. Nakagawa, B. Tamamushi and T. Isemura, "Colloidal Surfactants: Some Physicochemical Properties", Academic Press, New York, 1963.
3. B. W. Barry and G. M. T. Gray, J. Colloid Interface Sci., $\underline{52}$, 327 (1975).
4. M. J. Schick and D. J. Manning, J. Amer. Oil Chem. Soc., $\underline{43}$, 133 (1966).
5. M. J. Schick, J. Amer. Oil Chem. Soc., $\underline{43}$, 681 (1966).
6. G. I. Mukhayer and S. S. Davis, J. Colloid Interface Sci., $\underline{53}$, 224 (1975).
7. G. I. Mukhayer and S. S. Davis, J. Colloid Interface Sci., $\underline{56}$, 350 (1976).
8. H. R. Kruyt, Editor, "Colloid Science", Vol. 2, Elsevier, New York, 1949.
9. S. Razin, Biochem. Biophys. Acta., $\underline{265}$, 241 (1972).
10. A. Helenius and K. Simons, Biochim. Biophys. Acta., $\underline{415}$, 29 (1975).
11. R. A. Dennis, B. R. Eaton and E. A. Dennis, J. Biol. Chem., $\underline{250}$, 9013 (1975).
12. R. J. Robson and E. A. Dennis, Biochim. Biophys. Acta., $\underline{508}$, 513 (1978).
13. C. Tanford, Y. Nojaki, J. A. Reynolds and S. Makino, Biochemistry, $\underline{13}$, 2369 (1974).
14. C. Duve De, R. Wattiaux and M. Wibo, Biochem. Pharmacol., $\underline{2}$, 97 (1962).
15. G. Weissman and H. Keiser, Biochem. Pharmacol., $\underline{14}$, 97 (1965).
16. G. Weissman, Biochem. Pharmacol., $\underline{14}$, 1525 (1965).
17. G. Weissman, G. Sessa and S. Weismann, Nature, $\underline{208}$, 649 (1965).
18. K. Inone and T. Kitagawa, Biochim. Biophys. Acta, $\underline{426}$, 1 (1976).
19. G. Gale and J. D. Kadlec, J. Agr. Food Chem., $\underline{4}$, 426 (1956).
20. C. L. Gantt, N. Gochman and J. M. Dyniewicj, Lancet, $\underline{486}$, (1961).
21a. G. Baur, P. Rieckmann and W. Schanmann, Arjneimittel Forsch, $\underline{12}$, 487 (1962).
21b. K. Shinoda, Editor, "Solvent Properties of Surfactant Solutions", Vol. 2, Marcel Dekker, New York, 1967.
22. A. B. Mandal, S. Ray, A. M. Biswas and S. P. Moulik, J. Phys. Chem., $\underline{84}$, 856 (1980).
23. S. P. Moulik, A. B. Mandal and S. Ray, Ind. J. Chem., to appear.
24. F. M. Menger, Accts. Chem. Res., $\underline{12}$, 111 (1079).

25. K. L. Mittal, Editor, "Micellization, Solubilization and Micro-emulsions", Vol. 1, Plenum Press, New York, 1977.
26. S. P. Moulik, S. Ray and A. R. Das, J. Phys. Chem., $\underline{81}$, 1766 (1977).
27. S. P. Moulik, S. Ray and A. R. Das, Colloid & Polymer Sci., $\underline{257}$, 182 (1979).
28. M. J. Schick, Editor, "Nonionic Surfactants", Marcel Dekker, New York, 1967.
29. S. P. Moulik, S. Ghosh and A. R. Das, Colloid & Polymer Sci., $\underline{257}$, 645 (1979).
30. H. S. Frank and M. W. Evans, J. Chem. Phys., $\underline{13}$, 507 (1945).
31. P. Mukerjee and A. K. Ghosh, J. Phys. Chem., $\underline{67}$, 193 (1963).
32. S. P. Moulik and D. P. Khan, Indian J. Chem., $\underline{16A}$, 16 (1978).
33. R. M. Diamond, J. Phys. Chem., $\underline{67}$, 2513 (1963).

CASEIN MICELLES AND MICELLES OF κ- AND β-CASEIN

T. A. J. Payens and H. J. Vreeman
Physicochemical Department
Netherlands Institute for Dairy Research
P.O. Box 20, 6710 BA   EDE, the Netherlands

The tendency of proteins to associate in aqueous solution is well known. Most proteins form oligomers or undergo a series of consecutive association steps. A limited number, however, among which are κ- and β-casein, exhibit soaplike micellization.

Beta-casein forms micelles beyond 4°C. The association parameters have been collected by ultra-centrifugation, viscometry and light scattering. The degree of association is about 13 at I = 0.05 and increases to 23 at I = 0.2, indicating electro-static repulsion counteracting the hydrophobic effect. The influence of chemical and enzymic modification upon the HL-balance governing the micellization is reviewed.

The micelle formation of κ-casein, the protective colloid of the natural casein micelle, has been studied by ultracentrifugation and viscometry. It forms spherical, voluminous 30-mers, independent of ionic strength. The cmc has been determined from the Trautman plot in approach-to-equilibrium experiments and found to decrease with ionic strength. Micelle radii of about 11 nm are deduced from hydrodynamic data and the second virial coefficient. The size-limiting factor is discussed.

Together with the remaining α_s-caseins, κ- and β-casein constitute the natural casein micelle from

milk. Its precise structure is not known, but
interesting hypotheses have been put forward on the
role of $\varkappa$-casein in stabilizing the other, calcium
sensitive components against flocculation. These
will be summarized and some aspects of casein
associations and calcium phosphate in relation to
the stability of the micelle will be discussed.

INTRODUCTION

The physical chemist wondering about the significance of
micelle formation in biological systems will be inclined to
think, first of all, in terms of the micelle-forming properties
of lipids, phosphatides or bile salts, less in terms of
proteins. The tendency of proteins to associate in aqueous
solution is well recognized though[1,2] and is readily
understood from the diversity of the amino acid residues on
the particle's surface which can give rise to such different
interactions as hydrogen bonding, the hydrophobic effect and
the formation of salt linkages. By far the majority of proteins
form simple oligomers[3] or undergo a number of consecutive
association steps. The octamerization of β-lactoglobulin[4]
and the self-association of α_{s1}-casein[5] may serve as
examples. A restricted number of proteins, however, are known
to associate in a soaplike manner. Typical examples are
actin[6], ferritin[7], virus coat protein[8] and $\varkappa$- and
β-casein from milk. In the following we shall deal in
particular with the micelle formation observed with the latter
two proteins and discuss its implication for the stability of
the natural casein micelle.

It is at this point that we must recall Hartley's
apology[9] of "the grasping way in which physical chemists
of our kind took over a biologist's word "MICELLE" and used
it for something quite different". Indeed, when speaking of
the "natural casein micelle", we have in mind a colloidal
particle occurring in milk and giving rise to its white
appearance. This truly colloidal particle consists of about
7 percent of inorganic constituent, mainly calcium phosphate,
and 93 percent of a group closely related and firmly
associated phosphoproteins: the caseins. By now 4 different
casein species have been recognized, which, in order of
decreasing sensitivity toward precipitation by calcium ions,
were named α_{s2}-, α_{s1}-, β- and $\varkappa$-casein[10-13] (Table I). The
last mentioned casein is of particular interest, because it
remains stable at calcium concentrations up to 400 mM and, more
interesting, can stabilize the other, calcium-sensitive casein
components against flocculation. An example of this important
property of $\varkappa$-casein is shown in Figure 1.

Table I. Characteristic Properties of Bovine Caseins.

Type	No. of genetic variants	No. of ester phosphates	% of total casein	Mol. Wt.	soluble up to
α_{s2}	1	10-13	11	25,300	1 mM Ca^{++}
α_{s1}	4	8-9	38	23,600	2 mM Ca^{++}
β	7	5	38	24,000	9 mM Ca^{++}
$\varkappa$	2	1-2	13	19,000	400 mM Ca^{++}

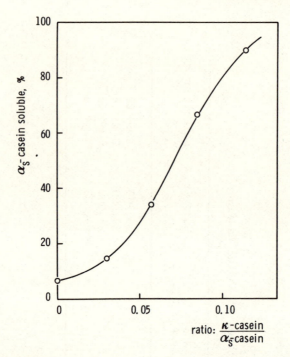

Figure 1.   Solubilization of α_{s1}-casein by increasing amounts
of $\varkappa$. Experimental conditions: α_{s1}-concentration 3 g/1;
0.02 M CaCl$_2$, pH 6.7, 30°C. After C. A. Zittle[14].

Rapid progress in our understanding of the factors that
determine the stability of the casein micelle was made since
the rediscovery of $\varkappa$-casein by Waugh and von Hippel in 1956[15].
It is now realized that their $\varkappa$-casein bears a close relation
to the micelle-protecting colloid isolated in the twenties
by Linderstøm Lang[16]. He described the separation of a
casein fraction that can stabilize the rest of the casein
in the presence of calcium ions and the protective action of
which is destroyed by milk clotting enzymes. A number of
micelle models based upon the idea of a protective colloid
surrounding the micelle have been proposed during the
years[4,17]. We shall come back to the appropriateness of such
models after a discussion of the micelle-forming properties
of the separate $\varkappa$- and β-casein.

Indeed, it is only when dealing with solutions of the
individual $\varkappa$- and β-casein that one can speak of casein
micelles in the sense not of biological particles of colloidal
dimensions, but of "aggregates formed spontaneously in

solutions of amphiphiles" to quote Hartley again. Actually, the
fact that casein "polymerizations bear a marked resemblance to
those responsible for the formation of soap micelles" was
already noted 25 years ago by von Hippel and Waugh[18] and long
before the amphiphilic character of the polypeptide chains of
х- and β-casein became evident from the amino acid
sequence[11,12].

Since the present overview is concerned mainly with the
thermodynamics of the micelle formation of х- and β- casein, we
shall forego the details of the always tedious purification of
the individual caseins. Likewise we refrain from a discussion
of the occurrence of the so-called minor casein components. For
such details the reader is referred to some recent reviews[4,17,19]
dealing with the chemistry and biochemistry of milk.

The methods to investigate the association of proteins are
well developed by now [1,2] In principle any property that is
a function of the degree of association can be used to monitor
the association. Thus UV-difference and fluorescence spectroscopy and the anomalies observed in transport processes like
sedimentation and electrophoresis have been applied to study
the association of the various caseins[17]. However, for
evaluation of the thermodynamic parameters the concentration
dependence of the apparent average molecular weight is the most
direct and reliable method. Since proteins are macromolecular
polyelectrolytes, interference from non-ideality effects is to
be expected. The necessary non-ideality corrections will be
dealt with when discussing the micellizations of х- and
β-casein below.

MICELLES OF β-CASEIN

The essential features of the association of β-casein can
already be recognized in the early work of von Hippel and
Waugh[18], Sullivan et al. [20] and Hawler[21] in the fifties.

The first authors concluded from the sedimentation pattern
of so-called soluble casein at pH 7 and I = 0.17 that β-casein
at low temperature dissociates into a species with a
sedimentation coefficient of about 1.3 S. On increasing the
temperature a second rapidly moving peak appears, the
sedimentation coefficient of which strongly increases with the
temperature chosen. They note that the β-casein "polymers"
center around a preferred size. This behavior was confirmed by
Sullivan et al., who found their β-casein to be completely
disassociated below 15°C. The sedimentation coefficient of the
polymers formed abruptly beyond that temperature was found to
be extremely concentration-dependent. Hawler, finally,

concluded from his light scattering experiments that the
association-dissociation reactions of β-casein are relatively
slow and only partially reversible. Later studies[22-24] have
confirmed these observations and moreover afforded insight into
the size and shape of the β-casein polymers formed. Before
discussing such evidence, we shall first present a picture of
the β-casein monomer as it appears from its amino acid sequence
and hydrodynamic and conformational studies under dissociating
conditions.

As was already noted by Waugh in 1954[25], -casein ranks
among the most hydrophobic proteins known. Its average
hydrdophobicity on the Tanford-Bigelow scale is 5.56 kJ per
residue and its non-polarity index is 0.47*. These are indeed
remarkable figures, the more so when the distribution of
hydrophobic and charged residues along the peptide chain is
inspected (Table II). This distribution suggests that the
unfolded peptide chain should exhibit soaplike properties. At
pH 7 its net charge is about -12 and this net charge,
originating from the ionization of 6 glutamic and 4 phosphoserine
residues is completely confined within the first 21 N-terminal
residues, the rest of the molecule having zero net charge.
On the other hand the average hydrophobicity increases toward
the C-terminal end from about 3.5 kJ to the extremely high
figure of 8.3 kJ per residue. A further remarkable figure of
β-casein is that one in six residues is a proline, a notorious
secondary structure breaker.

The comparison of β-casein with simpler amphiphiles stands
or falls by the tertiary structure that it will adopt in
aqueous solution. Simple theoretical considerations[26,27]
suggest already that the number of apolar residues in β-casein
is by far too large to be accomodated in the core of a
globular particle of molecular weight 24 000. More convincing
are the experimental arguments brought forward to demonstrate
that the β-monomer in aqueous solution behaves as a random coil
of considerable flexibility with its various side-chains well
accessible to the solvent. These can be summarized as follows.
1. There is a close agreement between the calculated and
    experimentally determined titration curve and also the 4
    tyrosines, 2 of which are located in the most hydrophobic
    C-terminal end, appear to be well accessible to titration[28].

---

* The residue hydrophobicity measures the free enthalpy of transferring the residue's side-chain from an aqueous to an ethanolic solution. Waugh's non polarity index simply counts the
  fraction of non polar residues such as tryptophan, isoleucine,
  tyrosine, phenylalanine, proline, leucine and valine [25,26].

Table II. Sequential Charge at pH 7 and Hydrophobicity in α_{s1}-, β- and κ-casein. [1]

Sequence	α_{s1} (B-variant)		β(A²-variant)		κ (B-variant)	
	Charge	Hydrophobicity (kJ/res)	Charge	Hydrophobicity (kJ/res)	Charge	Hydrophobicity (kJ/res)
1-20	+2.8	4.9	-9.6	3.5	-3	3.1
21-40	+1.0	6.3	-1.3	3.6	+3	7.6
41-60	-6.7	2.7	-2.5	4.3	+1	7.0
61-80	-10.2	3.0	0	6.8	+2	5.75
81-100	-1.0	5.3	0	6.3	+2	3.7
101-120	+1.7	5.8	+2.4	6.7	+1.5	5.9
121-140	+0.9	3.5	-2.6	5.1	-3	4.1
141-160²⁾	-2.0	7.1	+0.8	5.9	-5.7	4.6
161-180³⁾	-1.0	5.4	+1.0	5.9	-1	3.3
181-200	-3.0	4.8	0	6.4		
201-209			0	8.3		
total	-17.5	4.9	-11.8	5.7	-3.2	5.1

1) charge estimated at pH 7 with the electrostatic factor taken from Creamer[28]; hydrophobicities calculated as with Bigelow[26]
2) residues 161-169 with κ-casein
3) residues 181-199 with α_{s1}-casein

2. The intrinsic viscosity of the β-monomer measured at pH 7
   and low temperature, amounts to as much as 23 ml/g[20,22,29],
   whereas for compact, globular proteins a value of only
   3-4 ml/g is to be expected[30]. From this a radius of
   gyration of about 5.1 nm is readily calculated for the
   flexible coil in a good solvent. The experimental value
   found by small X-ray scattering[23] is slightly less
   (4.6 nm), but considerably smaller than the value
   calculated for the alternative of a rod (7.6 nm).
3. The intrinsic viscosity in 6 M guanidinium chloride, a
   notorius protein-unfolding medium, is 22.2 ml/g[29] and
   therefore not different from that in aqueous solution at
   pH 7.
4. The flexibility of the β-casein polypeptide chain is further
   substantiated by its well-resolved NMR-spectrum[23] and the
   similarity of its ORD-spectra in aqueous buffers and 6 M
   guanidium chloride[31]. In this connection it is also
   worthwhile to remember the abundancy of proline residues
   in β-casein and their structure-breaking role.

     Although all such evidence as well as the frictional
properties derived from sedimentation behavior[18,20,22] and
gel permeation chromatography[23] seem to support the idea
that the β-casein monomer is an expanded coil with its side-
chains well exposed to the solvent, some authors have
speculated whether the chain might yet be partially ordered.
Although this possibility cannot be ruled out with certainty,
the arguments brought forward do not sound very convincing.
Thus Garnier[32] estimates 11 percent of an α-helical and 12
percent of a polyproline II structure from the negative Cotton-
effects in the far ultraviolet. Comparable and even lower
α-helical contents are found from ORD or by the Chou-Fasman
structure predicting procedure[31,23]. Such low figures are
almost meaningless on account of the inherent inaccuracy of
the methods used. Also the conformational transition advanced
by Garnier to explain the temperature-dependent UV-difference
spectrum is not very persuasive. Such difference spectrum
could as well be explained by a more apolar environment of the
aromatic chromphores as the temperature-induced association of
β-casein proceeds. Pearce[33] indeed arrived at that conclusion
from his fluorescence studies.

     Let us now return to the association itself and the
evidence gathered by different authors to show that is indeed
of a micellar type. The association is readily demonstrated
in the ultracentrifuge by the sudden appearance of a second,
rapidly sedimenting peak when the temperature of the solution

is increased, say, beyond 4°C[**] (Figure 2A). As was mentioned
above, the sedimentation coefficient of this rapid peak is
extremely concentration dependent (Figure 3), which indicates
the necessity of making non-ideality corrections when
estimating the size of the polymers formed.

A number of arguments can be brought forward to demonstrate
that the association indeed leads to micelles without an
appreciable amount of intermediate species being formed. The
most convincing of these is the demonstration of the occurrence
of a critical micelle concentration (cmc) in the ultracentrifuge
(Figure 4) or by light scattering [35]. Also the Trautman plot
in approach-to-equilibrium experiments in the ultracentrifuge
is consistent with the occurrence of 2 species of widely
different molecular weight [22].

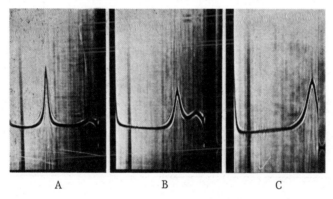

A   B   C

Figure 2. Sedimentation patterns of unmodified and acylated
β-casein at pH 6.86, I = 0.20 and 20°C after 64 mins. at
52.640 rpm.
A. Unmodified β-casein: 1.32 and 9.31 Sv.
B. Acetylated: 1.48 and 4.67 Sv.
C. Succinylated: 1.12 Sv.
After P.D. Hoagland [34].

[**] There appears some disagreement about the temperature at
which the micellization sets in [20,22-24]. It is likely that
such disagreement can be explained by the presence of
different genetic variants and/or impurities in the β-casein
preparations used.

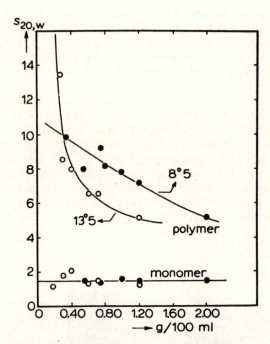

Figure 3. Concentration dependence of the sedimentation coefficients of β-casein monomers and polymers.
Experimental conditions: barbiturate buffer, pH 7.5, I = 0.2.

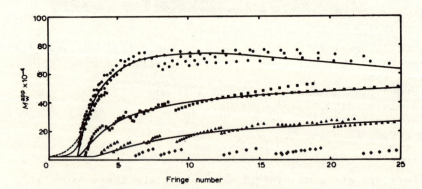

Figure 4. Apparent molecular weight of β-casein from sedimentation equilibrium vs. concentration (in fringes).
Experimental conditions: 0.2 M phosphate buffer, pH 6.7.
○, 20°C; □, 15°C; △, 10°C; ◇ , 2°C.
After K. Takase et al.[24].

In agreement with this the sedimentation pattern (cf. Figure 2A) shows two well-separated peaks with no intermediate species present and the sedimentation coefficient of the rapid peak only decreases with concentration. If appreciable amounts of intermediate species were formed, one would expect the sedimentation coefficient of this rapid peak to increase with concentration in the lower concentration range. Similar conclusions can be reached from the gel permeation pattern[23].

Also the fact that the radius of gyration of the polymers formed does not change appreciably with cencentration has been interpreted in terms of micelles of a well-defined size[23]. Finally, the equality of the van 't Hoff and calorimetric enthalpies suggests likewise that the association is a two-state transition with intermediate polymers being thermodynamically unstable[36].

Figure 5 presents a well-known picture of the concentration-dependence of the apparent molecular weight of β-casein at room temperature and different ionic strengths[37]. The non-ideality of the system is reflected in the appearance of a maximum in the apparent molecular weight. It is further evident that salt, as with simpler ionic detergents, strongly enhances the micellization, obviously by reducing the electrostatic repulsion between the monomers. We shall come back to such electrostatic effects when discussing the effect of chemical modification on the hydrophile-lipophile balance of β-casein.

The intricacies involved in unravelling the contributions of association and non-ideality to the apparent molecular weight have been clearly exposed by Eisenberg[38]. As stressed by this author, the experimental precision with plots such as those in Figure 5 is usually insufficient to complete a full analysis in terms of the type of association, the association constants and the non-ideality contributions of all the species present. A rather satisfactory approach is the following.

For the apparent molecular weight, M_a, from light scattering one finds[39,40]:

$$1/M_a = 1/\overline{M}_w + (2A_2/\overline{M}_w^2) \, c \, , \qquad (1)$$

where $\overline{M}_w$ is the weight-average molecular weight, c the solute concentration (g/l) and A_2 the second virial coefficient, defined as

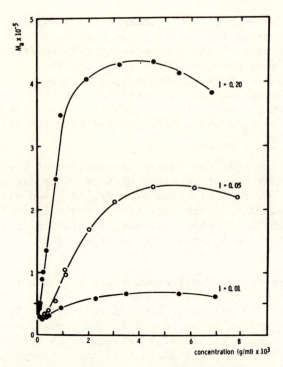

Figure 5. Concentration-dependence of the apparent molecular weight of β-casein as measured by light scattering. Experimental conditions: phosphate buffer, pH 7: 21°C.

$$A_2 = \sum_i \sum_j M_i M_j A_{ij} w_i w_j \qquad (2)$$

with w_i the weight-fraction c_i/c.
Furthermore the interaction parameter A_{ij} in Equation (2) is given by

$$A_{ij} = (1/2M_i)(\partial \ln \gamma_i / \partial c_j)_{\mu_o, T, c_k} \qquad (3)$$

where γ_i is the activity coefficient of component i and μ_o the solvent chemical potential.

With the assumptions that the contribution of the monomers to A_2 can be neglected (cf. Figure 3) and that the micelles are of uniform size Equation (1) becomes

$$1/M_a = 1/\bar{M}w + 2A_2c \ , \qquad\qquad (4)$$

in which A_2 is practically constant and equal to A_{22} on account of the relatively small contribution of the monomer to the weight-average molecular weight.

The condition of the maximum in Figure 5 can be reduced to the following cubic equation in the degree of polymerization[37] ;

$$(1/M_a)_{max} = \left\{ (c^2/M^1)(c_1 + n^2 c_n)/(c_1 + nc_n)^3 \right\}_{max} , \qquad (5)$$

where M_1 is the monomer molecular weight and c_1 and c_n the concentrations of monomer and micelle at the maximum.

By Equation (5) the degree of micellization, n, can easily be calculated, provided c_1 and c_n are known. In previous calculations these were taken from the peak areas of the sedimentation pattern. However, such estimates may be seriously in error on account of the Johnston-Ogston effect, especially in systems in which the sedimentation coefficient of the rapid peak is so highly concentration dependent (cf. Figure 3; ref. 41). We therefore prefer to use the cmc's as measured by light scattering[35] . They lead to the micelle parameters collected in Table III, which are to be compared to the recent figures of Takase et al.[24] and Evans et al.[36]. The former find n = 49 at 20°C and the considerably higher ionic strength of a 0.2 M phosphate buffer, pH 6.7. Their virial coefficient $(8.4 \times 10^{-5}$ ml.mol.g^{-2}) is of the same order as those given in Table III. Evans et al. estimate n from the temperature-dependence of extrapolated S-values, which are converted into molecular weights by the Mandelkern-Scheraga relation. They recognize that this is a risky procedure which could explain their relatively low value of n = 14 (phosphate buffer pH 7, I = 0.1, and 20°C).

The evidence presented above may suffice to demonstrate that the association of β-casein is indeed of the micellar type and to stress the similarity of this protein with simpler amphiphiles. Relatively little is known about the shape of the micelles formed. Buchheim and Schmidt[42] were able to freeze the equilibrium obtained at 20°C by rapid spray-freezing of solutions at -190°C. The electronmicrographs which were obtained from such spray-freezed samples nicely reproduced the bimodal distribution of monomers and polymers and showed the micelles to be spherical with a diameter of about 34 nm. Several authors [20,22,43] agree that the intrinsic viscosity of the polymers formed is considerably lower than that of the monomer.

Table III. Thermodynamic Parameters of β-casein Micellization at 21°C and Different Ionic Strengths.

I	$(M_a)_{max}$[1] $\times 10^{-5}$	C_{max}[1] (g/l)	cmc[2] (g/l)	n	$(M_w)_{max}$ $\times 10^{-5}$	$A_2 \times 10^5$ (ml·mol·g^{-2})
0.2	4.32	4.0	0.50	23	5.52	6.3
0.05	2.38	5.3	0.74	13	3.12	9.4

[1] From the curves of Figure 5.
[2] From ref.35.

This suggests that the micelles are more compact than the monomers from which they are formed.

The influence of the temperature on the micellization of β-casein leaves no doubt that the enthalpy is strongly positive and that therefore the driving force is a positive entropy change. The endothermicity of the association was confirmed by direct calorimetry by Evans et al.[36], who consider it "typical of hydrophobic bonding". Although the interpretation of thermodynamic data may be hazardous as Tanford points out[44], on account of the accompanying changes in the state of hydration of the charged groups, there are some further arguments in favor of hydrophobic bonding. Thus Thompson et al.[45] observed that the removal of the very last 3, hydrophobic, C-terminal residues by the action of carboxypeptidase A leads to a serious reduction of the association. This was confirmed by Berry and Creamer[46] who, moreover, found that the ability to associate is completely lost after removal of the last 20 C-terminal residues from the total of 209. Hydrophobic bonding is further suggested by the finding that β-casein depolymerizes under pressure up to 1000 atmosphere (Figure 6). It is interesting to note that the reversal of the dissociation which takes place beyond that pressure is also observed with ionic detergents such as sodium dodecyl sulphate and long-chain trimethylammoniumbromides[47,48]. The resemblance underlines again the similarity of the micelle formations of β-casein and simpler ionic amphiphiles.

Figure 6. Response of light scattering of β-casein to pressure changes. Experimental conditions: protein concentration 6.2 g/l; phosphate buffer pH 6, I = 0.2.

The delicacy of the HL-balance governing the micelle-formation of β-casein is further demonstrated by a number of experiments in which the charge of the protein was modified by acylation of the lysine residues[34], [49-51]. As Figures 2B and 2C show, complete acetylation, which nearly doubles the protein's net charge, leads to a drastic reduction of the association, whereas tripling the charge by succinylation completely inhibits it. Increasing the hydrophobicity of the acylating group, as Hoaglund[49] showed, can restore the ability to associate. One may wonder whether such chemical modification brings about conformational changes which affect the association. Evans et al.[50], however, by a comparison of the ORD-spectra of unmodified and acylated β-caseins were unable to detect such changes. Evans, Phillips and Jones[36] have collected evidence that also the enzymic removal of the 3 hydrophobic C-terminal residues does not lead to a gross perturbation of the conformation. It is therefore obvious that chemical and enzymic modification of β-casein can yield interesting information on the HL-balance governing the micellization.

MICELLES OF χ-CASEIN

When in 1956 Waugh and von Hippel described the isolation of a reasonably pure χ-casein[15], they also reported that it formed micelles in aqueous solutions, whose size did not depend on pH, temperature and concentration. More extensive physical characterization[52,53] showed that also the ionic strength and reduction and alkylation of the S-S bonds did not affect the micelles size. This last observation suggests that inter-molecular S-S bonds are not essential for micelle formation. It was shown only recently[54] that χ-casein micellization is accompanied by a critical micelle concentration (Figure 7). As this concentration is small, it was probably overlooked before or taken for a β-casein contamination. The micelles have a spherical geometry, which follows from the concentration-dependence of the reduced viscosity[55] and electron-microscopy[56].

The micelle formation as well as its role as a protective colloid (cf. Figure 1) have tempted several authors[4, 57] to liken χ-casein to a regular surface-active molecule. Accordingly, the natural casein micelle would be a particle in which Ca-insoluble α_{s1}-, α_{s2} and β-casein are solubilized by χ-casein. This picture, however, must be amended as unlike the situation with normal detergent solubilization, where the core of the micelle is not accessible to water, casein micelles turn out to be spongy and waterrich[58]. This is

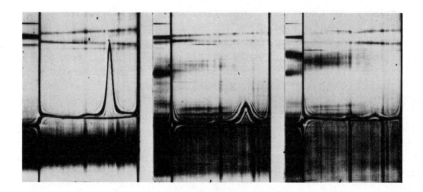

Figure 7. Sedimentation of ϰ-casein in a synthetic boundary
cell; the buffer contains 0.1 M NaCl, 0.005MEDTA,
0.001 DTT, pH 7.0. Centrifugal force is from left to right.
The total protein concentration is 5.1 g/l, 3.5 g/l and
1.4 g/l.

not a real obstacle for micelle formation, because protein
molecules are so large that they are able to form a sufficient
number of hydrophobic or hydrogen bonds without having to
exclude the water completely. The picture of the. micelle is
completed by assuming that ϰ-casein has a certain structure
which allows lateral interactions between the monomers in such
a way that the repellent part of the molecule is located on
the outside of the natural micelle.

   The primary structure of ϰ-casein does not contradict its
presumed role as a surface-active agent. The molecule can be
divided into two regions differing in charge and hydrophobicity
(cf. Table II). This the first 100 N-terminal residues have a
net positive charge and contain a strongly hydrophobic core
between residues 40 and 80. The remaining c-terminal part
carries a negative charge of -10, comparable to the hydrophilic
N-terminal part of β-casein (cf. Table II). Its hydrophobicity,
though not exceptionally low, is lower than that in the first
part of the chain. As mentioned in the Introduction, this
amphiphilic division is supported by the fact that milk-
clotting enzymes split the bond between the residues 105 and
106, whereby the protecting properties are completely lost.
The C-terminal end of 64 residues remains in solution, whereas
the N-terminal part of 105 residues rapidly coagulates.

Evidence for the occurrence of some kind of tertiary
structure in $\varkappa$-casein was provided by spectroscopic investigation. Leslie et al.[59] concluded from NMR that a
number of hydrophobic groups is restricted in their motion.
There is a considerable difference in the NMR-spectra of $\varkappa$-
and β-casein, that of the latter being typical of the denatured
protein. Similar conclusions were arrived at by Clarke and
Nakai[60] using spectrofluorimetry. They also revealed that
$\varkappa$-casein in very dilute solutions (0.1 g/1, i.e. below the cmc
as we shall see) has 4 hydrophobic regions per molecule. This
number decreases to 0.5 at high concentrations which suggests
that hydrophobic bonding plays a role in the association. The
structural elements in $\varkappa$ are probably not helical[31]. Recent
CD measurements[61] suggest that β-sheets may be more
important.

We shall now proceed with the micelle size and shape and
the cmc as found for $\varkappa$-casein with reduced S-S bonds. The
measurement of the concentration-dependence of the apparent
molecular weight was done in the SPINCO analytical ultracentrifuge, using the Archibald method[62]. The apparent
molecular weight is given by[63]

$$M_a = RT(dc/dr)_m / \{(\partial\rho/\partial c)_o \omega^2 r_m c_m\},\qquad(6)$$

where R is the gas constant, T the temperature, ω angular
velocity, r_m the distance of the meniscus from the center of
rotation and $(\partial\rho/\partial c)_o$ the density increment.

To determine the cmc and to smooth the data a so-called
Trautman plot is constructed whereby $(dc/dr)m/\omega^2$, which
by Equation (6) is proportional to $M_a c_m$, is plotted against
$c_o - c_m$, c_o being the initial concentration (Figure 8). It is
seen from Figure 8 that at low meniscus concentrations only
monomer exists and that polymers are formed only beyond a
certain concentration. The intersection of the two lines in
Figure 8 corresponds therefore to the cmc. An example of the
more familiar plot of M_a vs. c is given in Figure 9.

To correct for non-ideality in analytical ultracentrifugation the same basic equations (e.g. Equations (1) and (2))
as with light scattering can be used[39,40]. The interaction
parameter A_{ij} can be defined as[39]:

$$A_{ij} = (N_{av}/2M_iM_j)\int_0^\infty \{1-\exp(-V_{ij}/kT)\}4\pi r_{ij}^2 dr_{ij},\qquad(7)$$

where N_{av} is Avogadro's number, V_{ij} the intermolecular potential, k Boltzmann's constant and r_{ij} the distance between the
centers of the particles i and j. Since we will be concerned
mainly with hard-sphere potentials, Equation (7) reduces to

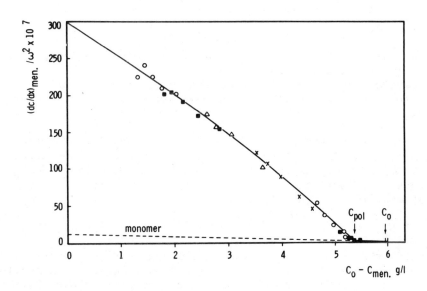

Figure 8. Trautman plot of ×-casein. The buffer composition is
given under Figure 7. Experiments performed at:
 o = 4800 rpm, ▣ = 6000 rpm, △ = 7200 rpm, x = 9000 rpm,
 o = 12 000 rpm and ▣ = 15 000 rpm.

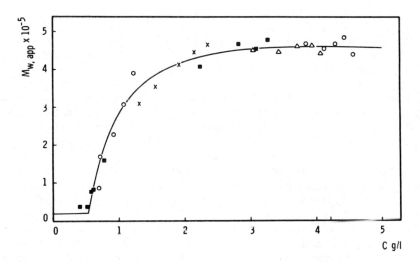

Figure 9. Apparent weight-average molecular weight of ×-casein
as a function of protein concentration. Experimental
circumstances, see Figure 8.

$$A_{ij} = 2\pi N_{av}(R_i + R_j)^3/3M_iM_j \qquad (8)$$

with R_i the radius of hard sphere i.
In the case of the micellization of $\varkappa$-casein we shall use the
following simplifications :
1. There are only 2 species present: monomer and micelle:
2. Both species are spherical and have equal specific volumes
   v.

The last proposition differs from the usual treatment of
the micellization in detergent solutions, where the monomer is
regarded as belonging to the electrolyte in the solvent medium
without contributing to the excluded volume. Combination of
Equations (1), (2) and (8) yields

$$1/M_a = (1 + 8 f v c)/\overline{M}_w \qquad (9)$$

in which the factor f depends on the aggregation number n and
the monomer and total protein concentration. For low aggregation
number f ⌐1 and Equation (9) is seen to reduce to the well
known expression for monodisperse hard spheres with the virial
coefficient proportional to 8 times the excluded volume. For
higher aggregation numbers, f decreases and the optimal values
of n and v can be calculated by an iterative procedure which
gives a least-square fit of calculated and measured apparent
molecular weights.

Some results at different ionic strengths are collected in
Table IV. It should be noted that the maximal value of M_a is
around 450,000, whereas the true micelle weight is 570,000
(n = 30) so that also with $\varkappa$-casein it appears worth while to
apply the non-ideality correction. In Table IV are also reported
the specific volume v found from the virial correction, the
intrinsic viscosity, the standardized sedimentation coefficient
extrapolated to zero micelle concentration, the cmc's and the
standard free energy of micellization per mole of monomer
calculated by $\triangle G° = RT \ln(cmc)$ (cmc in mole fraction units).

From the instrinsic viscosity and the sedimentation
coefficient the specific volume of the micelles is 6.5 and
5.7 ml/g respectively and the radius 11 nm[30] . The specific
volume from the virial coefficient (Table IV) is somewhat lower,
but in view of the inaccuracies involved in determining this
coefficient, the agreement is satisfactory. As found with ionic
detergents the cmc decreses with ionic strength. However, this
decrease amounts to only a few percent (1-2 kJ/mole monomer) of
the total standard free energy. This means that $\varkappa$-casein
micellization, in contrast to β-casein, is more akin to non-

Table IV. Characteristics of SH- ϰ- Casein Association.

Buffer M NaCl	n mon/pol	v * ml/g	cmc g/l	− ΔG° kJ/mol. mon
0.1	31	3.7	0.53	35.4
0.2	30	4.3	0.51	35.4
0.5	30	2.4	0.42	35.9
1.0	35	5.3	0.24	37.4

* The specific volumes calculated from [η] and S are 6.5 and
  5.7 ml/g respectively.

ionic than to ionic detergent behavior. The same conclusion
is reached from the constant value of n in Table IV.

A MODEL FOR THE ϰ-CASEIN MICELLE

From the review presented above it follows that ϰ-casein
indeed forms micelles of a discreet size. The micelle appears
to consist of 30 monomers independent of temperature,
concentration and ionic strength. The micelle volume is large
compared to a dry protein volume of about 0.75 ml/g. The
number of hydrophobic contacts is probably restricted to 4 per
monomer and at least part of the ϰ-casein molecule possesses
a tertiary structure.

Such micelle formation is strongly reminiscent of the
behavior of virus coat proteins, the assembly of which has
been described by Caspar and Klug[64]. Briefly, their reasoning
is, that if one wishes to arrange a number of identical and
asymmetric subunits on a spherical surface in such a way that
the subunits make the same specific contacts over and over
again, then the number of particles as well as their
arrangement appear to be very restricted. The possibilities,
given in Table V, are represented by cubic point groups because
all directions in space are equivalent. The association requires
built-in directions in the form of a structure unit with an
inherent set of specific bond sites. With virus self-assembly
the icosahedral symmetry appears to be the preferred choice.
As the ϰ-casein micelle consists of 30 subunits, the only way
to fit this protein into Table V is to assume that the
ϰ-monomer has a two-fold axis of symmetry. In that case 30
monomers are sufficient to be placed on a sphere in strict
equivalence (see Figure 10). This model, a ϰ-casein shell with

Table V. Number of Asymmetric and Identical Units Which can be
         Arranged in a Spherical Structure with Cubic Point
         Groups of Symmetry. The Regular Polyhedra Having These
         Elements of Symmetry are in the Last Column.

notation	rotation axes	asymmetric units	platonic solid
23	3 2-fold 4 3-fold	12	tetrahedron
432	6 2-fold 4 3-fold 3 4-fold	24	cube octahedron
532	15 2-fold 10 3-fold 6 5-fold	60	dodecahedron icosahedron

a hollow core, explains also the large hydration found for the
micelle. The tendency of x-casein to form stable shells wherein
insoluble casein can be packed and with a diameter not necessarily
restricted to the one for pure x-micelles, forms an attractive
working hypothesis to explain the formation and properties of
natural micelles.

Figure 10. Model of a x-casein micelle consisting of 30
monomers, each monomer having a two-fold axis of symmetry.
Views along the 2-fold axis of the icosahedral structure
(point group 532 of Table V).

DISCUSSION

The spontaneous formation of soaplike micelles has been
suggested in the solutions of a restricted number of pro-
teins[6-8], but it is only with $\varkappa$- and β-casein that the size
and shape of the micelles formed have been investigated into
some detail. At neutral pH and ionic strengths exceeding 0.1
the degree of micellization of $\varkappa$- and β-casein is fairly high
(30 and 23 at I = 0.2 respectively) and micelles were found to
be in equilibrium with monomers at a critical micelle concentration. The comparison with the behavior of simpler
amphiphiles suggests itself, especially in the case of β-casein
(cf. Table II).

The extreme delicacy of the HL-balance determining the
micelle parameters is impressively demonstrated by experiments
in which the charge and the hydrophobicity of the $\varkappa$-casein
molecule were enzymatically or chemically modified (cf.
Figure 2). Further as a comparison of the sequences of $\varkappa$- and
non-micellizing α_{s1}-casein (Table II) shows, it is not so much
the overall hydrophobicity as well the uneven distribution
of charged and apolar residues along the polypeptide chain
which determines the type of association. Both α_{s1} - and $\varkappa$-casein
have comparable overall hydrophobicities of about 5 kJ/res.,
which is among the highest found with proteins[26]. In line
with this figure both proteins have a strong tendency to
associate in aqueous solution, but their association behavior
is quite different. Kappa-casein, as we have seen, form globular
30-mers, α_{s1} on the other hand, undergoes a number of rapidly
equilibrating, consecutive association steps[4,5,35]. This is
most readily demonstrated by their different sedimentation
patterns (cf. Figures 7 and 11): the trailing edge of the
sedimenting boundary of α_{s1}-casein is typical for a polymer
undergoing a series of consecutive associations, not for
micelle formation.

The colloid chemist recognizing the amphiphilicity of both
$\varkappa$- and β-casein may wonder why only $\varkappa$ and not β acts as the
protective colloid of the natural casein micelle. The answer
to this question lies in the first place in the higher number
of ester-phosphate groups and the concomitant increased
calcium-sensitivity of β- in comparison to $\varkappa$-casein. Secondly,
the insensitivity of the $\varkappa$-casein micelle to temperature and
ionic strength contrasts with the behavior of the β-micelle,
whose size appears to depend strongly on both variables. This
suggests that the quality of the bonds in the $\varkappa$- and the
β-micelle is different, the bonds in the latter less specific
and more at random. Because of this $\varkappa$-casein is probably better
suited to form a stable and coherent layer around a core of

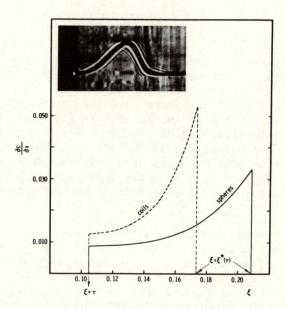

Figure 11. Comparison of experimental and theoretical boundary
spreading of α_{s1}-casein C in the ultracentrifuge after 3600 s
at 130 000 x g.
Experimental conditions: protein concentration 2.33 g/1;
barbiturate buffer pH 6.6, I = 0.2; 9°C. The theoretical
schlieren patterns were calculated assuming consecutive
association steps up to pentamerization and neglecting the
effect of diffusion on the shape of the boundary [63].

insoluble caseins in the natural micelle. The question now
arises by which mechanism $\varkappa$-casein stabilizes the other
calcium-sensitive components against flocculation: by
solubilization within a $\varkappa$-micelle or by the formation of nonmicellar stoichiometric complexes of less overall calcium-
sensitivity. Of course, this question can only be answered
by reliable experiments on the location of $\varkappa$-casein in the
natural micelle. So far the experiments have been rather
conflicting and led to two different micelle models: one in
which the $\varkappa$ is more or less evenly distributed through the
micelle and the other so-called coat/core models in which
$\varkappa$-casein is exclusively located in the surface[4,17,65]. It
appears to us that the theories in favor of the coat/core
model are somewhat more substantiated than those rejecting a
specific, surface-active role of $\varkappa$-casein. We shall just
mention 3 arguments to vindicate our preference.

The first of these is the important finding by Sullivan et al. [66] that there exists a strong, inverse correlation between the size and the $\varkappa$-casein percentage of natural micelles. This suggests that $\varkappa$-casein is indeed the component responsible for the dispersion of the caseins. Further, from the size and degree of micellization of the pure $\varkappa$-micelle (cf. Table IV) Vreeman[62] calculated the surface area of $\varkappa$-casein to be 1.7 m^2/mg. If one accepts that $\varkappa$ is exclusively located in the surface of the natural micelles with the same surface area, the amount of $\varkappa$-casein in milk can easily be calculated from the light scattering radii and Zimm distributions of micelle sizes [67,68]. From the data of 8 individual milks, one then finds an average $\varkappa$-content of 13.1 ($\pm$ 1.9) %, to be compared with the analytical figure of about 12.5%. The close agreement suggests that the amount of $\varkappa$-casein present in milk is indeed sufficient to be fitted in the surface of the natural micelles and is in line with its presumed role as a solubilizing amphiphile.

The most direct evidence about the surface location of $\varkappa$-casein, however, was recently obtained by Schmidt and Both (personal communication) in electronmicroscopic experiments with artificial micelles. If such micelles were prepared from Au-labelled $\varkappa$, unlabelled α_{s1} and CaCl$_2$, the staining of the electron micrographs is observed predominantly in the micelle surface (Figure 12). If on the other hand, only the α_{s1} is labelled, the gold is found in the micelle cores. Such experiments clearly show that, at least in reconstituted micelles, $\varkappa$-casein exerts its protecting role by solubilizing α_{s1} and suggests a similar mechanism of stabilization with the natural micelle.

The above considerations circumvent the important, but not fully understood, role of the 7% of colloidal calcium phosphate for the stability of the natural micelle. Since this overview is mainly concerned with the detergent-like properties of $\varkappa$- and β-casein, this omission seems justified. It should be kept in mind, however, that a small proportion of colloidal calcium phosphate can severely influence some of the micelle properties. This is most readily demonstrated with artificial micelles. Such micelles[4,69] can be prepared by bringing together Na-caseinate and CaCl$_2$ with or without Na-phosphate at 37°C. It is found, though, that in the presence of Na-phosphate the incorporation of colloidal calcium phosphate leads to an improved resistance against pressure and exhaustive dialysis, comparable to natural micelles [70,71]. Colloidal calcium phosphate is irreversibly removed by acidification to pH 5.9, which leads to a partial disintegration of the micelle[72]. The practical significance of such phenomena has been discussed in recent reviews [17,65].

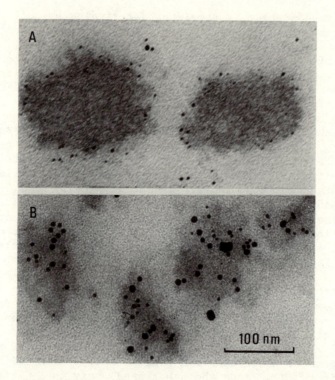

Figure 12. Thin section electron micrographs of gold-stained micelles. Experimental conditions: $1\varkappa/3\alpha_{s1}$ (w/w), 30 mM $CaCl_2$ A: $\varkappa(Au) - \alpha_{s1}$; B: $\varkappa - \alpha_{s1}(Au)$.

ACKNOWLEDGEMENT

        We are indebted to D. G. Schmidt and P. Both for providing us with Figure 12 prior to publication.

REFERENCES

1. L. W. Nichol, J. L. Bethune, G. Kegeles and E. L. Hess in "The Proteins", H. Neurath, Editor, 2nd edition, Vol. II, Ch. 9, Academic, New York, 1964.
2. J. R. Cann and W. B. Goad, "Interacting Macromolecules",

Academic, New York, 1970.

3. I. M. Klotz, D. W. Darnall, N. R. Langerman in "The Proteins", H. Neurath, Editor, 3rd edition, Vol. I, p. 293, Academic Press, New York, 1975.

4. H. A. McKenzie, Editor, "Milk Proteins. Chemistry and Molecular Biology", Vol. II, Academic Press, New York, 1971.

5. D. G. Schmidt, "On the Association of α_{s1}-Casein", Thesis University of Utrecht, 1969.

6. F. Oosawa and S. Asakura, "Thermodynamics of the Polymerization of Protein", Academic Press, New York, 1975.

7. R. R. Crichton, Angew. Chem. 85, 53 (1973).

8. R. A. Driedonks, P. C. J. Krijgsman, J. E. Mellema, J. Mol. Biol. 113, 123 (1977).

9. G. S. Hartley in "Micellization, Solubilization and Micro-emulsions", K. L. Mittal, Editor, Vol. I, p. 23, Plenum Press, New York, 1977.

10. J. C. Mercier, F. Grosclaude and B. Ribadeau Dumas, Eur. J. Biochem. 23, 41 (1971).

11. B. Ribadeau Dumas, G. Brignon, F. Grosclaude and J. C. Mercier, Eur. J. Biochem. 25, 505 (1972).

12. J. C. Mercier, G. Brignon and B. Ribadeau Dumas, Eur. J. Biochem. 35, 222 (1973).

13. G. Brignon, B. Ribadeau Dumas, J. C. Mercier, J. P. Pelissier and B. C. Das, FEBS-Letters 76, 274 (1977).

14. C. A. Zittle, J. Dairy Sci. 44, 2101 (1961).

15. D. F. Waugh and P. H. von Hippel, J. Am. Chem. Soc., 78, 4576 (1956).

16. K. Linderstrøm Lang, Compt. Rend. Trav. Lab. Carlsberg 17, 1 (1929).

17. D. G. Schmidt and T. A. J. Payens, in "Surface and Colloid Science", E. Matijevic, Editor, Vol. 9, Ch. 3, Wiley, New York, 1976.

18. P. H. von Hippel and D. F. Waugh, J. Am. Chem. Soc. 77, 4311 (1955).

19. R. McL. Whitney, J. R. Brunner, K. E. Ebner, H. M. Farrell, Jr., R. V. Josephson, C. V. Morr, H. E. Swaisgood, J. Dairy. Sci. 59, 785 (1978).

20. R. A. Sullivan, M. M. Fitzpatrick, E. K. Stanton, R. Annino, G. Kissel and F. Palermiti, Arch. Biochem. Biophys. 55, 455 (1955).

21. M. Hawler, Arch. Biochem. Biophys. 51, 79 (1954).

22. T. A. J. Payens and B. W. van Markwijk, Biochim. Biophys. Acta, 71, 517 (1963).

23. A. L. Andrews, D. Atkinson, M. T. A. Evans, E. G. Finer, J. P. Green, M. C. Phillips and R. N. Robertson, Biopol. 18, 1105 (1979).

24. K. Takase, R. Niki, S. Arima, Biochim. Biophys. Acta 622, 1 (1980).

25. D. F. Waugh, Adv. Protein Chem. 9, 326 (1954).

26. C. C. Bigelow, J. Theoret. Biolog. 16, 187 (1967).

27. H. F. Fisher, Proc. Natl. Acad. Sci. 51, 1285 (1964).
28. L. K. Creamer, Biochim. Biophys. Acta 271, 252 (1972).
29. M. Noelken and M. Reibstein, Arch. Biochem. Biophys. 123, 397 (1968).
30. C. Tanford, "Physical Chemistry of Macromolecules", Wiley, New York, 1961.
31. T. T. Herskovits, Biochemistry 5, 1018 (1966).
32. J. Garnier, J. Mol. Biol. 19, 586 (1966).
33. K. N. Pearce, Eur. J. Biochem. 58, 23 (1975).
34. P. D. Hoagland, J. Dairy Sci. 49, 783 (1966).
35. D. G. Schmidt and T. A. J. Payens, J. Colloid Interface Sci. 39, 655 (1972).
36. M. T. A. Evans, M. C. Phillips and M. N. Jones, Biopol. 18, 1123 (1979).
37. T. A. J. Payens, J. A. Brinkhuis and B. W. van Markwijk, Biochim. Biophys. Acta 175, 434 (1969).
38. H. Eisenberg, "Biological Macromolecules and Polyelectrolytes in Solution", Clarendon, Oxford, 1976.
39. H. Yamakawa, "Modern Theory of Polymer Solutions", Harper & Row, New York 1971.
40. R. J. M. Tausk, J. van Esch, J. Karmiggelt, G. Voordouw and J. Th. G. Overbeek, Biophys. Chem. 1, 184 (1974).
41. H. K. Schachman, "Ultracentrifugation in Biochemistry", Academic, New York, 1959.
42. W. Buchheim and D. G. Schmidt, J. Dairy Res. 46, 277 (1979).
43. R. Niki, K. Takase, S. Arima, Milchwissenschaft 32, 577 (1977).
44. C. Tanford, "The Hydrophobic Effect: the Formation of Michelles and Biological Membranes", Ch. 7, Wiley, New York, 1973.
45. M. P. Thompson, E. B. Kalan and R. Greenberg, J. Dairy Sci. 50, 767 (1967).
46. G. P. Berry and L. K. Creamer, Biochemistry 14, 3542 (1975).
47. T. A. J. Payens and K. Heremand, Biopol. 8, 335 (1969).
48. N. Nishikido, M. Shinozaki, G. Sugihara, M. Tanaka and S. Kaneshina, J. Colloid Interface Sci. 74, 474 (1980).
49. P. D. Hoagland, Biochemistry 7, 2542 (1968).
50. M. T. A. Evans, L. Irons, M. Jones, Biochim. Biophys. Acta 229, 411 (1971).
51. M. T. A. Evans, L. Irons, J. H. P. Petty, Biochim. Biophys. Acta 243, 259 (1971).
52. H. E. Swaisgood and J. R. Brunner, Biochem. Biophys. Res. Comm. 12, 148 (1963).
53. H. E. Swaisgood, J. R. Brunner and H. A. Lillevik, Biochemistry 3, 1616 (1964).
54. H. J. Vreeman, P. Both, J. A. Brinkhuis and C. A. van der Spek, Biochim. Biophys. Acta 491, 93 (1977).
55. H. E. Swaisgood, Crit. Rev. Food Technol. 3, 375 (1972–1973).
56. D. G. Schmidt and W. Buchheim, Netherl. Milk Dairy J. 30, 17 (1976).

57. R. J. Hill and R. G. Wake, Nature 221, 635 (1969).
58. R. K. Dewan, A. Chundgar, R. Head, V. A. Bloomfield and
    C. V. Morr, Biochim. Biophys. Acta 342, 313 (1974).
59. R. B. Leslie, L. Irons and D. Chapman, Biochim. Biophys.
    Acta 188, 237 (1969).
60. R. F. L. Clarke and S. Nakai, Biochim. Biophys. Acta
    257, 61 (1972).
61. M. H. Loucheux-Lefèbvre, J. P. Aubert and P. Jollès,
    Biophys. J. 23, 323 (1978).
62. H. J. Vreeman, J. Dairy Res. 46, 271 (1979).
63. H. Fujita, "Foundations of Ultracentrifuge Analysis",
    Chemical Analysis, Vol. 42, P. J. Ehrig and J. D.
    Wineforduer, Editors, Wiley, New York, 1975.
64. D. L. D. Caspar and A. Klug, Cold Spring Harbor Symp.
    27, 1 (1962).
65. T. A. J. Payens, J. Dairy Res. 46, 291 (1979).
66. R. A. Sullivan, M. M. Fitzpatrick and E. K. Stanton,
    Nature 183, 616 (1959).
67. C. Holt, Biochim. Biophys. Acta 400, 293 (1975).
68. C. Holt, T. G. Parker and D. G. Dalgleish, Biochim.
    Biophys. Acta 400, 283 (1975).
69. D. G. Schmidt, J. Koops and D. Westerbeek, Netherl.
    Milk Dairy J. 31, 328 (1977).
70. D. G. Schmidt and J. Koops, Netherl. Milk Dairy J.
    31, 342 (1977).
71. D. G. Schmidt, P. Both and J. Koops, Netherl. Milk
    Dairy J. 33, 40 (1979).
72. T. C. A. McGann and G. T. Pyne, J. Dairy Res. 27, 403
    (1959).

MICELLAR PROPERTIES OF GANGLIOSIDES

Mario Corti and Vittorio Degiorgio[+]
CISE S.p.A.,P.O.B.12081, Milano 20100,Italy
                    and
Riccardo Ghidoni and Sandro Sonnino
Department of Biological Chemistry,The Medical School
University of Milano, Milano, Italy

Gangliosides are amphiphilic biological lipids, having a hydrophilic part made of an oligosaccharide chain containing one or more molecules of sialic acid, and a hydrophobic part made of two long aliphatic chains belonging to a sphingosine and a fatty acid residue. The interactions of gangliosides with biological molecules and membranes may be considerably influenced by the state of aggregation of ganglioside molecules. In this review, the available experimental information about the micellar properties of gangliosides is collected and critically compared. The most significant data are the following: the probable value of the critical micelle concentration is in the range $10^{-10} - 10^{-8}$ M, the aggregation number is between 200 and 350, the hydrodynamic radius is about 60 Å, and the micellar shape is probably an oblate ellipsoid (disklike micelle) with an axial ratio about 2. The properties of mixed micelles with a non-ionic commercial amphiphile, Triton X-100, are also discussed.

[+] Researcher from the Italian National Research Council (CNR).

INTRODUCTION

Gangliosides are sialic acid-containing glycosphingolipids which display a marked amphiphilic character. They are known to be major lipid components of the nerve cell membranes to which they are tightly bound. They were first identified in brain forty years ago by Klenk who reported the first chemical data concerning their structure.[1,2]

It is well known that gangliosides are involved in a variety of cell membrane phenomena, although it is not possible in the present state of knowledge to precisely assess their physiological role. Because of their amphiphilic character, gangliosides may form micelles in aqueous solution and may be included, by their hydrophobic portion, in the bilayer of biological membranes. Since the interactions of gangliosides with biological molecules and membranes are influenced by their structural organization, it is necessary to get a detailed picture of their physicochemical characteristics in order to understand more deeply their function.

The purpose of this review is to collect and critically compare the available information about the micellar properties of gangliosides. As it will be shown there are several points still to be clarified.

The paper is organised as follows. The first Section describes the structure of ganglioside molecules and illustrates several biochemical mechanisms in which gangliosides are involved either in monomeric or micellar form. The second Section reports about measurements of the critical micelle concentration and of such micellar properties as the molecular weight, the sedimentation, and the diffusion coefficients. The last Section presents some recent light-scattering results on mixed micelles of ganglioside and Triton X-100.

STRUCTURE AND BIOCHEMICAL IMPLICATIONS OF GANGLIOSIDES

The ganglioside structure contains a molecule of sphingosine in which it is possible to identify two different sites of conjugation. The first is on the carbon in position 2, where a fatty acid residue is linked to the amino group, the second is on the carbon in position 1, which is glycosidically linked with an oligosaccharide chain where one or more molecules of sialic acid are always present (Figure 1).

The long aliphatic chains, belonging to the base and to the fatty acid residue, give the hydrophobic properties to the ganglio side molecule, while the polar carbohydrate portion is responsible for the high hydrophilicity of the molecule. Therefore, gangliosides can be represented as built from these two regions which are sepa-

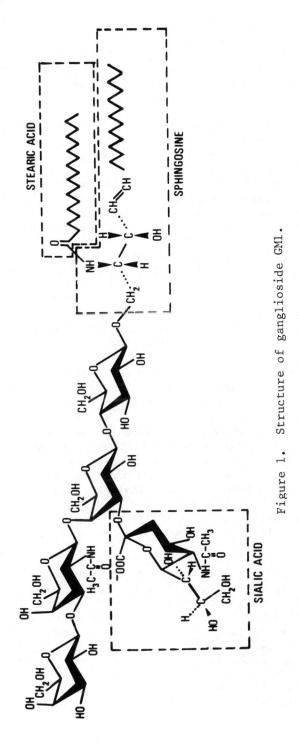

Figure 1. Structure of ganglioside GM1.

rated one from the other by the first three carbons of the long
chain base. This area of the molecule can be considered as a "bor-
der region" which feels the effects of both hydrophobic and hydrophilic parts even if, in principle, it should display a sensible
hydrophilicity, due to the possibility of the 3-hydroxyl group to
form inter and intramolecular hydrogen bonds.[3]

Sphingosines or, more correctly, long chain bases, found in
gangliosides from either nervous or extra-nervous tissues, are
always and only in the erythro configuration,[4] have typically 18
or 20 carbon atoms and display, except for a few per cent units,
an unsaturation site on carbon 4 (2D-amino-octadec-4-en-1,3-D-diol
and 2D-amino-eicos-4-en-1,3-D-diol, respectively). Owing to planar
placing, the double bond assigns a sensible rigidity to the molecule, preventing the possibility of free rotation on the C-C axis.

With regard to fatty acids, while in the nervous system at
least 70% is represented by stearic acid; whereas in extranervous
tissues also saturated and unsaturated fatty acids with a higher
aliphatic chain (22 and 24 carbon atoms) are present in considerable amounts. This feature, added to the differences in length and
unsaturation degree of sphingosine, gives heterogeneity to the lipidic portion of ganglioside molecules.

More complex is the situation concerning the saccharide core,
as till now about sixty gangliosides with distinct carbohydrate composition and/or type of linkage have been discovered. The structure
schematic formulas and the abbreviation used for the nomenclature[5,6]
of the major gangliosides are listed in Table I. In general, the
saccharide core contains neutral hexoses (glucose, galactose, fucose,
arabinose) and N-acetyl-hexosamines (N-acetyl-galactosamine and N-
acetyl-glucosamine), along with one or more residues of sialic acid,
meaning with this term all the biological derivatives of neuraminic
acid (5-amino-3,5-dideoxy-D-glycero-D-galacto-nonulopyranoside). The
most frequent sialic acids are N-acetyl-neuraminic acid and N-
glycolyl-neuraminic acid predominant in nervous and extranervous
districts respectively.

Ganglioside mixtures are currently prepared with procedures involving the lipid extraction from biological tissues with aqueous
chloroform/methanol or tetrahydrofurane/phosphate buffer.[7,8] The
presence of ions in the extraction medium allows the destruction of
non-covalent interactions between gangliosides and other membrane
components, as glycolipids or glycoproteins, favouring the extraction process. Single gangliosides, homogeneous from the point of
view of the carbohydrate part, are obtained from the ganglioside
mixture by purification through several silica gel and gel filtration chromatographic columns.[9-11]

Table I. Nomenclature and Schematic Formula of Gangliosides.

Schematic formula	IUPAC-IUB recommendations(5)	Nomenclature of Svennerholm(6)
NeuAcα2→3Galβ1→4Glcβ1→1'Cer	II^3αNeuAcLacCer	GM3
NeuAcα2→8NeuAcα2→3Galβ1→4Glcβ1→1'Cer	II^3α(NeuAc)$_2$LacCer	GD3
GalNAcβ1→4Gal(3←2αNeuAc)β1→4Glcβ1→1'Cer	II^3αNeuAcGgOse$_3$Cer	GM2
GalNAcβ1→4Gal(3←2αNeuAc8←2αNeuAc)β1→4Glcβ1→1'Cer	II^3α(NeuAc)$_2$GgOse$_3$Cer	GD2
Galβ1→3GalNAcβ1→4Gal(3←2αNeuAc)β1→4Glcβ1→1'Cer	II^3αNeuAcGgOse$_4$Cer	GM1
NeuAcα2→3Galβ1→3GalNAcβ1→4Gal(3←2αNeuAc)β1→4Glcβ1→1'Cer	II^3αNeuAcIV^{3}αNeuAcGgOse$_4$Cer	GD1a
Galβ1→3GalNAcβ1→4Gal(3←2αNeuAc8←2αNeuAc)β1→4Glcβ1→1'Cer	II^3α(NeuAc)$_2$GgOse$_4$Cer	GD1b
NeuAcα2→3Galβ1→3GalNAcβ1→4Gal(3←2αNeuAc8←2αNeuAc)β1→4Glcβ1→1'Cer	II^3α(NeuAc)$_2$IV^{3}αNeuAcGgOse$_4$Cer	GT1b

At the moment, no procedure has yet been described to obtain gangliosides homogeneous also in the lipidic portion. Therefore, the available products are always a complex family of different molecular species having exactly the same carbohydrate composition. Two aspects must be taken into account in handling these products. First, the purity regarding the oligosaccharide portion must be as high as possible. In fact, size and polarity differences in the carbohydrate core and presence of small amounts of contaminants can influence the global ganglioside hydrophilic properties. Second, the lipidic composition of gangliosides, with regard either to fatty acids or long chain bases, must be well known and unmodified in the course of the experiment. It has been in fact reported that, as it happens with other amphiphilic substances, a different lipidic composition of the ganglioside can influence its physico-chemical properties, for example the aggregation number in aqueous media.[12]

In aqueous solution, gangliosides can exist as monomers (or oligomers) at very low concentration and as micelles, above a critical concentration. There is no clear evidence about biological interactions of gangliosides as monomers becuase these investigations usually require labelled gangliosides with very high specific radioactivity. There is evidence about the capability of ganglioside monomeric form to adhere to all surfaces, nonbiological ones included.[13] More frequently studied are the interactions that gangliosides exhibit when they are in a micellar state.[14]

One interesting example about the influence of the state of aggregation on ganglioside interactions is given by the modifications of the Na^+, K^+ ATPase activity after incorporation of GM1 ganglioside in neuronal membranes. It has been observed that incubation of these membranes with micellar concentrations of GM1 ganglioside leads to an inhibition of Na^+, K^+ ATPase activity[15], while in the presence of nanomolar concentrations of GM1, probably in the monomeric form, the enzyme activity is significantly increased.[16]

Gangliosides, probably in micellar form, are involved in mediating the binding or the action mechanism of some biological molecules, as microbial toxins,[17] serotonin,[18] hormones,[19] interferon,[20] bilirubin,[21] wheat germ agglutinin[22] and lecithins[23].

The binding of gangliosides, either pure or mixed, with such molecules is consistent in many cases with a general ganglioside-protein interaction model recently worked out and verified by means of an investigation on the binding between GM1 ganglioside and bovine serum albumin (BSA).[24] These latter results have unequivocally proved the presence of at least three complexes: one of these is due to the interaction between BSA and a submicellar form of ganglioside, the other two are very likely due to the interaction between one micelle of GM1 and one albumine polypeptide chain and are related each other by a time-dependent dimerization process.

Another interesting field, investigated by many authors, concerns the ability of ganglioside molecules to interact with biological or artificial membranes. Such a binding process could be compatible either with monomeric or micellar ganglioside interactions. Up to now, there is no evidence in favour of one or the other interpretations. The role of gangliosides in such mechanisms is related to their contribution to membrane structuring and organization, and to enhance some peculiar membrane characteristics, as stability, permeability and recognization properties. This contribution surely depends on the chemical properties of gangliosides and on the influence they have in modulating protein-lipid interactions, in and out biological membranes.

GANGLIOSIDE MICELLES

Before entering into a detailed discussion of the available experimental results on ganglioside micelles, we briefly recall from Tanford's book[25] some general considerations about the aggregation properties of amphiphilic biological lipids.

The hydrocarbon chains of biological lipids are usually very long, and the predominant type of molecule contains two hydrocarbon chains per head group. The aggregate can be either a micelle or a vesicle depending on the length of the hydrocarbon chains and on the electric charge and the size of the head group.[26] Ionic double-chain amphiphiles having a large head group, as it is the case of gangliosides, are expected to aggregate as micelles with a very small value of the critical micelle concentration.

It is a general property of amphiphiles that the cmc decreases by increasing the alkyl chain length. The effect of having two separate hydrocarbon chains with a single head group has been also studied. The results demonstrate that the addition of the second chain is equivalent to lengthening the first chain by approximately 60% of the alkyl chain length of the second chain. By using this criterion Tanford predicted a cmc for dipalmitoyl phosphatidylcholine (a zwitterionic phospholipid with two C_{15} chains) in reasonable agreement with the measured value 4.7×10^{-10} M. [25]

An almost general feature of biological lipids is the presence of unsaturated fatty acids. For molecules with unsaturated hydrocarbon chains the melting point for ordered structures is expected to be below room temperature, whereas very long saturated hydrocarbon chains may have high melting temperatures. Therefore micellar structures formed by amphiphilic molecules with long saturated chains may have cores in which the chains form an ordered paracrystalline array at room temperature. This does not change however the order of magnitude of the cmc.

Cmc Measurements

We have reported in Table II the literature values for the cmc of gangliosides. The earlier studies assign the cmc to the concentration range $10^{-5} - 10^{-4}$ M. The more recent experiments, with the exception of Rauvala,[29,30] indicate that the cmc is lower by several orders of magnitude. Note that the light scattering experiment[33] could only assign an upper limit to the cmc because the scattered light intensity is too small to allow reliable measurements below the ganglioside concentration 10^{-6} M. It is very difficult to explain the discrepancy between the two groups of measurements. Although it is true that different techniques measure different properties, all the techniques employed have been cross-checked with many amphiphiles, and discrepancies in the order of magnitude of the cmc have never been found. Among the used techniques, the only one which lacks a clear interpretation and which does not work with all anionic amphiphiles is the triiodide method. However the results of Yohe and Rosenberg[28] have been confirmed by Rauvala[30] who has shown a crosscheck of the triiodide data by sedimentation analysis. It should also be noted that both Rauvala[30] and Formisano et al.[31] have measured the non-sedimentating radioactivity of labelled gangliosides solutions, and have found very different results.

A second point which should be examined is whether one can compare measurements at different temperature, ionic strength or pH. It is known that these parameters may influence the cmc of anionic amphiphiles. An example of this influence is given for GM1 solutions by Rauvala[30] showing a reduction of the apparent cmc by a factor of three going from pure water to 50mM sodium acetate buffer, pH 4.6. This example indicates that the effect is not large enough to explain the above mentioned discrepancy. Indeed, the data of Table II do not show any pattern concerning the dependence of the cmc on temperature, ionic strength or pH.

The fact that mixed gangliosides are employed instead of well characterized single species seems also to be irrelevant if one considers that distinct gangliosides show very similar cmc properties.

A technical problem which may have been overlooked in some of the published experiments is related to the ability of gangliosides to adsorb to glass surfaces. This may cuase the effective bulk concentration of gangliosides to be much smaller than anticipated.

The last, and very likely the most important, point is the effect of impurities. Particularly interesting is the case of amphiphilic impurities having a cmc much larger than the probable ganglioside cmc. According to the theory of mixed micelles[34], such impurities would be in monomeric form at very low concentrations, and would be progressively incorporated into the ganglioside micelle as the ganglioside concentration is increased. The concentration of im-

Table II. Literature Values for the cmc of Gangliosides.

cmc (M)	gangliosides	solvent	technique	temperature	Reference
1×10^{-4}	mixed	water	surface tension, conductivity	22°C 0°C	27
1×10^{-5}	mixed	water	conductivity	23°C	3
8.5×10^{-5} 7.5×10^{-5} 9.5×10^{-5}	GM1 GM2 GD1a	water	triiodide method	24°C	28
3×10^{-5} 8×10^{-5}	GM1 GM1	water+50 mM sodium acetate buffer,pH=4.6, water	neuraminidase, triiodide method,centrifufation	37°C 20°C	29,30
8.5×10^{-9} 7×10^{-9}	GM1 mixed	water−0.02 M Tris+0.1MNaCl pH=7.4	gel filtration, centrifugation in sucrose gradient, equilibrium dialysis		31
1×10^{-9}	GM1 GM2 GM3	water+ 10mM Tris/Hcl pH=7.5	ultracentrifugation	4°C	32
$<1 \times 10^{-6}$ $<1 \times 10^{-6}$	GM1 GD1a	water+ 25mM Tris/HCl pH=6.8	light scattering	37°C	33

purity monomers will show a saturation effect when the total concentration is sufficiently large (certainly much larger than the cmc
for the mixed micelle). If the saturation effect appears at concentrations around 10^{-5} - 10^{-4} M, it can be explained why measurements
sensitive to the monomer concentration, like those of Gammack,[27]
Howard and Burton,[3] and the sedimentation measurements of Rauvala[30]
find an increase in the monomer concentration up to the range 10^{-5} -
10^{-4} M, whereas methods sensitive to the presence of micelles, like
those of Formisano et al.[31], Mraz et al.[32], Corti et al.[33], indicate
that micelles are present well below the range 10^{-5} - 10^{-4} M.

Following this line of interpretation, one should guess that
Formisano et al.[31] were apparently able to eliminate completely impurities in their preparation of gangliosides, because they present
very low values of the nonsedimenting monomer concentration in
their boundary centrifugation experiment.

It should also be mentioned that Sattler et al.[35] and Ghidoni
et al.[36] have reported that at concentrations of 10^{-9} - 10^{-8} M
purified preparations of GM1, GM2 and mixed gangliosides in water
and in 0.1 M KCl aqueous solution were unable to cross a dialysis
membrane.

To conclude this Section, we can say that the cmc value of
gangliosides is probably in the range 10^{-10} - 10^{-8} M as suggested
by direct experimental evidence and by analogy with the information
available on double-chain phospholipids.

Size and Shape of Ganglioside Micelles

The literature data for the molecular weight M of ganglioside
micelles are reported in Table III. We have considered only the
most recent experiments (reference to earlier works can be found in
Gammack's paper[27]), because considerable advances in the preparation
methods and in the chemical characterization of gangliosides have
been achieved in the sixties.

Gammack[27] reports values of three micellar parameters, the sedimentation coefficient s, the diffusion coefficient D and the intrinsic viscosity $[\eta]$. He gives also the partial specific volume $\bar{v}$
of the mixed ganglioside micelle, $\bar{v}$ = 0.78 cm^3/g. The molecular
weight can be obtained from s and D by using the Svedberg relation

$$M = \frac{N\,k_B\,T\,s}{(1-\bar{v}\,\rho)D} \qquad (1)$$

where ρ is the density of the solvent, N the Avogadro number, T the
absolute temperature and k_B the Boltzmann constant. The micellar

weight can also be calculated from s and $[\eta]$, or from D and $[\eta]$ using the method of Scheraga and Mandelkern.[37] Static and transport coefficient of anionic micelles are expected to be concentration dependent in aqueous solution because of the strong electrostatic interactions due to micellar charge. The concentration dependence becomes less and less marked when the ionic strength is increased, since the interparticle Coulomb potential is screened more and more effectively by counterions [38]. Gammack[27] found indeed that s is a decreasing function of the ganglioside concentration c in pure water, and Yohe et al.[12] obtained a molecular weight almost independent of c in 0.1 M NaCl water. The values of M reported in Table III are calculated from Gammack's data by using the value of s extrapolated to small c, s = 11.8 S, whereas Gammack used the value s = 10.3 S corresponding to the 1% solution. The concentration dependence of D and $[\eta]$ is not given in reference 27, but it is presumably much smaller than for s.

Yohe et al.[12] have shown that the increase of sialic acid content decreases the micellar size (see Table III). The monosialogangliosides GM1 from GD1a and GM1 from GT1b are enzymatically prepared from GD1a and GT1b and differ from GM1 for the C_{20}-sphingosine content which is 37.3% for GM1, 56,5% for GD1a and 64.2% for GT1b. The data of Yohe et al. indicate that the length of the hydrophobic chains has a considerable effect on the micellar aggregation number.

The values of M obtained by laser-light scattering[33] are for both GM1 and GD1a larger than those reported in reference 12. The uncertainties in the absolute calibration and the differences in C_{20}-sphingosine content do not seem to explain completely the discrepancy between the two sets of data. In a successive experiment[39] the light intensity scattered by GM1 in water with 25 mM sodium phosphate buffer /5 mM disodium EDTA, pH 7.0, was measured as a function of the temperature in the range 15-42°C. The results are reported in Figure 2. The quantity I_r, which represents the scattered intensity normalized to the intensity scattered by the solvent, does not show large variations in the investigated temperature range, but a slight gradual decrease is found going from 30° to 40°C. The scattered intensity is related to M by the expression

$$I_r = A \left(\frac{dn}{dc}\right)_G^2 M (c - c_o) \tag{2}$$

where $(dn/dc)_G$ is the refractive index increment for the ganglioside solution, c_o is the ganglioside cmc, and A is a calibration constant. If we use the values A = 5.86 and $(dn/dc)_G$= 0.143 given in Reference 33 for the GM1 solution+ at 37°C, and we assume that

----

+ Due to a misprint the value of A actually appearing in Reference 33 is 8.34 instead of the correct value 5.86.

Table III. Molecular Weight M and Aggregation Number m of
           Gangliosides Micelles.

Ganglioside	Solvent	10^{-5} M (daltons)	m	Technique	Ref.
Mixed	Water,20°C	3.7±0.37	240	Sedim-Diffusion	27
	"	3.2±0.32	210	Sedim-Viscosity	27
	"	4.4±0.44	290	Diffusion-Viscosity	27
GT1b	Water+0.1MNaCl	2.5±0.25	120	Sedim-Equil.	12
GD1a	"	3.0±0.30	165	"	12
GM2	"	3.0±0.25	220	"	12
GM1	"	3.4±0.30	225	"	12
GM1 from GD1a	"	3.75±0.20	240	"	12
GM1 from GT1b	"	4.35±0.20	280	"	12
GM1	Water+0.025M Tris-HCl,37°C	5.32±0.53	352	Light scattering	33
GD1a		4.17±0.43	229	"	33
GD1a+10^{-3}CaCl$_2$		4.31±0.43	237	"	33

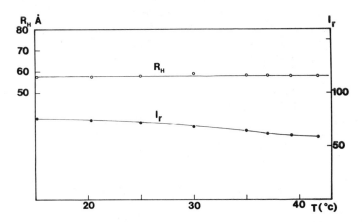

Figure 2. Behavior of the scattered light intensity I_r and of the hydrodynamic radius R_H of the GM1 ganglioside micelle as a function of the temperature in a 25 mM sodium phosphate/5 mM disodium EDTA (pH 7.0) aqueous solution.

both factors do not depend on T, from the data of Figure 2 the value of M is 500000 in the temperature range 15-30°C and decreases to the value 433000 at 42°C. The assumption that A is independent of T is reasonable, whereas it is possible that $(dn/dc)_G$ changes a little as a function of T.

The technique of quasielastic light scattering allows to measure quickly and accurately the diffusion coefficient D at a given concentration. This technique has been only recently employed for micellar solutions[40-41] and, in particular, for ganglioside solutions[33,39]. A useful feature of quasielastic light scattering is that it gives the full shape of the correlation function of concentration fluctuations. Such a function contains information not only on D, but also on the polydispersity of the micellar solution.

It is interesting to note that the ganglioside preparation of Reference 33 give appreciable polydispersities, whereas the data of Reference 39 show with very good reproducibility a monodisperse solution. We have reported in Figure 3 the time-dependent part of the intensity correlation function of scattered light measured at two distinct temperatures[39]. The evidence of small polydispersity is given by the exponential shape of the two curves. It is possible that the difference in polydispersity between the two ganglioside

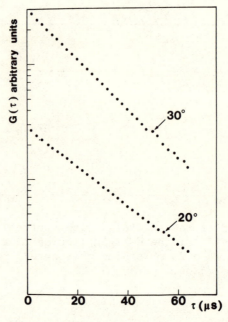

Figure 3. The time-dependent part $G(\tau)$ of the intensity correlation function of laser light scattered from 25 mM sodium phosphate/5 mM disodium EDTA (pH 7.0) aqueous solution of 0.8 mM GM1 at 20° and 30°C.

preparations is due to the fact that the GM1 used in Reference 33 was a mixture of salts (with ≃ 80% potassium salt), whereas the GM1 of reference 39 was a pure sodium salt.

The hydrodynamic radius R_H can be calculated from D through the Einstein-Stokes relation

$$D = \frac{k_B T}{6 N \eta R_H} \qquad (3)$$

where η is the shear viscosity of the solvent. We recall that $R_H = fR_e$ where R_e is the radius of the sphere having the equivalent volume, and f > 1 is a form factor. For a spherical particle f = 1.

The values of D reported by Corti et al.[33] are 4.97 x 10^{-7} cm^2/s and 5.34 x 10^{-7} cm^2/s for GM1 and GD1a, respectively, at 37°C. The only previously reported measurement of diffusion coefficient is

that of Gammack[27] who obtained D = 3.78 x 10^{-7} cm^2/s on a mixture of
gangliosides, at 20°C. This value is not too far from the data of
Reference 33, once the appropriate temperature correction is applied.
Indeed by considering that the ratio between the viscosity at 20°C
and that at 37°C is 1.45 for water, Gammack's diffusion coefficient,
corrected at 37°C, becomes 5.48 cm^2/s. The hydrodynamic radii of
GM1 and GD1a, calculated from the values of D given above[33], are
63.9 and 59.5 Å respectively. These radii are considerably larger
than the length of the monomer which is approximately 30 Å,[42] but
they are too small to be geometrically consistent with a vesicle
structure. This latter consideration is in agreement with the suggestion that ionic double-chain amphiphiles aggregate in micelles
when they have large head groups[26].

The knowledge of both m and R_H can be used to make a guess at
the shape of the ganglioside micelle, following a procedure proposed by Tanford[43] and subsequently used by several authors[44,45].
The physical model of a micelle is a hydrocarbon core formed by
the associated acyl chains with the sugar head groups projecting
out into the water. If the hydrophobic region is restricted to a
short dimension of the core equal to the length of the hydrophobic group, it is easy to see from our data that the ganglioside
micelle cannot be spherical. Indeed, taking m = 352 for GM1 and a
density 0.87 g/cm^3 for the core, the core volume is 341000 Å ^{3}. This
would correspond to a sphere of radius 43.2 Å, much larger than the
actual length of the hydrophobic group which is about 20 Å.
By assuming an oblate ellipsoid of revolution for the core shape
(disklike micelle), with minor semiaxis length of 20 Å, the major
semiaxis length comes out to be 64 Å. By adding a layer of 14 Å
(including the sugar head groups plus a hydration layer), the
disklike micelle would present an axial ratio 78/34 = 2.26, a radius
of the equivalent sphere R_e = 58.9 Å, a form factor f = 1.06, and
therefore a hydrodynamic radius R_H = 62.4 Å. By assuming instead
a prolate ellipsoid of revolution for the core shape (rodlike micel
le), we would calculate a major semiaxis length of 204 Å, an axial
ratio 218/34 = 6.41, R_e = 63.1 Å, f = 1.35, and therefore R_H=85.2 Å.
Clearly, the hydrodynamic radius calculated from the disklike model
is in much better agreement with the experimental result of 63.9 Å
than the radius calculated from the rodlike model. It is interesting
to note that this finding is in agreement with the prediction (see
Chapters 8 and 11 of Reference 25) that the micelle formed by mole
cules containing two hydrocarbon chains per head group is of the
bilayer type. The suggested axial ratio of the disklike micelle is
similar to the axial ratio about 2 proposed by Gammack[27] on the
basis of his viscosity and diffusion coefficient measurements.

The hydrodynamic radius of the GM1 ganglioside is independent
of the temperature in the temperature range 15-42°C, as shown by the
data reported in Figure 2.[39]

Measurements of the sedimentation coefficient of ganglioside micelles have been reported also by Formisano et al.[31], and by Mraz et al.[32]. The former experiment was performed with mixed gangliosides at concentrations between 2×10^{-8} and 10^{-5} M with buffer 0.02 M Tris, pH 7.4. The sedimentation rate was about 10 S at 20°C. The latter experiment gave, for a similar buffer and a similar concentration range, the rates 10.0, 7.5, and 5.3 S for GM1, GM2 and GM3 respectively.

Formisano et al.[31] find a slowly sedimenting species (s = 4.5 S) when the mixed gangliosides are first dissolved in dimethylsulfoxide and then diluted into buffer, or when the gangliosides dissolved in aqueous buffer are stored 15-20 days. Mraz et al.[32] also report a smaller sedimentation constant for GM_1 obtained from dimethylsulfoxide solution, and note that it remains to be determined whether or not the residual dimethylsulfoxide in water solution may influence the size of the ganglioside micelle.

A point about which conflicting statements can be found in the literature is the lifetime of the ganglioside micelle. Howard and Burton[3] report that dilution of a ganglioside solution results in a slow dissociation of micelles which is complete after 30 minutes. Formisano et al.[31] have observed in their equilibrium dialysis study of the monomer-micelle equilibrium with labelled gangliosides that there was no significant increase in radioactivity crossing the membrane between 0.5 and 50 hours. This could indicate that the dissociation rate is either smaller than 30 minutes, in agreement with Howard and Burton, or larger than 50 hours. Formisano et al. state that the dissociation of the ganglioside micelle may take several days, essentially because they have observed a difference in the trailing boundary of the gel filtration elution profile between a freshly prepared ganglioside solution and the same solution stored for 12 days at room temperature. However, Mraz et al.[32] have not found any significant alteration in the amount of sedimenting ganglioside after storing the aqueous gangliosides solution for weeks. During the light-scattering measurement of the molecular weight of GM1 micelles in the temperature range 15-42°C, it was observed that the equilibration time of the scattered intensity when the temperature was changed was never longer than half an hour[39].

MIXED MICELLES

The investigation of the capability of gangliosides to form in aqueous solution mixed micelles either with natural or synthetic detergents is interesting because the mixed micelle may be an useful tool to extend the use of gangliosides in pharmacological or immunological fields, and to investigate the behavior and the organization of gangliosides in a structure which may constitute a model for a biological membrane. The study of mixed micelles contain-

ing gangliosides is particularly important for its biochemical implications because it may give information about the ability of
enzymes to recognize gangliosides in different forms of aggregation.

Masserini et al.[46] have investigated the relation between
enzyme action and structural organization of gangliosides by using
galactose oxidase. This enzyme catalyzes the oxidation to aldehyde
of the primary alcoholic group C-6 carried by the galactose residue
terminally located in GM1. Galactose oxidase works poorly upon GM1
micelles, while the enzyme activity is considerably enhanced in the
presence of the nonionic amphiphile Triton X-100 which forms mixed
micelles with the ganglioside[39,46]. We note that a similar influence
of Triton X-100 upon the enzymatic reaction rate was observed by
Dennis[47] with the substrate lecithin, and by Yedgar et al.[48] with
spingomyelin as the substrate.

The order of magnitude of the critical micelle concentration
c_M for the formation of mixed micelles can be derived by the relation[34]

$$\frac{1}{c_M} = \frac{\alpha}{c_1} + \frac{(1-\alpha)}{c_2} \tag{4}$$

where c_1 and c_2 are the Triton and GM1 cmc, respectively, and α is
the molar fraction of Triton X-100.
Since $c_1 = 0.3$ mM is much larger than c_2, c_M is much smaller than
c_1 even when the molar ratio $\alpha/(1-\alpha)$ becomes as large as 100. The
theory of mixed micelles developed by Clint[34] can also be used to
calculate the monomer concentrations in the mixed micellar solution
as function of total amphiphile concentration. An interesting
result is that the concentration of Triton X-100 monomers does not
level off when the total concentration reaches c_M, but continues
to increase attaining the value c_1 when the Triton X-100 concentration is much larger than c_1. Such a behavior is indeed displayed by
the measurements of Masserini et al.[46] who give the surface tension
as a function of the Triton X-100 concentration both in absence
and in presence of 0.8 mM GM1. In the former case the surface tension decreases to about 30 dynes/cm and levels off when the Triton
X-100 concentration attains c_1. In the latter case the surface tension attains the same value of 30 dynes/cm, but only when the Triton X-100 concentration is about 10 times c_1.

The molecular weight M and the hydrodynamic radius R_H of the
micelles have been determined by laser-light scattering. We report
in Figure 4 the values of M and R_H obtained as function of Triton
X-100 concentration in aqueous solution containing 0.8 mM GM1 with
buffer 25 mM sodium phosphate/5 mM disodium EDTA (pH 7.0) at T=15°C.
The connection between M and the normalized scattered intensity I_r
is slightly different from Equation 2. By assuming that the two
amphiphiles form mixed micelles at all the investigated molar ratios,
the relative normalized scattered intensity I_r can be written as[49]

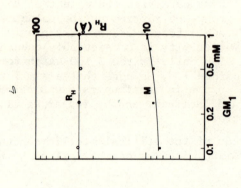

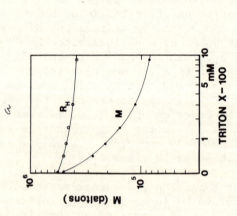

Figure 4a. The molecular weight M and the hydrodynamic radius R_H of mixed GM1-Triton X-100 micelles in the same buffer as for Figure 3 at 15°C as
a function of Triton X-100 molar concentration
with fixed 0.8 mM GM1 concentration.

Figure 4b. The same as for Figure 4a as a
function of GM1 molar concentration, with fixed
molar ratio 13.8:1 Triton X-100/GM1.

$$I_r = f \; A \; (\frac{dn}{dc})^2_G \; M \; (c - c_M) \tag{5}$$

where c is the total concentration and f is a dimensionless factor
given by

$$f = \frac{(1+\beta\gamma X)^2}{(1+\gamma X)^2} \tag{6}$$

where $\gamma = M_T/M_G$, M_T and M_G are the molecular weights of Triton and
GM1 monomers, $X = n_T/n_G$, n_T are the numbers of Triton and GM_1 monomers in the mixed micelle, and $\beta = (dn/dc)_T/ (dn/dc)_G$. In general
X will not coincide with the molar ratio $\alpha/(1 - \alpha)$ and will depend
on c because the concentration of Triton X-100 monomers depends on c.
However, when c is much larger than c_1, it is reasonable to put
$X = \alpha/(1 - \alpha)$ and to neglect c_M with respect to c.

    The data shown in Figure 4a indicate that, by adding increasing
amounts of Triton X-100 to a GM1 solution, M decreases gradually from
the value 5×10^5 typical of GM1 micelles to the value 8×10^4 typical
of Triton X-100 micelles, and correspondingly that R_H decreases from
56 to 38 Å. The data shown in Figure 4b refer to solutions in which
the total concentration is increased by keeping fixed the molar
ratio GM1/Triton X-100 at the value 1 : 13.8. The micellar size, as
expected, does not change by changing the concentration.

    Light scattering data on Triton-GM1 mixed micelles have been
obtained[39] also at temperatures and Triton X-100 concentrations
larger than those relative to Figure 4. Those data are however more
difficult to interpret because of the appearance of a new phenomenon,
critical concentration fluctuations. Aqueous solutions of Triton
X-100 are known to present a consolution curve (the cloud curve)
with a lower consolution point at $T_c \simeq 64°C$. The approach to the
critical point is characterized by an increase of the range of concentration fluctuations with a consequent divergence of the light
scattering intensity and of the fluctuations decay time[40]. As shown
by Masserini et al.[46], the addition of the buffer and of 0.8 mM GM1
to the H_2O-Triton X-100 solution shifts the critical point toward
a much lower temperature ($T_c \simeq 39°C$), so that the effect of critical
concentration fluctuations becomes very large at 37°C, and is already detectable at 15°C when the Triton concentration is larger than
10 mM.

                              CONCLUSIONS

    We summarize below the main information available about the
micellar properties of gangliosides. Clearly, further measurements

are needed to clarify the role of impurities, to fix more precisely the micellar size, to measure the micellar lifetime, and to make a systematic study of mixed micelles.

The critical micelle concentration of gangliosides in water
is in the range 10^{-10} - 10^{-8} M, as shown by several techniques which
recognize the presence of micelles. The precise value of the cmc will
depend, of course, on the structure of the ganglioside molecule,
and on the physicochemical characteristics (temperature, pH, ionic
strength) of the aqueous solution. The earlier experiments which
assigned the cmc to the range 10^{-5} - 10^{-4} M have used techniques
sensitive to the presence of monomers, and therefore more easily
influenced by the presence of impurities.

The aggregation number m of the ganglioside micelle is between
200 and 350, and it is dependent, similarly to the cmc, on the structure of the ganglioside molecule. The physicochemical characteristics
of the aqueous solution do not seem to influence markedly m (see,
for instance, Figure 2), but a systematic investigation of this
point is still lacking.

The hydrodynamic radius is about 60 Å, much larger than the
length of the gangliosides molecule. This fact suggests that the
micelle is not spherical. The quantitative analysis of light scattering data indicates that the micellar shape is probably disklike
with an axial ratio about 2.

Gangliosides form mixed micelles with the nonionic detergent
Triton X-100 in a wide range of molar ratios. The properties of
such mixed micelles have been investigated by surface tension, viscosity and light scattering measurements, and correlated with
the behavior of the enzymatic activity.

ACKNOWLEDGEMENTS

We thank G.Tettamanti for many illuminating discussions.
This work was supported by CNR-CISE contract n.80.00016.02.

REFERENCES

1. E.Klenk, Z.Physiol.Chem., 235, 24 (1935).
2. E.Klenk, Z.Physiol.Chem., 273, 76 (1942).
3. R.E.Howard and R.H.Burton, Biochim.Biophys.Acta, 84, 435 (1964).
4. W.Stoffel, Ann.Rev.Biochem., 40, 57 (1971).
5. IUPAC-IUB Commission on Biochemical Nomenclature Lipids, 12, 455 (1977).
6. L.Svennerholm, J.Neurochem, 10, 613 (1963).
7. J.Folch-Pi, M.Lees and G.H.Sloane-Stanley, J.Biol.Chem.,226, 497 (1957).
8. C.Tettamanti, F.Bonali, S.Marchesini and V.Zambotti, Biochim. Biophys.Acta, 296, 160 (1973).
9. R.Ghidoni, S.Sonnino, G.Tettamanti, H.Wiegandt and V.Zambotti, J.Neurochem., 27, 511 (1976).
10. S.Sonnino, R.Ghidoni, G.Galli and G.Tettamanti, J.Neurochem.,31, 947 (1978).
11. R.Ghidoni, S.Sonnino, G.Tettamanti, N.Baumann, G.Reuter, R.Schauer, J. Biol. Chem., 255, 6990 (1980). .
12. H.C.Yohe, D.E.Roark and A.Rosenberg, J.Biol.Chem.,251, 7083 (1976).
13. G.Toffano, D.Benvegnù, A.C.Bonetti, L.Facci, A.Leon, P.Orlando, R. Ghidoni and G. Tettamanti, J. Neurochem, 35, 861 (1980).).
14. B.Cestaro, G.Ippolito, R.Ghidoni, P.Orlando and G.Tettamanti, Bull.Mol.Biol.Med., 4, 240 (1979).
15. H.McIlvain, "Chemical Exploration of the Brain", Elsevier Pub. Co., Amsterdam, 1963.
16. A.C.Bonetti, D.Benvegnù, A.Leon, L.Facci, G.Toffano and G.Tettamanti, "Glucoconjugates", Proceedings of the Fifth International Symposium, Kiel, Fed.Rep.of Germany, 1979, Edited by R.Schauer, P.Boer, E.Buddecke, M.F.Kramer, J.F.G.Vliegenthart, H.Wiegandt, pp.576-577.
17. H.Wiegandt in "Advances in Cytopharmacology", B.Ceccarelli and F.Clementi Editors, Vol.3, Reven Press, New York, 1979.
18. E.Ochoa and A.Banbham, J.Neurochem., 26, 1193 (1976).
19. S.M.Aloj, L.D.Kohn, G.Lee and M.F.Meldolesi, Biochim.Biophys. Res.Commun., 74, 1053 (1977).
20. V.Vengris, F.Reynolds, M.Hollenberg and P.Pitha, Virology, 72, 486 (1976).
21. I.Kahan, M.Timar and M.Foldi, Acta Paediatr.Acad.Sci.Hung, 9 , 121 (1968).
22. W.Redwood and T.Polefka, Biochim.Biophys.Acta, 455, 631 (1976).
23. R.Maget-Dana, A.C.Roche and M.Monsigny, FEBS Lett., 79, 305 (1977).
24. M.Tomasi, L.G.Roda, C.Ausiello, G.D'Agnolo, B.Venerando,R.Ghidoni, S.Sonnino and G.Tettamanti, Eur. J. Biochem. 111, 315 (1980)
25. C.Tanford, "The Hydrophobic Effect : Formation of Micelles and Biological Membranes", Chap. 11, J. Wiley, New York, 1980.

26. R.Nagarajan and E.Ruckenstein, J.Colloid Interface Sci., 71, 580 (1979).
27. D.Gammack, Biochem.J., 88, 373 (1963).
28. H.C.Yohe and A.Rosenberg, Chem.Phys.Lipids, 9, 279 (1972).
29. H.Rauvala, FEBS Lett., 65, 229 (1976).
30. H.Rauvala, Eur.J.Biochem., 97, 555 (1979).
31. S.Formisano, M.L.Johnson, G.Lee, S.M.Aloj and H.Edelhoch, Biochemistry, 18, 1119 (1979).
32. W.Mraz, G.Schwarzmann, J.Sattler, T.Momoi, B.Seemann and H.Wiegandt, Hoppe-Seyler's Z.Physiol.Chem., 361, 177 (1980).
33. M.Corti, V.Degiorgio, R.Ghidoni, S.Sonnino and G.Tettamanti, Chem.Phys.Lipids, 26, 225 (1980).
34. J.H.Clint, J.Chem.Soc., 71, 1327 (1975).
35. J.Sattler, G.Schwarzman, J.Staerk, W.Ziegler and H.Wiegandt, Hoppe-Seyler's Z.Physiol.Chem., 358, 159 (1977).
36. R.Ghidoni, S.Sonnino and G.Tettamanti, Lipids, 13, 820 (1978).
37. H.A.Scheraga and L.Mandelkern, J.Am.Chem.Soc., 75, 179 (1953).
38. M.Corti and V.Degiorgio in "Light Scattering in Liquids and Macromolecular Solutions", V.Degiorgio, M. Corti and M. Giglio, Editors, p.109, Plenum, New York, 1980.
39. M.Corti, V.Degiorgio, S.Sonnino, R.Ghidoni, M.Masserini and G.Tettamanti,Chem.Phys.Lipids, in press.
40. M.Corti and V.Degiorgio, Opt.Commun. 14, 358 (1975).
41. N.M.Mazer, G.B.Benedek, and M.C.Carey, J.Phys.Chem., 80, 1075 (1976).
42. W.Curatolo, D.M.Small and G.Shipley, Biochim.Biophys.Acta, 468, 11 (1977).
43. C.Tanford, J.Phys.Chem., 78, 2469 (1974).
44. R.J.Robson and E.A.Dennis, J.Phys.Chem., 81, 1075 (1977).
45. M.Corti and V.Degiorgio, Chem.Phys.Lett., 53, 237 (1978).
46. M.Masserini, S.Sonnino, R.Ghidoni and G.Tettamanti, Biochim. Biophys.Acta, 601, 282 (1980).
47. E.A.Dennis, J.Lipid.Res.14, 152 (1973).
48. S.Yedgar, Y.Barenholz and V.G.Cooper, Biochim.Biophys.Acta, 363, 98 (1974).
49. M.Corti and V.Degiorgio (to be published).

MICELLIZATION, SOLUBILIZATION AND MICROEMULSIONS IN AQUEOUS BILIARY LIPID SYSTEMS

N. A. Mazer, M. C. Carey and G. B. Benedek
Massachusetts Institute of Technology
Cambridge, Massachusetts   02139
Peter Bent Brigham Hospital
Boston, Massachusetts   02115

We have employed laser light scattering methods to deduce the size, shape, structure and polydispersity of the macromolecular complexes formed in aqueous systems containing: bile salts, lecithin and cholesterol. Such studies have revealed an extraordinary variety in the size and structure of the aggregates as well as their patterns of aggregation. Bile salts form micelles whose size and shape varies from globular (radius$\sim$10Å) to elongated (length$>$200Å) as functions of concentration, bile salt species, temperature and added NaCl. The solubilization of lecithin by bile salts involves a unique mixed micellar structure that is disc shaped. The radii of these discs increase non-linearly ($20 \rightarrow 300$Å) with the L/BS ratio and appear to diverge as the mixed micellar phase limit is approached. Above this limit the discs may transform into metastable liposomal structures. The solubilization of cholesterol is achieved by its incorporation into bile salt and bile salt-lecithin micelles. The solubilized molecules are in equilibrium with cholesterol monomers whose concentration becomes equal to the monomer solubility at the solubilization limit. In supersaturated systems, cholesterol micro-precipitates form which are globular with radii from 600 to greater than 10,000Å. Such systems appear to resemble microemulsions. These aggregative phenomena provide new insights into the behavior of amphiphilic molecules in aqueous solution and have important implications in the physical chemistry of bile and the mechanisms of cholesterol gallstone formation.

595

INTRODUCTION

Bile salts, lecithin and cholesterol - the three major lipid components of bile - exhibit a rich variety of aggregative phenomena when dissolved either individually or in combination with eachother in aqueous solution.[1] An understanding of these phenomena is vital for elucidating the molecular mechanisms by which these lipids are secreted and transported in bile, how they function in fat absorption, and for understanding the molecular basis of cholesterol gallstone formation and dissolution. For these reasons we have been actively investigating[2-5] the aggregative behavior of aqueous biliary lipid systems using the technique of quasielastic light scattering (QLS). This technique[6,7] provides information on the size, shape and polydispersity of the aggregates formed in these solutions and is particularly well suited for studying solutions at the lipid concentrations of physiological importance (1-10 g/dl).

In this chapter we will present a review of our experimental findings on aqueous biliary lipid systems that will be divided into three sections:

1) Simple Micelle Formation in Bile Salt Solutions

2) Mixed Micelle Formation in Bile Salt-Lecithin Systems

3) Cholesterol Solubilization and Precipitation in Model Bile Systems

In conjunction with these experimental studies we have also developed a quantitative theoretical model[2-5] of the aggregative bahavior of the biliary lipids and will present the relevant aspects of this model in the appropriate sections listed above. Where possible the similarities between aqueous biliary lipid systems and other aqueous and non-aqueous amphiphile systems will be discussed. In this manner we hope to demonstrate that the aggregative behavior found in aqueous biliary lipid systems encompasses the broad range of micellization, solubilization and microemulsion phenomena exhibited by many different amphiphilic molecules,[8] and thus provides an interesting system for both experimental investigation and theoretical analysis.

MATERIALS AND METHODS

Details of the purity and methods of preparing the aqueous bi-

liary systems have been published previously.[2,4] A description of
our laser light scattering apparatus, data analysis methods and the
relevant equations and assumptions employed in our deductions of the
mean hydrodynamic radius ($\bar{R}_h$), shape and polydispersity of the biliary lipid aggregates can also be found in our previous publications.[6,7]

RESULTS AND DISCUSSION

Simple Micelle Formation in Bile Salt Solutions

We have studied[3] the micellar properties of the four common bile
salts of man, as the taurine conjugated species: taurocholate (TC),
taurodeoxycholate (TDC), taurochenodeoxycholate (TCDC) and taurourso-
deoxycholate (TUDC). These molecules differ from eachother in the
number and location of the hydroxyl groups that are attached to the
hydrophilic surface of the steroid nucleus; the TC species possessing
three hydroxyl groups and the remaining dihydroxyl bile salts possessing two groups.

As shown in figure 1, the mean hydrodynamic radii ($\bar{R}_h$) of bile
salt micelles (measured at 10 g/dl concentrations) shows the following dependence on bile salt species: TDC>TCDC>TUDC>TC, with sizes
ranging from 10Å to greater than 60Å depending on temperature and added NaCl concentration. The influence of bile salt concentration on
$\bar{R}_h$ is shown in figure 2 for TDC and TC micelles. At physiologic
NaCl concentration (0.15M) figure 2A shows a very weak dependence of
$\bar{R}_h$ on bile salt concentration for both species, indicating that there
is little or no micellar growth at concentrations greater than the
CMC. The small negative slope seen for TC is consistent with the influence of repulsive micellar interactions on the micellar diffusion
coefficients[6,7] (from which $\bar{R}_h$ values are derived) and should not be
interpreted as an actual decrease in micellar size. At high NaCl
concentrations (0.6M), $\bar{R}_h$ increases appreciably with concentration
for the TDC species indicating a strong effect of detergent concentration on the micellar size distribution above the CMC. The extent of
this micellar growth is also seen to be temperature dependent. Conversely, as the CMC is approached the $\bar{R}_h$ of both species fall in the
range 12-19Å for all temperatures and NaCl concentrations. The corresponding mean aggregation numbers ($\bar{n}$) for the bile salt micelles
shown in figures 1 and 2 vary from about 5 (TC near the CMC) to greater than 100 (TDC in 0.6M NaCl). These values correspond to a rod-like
micellar shape that was deduced from measurements of the temperature
dependence of the scattered intensity for TDC micelles.[3] In conjunction with these results we have developed a quantitative model of bile
salt aggregation based on the primary-secondary micelle hypothesis proposed by Ekwall[8] and Small.[9] As shown schematically, in figure 3, bile

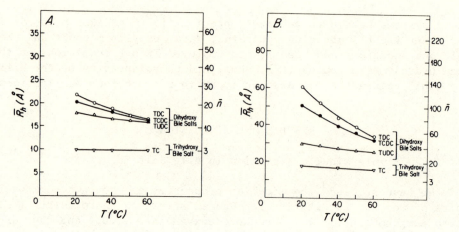

Figure 1.   Mean hydrodynamic radii, $\bar{R}_h$, and aggregation numbers, $\bar{n}$, of bile salt micelles as functions of temperature in 10 g/dl solutions containing (A) 0.15M NaCl and (B) 0.6M NaCl.   Bile salt species: TDC (o), TCDC (●), TUDC (Δ), and TC (∇).

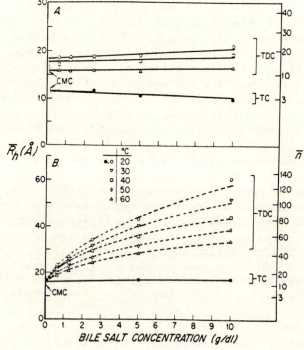

Figure 2.   Mean hydrodynamic radii, $\bar{R}_h$, and aggregation numbers, $\bar{n}$, of TDC and TC micelles as functions of bile salt concentration and temperature in (A) 0.15M NaCl and (B) 0.6M NaCl.   Dashed curves in (B) are derived from theory.

salts are presumed to associate hydrophobically at the CMC to form
small globular aggregates termed primary micelles which consist of
∿5-10 bile salt molecules oriented with their hydrophobic surfaces
toward the micelle interior and hydrophilic surfaces toward the solvent. At concentrations greater than the CMC these micelles may
polymerize in a linear fashion to form rod-like secondary micelles.
We have modeled[3] the thermodynamics of secondary micelle formation
by a stepwise addition process of the primary micelles ($S_n + P_1 \underset{\leftarrow}{\rightarrow} S_{n+1}$)
characterized by the polymerization constant K(T) which is assumed
to be the same for each reaction (independent of n).

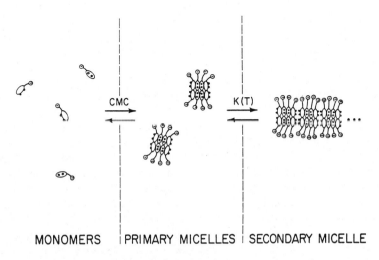

MONOMERS   ┊PRIMARY MICELLES┊ SECONDARY MICELLE

Figure 3. Schematic diagram of bile salt aggregation based on the
primary-secondary micelle hypothesis.

The model provides an excellent fit to the concentration dependence
of $\bar{R}_h$ measured for TDC micelles in 0.6M NaCl (as shown in figure 2)
and thereby permits deductions of the polymerization constant K as
a function of temperature, NaCl concentration and bile salt species.[3]
From these deductions we have concluded that the thermodynamic driving force for secondary micelle formation is actually a further
manifestation of hydrophobic interactions, in that a significant
area of hydrocarbon/water contact on the surface of the primary
micelle is eliminated by the formation of secondary micelles.[3] This
view is different than that of Ekwall and Small who originally proposed[8-9] that hydrogen bonding between the hydroxyl groups caused the
polymerization of micelles, but is found to provide a more coherent
understanding of the effects of bile salt species, and of the influence of additives (such as urea) on the thermodynamics of bile salt

micelle formation.[3]   In this regard it is important to recognize that
despite the unusual amphiphilic structure of bile salt molecules,
their micellar properties show many similarities to the properties
of ionic alkyl chain detergents,[6,10,11] such as the growth of micelle
size with increasing NaCl concentration and detergent concentration,
and the decrease of micellar size with increasing temperature and
added urea.   Although our quantitative description of micellar growth
in the bile salt system (primary-secondary micelle hypothesis) differs
from the model of the sphere-rod transition which has been used to
analyse the thermodynamics of alkyl sulfate micelles,[7,10,11] we have
nevertheless found that our quantitative deductions concerning the
thermodynamic properties of the hydrophobic interaction and its influence on micellar growth are in good agreement for bile salt and
alkyl sulfate systems.[3,11]   Thus it would appear that the role of
hydrophobic interactions in both systems is quite similar.

Mixed Micelle Formation in Bile Salt-Lecithin Solutions

     The ability of bile salts to solubilize the lamellar liquid
crystalline structures formed by lecithin and other membrane lipids
in aqueous solution[12] is believed to play a vital role in the mechanism of bile formation, and is also employed widely in the study
of cellular membranes.   Small postulated[13] that bile salts solubilize lecithin bilayers by dispersing them into mixed micellar aggregates whose structure is shown in figure 4.   According to Small's
model, the mixed micelle consists of a lecithin bilayer disc surrounded on its perimeter with bile salts, oriented with their hydrophilic surfaces facing the aqueous solvent.   An interesting feature
of this model is its prediction[13] of a linear increase of the disc
radius (r), as a function of the ratio of lecithin-to-bile salt molecules in the mixed micelle (n_L/n_{BS}).

$$r = \left(\frac{2\rho}{\sigma}\right)\frac{n_L}{n_{BS}} \qquad (1)$$

σ is the number of lecithins per unit area of bilayer and ρ is the
number of bile salts per unit length of the disc perimeter.   The
ratio $\dfrac{n_L}{n_{BS}}$ is related to the molar concentrations of lecithin, C_L,
and bile salt, C_{BS}, and to the intermicellar concentration of bile
salts, IMC, by:[4]

$$\frac{n_L}{n_{BS}} = \frac{C_L}{C_{BS} - IMC} \qquad (2)$$

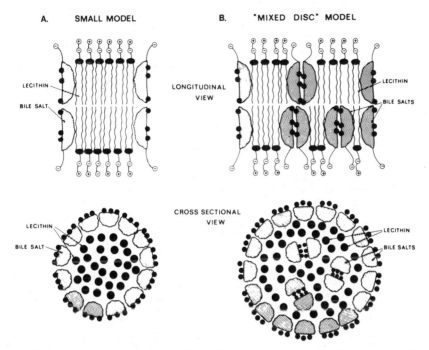

A.   SMALL MODEL   B.   "MIXED DISC" MODEL

LONGITUDINAL VIEW

CROSS SECTIONAL VIEW

Figure 4.   Schematic models for the structure of the bile salt-
lecithin mixed micelle, shown in longitudinal and cross section.
(A) Small's model, (B) Mixed Disc model.

In the limit when $C_{BS} \gg$ IMC (which is typically comparable in magnitude to the CMC of the pure bile salt solution) equations (1) and
(2) predict that r should increase linearly with C_L / C_{BS} (the lecithin-to-bile salt molar ratio in solution, L/BS). Our experimental
test of this prediction[2,4] is shown in figure 5 where QLS measurements of $\bar{R}_h$ are plotted as a function of L/BS ratio using the four
bile salt species studied previously. At low L/BS ratios (≤ 0.5),
the $\bar{R}_h$ values show different behavior depending on bile salt species.
A detailed analysis[4] of this regime suggests that both simple and
mixed micellar aggregates coexist in varying proportions at these
low L/BS ratios. However, at high L/BS ratios (> 0.6) only mixed
micelles are present and their sizes deviate markedly from the predictions of the Small model as the L/BS ratio increases. In fact,
the $\bar{R}_h$ values increase non-linearly and appear to diverge ($\bar{R}_h \to \infty$) as
the L/BS ratios approach the phase limits for maximum lecithin solubilization appropriate to each system. This "divergence phenomenon"
is further illustrated in figure 6A where the influence of total lipid concentration as well as L/BS ratio on $\bar{R}_h$ is shown.

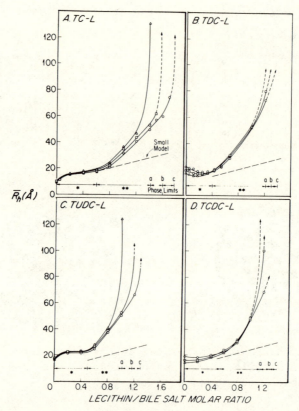

Figure 5. Mean micellar hydrodynamic radii, $\bar{R}_h$ in four bile salt-lecithin systems, plotted as a function of lecithin-bile salt (L/BS) molar ratio at (○) 20, (□) 40 and (△) 60°C; total lipid concentration 10 g/dl. At low L/BS ratio(*) systems contain simple and mixed micelles, whereas at high L/BS ratios (**) only mixed micelles are present.

With decreases in total lipid concentration, the L/BS ratio corresponding to the micellar phase limit decreases and the $\bar{R}_h$ values are thus seen to "diverge" earlier. Dilution thus leads to a large increase in mixed micellar size, the opposite of what was seen in pure bile salt systems.[3] Although the simple disc model proposed by Small is clearly incompatible with these data, a deduction of mixed micellar shape using scattered intensity measurements suggests that the large mixed micelles are nevertheless disc-like.[4] It is thus necessary to explain why the radii of the mixed micellar discs exceed the

predictions of the Small model and furthermore to understand the
apparent divergence of micellar size at the phase limit.

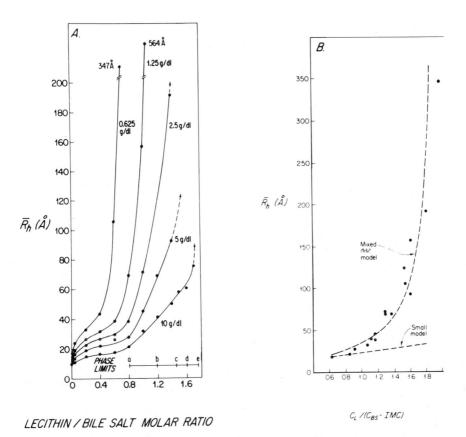

LECITHIN / BILE SALT MOLAR RATIO

$C_L /(C_{BS}-IMC)$

Figure 6 A and B. Mean hydrodynamic radii, $\bar{R}_h$, in TC-L systems
(20°C) as a function of L/BS ratio and total lipid concentration
(0.625-10 g/dl). In B data have been plotted as a function of $C_L/$
(C_{BS}-IMC) and compared with theoretical curves based on Small model
and Mixed Disc model.

Considerations based on the Small model show that both questions
can be answered if one postulates that bile salts not only coat the
perimeter of the mixed micelle but are also incorporated within the
interior of the lecithin bilayer in a fixed stoichiometry (see figure 4B) -   "mixed disc" model.[3,4] If α represents the ratio of
lecithin-to-bile salt molecules within the bilayer of the mixed micelle, it can then be shown that the disc radius, r, will depend
on C_L and C_{BS} as follows:[4]

$$r = \frac{\left(\frac{2\rho}{\sigma'}\right)(C_L/(C_{BS} - IMC))}{1 - \alpha^{-1}(C_L/(C_{BS} - IMC))} \qquad (3)$$

where σ' is the number of lecithins per unit area of a mixed bilayer (containing bile salts). From equation (3) it is seen that the "mixed disc" model of micellar structure predicts a divergence in r when C_L and C_{BS} satisfy the relationship:

$$\frac{C_L}{C_{BS} - IMC} = \alpha \qquad (4)$$

Physically this corresponds to the situation when all of the bile salt molecules (excluding the IMC) are included within the bilayer, leaving no additional bile salts to form the disc perimeters that are needed to solubilize the bilayer. In this way, the mixed disc model explains both the apparent divergence of the mixed micelle size and the origin of the phase limit. At L/BS ratios greater than the phase limit, our experimental results[4,5] suggest that the bilayer structures can exist as metastable liposomes, a phenomenon that has been employed to produce model liposomel systems.[14,15]

Quantitative support for the mixed disc model has come from the success of fitting the experimental data of figures 5 and 6 with theoretical predictions based on equation (3). This is illustrated in figure 6B, where the data of figure 6A, obtained at various total lipid concentrations, are replotted as a function of $C_L/(C_{BS}-IMC)$. The data are now seen to fall on a single functional relationship which can be fit quite well by the mixed disc model. Moreover, the resulting deductions of the parameters: $\frac{2\rho}{\sigma'}$ (17.5Å), α (2.0 at 20°C) and IMC (3.2 mm for large mixed micelles at 20°C) are found to be in excellent agreement with independent estimates[4] based on molecular models and other experimental data.

It is interesting to point out that the solubilization pheno-mena observed in aqueous bile salt-lecithin systems are similar in many respects to the water-in-oil (W/O) microemulsion behavior of the AOT-Water-Hexane system studied by Zulauf and Eicke.[16] They employed QLS methods to deduce the $\bar{R}_h$ values of the microemulsion particles and have found that at low temperature, the dependence of $\bar{R}_h$ on the Water/AOT ratio is consistent with a spherical struc-ture in which a droplet of water is coated on its surface by the AOT detergents. Such a picture could be considered a three dimen-sional equivalent of the Small model[9] in which the AOT molecules play the role of the bile salt perimeter, and the water droplet is

analogous to the lecithin bilayer. Zulauf and Eicke have further
shown that with increasing temperature the $\bar{R}_h$ value for the microemulsion droplets increase dramatically until a phase separation
occurs.[16] Such a behavior could be explained by analogy to the
mixed disc model by postulating that at higher temperatures the AOT
molecules become dissolved within the water droplet interior, thus
reducing the number of molecules available for the droplet surfaces
and necessitating the formation of larger droplets. Such an explanation has, in fact been suggested.[16]

Cholesterol Solubilization and Precipitation
in Model Bile Systems

Because of its relevance to the problem of cholesterol gallstone formation, we have systematically investigated the process
of cholesterol solubilization in bile salt and bile salt-lecithin
solutions and in addition have studied the evolution of cholesterol
precipitation from supersaturated systems.[2,5] In figures 7 and 8,
the influence of solubilized cholesterol on $\bar{R}_h$ is shown for simple
(TC) and mixed (TC-lecithin) solutions. The small TC micelles
increase only slightly $10 \rightarrow 11.5 \text{Å}$ as the cholesterol mole fraction
reaches 4% and show no abrupt changes as the limit of solubiliza-
tion is reached and exceeded. Similarly, in solutions where simple and mixed micelles coexist (L/TC = 0.25), only a modest increase in size (2-3Å) occurs as up to 12% cholesterol is solubilized. These data suggest that the incorporation of cholesterol
into simple and mixed micelles causes only small alterations of
micellar size, and does not require any significant reorganization
of micellar structure. On this basis we have analysed[5,17] cholesterol solubilization in terms of binding equilibria, in which the
simple TC micelles possess a single binding site and the mixed
TC-L micelles contain multiple sites whose number depends on the
mixed micellar size. By coupling the binding equilibria to the
equilibrium that exists between cholesterol monomers and precipitates, one obtains the model of cholesterol solubilization shown
in figure 9.[5] This model implies that the limit of cholesterol
solubilization is reached when the concentration of cholesterol
monomers becomes equal to the aqueous solubility of the cholesterol
monomer. By quantitatively analysing the extensive solubilization
data of Carey and Small,[12] we have been able to deduce values[5,17]
for the cholesterol binding constants in simple TC micelles (K_1
(30°C) = 1.3×10^6 liter/mole) and mixed micelles ($K_2(30^\circ$C) = 1×10^7
liter/mole). From these values we estimate that when the solubi-
lization limit is reached, less than 20% of the simple micelle
binding sites and < 60% of the mixed micelle binding sites are
occupied, a consequence of the very low monomeric solubility of
cholesterol ($< 10^{-7}$ moles/liter).

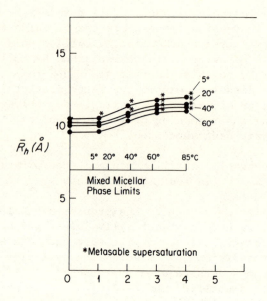

CHOLESTEROL MOLE FRACTION (%)

Figure 7. Mean hydrodynamic radii, $\bar{R}_h$, in TC-Ch systems as a function of the mole fraction of solubilized cholesterol and temperature. Total lipid concentration is 10 g/dl.

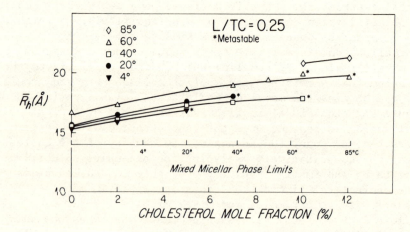

CHOLESTEROL MOLE FRACTION (%)

Figure 8. Mean hydrodynamic radii, $\bar{R}_h$, in TC-L-Ch systems as a function of the mole fraction of solubilized cholesterol. L/TC ratio = 0.25, and total lipid concentration is 10 g/dl.

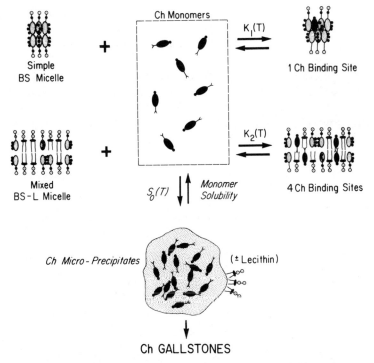

Ch GALLSTONES

Figure 9. Schematic model of cholesterol solubilization and precipitation in bile salt-lecithin systems. Cholesterol monomers
can bind to simple and mixed micelles and are also in equilibrium
with cholesterol precipitates.

From the model depicted in figure 9, we can also understand the
temperature dependence of cholesterol solubilization and the use of
temperature variations to study cholesterol precipitation.[2,5] At
high temperature ($> 60°C$) one is able to solubilize the maximum
amount of cholesterol in mixed micellar solution by virtue of the
increase in monomeric solubility with temperature and the increased
affinity of the binding sites. When the temperature of such a system is rapidly lowered, the concentration of cholesterol monomers
will instantaneously exceed its maximum solubility. If this degree
of monomeric supersaturation is greater than the critical degree
needed for nucleation, a rapid homogeneous precipitation of cholesterol from the monomeric phase will occur.[18] Solubilized cholesterol will then be released from the micelles in order to re-
populate the monomer concentration, leading to further precipitation. In effect then, a flow of cholesterol from micelles $\longrightarrow$
monomers $\longrightarrow$ precipitate occurs. Experimental studies[5] of such

precipitation phenomena are illustrated in figure 10 where we have monitered the scattered intensity I(t) and the $\bar{R}_h$ values of the micro-precipitates as a function of time after making temperature "drops" ΔT of varying depth. From this data we observe an induction time t_{ind} associated with the initiation of precipitation that varies inversely with ΔT (i.e. t_{ind} becomes larger as the degree of supersaturation becomes smaller). In addition we see that the final size of the micro-precipitates also varies inversely from 500Å to 1900Å with ΔT. Such findings are consistent with a homogeneous nucleation process.[18]

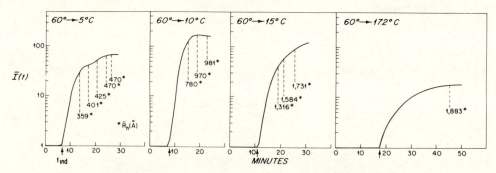

Figure 10. Temperature "drop" studies of cholesterol precipitation in model bile solutions containing 10 g/dl total lipids, L/TC = 0.25, and cholesterol mole fraction, 7.5%. Curves show scattered intensity, I(t), and $\bar{R}_h$ values of micro-precipitates as a function of time after changing temperature. Note induction times t_{ind} for reaction to occur.

By employing nucleation theory to the data,[5,18] we have been able to deduce the interfacial surface energy, E_i, between precipitate and solution. In the absence of lecithin E is estimated to be greater than 12.8 ergs/cm² whereas in the presence of lecithin E_i is ~5 ergs/cm². These values can account for the relative metastability of supersaturated solutions containing no lecithin, and suggest that when present, lecithin may act to lower the interfacial energy by coating the surface of the micro-precipitate.[5] By this coating mechanism the cholesterol precipitates can also remain dispersed in solution, in a manner analogous to an O/W microemulsion system.[8] Such phenomena, if occurring in native bile, may have profound implications in the mechanisms of cholesterol transport and precipitation in bile.

CONCLUSION

We have employed laser light scattering methods to systematically investigate the aggregative properties of aqueous biliary
lipid systems. These studies reveal an extraordinary range of
phenomena showing close similarities to the micellization, solubilization and microemulsion behavior seen in other aqueous and
non-aqueous amphiphile systems. We believe that an understanding
of such phenomena may provide important new insights into the
physiology of bile, and the formation of cholesterol gallstones.

ACKNOWLEDGEMENTS

Research support provided by N.I.H. grants AM18559 and AM00195
and N.S.F. grants DMR768095-A02 and 7707666-CHE. Dr. Mazer wishes
to thank Professor Werner Känzig and the department of Solid State
Physics at the Eidgenossiche Technische Hochschule, Zürich, Switzerland for providing him a research fellowship during which this
manuscript was prepared. We also thank Ms. Debi Yeh for her care-
ful typing of this paper.

REFERENCES

1. M. C. Carey and D. M. Small, Am. J. Med., $\underline{49}$, 590, (1970).
2. N. A. Mazer, M. C. Carey, R. F. Kwasnick and G. B. Benedek,
    in "Micellization, Solubilization and Microemulsions", Vol. 1 ,
    K. L. Mittal, Editor, p. 383, Plenum Press, New York, 1977.
3. N. A. Mazer, M. C. Carey, R. F. Kwasnick and G. B. Benedek,
    Biochemistry, $\underline{18}$, 3064, (1979).
4. N. A. Mazer, M. C. Carey and G. B. Benedek, Biochemistry, $\underline{19}$,
    601, (1980).
5. N. A. Mazer, Ph.D. Thesis, Massachusetts Institute of Tech-
    nology, (1978).
6. N. A. Mazer, G. B. Benedek and M. C. Carey, J. Phys. Chem.,
    $\underline{80}$, 1075, (1976).
7. N. A. Mazer, G. B. Benedek and M. C. Carey, in "Micellization
    Solubilization and Microemulsions," Vol. 1, K. L. Mittal, Ed-
    itor, p. 359, Plenum Press, New York, 1977.
8. P. Ekwall, K. Fontell and A. Sten: in "Proceedings Second
    International Congress of Surface Activity, Vol. 1", pp.357-
    373, Butterworth Sci. Publishers, London, 1957.
9. D. M. Small, Adv. Chem. Series, $\underline{84}$, 31, (1968).
10. P. J. Missel, N. A. Mazer, C. Y. Young, G. B. Benedek and M.
    C. Carey, J. Phys. Chem., $\underline{84}$, 1044, (1980).

11. P. J. Missel, N. A. Mazer, M. C. Carey and G. B. Benedek, Proceedings of this Symposium.
12. M. C. Carey and D. M. Small, J. Clin. Invest., 61, 998, (1978).
13. D. M. Small, Gastroenterology, 52, 607, (1967).
14. J. Brunner, P. Skrabaal and H. Hauser, Biochem Biophys. Acta, 455, 322, (1976).
15. M. Milsmann, R. Schwendener and H.-G. Weder, Biochem Biophys. Acta, 512, 147, (1978).
16. M. Zulauf and H. F. Eicke, J. Phys. Chem., 83, 480, (1979).
17. N. A. Mazer and M. C. Carey, Gastroenterology Abst., Nov. 1978.
18. A. S. Walton, "The Formation and Properties of Precipitates", Interscience Publishers, New York, 1967.

STUDY ON THE MICELLE FORMATION OF SODIUM DEOXYCHOLATE

Yoshio Murata, Gohsuke Sugihara
Nagamune Nishikido, Mitsuru Tanaka
Department of Chemistry, Faculty of Science
Fukuoka University
Nishi-ku, Fukuoka 814, Japan

The micelle formation of sodium deoxycholate
(NaDC) in aqueous solution with addition of NaCl and
in a buffer solution (pH = 7.78) has been investigated
by means of light scattering, circular dichroism,
viscosity, density and solubilization of cholesterol.
In the both solution systems of the added NaCl and the
borate buffer it was clearly seen that the shape and
size of aggregate at the lower concentration range are
quite different from those at the higher concentration.
The time dependence in the size and shape of the
aggregate was so remarkable that all experiments had
to be made until the systems observed reached their
time equilibria. In the system with addition of NaCl
the association number of spherical micelle, formed
in the relatively higher range of NaDC concentration,
increases with increasing the concentration of added
NaCl and with lowering temperature. Also the association number in pure water at each temperature was
estimated by extrapolating to the zero concentration
of NaCl added. The rod like shape of the aggregate,
formed in the lower concentration range, was found by
a combination of the coagulation theory by von Smoluchowski and the correction factor calculated by Doty
and Steiner. In the buffer solution system also it
was confirmed that there exist highly assymetric and
more ordered (helically) aggregates at the concentration range below 0.01 g/ml, and that their shape
and size are much different from those of the micelles
formed above that concentration of NaDC. The existence

of different types of aggregation was elucidated by
all experimental results obtained through the measurements of dissymmetry Z_{45}, molecular elipticity,
reduced viscosity, apparent molar volume, and amounts
of solubilized cholesterol. If the micelles, formed
at the higher concentration, solubilize the cholesterol molecule, they increase their association
number and become more stable.

INTRODUCTION

The first mention of the micellar properties of the aqueous
solution of bile salts was made by MacBain et al.[1,2] Studies
carried out in the 1940's proved that the bile salts are association
colloids.[1-4] Per Ekwall summerised in his literature[5] how certain
properties of sodium cholate (NaC) and sodium deoxycholate
(NaDC) solutions vary with the concentration. Some abrupt or
discontinuous changes in various property behaviours were found.
Ekwall's concern for the bile salt solution was focused on the
indication of the change of physicochemical properties accompanied
by the change of *concentration limits*. Ekwall's investigation
has been taken over by Fontell up to now. Fontell revealed
micellar behaviors in solutions of bile salts from the experiment
of vapor pressure of the aqueous solutions and the osmotic activity
of the bile salts,[6] through the light scattering measurements,[7]
the viscosity measurements[8] and the X-ray measurements.[9,10] In his
light scattering study the micellar weights between 1200 and 3000
for NaC and between 3000 and 4000 for NaDC were obtained for the
solution without supporting electrolyte, on the assumption that
association begins above 0.013 M for NaC and above 0.004 M for
NaDC. The X-ray diffraction studies by Blow and Rich showed that
the fibvous aggregate has an elongated helical configuration.[10,11]
Fontell's results of X-ray study indicated the existence of
micellar aggregate; these have a radius of ca 20 Å in NaDC solution
above 6.5×10^{-3} M and ca. 17Å in NaC solutions above 8.5×10^{-3} M.[9]
With these radii Fontell estimated the association number 24 for
NaDC and 16 for NaC. Through the viscosity study Fontell pointed
out that micelles at higher concentrations were voluminous and
anisometric, and that there were indication of a secondary structure
where the micelles might be interlinked. Preceeding Fontell, Blow
and Rich had made viscometric measurements in the study of the
conditions favoring the formation of helical complex (aggregate)
and observed thixotropic behavior.[11] More detailed studies on the
viscosity of NaDC were performed by Vochten et al.[12] and by us.[13,14]
These papers all had pointed out the time dependent behavior in
the viscosity, while Fontell did not mention about it. With
respect to the time dependent behavior in the light scattering
also we have reported a little.[13,15]

The characteristecs of aqueous NaDC solution lies in the remarkable time dependency in the association state, the specific structure of aggregate which is formed with aid of hydrogen bonding by hydrolyzed species,[16,17] and the concentration limits that have been indicated by aforementioned researchers. These characteristic figures of NaDC, a surfactant in vivo, will be revealed and high-litened as a contrast to synthetic surfactants.

EXPERIMENTAL

NaDC purchased from E. Merck and Nakarai Co. was three to seven times recrystallized from the ethanol solution and dried at 110°C in vacuo for 1 to 5 days. The purity of NaDC was found to be higher than 99.9% by elemental analysis. Cholesterol (E. Merck) was recrystallized from ethanol and purified cholesterol was stored in the darked desiccator along with N_2 gas to avoid its oxidation. Other chemicals were of guaranteed reagent grade and used without further purification except NaCl which was recrystallized several times from pure water. The thrice distilled water was used through all experiments.

Instruments used are as follows. For the light scattering and the refractive index measurement; Shimazu Light Scattering Photometer PG-21 and Shimazu Refractometer DR-3 respectively, for the density (thus, partial molar volume) measurement; Anton Parr Densitometer Model 02C. For the electroconductivity measurement; Yanagimoto Conductivity Outfit, Model MY-8, for viscocity measurements; a modified Ostwald type viscometer and for the circular dichroism measurements; Jasco Authomatic Recording Spectropolarimeter J-40A. The amount of cholesterol solubilized by NaDC was measured by the use of Hitachi Spectrophotometer 124 (wave length 430 nm) according to Liebermann-Burchard reaction.

The temperatures in the measurements were controled by the circulation of thermostated water; for the density measurement the accuracy was within ± 0.001°C and for the others within ± 0.01°C.

RESULTS AND DISCUSSION

(I) System with Addition of NaCl

In general it is well known that the following Debye's relation holds for such a solution system of micelles as are much smaller than wave length of light.

$$\frac{K_{90}(C - C_0)}{R_{90} - R_{90}^o} = \frac{1}{M} + 2B(C - C_0) \tag{1}$$

where M is the micellar weight, B is the second virial coefficient,
C and C_0 are the total concentration of surfactants in g/ml and
the critical micelle concentration (CMC), respectively. R_{90} and
R_{90}° are Reyleigh ratios (at the angle 90°) at concentrations C
and CMC, respectively, and K_{90} is a function of refractive index
increment, wave length, etc.

At first the effect of setting time on the association should
be mentioned. Figure 1 shows an example of time dependency of
$K_{90}C/R_{90}$ for each concentration of NaDC with addition of 0.15 M
NaCl, and tells us that it takes the longer time to reach an equilibrium, the smaller the concentration of NaDC. The fact suggests
that an investigation of the property of aqueous NaDC solution
should not disregard the factor of setting time. All data described below are those obtained by continuing the measurement until
the solution reaches a time-equilibrium. In order to apply the
Debye's relation (Equation 1) to the surfactant system we have
to know the value of C_0. For the purpose to determine the CMC of
NaDC solution with addition of NaCl, the electroconductivity of the
various concentrations of NaDC solutions was measured. The solutions were prepared batchwisely by the use of NaCl solution, as a
solvent, of which concentration was fixed, and they were allowed
to stand for a day at a constant temperature desired. In this
experiment the strange aggregate appeared at the very low concentration and thus the CMC could not be determined precisely.
However considering that the strange macromolecular aggregate is
one of the secondary micelle composed of the smaller primary
micelle, the CMC of the primary micelle should be lower than the
concentration range of bigger aggregate and thus it seems to range
between 1×10^{-4} and 1×10^{-3} g/ml ($2.5 - 25.0 \times 10^{-4}$ mol/l).
This small value is within experimental error, so that C_0 is
negligible and R_{90}° is negligible too. Figure 2 shows the result
of Debye plot at 20°C. Those at different temperatures (27.0°C
and 36.5°C) are almost similar to Figure 2. Generally speaking
the plot of $K_{90}C/R_{90}$ vs C does not give a good straight line,
because large deviations from the extrapolated line take place
especially at the lower range of the NaDC concentration, where
the solutions are unstable; many visible flocculates which look
like thin fibers appear in the bulk, or a jelly-like layer (lump)
rises to the surface of the solution. Further at the lower concentration range, the time-change in both of scattered light intensity
and dissymmetry Z_{45} is much more remarkable. On the process of
flocculation or gelation a remarkable increase in both of R_{90} and
Z_{45} has often been observed. This leads to a deviation from the
extrapolated line in the Debye plot to the lower side. Sometimes
after the increase in R_{90} and Z_{45}, a gradual decrease of them has
been observed with setting time because the formed jelly layer
traverse the light path while it goes up near to the surface of
the solution. This leads to a upper deviation from the extrapolated

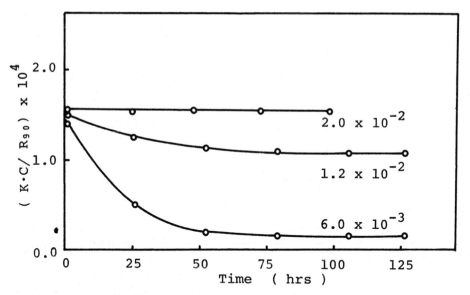

Figure 1.   The time dependency of $K_{90}D/R_{90}$ for solutions of
different NaDC concentrations with addition of 0.15 M NaCl.
Numerical volues indicate NaDC concentration in g/ml, at 36.5°C.

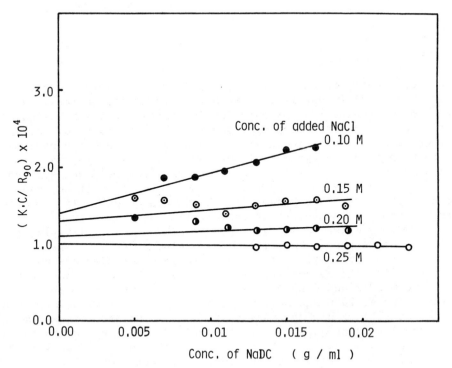

Figure 2.   Debye plots for the systems with addition of NaCl at 20°C.

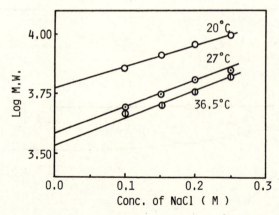

Figure 3. The plot of logarithm of micellar weight as a function of the concentration of added NaCl at various temperatures, O;20°C, ◉;27°C, ⦻;36°C.

line. Apparently the state of aggregation in the lower concentration range is different from that in the higher concentration. Regarding the unstable aggregate-forming range, in which a kind of salting out of hydrated aggregates may occur, the ratio of the concentration of added inorgamic salt to that of NaDC may have a key to be solved, though details are not yet known. Anyway this concentration range corresponds to that on which we[16] and Rich and Blow[10,11] studied associated with the sol - gel transition, and the aggregation at this range will be discussed soon. It is noteworthy that the dissymmetry of the micelles at higher concentration range are very close to unity. This enables us, in principle, to apply the Debye plot (see Figure 2). Also it is interesting that the slope of Debye plot is conveted into negative one as the concentration of added NaCl is inreased, and when NaCl concentrations are 0.20 M and 0.15 M, the Debye plots give nearly zero value of the slope at 20°C and 36.5°C, respectively. The micellar weight for the micelle at higher concentration range of NaDC was estimated from each intercept, and the micellar weight and association number are plotted as a function of the concentration of added NaCl (see Figure 3). An extrapolation to zero concentration of NaCl may give the micellar weight in pure water. (The intensity of light scattered from the NaDC micelle in pure water was too weak to detect by means of our apparatus.) The extrapolated valued are in fairly good agreement with those given by Fontell[7] and Cardinal.[18] The extrapolated values at different temperatures are listed in Table I. Figure 3 indicates that the micellar weight or association number increases with an increase in the concentration of added salt, and decreases with raising temperature.

Table I. The Micellear Weight and Association Number of Micelle in Water Estimated from Figure 3 by Extrapolation at Various Temperature.

Temp.	20°C	27°C	36.5°C
M.W. x 10^{-3}	6.0	3.8	3.3
A.N.	14.5	9.1	8.0

With respect to a sample of the lower concentration range where flocculation or gelation takes place, in order to measure the rate of aggregation the time change of scattered light intensity at angles 45°, 90° and 135° was measured just after preparation and filteration of solutions. According to the coagulation theory of von Smoluchowski, scattering with iso-dispersed sol with ν_0 particles, each of volume v_1, the scatered light will be given by

$$I_r = I_0 K \nu_0 v_1^2 \tag{2}$$

where I_0 designates the intensity of incident light, I_r, that of scattered light at an angle and K, a constant. After a certain time t, the number of primary, secondary and other multiple particles will be described by the theory of von Smoluchowski.[20] The statistical consideration leads to the following expression,

$$I_r(t) = I_0 K \nu_0 v_1^2 \left(1 + \frac{2t}{T} \right) \tag{3}$$

which means that the scattered light increases linearly with time and $I_r(t)$ is three times the original value after "time of coagulation T", defined by him. Whereas the shape of coagulates in Smoluchouski's theory is spherical and his theory lacks a consideration for the destructive interference due to the large growth of coagulate the aggregate of NaDC may have a big rod shape. So that the correlation between the intensity of the scattered light and dimension and/or the shape has to be considered. One can apply to the NaDC system in which the dissmmmetry coefficient may be used also to correct the scattered light intensity observed at 90° for the effects of destructive interference. And one finds that the

relation between $1/P(90°)$ and $[Z_{45}]$ will depend on the particle
shape as the dimension of the particles exceeds a certain limit.
The correlation plotted from the values calculated by Doty and
Steiner[21] show that estimates of $1/P(90°)$ will require the information on the shape scattering molecule for $[Z_{45}] = 1.4$. It is
regarded that the scattered intensity I_r at any angle is the same
in the procedure of Smoluckowski. Thus, if only I_r is settled for
the intensity at 90° from which the interference effect is excluded,
the apparent intensity (measured value) at 90°, I_{90}^a, is corrected
as

$$I_{90} = I_{90}^a/P(90°) \tag{4}$$

by using the correction factor evaluated by Doty and Steiner. The
dependence of $1/P(90°)$ on the dissymmetry $[Z_{45}]$ is illustrated
for (a) monodispersed coil, (b) coils with a normal chain length
distribution, (c) rods, and (d) spheres, respectively, in their
paper. Of these corrections by a curve of $[Z_{45}]$ vs. $1/P(90)$ plot,
only one that leads to a straight line of I_{90} is of (c) rods. This
result is shown in Figure 4. The smaller circles on the broken
line are the observed values of I_{90}^a, and these deviations from
linearity are shown by a thin straight line. The larger circles
which ride on a solid line are values of I_{90} corrected for I_{90}^a.
The good linearity of I_{90} means indirectly that the shape of NaDC
aggregate in the lower concentration of NaDC with supporting electrolyte is of rod-type, and affords the accurate coagulation time
T. The result illustrated in Figure 4 shows that aggregation rate
and the shape of aggregate both are determined by a combination of
the coagulation theory of von Somoluchouski with the correction
factor for the destructive interference of scattered light clculat-
ed by Doty and Steiner.

(II) System in the Buffer Solution

It has been pointed out that the pH dependence in the solution
behavior or the association state of NaDC is larger than that of
common surfactants,[11-15] and the pH itself of NaDC solution change
with its concentration due to the specific hydrolysis.[15] Accordingly it is desirable to carry out the study by the use of a buffer
solution as a solvent whose ionic strength is kept constant as well
as pH. We used the Palitzsch's borate buffer (pH = 7.78) through
all experiments described hereinafter. And the solutios in this
section were stood for at a constant temperature (30°C) for a day
in order to make them reach the equilibulium. In the buffer solution system also the higher dissymmetry coefficient Z_{45} was found
at the lower concentration range as seen in Figure 5. Over the
range above 0.01 g/ml the Z_{45} is close to unity, and should be
noted that the time dependence in Z_{45} at the lower concentration
range is remarkable but the change is hardly observed at the higher

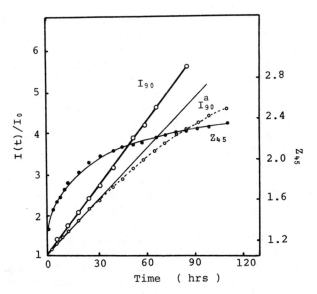

Figure 4. The increase of intensity ratio of scattered light
$I(t)/I_0$ and dissymmetry Z_{45} with setting time and the determination
of coagulation time T. (NaDC 0.004693 g/ml, 0.5 M NaCl added, 20°C)

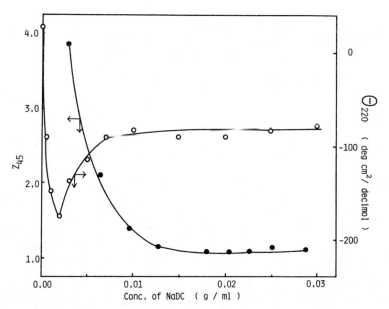

Figure 5. The concentration dependence of dissymmetry Z_{45} and
molecular ellipticity Θ_{220} for the NaDC - buffer solution systems
(pH = 7.78, 30°C).

concentration range where stable and nearly spherical micelles can
exist. In order to confirm the existence of asymmetric micelles a
circular dichroism (CD) measurement was carried out (wave length
from 250 - 210) and its result at wave length 220 nm is shown in
Figure 5 together with Z_{45}. The molecular ellipticity Θ of other
wave length behaved simirally to that at 220 nm. The increase in
Θ_{220} at the lowest concentrations may correspond to monomeric
dispersion. From Figure 5 it is obvious that the aggregates at the
lower concentration range have more ordered structure than those at
the higher concentration, and Z_{45} and CD correspond to each other.

    Futher we measured the viscosity which reflects well the shape
and size of aggregate. As mentioned above the viscosity of NaDC
solution has the characteristic time dependence in the field of
capillary flow, where the formation or degradation of aggregate
takes place. Therefore the measurements were carried out so as to
avoid the repeated flow in capillary. As shown in Figure 6 the
reduced viscosity, $\eta s/C'$, (C' in g/dl), decreases gradually with
increase in concentration up to 0.01 g/ml and then becomes almost
constant. Ferthermore as mentioned below we measured the partial
molar volume of NaDC (330 cm^3/mol at micellar states) so that the
volume fraction of NaDC, Ψ, is caluculated from Equation (5)

$$\Psi = \frac{C \cdot 330}{330 \cdot C + (1/d_0) \cdot 1000} \tag{5}$$

where d_0 is the density of solvent (buffer). And if aggregates
had ellipsoidal shape, specipic viscosity ηs would be related to
volume fraction Ψ by Equations (6) and (7).

$$\eta s = 2.5 \ \Psi \ (f/f_0) \tag{6}$$

where

$$2.5(f/f_0) = [\ \frac{J^2}{15(Ln \ 2J - 1.5)} + \frac{J^2}{5(Ln \ 2J - 0.5)} + \frac{14}{15} \ ] \tag{7}$$

In Equation (7), $J = A/B$, A is the radius of apsis, B is the radius
of minor axis. From Equation (6) and (7), the axis ratio, J was
calculated by using a computer and the result is shown in Figure 6.
In Figure 6 also $\eta s/C'$ and J both show that there exist polymer-like
aggregates at the lower concentration range. At the higher concentration range, the J obtained by means of dynamic measurement
(viscosity) is ca. 2.9, whereas the dissymmetry Z_{45} determined
statically (light scattering) is very colse to unity. This suggest
that the shape of the aggregate formed at the higher concentration
range might be elipsoidal though we have used the term spherical
up to now.

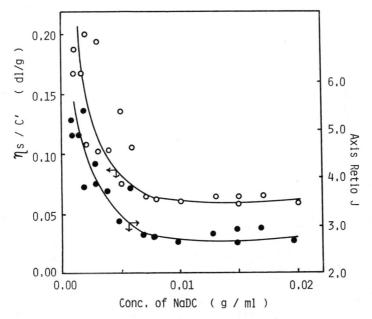

Figure 6. The plot of reduced viscosity $\eta s/C'$ and axis ratio J of the aggregate as a function of the concentration of NaDC (pH = 7.78, 30°C).

The change of apparent molar volume, Φ_V, with concentration is illustrated in Figure 7. The measured points at the lower concentration disperse widely because the solutions were prepared batchwisely and probably because the aggregates are too sensitive to a small difference in the conditions and the aggregates might show the polydispersion, but it can be regard that the higher the values, the lower the concentration. In Figure 7 the amount of solubilized cholesterol is plotted as a function of NaDC concentration along with the apparent molar volume. The cholesterol solubilization curve is one of our data which was obtained in order to determine not only the amount solubilized cholesterol but also CMC as a function of pH, pNa and temperature. But it turned out that the solubilization method to determine the CMC of NaDC did not give the first CMC (of the primary micelle) and was difficult to obtain precise value. The break point might correspond to the transition point from helical aggregate to spherical one, because spherical micelles are stabilized by the cholesterol so that the transition point, a kind of CMC, shifts to the lower concentration. Compared Figure 7 with Figures 5 and 6, it is seen that break points (0.0007 mol/l = 3 x 10^{-3} g/ml) in the curves of Φ_V and solubilization are within the range of non-spherical micelles (below 0.01

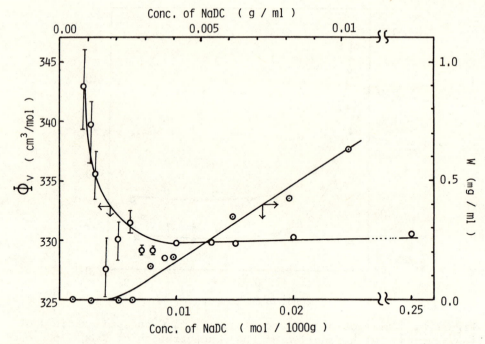

Figure 7. The concentration dependence of apparent molar volume
of NaDC and of the amount of solubilized cholesterol (pH = 7.78,
30°C).

g/ml). With respect to the solubilization of cholesterol we will
discuss later.

As is shown in Figures 5,6 and 7 the aggregates at the lower
concentration range between a certain critical concentration of the
primary micelle formation and 0.01 g/ml must have some ordered
structure and give a viscous solution. From all these facts
together with those described in section 1 it is concluded that the
aggregates formed at "the lower concentration range" have helical
structure and they change gradually into spherical micelles as the
concentration increases. Since the every property for the aggregate does not show a discrete change but a gradual change over
that range, the size may change gradually, and also size distribution may be wide. The stepwise formation of micelles for bile salts
has been considered by many researchers[22-27] but such a phemomenon
as the stepwise deformation (degradation) with increase in the
concentration has not yet been reported and considered. It is known
that the dissymmetric and ordered structure of the aggregate (or
gel) is formed more easily in the lower pH than in the higher
pH[11,15] and the micellization or aggregation of NaDC is accompanied
by a decrease of hydrogen ion concentration, ie., a specific hydrol-

ysis of NaDC.[11,15] If the dissymmetric and ordered aggregates were
helical even in the aqueous solution as pointed out by Rich and
Blow,[10,11] the intermolecular hydrogen bonding between the hydrolized
carboxyl group and hydroxyl group of the other molecule should play
an important role to form the aggregate. The species which has an
undissociated carboxyl group is expected to become an initiator of
aggregation because of its low solubility and to be solubilized by
the species with dissociated carboxyl group. Taking account into
that the polymer-like aggregate (coagulate, gel) is formed in the
solvent of which concentration of added salt is ralatively high as
compared with the concentration of NaDC, the aggregate must be
subject to the salting out or dehydration and the aggregate exists
in the state between the precipitation and dissolution. The reason
why the aggregate becomes smaller with an increase in the concentration of NaDC may be due to the redissolution by the added NaDC
itself. At the higher concentration range the nearly spherical
micelles can exist stably keeping a balance among the concentrations
of added salts and NaDC itself, and pH. As a contrast to synthetic
surfactant it is interesting to describe the concentration dependence
of the aggregation. Kratohvil et al.[28] and Ikeda et al.[29] have
reported with respect to the concentration dependent micellar growth
of sodium dodecyl sulfate at high conterion concentrations as the
micelles at high concentration of NaCl are spherical at CMC, but
they gradually convert into larger rod-like micelles with increasing
surfactant concentration. The result for NaDC seems to be contrary
to that of SDS at least within the concentration range studied, but
in the case of NaDC too the micelles may have larger rod-like shape
again at much higher concentration than that studied.

(III) Cholesterol - Solubilizing System

As discribed already the micelle of NaDC at the concentration
above 0.01 g/ml has a stable and almost spherical shape in the
solution with addition of only NaCl and the buffer solution both.
Here the light scattering measurements in this section were carried
out for each solution made by the dilution of concentrated solutions
over the spherical micellar reagion. When we made NaDC micelle
solubilize choesterol, we found the micelle with choesterol are more
stable (hardly independent of the setting time) than that without
cholesterol, and also no change in Z_{45} appeared by dilution (see
Figure 8). It has been confirmed that the cholestrol - NaDC mixed
system which has reached a solubilization equilibrium once shows
little change in its equilibrium by some purturbation, such as
dilution, temperature change etc. These facts suggest that we can
use the Debye plot for the estimation of micellar weight and for it
we can apply not only the batchwise method but also dilution method
by the use of a deep cylindorical cell. Figure 9 shows the Debye
plots for the systems in the Palitsch buffer solution with and

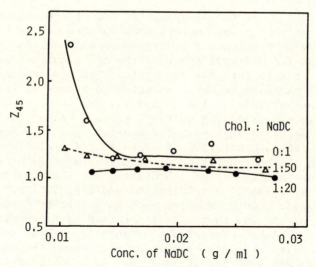

Figure 8. The change in the dissymmetry Z_{45} accompanied by the dilution of NaDC - buffer solution with and without solubilized cholesterol.   (pH = 7.78, 30°C)

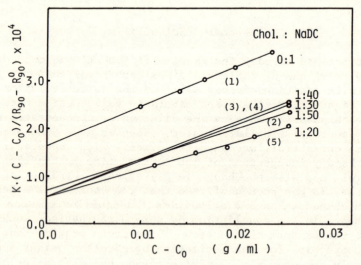

Figure 9.   The Debye plots for cholesterol solubilizing systems. Numerical volues indicate the molar ratio of cholesterol to NaDC (pH = 7.78, 30°C).

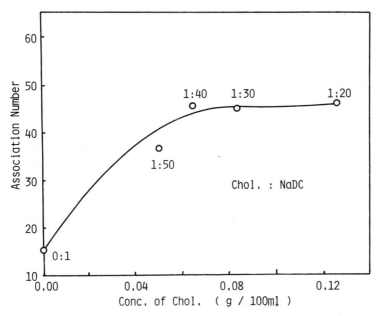

Figure 10. The correlation of the association number of NaDC micelle
with the concentration of cholesterol (pH = 7.78, 30°C).

without cholesterol. In Figure 9 the curvel 1 is for the pure NaDC
and obtained by means of dilution method. At the concentration
range measured, it was confirmed beforehand that the pure NaDC system
also did not show the time dependence in association state. In the
cases of curve 2 - 5 various amounts of cholesterol are solubilized
respectibely by fixed amount of NaDC (0.027 g/ml). Each amount
of the solubilized cholesterol is below the maximum (saturated)
amount for the solubilizer NaDC. The maximum amount was determined
from the slope of liner part in Figure 7 and it was concluded that
one cholesterol molecule is solubilized by 16 NaDC molecules. Here
it should be noted that the ratio of cholesterol amount to NaDC
amount is not changed by diluting the originally prepared solution,
and thus the composition of the micelle determined by the extrapolation to the zero concentration can be regarded the same as that of
original solution. In Figure 10 the average association number is
shown as a function of the amount of the solubilized cholesterol by
a fixed amount of NaDC. The Figure 10 tells us that the micellar
size increases with an increase in cholesterol concentration and then
reaches a certain value (association number ca. 45). The point
measured for the highest concentration is of the ratio of one
cholesterol molecule to 20 NaDC molecules, which is close to that
of the maximum solubilization (1 : 16), and accordingly suggests
that the micelle saturated with cholesterol may be almost the same

in size and the shape as that mentioned above. It seems that 2 or 3 cholesterol molecules are solubilized in a NaDC micelle at maximum solubilization. It is interesting that the cholesterol solubilizing micelle has almost the same size irrespective of the number of solubilized cholesterol molecules. At the lowest point measured within the concentration range which gives the association number ca. 45, the molar ratio of cholesterol to NaDC is 1 : 40. So that each micelle solubilize at least one cholesterol molecule. On the other hand the association number at the maximum solubilization seems to be about 45 - 50 from Figure 10 and the number of solubilized cholesterol molecule per one NaDC micelle is 2 - 3. It is noteworthy that if only the micelle solubilize a cholesterol molecule, its association number becomes large abruptly and almost equal to the association number of maximum solubilizing micelle, and that the micelle which has still a room for the cholesterol is not different in the size from those which are saturated with cholesterol.

SUMMARY

From all results mentioned above it can be regarded that there exist different types of aggregate, so that the solution state seems to be separated into several regions, i.e., (I) singly dispersed, (II) primary micellar (dimer, trimer, tetramer...), (III) polymer-like (helical), (IV) nearly spherical (ellipsoidal?) and so on. The association number of the micelle(IV) increases with increasing NaCl concentration and with lowering temperature. When the micelle of region(IV) solubilizes cholesterol, the structure of the micelle becomes stable and large compared to the micelle without cholesterol.

ACKNOWLEDGEMENTS

We would like to acknowledge helpful discussion and encouragement by Prof. E.J. Fendler, Prof. R. Matuura and Prof. I. Satake. We are indebted to Mrs. T. Taka, and our co-workers for experimental assists. The present work has been performed within a research program sponsored by the Institute of Advance Research, Fukuoka University.

REFERENCES

1. S. A. Johnston and J. W. McBain, Proc. Roy. Soc., (London) 181, 199 (1942).
2. C. R. Merill and J. W. McBain, J. Phys. Chem., 46, 10 (1942).
3. P. Ekwall, Acta Acad. Aboensis. Math. et Phys., 17, 8 (1951).
4. P. Ekwall, K. Setälä and L. Siöblom, Acta Chem. Scand., 5, 175 (1951).

5. P. Ekwall, J. Colloid Sci., 9, (Suppl. 1), 66, (1954).
6. K. Fontell, Kolloid·Z. u. Z. Polymere, 244, 246 (1971).
7. K. Fontell, Kolloid·Z. u. Z. Polymere, 244, 253 (1971).
8. K. Fontell, Kolloid·Z. u. Z. Polymere, 246, 614 (1971).
9. K. Fontell, Kolloid·Z. u. Z. Polymere, 246, 710 (1971).
10. A. Rich and D. M. Blow, Nature, 182, 423 (1958).
11. D. M. Blow and A. Rich, J. Am. Chem. Soc., 82, 3566 (1960).
12. R. Vochten and P. Joos, J. Chim. Phys., 67, 1373 (1970).
13. G. Sugihara, K. Motomura and R. Matuura, Memoirs Fac. Sci.
    Kyushu Univ. Ser. C, 7, 103 (1970).
14. G. Sugihara, M. Tanaka and R. Matuura, Bull. Chem. Soc. Jpn.,
    50, 2542 (1977).
15. G. Sugihara and M. Tanaka, Hyomen, 13, 537 (1978).
16. G. Sugihara and M. Tanaka, Bull. Chem. Soc. Jpn., 49, 3457
    (1976).
17. G. Sugihara, T. Ueda, S. Kaneshina and M. Tanaka, Bull. Chem.
    Soc. Jpn., 50, 604 (1977).
18. J. R. Cardinal, (1980), parsonal communication.
19. M. C. Carey and D. M. Small, Arch. Intern. Med., 130, 506
    (1972).
20. H. R. Kruyt, "Colloid Science," Elsevier Publishing Co., Vol.
    I, P. 296, 1952.
21. P. Doty and R. F. Steiner, J. Chem. Phys., 18, 1211 (1950).
22. E. J. Fendler and N. Rosenthal, in "Solution Chemistry of
    Surfactants," K. L. Mittal, Editor, Vol. 1, pp. 455-472.
    Plenum Press, New York, 1979
23. A. Djavanbakht, K. M. Kale and R. Zana, J. Colloid Interface
    Sci., 59, 139 (1977).
24. Y. Chang and J. R. Cardinal, J. Pharm. Sci., 67, 994 (1978).
25. B. Lindman, N. Kanenka, H. Fabre, J. Ulmius and T. Wieloch,
    J. Colloid Interface Sci., 73, 556 (1980).
26. P. Mukerjee and J. R. Cardinal, J. Pharm Sci., 65, 882 (1976)
27. D. G. Oakenfull and L. R. Fisher, J. Phys. Chem., 81, 1838
    (1977).
28. B. L. Newkirk and J. P. Kratohvil, Abstracts of ACS/CSJ Chemi-
    cal Congress, Coll. 142, Honolulu, 1979.
29. S. Ikeda and S. Hayashi, Abstracts of ACS/CSJ Chemical Congress,
    Coll. 143, Honolulu, 1979.

THERMODYNAMICS OF BILE SALT INTERACTIONS WITH LIPIDIC SUBSTANCES

Charles H. Spink and Stephen Colgan

Department of Chemistry
State University of New York
Cortland, NY   13045

Solubilization by bile salts is a fundamentally
important process in lipid biochemistry. The interaction of long-chain, aliphatic compounds and other
lipidic substances with bile salt micelles to produce solubilized aggregates provides a transport
mechanism for the absorption of the fatty materials
in the small intestine. The basic energetics of
formation of the aggregates determines their stability and solution characteristics, and thus are
important in understanding the behavior of the bile
salts in the solubilization process. This paper
presents a summary of the thermodynamics of transfer of a series of fatty alcohols from aqueous to
the bile salt micelle phase. Free energy, enthalpy,
entropy, and heat capacity effects are presented,
and analyzed in terms of the additive contributions
to the properties of the solutes. A comparison of
bile salt behavior with other solubilizing agents
shows some similarities, but also differences that
seem to relate to the aggregation characteristics
of the surfactants themselves. The thermodynamic
data indicate an increasing enthalpic component to
the stability of longer chain, aliphatic substances,
and a relatively constant entropic contribution.
Heat capacities of transfer are typical of hydrophobic compounds, showing large decreases in Cp
in transferring from the aqueous to micellar phase.
Projection of these results to the behavior of

629

physiologically important compounds leads to specula-
tion that the stability of aggregates of bile salts
and lipid materials is largely enthalpic, and relatively independent of media characteristics.

INTRODUCTION

   Bile salts are physiological surfactants which are involved in a number of fundamental processes relating to lipid biochemistry. They act as emulsifying agents for triglyceride fats
in the small intestine, and provide a mechanism for solubilization of the products of fat hydrolysis, the fatty acids and
monoglycerides. In addition, bile salt solubilization has been
shown to be important in the stability of bile itself, which is
a complex mixture of lecithin, cholesterol, and bile salts, as
well as other minor components. Thus, the bile salts are detergents of considerable importance to living systems, their importance largely related to the ability of the salts to solubilize
lipidic substances.

   Solubilization by surfactants is generally considered to
occur through the formation of comicellar aggregates of the
detergent and specific solubilizate.[1] The basic process may be
considered as dissolution of the solute into or onto the surface
of micelles of the surfactant.[2,3] The interactions between
lipidic substrate and the surfactant can be formalized in terms
of a basic two-phase distribution process in which the solute is
in equilibrium with a micellar aggregate phase and an aqueous
medium.[3]

   In the case of bile salt solubilization complexities in the
solubilization process have been shown in several studies.[4,5,6]
Based on solubility data for naphthalene in sodium cholate solutions, Mukerjee showed that the solubilization behavior of the
bile salt is different from flexible chain detergents, such as
sodium dodecyl sulfate (SDS).[4] Although the bile salts do exhibit
a critical micelle concentration (cmc) typical of aggregating
surfactants, their behavior above the cmc is quite different from
classical detergents, showing more gradual changes in solution
properties used to characterize the cmc and the aggregation process.[7] Fisher and Oakenfull have demonstrated further subtleties
in solubilizing behavior of bile salts.[6] They found that small,
planar molecules show free rotation within bile salt aggregates,
while larger and nonplanar species are markedly restricted in
their motion in the micellar phase. These results, based on
fluorescence and electron spin probe measurements, indicated the
special character of the bile salt aggregates responsible for
their solubilizing behavior.

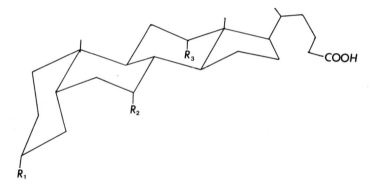

Figure 1.   Structures of some common bile acids.

$R_1=R_2=R_3-OH$:   Cholic acid

$R_1=R_2=OH$, $R_3=H$:   Chenodeoxycholic acid

$R_1=R_3=OH$, $R_2=H$:   Deoxycholic acid

The specific properties of the micelles of bile salts have been reviewed by Small.[8,9] At least a part of their unique solutions characteristics are a result of the of the basic structure of the molecule. Figure 1 shows the structural features of the common bile acids. The usual physiologically important molecules occur with the carboxyl group conjugated with either glycine or taurine. Clearly, with the rigid, steroid skeletal system, and the presence of -OH groups in the backbone of the molecule, these structures are not typical of the usual surfactant. Light scattering data have been interpreted to indicate that primary association of the bile salts in aqueous solutions occurs through aggregation of the nonpolar sides of the steroid backbone in such a geometry that the -OH groups are exposed to the aqueous phase.[9,10] As concentration of surfactant increases the primary aggregates are then thought to associate into larger multiple structures through interactions of the -OH groups on the exposed outer surface of the primary micelles.[10] Because of the complexities of the

fundamental aggregation process, one might expect solubilization
by bile salt micelles to reflect these complex interactions, and
as mentioned above, there are some indications that interactions
between solutes and bile salt micelles are, indeed, not simple.

The basic thermodynamics of solubilization interactions have
been discussed by Mukerjee.[1,3] Unfortunately, relatively few
thermodynamic data are available for analysis of the properties
of solutes which undergo transfer from an aqueous to micellar phase.
In order to sort out various effects of the aqueous medium, surfactant concentration, temperature, micellar structure, and solute
characteristics, thermodynamic transfer data are needed for a wide
variety of conditions. From distribution coefficients between
aqueous and micellar phase the free energy change for transfer to
the micelle can be evaluated, and the temperature dependence of
the fraction solubilized provides data from which enthalpy effects
can be calculated, although direct calorimetric measurements are
preferred in such complicated systems. The entropy change and
particularly, heat capacity effects are useful properties, since
they frequently indicate the nature of the basic interactions
involved, i.e., whether large media effects are involved in the
transfer process.

Some thermodynamic data are available for the solubilization
of alcohols in SDS micelles,[11,12] and for hydrocarbon transfer
from aqueous to SDS aggregates.[13] Menger reported equilibrium
constants for the binding of some p-nitrophenol esters to bile
salt micelles, the data actually obtained from kinetics of hydrolysis of the esters.[5]

Because of the lack of any systematic thermodynamic studies
on bile salt interactions with various solutes, we have undertaken a program of investigation of these systems with the purpose
to obtain thermodynamic properties of transfer of solutes from
aqueous media to bile salt micelles under a variety of conditions.[14,15] These data are intended not only to provide properties
of the solute as it distributes between the phases, but also to
generate some insight into the behavior of the bile salts acting
in their critical role as solubilizing agents. In this paper we
present an overview of the thermodyanmic data now available for
the transfer of a series of aliphatic alcohols from aqueous to
bile salt micellar phase.[14,15] The alcohols were chosen as a
representative solute with aliphatic chain and a polar functional
group in the molecule. Also, because some data are available for
the interaction of SDS micelles with the alcohols, this group of
molecules is a useful place to start examination of the solubilization process with bile salts.

In the summary which follows thermodynamic data will be presented first for the transfer of alcohol solutes from aqueous media to bile salt micellar aggregates. The results then will be discussed in terms of comparisons with other published data on solubilization by micelles. Attempts will be made to distinguish the factors responsible for the over-all behavior of the solutes, and to evaluate the inherent properties of bile salt aggregates in relation to their solubilizing behavior toward the alcohol solutes.

THERMODYNAMIC RESULTS

Free Energies

The free energy data for transfer of alcohol from aqueous to micellar phase were obtained by a vapor pressure technique.[11,15] The method consists of analysis by gas chromatgraphy of the amount of alcohol in a vapor space in equilibrium with aqueous buffer solution containing bile salt, and the amount in the vapor in contact with buffer solution alone. From the vapor pressure depression in the presence of bile salt the fractions of the total alcohol in aqueous phase and in the micellar phase can be evaluated. If the two phase distribution model is used, the equilibrium constant, K, is determined by,

$$K = \frac{Xm}{Xa} \quad (1)$$

where,

$$Xa = \frac{Ma}{55.55} \quad (2)$$

and,

$$Xm = \frac{Mm}{(C_s - cmc) + Mm} . \quad (3)$$

In Equation (2) and (3), Ma is the molar concentration of alcohol in the aqueous phase, Mm the concentration in the micellar phase, and the quantity $(C_s - cmc)$ is the total surfactant concentration minus the cmc value for the conditions. This latter term represents the total amount of bile salt in the micelle phase. The free energy change evaluated from K by the usual logarithmic relationship corresponds to the desired transfer process, provided the micellar phase can indeed be treated as a unique, definable phase, and activity coefficients in the two phases are unity.

Figure 2 shows the behavior of the fraction in the micelle phase for several alcohols, as the concentration is increased for the bile salt, sodium deoxycholate. These are two major points to be made from these data. First, as has been observed with alcohol binding to SDS micelles,[11] as the aliphatic chain-length

in the alcohol increases, a greater fraction is solubilized in the
micellar phase. However, it is clear that as the concentration of
bile salt is increased above the critical micelle concentration
(which is 2.0 mM under the prevailing conditions), the fraction
bound is not constant, but increases to a more or less constant
value when the deoxycholate concentration reaches about 100 mM.   If
this system is to be treated according to the two-phase model, the
data in Figure 2 indicate that the bile salt concentration must be
specifically defined. On the basis of the observed leveling above
100 mM bile salt, we have chosen to analyze the thermodynamic
properties at concentrations of 0.2 m sodium deoxcholate.   At this
concentration of bile salt, a more or less constant distribution
process is expected over a range of bile salt compositions.
Also, of importance in defining the conditions for the distribution process is the presence of counterions in the micellar
medium.   Table I shows the fraction in the micelle phase for 0.1 M
sodium deoxycholate and the three alcohols, butanol, pentanol, and

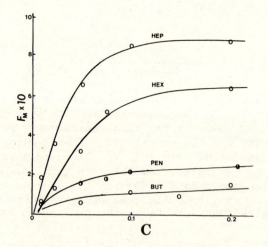

Figure 2.   Fraction of alcohol in micelle phase, Fm, plotted
versus molar concentration of sodium deoxycholate.   BUT=butanol,
PEN=pentanol, HEX=hexanol, HEP=heptanol.

hexanol with varying concentrations of NaCl added to the medium.
Clearly, from these data there is virtually no effect of sodium
chloride concentration in the range shown. Since physiological
conditions are near 0.15 M NaCl, the medium which we chose for
evaluation of the equilibrium constants is 0.15 M NaCl and 0.20 M
sodium deoxycholate. The pH of the solution is critical in
defining the solubility of the bile salts.[8] In order to eliminate
the formation of the insoluble gel phases that form at lower pH
values, the medium was buffered at pH=8.20 $\pm$ 0.05 with 0.01 M TRIS
for all solutions studied.

Table I. Fraction of Alcohol in Micelle Phase as NaCl Concentration
is Increased in 0.1M Sodium Deocycholate.

Alcohol	Fm^a		
	0.01 M NaCl	0.05 M NaCl	0.15 M NaCl
Butanol	0.15	0.15	0.14
Pentanol	0.24	0.21	0.20
Hexanol	0.49	0.51	0.47

[a]Fraction of total alcohol in micellar phase.

     With the above conditions specified, the equilibrium constants
for distribution between the aqueous and micellar phase can be
calculated, and converted to the free energy of transfer between
the phases. Figure 3 shows a plot of the free energy data for
the C_4 to C_7 alcohols, along with similar data for SDS.[11] For
the bile salt case the three higher alcohols fall on a straight
line with butanol slightly above the line. The slope of the line
is -3.30 kJ/mole per $-CH_2-$.[15] Thus, the behavior of the alcohols
with bile salt micelles is fairly typical of hydrophobic processes,
the solutes showing increased preference for the nonpolar micellar
phase as more $-CH_2-$ groups are added to the molecule. While the
stability in the micelle phase for the alcohols studied is greater
in SDS micelles, the rate of increase in stability with increased
chain length is greater for bile salt micelles.

     The fact that butanol does not fit exactly on the line in
Figure 3 could be related to the behavior of the lower alcohols
in general.[12] The C_1 - C_3 alcohols, and to some extent the C_4,
show little change in their partial molal volumes in solutions
containing SDS micelles compared with their aqueous solution
volumes. These results, and the effects of alcohols on the cmc
behavior of SDS, indicate that the lower alcohols are not solu-

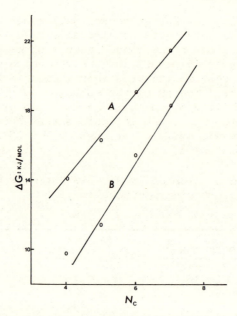

Figure 3. Free energy of transfer of alcohols from aqueous to sodium dedecyl sulfate (A), and sodium deoxycholate (B) micelles versus number of carbon atoms in alcohol aliphatic chain.

bilized to a great extent, and exhibit their influence on the micelles through media induced changes.[17] Butanol seems to be on the borderline, being slightly solubilized (See Figure 2), but also showing somewhat atypical behavior.[17]

Before leaving the free energy data, it is informative to compare the solubilizing behavior of other bile salts for the alcohols. In addition to the deoxycholate, a dihydroxy bile salt, sodium cholate is a physiologically common salt, and is a tri-hydroxy compound. Figure 4 shows the fraction heptanol solubilized in the micellar phase for sodium cholate (C), sodium deoxycholate (B), and sodium dodecyl sulfate(A), as the concentration of sur-factant is changed.[15] Two trends are apparent in these data. First, for lower amounts of surfactant in solution there are clear differences in solubilizing behavior in the three cases. There must be inherent differences in the properties of the micellar aggregate phases to account for the rather large difference in the vicinity of 0.05 M surfactant. Equally significant is the fact that at higher concentration of the salts all three seem to reach a limiting fraction of heptanol solubilized of about 0.90. While the three micellar phases reach this limiting value at different concentrations of surfactant, the fraction solubilized is the same, suggesting that all of the surfactants reach a point at which the

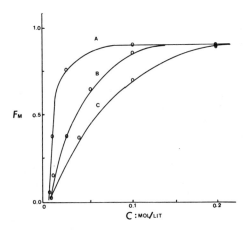

Figure 4. Fraction of heptanol in micelle phase for sodium dodecyl sulfate (A), sodium deoxycholate (B), and sodium cholate (C), versus concentration of surfactant.

micellar phases are quite similar with respect to solubilizing alcohols. In such a case the distribution of the alcohol is dependent only on the difference in chemical potentials between the aqueous phase and a nonpolar micelle phase.

Enthalpies and Entropies

In order to better understand the energetic factors responsible for the stability of the micellar aggregates, it is important to examine the enthalpy and entropy contributions. Enthalpies of transfer of the alcohol solutes from aqueous to bile salt micellar phases have been evaluated from heat of solution data.[14] Transfer enthalpies are obtained from the differences in heat of solution into bile salt solutions and that for the buffer solution containing no micellar phase. Because some of the alcohols are not completely bound into the micelles, the heat effects have to be corrected for the actual amount transferred to the nonpolar phase.[14] Figure 5 shows the ΔH of transfer of some alcohols from aqueous buffer to micelle phase for sodium deoxycholate micelles and for dodecyl sulfate micelles, the latter data obtained

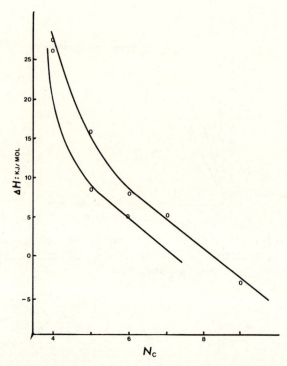

Figure 5. Enthalpy of transfer of aliphatic alcohols from water to sodium deoxycholate micelles (upper curve) and to sodium dodecyl sulfatemicelles (lower curve) versus number of carbon atoms in alcohol.

from the study of Aveyard and Lawrence.[18] The SDS enthalpies have been corrected for the fraction solubilized in the micellar phase.[15,18] The corrected enthalpy change for butanol shows a fairly large endothermic contribution and there is progressively more exothermicity with increased chain length, implying that the $-CH_2-$ groups provide a stabilizing effect in the micellar phase. The slope of the enthalpy of transfer for the C_6 to C_9 compounds is about -3.7 kJ/mol per $-CH_2-$ group for the bile salt case. It appears that the SDS curve would have a similar slope for the longer chain length.

With a fixed concentration of sodium deoxycholate in solution it was found that $\Delta H(tr)$ was independent of the total amount of alcohol in solution.[14] These data imply that the fraction entering the micelle phase is independent of the alcohol concentration in the micelle. The ratio of bile salt to alcohol was varied from 30:1 to 2:1, so that in this range of composition there appears to be little evidence of non-ideality that is concentration dependent. In addition, there was no effect on the transfer enthalpies from varying the NaCl concentration between 0.01 and 0.15 M.[14] It was found, however, that the bile salt concentration did have significant effect on the enthalpy difference between aqueous and micellar phase. For example, the value for pentanol varied from 4.1 to 2.2 kJ/mol as bile salt concentration decreased from 0.20 to 0.05 M. This effect is a result of a shift in the binding equilibrium with concentration as was shown above in Figure 2. If the transfer enthalpies are corrected for the fraction actually transferred to the micelles, they are constant to within the experimental error.[14]

With enthalpy data available it is now possible to evaluate the entropy of transfer of alcohols between aqueous and sodium deoxycholate micelles. Table II gives a summary of the thermodynamic transfer data for the alcohols.

Table II. Thermodyanmic Transfer Properties of Aliphatic Alcohols Between Aqueous and 0.20 M Sodium Deoxycholate Solution.

Alcohol	K^a	$- \Delta G^b$	ΔH	ΔS
Butanol	52	9.8	27.6	126
Pentanol	100	11.4	15.8	91
Hexanol	482	15.3	7.8	78
Heptanol	1934	18.7	5.1	80
Nonanol	-	-	-3.3	-

[a] Distribution ratio between the phases as defined by Equation 1. Data are from reference (15).
[b] Units are kJ/mol for ΔG and ΔH, and J/K-mol for ΔS.

The striking feature of these data is that a relatively large, positive entropy effect decreases and eventually becomes constant as the alcohols become larger. The major consequence of this behavior is that as the chain length increases, changes in the enthalpy term will essentially determine the increased stability of the alcohols in the micellar phase. In the previous section it was observed that the $-CH_2-$ increment in the free energy is about -3.3 kJ/mol, and since the enthalpy increment is -3./ kJ/mol, it is obvious that beyond the $C_5 - C_6$ alcohols the alkyl chain contribution to stability is largely determined by the energy differences between aqueous and micelle phase.

Benjamin has pointed out a similar trend in the thermodynamics of solution of alcohols in water.[19] From his compilation in the range of $C_6 - C_{10}$ alcohols the free energy $-CH_2-$ increment for the

transfer from aqueous to pure liquid phase is -3.4 kJ/mol, very
close to the value for transfer to the deoxycholate micelles.
Also, as found with the bile salts, the enthalpy increment is a
significant part of the stabilizing effect of the methylene group,
the value being -2.5 kJ/mol in this case. The similarities in the
thermodynamics of transfer of the alcohols from water to pure
liquid and to bile salt micelles at the longer chain lengths suggests that the internal environment of the micelles is similar to
that of pure liquid alcohols. More on the consequences of this
behavior will be presented in the Discussion below.

Heat Capacities

The apparent excess heat capacity in aqueous solution associated with nonpolar molecules, and particularly with aliphatic
substances, has been well-documented.[20-24] It is thus important to
examine heat capacity changes in the course of transfer of the
aliphatic alcohols from water to the bile salt micelles. Relatively
large heat capacity decreases have been observed for other binding
processes involving aqueous to nonpolar transfer.[25,26] From the
temperature dependence of the enthalpies of transfer from water to
bile salt micelles, heat capacities of transfer have been evaluated.[14] Results for transfer to 0.2 M sodium deoxycholate micelles
are presented in Table III. Also shown in the Table for comparison

Table III. Heat Capacities of Transfer of Aliphatic Alcohols from
Aqueous Buffer to 0.20 M Sodium Deoxycholate Micelles and to Pure
Liquid Phase[a].

Alcohol	$\Delta Cp(mic)$[b]	$\Delta Cp(p.l.)$[c]	$\Delta Cp(R-)$[d]
Butanol	-40	-290	-322
Pentanol	-130	-350	-390
Hexanol	-250	-400	-450
Heptanol	-400	-460	-520
Nonanol	-580	-590	-650

[a]Values are in J/K-mol, and are from Reference (14).

[b]Heat capacity of transfer from aqueous buffer to 0.20 M sodium
deoxycholate micelles.

[c]Heat capacity of transfer from water to pure liquid alcohol.

^{d}Heat capacity of transfer of aliphatic chain from aqueous to non-
polar environment, calculated using the additivity rules of
Reference (21).

are corresponding data for transfer to the pure alcohol phase. In
addition, values are presented for the transfer of the aliphatic
group in each case from water to nonpolar phase, calculated using
the partial molal heat capacity additivity rules of Nichols, et
al.[21] The larger alcohols show the expected large decrease in heat
capacity upon transfer to the bile salt nonpolar environment, with
heptanol and nonanol relatively close to the pure liquid values.
Butanol and pentanol, and to some extent hexanol show anomalously
small decreases in Cp. These results suggest that the aliphatic
chain of the smaller alcohols is not removed completely from the
aqueous solution, so that the excess heat capacity still remains
for a portion of the molecule. Alternately, butanol may be
specifically binding in a way that leads to changes in conformation
of the micellar aggregate. The rather high enthalpy of binding
shown above also supports that idea that the lower alcohols are
behaving atypically.

The transfer of the R- group of the alcohol to a nonpolar
medium from water leads to larger heat capacity decreases than are
observed for the bile salt cases, based on comparison of the
expected values in column 3 of Table III with the observed micellar
transfer values. The -OH group has a small effect on aqueous heat
capacities,[21] so the somewhat smaller ΔCp for transfer to bile
salt micelle must be a consequence of either specific interactions
within the micelles or that the R- group is not completely transferred to the nonpolar core of the micelle phase. For heptanol
and nonanol about one -CH$_2$- group not entered into the nonpolar
medium of the core would account for the differences between
expected R-group transfer heat capacities. With the alcohols
considered to have the -OH groups in contact with the aqueous
medium, it would be possible that a methylene next to the -OH might
also be in contact with water. On the other hand, it is reasonable
to consider the internal core of the micelle to be quite similar
to the environment of pure liquid alcohols, and that the transferred
alcohols are completely removed from contact with water. The
similarities between all of the transfer properties, including heat
capacity changes, for the aqueous to pure liquid and aqueous to
micelle phases supports this view of alcohols bound into the micellar core. From thermodynamic data alone it is not possible to
distinguish the possible physical status of the alcohol.

DISCUSSION

The thermodynamic data presented in the previous section can provide important information about the factors responsible for stability of bile salt complexes with polar, nonionic solutes. The information relies upon the suitability of the two-state model, and whether activity coefficient effects are negligible in these systems. Let us first examine the activity coefficient problem. Three experimental factors offer support to the idea that nonideal behavior is minimal or at least constant in the concentration ranges studied.[14,15] First, in the distribution studies it was observed that Henry's law was obeyed over the alcohol compositions involved.[15] Secondly, the fact that the enthalpies of solution into the bile salt micellar solutions was constant over a wide range of bile salt to alcohol ratios adds corroborative evidence that nonideality is at least constant in these mixtures.[14] Both the Henry's law behavior and the enthalpy results are likely a consequence of the small amount of alcohol relative to total bile salt concentration. In most of the studies the bile salt solutions were 200 mM in sodium deoxycholate and just a few mM (1-5 mM) in alcohol. Thus, it is not surprising that the laws of dilute solutions would be valid, and the assumption of activity coefficients of unity in the micellar phase is reasonable. Although activity coefficients in the aqueous medium surrounding bile salt micelles might be diffi- cult to predict, the ionic salt contribution can be estimated using Long-McDevitt equations.[27,28] The effect on the free energy would be only a few percent, which is close to the experimental uncer- tainties in the distribution method.[15]

One further piece of evidence shows that the presence of alcohol in the micelle phase produces no major composition depen- dent effects on the chemical potential of the bile salt. It was found that the cmc of sodium deoxycholate, as determined by surface tension measurements, was not altered significantly in the presence of up to 5 mM heptanol.[15] Similar studies with SDS micelles showed about a 10% decrease in cmc for similar amounts of heptanol.[29] For the bile salt case it appears that the structural features of the aggregates are such as to accomodate these small amounts of alcohol with little effect on the thermodynamic behavior of the bile salt. SDS, being a spherical, flexible chain micelle, is known to undergo changes in cmc with the binding of nonionic solutes, presumably a result of the lowering of electrostatic repulsive forces at the surface of the micelle.[1,29]

The use of the two-phase distribution model requires that the standard state chemical potential of the micellar phase be a con- stant at a specific temperature and pressure, and independent of the amount of bile salt. The binding data in Figures 2 and 3

clearly show that solubilization is dependent on the concentration
of surfactant, at least until higher concentrations are reached.
These results strongly infer that changes in surfactant properties
occur in the composition region between the cmc and the point at
which levelling is observed in the binding curves. Work by
Fontell[31] and Murata, et. al.[32] has indicated that the bile salts
form primary micelles which have an elongated, helical structure,
and that these primary micelles undergo transformation to more
spherical or ellipsoidal shape at higher concentrations of bile
salt. It is interesting that this transformation occurs in the
approximate range of deoxycholate concentration that the binding
curves in Figures 2 and 3 are changing from virtually zero binding
to the maximum in each case. One could interpret the increases in
solubilization as a consequence of higher efficiency of binding the
alcohols for the secondary micelles which form at higher concentrations. The helical, fibrous primary micelles may not have well-
developed nonpolar regions for solubilization of the alcohols.
Examination of the solubilization model is in progress, but must be
reconciled with the mass action principles formulated by Hall and
Pethica.[30] The standard chemical potentials of the various
micellar aggregates must be defined in terms of the mole fraction
of each aggregate phase. It is possible that the data of Fontell[31]
and Murata[32] can provide considerable insight into the solubilization equilibria for nonionic solutes.

One final observation on the thermodynamics of transfer of
the alcohols to bile salt micelles should be made. Values of the
transfer properties for the aliphatic chain or -CH_2- group are
important in understanding the contribution of the hydrophobic
effect to stability of the micellar aggregates.[20] Table IV
summarizes data for -CH_2- transfer from aqueous to sodium deoxycholate micelles along with corresponding data for aqueous to pure
liquid. Also shown are gas phase transfer properties, which provide a basis for comparing interactions in the various phases.
The entries above the line are based on the C_6 and higher alcohol
homologs, while the two below are based on C_3 to C_6 alcohols.[33,34]

Examinations of the aqueous-to-bile salt or aqueous-to-pure
liquid alcohol properties for the higher homologs reveals that the
enthalpy term is dominant in both cases. It is clear from the gas
phase processes that the enthalpy effect results largely from the
considerably larger enthalpy of transfer into the nonpolar media
of bile salt or pure liquid phases than into water. Although there
are some small differences in entropy change, the aqueous phase
being more negative than the other two, the 2.5 to 3.0 kJ/mol
enthalpy difference provides the major favorable free energy
component for the CH_2-group in a nonpolar environment. Thus, one
concludes that the aqueous-to-nonpolar medium transfers are
essentially lipophilic rather than hydrophobic on the basis of the

Table IV. Transfer Properties of CH_2-group Between Various Phases from Aliphatic Alcohol Data.

Process[a]	kJ/mol		
	ΔG	ΔH	$T\Delta S$
AQ $\longrightarrow$ BILE SALT	-3.3	-3.7	-0.4
AQ $\longrightarrow$ PURE LIQ	-3.4	-2.5	+0.9
GAS $\longrightarrow$ AQ	+0.4	-2.5	-2.9
GAS $\longrightarrow$ BILE SALT	-2.9	-5.5	-2.6
GAS $\longrightarrow$ PURE LIQ	-2.9	-5.0	-2.1
AQ $\longrightarrow$ PURE LIQ	-2.7	-0.9	+1.8
GAS $\longrightarrow$ AQ	-0.2	-4.1	-3.9

[a]Transfer properties obtained from data in References (15) and (19). Values above line are based on C_6 and higher alcohols, while those below line are for C_3 to C_6 homologs from References (33) and (34).

the data for the larger alcohol homologs.

    In examining data in the literature for CH_2-group transfers based on the smaller alcohols,[33,34] one obtains a rather different picture. The aqueous-to-pure liquid transfers below the line in Table IV show a rather different trend. In this case the positive entropy change is almost double that for the corresponding transfer obtained from the larger alcohols. This leads to an almost reversed analysis of the factors responsible for the stability of the CH_2-group in nonpolar media. Although the free energy change is not too different in the two cases, one concludes that the entropy effect is dominant, and the favorable conditions for transfer to pure liquid are a result of a hydrophobic, entropic term. Clearly, the two examples provide an interpretive dilemma.

    There is considerable evidence that the smaller alcohols,[15,33] and even hydrocarbons,[35] show influences of the functional group attached to the aliphatic chain, and that this influence is transmitted far down the chain. Polar groups have significant hydration contributions to the thermodynamic properties in aqueous media.[15] Even a methyl group attached to an aliphatic chain has a significantly higher partial molal heat capacity[21] and chemical potential[20] than a methylene. These "end" effects must certainly influence the behavior of CH_2-groups for some distance away from the functional group, so that increments in thermodynamic properties based on the smaller aliphatic compounds contain not only the inherent property of the methylene, but also a contribution from the groups attached to the methylenes. With this in mind it would seem that the increment values shown in the top of Table IV more closely represent the "true" methylene transfer properties, devoid of perturbations from the ends of the aliphatic chains. Further, the usually defined hydrophobic effect, which contains additional entropic components from the end effects, is a composite effect whose value may depend significantly on the nature of the functional groups attached to the aliphatic chain.

In conclusion, the thermodynamic analysis of interaction of bile salts with aliphatic alcohols has provided new information on the nature of the factors responsible for the stability of aggregates of aliphatic compounds in nonpolar environments that are in equilibrium with aqueous solution. The partitioning of the methylene contribution into the enthalpic and entropic components has shown that caution must be exercised in how the data are used in an interpretive sense. More work on the influences of functional groups and ionic components on the stability of bile salt aggregates should give a more firm basis to understanding the behavior of lipidic substances in these systems.

ACKNOWLEDGEMENTS

A major portion of the work reported here was supported by a grant from the National Institute of Health under Grant #AM20946.

REFERENCES

1. P. Mukerjee, Adv. Colloid Interface Sci., 1, 241 (1967).
2. M.E.L. McBain and E. Hutchinson, "Solubilization and Related Phenomena", Academic Press, New York, 1955.
3. P. Mukerjee, J. Pharm. Sci., 60, 1531 (1971).
4. P. Mukerjee and J.R. Cardinal, J. Pharm. Sci, 65, 882 (1976).
5. F.M. Menger and M.J. McCreery, J. Amer. Chem. Soc., 96, 121 (1974)
6. L. Fisher and D. Oakenfull, Austral. J. Chem. 32, 31 (1979).
7. R. Zana, J. Lang, S.H. Yiv, A. Djavanbakht and C. Abad, in "Micellization, Solubilization, and Microemulsions", K. Mittal Ed., Vol. 1, pp. 291-304, Plenum Press, New York, 1977.
8. M.C. Carey and D.M. Small, Amer. J. Med., 49, 590 (1970).
9. D.M. Small, in "The Bile Acids", P.P. Nair and D. Kritchevsky, Eds., Plenum, New York, 1971, chap. 8.

10. N.A. Mazer, M.C. Carey, R.F. Kwasnick, and G.B. Benedek,
     Biochemistry, 18, 3064 (1979).
11. K. Hayase and S. Hayane, Bull. Chem. Soc. Japan, 50, 83 (1977).
12. M. Manabe, K. Shirahama, and M. Koda, Bull. Chem. Soc. Japan,
     49, 2904 (1976).
13. A. Wishnia, J. Phys. Chem., 67, 2079 (1963).
14. C.H. Spink and R. Stedwell, J. Phys. Chem., in press.
15. C.H. Spink, C. Missack, and S. Colgan, J. Phys. Chem.,
     submitted for publication.
16. C. McAuliffe, Nature, 200, 1092 (1963).
17. M. Manabe and M. Koda, Bull. Chem. Soc. Japan, 51, 1599 (1978).
18. R. Aveyard and A.S.C. Lawrence, Trans. Fara. Soc., 60, 2265 (1964).
19. L. Benjamin, J. Phys. Chem., 68, 3575 (1964).
20. C. Tanford, "The Hydrophobic Effect", John Wiley, New York, 1973.
21. N. Nichols, R. Skold, C. Spink, J. Suurkuusk and I. Wadso,
     J. Chem. Thermodyn., 8, 1081 (1976).
22. C. Spink and I. Wadso, J. Chem. Thermodyn., I, 561 (1975).
23. R. Skold, J. Suurkuusk, C. Spink and I. Wadso, J. Chem.
     Thermodyn., 8, 993 (1976).
24. J. Konicek and I. Wadso, Acta Chem. Scand., 25, 1541 (1971).
25. J.M. Sturtevant, Proc. Natl. Acad. Sci. USA, 74, 2236 (1977).
26. G.C. Kresheck, in "Water: A Comprehensive Treatise",
     F. Franks, Ed., Vol. 4, Plenum, New York, 1975, pp. 145-157.
27. F.A. Long and W.F. McDevitt, Chem. Rev. 51, 119 (1952).
28. N.C. Deno and C.H. Spink, J. Phys. Chem., 67, 1347 (1963).
29. M. Manabe and M. Koda, Memoirs of the Niihama Technical College,
     13, 57 (1977).
30. D.G. Hall and B.A. Pethica, in "Nonionic Surfactants", M.J.
     Schick, Ed., Marcel Dekker, New York, 1967.
31. K. Fontell, Kolloid Z.u. Z. Polymere, 246, 710 (1971).
32. Y. Murata, G. Sugihara, N. Nishikido and M. Tanaka, in
     "Solution Behavior of Surfactants: Theoretical and Applied
     Aspects". (This proceedings volume).
33. G.L. Amidon and S.T. Anik, J. Phys. Chem., 84, 970 (1980).
34. D.J.J. Hill and L.R. White, Austr. J. Chem., 27, 1905 (1974).
35. A. Ben Naim and J. Wilf, J. Phys. Chem., 84, 583 (1980).

THE CONFORMATION OF THE GLYCERYLPHOSPHORYLCHOLINE GROUP IN

PHOSPHOLIPID FORMING SMALL MICELLES

Helmut Hauser and Irmin Pascher

Department of Biochemistry, ETH Zurich, Zurich,
Switzerland and Department of Structural Chemistry
University of Goteborg, Goteborg, Sweden

The conformation of the glycerylphosphorylcholine
group of various phosphatidylcholines (PC) forming small
micelles in H_2O has been studied by NMR in the absence
and presence of lanthanide ions. Both in the absence
and presence of lanthanides the motionally averaged
polar group conformation of PC in micelles is similar
to that in bilayers. This conformation is found to be
independent of the state of aggregation, i.e., the main
features are the same below and above the cmc. The determining factor must therefore be the intramolecular
energetics. Within the experimental accuracy the polar
group conformation of diacylPC is the same as that of
dialkylPC indicating that the replacement of the two
ester linkages by ether bonds has no effect on the polar
group conformation. Lanthanide ions induce a conformational change leading to a reorientation of the OP-N
dipole. This reorientation produces a more extended
disposition of the polar group along the surface normal.
Conformational details in the absence and presence of
lanthanides are compared.

INTRODUCTION

The knowledge of the conformation of the head group of lipids
is important for an understanding of the interaction of ions, small
molecules and amphipathic substances at the lipid interfaces. Here
we have studied by NMR the conformation of the zwitterionic phosphorylcholine group of various phosphatidylcholines (PC) such as
egg lyso PC, 3-lauroylpropandiol-1-phosphorylcholine (LPPC), di-

hexanoyl PC (ester) and dihexyl PC (ether). These lipids are known
to form small micelles in H_2O above the critical micellar concentration (cmc). By reducing the concentration below the cmc the
effect of aggregation on the polar group conformation can be examined. Similarly, by replacing H_2O by organic solvent information
on the effect of solvation can be obtained. Lipids present in
micellar aggregates have a great deal of molecular and segmental
motion at room temperature and consequently, the conformation derived is a motionally averaged conformation. The NMR data will
be compared with single crystal structures.

EXPERIMENTAL

     Egg PC and lyso PC were purchased from Lipid Products (South
Nutfield, Surrey, UK). Dihexanoyl PC was obtained from Applied
Science Labs (State College, PA). Bioleyl PC (ether) and dihexyl PC
(ether) were synthesized according to the method of Hirt and Berchtold.[1] 3-Lauroylpropandiol-1-phosphorylcholine (LPPC) was synthesized and crystallized as described before.[2] Lanthanide nitrates
were purchased from E. Merch. Titration experiments with lanthanide
nitrates were carried out by adding small aliquots of stock solutions of these compounds in D_2O (nominal pH 5-6) to solutions or
micellar dispersions of the lipids.

     The critical micellar concentration (cmc) was determined ac-
cording to methods given previously[3] and the following values were
obtained: $10 + 3 \times 10^{-6}$ M for egg lysoPC consistent with data in the
literature,[4] 0.33 ± 0.02 mM for LPPC, 15.2 ± 1 mM for dihexanoylPC
and $6.6 + 0.6$ mM for dihexylPC. The micelle weights of egg lyso
PC[5] and LPPC[6] determined by analytical untracentrifugation are
116×10^3 and 28.5×10^3, respectively. The apparent Stokes diameter of egg lysoPC and dihexanoylPC micelles determined by gel filtration on Sepharose 4B are 77 ± 5 and about 25 Å, respectively.

     ^{1}H NMR spectra were recorded on a Bruker HXS-360 Fourier trans-
form spectrometer (digital resolution 0.18 Hz/point). [13]C and [31]P
NMR spectra were obtained at 100.6 MHz on a Bruker WH-400 and at
36.4 MHz on a Bruker HXE-90 spectrometer, respectively. H-H, H-C
and H-P coupling constants were derived from computer simulations
of the spectra using the Nicolet ITRCAL version of the LAOCN3 program on a Nicolet B-NC 12 computer equipped with a NIC-294 disk
memory. Experimental spectra were fitted satisfactorily using
Lorentzian line shapes. Spin coupling constants thus derived were
accurate to within 0.2 Hz. The fractional populations of the three
possible, staggered conformations of minimum free energy were computed from the spin coupling constants as discussed previously[6]
and were accurate to within 10%. Spin-lattice relaxation times (T_1)
were measured by means of a 180°- -90° pulse sequence.

RESULTS AND DISCUSSION

^1H, ^{13}C and ^{31}P NMR spectra of the following compounds dissolved in D_2O were recorded at 360 MHz, 100.6 MHz and 36.4 MHz, respectively: dihexanoylPC, dihexylPC, LPPC and egg lysoPC. The short chain phosphatidylcholines have relatively high critical mciellar concentrations (cmc) and spectra below the cmc were easily obtained. For comparison ^1H and ^{31}P NMR spectra of the above compounds dissolved in CD_3OD were also recorded. The assignment of the resonances was made on the basis of intensity measurements, homo- and heteronuclear double-resonance experiments, changes in chemical shift induced by shift probes of the lanthanide series and line broadening in the presence of Gd^{3+}. The above compounds form either monomeric solutions or small micelles in the solvents used in this work. Consequently narrow lines were obtained in the NMR spectra which show hyperfine splitting due to spin coupling. (Some of the NMR spectra together with the assignment have been published before[3,6,7]). Spin coupling constants were derived from computer simulations of the experimental spectra as reported before[6,7]. The vicinal spin coupling constants thus derived are the starting point of our conformational analysis. The prinicple underlying this analysis and the assumptions involved have been discussed previously.[6] As a result fractional populations for the C-C and C-O bonds of the glycerylphosphorylcholine moiety of PC are obtained as summarized in Table I. We wish to stress that for short chain PC (dihexanoylPC and dihexylPC) the spin coupling constants were very similar below and above the cmc. This result indicates that the aggregation of monomers is not accompanied by a conformational change of the polar group. Furthermore, it strongly suggests that the polar group conformation of PC is determined by intramolecular energetics.[6]

When the compounds of Table I were dissolved in CD_3OD and the same conformational analysis was carried out, spin coupling constants similar to those in Table I were obtained. This finding indicates that replacement of water of hycration by CD_3OD had no significant effect on the motionally averaged conformation. It is clear from Table I that replacement of the two ester linkages in PC by ether bonds does not affect the polar group conformation.[10] Within the experimental accuracy all four compounds (Table I) have similar α-torsion angles. Both mono- and diacylPC have similar motionally averaged conformations in the clycerylphorylcholine group. This conformation is characterized as follows: 1) Except for the C1-C2 (glycerol) bond (torsion angles θ_1 and θ_2) there is no free rotation about the C-C and C-O bonds of the glycerylphosphorylcholine group. This group is therefore characterized by a preferred conformation. 2) The choline group (O-C-C-N bone, α_5) is practically locked in the $\pm$ syn-clinal conformation. The preferred conformation of α_1 and α_4 is anti-periplanar. Our analysis using spin coupling does not give any information about torsion angles α_2 and α_3. 3) In diacylPC the conformation of the glycerol

Table 1. Fractional Populations of Minimum Free Energy Conformations About the C-C and C-O Bonds of the Glycerylphosphorylcholine Group of Various Phosphatidylcholines.

bond [a]	torsion angle [b]	staggered confirmation [c]	dihexanoylPC [d]	dihexylPC	egg lysoPC	LPPC
R_1OCH_2-CHO (R_1OCH_2-CH_2)	$\theta_3(\theta_4)$	+sc (-sc) ap (+sc) -sc (ap)	0.33 0.60 0.03	0.44 0.50 0.06	0.42[e](0.53) 0.50 (0.05) 0.08 (0.42)	0.32 0.36 0.32
OCH-CH_2OP (CH_2-CH_2OP)	$\theta_1(\theta_2)$	-sc (sc) ap (-sc) +sc (ap)	0.48 (0.53) 0.37 (0.13) 0.15 (0.34)	0.44 (0.49) 0.37 (0.15) 0.19 (0.36)	0.43 (0.48) 0.39 (0.14) 0.18 (0.38)	0.35 0.30 0.35
CHCH_2-OP (CH_2CH_2-OP)	α_1	± sc ap	0.26 0.74	0.16 0.84	0.20 0.80	0.32 0.68
PO-CH_2CH_2	α_4	± sc ap	0.26 0.74	0.24 0.76	0.22 0.78	0.22 0.78
POCH_2-CH_2N	α_5	± sc ap	0.98 0.02	1.00 0.0	1.00 0.0	1.00 0.0

Legend to Table I

a The bond in parenthesis refers to LPPC

b The notation of the torsion angles and the numbering of the atoms are as described [8].

c For the description of approximate torsion angles the terminology of Klyne and Prelog is used [9].

d All compounds were dissolved in D_2O at concentrations >cmc.

e Two sets of fractional populations are given when the vicinal spin coupling constants could not be assigned.

The abbreviations used are: sc = syn-clinal, ap = anti-periplanar.

is determined by the parallel stacking of the two hydrocarbon chains. In the two short chain PCs (Table I) about 95% of the molecules have conformations about the C2-C3 (glycerol) bond (torsion angles θ_3 and θ_4) which readily allow the parallel alignment of the two hydrocarbon chains. About 50-60% of the molecules have a conformantion which is consistent with the unique conformation of that bond in single crystal structures.[11-13] It is interesting to note that the two mono-acyl compounds (Table I) differ in the conformation of that bond. While there is no preferred ocnformation in LPPC, the conformation of egg lysoPC is similar to that of diacylPC. We believe that this difference is due to the free OH-group which is probably involved in hydrogen bonding stabilizing the conformation about the C2-C3 bond. 4) Torsion angles θ_1 and θ_2 determine the orientation of the phosphorylcholine group relative to the hydrocarbon chain(s). All compounds are quite flexible about this bond, particularly LPPC. In this molecule there is free rotation about the C1-C2 glycerol bond generating equally populated rotamers (Table I).

The average polar group conformation of phosphatidylcholine micelles in H_2O as derived from the spin coupling analysis is in good agreement with single-crystal structures of phosphatidylcholines[12,13] and with the conformation of fully hydrated, liquid-crystalline phosphatidylcholine bilayers.[14] If we assume that in micelles torsion angles α_2 and α_3 are in the $\pm$ syn-clinal range like in the crystal and liquid-crystalline state then the orientation of the OP-N dipole is parallel to the plane of the interface. From a comparison of micelles with planar bilayers in crystals and liquid crystals it is clear that the large curvature of the lipid-H_2O interface in micelles has no significant effect on the polar group conformation.

The notion that the structure and dynamics of PC in micelles and bilayers are similar is supported by spin lattice T_1 measurements (Figure 1). In Figure La the plot of T_1 vs. approximate position of the proton within the lipid molecule is given for egg lysoPC micelles. This is compared to the corresponding plot of T_1 vs. ^{13}C-position for sonicated egg PC vesicles (Figure 1b, from Godici and Landsberger[15]). Qualitatively the [1]H T_1 measurements are in good agreement with the ^{13}C NMR experiments using single-bilayer egg PC vesicles. In both cases the T_1 (or NT_1) increases from the glycerol group (-CO carbon) to the terminal CH_3 and also to the choline group. In both micelles and bilayers there is a motional gradient from the relatively immobilized glycerol backbone and ester carbonyls toward the terminal CH_3 and the choline group. This trend has been established for phosphatidylcholine bilayers from both spin label and NMR studies.

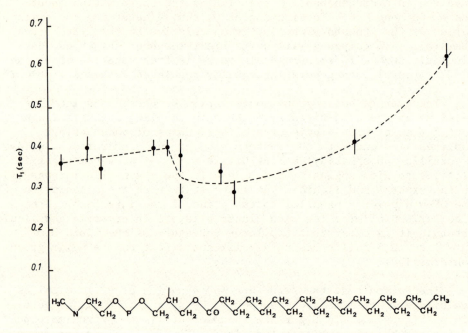

Figure 1a. ^{1}H spin-lattice relaxation times (T_1) of each clearly discernible signal of egg lysoPC micelles in D_2O (40-100 mM) as a function of the approximate position of the proton.

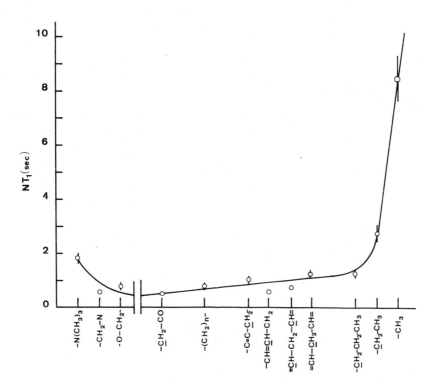

Figure 1b. NT_1 as a function of the approximate position of the ^{13}C nuclei of egg PC. N is the number of protons bonded to the ^{13}C nucleus. Sonicated, aqueous dispersions of the lipid at concentrations of 25 mM were used. Because of the heterogeneity of the esterified fatty acids there is some ambiguity in the exact position of the nuclei. The size of the symbol or the bar represent the stand. dev. (from Godici and Landsberger[15]).

THE INTERACTION WITH LANTHANIDES

   Figures 2 and 3 show the changes in chemical shift induced by
Pr^{3+} in the 360 MHz ^{1}H NMR spectra of egg lysoPC and dihexylPC
(ether) micelles. Two points should be noted: (I) all the resonances including those from the hydrocarbon chains of dihexylPC undergo shift changes while in the ^{1}H NMR spectra of egg lysoPC only
the polar group singlas were affected to any significant extent.
Consistent with dihexylPC a very small upfield shift was observed
for those CH_2 groups of egg lysoPC which are close to the glycerol
backbone.[16] (II) In case of a shift change, all of the signal intensity is affected, i.e., the total peak is shifted. This is con-
trasted by the behavior of small, single-bilayer vesicles; with the
 latter structures only part (about 2/3) of the total signal intensity arising from the molecules on the external layer of the bilayer
(exposed to the lanthanide ion) is shifted. DihexanoylPC (ester)
micelles gave "titration curves" in the presence of $Pr(NO_3)_3$ similar to those of dihexylPC ether (Figure 3). Consistent with the
shift changes observed in the presence of $Pr(NO_3)_3$, $Gd(NO_3)_3$ added
to dihexanoylPC or dihexylPC micelles broadened all resonances and
also caused an increase in the spin-lattice relaxation rate $(1/T_1)$
of all resonances including those of the hydrocarbon chains.

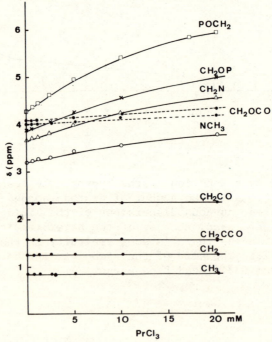

Figure 2. [1]H chemical shifts δ(ppm) induced by $PrCl_3$ in the spectrum of egg lysoPC micelles in D_2O. Lipid concentration: ~25 mg/ml
(50 mM).

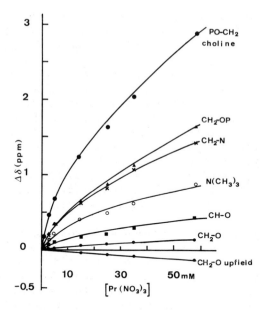

Figure 3a. ^{1}H chemical shift changes $\Delta\delta$(ppm) induced by Pr(NO$_3$)·5H$_2$O in the spectrum of dihexylPC micelles in D$_2$O.

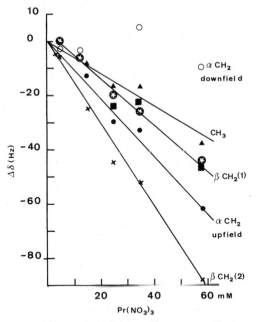

Figure 3b. Shift changes $\Delta\delta$(Hz) for the hydrocarbon chain signals. Lipid concentration ~40 mg/ml (90mM). Upfield shifts are negative, downfield shifts are positive. (o) downfield α-CH$_2$, (●) upfield α-CH$_2$, (✗) β-CH$_2$ (β-chain), (⊗) β-CH$_2$ (γ-chain), (■) (CH$_2$)$_n$, (▲) term. CH$_3$.

The absolute changes in chemical shift induced by $Pr(NO_3)_3$ were in the order lysoPC micelles > dihexylPC micelles > dihexanoyl-PC micelles > dihexanoyl PC monomers. These changes reflect the affinity of the lanthanide ion to the micellar surface. Since $La(NO_3)_3$ had no perturbing effect on the ^{1}H NMR spectra of the compounds in Table II we concluded that the shifts observed with lanthanide ions were due to paramagnetic perturbations alone. The relative shift changes standardized to the shift change induced in the $OPCH_2$ (choline) signal are summarized in Table II. For all compounds used the two CH_2 groups next to the phosphorous exhibited the largest shift changes. Consistent with that finding, line broadening and T_1 measurements in the presence of $Gd(NO_3)_3$ indicated that the nearest protons to the metal binding site are those of the CH_2OP (glycerol) and $POCH_2$ (choline) groups.

Furthermore, within experimental error the relative shift changes of the different ^{1}H signals were independent of the lanthanide ion indicating that the induced shifts are pseudo-contact in origin. Inspection of Table II shows that the relative shifts or pseudo-contact shift ratios measured with micellar PC solutions are in good agreement. Within experimental accuracy these shift ratios also agree well with those reported for single-bilayer vesicles of egg PC,[5,17] dioleoylPC (ester)[10] and dioleylPC (ether).[10] That the shift ratios of PC micelles are consistent with those of PC bilayers indicates that the mode of lanthanide binding and the conformation in the presence of lanthanides are the same in the two structures. The curvature of the micellar surface does not seem to affect these properties. The conclusions which have been drawn from the analysis of (lanthanide ion – PC bilayer) interactions[5,16,17] are also applicable to lanthanide – micelle interactions[7]: (I) Binding of lanthanide ions to the PC molecule occurs at the phosphate group. (II) Lanthanide ions induce a conformational change. (III) The conformation of the PC polar group in the presence of lanthanides is characterized by the following average torsion angles: $\alpha_1 = 170° \pm 30°$; $\alpha_2 = 0° \pm 35°$; $\alpha_3 = 170° \pm 15°$; $\alpha_4 = 155° \pm 30°$; $\alpha_5 = 150° \pm 40°$. The error represents the torsion angle range which is consistent within 20% with the experimental shift ratios. Torsion angles α_3 and α_5 change in the presence of lanthanides from $\pm$ synclinal to antiperiplanar. As a result the orientation of the OP–N dipole changes from an alignment approximately parallel to the bilayer to one of about 45°. This realignment of the OP–N dipole gives rise to a more extended disposition of the polar group along the bilayer normal.

A comparison of dihexanoylPC (ester) and hihexylPC (ether) (Table II) shows that ester and ether PC have similar conformations. Table II shows that the pseudo-contact shift ratios measured in monomeric solutions of dihexanoylPC in D_2O or CD_3OD are significantly different from those obtained in the aggregated state. It can be shown that the mode of ion binding to monomeric dihexanoylPC

Table II. Relative Shifts $\Delta\delta$ Induced by $Pr(NO_3)_3$ in the ^1H NMR Spectra of Various Phosphatidyl-cholines. The Shifts are Standardized to the Largest Shift Induced in the $OPCH_2$ (Choline) Signal.

signal	lysoPC in H_2O > cmc	dihexylPC in H_2O > cmc	dihexanoylPC in H_2O > cmc	dihexanoylPC in H_2O < cmc	dihexanoylPC in CD_3OD
glycerol ($-CH_2-O$ upfield	0.10 ± 0.04	-0.04 ± 0.01[a]	0.051 ± 0.003	0.18 ± 0.01	0.17 ± 0.02
(downfield		$+0.05 \pm 0.01$	0.093 ± 0.005	0.17 ± 0.01	0.13 ± 0.01
($-CH-O$	0.18 ± 0.04	0.15 ± 0.01	0.17 ± 0.01	0.33 ± 0.02	0.34 ± 0.03
($-CH_2-OP$	0.59 ± 0.05	0.56 ± 0.04	0.58 ± 0.02	0.78 ± 0.02	0.79 ± 0.05
choline ($-OPCH_2$	1.00	1.00	1.00	1.00	1.00
($-CH_2N$	0.53 ± 0.03	0.52 ± 0.03	0.51 ± 0.02	0.37 ± 0.03	0.38 ± 0.03
($-N(CH_3)_3$	0.33 ± 0.03	0.32 ± 0.02	0.30 ± 0.02	0.17 ± 0.02	0.13 ± 0.01

[a] Downfield shifts are positive, upfield shifts are negative.

is dependent on the nature of the lanthanide ion. These results suggest that the geometry of the lanthanide ion - PC complex is (I) different and (II) less well defined than in PC aggregates. Spin-lattice (T_1) measurements of dihexanoylPC in CD_3OD in the presence of increasing quantities of $Gd(NO_3)_3$ lend support to this notion. The relative distances derived from these T_1 measurements in mono-meric solutions differ from those derived from micelles and bilayers (data not shown).

Further evidence in support of the notion that the conformation of diacylPC in micelles (in the presence and absence of cations) is similar to that in bilayers is provided by experiments with shift and broadening probes. As discussed above, a significant proportion of the dihexanoylPC molecules have a conformation about the C2-C3 bond (torsion angles θ_3, θ_4) which is consistent with that found in crystal structures of phospholipies.[11-13] This conformation is as-sociated with the tuning fork-type arrangement of the two fatty acyl chains. The glycerol carbons form a continuous zig-zag with the fatty acid linked to glycerol C3; the fatty acid attached to gly-cerol C2 is first oriented parallel to the bilayer plane and makes a sharp bent at the second C-atom along the chain. In such an ar-rangement the α-CH_2 groups of the two hydrocarbon chains are expected to be non-equivalent; furthermore, the α-CH_2 group of the fatty acid esterified to glycerol C2 is expected to be closer to the lipid-H_2O interface. These expectations are borne out by experiment. ^1H and ^{13}C NRM measurements using dihexanoylPC micelles show that the two α-CH_2 groups have different chemical shifts. The α-CH_2 group attached to glycerol C2 gives proton and ^{13}C shifts[18] that are down-field with respect to the shift of the other α-CH_2 group is, as ex-pected, closer to the Gd^{3+} binding site than the other -CH_2 attached to glycerol C3. This finding confirms that the type of chain stacking which is typical for the solid state and for liquid-crystalline phospholipid bilayers is also maintained in micellar aggregates.

The experiments depicted in Figures 2 and 3 are pertinent to the question of lipid exchange between monomers and micelles. The fact that in the presence of lanthanides a single shifted resonance for each proton group is observed and the induced shift changes are frequency independent points to the exchange rate being fast on the NMR time scale. This conclusion is further supported by the obwervation that the pseudo-contact shift ratios are independent of the lanthanide ion. The result that in the presence of lanthanides all hydrocarbon chain signals of the short chain PCs in micelles (figure 3) are shifted while those of egg lysoPC are not affected is explained in terms of fast exchange; due to the much larger cmc (by a factor of 10^3) of the short chain PCs, the proportion of mole-cules in the monomeric state is significantly larger; it is assumed that the monomeric molecule exposed to the lanthanide solution gives rise to the shift changes in the hydrocarbon resonances. The packing of dihexanoyl (dihexyl)PC micelles is not drastically different from that of egg lysoPC and hence the affinity of the lanthanide ion for the micellar surface of these compounds is also not significantly different. The data in Figures 2 and 3 cannot therefore be interpreted in terms of differences in binding properties or differences in the H_2O and/or ion penetration of the micelle.[19] If ion penetration was responsible for the shifts induced in the hydrocarbon chain resonances then one would expect both kinds of micelles to be affected to a similar extent.

ACKNOWLEDGEMENTS

This work was supported, in part, by the SWISS NSF (grant No. 3.570-0.79).

REFERENCES

1. R. Hirt and R. Berchtold, Pharm. Acta Helv. 33, 349 (1958).
2. H. Hauser, I. Pascher and S. Sundell, J. Mol. Bio. 137, 249 (1980).
3. H. Hauser, W. Guyer, I. Pascher, P. Skrabal and S. Sundell, Biochemistry 19, 366 (1980).
4. M. E. Haberland and J. Reynolds, J. Biol. Chem. 250, 6636 (1975).
5. H. Hauser, J. Colloid Interface Sci. 55, 85 (1975).
6. H. Hauser, W. Guyer, M. Spiess, I. Pascher and S. Sundell, J. Mol. Biol. 137, 265 (1980).
7. H. Hauser, W. Guyer, B. Levine, P. Skrabal and R. J. P. Williams, Biochim. Biophys. Acta 508, 450 (1978).
8. M. Sundaralingam, Ann. N. Y. Acad. Sci. 195, 324 (1972).
9. W. Klyne and V. Prelog, Experientia 16, 521 (1960).
10. H. Hauser, W. Guyer, F. Schwarz and F. Paltauf, Biochemistry, submitted for publication.
11. P. B. Hitchcock, R. Mason, K. M. Thomas and G. G. Shipley, Proc. Natl. Acad. Sci. USA, 71, 3036 (1974).
12. R. Pearson and I. Pascher, Nature 281 499 (1979).
13. H. Hauser, I. Pascher, R. H. Pearson and S. Sundell, Biochim. Biophys. Acta, submitted for publication.
14. J. Seelig, H.-U. Gally and R. Wohlgemuth, Biochim. Biophys. Acta 467, 109 (1977).
15. P. E. Godici and F. R. Landsberger, Biochemistry 13, 362 (1974).
16. H. Hauser, M. C. Phillips, B. A. Levine and R. J. P. Williams, Eur. J. Biochem. 58, 133 (1975).
17. H. Hauser, M. C. Phillips, B. A. Levine and R. J. P. Williams, Nature 261, 390 (1976).
18. R. A. Burns, Jr. and M. F. Roberts, Biochemistry 19, 3100 (1980).
19. B. Lindman and H. Wennerstrom, "Topics in Current Chemistry", pp. 1-83, Springer-Verlag, Berlin, 1980.

CONDENSATION OF SURFACTANT MICELLES ON A POLYMER

MOLECULE IN AQUEOUS SOLUTION

B. Cabane
Physique des Solides, Universite Paris Sud
91405 - Orsay, France
R. Duplessix
C. R. M., 6, rue Boussingault, 67083 - Strasbourg, France

Adding a polymer to a surfactant solution induces the formation of well defined aggregates; this paper presents a discussion
of the structure of aggregates formed with a collection of small
surfactant molecules associated with one nonionic macromolecule.
These aggregates have some remarkable properties (stoichiometry,
critical micelle concentration) suggesting that there is more than
a simple adsorption (preferential solvation) (Figure 1) of the
surfactant molecules along the polymer chain. Indeed, NMR indi-

Figure 1.

cates that the aliphatic tails of the surfactant molecules are
segregated from water, and therefore that some type of micelles
are formed, with the polymer adsorbed on the surface of these
micelles (Figure 2). At first, small polymers were used, such
that the number of surfactant molecules associated with one polymer
molecule was just enough to form a spherical micelle. In this
case, the polymer + surfactant aggregate can be described as a
micelle coated with a polymer layer. With large polymers, two
possible alternatives were contemplated: either each polymer

661

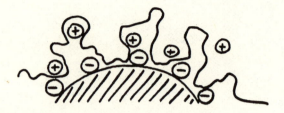

Figure 2.

molecule could still be adsorbed on a single small micelle, or it would induce a growth of this micelle (Figure 3). In fact, neutron

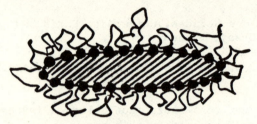

Figure 3.

scattering has revealed that large polymers induce a different type of organization: each aggregate is formed of a cluster of small micelles attached to one polymer molecule (Figure 4).

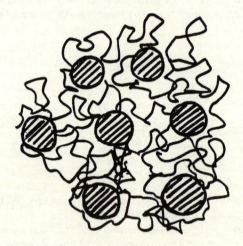

Figure 4.

This neutron scattering study was based on the use of selective deuteration of one component of the scattering particles. In our case, the surfactant is deuterated sodium dodecylsulfate (SDS), and the polymer is protonated poly(ethylene oxide) (PEO).

Using H_2O/D_2O mixtures of appropriate ionic strengths as solvents, we find that the scattering curves depend markedly upon the scattering length of the solvent; this shows that the contrast variation method works well in our case (Figure 5). When the solvent

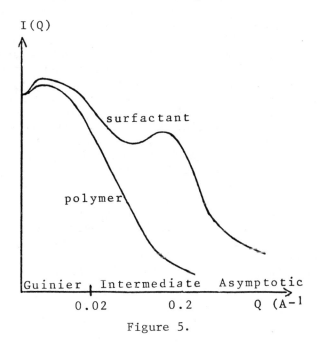

Figure 5.

is D_2O, the configuration of the polymer in the aggregates can be observed: it shows up as a swollen random coil (in the intermediate range, $I(q) \propto q^{-1.46}$ compared with $q^{-1.75}$ for the polymer alone in water). On the other hand, the contrast of the polymer is cancelled by using 82% H_2O + 18% D_2O as a solvent; then the scattering curve of the surfactant in the aggregates can be observed. It can be analyzed into 3 parts:

- The small angle limit ($q = 0.02$ $\overset{\circ}{A}^{-1}$) yields a radius of gyration which is somewhat smaller than that of the polymer, but of comparable magnitude (typically, $R \sim 200$ $\overset{\circ}{A}$ if the polymer has a molecular weight of 10^5). This implies that the surfactant particle fills the whole polymer coil.

- The intermediate scattering indicates that this surfactant particle must be formed of subunits; the peak observed at $q = 0.08$ $\overset{\circ}{A}^{-1}$ corresponds to interferences between these subunits (distance ~ 80 $\overset{\circ}{A}$).

- At larger scattering angles, the structure of these subunits is observed, and their surface/volume ratio can be deduced

from the asymptotic properties of the scattering function. We
find that these subunits are similar to regular surfactant micelles.

These data show that the surfactant molecules must be assembled in small spherical micelles, and that there must be many
such micelles within each polymer + surfactant aggregate; the peak
observed at $q = 0.08 \text{ Å}^{-1}$ corresponds to the distance between these
micelles. This distance probably is a result of the competition
between the free energy of the polymer, which tends to keep the
individual micelles close together, and the electrostatic repul-
sions between these micelles. Indeed, we have observed that a
change in the ionic strength of the solvent produces a variation
in the position of the interference peak. Furthermore, this peak
would not be observed unless the distance between the micelles
was fairly uniform within the aggregate. In this respect, the
cluster of micelles is similar to a small droplet of concentrated
micellar solution. Indeed its scattering function can be re-
constructed through a convolution of the scattering of a concentrated micellar solution by the form factor of the aggregate.
Thus the effect by the polymer on the surfactant solution can be
described as a condensation of the micellar "gas" (i.e. the
dilute solution of micelles) into droplets of micellar "liquid"
(i.e. concentrated micellar solution), each droplet being nuc-
leated by a polymer molecule.

POLYMER-SURFACTANT INTERACTIONS BY SURFACTANT SELECTIVE ELECTRODES

Kalidas Kale, Gordon C. Kresheck and
James Erman
Department of Chemistry
Northern Illinois University
DeKalb, Illinois 60115

The interaction between ionic surfactants and
several polymers was investigated using surfactant
ion and counterion selective electrodes. Four block
polypeptides containing either alanine-lysine or
alanine-glutamic acid were observed to bind a number
of oppositely charged surfactant ions, dodecyl
sulfate and dodecyltrimethylammonium ions, respectively. The binding ratios, corresponding to the
net charge on the peptides, were similar to those
found previously using titration calorimetry. Also
studied were polyvinylpyrrolidone, which exhibited
complex dodecyl sulfate binding, and cytochrome c
peroxidase. The later strongly bound a number of
dodecyl sulfate ions which was also approximately
equal to the number of basic amino acid residues
present in the protein. All six polymers reduced
the critical micelle concentration from its value
in the absence of the polymers whenever appreciable surfactant binding occurred.

INTRODUCTION

The study of surfactant-polymer interactions is of great
interest for many physico-chemical as well as biological phenomena.
Surfactant solutions are used to lower the interfacial tension
between oil and rock during enhanced oil recovery, and polymer
solutions are then added to control the mobility of the resultant
sludge. It is very likely that interactions of the polymers with
the surfactants alter the rheological properties of the mixtures.

665

In biological systems the frequent use of surfactants to isolate
membrane bound proteins, to characterize macromolecules as well as
to serve as simplified model membranes are examples where surfactant polymer interactions play a significant role.

A number of different techniques such as calorimetry[1,2] dye
solubilization,[3] surface tension,[3] dialysis,[4] conductivity,[5]
viscosity,[5] and gel electrophoresis[6] are employed to study these
interactions. All of the methods listed either reflect the properties of the high molecular weight species present or the combined
contribution of aggregates, surfactant monomers and counterions.
In contrast surfactant ion electrodes provide a direct measure of
surfactant monomer activity alone. When used with counterion
electrodes this technique provides data that is difficult to
obtain by other methods.

Birch et al.[7] have studied sodium dodecyl sulphate-polymer
interactions with a dodecyl sulphate liquid membrane electrode
containing the complex, cetyltrimethylammonium-dodecyl sulphate as
an ion exchanger. Recently Kale, Cussler and Evans have shown that
surfactant selective electrodes based on cetyltributylammonium
bromide-anionic surfactant and sodium cholanate-cationic surfactant
complexes as ion exchangers behave as well as a plasticized polymeric
membrane electrode in micellar solutions.[8] In this paper we have
used these electrode systems to study the interactions of sodium
dodecyl sulphate and dodecyltrimethylammonium bromide with alanine
and lysine containing cationic block polypeptides, alanine and
glutamic acid containing anionic block polypeptides, polyvinylpyrrolidone (a water soluble nonionic polymer) and cytochrome c
peroxidase (a globular protein).

MATERIALS AND METHODS

Two cationic block polypeptides, $(Lys)_{11-n}-(Ala)_{13}-(Lys)_n$ (LAL)
and $(Ala)_{16}-(Lys)_{13.5}$ (AL), and two anionic block polypeptides,
$(Glu)_{18-n}-(Ala)_{20}-(Glu)_n$ (GAG) and $(Ala)_{14.5}-(Glu)_{15}$ (AG), were
chosen because they were synthesized in our laboratory and are
well characterized[1] by amino acid analysis, sedimentation equilibrium centrifugation, and circular dichroism. The interactions of
these polypeptides with sodium dodecyl sulphate, dodecyl pyridinium bromide and Lubrol were previously studied by calorimetric
titrations.[1] Polyvinylpyrrolidone (PVP) with a molecular weight
of 40,000 (Schwarz/Mann) is a nonionic water soluble polymer. It
was chosen due to its similarity with proteins and its widespread
use as a protective colloid and suspending agent, dye receptive
agent, binder and stabilizer, detoxicant and complexing agent. Cytochrome c peroxidase (CcP) was chosen as it is well characterized[9]
and has been studied in this laboratory for the last ten years.

Specially pure grade sodium dodecyl sulphate (SDS) was from B.D.H.
and dodecyltrimethylammonium bromide (DTAB) was purchased from
Sigma. The surfactants were used as received. All the studies
were done in 0.1 mM EDTA, 10 mM Tris-HC1 buffer at pH 7.4 (Tris-
EDTA) except PVP which was studied in aqueous solution.

     Sodium and bromide selective solid membrane electrodes and the
reference calomel electrode were purchased from Orion Research. Emf
measurements were done with an Orion Research analyzer model 801 with
a model 605 manual electrode switch to allow simultaneous measurement of six electrodes. The preparation of dodecyltrimethylammonium
(DTA^+) and dodecyl sulphate (DS^-) selective electrodes and emf
measurements were as given by Kale et al.[8]. Calibrations experiments to determine ionic concentrations consisted of placing 10 to
20 ml of buffer solution in a cell thermostated at 25°C and progressively increasing the surfactant concentration by adding small
aliquots of concentrated surfactant solution. By this method, the
emf of the counterion and surfactant ion were measured as a function
of concentration. In the polymer experiments a fixed amount of
polymer was dissolved in 10 to 20 ml of solution, added to the sample
cell, and titrated with concentrated surfactant solution as described
for the calibration experiments.

RESULTS AND DISCUSSION

     Figure 1a contains a plot of emf versus log [SDS] in Tris-EDTA
buffer. The DS^- and Na^+ plots are linear up to the critical micelle
concentration, (CMC), with a slope of 57 mV/dc and 59 mV/dc, respectively. These values are very close to the value given by Nernst
law of 59.16 mV/dc at 25°C showing that the electrodes behave ideally.
The breaks in these plots correspond to the CMC.[8] The DS^- and Na^+
electrodes give values for the CMC of SDS in Tris buffer of 3.5 and
7.5 mM, respectively. This is lower than the value 8 mM for SDS in
aqueous solution. The lower CMC value obtained by the DS^- electrode
compared to that obtained by Na^+ is likely due to the fact that the
DS^- electrode is sensitive to premicellar aggregation, while Na^+
is not.

     Figure 1b contains a plot of emf versus log [SDS] in buffer
containing an initial concentration of 1.55 mg/ml LAL. The Na^+
curve exhibits no change from that of Figure 1a except that the CMC
is increased, indicating the lack of detectable binding to LAL.
However, the DS^- curve shows a markedly different behavior. The emf
is almost constant up to a SDS concentration of 2 mM, and then
decreases very rapidly before it levels off at 8 mM. This suggests
that a very strong initial binding occurs followed by a region of
possible binding. The final leveling of the curve is characteristic
of micelle formation.[8] The titration of LAL with DTAB was identical

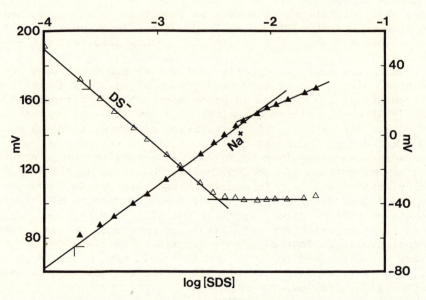

Figure 1a. Emf versus log SDS concentration in pH 7.4 Tris–EDTA
buffer.

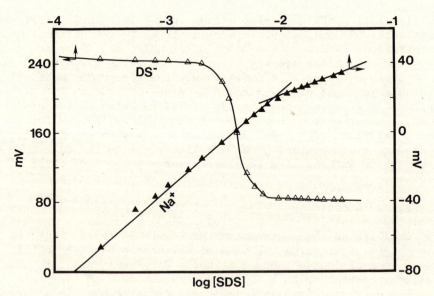

1b. In the presence of 1.55 mg/ml initial concentration of
$(Lys)_{11-n}-(Ala)_{13}-(Lys)_n$.

to that of the calibration experiment indicating that DTAB does not bind to LAL. The results obtained for titrating AL with SDS and DTAB were similar to those described for LAL, i.e., apparent DS⁻ binding but not DTA⁺ or Na⁺.

Figure 2a contains a plot of emf versus log [DTAB] in buffer. The bromide electrode gave a slope of 54 mV/dc and the dodecyltri- methylammonium electrode gave a slope of 47 mV/dc below the CMC. This could indicate that there is premicellar aggregation in DTAB. The CMC value obtained from the DTA⁺ and Br⁻ electrodes in buffer are 1×10^{-2} M and 1.4×10^{-2} M, respectively. Figure 2b shows a plot of emf versus log [DTAB] containing 1.09 mg/ml initial con- centration of GAG. The bromide electrode shows a slope of 19 mV/dc in the concentration range of 1×10^{-4} to 1×10^{-3} M, and then a slope of 46 mV/dc up to the CMC. When these data were analyzed for bromide binding to GAG, only negative values were obtained due to the poisoning of the bromide electrode by GAG. The structurally related peptide, AG, also poisoned the bromide electrode.

The DTA⁺ electrode gave a slope of 15 mV/dc in the DTAB con- centration range of 1×10^{-4} to 1×10^{-3} M, followed by a slope of 58 mV/dc, and the apparent CMC was higher than that obtained in absence of GAG. This suggests that DTA⁺ binds to GAG in two steps. Binding in the initial stage appears to be less strong compared to the initial binding of SDS to LAL. It may be followed by secondary binding, and the additional slope change at 1×10^{-2} M again corresponds to micelle formation.

The binding isotherm, i.e., plot of the ratio of bound deter- gent to polymer concentration as a function of free detergent con- centration, should give a better idea of the binding patterns. Figures 3 to 6 are the binding isotherms for these block polypep- tides. Figure 3 is the binding isotherm of SDS to LAL. The initial vertical portion of the isotherm indicates a very strong interaction between LAL and SDS, which levels off at the [DS⁻]b/ [LAL] ratio of about 9.5 ± 0.5. This value is in agreement with our previous calorimetric value of 7.5 ± 1.5 for SDS binding to LAL. Since LAL contains 11 lysine residues, it suggests that each lysine residue binds one DS⁻. Furthermore, the lack of interaction of LAL or AL with DTAB suggests than an electrostatic interaction is a predominant force in these types of complexes. There is no evidence of Na⁺ binding below the region of micelle formation. It is interesting to note that the isotherm containing the highest amount of LAL shows the lowest CMC value. Thus these polymers behave like additives in decreasing the CMC of surfactants, suggesting a mixed micelle type of structure for the SDS-LAL complex at high concentrations of SDS.

Although the binding isotherms for DS⁻ to LAL and AL resemble those previously reported by Satake and Yang[10] for DS⁻ binding to

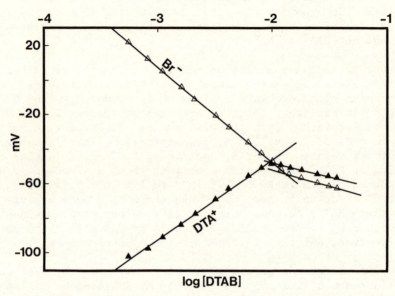

Figure 2a.   Emf versus log DTAB concentration in pH 7.4 Tris–EDTA
             buffer.

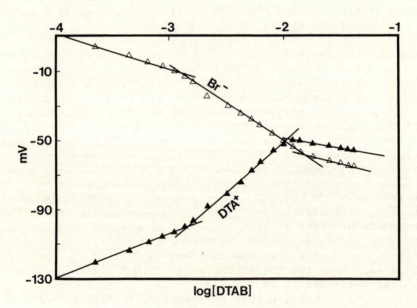

2b.   In the presence of 1.09 mg/ml initial concentration of
      $(Glu)_{18-n}-(Ala)_{20}-(Glu)_n$.

poly(Orn) and poly(Lys), it does not appear that the block polypep-
tides-DS⁻ complexes consist of micelle-like clusters as suggested
for the structure of the homopolymer complexes. The major evidence
for this interpretation is the apparent lack of Na^+ binding until
SDS concentrations approaching the CMC are reached.

Figure 4 represents the binding isotherm of AL-SDS. This is
very similar to the LAL-SDS isotherm, i.e., first it rises almost
vertically to a binding ratio of 8.5 ± 0.5, levels off, and increases
sharply near the CMC. The insert contains the lower part of the
curve which is plotted on an expanded scale. It indicates a break
at a binding ratio of 4. Thus, AL-SDS binding also have two distinct regions. In the initial step, 4 moles of surfactants are
bound to AL, and 8.5 ± 0.5 moles of SDS are bound to AL in the
secondary region. These values are slightly lower than the calorimetric values (5 ± 1 and 11 ± 2) obtained previously. The reason
is due to the fact that the calorimetric analysis assumed all the
added surfactant is bound, while electrode measurements can distinguish between bound and free surfactant.

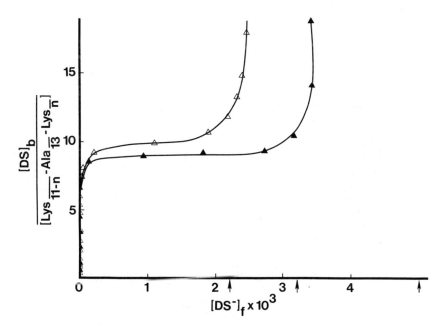

Figure 3.   Binding isotherm of DS⁻ to $(Lys)_{11-n}-(Ala)_{13}-(Lys)_n$
in Tris-EDTA buffer with initial peptide concen-
tration of 5.1 mg/ml (open) and 1.55 mg/ml (filled).

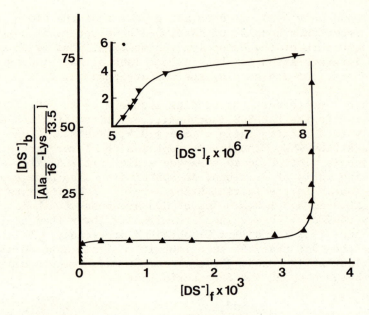

Figure 4.   Binding isotherm of DS$^-$ to $(Ala)_{16}$-$(Lys)_{13.5}$ in Tris-
EDTA buffer with an initial peptide concentration of
1.19 mg/ml.

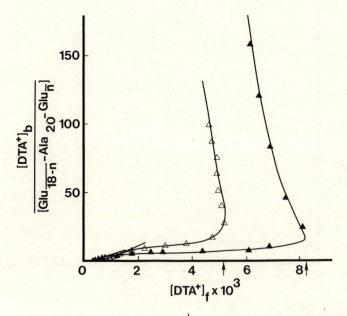

Figure 5.   Binding isotherm of DTA$^+$ to $(Ala)_{14.5}$-$(Glu)_{15}$ in
Tris-EDTA buffer with an initial peptide concen-
tration of 2.46 mg/ml.

Figure 5 represents the binding isotherm of AG-DTAB. The binding ratio increases slowly to a value of 5 ± 1 where it levels off and again increases sharply as it approaches the CMC. The significantly smaller slope in the initial region compared to the LAL-SDS or AL-SDS binding isotherms indicates that the equilibrium constant for binding between AG-DTAB and GAG-DTAB is significantly lower than that of AL-SDS and LAL-SDS. This may be due to a head group effect of the surfactants.

Figure 6 is the binding isotherm of GAG-DTAB. The two curves represent two different initial concentrations (2.7 mg/ml and 1.09 mg/ml) of polypeptides. These two curves rise gradually up to a binding ratio of 6 ± 1, level off, and rise again as they approach the CMC. The curve corresponding to the higher concentration of GAG again has a lower apparent CMC as found in the case of LAL-SDS.

Figure 7 contains a plot of the emf as a function of log [SDS]. The filled and open points correspond to DS⁻ activity in the absence and presence of 10.16 mg/ml initial concentration of PVP. The curve for the solution containing PVP shows four regions of binding. The first region up to 1.2×10^{-3} M is almost parallel to the reference experiment, indicating little if any binding. Then from 1.2×10^{-3} to 1.25×10^{-2} M, the emf is almost constant with a slightly negative slope. Thereafter, it decreases and finally has a slightly positive slope. These results are very similar to those of Birch et al.[7]

Figure 8 represents a binding isotherm of SDS to PVP. This curve may be divided into three distinct regions. In the first concentration region it shows no binding. In the second region from 1.26 mM to 4.5 mM of free surfactant concentration the binding isotherm increases linearly up to the binding ratio of 0.325. In this region SDS binds to PVP in the form of clusters of premicellar aggregates according to Fishman and Eirich[4,5] from conductivity, viscosity, and equilibrium dialysis measurements. Counterion binding studies could not be used to test this mechanism since PVP poisoned the Na⁺ electrode. At 4.5 mM free SDS, the binding isotherm again increases rapidly. This is the region where mixed micelles are apparently formed. The decrease in CMC from 6.5 mM to 4.5 mM is evidence that PVP and SDS form mixed micelles. The similarity between the binding isotherms reported by Fishman and Eirich and our studies is further evidence that the surfactant electrodes are behaving properly. Titration of PVP with DTAB did not show any evidence of binding.

Figure 9 is the binding isotherm of cytochrome c peroxidase with SDS in buffer solution. The initial concentration of CcP was 3.01 mg/ml. The emf versus log [SDS] plot was similar to the PVP-SDS system. The binding isotherm shows no binding until a free surfactant concentration of 0.16 mM is reached. Then it

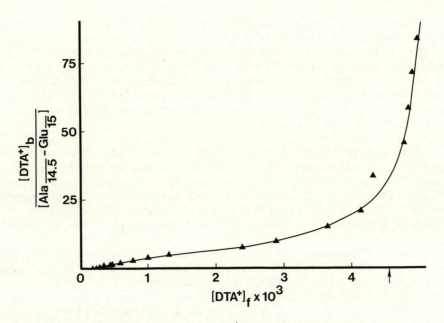

Figure 6.   Binding isotherm of DTA$^+$ to (Glu)$_{18-n}$-(Ala)$_{20}$-(Glu)$_n$
            in Tris-EDTA buffer with initial peptide concentrations
            of 2.72 mg/ml (open) and 1.09 mg/ml (filled).

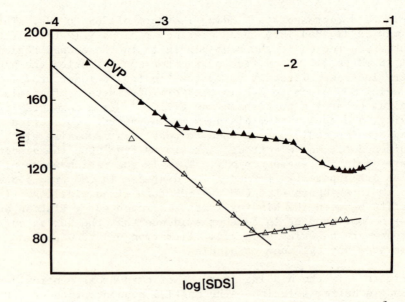

Figure 7.   Emf versus log SDS concentration in aqueous solution
            (filled) and an aqueous solution containing an initial
            PVP concentration of 10.16 mg/ml (open).

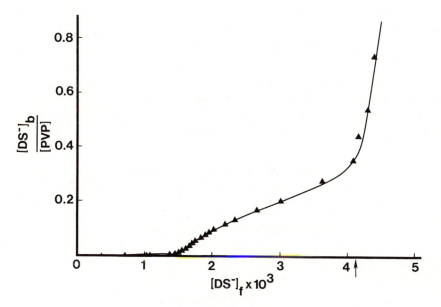

Figure 8. Binding isotherm of DS⁻ to PVP with an initial concentration of 10.16 mg/ml.

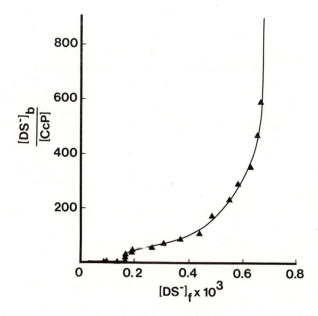

Figure 9. Binding isotherm of DS⁻ to CcP in Tris-EDTA buffer
with an initial protein concentration of 3.01 mg/ml.

rises vertically up to a $[DS]_b/[CcP]$ ratio of about 35, when it
levels off. At $[DS]_{free}$ about 0.63 mM, it rises sharply. The
CcP contains 23 lysine and 10 arginine residues which may be sites
of SDS binding in the lower binding region. CcP also lowers the
true CMC of the SDS from 6 mM to 0.63 mM. The titration of CcP
with DTAB in Tris-EDTA buffer did not show any change in slope
from the reference experiment but the apparent CMC was increased
by 1 mM. This indicates that the CcP interaction with DTA^+ is
weak. Analysis of the binding indicates five DTA^+ ions bind to
CcP below the CMC.

This study confirms the report of Birch et al.[7] that surfactant
ion binding to polymers may be rapidly determined by this method with
results which are comparable to those obtained by other less convenient ones. In addition, it gives a measure of free monomer ion
concentrations, which reveals the true effect of the polymers on
the CMC. Counterion studies provide important supplemental information when such measurements are possible.

ACKNOWLEDGMENTS

This work was supported in part by grants GM 18648-08 and
GM 00249-04 from the National Institutes of Health.

REFERENCES

1. K.M. Kale, L. Vitello, G.C. Kresheck, G. Vanderkooi, and
    R.J. Albers, Biopolymers, 18, 1889 (1979).
2. G. Vanderkooi, K.M. Kale, L. Vitello, G.C. Kresheck, and
    R.J. Albers, in "Proc. International Symposium on Biomolecular
    Structure, Conformation, Function, and Evolution, Madras,
    India," R. Srinivasan, Editor, pp. 499-, Pergamon Press, 1980.
3. H. Arai, M. Murata, and K. Shinoda, J. Colloid. Interface
    Sci., 37, 223 (1971).
4. M.L. Fishman and F.R. Eirich, J. Phys. Chem., 75, 3135 (1971).
5. M.L. Fishman and F.R. Eirich, J. Phys. Chem., 79, 2740 (1975).
6. T. Takagi, K. Tsugi, and K. Shirahama, J. Biochem., 77,
    939 (1975).
7. B.J. Birch, D.E. Clarke, R.S. Lee, and J. Oakes, Anal. Chim.
    Acta, 70, 417 (1974).
8. K.M. Kale, E.L. Cussler, and D.F. Evans, J. Phys. Chem.,
    84, 593 (1980).
9. T.L. Poulos, S.T. Freer, R.A. Alden, S.L. Edwards, U. Skoglund,
    K. Takio, B. Eriksson, N. Xuong, T. Yonetani, and J. Kraut,
    J. Biol. Chem., 255, 575 (1980.
10. I. Satake and J.T. Yang, Biopolymers, 15, 2263 (1976).

THERMOMETRIC AND SURFACTANT SELECTIVE POTENTIOMETRIC TITRATION

STUDIES OF SURFACTANT BINDING TO PHOSPHOLIPID VESICLES

Gordon C. Kresheck, Kalidas Kale and
James Erman
Department of Chemistry
Northern Illinois University
DeKalb, Illinois 60115

The interactions between sodium dodecyl sulphate
and dodecyltrimethylammonium bromide with Asolectin
(phospholipid extract from soybeans) vesicles has been
studied using titration calorimetry, potentiometry
using surfactant selective electrodes, and gel filtration chromatography. Exothermic heat changes were
observed on mixing which depend on the concentration
of Asolectin. The emf data were also observed to be
related to the concentration of phospholipid. At low
ratios of surfactant to Asolectin, the data were consistent with a mechanism in which there is a steady
amount of surfactant bound to the vesicles until the
apparent critical micelle concentration is reached.
The free surfactant at that concentration, or the
true critical micelle concentration, is always less
than the critical micelle formation without Asolectin.
All of the evidence points to the formation of mixed
surfactant-phospholipid micelles when the apparent
critical micelle concentration is reached.

INTRODUCTION

Lipid vesicles (unilamellar liposomes) have proven to be
useful model systems for interpreting membrane phenomena that
occur in biological systems.[1] A recent application has involved
the investigation of the interaction of surfactants with liposomes to provide a background for understanding the effects of
surfactants on membranes.[2] Surfactants have been used during the

677

isolation of membrane proteins[3],[4] and to restore the biological
activity of certain membrane proteins once delipidated.[5] It has
also been demonstrated that surfactants can increase the conductivity of liposomes and bilayer membranes to ions and non-electrolytes at surfactant concentrations much below their critical
micelle concentration (CMC).

One important though mainly neglected aspect of previous
research has been the lack of systematic thermodynamic studies of
binding low molecular weight substances to biological membranes.
Notable exceptions include the work of Diamond,[6] Stone,[7] and
Vilallonga.[8] Zaslavsky et al.[9] have recently described a new
approach to the study of lipid-protein interactions in the structure
of biological membranes. It involves following the solubilization
of liposomes with surfactants by turbidity measurements. We have
shown that titration calorimetry[10] is also an effective way to
study the solubilization of vesicles with surfactants. Our previous
thermodynamic studies of micelle formation[11] have provided a model
system with which to compare such results. The current studies are
an extension of this work.

EXPERIMENTAL

Crude soybean phospholipid acquired from Associated Concen-
trates (Asolectin) was dispersed in pH 7.4, 10 mM Tris-HCl buffer
containing 0.1 mM EDTA, dialyzed, sonicated for 30 min with a
Branson Sonifier, and then centrifuged at 48,300 x g for 1 hr to
remove nondispersed material and small metallic pieces from the
tip of the probe. The concentration of the resulting material was
determined by weight after drying. An average value of 775 g/mol
was used for the molecular weight of the phospholipid. The average
composition of soybean phospholipids has been previously given.[12]
Commercial samples of sodium dodecyl sulfate (SDS) (BDH Chemicals
Ltd.) and dodecyltrimethylammonium bromide (DTAB) (Sigma) were
used as received. All solutions contained the same buffer used
to dissolve the Asolectin.

The calorimetric measurements were made at 25°C with the
titration calorimeter previously described[10],[11] using 3.0 ml samples
with a buret which delivered the titrant at a rate of 37.5 μl/min.
The enthalpy change, ΔH, was calculated from Equation (1)[10]

$$\Delta H = -\frac{Cp}{M_2} \left[\left(\frac{dT}{dV} \right)_2 - \left(\frac{dT}{dV} \right)_1 \right] \qquad (1)$$

where Cp and M_2 represent the heat capacity of the system and
molarity of the titrant, and $(dT/dV)_2$ and $(dT/dV)_1$ correspond to
the slope of the titration curve above and below the point where

a slope change occurs during a titration. The temperature, T, is monitored continuously with a thermistor as the volume of the titrant, V, is increased.

The liquid ion exchange electrode systems defined by Kale, Cussler and Evans[13] were used to selectively monitor the surfactant ion concentrations, either dodecyl sulfate (DS^-) or dodecyltrimethyl-ammonium (DTA^+). The counterions were determined with commercial electrodes (Orion). The emf was determined with an Orion Research Meter (Model 801A) and accompanying Model 605 manual electrode switch. The samples ranging from 10-20 ml were placed inside a water jacket maintained at 25°C. The experimental procedures followed that of Kale et al.[13] The emf below the critical micelle concentration (CMC) in the absence of Asolectin was used as an empirical measure of surfactant or counterion concentration. The concentration dependence always was within experimental error of the value expected from the Nernst equation. Asolectin did <u>not</u> alter the time required for the electrodes to respond to concentration changes.

Gel filtration chromatography was performed with a sample size of 0.5 ml on a 2.5 x 17 cm column of Sepharose 6B, which was packed and eluted with the previously described buffer containing 0.1 M NaCl. All experiments were performed at room temperature, and an ISCO UA-5 absorption monitor operated at various wavelengths was used to follow the elution profile. Methyl yellow was added as a tracking dye to follow the SDS micelles, and the void volume and internal volume were determined using blue dextran and DNP alanine, respectively.

RESULTS AND DISCUSSION

<u>Sodium Dodecyl Sulphate</u>. The results of enthalpy titrations of Asolectin with 0.6 M SDS at various concentrations is given in Figure 1. The dilution in the absence of phospholipid is endothermic as previously observed[11] in the absence of buffer. All three curves with Asolectin show an initial nearly linear exothermic region followed by a more gradual change. The curve with 5.46 mM Asolectin becomes endothermic at higher concentrations as is characteristic of ionic surfactants above the CMC.[11] All three Asolectin solutions were free of turbidity, which is characteristic of solutions containing vesicles, at the end of the experiments.

The concentration dependence of the emf in the absence and presence of Asolectin is given in Figures 2a and 2b. In agreement with previous results, without Asolectin, the DS^- and Na^+ curves are linear with a slope of about 59 mV over a 10 fold range of concentration, and exhibit an abrupt leveling at the CMC.[13] With

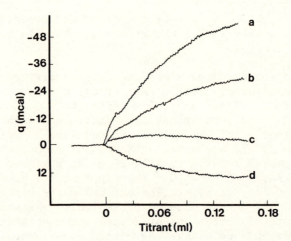

Figure 1.   Titration calorimetry of Asolectin with SDS in pH 7.4
Tris-EDTA buffer for initial Asolectin concentrations of
(a) 21.83 mM, (b) 14.55 mM, (c) 5.46 mM, and (d) zero.

Asolectin, however, obvious deviation from linearity is observed at
low SDS concentrations, and the apparent CMC is increased (from
about 5 to 14 mM). Using the data without phospholipid to find the
concentration of free and bound surfactant ion, $[DS^-]_f$ and $[DS^-]_b$,
respectively, a binding isotherm was constructed and the results
for two Asolectin concentrations are given in Figure 3.   The
apparent CMC, CMC_{app}, noted in the emf plot corresponds to an
actually $[DS^-]_f$ of 2.8 mM and 3.5 mM, for the high and low Asolectin concentrations, which indicates the opposite effect of
Asolectin on the CMC as would be concluded from the raw data. A
reduction of the CMC of dimethyldecylphosphine oxide in the presence
of Asolectin has also been noted by Kresheck and Jones by [31]PMR.[14]
The initial linear region of binding shown in the insert correlates
with the initial linear region of the calorimetric titration curve
which ends at a stoichiometric ratio of [SDS]/[Asolectin] of 0.1.
The arrows shown in the bottom of Figure 3 represent the $[CMC]_{app}$
in the presence (lower two) and absence of Asolectin. All solutions
became clear indicating solubilization of the vesicles at the CMC,
which in the present case occurred at a mole ratio of SDS/Asolectin
of about 1.   The DS$^-$ binding data above the linear region were
plotted according to Klotz[15] for a multiple binding mechanism with
a large number of equivalent sites, and the results are given in
Figure 4. Deviations from linearity are noted at high DS$^-$ concentrations but a value of about 1000 1/mol would be estimated from

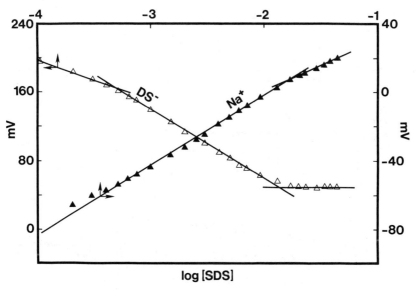

Figure 2a.   EMF versus log SDS concentration in pH 7.4 Tris-EDTA buffer.

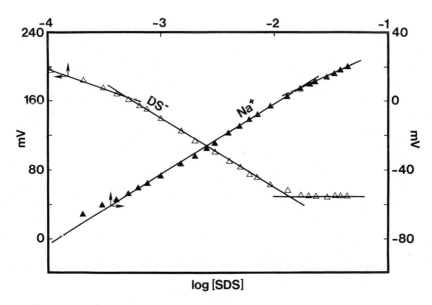

2b.   In the presence of 18.5 mM initial Asolectin.

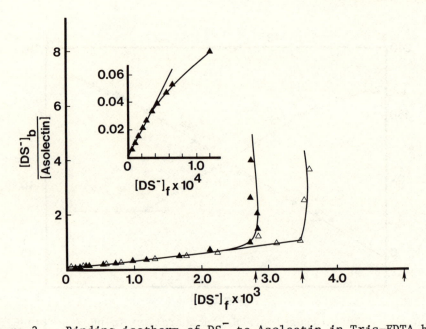

Figure 3.   Binding isotherm of DS$^-$ to Asolectin in Tris–EDTA buffer
for initial Asolectin concentrations of 18.05 mM (filled) and
4.51 mM (open).

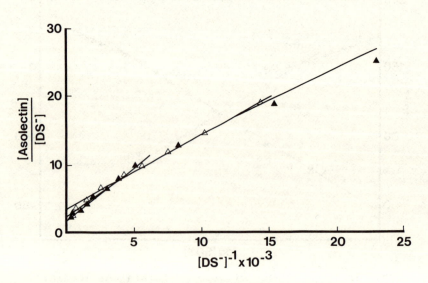

Figure 4.   Klotz plot for DS$^-$ binding to Asolectin.

the near linear region for the equilibrium constant of the process consuming DS$^-$ between the initial strong binding region and the CMC (assumed to be binding to the vesicles).

The concentration of free and bound Na$^+$ was also determined as described for DS$^-$ binding, and the resulting binding isotherm is given in Figure 5. A gradual increase in bound sodium ion, $[Na^+]_b$, may be noted as the concentration of free ion, $[Na^+]_f$, is raised. The arrow at the bottom of the figure represents the free sodium ion concentration at the apparent CMC. In the case of the counterion, unlike that of DS$^-$, the isotherm does not depend on varying Asolectin concentrations up to 18.5 mM. The gradual change in binding up to the CMC$_{app}$ reflect a rather large amount of counterion associated with the Asolectin-DS$^-$ complex.

Gel filtration chromatography experiments were performed to get an indication of particle size and heterogeneity, and these results are given in Figure 6. The void volume, V_o, and total liquid volume, V_t, are noted at the bottom of the figure. Asolectin vesicles without SDS may be seen to elute at the void volume, whereas the lower molecular weight SDS micelles require a greater volume for their elution. Above CMC$_{app}$ (9 mg/ml Asolectin plus 25 mM SDS), the material is very heterogeneous in size, and the bulk of it is intermediate in size between the vesicles and bilayers. This material undoubtedly consists of mixed SDS-Asolectin micelles. At lower SDS concentrations (1 mM SDS and 9 mg/ml Asolectin) the curve resembles that of Asolectin vesicles without SDS. The significance of the small amount of additional tailing is uncertain.

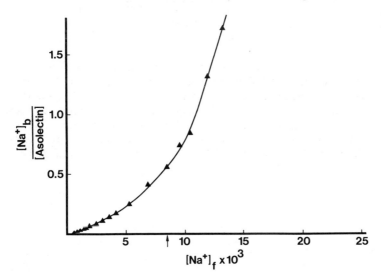

Figure 5.   Binding isotherm of Na$^+$ to Asolectin in Tris-EDTA buffer with an initial Asolectin concentration of 18.05 mM.

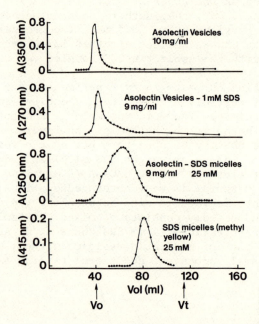

Figure 6.   Gel Filtrration on Sepharose 6B with a 2.5 x 19 cm column
in Tris–EDTA buffer with 0.1 M NaCl. Since the turbidity of the
vesicle solutions decreased upon the addition of SDS, wavelengths for
detection were selected to give comparable absorbance values for the
fractions containing the most concentrated solutions. The elution
volume of the SDS micelles without phospholipid was determined by
the absence of methyl yellow (415 nm), which was solubilized by the
micelles.

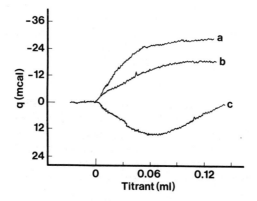

Figure 7.   Titration calorimetry of 10.92 mM Asolectin with SDS in Tris-EDTA buffer supplemented with (a) 0.1 M NaCl, (b) none, and (c) 6 M urea.

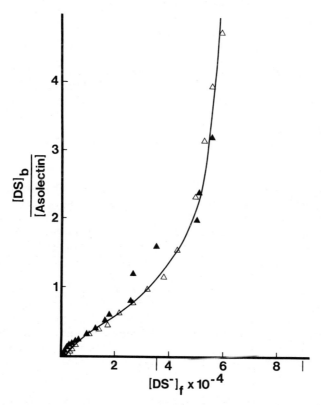

Figure 8.   Binding of isotherm of DS$^-$ to Asolectin in Tris-EDTA buffer with 0.1 M NaCl with initial Asolectin concentrations of 6.15 mM (open) and 12.29 mM (filled).

Optical absorbance studies were also performed as Asolectin was titrated with SDS. A steady decrease in absorbance at 410 nm with increasing SDS concentration was noted, whereas the addition of buffer only yielded small absorbance increases. This could reflect the decrease in light scattering due to the decreased size of the SDS-vesicle complex.

The results of enthalpy titrations of 10.92 mM Asolectin with SDS in buffer alone and buffer containing 0.1 M NaCl or 6 M urea is given in Figure 7. The titration in the presence of salt is more exothermic and levels off at a lower concentration than the titration in buffer. The curve in the presence of urea is endothermic and then exothermic. These solvent effects resemble those previously noted for micelle formation of SDS. [11] Binding isotherms were constructed for DS$^-$ binding, and these are given in Figures 8 and 9. In the presence of NaCl, CMC$_{app}$ is reached at a much lower concentration of free surfactant (arrow at 0.35 mM). This is again lower than the CMC with Asolectin (arrow at 0.9 mM). There does not appear to be a significant Asolectin concentration effect in 0.1 M NaCl, and the binding ratio at CMC$_{app}$ is about the same as in buffer without salt. However, in 6 M urea, the binding isotherm again depends on phospholipid concentration, but the binding ratio at CMC$_{app}$ (arrows at two lower concentrations) is reduced from that in buffer alone to about 0.5. The concentration of free DS$^-$ at the CMC$_{app}$ is again less than without Asolectin (arrow at 9 mM). The difference between the value for [DS$^-$]$_f$ in the presence and absence of Asolectin is thus not as great in 6 M urea as it is in buffer alone or buffer with 0.1 M NaCl. One other interesting difference noted was the apparent absence of Na+ binding below CMC$_{app}$ in 6 M urea.

Dodecyltrimethylammonium bromide. The results of enthalpy titrations of Asolectin with 0.656 M DTAB at various concentrations is given in Figure 10 for three Asolectin concentrations. Whereas the dilution in buffer is endothermic, (approximate CMC indicated with the arrow) all three curves with Asolectin are first exothermic and then resemble the lower one for demicellization followed by micelle dilution. The solution was still cloudy at the conclusion of the titration with 24.65 mM Asolectin, and it was titrated with a second buret full of titrant. There was only a slight gradual cooling, and the solution was now clear at the end of the second titration indicating the CMC$_{app}$ had been reached. The end point for the initial exothermic portions is obviously concentration dependent, and corresponds to a stoichiometry of 0.25 [DTAB]/ [Asolectin].

The results of the emf determination for DTAB in the presence and absence of Asolectin are given in Figures 11a and 11b, and the results are similar to those for the addition of SDS except much stronger DTA+ binding at low DTAB concentrations is indicated. The

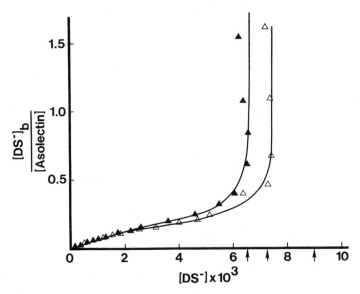

Figure 9.   Binding isotherm of DS⁻ to Asolectin in Tris-EDTA buffer with 6.0 M urea with initial Asolectin concentrations of 21.8 mM (filled) and 10.9 mM (open).

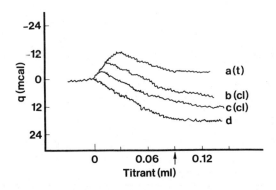

Figure 10. Titration calorimetry of Asolectin with DTAB in Tris-EDTA buffer for initial Asolectin concentration of (a) 24.85 mM, (b) 12.43 mM, (c) 6.24 mM and (d) none. The solutions containing Asolectin were either clear (Cl) or turbid (t) at the end of the titrations.

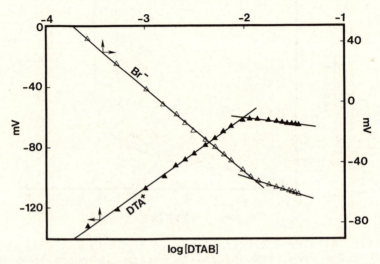

Figure 11a.   Emf versus log DTAB concentration in Tris–EDTA buffer.

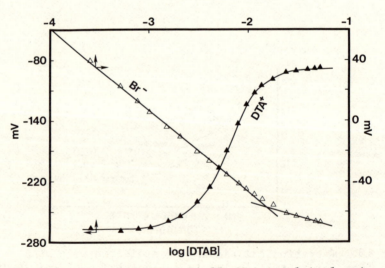

11b.   In the presence of 24.85 mM initial Asolectin.

concentration at the linear portion approximately corresponds to the concentration of DTAB at the end of the exothermic portion of the calorimetric titration curves. The binding isotherm for DTA^+ is given in Figure 12. The slope below the CMC_{app} (arrows at two lowest concentrations) is not as great for DS^- binding, and the $[DTA^+]_b/[Asolectin]$ binding ratio is also less than for DS^- binding. The concentration of free DTA^+, $[DTA^+]_f$, at the CMC_{app} again shows a dependence on Asolectin concentration and is less than the CMC in buffer (arrow at 9 mM). There was no evidence of counterion binding below the CMC_{app} with DTAB.

Comparisons. A comparison of thermodynamic parameters for micelle formation and vesicle binding from this study with those previously reported[10] for DDePO binding are given in Table I. The only free energy change included for ionic surfactants (line 3) is based on the data in Figure 4 for weak DS^- binding. In all cases, the enthalpy change for surfactant binding to the vesicles is more exothermic. The binding enthalpies do not show as large a solvent effect as the ones for micelle formation. It is tempting to attempt to estimate entropies of binding from compensation plots,[16] but the data for DDePO show that this is not justified. Further emf studies at very low surfactant concentrations would be required to obtain this information. Otherwise, the values are not too different for binding and micellization.

Table I.   Comparison of Thermodynamic Parameters for Micelle Formation and Vesicle Binding at 25° in Tris-EDTA Buffer.[a]

Surfactant	ΔG° (kcal/mol)		ΔH° (kcal/mol)		ΔS° (cal/mol-deg)	
	Micelle	Vesicle	Micelle	Vesicle	Micelle	Vesicle
DDePO	−3.1	−4.3	2.0	−1.7	17	8
SDS	−3.1	----	−0.2	−2.1	10	----
	−3.1	−4.1	−0.2	−0.5	10	12
DTAB	−2.4	----	−0.5	−1.9	6	----
SDS						
0.1 M NaCl			−0.7	−2.1		
6 M Urea			−2.8	−1.8		

[a]Thermodynamic values and the binding of dimethyldecylphosphonium oxide (DDePO) were determined as described in reference 10. The two sets of values given for SDS refer to the primary (strongest) and secondary (weakest) binding.

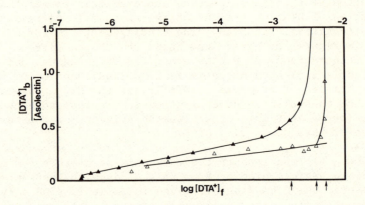

Figure 12.   Binding isotherm of DTA^+ to Asolectin in Tris–EDTA buffer with initial Asolectin concentrations of 24.85 mM (filled) and 6.21 mM (open).

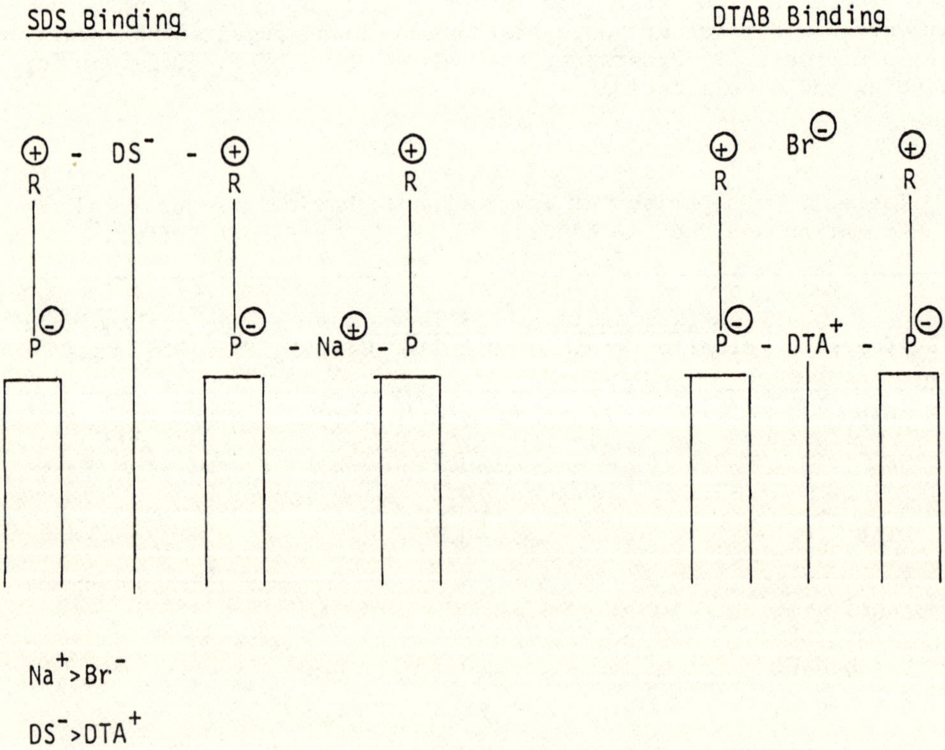

SDS Binding   DTAB Binding

$Na^+ > Br^-$

$DS^- > DTA^+$

Figure 13.   Possible binding mechanism for SDS and DTAB to Asolectin vesicles.

Based upon the results of this investigation, the following scheme is proposed as a possible binding mechanism for the interactions of SDS and DTAB with Asolectin vesicles (Figure 13). Since 2/3 of the phospholipids in Asolectin are Zwitterionic[12] (the group attached to phosphorus bears a positive charge and orthophosphate bears a negative charge at pH 7.4), there would appear to be mainly two ionic binding sites on the vesicle surface in addition to the hydrophobic one in the bilayer interior. The alignments given in the figure reflect favorable electrostatic attractions and the hydrophobic contacts. The results from the counterion electrodes show more favorable Na^+ than Br^- binding, and the binding isotherms show stronger DS^- binding and larger binding ratios than for at least the intermediate region of DTA^+ binding. Differences in the amount of Na^+ and Br^- binding might influence the magnitude of the binding ratio as the CMC_{app} is reached. The lower values of free surfactant ion at the CMC_{app}, gel filtration chromatography differences, dependence of CMC_{app} on [Asolectin], and the solvent effects for binding which parallel those found for micelle formation, all support the existence of mixed micelles above CMC_{app}. The absence of Br^- binding below the CMC_{app} would argue against mixed micelle formation below the CMC_{app}. The same might be true with SDS binding, but the evidence is not unambiguous.

The next stage in our studies would be to investigate the temperature dependence of the enthalpy of binding to determine heat capacity changes for comparison with those for micelle formation, and to continue these studies with homologous series of surfactants using purified phospholipids.

ACKNOWLEDGMENTS

This work was supported in part by grants GM-18648-08 and GM 00249-04 from the National Institutes of Health.

REFERENCES

1. A.D. Bangham, Ann. Rev. Biochem., 41, 753 (1972).
2. J. Sunamoto, H. Kondo and A. Yoshimatso, Biochim. Biophys. Acta, 510, 52 (1978).
3. A. Helenios and K. Simons, Biochim. Biophys. Acta, 415, 29 (1975).
4. H.H. Kamp, K.W.A. Wirtz, and L.L.M. Van Deenen, Biochim. Biophys. Acta, 398, 401 (1975).
5. C.A. Yu, L. Yu and T.E. King, J. Biol. Chem., 240, 1383 (1975).
6. Y. Katz and J.M. Diamond, J. Membrane Biol., 17, 101 (1974).
7. S.A. Simon, W.L. Stone, and P. Busto-Latorre, Biochim. Biophys. Acta, 468, 378 (1977).

8. F.A. Vilallonga, E.R. Garrett, and J.S. Hunt, J. Pharm. Sci.,
    66, 1229 (1977).

9. R.Y. Zaslavsky, A.A. Borovskaya, A.Y. Lisichkim, Y.A.
    Davidovich and S.V. Rogozhin, Chem. Phys. Lipids, 24, 297
    (1979).

10. G.C. Kresheck, K. Kale and M.D. Vallone, J. Colloid. Interface
    Sci., 73, 460 (1980).

11. G.C. Kresheck and W.A. Hargraves, J. Colloid. Interface Sci.,
    48, 481 (1974).

12. Y. Kagawa, A. Kandrach and E. Racker, J. Biol. Chem., 248,
    676 (1973).

13. K.M. Kale, E.L. Cussler and D.F. Evans, J. Phys. Chem., 84,
    593 (1980).

14. G.C. Kresheck and C. Jones, J. Colloid. Interface Sci.,
    77, 278 (1980).

15. I.M. Klotz, in "The Proteins" H. Neurath and K. Bailey,
    Editors, Vol. 1B, pp. 727, Academic Press, New York, 1953.

16. R. Lumry and S. Rajender, Biopolymers, 9, 1125 (1970).

HYDROPHOBIC INTERACTIONS OF AROMATIC HYDROCARBONS INDUCED BY SURFACTANTS AND POLYELECTROLYTES

Peter A. Martic, Susan E. Hartman, Jack L. R. Williams,
Samir Farid
Research Laboratories
Eastman Kodak Company
Rochester, New York 14650

The microenvironment of charged molecules can be significantly altered in the presence of ionic molecules such as surfactants, lipids, and polyelectrolytes. Such a change in the microenvironment of aromatic hydrocarbon chromophores can be conveniently studied spectroscopically. The interactions in aqueous solutions of cationic as well as anionic derivatives of pyrene and anthracene such as N-[-4-(1-pyrenyl)butyryloxyethyl]-N,N,N-trimethylammonium methosulfate (1), sodium 4-(1-pyrenyl)butyrate (2), and sodium 3-(9-anthryl)propionate (3)

were studied by absorption and emission spectroscopy. At low concentrations ($\leq 2 \times 10^{-5}$M) of these compounds there is, as expected, no indication of a ground-state interaction and

virtually no excimer emission. However, in the presence of
oppositely charged surfactants such as sodium dodecylsulfate (SDS)
and dodecyltrimethylammonium bromide (DTAB) at concentrations some
two orders of magnitude below their critical micelle concentration,
(cmc) there is a profound interaction among these aromatic hydrocarbons in the ground state. Similarly, the presence of oppositely
charged polyelectrolytes 4 and 5 induced the ground-state interactions among these hydrocarbons.

$$
\begin{array}{cc}
\left(CH_2-\underset{\substack{CO \\ | \\ O \\ | \\ (CH_2)_3 \\ SO_3^{2-}Na^+}}{\overset{CH_3}{\underset{|}{C}}}\right)_n
&
\left(CH_2-\underset{\substack{CO \\ | \\ O \\ | \\ (CH_2)_2 \\ {}^+N(CH_3)_3}}{\overset{CH_3}{\underset{|}{C}}}\right)_n \\
& CH_3SO_4^- \\
4 & 5
\end{array}
$$

This hydrophobic interaction is evident from a large decrease in
resolution of the vibrational structure accompanied in some instances by a shift of a few nanometers to the red (Figure 1).
Further evidence for such a ground-state interaction is obtained
from emission data (Figure 2). The addition of oppositely charged
surfactants or polyelectrolytes to the aqueous solutions of 1 and
2 leads to the appearance of a pronounced excimer band in their
emission spectra. The excitation spectra for the residual monomer
fluorescence and that for the excimer band are distinctly
different (Figure 2). The excitation spectrum monitored at the
monomeric fluorescence band is vibrationally well resolved, but
the excitation spectrum monitored at the structureless excimer
band (~500 nm) is poorly resolved.

Addition of the oppositely charged surfactants to 1 and 2 at
concentrations above the cmc leads to normal micellar behavior
with no indication of ground-state interactions. Also, in the
case of hydrophobic interaction between aromatic hydrocarbon
chromophores in 1 and 2 induced by the polyelectrolyte, the
addition of a surfactant of the same charge as that of the pyrene
chromophore, i.e., of opposite charge to that of the polyelectrolyte, eliminates this ground-state interaction. Exchange of some
of the counterions on the polyelectrolyte by the surfactant will
create hydrophobic micellar sites in which the pyrene chromophore
can be incorporated. Once the chromophore is in such a lipophilic
medium, "shielded" from the ionic sites, the driving force for the
ground-state pyrene-pyrene interaction will be eliminated.

Polyelectrolyte 6 has few pyrene chromophores covalently attached, in an apparently random distribution, to the polymer chain. The absorption spectrum of a dilute aqueous solution of 6 shows poor resolution of the vibrational structure. Also in this case the decreased resolution is attributed to a ground-state hydrophobic interaction among the pyrene chromophores. As expected, addition of SDS (surfactant/ionic sites on 6 = 0.1 - 0.5) leads to a breakdown of the pyrene-pyrene interaction by creating lipophilic micellar environment for the pyrene chromophore.

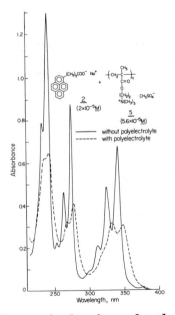

Figure 1. Influence of oppositely charged polyelectrolytes on the Pyrene derivative 2.

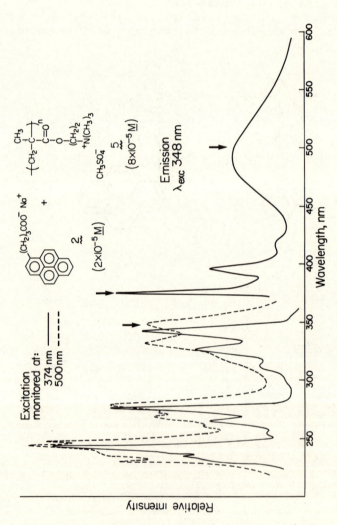

Figure 2. Fluorescence excitation and emission spectra of the pyrene derivative 2 in the presence of oppositely charged polyelectrolyte 5.

STRUCTURE AND HYDROPHOBIC BONDING:

CONCEPTS AND APPLICATIONS TO ANESTHESIA

Mohammad Abu-Hamdiyyah
Chemistry Department
University of Kuwait
Kuwait

Hydrophobic bonding is related to the three dimensional hydrogen-bonded structure in liquid water. This
skeletal structure allows the existence of cavities
capable of accommodating small non-polar moieties and
also the formation of cavities by the larger non-polar
groups on dissolution. The limit of this interstitial
dissolution at a given temperature is the onset of hydrophobic bonding such as micellization, saturation solubility or the intramolecular aggregation of non-polar side
chains in proteins. The stronger the skeletal structure
the more stable the natural cavities and the higher the
solubility of small non-polar molecules. Weaker skeletal
structures accommodate relatively large non-polar
molecules (moieties) better than the stronger skeletal
structures. This explains the solubility of argon,
hydrocarbons, amino acids and micellization in light
water, heavy water and in aqueous urea solutions.

Additives with non-polar moieties which also dissolve interstitially in water strengthen hydrophobic bonding hence the reduction in the critical micelle concentra-
tion(cmc) of a surfactant or the increased intramolecular
aggregation-coaggregation in proteins (stablization of
proteins) at low concentrations of the additive. Comparison with the effects of anesthetic agents on cell
membranes suggests that the action of anesthetic agents
at the site in nerve cell membranes is akin to

micelle formation. Therefore it is proposed that the
micellization process be used as a model for the anesthetic action with the effect of anesthetic agent on
the micellization parameters of a surfactant (such as
the reduction of the cmc, the increase in surface pressure prior to micelle formation or the distribution coe-
ficient between the aqueous phase and the micelle), as
indices of potency. Available data confirm this. A
molecular mechanism of anesthesia is proposed.

INTRODUCTION

Hydrophobic bonding phenomena occur whenever non-polar
substances or substances containing non-polar moieties are dissolved in water (aqueous solutions) particularly at low temperatures. Because water is the solvent in biological systems, hydrophobic bonding is expected to have a major role in the processes
occuring in these systems. In this work we discuss first what
is believed to be the fundamental relationship of water structures to hydrophobic bonding. Then the differences in the
strength of hydrophobic bonding in light and heavy water and in
aqueous urea solutions are discussed in terms of the strength
of the skeletal hydrogen-bonded structures in these solvent
systems explaining the apparent discreparencies in the behaviour
of small and large solutes. Then it is pointed out that the
effects of non-polar and amphiphilic additives at low concentration on hydrophobic bonding and the effects of anesthetic agents
at the site of action in nerve cell membranes are analogous, and
it is suggested to use the micellization process as a model to
simulate the site of action in nerve cell membranes. This
provides a basic molecular mechanism of anesthesia.

WATER STRUCTURE AND HYDROPHOBIC BONDING

Hydrophobic bonding, the full or partial removal of non-
polar groups (moieties) from bulk water as in the aggregation
of monomer surfactant molecules (ions) to form micelles or the
limited solubility of hydrocarbons, inert gases etc. or the
intramolecular aggregation of non-polar side chains of amino
acids in proteins, is a direct consequence of the strong water-
water interactions[1-4]. The structure of liquid water is
characterized by the three dimensional hydrogen-bonding[4-5] which
is often referred to as a skeletal structure. This dynamic
skeletal structure allows the existence of dynamic interstices

and cavities of certain sizes[3,6] and also allows the formation of
cavities by the relatively large non-polar groups on dissolution.
As a result of the strong hydrogen-bonding between the water
molecules, non-polar groups tend to dissolve interstitially in
liquid water, the stability of the interstitial solution depends
on the size of the solute and that of the cavity[3]. A small
sized solute does not stabilize a relatively large dynamic cavity.
This can be inferred from the solubility pattern of inert gases
which shows increasing solubility in going from helium to
radon[7,8], at 25°C, suggesting filling of already existing cavities. However, when the size of the solute is such that it could
not be accommodated in a natural cavity, a suitable cavity is
formed[4,6] but this step requires work and hence a decrease in
solubility occurs, despite the increase in polarizability. This
can be inferred from the solubility pattern of hydrocarbons[8]
whose solubility at 25°C increases in going from methane to ethane
then it decreases slightly in going to propane and the solubility
decrease further in going to n-butane etc.

Hydrophobic bonding sets in as the limit of interstitial
solubility is attained. Comparison of the standard free energy of
solution (micellization) of a given solute (surfactant) in a
series of solvents such as those we are interested in, gives the
relative strength of hydrophobic bonding in these solvents. The
greater the solubility or the cmc, both in mole fraction units,
the weaker the hydrophobic bonding. It is clear from the above
that the size of the solute is a factor in hydrophobic bonding.
Another factor is the temperature. For example the standard
solubility of helium decreases with temperature until it reaches
a minimum about 23°C above which the solubility starts to
increase[9]. Other non-polar gases behave similarly but the minimum shifts to higher temperatures depending on the size of the
solute[9,10]. Increasing the temperature increases the motion of
the water molecules which tends to destabilize the natural cavities, however the work necessary to create a cavity becomes less.
At low temperatures, interstitial dissolution in the natural
cavities is predominant whereas dissolution by making cavities
is dominant at high temperatures. It is thus obvious that the
strength of the skeletal structure would also be a factor in
hydrophobic bonding. Strengthening the skeletal structure in
water, at a given temperature, would increase the stability of
the natural cavities whereas it would increase the work required
to create a relatively larger cavity. These two tendencies predict an increase in the solubility of non-polar solutes that can
be accommodated in natural cavities and a decrease in the solubility of the relatively large solutes. On the other hand weakening of the skeletal hydrogen-bonded structure in solution would

have exactly the opposite trend. The stability of natural cavities would decrease, while the work required to create larger
cavities become less, thus it is expected that the solubility
of small non-polar solute would decrease and the solubility of
relatively large non-polar solutes would increase as the skeletal
structure is weakened.

When hydrophobic bonding sets in and a non-polar moiety is
transferred from bulk water to an aggregate, an expansion of
volume occurs[11-13] and the moiety becomes less restricted[7]. Application of pressure reverses the aggregation tendency (for example
the cmc is increased[14-15]). If a non-polar or amphiphilic additive is added at low concentrations to the system, co-aggregation
(solubilization) occurs because all non-polar moieties tend to
dissolve interstitially and thus a change in the limit of interstitial dissolution[16]. In a micellar system this is manifested
by a decrease in the cmc[16] or by a decrease in the surface tension
of the solution prior to micelle formation even if the additive
is non-surface active[17,18]. If the system is a protein solution,
then at low concentration of the additive and at low temperatures,
stabilization of the native state occurs[19]. The strengthening of
hydrophobic bonding resulting from the addition of a non-polar or
amphiphilic substance occurs by both competition for cavities
and by participation in aggregation. The latter occurs as the
additive distributes itself between the aqueous phase and the
aggregate (e.g.micelles). This distribution is dependent on the
size of the non-polar moiety of the additive and the chain length
of the surfactant molecule (ion) forming the aggregate. For a
given surfactant solution the maximum concentration that could be
osolubilized in a homologous series of additives or solubilizates
(e.g., hydrocarbons) depends on the chain length of the additive.
The amount solubilized in moles per mole of surfactant decreases
as the chain length of the additive increases[20]. This tendency of
"cut-off" in solubilization has been noted in the aqueous solutions of dodecylammonium chloride, where it was found[21] that
heptadecane and octadecane did not have any effect on the cmc.

We have described above qualitatively what we believe to be
the physical basis of hydrophobic bonding and its relationship
to water structure. Ben-Naim[22] on the other hand has devised a
quantitative model for the study of hydrophobic bonding (interaction), HI, which he defines as the indirect part of the work
required to bring two solute particles (e.g. two methane molecules) from fixed positions at infinite separation in the solvent
to a small distance from each other (e.g. the distance equal to
the length of C-C bond in ethane). This indirect work of bringing two molecules together so they are fused to form some sort of

a "dimer", $2CH_4 \rightarrow C_2H_6$, has been approximated by the difference in the standard free energy of solution of the "dimer" e.g. ethane and that of the two monomers, e.g. methane. The conclusions of this model sometimes disagree with those using the conventional method, the standard free energy of transfer, as has been pointed out by the author[23], himself. Recently the application of this model has been extended to the problem of intramolecular hydrophobic (pair) interactions[24]. Ben-Naim and Tenne[25] combined the scaled particle theory (SPT) with his model to calculate the hydrophobic interaction when bringing m solute particles from fixed positions at infinite separations from each other in the solvent to a closed packed configuration where they are confined to a spherical region of a suitable diameter. Applied to methane it was found that HI increases with temperature and at constant temperature HI increases with m. However, it was found that HI increases monotonically with pressure which is opposite to what is expected for an aggregation (micellization) process in water since pressure increases the cmc i.e. weakens HI[14], in the pressure range considered.

HYDROPHOBIC BONDING IN HEAVY WATER AND IN AQUEOUS UREA

It is generally accepted[26] that the "hydrogen-bond" in heavy water is slightly stronger than that in light water thus the skeletal hydrogen-bonded structure in D_2O is stronger than in H_2O. This difference should be reflected in the solubilities of small and relatively large non-polar solutes according to the qualitative picture sketched earlier which predicts that D_2O favors small while H_2O favors the relatively large solute particles. The solubilities of argon[27], methane, ethane, propane and butane[28,29] as well as the solubilities of benzene[28], toluene, xylenes and naphthalene[30] have been measured in light and heavy water. At 25°C the (mole fraction) solubility of argon, methane, ethane and propane is greater in heavy than in light water, with the standard free energy of transfer from light to heavy water getting less negative as the size of the solute gets larger. The solubility of butane[28] was found to be greater in light than heavy water. The reverse is reported in reference 29 but when all the data are taken together, say at 25°C, the trend is unmistakable and the conclusion of ref. 28 regarding butane is consistent with the trend which predicts that pentane, hexane and higher hydrocarbons should have less solubility in heavy than in light water. For benzene and the other aromatic compounds[30] it was found that heavy water is less favorable than light water, the standard free energy of transfer from light to heavy water being positive for benzene and becomes more positive for the larger compounds. (The data for biphenyl in reference 28 is against the expected trend).

Using compounds with functional groups introduces other factors which complicate the analysis. Ketones have the carbonyl group which is a good hydrogen-bonding acceptor and since the only difference between light and heavy water is the strength of the "hydrogen-bond" it is expected that the carbonyl group would favor heavy water. However the data obtained by Dahlberg[30] and by Jolicoeur and Lacroix[31] on ketones do not agree and are difficult to interpret although introduction of very bulky substituents makes the standard free energy of transfer from light to heavy water positive.

On the other hand, the solubility studies of amino acids[29] show that for glycine, alanine and α-aminobutyric acid, heavy water is the better solvent. The converse is true for amino acids with larger side chains: norvaline, norleucine and L-phenylalanine. Finally the critical micelle concentration of several surfactants, dodecyltrimethylammonium bromide[32], dodecylpyridinium iodide[29], and hexadecyltrimethylammonium carboxylates[33], were measured in heavy and light water. All have lower cmc's in heavy water indicating stronger hydrophobic bonding in heavy water. The results of amino acids and those of micellization are in accord with the expectations of our qualitative picture. This does not mean that ionic heads having no effect, but it must be due to some kind of self-compensating effects occurring.

Urea is able to hydrogen-bond with water in three dimensions[3,34]; however, the skeletal hydrogen-bonded structure is more labile, irregular and weaker than that in light water as can be inferred from various studies[34-36]. This is reflected in the positive values of transfer of partial molal volumes and of enthalpy of solutions of non-polar moieties from water to aqueous urea solutions[35,37,38]. Thus according to our picture, small non-polar solutes would favor water and relatively large non-polar solute would favor aqueous urea solutions. Solubility studies of hydrocarbons[39] show that methane and ethane (at 25°C) are more soluble in light water than in aqueous urea, and the converse is true for higher hydrocarbons, which is the expected pattern. Thus in the three solvent systems discussed the strength of the skeletal hydrogen-bonded structure follows the order $D_2O > H_2O >$ aqueous urea. The transfer free energy from light water to heavy water and from light to aqueous urea have opposite trends, as seen in Figure 1.

The isotopic effect in hydrophobic bonding has also been treated by Ben-Naim[25,28] using his model as it was also treated by Lucas and Bury[40] using SPT. The conclusion of Ben-Naim and Yaacubi[23] that "increasing the structure of the solvent leads to a decrease of the strength of HI" leads to anomalies regarding the prediction of the HI in light and in heavy water for small and large sized non-polar solutes.[29,33] Lucas and Bury[40] treated the isotopic effect as a function of the non-polar hard-sphere solute size using the Stillinger amendment of SPT. They found that the transfer free energy from light to heavy water is negative for small sized solutes and dominated by entropy and that it is increasingly positive and dominated by enthalpy for larger sizes (Figure 2 of reference 40).

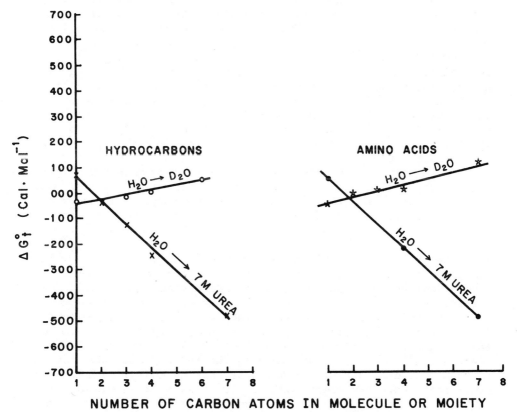

Figure 1: Transfer free energy of hydrocarbons[28,29,39] and of amino acids[29,39] from light water to heavy water and to 7M aqueous urea solutions at 25°C.

HYDROPHOBIC BONDING AND THE MOLECULAR MECHANISM OF ANESTHESIA

It is now widely accepted that anesthetic agents, which are all non-polar or amphiphilic, induce anesthesia by acting at a hydrophobic site in the nerve cell membrane[41-47]. The hydrophobic

site could be in the lipid bilayer or it could be part of a protein
in the membrane[41,43,47-51]. Solvent models used to stimulate the
site, assuming it is in the lipid bilayer,were olive oil, octanol,
benzene, etc[41]. Monolayers[41]and black film phosphatidylcholine-
cholesterol bilayers[46] were also used. Proponents of the protein
as the action site of anesthetic agents used water soluble proteins
as models [47,50,51]. On the other hand Pauling and Miller independently suggested that the aqueous phase in the central nervous
system as the action site where the anesthetic agents form ice
microcrystals[52] and icebergs[53] respectively. They related the
potency of anesthetic agents to the dissociation pressure of the
agents clathrates at O^OC. However, there seems to be no further
interest in this theory). Recent experimental evidence strongly
suggest the unlikelihood of the lipid bilayer being the action site
and points to the protein as the logical site[48,49,54,55]. Thus
an explanation of the mode of action of anesthetic agents must be
sought in terms of the effect of these agents on the protein of
the excitable cell membrane. This is what the protein conformational
change (PCC) theory proposes to do. Before proceeding to discuss
the PCC theory, it must be pointed out[41] that any theory of anesthesia must explain the non-specificity of anesthetic agents, the
volume expansion of the membrane when exposed to anesthetic agents,
the increased fluidity of the membrane, pressure reversal of anesthesia and the "cut-off" in potency in a homologous series of anesthetic agents as the non-polar chain increases above a certain
value[42-44].

     The proponents of PCC theory propose that anesthetic agents
combine with the hydrophobic interior of the protein(s) and
unfold them so that the hydrophobic side chains which were
burried in the interior are exposed to water and thus undergo
"hydrophobic" hydration. Simultaneously the ionic charges which
were exposed to the solvent (water) disappear by neutralization
releasing electrostricted water[47,50,51,56,57]. This theory which has
been termed[48] the "protein unfolding theory" explains the increase
in volume as due to neutralization of charges and hydrophobic
hydration. However, comparison of the effects of non-polar and
amphiphilic additives at surgical concentrations as well as the
effect of hydrostatic pressure on globular proteins and on
micelles with the corresponding effects of anesthetic agents
suggests the occurrence of aggregation of non-polar side chains
of proteins in nerve cell membranes rather than unfolding as,
can be seen from the following:

     In the native state of globular proteins the tendency for
non-polar side chains to contact water is minimized by forming
intramolecular aggregates. i.e. folding[24]. An equilibrium exists

between the side chains still projecting into water and those
that have aggregated. On denaturing of proteins side chains
which were burried inside are exposed to the solvent i.e. unfolding occurs[2,4]. Denaturing can occur by pressure, temperature
or by additives such as urea or high concentrations of amphiphilic
additives. Densitometric and dilatometric volume changes have
been measured for numerous denaturing reactions and found to be
negative[2] (a decrease of about 0.5% of the total molar volume).
Pressure denaturation showed also a small volume decrease
for many different proteins[2]. Others[58-60] found also a
volume decrease in going from the native to the denaturated
states i.e. from folded to unfolded states. This means exposure
of hydrophobic residues to solvent during denaturation contributes negatively to the volume change. Recently French and
Gosline[61] estimated the transfer of one mole of an average non-
polar amino acid side chain from hydrophobic interior into contact with water, as a result of pressure denaturation, to be
about (-6) ml.

It has already been noted that addition of non-polar or
amphiphilic substances at very low concentrations (comparative
to surgical concentrations) to protein solutions stabilizes them
and does not denature them. In a micellar system, non-polar
moieties (singly) dispersed in water are in equilibrium with the
micelles. The main characteristics of this equilibrium are: a
volume increase on micellization[11-13], a fluid hydrocarbon interior, micellization reversal by hydrostatic pressure[14-15]
(i.e. an increase in the cmc), a cmc decrease by non-polar gases[17,18]
(and liquids[21]) and by amphiphilic additives at low concentrations[16]
and a decrease in surface tension by (non-surface active) non-
polar additives prior to micelle formation[17,18]. The above shows
that pressure weakens hydrophobic bonding, i.e. shifts the equilibrium from the aggregates to the monomer (unaggregated side chains
in proteins) and since the pressure reverses the action of anesthetic agents, the latter step looks like an aggregation step.
This is in line with the stabilization of proteins by anesthetic
agents at low concentration[41]. Stabilization means increased
aggregation and/or coaggregation which is equivalent to a reduction in the cmc of a surfactant solution on addition of non-
polar or amphiphilic substances at low concentrations and low
temperatures.

Furthermore comparing the effect of anesthetic agents on
the stability of erythrocyte membranes[41] against hemolysis, of
lysosomes[41] against relative release of hydrolases, or of cate-
cholamin granules[41] against the release of noradrenaline and the
effect of amphiphilic additives on the cmc of sodium larylsul-
fate[16] over relatively wide concentration range we see stabilization of the membranes corresponding to strengthening of hydro-
lysosomes[41]

phobic bonding at low concentrations and destabilization of the
membranes corresponding to the disruption of the micelles at
higher concentrations.

Finally the decreasing solubility of hydrocarbons in micelles
as the chain length of the hydrocarbon increases parallels the
decrease in the anesthetic effect in homologous hydrocarbons[41,42,62].
All these observations suggest that anesthetic agents on dissolving in the aqueous phase in the CNS at clinical concentrations induce aggregation and/or coaggregation of non-polar side
chains of the polypeptides or proteins projecting out in the
aqueous phase. This aggregation and/or coaggregation is considered to be the primary action of anesthetic agents. The
action of anesthetic agents at the hydrophobic site in the nerve
cell membrane is thus akin to micelle formation and therefore we
propose the use of the micellization process as a model for the
study of the effects of anesthetic agents at the site in nerve
cell membranes.. The effectiveness of an agent in reducing the
cmc of a given surfactant, its distribution coefficient between
the micelle and aqueous phase or its effectiveness in reducing
the surface tension of a surfactant solution prior to micelle
formation should all be useful indices of potency.

Available data in the literature have been used to test
the model, Figures 2-4. The results clearly support our contention.

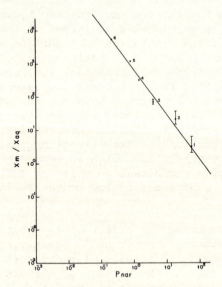

Figure 2: The distribution of inhalational anesthetics between
the micelle and the aqueous phase in NaLS[63,64] versus the gaseous
pressure in atmospheres needed for narcosis[62]. 1,helium; 2,argon;
3,methane; 4,ethane; 5,propane; 6,butane.

Figure 3 shows that for a given alcohol nerve-blocking concentration, the ability of inducing aggregation-coaggregation increases as the chain length of the micelle-forming monomer decreases as seen from the increasing rate of cmc reduction. In Figure 4 the difference between the chain lengths of the monomers is not sufficiently great, for this tendency to be very distinct. The deviations from linearity shown by nonanol in Figure 3 means decreasing ability of the alcohol to induce aggregation-coaggregation. If these points are real then they indicate the beginning of a "cut-off" in anesthetic potency, however, no such deviations appear in Figure 4. It is important to extend the measurements to the common anesthetic agents using various surfactant solutions with different monomer chain lengths.

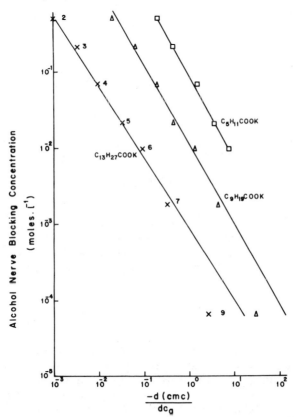

Figure 3: The alcohol nerve-blocking concentration[41] in moles.1^{-1} plotted against the initial rate of the decrease of the cmc of the surfactant with alcohol concentration[65]. The alcohols are: 2,ethanol; 3,1-propanol; 4,1-butanol; 5,1-pentanol; 6,1-hexanol; 7,1-heptanol; 9,1-nonanol. The surfactants are: X,$C_{13}H_{27}COOK$; Δ, $C_9H_{19}COOK$; $\square$, $C_5H_{11}COOK$.

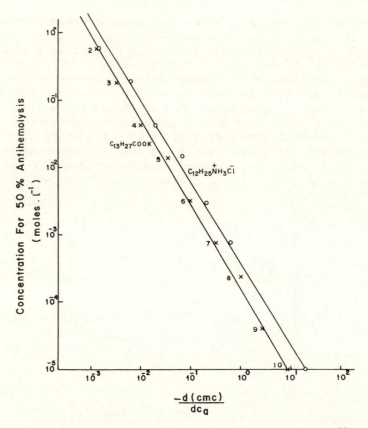

Figure 4: Alcohol concentration for 50% antihemolysis[41] plotted against the initial rate of the decrease of the cmc with alcohol concentration[65]. The alcohols are n-alkanols from ethanol to decanol. The surfactants are X, $C_{13}H_{27}COOK$ and O, $C_{12}H_{25}\overset{+}{N}H_3\overset{-}{C}l$.

Figure 5 shows a crude sketch of one of many possible pictures depicting what is thought to be the basic molecular mechanism of anesthesia viz: the aggregation-coaggregation of the interstitially dissolved non-polar side chains of amino acids in the aqueous phase (the channel) when the anesthetic agent (moiety) dissolves also interstitially in the aqueous phase (the channel) in the nerve cell membrane. This aggregation-coaggregation blocks the channels which allow, when open, the translocation of ionic and other hydrophilic species necessary for the awake state or nerve conduction. This type of conformational change, the aggregation-coaggregation seems to be basic to conduction in all types of excitable cell membranes.

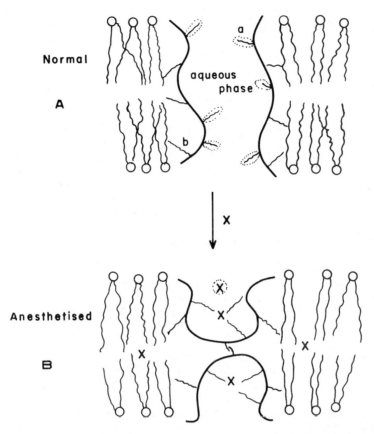

Figure 5: A model depicting the inducement of side chain aggrega-   709
tion-coaggregation when anesthetic agents are dissolved in the
aqueous phase of nerve cell membranes (the ionic or hydrophilic
channels). A depicts, the normal state with the polypeptides
having some side chains projecting in the aqueous phase (marked a)
and side chains that are associated with the bilayer (marked b).
B depicts the anesthetized state where aggregation-conaggregation
occurs. Side chains which were projecting in the aqueous phase
are aggregated. Some of the side chains are still associated
with the bilayer.

The micellization model predicts also that at very high pressure hydrophobic bonding starts to increase again (the cmc starts to decrease after passing through a maximum[14]). A similar trend has also been noted for the effect of hydrostatic pressure on the potency of anesthetic agents[66] with weakening at relatively low pressures and enhancement at relatively high pressures. Agents such as urea which increase the cmc and denature proteins (unfold them) should also antagonize the action of anesthetic agents according to the proposed mechanism.

REFERENCES

1. G.S. Hartley, "Aqueous Solutions of Paraffinic Chain Salts", Herman and Cie, Paris, 1936.
2. W. Kauzmann, Advances in Protein Chem., $\underline{14}$, 1 (1959).
3. M. Abu-Hamdiyyah, J. Phys. Chem., $\underline{69}$, 2720 (1965).
4. C. Tanford, "The Hydrophobic Effect", J. Wiley and Sons, New York, 1973.
5. J.A. Pople, Proc. Roy. Soc. (London), $\underline{A205}$, 163 (1951).
6. D.D. Eley, Trans. Farad. Soc., $\underline{35}$, 1281 (1939).
7. O.W. Howarth, J. Chem. Soc., Faraday Trans. 1, $\underline{71}$, 2303 (1975).
8. M.H. Abraham, J. Am. Chem. Soc., $\underline{101}$, 5477 (1979).
9. E. Wilhelm and R. Battino, Chem. Rev., $\underline{73}$, 1 (1973).
10. D.M. Himmelblau, J. Phys. Chem., $\underline{63}$, 1803 (1959).
11. L. Benjamine, J. Phys. Chem., $\underline{70}$, 3790 (1966).
12. M.E. Friedman and H.A. Scheraga, J. Phys. Chem., $\underline{69}$, 3795 (1965).
13. K. Shinoda and T. Soda, J. Phys. Chem., $\underline{67}$, 2072 (1963).
14. S.D. Hamann, J. Phys. Chem., $\underline{66}$, 1354 (1962).
15. R.E. Tuddenham and A.E. Alexander, J. Phys. Chem., $\underline{66}$, 1839 (1962).
16. M. Abu-Hamdiyyah and L. Al-Mansour, J. Phys. Chem., $\underline{83}$, 2236 (1978).
17. I.J. Lin and A. Metzer, J. Phys. Chem., $\underline{75}$, 3000 (1971).
18. P. Somasundaran and B.M. Moudgil, J. Colloid Interfac. Sci., $\underline{47}$, 290 (1974).
19. D. Eagland in "Water", F. Franks, Editor, Vol. 4, Plenum Press, New York, 1974.
20. P.H. Elworthy, A.T. Florance and C.B. Macfarlane, "Solubilization", Chapman and Hall, London, 1968.
21. K. Shinoda in "Colloidal Surfactants", Academic Press, New York, 1963.
22. A. Ben-Naim, J. Chem. Phys., $\underline{54}$, 1387 (1971).
23. A. Ben-Naim and M. Yaacobi, J. Phys. Chem., $\underline{78}$, 170 (1974).
24. A. Ben-Naim and J. Wilf, J. Chem. Phys., $\underline{70}$, 771 (1979).
25. A. Ben-Naim and R. Tenne, J. Chem. Phys., $\underline{67}$, 627 (1977).
26. A. Ben-Naim, J. Chem. Phys., $\underline{42}$, 1512 (1965).
27. A. Ben-Naim, J. Phys. Chem., $\underline{79}$, 1268 (1975).

28. A. Ben-Naim, J. Wilf and M. Yaacobi, J. Phys. Chem., 77, 95 (1973).
29. G.C. Kresheck, H. Schneider and H.A. Scheraga, J. Phys. Chem., 69, 3132 (1965).
30. D.B. Dahlberg, J. Phys. Chem., 76, 2045 (1972).
31. C. Jolicoeur and G. Lacroix, Can. J. Chem., 51, 3051 (1973).
32. M.F. Emerson and A. Holtzer, J. Phys. Chem., 71, 3320 (1967).
33. D. Oakenfull and D.E. Fenwick, Aust. J. Chem., 28, 715 (1975).
34. D.W. James, R.F. Armishaw and R.L. Frost, J. Phys. Chem., 80, 1346 (1976).
35. G.C. Kresheck and L. Benjamine, J. Phys. Chem., 63, 2426 (1964).
36. E.G. Finer, F. Franks and J.J. Tait, J. Am. Chem. Soc., 94, 4424 (1972).
37. W.A. Hargraves and G.C. Kresheck, J. Phys. Chem., 73, 3249 (1969).
38. A. Shehab-El-Din, M.S. Thesis, University of Kuwait, Kuwait, 1980.
39. D.M. Wetlaner, S.K. Malik, L. Stoller and R.L. Coffin, J. Am. Chem. Soc., 86, 508 (1964).
40. M. Lucas and R. Bury, J. Phys. Chem., 80, 999 (1976).
41. P. Seeman, Pharmacol. Rev., 24, 583 (1972).
42. E.B. Smith in "Molecular Mechanisms in General Anesthesia", M.J. Halsey, R.A. Millar and T.A. Sutton, Editors, pp. 112-130, Churchill-Livingston, London, 1974.
43. P. Seeman in "Molecular Mechanism of Anesthesia", B.R. Fink, Editor, Progress in Anesthesiology, Vol. I, pp. 243-251, Raven Press, New York, 1975.
44. R.R. Trudell, Anesthesiology, 46, 5 (1977).
45. H. Schneider, Biochem. Biophys. Acta, 163, 451 (1968).
46. D.A. Haydon, B.M. Hendry, S.R. Levinson and J. Requena, Nature, 268, 256 (1977).
47. J.W. Woodbury, J.D. D'Arrigo and H. Eyring in "Molecular Mechanism of Anesthesia", B.R. Fink, Editor, Progress in Anesthesiology, Vol. I., pp. 253-275, Raven Press, New York, 1975.
48. P. Seeman, Anesthesiology, 47, 1 (1977).
49. J.C. Hsia and J.M. Boggs in "Molecular Mechanism of Anesthesia", B.R. Fink, Editor, Progress in Anesthesiology, Vol. I., pp. 327-338, Raven Press, New York, 1975.
50. I. Ueda, J. Mashimo and D.D. Shieh, Anesthesiology, 51, 514 (1979).
51. H. Kamaya and I. Ueda, Anesthesiology, 51, S 15 (1979).
52. L. Pauling, Science, 134, 15 (1961).
53. S.L. Miller, Proc. Nat. Acad. Sci. U.S.A., 47, 1515 (1961).
54. N.P. Franks and W.R. Lieb, Nature, 247, 339 (1978).
55. M.J. Conrad and S.J. Singer, Proc. Nat. Acad. Sci. U.S.A., 76, 5202 (1979).
56. I. Ueda and H. Kamaya, Anesthesiology, 38, 423 (1973).

57. I. Ueda, H. Kamaya and H. Eyring, Proc. Nat. Acad. Sci.
     U.S.A., 73, 481 (1967).
58. D.N. Holcombe and K.E. Van Holde, J. Phys. Chem., 66,
     1999 (1962).
59. J.E. Brandt, R.J. Oliveir and C. Westort, Biochemistry,
     9, 1038 (1970).
60. S. Hawley, Biochemistry, 10, 2436 (1971).
61. C.J. French and J.M. Gosline, Biochem. Biophys. Acta,
     537, 286 (1978).
62. L.J. Mullins, Chem. Rev., 54, 289 (1954).
63. I.B.C. Matheson and A.D. King, Jr., J. Colloid Interfac.
     Sci., 66, 464 (1978).
64. A. Wishnia, J. Phys. Chem., 67, 2079 (1963).
65. K. Shinoda in "Colloidal Surfactants", K. Shinoda,
     T. Nakagawa, B.I. Tamamushi and I. Isemura, Academic
     Press, New York, 1963.
66. S.H. Roth in "Molecular Mechanisms of Anesthesia", B.R. Fink,
     Editor, Progress in Anesthesiology, Vol. I., Raven Press,
     pp. 405-420, New York, 1975.

DISCUSSION

On the paper by G. Kegeles

B. Lindman, *University of Lund, Lund, Sweden* : What are the exact differences between your approach and that of Aniansson and Wall as regards basic assumptions and results? In particular it would be appreciated if you could comment on differences regarding the aggregate size distribution, e.g., the location and depth of the minimum.

G. Kegeles: The major difference between the Aniansson and Wall theory and mine is that they have begun by attacking directly the problem of the relaxation kinetics, assuming a priori a sharp pre-existing distribution of micellar material, whereas I have begun by focusing on the distribution and trying to establish some kind of a modified mass-action law model for the equilibrium between all species. Thus Aniansson and Wall have originally searched for tractable closed solutions for both the fast and slow time domains, making physical approximations where necessary so that the mathematics can be handled. I have been more concerned with questions involved in relating the rate constants consistently to the modified mass-action equilibrium constants, and in relating perturbations of the local rate constants in relaxation processes precisely to a shift between two neighboring equilibrium situations. Thus, I have a unique closed solutions relating monomer perturbation and perturbation of the intrinsic equilibrium formation constant. While Aniansson and Wall have developed a closed solution for both the fast time domain and the slow time domain, I have a closed solution for only the intitial time, which seems to be in qualitative agreement with theirs, but which extends down through the CMC all the way down to infinite dilution. I have worked directly with the coupled rate equations of chemical kinetics, and my formulations have used only very simple mathematics. My treatment of the slow

time domain is only developed by means of direct numerical
analysis. As such, it is essentially exact and free of all
special physical assumptions other than those of the original
distribution model. It suffers from the common defect of all
numerical analysis methods, that an all-inclusive picture is obtained only by a thorough systematic variation of all possible
parameters, which still remains to be completed.

With respect to basic assumptions, Aniansson and Wall chose
a model either Gaussian or nearly Gaussian in form, with an
arbitrary deep valley between monomer and micelles, generated by
arbitrary step-by-step upward adjustment of the dissociation rate
constant for a whole sequence of small oligomers. In the range of
"proper micelles" they now adopt either a constant or a linearly
increasing dissociation rate constant with degree of polymerization, and adjust the association rate constant to be consistent
with assumed micellar distribution, an approximately linear
choice[16]. It might be pointed out that for my model, the association rate constant contains a quadratic term in degree of polymerization, which, according to Almgren et al.[15] tends to give
rise to a mixing of relaxation times. The choice of the depth or
shape of the minimum in the distribution appears to be rather
arbitrary, since concentrations much less than 10^{-3} of that of
the sample are generally inaccessible at present to direct equilibrium measurement. For example, sedimentation equilibrium
studies of size distributions even in a non-reequilibrating
system using Rayleigh interferometric optics, which presently
appears to be the most precise static technique, would hardly be
expected to provvide data of any accuracy for species present at
much less than 1% of the total sample concentration. The precise
shape of the deep valley is thus currently inferred, with
possibly the only information deriving from the Aniansson and
Wall model for the slow time domain. It has been most convenient
for me to select a single nucleation factor between monomer and
dimer, so that the dimer becomes suppressed, and acts as the
nucleus for all further polymerization. When this nucleation
factor f is 10^{-2} or larger, my model gives unsatisfactory predicted equilibrium CMC behavior. For a factor f of 10^{-4} or less,
equilibrium behavior becomes more satisfactory, predicting more
closely what the experimenter might find with single parameter
weight average molecular weight measurements. The smaller the f
factor becomes, and the larger the maximum possible globular
micelle size in my model, the more cooperative is the micelle
formation, and the larger is the relative kinetic contribution to
monomer buildup from direct exchange, as compared to complete
sequential dissociation. It appears now that the precise location, i.e. oligomer number, of the assumed minimum in my distribution is of trivial importance, the location of that minimum not
controlling its depth.

With respect to shifts in the distribution of micellar species, I believe that my prediction in Figure 9 for the simultaneous rebuilding of large micelles, together with the building of small micelles, at the expense of micelles near the distribution peak, is a transient phase of the kinetics which has not been previously described.

N. Mazer, MIT : Could you discuss qualitatively, what kinetic phenomena would be expected for the highly skewed micellar size distributions corresponding to the sphere-to-rod transition? Has the kinetic data been measured at high salt concentration when such distributions exist?

G. Kegeles: Since I have not followed the literature on the sphere-to-rod transition, and my equilibrium and kinetic models do not extend to the conditions of this transition, I would prefer not to make uneducated guesses. About all that I can say is that if the model for the rod is two saturated hemispherical end caps connected by a straight portion, the kinetics for the spherical portions alone might be expected to be determined by the vacancy rate, essentially independent of concentration. Thus, this component might be represented by $1/\tau = Nk_b$, where N is the maximum number of monomers which can enter the globular micelle, and k_b is the intrinsic dissociation rate constant. Since you have a model for the equilibrium distribution, it should be a straightforward matter to select rate constants consistent with this model, and to integrate the coupled rate equations numerically by an iterative computation similar to that which I have presented.

R. Zana, CNRS, Strasbourg, France : This is more a comment than a question. In your treatment the size distribution function is supposed to go through a minimum for the dimer (or the trimer), while in Aniasson's theory the minimum occurs for a larger associated specie with an aggregation number of about 8. Because of your choice of the dimer as the least concentrated aggregate, the minimum in your size distribution function is much more shallow than in the distribution used by Aniansson. This explains why your theory yields in the course of the time evolution of the system, right after the perturbation, the sequence of events that you have described, that is the complete dissolution of some micelles into (or their formation from) monomers, even after very short time after the perturbation: the monomer exchange and the micelle dissolution are kinetically coupled in your scheme. If you had set the size distribution minimum at a higher aggregation number, the sequence of events would have been different and the exchange process would have completely decoupled from the micelle formation-dissolution process, for all practical purposes.

We believe that your model may apply to systems with a
shallow minimum in the distribution curve, where the average
aggregation number shifts to higher values with increasing concentration. Such systems should be found to test your theory, and
if so, your model may prove valuable. We believe, however, that
it does not apply to classsical detergents for which both the
theory andd the experiments indicate:

    1) no shift of the average aggregation number, and
    2) a minimum of the size distribution function at an
       aggregation value well above 3.

G. Kegeles: Your second sentence of your Comment states that my
size distribution function goes through a minimum for dimer or
trimer, while in Aniansson's theory the minimum occurs for a
larger oligomer, with an aggregation number of about 8, which is
true. In your next sentence you state that because of my choice
of the dimer as the least concentrated aggregate, the minimum in
my size distribution function is much more shallow than that in
the distribution by Aniansson. This is not a correct description
of my model.

    In the accompanying Figure 11, I have computed a shell model
equivalent concentration distribution function for the case N =
200, $K[A_o]$ = 2.0, f = 10^{-18}, as shown by the unfilled triangles.

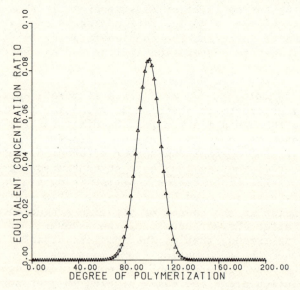

Figure 11. Initial equilibrium ratćo of equivalent concentration of
each species to that of the monomer. Unfilled triangles are for the
shell model, n = 200, $K[A_o]$ = 2.0, f = 10^{-18}. Continuous curve is for
the theoretical corresponding Gaussian Distribution$\sqrt{2}$ $(10)^{-18}$ (2/
$\sqrt{e}$)$\frac{2}{1}$00 e^{-x^2} $/200$, where x is the distance, in number of monomer
units, from the peak position. $C^o/[A_o]$ = 3.12.

The superposed continuous curve is the corresponding theoretical
Gaussian distribution function $\sqrt{2}(10)^{-18} (2/\sqrt{e})^{200} e^{-x^2/200}$,
where x is the distance, in number of monomer units, from the
peak position. The standard deviation σ for this corresponding
Gaussian distribution function is 10, out of a total span of
polymerization from 2 to 200. The fit between the two models is
astonishingly good, the slight skewing in the shell model corresponding to an x^3 term in the exponent. Moreover, the ratio of
the peak equivalent concentration term to the minimum of the
shell model (at dimer) is $4.2(10)^{16}$, and one must go through the
first 49 oligomers before one reaches an equivalent concentration
as large as 10^{-5} of that at the maximum. This is then a much
more cooperative system with a much deeper minimum than the one
just described by Wall and Aniansson[16]. Thus the shallowness of
the minimum to which you have referred is not at all an inherent
property of my distribution model, and it is not controlled by
the location of the absolute minimum of the distribution.

Your Comment is reasonable that the minima are relatively
shallow for kinetics cases which I have selected in Figures 5-10
for presentation in the Symposium. In the next two sentences of
your Comment, you state that "the shallowness of the minimum in
(my) size distribution accounts for the sequence of events that I
have described, that is, the complete dissolution of some
micelles into (or their formation from) monomers, even after very
short time after perturbation: the monomer exchange and the
micelle dissolution are kinetically coupled in (my) scheme. If
(I) had set the size distribution minimum at a higher aggregation
number, the sequence of events would have been different and the
exchange process would have been completely decoupled from the
micelle-dissolution process, for all practical purposes".

To see whether your intuitive analysis is correct, I now
offer a detailed quantitative analysis of the rates of the processes for the actual case shown in Figures 3 and 9, for N = 100
and $K[A_0]$ = 1.5, with f = 10^{-4}, specifically at 100 microseconds
after perturbation. From Figure 3, at 100 microseconds we find
that the overall rate of monomer production is about 10^{-7} moles
per liter per microsecond, directly from the ordinate reading.
This also must be the net difference between areas of the
negative and positive loops in Figure 9, computed as rate of
change of equivalent concentration. Also, from Figure 9, we
observe that the maximum rate of loss of any single micelle size
alone develops a rate of monomer output of $3(10)^{-8}$ moles per liter
per microsecond, and the maximum rate of gain of any single micelle
size alone develops a monomer requirement of $1(10)^{-8}$ moles per liter
per microsecond. Thus, the phenomenon shown in Figure 9, the
simultaneous buildup of small and large micelles, with the loss
of micelles near the peak, requires net excess monomer production
at a rate of 10^{-7} moles per liter per microsecond. I have now
computed the rate of transfer of micellar material through the
distribution minimum, taking everything from trimer up as a

micelle. (Although there is no problem with doing this calculation, this choice introduces a _semantic_ problem, which I will
discuss further below). This computation shows that in the neighbor-
hood of 100 microseconds after perturbation, the loss of moles of
micelles per liter per microsecond is only $5(10)^{-11}$, which can
account for $1.5(10)^{-10}$ moles of monomer per liter per microsecond made available through the pathway of sequential transfer
through the minimum. The _semantic_ problem referred to above
occurs here: are we content to substitute, for example, an
octamer for a more abundant micellar species, say a 30-mer, and
call this an exchange process? If not, then the semantic difficulty is accentuated when the distribution minimum is at dimer.
However, even if we insist on multiplying the number of moles per
liter per microsecond of micelles being lost by the degree of
polymerization at the distribution maximum in order to arrive at
a figure representing the output of monomer due to micelle
dissolution, we obtain $1.5(10)^{-9}$ moles of monomer per liter per
microsecond as the maximum attributable to "dissolutiion". Even
this extreme estimate is approximately two orders of magnitude
smaller than the net _difference_ between monomer due to micelle
disappearance and micelle production shown in Figure 9, and much
smaller still than either the rate of monomer output alone, or
the rate of monomer uptake alone. Thus we see that, "coupling"
of the "two kinetic processes" notwithstanding, at early times,
the production of monomer by dissolution is many order of magnitude too small to explain the phenomena shown in Figure 9. What
we have, then, in Figure 9 is a transient monomer exchange
process of a complicated type, not discussed in the Aniansson and
Wall theory.

It should also be pointed out that the kinetics experimenter
following monomer concentration to study a system like the one
presented in Figures 3, 8, 9 and 10 is inherently completely unable to detect even the existence of the phenomena shown in Figure 9. Figure 3 shows that at 100 microseconds after perturbation, when large and small micelles are being formed simultaneously at the expense of micelles in the peak vicinity, the monomer kinetics will indicate nothing but the same single average
fast relaxation time which has been in effect since the end of
the perturbation!

If the _equilibrium_ properties of the types of micellar
systems with which you work are precisely as described in your
final paragraph, my model can also reasonably simulate the behavior of such systems, as suggested by Figure 11. I believe that
the relatively simple, exact and inexpensive computational
approach which I have described here can be used fruitfully to
predict and uncover subtle details of the kinetics processes not
heretofore discussed. This approach is completely divorced from

and independent of preconceived physical approximations about the
overall sequence of events in the kinetics. Once experimental
methods are devised to follow the fine details of size distribution shifts in very short periods of time, such predictions can
be subjected to direct experimental tests, which may help to
provide further understanding.

Editors' Note: Figure numbers 1-10 refer to Figures in the text.

On the paper by B. Jönsson, G. Gunnarsson
and H. Wennerström

R. G. Laughlin, *Procter & Gamble Company, Cincinnati*
    1.   Can the theory governing association be extended to
cover the other two major phase phenomena observed in surfactant/
water systems - the miscibility gaps and the Krafft boundary?
    2.   Is there sufficient water in a lamellar liquid cyrstal
to allow dissociation of counterions in the same sense as in
dilute solution?

H. Wennerström:
    1.   An underlying assumption in the theory presented above
is that the surfactant behaviour in the aggregates is liquid-
like. The Krafft boundary represents the equilibrium with a solid
crystalline phase for which it seems, at present, difficult to
develop a free energy expression. However by knowing from experiment the heat capacities and the equilibrium, at one temperature,
between the crystals and an isotropic or liquid crystalline phase
the full phase boundary to the crystals can be calculated.
    Regarding the miscibility gaps, these typically occur for
nonionic surfactants, and they are usually not observed for ionic
surfactants. The theory does account for the latter observation,
which can be inferred from curve 1 in Figure 7. If a miscibility
gap exists the curve has to make a closed loop, where the point
of intersection corresponds to the two isotropic solutions in
equilibrium at that particular temperature.
    2.   This depends on the particular system and on the com-
position. In a very swollen lamellar phase as in the AOT-water
system there is a considerable excess of water in the sense that
the molar ratio H_2O/AOT is large. For the series of potassium
carboxylates, for which data are presented in Figure 3 there is
roughly just enough water for a first hydration shell.

K. D. Cook, *University of Illinois, Champaign-Urbana* : Could you amplify on your slide showing activities of surfactant and counterion, and also total activity, as functions of surfactant concentration?

H. Wennerström: Figure 6 in the text shows that as the amphiphile concentration is increased above the CMC, the counterion activity increases, although less steeply than before the CMC, while the mean activity of the neutral salt increases only slightly in a way similar to a nonionic surfactant. The, perhaps somewhat unexpected, marked decrease in the surfactant ion activity is then a trivial consequence of the more familiar of the counterion and mean activities since $A^{\pm}=(a^{+}a^{-})^{1/2}$. The behavior of the surfactant ion activity can also be interpreted in a more intuitive way. Particularly at low salt concentrations, and thus for surfactants with low CMCs, it is the entropy of the ion binding (eq. 7) that gives the dominant contribution to the electrostatic free energy of micelle formation. Since only a fraction of the counterions are "bound" to the micelle, the average concentration of "free" counterions increases as the surfactant ion concentration is increased. Thus the entropy loss on binding the counterions to the micelles is decreased, so that the surfactant ions in the micelles can be in equilibrium with bulk surfactant ions at lower activity. This argument can also easily be formulated in terms of the law of mass action. One can also note that although Figure 6 refers to activities there is a similar behaviour of the concentrations of the monomeric species. There are thus substantial errors involved in making the assumption that the free surfactant ion concentration is constant above the CMC.

On the paper by J. E. Desnoyers, D. Roberts
and G. Perron

B. Yarar, *University of British Columbia, Canada*:   What is the critical distance for hydrophobic interaction?

J. E. Desnoyers: The term hydrophobic interactions is used by many authors to define different processes. Tanford referes to the passage of an hydrophobic molecule from a non-aqueous medium to an aqueous medium. Ben-Naim is interested in the interaction when two hydrophobic molecules go from an infinite separation to the formation of a contact pair. Franks and Friedman calls hydrophobic interactions any interaction arising when two hydrophobic

solutes approach each other to some critical distance which is
not necessarily the contact distance. I like to call these three
effects hydrophobic hydration, hydrophobic bonding and hydrophobic interactions. These latter interactions are measured
through the concentration dependence of the thermodynamic quantities (second virial coefficients). In terms of a molecular
picture the smallest distance reached by the solutes before
hydrophobic bonding occurs is probably the two solutes separated
by a water molecule as in the case of a clathrate hydrate.

D. Balasubramanian, *University of Hyderabad, India* : Can you use
your techniques to study reverse micelles?

J. E. Desnoyers: We can use thermodynamic techniques to study
transitions if the thermodynamic properties of the system in the
initial and final state are different. In the case of micellization there are large changes in properties due to the destruction of hydrophobic hydration of the surfactant molecules when
they associate. With reverse micelles the changes will be much
smaller. Experiments are underway in our laboratory and elsewhere
to investigate this, but we have little results up to now mostly
because we need anhydrous non-aqueous systems as references and
this is not always easy to achieve experimentally.

N. A. Mazer, *MIT* : Can you evaluate the heat of micellization
from your heat capacity data?

J. E. Desnoyers: If we use a phase transition model we can show
that the relaxational contribution is a function of ΔH_m^2 . However, a phase transition model is not a very good representation
of micellization and we can readily show that there are large
derivatives from this model with our systems. In the case of
simple association or dimerization, Jolicoeur, et al. (J. Phys.
Chem.) have shown that it is possible to extract the enthalpy of
the process from the relaxational contribution. It should be
possible to do the same with an association model for micellization, but we have not succeeded yet.

C. Jolicoeur, *Universite de Sherbrooke* : (Comment following the
question by Charles Spink) With regards to the extraction of ΔH
of micellization from the maximum in the $\bar{C}_p$ vs. concentration
curve, as inquired by Dr. Spink, I wold like to add that this is
possible in simpler systems. For example, heat capacity measurements in solution containing cation-cyclic polyether complexes,
carried out with different cation/complexant ratios, show a
similar maximum from which the ΔH, and sometimes the equilibrium
constant, for the complexation (J. Phys. Chem. <u>83</u>, 2806 (1979))
can be obtained.

On the paper by P. J. Missel, N. A. Mazer,
G. B. Benedek and M. C. Carey

J. E. Desnoyers, *Université de Sherbrooke, Canada* : Some of your measurements with sodium dodecylsulphate seem to extend below the Krafft temperature and in addition the solubility of such a surfactant decreases rapidly in the presence of NaCl. I therefore have trouble seeing how you were able to measure the sphere-to-rod transition unless you were working in the supersaturated region. Can you clarify this?

P. J. Missel: Thank you for your question. Indeed, some of our measurements were taken below the Krafft temperature in the supersaturated region. Nevertheless, it is our experience that when the alkyl sulfate detergent solutions were made clean by filtration and centrifugation, the solutions could remain clear at temperatures 5-10°C below the Krafft temperature for a substantial period of time ranging from a few minutes to hours. For all our data, we monitor the scattered light intensity, taking QLS measurements only fater obtaining a constant intensity reading for at least ten minutes, and after taking QLS data, a process which takes from 1-5 minutes, we would check the scattered intensity again. The data is reported only if the intensity is constant throughout. Since we saw no discontinuous behavior in micellar size or in scattered light intensity as we crossed below the Krafft temperature, we concluded that the micellar state is metastable below the Krafft temperature. This conclusion is in agreement with the conductimetry and ^{13}C NMR studies of E. I. Franses, et al., J. Phys. Chem. $\underline{84}$, 2413 (1980), who concluded that the aggregates present in supersaturated solutions of SDS in 0.6M NaCl resemble micelles rather than microdispersions of the hydrated crystal.

On the paper by N. A. Mazer, G. B. Benedek
and M. C. Carey

K. D. Cook, *University of Illinois, Champaign-Urbana* : Could you incorporate metal atom labels and investigate their location in your microscopy in order to test your theory of, for example, cholesterol location?

N. A. Mazer: It would certainly be helpful to conduct additional microscopic investigations on these mixed micellar systems in the hope of validating the structures deduced from light scattering. The use of labeled molecules might be a clever way to determine the location of cholesterol and bile salt molecules in the large "mixed disc" micelles.

On the paper by Y. Murata, G. Sugihara,
N. Nishikido and M. Tanaka

R. Zana, *CNRS, Strasbourg, France*:

Y. Murata: Your first question concerns the purity of our sample
of deoxycholate. The purity was checked by the elemental analysis
(Yanagimoto C,H,N, coder MT2 type) in our reported paper.
    The purity was again checked by the thin-layer chromato-
graphy and the surface tension measurement after returning from
the symposium. The thin-layer chromatography was carried out by
means of T. Usui (J. Biochem., 54, 283 (1963)) and got a single
spot. The surface tension measurement was carried out for the
borate buffer solution (pH = 9.3, ion strength = 0.35) at 30°C by
means of Wilhelmy's surface balance (Kyowa CBVP Surface Tensiometer A3). The solutions were prepared by dilution method
keeping the constant ion strength. The curve of surface tension
vs. log(concentration) shows no minimum as shown in Figure 11 in
which the accuracy was within ± 0.1 dyne/cm.
    From these results the purity of our sample is considered to
be sufficiently high for the study of the nature of bile salt
solutions.

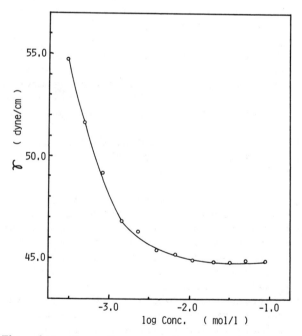

Figure 11. The plot of surface tension as a function of the
logarithm of concentration of NaDC, pH = 9.3, ion strength = 0.35
at 30°C.

The second one concerns the apparent molal volume in very low concentration range. We agree with your saying that the values of the apparent molal volume have large errors in the range of lower concentration. But, Figure 7 (see text) simply shows dependence of the apparent molal volume on the increase of concentration. We do not intend to say that the amount of decrease of the apparent molal volume on micellization may be determined from this Figure.

In order to do the quantitative thermodynamic discussion about the volume change on micellization, we must determine the partial molal volume from the more detailed measurement of the apparent molal volume which will be done in near future.

On the paper by M. Abu-Hamdiyyah

B. Yarar, *University of British Columbia, Canada* : Please comment on the nature and range of the forces leading to hydrophobic association.

M. Abu-Hamdiyyah: The forces leading to hydrophobic association are primarily those that are responsible for the strong water-water interaction since it is the inability of the non-polar moiety to dissolve regularly in liquid water that leads to association of the non-polar moieties, plus those forces that are responsible for maintaining the aggregate in aqueous surroundings namely ionic (dipole)-dipole interactions of the heads with water and with each other and the dispersion forces between the non-polar moieties in the aggregate. Thus there are no special forces and the existing forces operate at the usual ranges.

N. Mazer, *MIT* : Does your data and/or theoretical analysis suggest how the magnitude of the hydrophobic interaction, itself, varies as a function of pressure?

M. Abu-Hamdiyyah: It is found experimentally (references 13-15) that the hydrophobic interaction (HI) is weakened as pressure is increased reaching a minimum and then starts to increase. It is obvious that two opposing factors are involved: one tending to decrease and the other to increase HI. The factor that weakens HI is probably the weakening of the skelatal structure in liquid water (becoming easier to accommodate non-polar moiety in it). The factor that increases HI probably is the breakdown of some of the skeletal structure as the pressure is increased. The first is dominant at relatively lower pressure while the other factor is dominant at higher pressures.

GENERAL DISCUSSION

N. A. Mazer, *MIT*   :   What is the effect of pressure on hydrophobic interactions?

J. Desnoyers, *Université de Sherbrooke* : To answer this question you have to define what is meant by hydrophobic interactions. In general

$$(\partial \Delta G/\partial P)_T = \Delta V \text{ and } (\partial \Delta V/\partial P)_T = -\Delta K$$

where K is the isothermal compressibility. In the pre-micellar region ΔV is negative, i. e. the apparent or partial molal volume of non-ionic surfactants decreases with concentration. Therefore, at low pressures, the hydrophobic interaction should increase (ΔG more negative) with pressure. On the other hand, if we refer to the micellization process, then ΔV is positive and the hydrophobic interaction now decreases (ΔG less negative) with pressure. At high pressures, this trend reverses because ΔK of micellization is positive.

E. Fendler, *Texas A&M University* : How much does water penetrate into the micellar core?

B. Cabane, *Université Paris Sud, Orsan, France:*
    First there is the problem of the geometrical frame of reference used to measure water penetration. Some workers have used the molecule as a frame of reference. For example, they remark that the first 3 CH_2 groups of the surfactant molecules are hydrated, and conclude that water penetrates about 1/3 of the micellar core. I believe that this conclusion would only be correct if the chains would extend radially from the center of the micelle to its surface. There is considerable evidence that they do not; a typical order parameter for the surfactant chains in micelles is 0.2, which implies that they have rather few radial segments[1] . For this reason, we do not know what is the location of, say, the 3rd CH_2 group of a surfactant chain within the micellar core; it might well be right at the surface. In other words, because of the great variations in the configuration of the surfactant molecules in the micelles, a molecular frame of reference is useless for this purpose; the only acceptable frame of reference is the micellar frame (i.e. distances measured from the center or from the charged surface.[2])
    Secondly, if we compare a micelle with no water penetration to a micelle with water penetration into the core, we can make the following statements:

   - The micelle with no water penetration can be pictured as
     a hydrocarbon droplet with about 1/3 of its surface
     covered by polar groups; 2/3 of its surface remains
     exposed to water; this implies that 15 to 30% of the
     CH_2 groups are in contact with water[3].
   - The micelle with water penetration (random penetration
     or "fjords") has even more hydrocarbon in contact with
     water. I believe that, because of the hydrophobic
     interaction, this second micelle will be less stable than
     the first one.

1. J. Eriksson, U. Henriksson, L. Odberg, These proceedings, Vol.2.
2. B. Cabane, J. de Physique (1981) to be published.
3. B. Cabane, J. Phys. Chem. <u>81</u>, 1639 (1977).

C. Jolicoeur, *Université de Sherbrooke*:
     Comment on the topic of water penetration in micelles. If
the hydrocarbon core of a micelle resembles, in its physical
properties, a liquid hydrocarbon, the presence of water molecules
in this core would seem to pose either a conceptual, or an experimental detection problem. Conceptually, if a single water
molecule is present in the core of a spherical micelle of say
SDS, the local concentration of water in the hydrocarbon will be
of the order of 10^{-1} Molar, that is a few orders of magnitude
higher than the solubility of water in liquid hydrocarbons. If,
on the other hand, one assumes a water solubility in the micelle
of 10^{-3} M, then one liter of a 0.5M solution of SDS could
dissolve (based on the volume fraction of the hydrocarbon core),
approximately 10^{-4} moles of water. Clearly, measurements of the
properties of this amount of water in the presence of 55 moles
of water solvent will require highly discriminant and sensitive
methods.

J. B. Nagy, *Facultés de Universitaires Namur, Namur, Belgium*:
     Can you comment more and give quantitative data concerning
the importance of through space electric field effects on
micellar aggregation?

C. Jolicoeur, *Université de Sherbrooke*:
     The mangitude of "charge transmission" effects in the
hydrocarbon chains of n-alkylcarboxylates had been discussed
earlier by Everett (Disc. Faraday Soc. <u>24</u>, 220 (1957)) and
theoretical basis for such effects have been reported by P.
Pyykkö in Turku (Åbo akademi) (Report B97, 1 (1978)). I'm not
aware that the details of these effects have been incorporated in
electrostatic theories of ionic micelles, but I would assume that
the charge transmission effects would add chain-chain repulsion
within the micelle, thus increasing its free energy, i.e. raise
the CMC.

Somebody from the audience::
     There is no evidence (to my knowledge) for premicellar
aggregates and certainly not at a concentration of 3.5 mM SDS. A
possible explanation for the different CMC indicated by the DS$^-$
and Na$^+$ electrodes might be an interaction between TRIS and DS$^-$,
but this is not the same as premicellar aggregation.

K. Kale, *Northern Illinois University*:
     Here we are not comparing the CMC of SDS in aqueous solution
(8mM) to that in TRIS buffer (3.5 mM). Certainly this decrease
in CMC can be understood as a general salt effect.
     In our case we are interested in the different CMC value
determined by the detergent electrode compared to the counterion
electrode in the same solvent (with or without buffer). We have
observed this difference in all the experiments we have performed. Our interpretation of this difference reflects the sensitivity of the surfactant electrode to premiceller aggregation,
dimer, trimer etc: that counterion electrodes do not detect since
an appreciable amount of counterions may not bound until an
aggregate size approaching that of the micelle is reached.

ABOUT THE CONTRIBUTORS

Here are included biodata of only those authors who have contributed to this volume. Biodata of contributors to Volume 2 are
included in that volume.

Mohammed Abu-Hamdiyyah is currently in the faculty of the
University of Kuwait, Kuwait. He received his Ph.D. in 1965 from
the University of Southern California followed by four years at
duPont. He was also associated (1969-1973) with the University of
Petroleum and Minerals, Dhahran, Saudi Arabia.

George B. Benedek is the Alfred H. Caspary Professor of Physics
and Biological Physics at the Massachusetts Institute of Technology
and a member of the faculty of the Harvard-M.I.T. Division of
Health Sciences and Technology. His research interests include:
laser light scattering, the thermodynamics of aggregating systems
and the pathophysiology of cataract disease. He was recently elected
a member of the National Academy of Sciences.

Arieh Y. Ben-Naim is Professor of Physical Chemistry, Hebrew
University of Jerusalem. He received his Ph.D. degree in 1964
followed by a number of teaching and research appointments. He has
been a Visiting Scientist/Professor at various institutions, the
most recent being at Bell Laboratories. His research interests include theoretical and experimental aspects of the structure of
water, aqueous solutions and the problem of hydrophobic interaction.
He has authored two monographs Hydrophobic Interactions (1980) and
Water and Aqueous Solutions (1974).

Kulbir S. Birdi is Assistant Professor at the Technical University
of Denmark, Lyngby, Denmark. His research interests are monolayers,
micelle formation, solubilization, and microemulsions.

J. O-M. Bockris has been Professor of Chemistry. Texas A & M
University since 1978. He received his Ph.D. degree from London
University in 1945 followed by a number of academic appointments,
including Directorship of the Electrochemistry Laboratory, Univ-

ersity of Pennsylvania (1962-1972). He is a very prolific author as he has authored / edited many monographs and has about 560 papers to his credit. He is a member of the Editorial Boards of a number of journals and has served on many commissions, committees, etc. He has been invited to about 100 international conferences (including 14 Gordon Conferences) and has visited and lectured, by invitation, in most of the technologically advanced countries. He has been a recipient of a number of prestigious awards, the latest being the Chemical Lecture Award, Swedish Academy, 1979. His published work is very frequently cited and his research interests include all aspects of electrochemistry.

Bernard Cabane is Charge de Recherche, CNRS, at the Universite Paris Sud, Orsay, France. He obtained his Ph.D. degree from Orsay, France. His research interests include NMR study of micelles.

Martin C. Carey is Associate Professor of Medicine at Harvard Medical School, and Lawrence J. Henderson Associate Professor of Health Sciences and Technology in the Harvard University-Massachusetts Institute of Technology Division of Health Sciences and Technology. He also serves as a physician in the Department of Medicine at Brigham and Women's Hospital in Boston. He obtained his M.D. degree from the National University of Ireland in 1962. His research interests extend to all aspects of biological colloid chemistry. He serves as Associate Editor of the J. Lipid Research and on the Editorial Boards of a number of international journals.

Dipti K. Chattoraj is Professor in the Department of Biochemistry and Biophysics, University of Kalyani, West Bengal, India. His research interests are physical biochemistry, adsorption,surface excesses, and micelles.

Michel Che is currently Professeur at the Universite Pierre et Marie Curie in Paris, France. Before his current position, he was at the Institut de Recherches Sur la Catalyse at Villeurbanne, France. He graduated from Ecole Superieure de chimie Industrielle de Lyon in 1964 and obtained his Doctorat es Sciences in 1968. His research interests include adsorption, catalysis and spectroscopy.

Stephen Colgan is presently a graduate student at Northeastern University. He received his B.S. from SUNY-Cortland.

Mario Corti is affiliated with the Quantum Optics Section of CISE (Segrate - Milano, Italy). He is also Professor at the Istituto de Fisica dell'Universita di Milano. In the last seven years, he has been working on quasielastic light scattering from pure fluids and micellar solutions.

S. U. Dalsager is with the Fysisk-Kemisk Institut, Technical University of Denmark, Lyngby, Denmark.

Valfredo Tadeu DeFávere is Instructor in Chemistry at the Universidade Federal de Santa Catarina, Florianópolis, Brazil. He received his M.S. in Chemistry in 1980. His research interests are in the area of surface chemistry.

Vittorio Degiorgio is a Senior Researcher of the Italian National Research Council (CNR), and Professor of Quantum Electronics at the University of Pavia. He has published in the areas of quantum optics and statistical physics. His current research interests are in the applications of laser-light scattering techniques to micellar and macromolecular solutions, and in phase transitions and instabilities in open systems.

Y. DeGrandpré is a Ph.D. student at Universite de Sherbrooke, Canada.

Rosario DeLisi is Invited Professor at the Universite de Sherbrooke where he is on leave from Istituto di Chimica Fisica, Palermo, Italy. He received his Ph.D. in 1967 from the University of Palermo.

Jacques E. Desnoyers is Professor of Chemistry, Universite de Sherbrooke, Canada. He received his Ph.D. degree in 1961 from the University of Ottawa.

R. Duplessix is with C.R.M. 6, Strasbourg, France.

James E. Erman is Associate Professor of Chemistry at Northern Illinois University which he joined in 1970. He received his Ph.D. degree in Physical Chemistry from MIT. He is currently working principally in the area of structure-function relationships of heme proteins and has authored or coauthored 30 research publications.

Samir Farid is Research Associate and Group Leader at the Research Laboratories of Eastman Kodak Company which he joined in 1969. He received his Ph.D. degree in 1967 from Gottingen University. Current research activities are preparative and mechanistic organic photochemistry, exciplex and electron-transfer reactions, light-sensitive polymers, photopolymerization, and photochemistry in polymeric matrices.

Eleanor J. Fendler,* is presently employed at the Kimberly-Clark Corp., Neenah, WI. Before her present position, she was Associate Professor of Chemistry at Texas A&M University. She obtained her Ph.D degree in 1966 from the University of California, Santa Barbara. She was

*As the Coeditor of this two-volume set.

an NIH research Career Development Awardee from 1971-1976. She has
published more than 70 papers in the areas of micellar catalysis;
NMR spectroscopy; and physical, organic, bioorganic and radiation
chemistry. Also, she is co-author (with J. H. Fendler) of the book
Catalysis in Micellar and Macromolecular Systems published in
1975. Her research interests include biomedical functions of
surfactants.

Riccardo Ghidoni is Assistant Professor of Biological Chemistry at the University of Milan, where he received his degree in
Chemistry in 1974. In the same year he was guest at the University
of Marburg in West Germany. His research work deals with chemical
and structural studies on gangliosides.

Charles H. Giles is presently Honorary Research Fellow, University of Strathclyde, Glasgow, Scotland. He worked as a chemist
for Imperial Chemical Industries, 1933-1946. He has been a
Visitive Professor, Universisty of New South Wales (1965) and
University of Bombay (1966).

Muriel Goyer is a staff member of the Bio/Medical Sciences
Section of Arthur D. Little, Inc., with extensive experience in
many aspects of biological sciences. Her area of specialization
encompasses the evaluation of the toxic effects of chemical
pollutants to man and other biota. She received her M.S. degree in
pharmacology in 1971 from Northeastern University.

Reid B. Grigg is presently at the University of Lethbridge,
Canada to do research on solution thermodynamics with applications
to recovery of bitumen and heavy oils. He received his Ph.D. in
Physical Chemistry from Brigham Young University.

Gudmundur Gunnarsson is a graduate student at the Lund
Institute of Technology, Lund, Sweden.

Susan E. Hartman has been a Research Chemist since 1972 in
the Research Laboratories of Eastman Kodak Company. She received
her B.S. in Chemistry in 1972 from Juiata College. She has coauthored
5 publications, and is the coinventor on several patents in the synthesis and polymerization of specialty monomers.

Helmut Hauser is in the faculty of the Department of Biochemistry, ETH Zurich. He received his Ph.D. in Chemistry and
D.Sc. in Pharmacy. He is the author of 85 publications.

Ulf Henriksson is a Research Associate at the Royal Institute
of Technology, Stockholm, and received a Doctor of Technology
degree in 1975. Publications deal with applications of NMR spectroscopy in surfactant-containing systems.

Loren G. Hepler is Professor of Chemistry and also Research Professor for the Alberta Oil Sands Technology and Research Authority in the University of Lethbridge, Lethbridge, Alberta, Canada. He is interested in applications of thermodynamics to problems in both "pure" and "applied" science, with particular emphasis on solutions.

Lavinel G. Ionescu is Professor of Physical Chemistry at the Universidade Federal de Santa Catarina, Florianópolis, Brazil. Before his present position he had faculty appointments at New Mexico Highlands University, Las Vegas and the University of Detroit. He received his Ph.D. in Physical Chemistry from New Mexico State University, Las Cruces and had postdoctoral experience at the University of California, Santa Barbara. His research interests are properties of surfactants, micelles and liquid crystals, micellar catalysis, membrance models, respiratory pigments, clathrates or gas hydrates, chemistry of noble gases and history of science. He is fluent in at least ten European languages and has published over 50 scientific articles.

Carmel Jolicoeur is Professor of Chemistry, Universite de Sherbrooke, Sherbrooke, Canada.

Bengt Jönsson is a graduate student at the Lund Institute of Technogy, Lund, Sweden.

Kaldas M. Kale is currently a Research Chemist at the Experimental Station, E. I.du Pont de Nemours & Co., Wilmington, DE. Prior to joining du Pont,he was Instructor of Chemistry at Northern Illinois University, DeKalb, IL. He received his Ph.D. degree in 1974 from National Chemical Laboratory, Pune, India, followed by postdoctoral research at Centre de Recherches sur les Macromolecules, Strasbourg, France, and Carnegie-Mellon University Pittsburgh. He is coauthor of about 18 publications.

Shoji Kaneshina is Associate Professor, College of General Education, Kyushu University, Japan. He obtained his Ph.D. degree from Kyushu University. His research interests include effect of pressure on the solution behavior of aqueous surfactants.

Gerson Kegeles has been Professor, Section of Biochemistry & Biophysics, University of Connecticut, Storrs since 1968. He received his Ph.D. degree in 1940 from Yale University and since then has had many research and teaching assignments. Since 1939, he has published about 90 papers mostly in the field of macromolecular and biophysical chemistry. More recently he has published in the area of micelles.

Tomas Klasson is a graduate student in physical chemistry at the Royal Institute of Technology, Stockholm, Sweden.

Gordon C. Kresheck is currently Professor of Chemistry and Director of the Center for Biochemical and Biophysical Studies at Northern Illinois University. He received his Ph.D. in 1961 from Ohio State University. He is coauthor of about 30 publications and chapters in monographs dealing with surfactants and calorimetry of bacterial and mammalian cells. He has also contributed sections to the Handbook of Biochemistry, and Bulletin of Thermodynamics and Thermochemistry.

D. D. Lasic received a Ph.D. degree in Chemistry in 1979 from the University of Ljubljana, Yugoslavia. Research interest is in liquid crystals.

Yvan Lavigne is currently working for Bombardier, Valcourt, Quebec, and received an M.SC. in 1979 from the Universite de Sherbrooke, Canada.

L. L. Lemelin is a Research Assistant at the Universite de Sherbrooke, Canada.

Israel J. Lin is Associate Professor of Mineral Engineering and Head of the Mineral Engineering Research Center at the Technion - Israel Institute of Technology, where he received his D.Sc. degree in 1968. He was a Visiting Professor at Henry Krumb School of Mines, Columbia University (1970-1971) and Visiting Principal Scientist at the National Institute for Metallurgy, Johannesburg, South Africa. Among his research interests are applied surface and colloid chemistry, mineral beneficiation techniques, hydrocycloning and mechanochemistry. He is the author/coauthor of over 150 publications.

Björn Lindman is Professor of Physical Chemistry, University of Lund, Sweden. His research interests are in the fields of micelles, microemulsions, emulsions and other surfactant systems, ion binding to polyelectrolytes and biomacromolecules and applications of NMR spectroscopy to physico-chemical biological problems.

Ashit B. Mandal is currently a Scientist in the Central Leather Research Institute, Madras, India. He carried out research in the Department of Chemistry of Jadavpur University on micellar and mixed micellar systems and submitted a thesis for Ph.D. in 1980.

Peter A. Martic is affiliated with the Research Laboratories of Eastman Kodak Company which he joined in 1968. He received his M.S. in Physical Chemistry in 1965 from Oklahoma State University. He has coauthored several papers, and his current interests are induced aggregation of aromatic hydrocarbons by polyelectrolytes and surfactants.

Norman A. Mazer is a Research Associate at the Massachusetts Institute of Technology and Harvard Medical School. He received his Ph.D. in Physics and M.D. degree from these institutions in 1978 and has been interested in applying the methodology and concepts of the physical sciences to problems in medicine and biology. His specific research activities concern laser light scattering and its application to micellar systems.

Paul Joseph Missel is currently a Research Assistant in the Physics Department at MIT working toward a Ph.D. degree, where he received his S.B. degree in 1977.

Kashmiri Lal Mittal, * is presently employed at the IBM Corporation in Hopewell Junction, NY. He received his M.Sc. (First Class First) in 1966 from Indian Institute of Technology, New Delhi, and Ph.D. in Colloid Chemistry in 1970 from the University of Southern California. In the last seven years, he has organized and chaired a number of very successful international symposia and in addition to this two-volume set, he has edited nine more volumes as follows: Adsorption at Interfaces, and Colloidal Dispersions and Micellar Behavior (1975); Micellization, Solubilization, and Microemulsions, Volumes 1 & 2 (1977); Adhesion Measurement of Thin Films, Thick Films, and Bulk Coatings (1978); Surface Contamination: Genesis, Detection, and Control, Volumes 1 & 2, (1979); Solution Chemistry of Surfactants, Volumes 1 & 2 (1979). In addition to these volumes he has published about 50 papers in the areas of surface and colloid chemistry, adhesion, polymers, etc. He has given many invited talks on the multifarious facets of surface science, particularly adhesion, on the invitation of various societies and organizations in many countries all over the world, and is always a sought-after speaker. He is a member of many professional and honorary societies, is a Fellow of the American Institute of Chemists and Indian Chemical Society, is listed in American Men and Women of Science and Who's Who in the East. He is or has been a member of the Editorial Boards of a number of scientific and technical journals.

Satya P. Moulik is in the Faculty of Chemistry of Jadavpur University, Calcutta, India, which he joined in 1973. He received his Ph.D. and D.Sc. degrees in 1963 and 1976 respectively from Calcutta University, India. He has had a number of research appointments and has published 65 research papers.

Stefan C. Müller is in the Department of Chemistry, Stanford University on a Fellowship supported by the Deutsche Forschungsgemeinschaft. He received the Diploma in Physics in 1975 and the Doctor's degree in 1978 both from the University of Gottingen, W. Germany. Presently he is carrying out research in various chemical instability phenomena.

*As the coeditor of this two-volume set.

Yoshio Murata is working in Physical Cehmistry Laboratory, Department of Chemistry, Fukuoka University from which he graduated. He obtained his M.S. from Kyushu University, Japan.

Nagamune Nishikido is teaching Physical Chemistry as an Instructor (Lecturer) in the Department of Chemistry, Fukuoka University. He obtained his Ph.D. from Kyushu University, Japan.

Jean Paquette is currently working for Atomic Energy of Canada, Pinawa, Manitoba. Received Ph.D. degree in 1978 from Université de Sherbrooke, Canada.

Irmin Pascher is Reader at the University of Göteborg, Sweden, and has a Ph.D. in Chemistry.

L. K. Petterson is currently Associate Faculty Fellow in the Radiation Laboratory and Chemistry Department, University of Notre Dame. He received his Ph.D. degree from Kansas State University and was a Postdoctoral Fellow at the Royal Institution of Great Britain. For over ten years, he has been involved with radiation chemistry in micellar systems.

T. A. J. Payens is Head of the Department of Physical Chemistry at the Netherlands Institute for Dairy Research (NIZO) which he joined in 1956. He received his Ph.D. degree in 1955 under the direction of J. Th. G. Overbeek. He served as a Visiting Professor at the Universities of Illinois and Wageningen. He is a member of the Advisory Board of European J. Biochem., and his research activities deal with the physical chemistry of proteins and polysaccharides and enzyme coagulation reactions.

Gerald Perron is a Research Associate at the Universite de Sherbrooke, Canada. He obtained his B.Sc. (1968) and M.Sc. (1974) from the same university.

Joanne Perwak is a staff member of Arthur D. Little's Bio-Enviro Systems Section with particular expertise in the area of environmental management. She holds an M.S. degree in Environmental Sciences from Harvard University. She is currently carring on studies in risk management related to chemicals.

Reinhard Pottel has since 1973 been Professor in the Department of Physics and Leader of the Section for Physics of Molecular Relaxation Processes in the Drittes Physikalisches Institut of the University of Gottingen. He received Diploma and Doctor's degree in Physics from the University of Gottingen, W. Germany in 1955 and 1957 respectively. He has published on dielectric relaxation spectroscopy of aqueous systems.

T. V. Reddy has since 1977 been Visiting Fellow and Visiting Associate in the Laboratory of Carcinogen Metabolism, National Cancer Institute. Received a Ph.D. in Biochemistry from the University of Delhi, India, followed by a number of research appointments. Has about 10 publications.

David Roberts is a Postdoctoral Fellow at the Universite de Sherbrooke, Canada. He obtained his Ph.D. degree in 1979 from the University of Leicester, United Kingdom.

Jarl B. Rosenholm is in the Department of Physical Chemistry, Abo Akademi, Abo (Turku), Finland. He spent two years on research leave in Canada, working in Lethbridge and Sherbrooke. He is interested in the applications of thermodynamics to problems in both "pure" and "applied" science, with particular emphasis on solutions.

M. Schara is Scientific Advisor, J. Stefan Institute and Associate Professor of Chemical Physics at the E. Kardlej University of Ljubljana, Yugoslavia. He received his Ph.D. degree in 1965 from the University of Ljubljana. His present fields of research are membrane biophysics and liquid crystals (EPR technique) and he has published about 60 papers.

Lawrence A. Singer is Professor of Chemistry, University of Southern California, Los Angeles. He received his Ph.D. degree in 1962 from UCLA and was a Postdoctoral Fellow at Harvard (1962-1964). He was an Alfred P. Sloan Fellow, 1972-1974. His current research interests include excited state complexes, chemiluminescence, photophysical processes in micellar systems, and he has published over 50 papers.

Andrew Sivak is Vice President and Manager of the Bio/Medical Sciences Section of Arthur D. Little, Inc. He received his Ph.D. degree in 1960 from Rutgers University. His areas of specialization include cell biology, biochemistry, microbiology and toxicology with special interest in carcinogenesis and mutagenesis. He is the author of more than 50 scientific publications and co-editor of a monograph on Mechanism of Cocarcinogenesis and Tumor Promotion.

Sandro Sonnino is Assistant Professor of Biological Chemistry at the University of Milan. He was graduated in Chemistry from the same University, in 1974, and spent some months in 1979 at the Institute Pasteur of Paris. His present interests concern the studies on the physiological role of gangliosides.

Charles H. Spink is Professor of Chemistry, SUNY-Cortland. He received his Ph.D. in 1962 from Pennsylvania State University. His most recent research activities have been in solution thermo-

dynamics and the application of calorimetry to problems in
solution structure and the behavior of bile salts as solubilizing
agents for lipidic substances.

Gohsuke Sugihara is Associate Professor, Fukuoka University,
Japan. He was a Visiting Associate Professor, School of Pharmacy,
University of Wisconsin-Madison from 1979 to 1980. He graduated in
applied physics from the Defence Academy of Japan and received a
Ph.D. degree from Kyushu University.

R. D. Swisher retired from Monsanto Company in 1975 which he
had joined upon receiving his Ph.D. in Pharmaceutical Chemistry in
1934 from the University of Michigan. He received the 1976 Award
for Outstanding Achievement in Environmental Chemistry presented
by the Synthetic Organic Chemical Manufacturers Association. He
has authored over two dozen research publications and the treatise
Surfactant Biodegradation, and is the holder of about a dozen
patents. He served with the international Group of Experts of the
OECD in the development of surfactant biodegradation test methods, and is now chairman of the Joint Task Group -- Surfactants of
"Standard Methods for the Examination of Water and Wastewater."

Youne Ben Taarit is presently Maitre de Recherche in charge
of the NMR facilities at IRC, and Assistant Manager of the Zeolite
Research Project. He received his Ph.D. degree from Claude Bernard
University - Lyon, France followed by NSF Postdoctoral Fellowship
at Texas A & M University. He has recently coedited a book
Catalysis by Zeolites and has published about 60 papers covering
various topics including the use of EPR and NMR in the characterization of surface species, and zeolites.

Mitsuru Tanaka is Professor and Head of Physical Chemistry
Laboratory, Fukuoka University. He also has been teaching at
Tokushima University since he received his Ph.D. from Kyushu
University. He has contributed in the area of effect of pressure
on surfactant solutions.

Philip Thayer is Vice President and Senior Staff member of
Life Sciences Group of Arthur D. Little, Inc. Since joining
Arthur D. Little, Inc., in 1955, he has been, among other things,,
involved in studies of growth (algae, protozoa, bacteria and
molds) and the production and isolation of specific fungal and
bacterial enzymes and other products. He received his Ph.D. degree
in Biochemistry in 1952 from the California Institute of
Technology.

H. Ti Tien is Professor and Chairman of the Department of
Biophysics at Michigan State University, East Lansing. He received
his Ph.D. degree in Chemistry and has had a number of industrial
and teaching appointments before coming to Michigan State. His

research interests include membrane phenomena in general with
special emphasis on membrane biophysics, physics and chemistry of
BLM, interfacial chemistry, immuno-chemical reactions and solar
energy conversion. From 1975 to 1976, he served as a UNESCO consultant in Hungary. September – December 1978 he was invited by
the Chinese Academy of Sciences to give a series of lectures, and
was made an honorary professor of the Institute of Photochemistry,
Beijing.

H. J. Vreeman is with the Netherlands Institute for Dairy
Research (NIZO) which he joined in 1968. He received his Ph.D. in
1968 under the direction of J. Th. G. Overbeek. From 1960-1968 he
was a member of the scientific staff of the Van't Hoff Laboratory,
Utrecht. His present interests are in the association, denaturation and fluorescence properties of proteins.

Elizabeth K. Weisburger has since 1973 been Chief, Laboratory
of Carcinogen Metabolism, National Cancer Institute, Bethesda, MD.
She received her Ph.D. in Organic Chemistry from the University of
Cincinnati followed by a number of research appointments. She
received the PHS Meritorious Service Medal in 1973.

Hakan Wennerström is Professor of Physical Chemistry at the
University of Stockholm. He received his Doctor of Technology in
1974 from the Lund Institude of Technology. His publications deal
with theories of amphiphile – water systems, the applications of
NMR to amphiphilic systems, and the application of quantum
mechanics and Monte Carlo simulations to chemical problems.

Jack L.R. Williams is currently a Senior Laboratory Head in
charge of the Organic Photochemistry Laboratory of the Eastman
Kodak Company which he joined about 30 years ago. He received his
Ph.D. in Organic Chemistry in 1948 from the University of Illinois
under the direction of Prof. C. S. Marvel. Areas of research at
Kodak have included monomer synthesis, stereo-specific polymerization, high-pressure chemistry, organic and polymer photochemistry,
and organoboron compounds.

Raoul Zana is Maitre de Recherches at the Centre de Recherches sur les Macromolecules, CNRS, Strasbourg, France. He received
his D. Sc. in 1964 from the University of Strasbourg. He has
published in the field of fast kinetics in solutions of synthetic
and natural biopolymers and of micellar solutions as well as in
ion-solvent interactions. His current research interests are on
polyion-counterion interactions and properties of micellar
solutions and microemulsions.

Y. Zimmels is with the Mineral Engineering Research Center,
Technion-Israel Institute of Technology, Haifa, Israel.

SUBJECT INDEX